MAKING
*the Nonprofit Sector
in the United States*

Philanthropic Studies

DWIGHT F. BURLINGAME AND DAVID C. HAMMACK, GENERAL EDITORS

Albert B. Anderson. *Ethics for Fundraisers*

Karen J. Blair.
The Torchbearers: Women and Their Amateur Arts Associations in America

Dwight F. Burlingame, editor. *The Responsibilities of Wealth*

Dwight F. Burlingame and Dennis Young, editors.
Corporate Philanthropy at the Crossroads

Marcos Cueto, editor.
Missionaries of Science: The Rockefeller Foundation and Latin America

Gregory Eiselein. *Literature and Humanitarian Reform in the Civil War Era*

David C. Hammack.
Making the Nonprofit Sector in the United States: A Reader

Jerome L. Himmelstein.
Looking Good and Doing Good: Corporate Philanthropy and Corporate Power

Warren F. Ilchman, Stanley N. Katz, and Edward L. Queen, II, editors.
Philanthropy in the World's Traditions

Thomas H. Jeavons.
When the Bottom Line Is Faithfulness: Management of Christian Service Organizations

Ellen Condlith Lagemann.
Philanthropic Foundations: New Scholarship, New Possibilities

Mike W. Martin. *Virtuous Giving: Philanthropy, Voluntary Service, and Caring*

Mary J. Oates. *The Catholic Philanthropic Tradition in America*

J. B. Schneewind, editor. *Giving: Western Ideas of Philanthropy*

David H. Smith. *Entrusted: The Moral Responsibilities of Trusteeship*

Bradford Smith, Sylvia Shue, Jennifer Lisa Vest, and Joseph Villarreal.
Philanthropy in Communities of Color

MAKING
the Nonprofit Sector
in the United States

A READER

Edited with introductions by
David C. Hammack

Indiana
University
Press

BLOOMINGTON & INDIANAPOLIS

Publication of this book is made possible in part
with the assistance of a Challenge Grant from
the National Endowment for the Humanities,
a federal agency that supports research, education,
and public programming in the humanities.

This book is a publication of

Indiana University Press

601 North Morton Street
Bloomington, Indiana 47404-3797 USA

www.indiana.edu/~iupress

Telephone orders 800-842-6796
Fax orders 812-855-7931
Orders by email iuporder@indiana.edu

The paper used in this publication meets the minimum
requirements of American National Standard for Information
Sciences—Permanence of Paper for Printed Library
Materials, ANSI Z39.48-1984.

Manufactured in the United States of America

Library of Congress Cataloging-in-Publication Data
Making the nonprofit sector in the United States : a reader / edited
with introductions by David C. Hammack.
p.   cm. — (Philanthropic studies)
Includes bibliographical references and index.
ISBN 0-253-33489-6 (alk. paper)
!. Nonprofit organizations—United States—History.
2. Endowments—United States—History. 3. Charities—United States—History
I. Hammack, David C.   II. Series.
HD2769.2.U6M35   1998   98-7117
ISBN 0-253-21410-6 (pbk : alk. paper)

3 4 5 6 7 05 04 03 02 01 00

For My Mother, Dorothy Morgan Hammack

CONTENTS

Acknowledgments / xi

Introduction: The Growth of the Nonprofit Sector in the United States / xv

British and Colonial Patterns

ONE
Colonial Theory: Established Churches

1. *The Statute of Charitable Uses,* 1601   5
2. *The Elizabethan Poor Law,* 1601   9
3. Brother Juan de Escalona,
   Report to the Viceroy of Mexico on Conditions at Santa Fe, 1601   14
4. John Winthrop, *A Model of Christian Charity,* 1630   19
5. Virginia General Assembly, *Laws Regulating Religion,* 1642   28
6. Hugh Peter and Thomas Weld, *New England's First Fruits,* 1643   30
7. Claude Jean Allouz, S.J.,
   Account of the Ceremony Proclaiming New France, 1671   34

TWO
Colonial Reality: Religious Diversity

8. Inhabitants of Flushing, Long Island,
   Remonstrance against the Law against Quakers, 1657   39
9. Roger Greene, *Virginia's Cure,* 1662   42
10. William Penn, *The Great Case of Liberty of Conscience,* 1670   46
11. Cotton Mather, *Bonifacius: Essays to Do Good,* 1710   50
12. William Livingston,
    Argument against Anglican Control of King's College (Columbia), 1753   61
13. Charles Woodmason, *Journal of the Carolina Backcountry,* 1767-68   64
14. Benjamin Franklin,
    Autobiography: Recollections of Institution-Building, 1771-84   70

The American Revolution: Sources of the Nonprofit Sector

THREE
To the Constitution: Limited Government and Disestablishment

15. John Trenchard and Thomas Gordon,
     Cato's Letters: Arguments against a Strong Central Government, 1720   91
16. Isaac Backus,
     Argument against Taxes for Religious Purposes in Massachusetts, 1774   97
17. Thomas Jefferson, *Virginia Act Establishing Religious Freedom,* 1786   100
18. James Madison, *The Federalist, No. 10,* 1787   103
19. The *Constitution of the United States,* excerpts, 1789,
     and *The First and Tenth Amendments,* 1791   111

FOUR
Voluntarism under the Constitution

20. Lyman Beecher, *Autobiographical Statement on the 1818
     Disestablishment of the "Standing Order" in Connecticut,* 1864   118
21. *The Dartmouth College Case*:
     Daniel Webster, *Argument before the U.S. Supreme Court,* 1818;
     Chief Justice John Marshall, *Decision,*
     and Joseph Story, *Concurring Opinion,* 1819   123
22. Alexis de Tocqueville,
     Political Associations in the United States, 1835, and
     *Of the Use Which Americans Make of Public
     Associations in Civil Society,* 1840   142

Uses of Nonprofit Organizations

FIVE
Varieties of Religious Nonprofits

23. Organized Activity among Slaves: Henry Bibb,
     The Suppression of Religion among Slaves, 1849,
     and Daniel A. Payne, *Account of Slave Preachers,* 1839   159
24. Robert Baird, *The Voluntary Principle in American Christianity,* 1844   163
25. Peter Dobkin Hall,
     Institutions, Autonomy, and National Networks, 1982   174
26. Jay P. Dolan, *Social Catholicism,* 1975   188
27. Arthur A. Goren, *The Jewish Tradition of Community,* 1970   203

SIX
Nonprofit Organizations as Alternative Power Structures

28. Suzanne Lebsock,
    Women Together: Organizations in Antebellum Petersburg, Virginia, 1984   224
29. Kathleen D. McCarthy,
    Parallel Power Structures: Women and the Voluntary Sphere, 1990   248
30. W. E. B. Du Bois, Economic Cooperation among Negro Americans, 1907   264

Nonprofit Structures for the Twentieth Century

SEVEN
Science, Professionalism, Foundations, Federations

31. Debate over Government Subsidies: Amos G. Warner,
    Argument against Public Subsidies to Private Charities, 1908;
    Everett P. Wheeler, The Unofficial Government of Cities, 1900   286
32. David Rosner,
    Business at the Bedside: Health Care in Brooklyn, 1890-1915, 1979   309
33. Frederick T. Gates,
    Address on the Tenth Anniversary of the Rockefeller Institute, 1911   320
34. David C. Hammack,
    Community Foundations: The Delicate Question of Purpose, 1989   329
35. John R. Seeley et al., Community Chest, 1957   354
36. David L. Sills, The March of Dimes: Origins and Prospects, 1957   373

EIGHT
Federal Regulation and Federal Funds

37. Pierce v. Society of the Sisters:
    William D. Guthrie and Bernard Hershkopf, Brief for Private Schools;
    Justice McReynolds, Decision of the U.S. Supreme Court, 1925   404
38. Debate over a Great Society Nonprofit Organization in Mississippi:
    Senator John Stennis and Attorney Marian Wright, Testimony on
    the Child Development Group of Mississippi and the
    Head Start Program, 1967   422
39. The Filer Commission, The Third Sector, 1974   439
40. Steven Rathgeb Smith and Michael Lipsky,
    The Political Economy of Nonprofit Revenues, 1993   454
41. Rust v. Sullivan: Chief Justice William Rehnquist,
    Decision of the U.S. Supreme Court, 1991   474

ACKNOWLEDGMENTS

I must begin by acknowledging my debt to the Mandel Center for Nonprofit Organizations at Case Western Reserve University. As a member of the 1986 faculty committee that launched the Mandel Center's master's degree program, I agreed to offer the course, "Introduction to the Nonprofit Sector," for which I have prepared these readings. Many of my faculty colleagues at the Mandel Center—especially Dennis R. Young, John Yankey, Paul Salipante, Laura Chisolm, Al Abramowitz, Pranab Chatterjee, Tom Bogart, Margaret Wyszomirski, James Strachan, Paul Feinberg, and most recently John Palmer Smith—have taught me a great deal about nonprofit organizations and their management. The nearly five hundred students, many of whom were already experienced senior managers, who have taken my Mandel Center course have taught me much about the realities that a contemporary nonprofit leader must face. Mandel Center students have also pushed me to edit these selections for clarity and brevity and to provide succinct introductions explaining how each reading, including several from the 1600s and 1700s, is relevant today. Thus this collection is designed for the practical nonprofit leader, even as it is edited in the light of the best current historical and policy scholarship.

Several students in Case Western Reserve University's Social Policy History Ph.D. Program helped put this collection together. Dr. Qiusha Ma, Lori Ferguson, Christopher Cronin, and Marta Hokenstad all helped locate important readings that were new to me. Michael FitzGibbon, Martha Gibbons, Stephanie Hiedemann, Daniel Kerr, Stuart Mendel, and Amy Powers made valuable contributions as students and as teaching and research assistants.

History is the discipline through which I began my approach to the nonprofit world, and I am personally indebted to several historians for showing me the way. I learned a great deal about the significance of the American Revolution and the impact of the Constitution in the classes of Bernard Bailyn and through working with John M. Murrin. Readers familiar with their work will be aware of my debt to two editors of documentary histories of religion in America, Joseph L. Blau and Edwin S. Gaustad. From David Tyack and Carl Kaestle's studies of public schools I have learned much about the roles of private institutions. Stuart Bruchey taught me a great deal about the development of the American economy and of American business, lessons that have shaped my understanding of nonprofit as well as profit-seeking activity; more recently, he has edited a very useful set of reprints in the nonprofit field. Barry D. Karl and Stanley N. Katz have emphasized the central political roles played by nonprofit organizations in the American system; Ellis W. Hawley has shown how nonprofits provided "private governments" and extended the powers of government officials as long ago as the 1920s. Ellen Condliffe Lagemann and Steven Wheatley have shown how those insights worked out as foundations sought to shape operating nonprofits in such fields as education and medical education. I have learned a great deal about nonprofit health care organizations from conversations with David Rosner as well as from his publications. Suzanne Lebsock, Kathleen McCarthy, Ann Firor Scott, Lori Ginsberg, and others have contributed greatly to our understanding of the ways women have used nonprofits. As long ago as 1907 W.E.B. Du Bois showed how African Americans used nonprofits to meet community needs; I am indebted to Kimberly Phillips for bringing his work to my attention, and also to Adrienne Lash Jones for teaching me many things about philanthropy in the African American experience. Peter Dobkin Hall has both provided stimulating scholarship on the field as a whole and offered me remarkably generous suggestions, some of them derived from his own comprehensive assemblage of historical documents relating to the sector. In all my historical work I have been influenced by Sigmund Diamond's insistence that we ask the hard practical questions.

In shaping this collection I have drawn on the insights of other disciplines in addition to history. My own understanding of the nonprofit sector has been shaped by the writing and conversation of political scientists Herbert Kaufman, David B. Truman, Wallace Sayre, Nelson Polsby, Byron Shaffer, and E. E. Schattschneider; by sociologists as diverse as Robert K. Merton, Edward Shils, David A. Sills, John Seeley, Paul DiMaggio, Bradford Gray, and Carl Milofsky; and by several economists, including Burton Weisbrod and Richard Steinberg. A good deal of what I know about the nonprofit sector derives from my work with sociologist and law professor Stanton Wheeler on *Social Science in the Making* and with economist Dennis R. Young on *Nonprofit Organizations in a Market Economy.*

Several analysts of contemporary nonprofits have also shaped my understanding of the sector. John Simon, Walter W. Powell, and others associated with Yale's Program on Nonprofit Organizations have contributed greatly to our comprehension of the sector as a whole. The data gathered by Virginia Hodgkinson and her associates and successors at Independent Sector and the National Center for Charitable Statistics are essential. I have relied on Lester Salamon's *America's Nonprofit Sector: A*

Primer, as well as on his continuing work on the impact of the federal government in the last three decades. Emmett Carson's essays have taught me much about African American philanthropy. And I am much indebted to studies of the current roles of nonprofits by Julian Wolpert, Kirsten Gronbjerg, and Steven Rathgeb Smith and Michael Lipsky.

I also want to acknowledge my debt to many nonprofit leaders with whom I have had extended discussions of both individual nonprofits and the sector as a whole: William Bowen and Neil Rudenstine when I was teaching at Princeton in the 1970s; Mary Douglas, James Douglas, Marshall Robinson, Peter de Janosi, Bernard Gifford, and Alida Brill at the Russell Sage Foundation in the early 1980s; Robert Fisher of the San Francisco Foundation and Richard Magat through the Council on Foundations; Norman Edelman, Dean of the School of Medicine at the State University of New York in Stony Brook; Dudley Hafner of the American Heart Association; Thomas Jeavons of the Philadelphia Yearly Meeting of the Society of Friends; James Fisher of the Union Institute; Steven Minter, Richard Shatten, Eric Fingerhut, Richard Jones, Robert Dietz, Robert Lewis, and others in Cleveland; and Anita Plotinsky at the Association for Research on Nonprofit Organizations and Voluntary Action. And I have also learned much through conversations with Loren and Judy Wyss of Portland, Oregon, Vic Samuels of Houston, Harold Wechsler of Rochester, and Deborah Gardner of New York City.

When I started this project ten years ago I was supported in part by a Guggenheim Fellowship. Since then I have benefitted from support by the College of Arts and Sciences and the Mandel Center for Nonprofit Organizations at Case Western Reserve. Yale University's Program on Non-Profit Organizations has provided perfect conditions for completing the work. The collection has been significantly improved by opportunities to present ideas at the Indiana University Center on Philanthropy, at the Center for the Study of American Culture and Education at New York University's School of Education, and at the Independent Sector Research Forum. Dwight Burlingame of the Indiana University Center on Philanthropy has made many contributions to the final completion of this collection and encouraged me at every step. At Indiana University Press Robert Sloan has made several thoughtful suggestions as Sponsoring Editor, and Roberta L. Diehl has been an exemplary copyeditor. My daughter, Elizabeth, served as an essential assistant at many points. My wife, Loraine Shils Hammack, knows how much this work owes to her.

I am indebted to all of those who contributed directly or indirectly, to the creation of this work. I alone am responsible for its organization, its selections, and its introductions.

INTRODUCTION

The Growth of the Nonprofit Sector in the United States

Americans conduct almost all of their formally organized religious activity, and many cultural and arts, human service, educational and research activities, through private nonprofit organizations. American nonprofits have always received substantial support from local, state, and federal governments, and from fees paid by those who use their services, but they have also always relied on donations and voluntary service. American nonprofits have always pursued their particular missions, enjoying considerable independence from government. To carry out their diverse missions, the largest American nonprofits have amassed remarkable resources. They have acquired some of the most impressive hospital, university, performing arts, and museum facilities and collections in the world. They have also amassed a considerable number of large endowments, including many that surpass one billion dollars. Americans also work through hundreds of thousands of small nonprofits, most of which have no tangible resources at all.

No other nation manages its religious, cultural, social service, health care, and educational activities in this way (although in recent years Great Britain, Canada, Israel, and a few other nations have moved in this direction). "Nongovernmental," nonprofit human service organizations exist in many other countries, but nowhere do they employ anything like 10% of the labor force, a reasonable estimate of their share of the U.S. labor force. Nowhere else do nonprofits own such impressive facilities, or hold such large endowments. In most of the world, governments and tax-supported religious groups continue to provide all—or nearly all—social service, higher education, health care, and opera, orchestral music, and museum exhibitions.

How did the United States come to rely so heavily on nonprofits? Why has it continued to do so? What are the consequences? What purposes do Americans seek to advance through their use of nonprofits? Whose purposes do nonprofits best serve? How have Americans sought to control nonprofits? How have the expansions of both state and federal government in twentieth-century America affected nonprofits?

These questions are of pressing interest to those who lead nonprofit organizations, to those who are concerned about the contributions and potential problems and abuses of nonprofit activity, and to those interested in American political and social life in general. They suggest the length and the complexity of the history of nonprofit organizations in the United States. This reader presents some of the classic documents from that history, and some of the most important interpretations by recent scholars of nonprofit organizations and of the nonprofit sector as a whole.

In assembling this collection, I have been concerned to include items that clarify the most important questions that face the nonprofit sector today. Most are original statements, often delivered at the launching of great enterprises or in the midst of heated controversy, by very human men and women—people who were often the leaders of important organizations as they wrote. To a remarkable extent, the men and women who made these statements have been engaged in a single extended conversation for nearly four hundred years. From generation to generation, the leading participants in this conversation have known one another, have grown up under their predecessors' influence, have worked with and against one another. In many ways these men and women were taking part in the effort to define America and American possibilities even as they have shaped what we now call the nonprofit sector.

This collection includes several essays by recent historians and social scientists as well as statements by participants in some of the leading phases in the growth and development of the nonprofit sector. The scholars' essays have the advantage of surveying important issues and periods for us in a concise way. The essays I have chosen are also distinguished by the way they give voice to past contributors to the American debate about voluntary associations and private institutions, contributors whose views would otherwise be difficult for a contemporary reader to find or to comprehend. And, of course, scholars are themselves deeply engaged in the conversation.

I have included many historical documents and historical essays not simply because history is my own discipline, or even because historians have made some of the most careful and extensive studies of the field, but because the American nonprofit sector is a distinctive product of American history. In a fundamental sense American nonprofit organizations owe their existence to the American constitutional system, with its separation of church and state and its limits on government activity.

America's nonprofit organizations are also distinguished, in part, by the fact that they have always obtained the bulk of their resources from fees paid by those who use their services and from governments. Nonprofits have never depended chiefly on donors. Many of the best historians of schools, of colleges and universities, of hospitals and clinics, of libraries and museums, of orchestras and opera companies have been well aware of this fact, and have paid close attention to efforts to maintain good relations both with customers and with governments. For much of American history the nonprofit sector seems to have grown as fast as the American economy as a whole. In the past thirty years it has grown much faster. This record of growth is the result, not merely of philanthropy, but of increased national wealth, effective marketing, and greatly increased government subsidies.

Accordingly, I have divided this collection chronologically into four large sections that reflect key constitutional, political, and economic developments, and I have further divided each section into two parts that explore enduring themes relevant not just to the period but to nonprofit organizations as well.

The first section of this reader includes material on British and Colonial patterns of activity, including the controversies that arose around the relation between church and state. These patterns and controversies provided the matrix out of which Americans developed their nonprofit organizations, and they will resonate with anyone concerned with debates over the proper relation of church and state today. As the selections in Part One show, the established churches that were integral to imperial governance held sway throughout the 1600s, leaving no space for independent institutions. The selections in Part Two demonstrate that religious diversity and conflict over the relationship between government and religion (and religious taxes) became significant to colonial society after 1700, and in fact played a leading part in the developments that led to the American Revolution.

The second section includes basic material on the way in which the political debates of the Revolution and the Constitution created the opportunity to develop independent, nonprofit, nongovernmental organizations in the United States. Those who framed the U.S. Constitution hoped to control the abuse of power through religious as well as other institutions, as the selections in Part Three make clear.

In many ways the Constitution marked a sharp break with the past. It is among the world's oldest active frames of government, so that much of American life today, including important aspects of nonprofit activity, is governed by legal rules and precedents that are now two hundred years old. Some of these are especially important to nonprofit organizations. The First Amendment ("Congress shall make no law respecting an establishment of religion, or prohibiting the free exercise thereof; or abridging the freedom of speech, or of the press, or the right of people peaceably to assemble, and to petition the government for the redress of grievances") is in many ways the fundamental American law for nonprofits. Part Four of this reader contains key documents in the implementation of the First Amendment and other fundamental legal rules, notably the U.S. Supreme Court's decision, in the *Dartmouth College Case*, that corporate charters represent contracts and, under the Constitution, cannot be changed unilaterally by the legislatures or officials of the states that grant them. Alexis de Toqueville saw the practical implications of the constitutional system for both political and social institutions, and his famous essays belong in this part as well.

The third section of the reader concerns the uses Americans have made of nonprofit organizations. It includes materials from the nineteenth century because it was then that American nonprofits took on their characteristic form, because the nineteenth century is now sufficiently far in the past that we are able to discuss its conflicts openly, and because scholars have written many notable discussions of nineteenth-century organizations. Having created the largely independent nonprofit corporation, Americans made many uses of it. As Toqueville saw, all nonprofit organizations play roles in the American political system. Through much of the nineteenth century state legislatures viewed each new nonprofit corporation as an agent of state power, as an institution to carry out state purposes, or at least purposes endorsed by the state. During the Civil War the federal government used the nonprofit United States Sanitary Commission to provide essential health care services to Union soldiers. In the 1920s, Secretary of Commerce Herbert Hoover and other federal officials used nonprofit organizations to coordinate commercial activities in the interest of national efficiency; one of Hoover's chief collaborators for a time was Franklin Delano Roosevelt.

But most nonprofit organizations have always sought not to advance official policy but to change it, or to conduct activities entirely outside the arena of official government. Part Five of this reader includes accounts of nonprofit religious organizations, including not only those of mainstream Protestants, but of Catholics and Jews as well. Slaves lacked the legal status to create and defend corporations, of course, and one of the selections in this part describes the consequences. Part Six includes three accounts of the ways in which women and African Americans, long excluded from voting and equal use of the courts, used nonprofit organizations to create alternative power structures for their own purposes.

The final section of this reader emphasizes the major changes that the nonprofit sector has undergone in the twentieth century. Part Seven reflects the view that what *was* new in the first third of the twentieth century was the rise of science and of professionalism, and the need to find resources to provide services in the newly large metropolitan markets. Some recent writers have objected to what they take to be a recent increase in government control of American nonprofit organizations. Part Eight contains readings that suggest that what is really new is the increase in federal funds and in direct federal regulation.

BRITISH AND COLONIAL PATTERNS

ONE

Colonial Theory: Established Churches

Very few independent, nongovernmental, nonprofit organizations were to be found in the American colonies. Under the theory of British rule at the beginning of the colonial period—and under Spanish rule in Florida and the Southwest, and under French rule in Canada and Louisiana—an established church had the legal responsibility of providing nearly all religious, cultural, human service, and educational activities.

The British theory found legislative expression in two laws, the *Statute of Charitable Uses* and the *Poor Law,* passed at the end of the reign of Queen Elizabeth I in 1601. Elizabeth had devoted her long reign to defining the character of the Church of England and its relation to the British government. When her predecessor, Henry VIII, assumed the throne in 1509, England, Scotland, and Wales had been Catholic countries in which Catholic institutions had provided education and social welfare facilities and the Church had patronized many artists and musicians. Henry's break with the Catholic Church during the 1530s and his seizure of the property of the monasteries disrupted these arrangements, creating practical problems for many schools and hospitals. Elizabeth adopted a middle course between Catholics and Protestants, refusing to tolerate either Catholics or dissenting Congregationalists and favoring the idea that her kingdoms would retain an established—and moderate—church.

1601 was also the year of a vivid critique of the actions of a Spanish official in the area that became Santa Fe, New Mexico, by a Catholic friar. For the next one hundred years, everywhere except in Rhode Island and Pennsylvania, both the European rulers in the Americas and the Europeans they ruled agreed with the theory that there was one true religion and that it should be established by government.

It followed, in the mind of almost every European living in the 1600s who expressed an opinion on the subject, that religious institutions should be supported by taxes, and that the church should control education and social services. Thus the activities later undertaken by American nonprofits were conducted, during the colonial period, by established, tax-supported churches and church agencies that were in a very real sense instruments of government. Certainly the early legislatures of both Massachusetts and Virginia made concerted efforts to put these ideas into practice. John Winthrop, the founding governor of the Massachusetts Bay Colony, expressed this idea vividly in his lay sermon, *Model of Christian Charity,* one of the most influential statements in all of American history. A similar view prevailed among the Catholics who proclaimed the power of New France in the region that reached as far west as the Great Lakes in 1671.

1

The Statute of Charitable Uses, 1601

In 1601, just before the end of her reign, Elizabeth I accepted two laws that put into effect key elements of the new relationship between church and state. These laws continued in effect throughout the colonial period, and they continued to affect both legislation and court decisions long after the American Revolution.

The *Statute of Charitable Uses* addressed problems familiar to modern American readers despite its old-fashioned language (it was written at a time when Shakespeare was still producing new plays in London and when scholars were completing the King James translation of the Bible) and its use of bishops to enforce civil law. The complex description of legal authorities in its fourth paragraph reflects the intricate complexities of British government, in which distinct legal officials served in effect as Lord Chancellor for separate parts of the realm, playing the part that an attorney general plays in the government of a state in the United States. The last three paragraphs of the act reflect a phenomenon not unknown in modern America: the granting of exceptions to favored institutions, in this case Oxford and Cambridge, several notable secondary schools, and certain churches, cities and towns, etc.

The *Statute of Charitable Uses* is important to students of America's nonprofit sector for several reasons. It reflected the dominant position of the established church in Britain and hence (in theory at least) in the American colonies: consider, for example, the implications for religious dissenters (Presbyterians, Congregationalists, Dutch Reformed, Quakers, Baptists) of the provision that a bishop of the Church of England head every investigation into allegations—including allegations of religious irregularity—against charitable boards and directors. Many colonists found this power of the established church oppressive and were glad to get rid of religious establishment after the American Revolution.

The *Statute of Charitable Uses* included, in its second paragraph, a list of the legitimate objects of charity that continued to influence U.S. courts and legislatures into the twentieth century. Even more generally, the *Statute* acknowledged the fact that the trustees and officials of charitable institutions sometimes misused assets under their care and established a means by which they could be forced to be accountable to the public.

QUEEN AND PARLIAMENT OF GREAT BRITAIN

The Statute of Charitable Uses

AN ACT TO REDRESS THE MISEMPLOYMENT OF LANDS, GOODS, STOCKS, AND
MONEY HERETOFORE GIVEN TO CHARITABLE USES

1601

Whereas lands, tenements, rents, annuities, profits, inheritances, goods, chattels, money, and stocks of money have been heretofore given limited appointed and assigned, as well by the Queen's most excellent majesty and her most noble progenitors, as by sundry other well disposed persons.

Some for relief of aged, impotent, and poor people, some for maintenance of sick and maimed soldiers and marines, schools of learning, free schools, and scholars in universities, some for repair of bridges, ports, havens, causeways, churches, seabanks, and highways, some for education and preferment of orphans, some for or towards relief stock or maintenance for houses of correction, some for marriages of poor maids, some for support, aid and help of young tradesmen, handicraftsmen, and persons decayed, and others for relief or redemption of prisoners or captives, and for aid or ease of any poor inhabitant concerning payment of Fifteens [a tax], setting out of soldiers and other taxes.

Which land, tenements, rents, annuities, profits, inheritances, goods, chattels, money, and stocks of money nevertheless have not been employed according to the charitable intents of the givers and founders thereof, by reason of fraudulant breeches of trust and negligence in those that should pay, deliver, and employ the same:

For redress and remedies whereof, be it enacted by authority of this present Parliament, that it shall and may be lawful to and for the Lord Chancellor or keeper of the great seal of England for the time being, and for the Chancellor of the Duchy of Lancaster for the time being for lands within the county Palantine of Lancaster, from time to time to award commissions under the great seal of England, or the seal of the county, Palatine, as this case shall require, into all or any part or parts of this realm respectively, according to their several jurisdictions as aforeside, to the Bishop of every several Diocesse and his Chancellor, in case there shall be any bishop of that Diocesse at the time of awarding of the same commissions, and to other persons of good and sound behavior.

Authorizes them thereby, or any fewer or more of them, to inquire, as well by the oathes of twelve lawful men or more of the counts as by all other good and lawful ways and means, of all and singular such gifts, limitations, assignments, and appointments aforeside, and of the abuses, breaches of trust, negligences, misemployments, not employing concealing, defrauding, misconverting, or misgovernments, of any land, tenements, rents, annuities, profits, inheritances, goods, chattels, money, stocks of money heretofore given limited appointed or assigned, to or for any the charitable and godly uses before rehearsed.

And after the said commissioners or any fewer or more of them, upon calling the parties intrested in any such lands, tenement, rents, annuities, profits, goods, chattels, money, and stocks of money, shall make inquiry by the oaths of twelve men or more of the said county, whereunto the said parties interested shall and may have and take their lawful challenge and challenges.

And upon such inquiry hearing and exchanges thereof set down such orders, judgements, and decrees, as the said lands, tenements, rents, annuities, profits, goods, chattels, money, and stocks of money may be duly and faithfully employed, to and for such of the charitable uses and intents before rehearsed respectively, for which they were given limited assigned or appointed by the donors and founders thereof.

Which orders, judgements, and decrees, not being contrary or repugnant to the orders, statutes, or decrees of the donors or founders, shall by the authority of this present Parliament stand firm and good according to the tenor and purport thereof, and shall be executed accordingly, until the same shall be undone or altered by the Lord Chancellor of England or lord keeper of the great seal of England, or the Chancellor of the county, Palatine of Lancaster, respectively within their several jurisdictions, upon complaint by any party grieved, to be made to them.

Provided always, that neither this act, nor any thing therein contained, shall in any way extend to any land, tenements, rents, annuities, profits, goods, chattels, money, or stocks of money, given, limited, appointed, or assigned, or which shall be given, limited, appointed, or assigned, to any college hall or house of learning within the Universities of Oxford or Cambridge, or to the College of Westminster, Eton, or Winchester, or any of them, or any cathedral collegiate church within this realm.

And provided also, that neither this act nor anything therein shall extend to any city or town corporate, or to any of the land or tenements given to the uses aforesaid within any such city or town corporate, where there is a special governor or governors, appointed to govern or direct such land, tenements, or things disposed to any the uses aforesaid; neither to any college hospital or free school which special visitors or governors or overseer appointed them by their founders.

Provided also and be it enacted by the authority aforesaid, that neither this act nor anything therein contained shall be anyway prejudicial or hurtful to the jurisdiction or power of the ordinary; but that may be lawful in every cause, execute, and perform the same as though this act had never been made.

2

The Elizabethan Poor Law, 1601

The *Elizabethan Poor Law,* which dates from the same year as the *Statute of Charitable Uses,* attempted to deal with one of the great social problems of its time, the massive relocation of people from long-established rural communities. Driven from ancient homes by the conversion of common lands into "enclosed" fields for the local lord's sheep and by the increase of population, and attracted to rapidly growing port towns and cities by the opportunity for work, thousands of English families found themselves at the beginning of the seventeenth century far from their places of birth and unable to support themselves. To a modern reader one of the striking features of the *Poor Law* is the fact that it treated church parishes as agencies of the national government and empowered parish officials to secure court orders to enforce their decisions.

The *Poor Law* stated that church parishes must care for those who were unable to care for themselves. In the first instance, the churchwardens and overseers of the poor were to place them at work, in service or in an apprenticeship. If sufficient work was lacking, or if a person was unable to work, the law (section VII) required that he or she be placed under the care of relatives. In the last resort, the law required that the taxpayers of each parish must pay what was necessary, or be liable to have their property seized and sold (section IV).

The Poor Law also stipulated that each parish was responsible only for those who were "settled," usually by birth, within its borders. In effect, church authorities enforced a system of residential permits. It seemed practical to assign this task to the churches, because they also served as public records offices: each Church Register was supposed to note every christening, marriage, and death that occurred in the parish.

QUEEN AND PARLIAMENT OF GREAT BRITAIN

The Elizabethan Poor Law

1601

Be it enacted by the authority of this present Parliament, that the church-wardens of every parish, and four, three or two substantial household-ers there, as shall be thought meet, having respect to the proportion and greatness of the same parish and parishes, to be nominated yearly in Easter week, or within one month after Easter, under the hand and seal of two or more justices of the peace in the same county, whereof one to be of the *Quorum,* dwelling in or near the same parish or division where the same parish cloth lie, shall be called overseers of the poor of the same parish: And they, or the greater part of them, shall take order from time to time, by, and with the consent of two or more such justices of peace as it aforesaid, for setting to work the children of all such whose parents shall not by the said churchwardens and overseers, or the greater part of them, be thought able to keep and maintain their children: And also for setting to work all such persons, married or unmarried, having no means to maintain them, and use no ordinary and daily trade of life to get their living by: And also to raise weekly or otherwise (by taxation of every inhabitant, parson, vicar and other, and of every occupier of lands, houses, tithes impropriate, propriations of tithes, coal-mines, or saleable underwoods in the said parish, in such competent sum and sums of money as they shall think fit) a convenient stock of flax, hemp, wool, thread, iron, and other necessary ware and stuff, to set the poor on work: And also competent sums of money for and towards the neces-sary relief of the lame, impotent, old, blind, and such other among them, being poor, and not able to work and also for the putting out of such children to be apprentices, to be gathered out of the same parish, ac-cording to the ability of the same parish, and to do and execute all other things as well for the disposing of the said stock, as otherwise concern-ing the premisses, as to them shall seem convenient:

II. Which said churchwardens and overseers to be nominated, or such of them as shall not be let by sickness or other just excuse, to be allowed by two such justices of peace or more as is aforesaid, shall meet together at the least once every month in the church of the said parish, upon the Sunday in the afternoon, after divine service, there to con-sider of some good course to be taken, and of some meet order to be set down in the premisses; (2) and shall within four days after the end of their year, and after other overseers nominated as aforesaid, make and yield up to such two justices of peace, as is aforesaid, a true and perfect account of all sums of money by them received, or rated and assessed, and not received, and also of such stock as shall be in their hands, or in the hands of any of the poor to work, and of all other things concerning their said office, (3) and such sum or sums of money as shall be in their hands, shall pay and deliver over to the said churchwardens and overseers newly nominated and appointed as aforesaid; (4) upon pain that every one of them absenting themselves without lawful cause as aforesaid, from such monthly meeting for the purpose aforesaid, or being negligent in their office, or in the execution of the orders aforesaid, being made by and with the assent of the said justices of peace, or any two of them before-mentioned, to forefeit for every such default of absence or negligence twenty shillings.

III. And be it also enacted, that if the said justices of peace do perceive, that the inhabitants of any parish are not able to levy among themselves sufficient sums of money for the purposes aforesaid; that then the said two justices shall and may tax, rate and assess, as aforesaid; any other of other parishes, or out of any parish, within the hundred where the said parish is, to pay such sum and sums of money to the churchwardens and overseers of the said poor parish, for the said purposes, as the said justices shall think fit, according to the intent of this law: (2) And if the said hundred shall not be thought to the said justices able and fit to relieve the said several parishes not able to provide for themselves as aforesaid; then the justices of peace, at their general quarter-sessions, or the greater number of them, shall rate, and assess as aforesaid, any other of other parishes, or out of any parish within the said county, for the purposes aforesaid, as in their discretion shall seem fit.

IV. And that it shall be lawful, as well for the present as subsequent churchwardens and overseers, or any, of them, by warrant from any two such justices of peace as is aforesaid, to levy as well the said sums of money and all arrearages, of every one that shall refuse to contribute according as they shall be assessed, by distress and sale of the offenders goods, as the sums of money or stock which shall be behind upon any account to be made as aforesaid, rendering to the parties the overplus, (2) and in defect of such distress, it shall be lawful for any such two justices of the peace, to commit him or them to the common gaol of the county, there to remain without bail or mainprize, until payment of the said sum, arrearages and stock: (3) And the said justices of peace or any one of them, to send to the house of correction or common gaol, such as shall not employ themselves to work, being appointed thereunto as aforesaid: (4) And also any such two justices of peace to commit to the said prison every one of the said churchwardens and overseers, which shall refuse to account, there to remain without bail or mainprize, until he have made a true account, and satisfied and paid so much as upon the said account shall be remaining in his hands.

V. And be it further enacted, that it shall be lawful for the said churchwardens and overseers, or the greater part of them, by the assent of any two justices of the peace aforesaid, to bind any such children, as aforesaid to be apprentices, where they shall see convenient, till such man-child shall come to the age of four and twenty years, and such woman-child to the age of one and twenty years, or the time of her marriage; the same to be as effectual to all purposes as if such child were of full age, and by indenture of covenant bound him or her self. (2) And to the intent that necessary places of habitation may more conveniently be provided for such poor impotent people; (3) Be it enacted by the authority aforesaid, that it shall and may be lawful for the said churchwardens and overseers, or the greater part of them, by the leave of the lord or lords of the manor, whereof any waste or common within their parish is or shall be parcel, and upon agreement before with him or them made in writing, under the hands and seals of the said lord or lords, or otherwise, according to any order to be set down by the.justices of peace of the said county at their general quarter sessions, or the greater part of them, by like leave and agreement of the said lord or lords in writing under his or their hands and seals, to erect, build, and set up in fit and convenient places of habitation, in such waste or common, at the general charges of the parish, or otherwise of the hundred or county, as aforesaid, to be taxed, rated and gathered in manner before expressed, convenient houses of dwelling for the said impotent poor; (4) and also to place inmates, or more families than one in one cottage or house; one act made in the one and thirtieth year of her majesty's reign, intitled, *An Act against the erecting and maintaining of Cottages,* or any thing therein contained, to the contrary not withstanding: (5) Which cottages and places for inmates shall not at any time after be used or employed to or for any other habitation, but only for impotent and poor of the same parish, that shall be there placed from time to time by the churchwardens and overseers of the poor of the same parish, or the most part of them, upon the pains and forfeitures contained in the said former act made in the said one and thirtieth year of her majesty's reign.

VI. Provided always, that if any person or persons shall find themselves grieved with any sess or tax, or other act done by the said churchwardens, and other persons, or by the said justices of peace; that then it shall be lawful for the justices of peace at their general quarter sessions, or the greater number of them, to take such order therein as to them shall be thought convenient; and the same to conclude and bind all the said parties.

VII. And be it further enacted, that the father and grandfather, and the mother and grandmother, and the children of every poor, old, blind, lame, and impotent person or other poor person not able to work, being of sufficient ability, shall, at their own charges, relieve and maintain every such person in that manner, and according to that rate, as by the justices of peace of that county where such sufficient persons dwell, or the greater number of them, at their general quarter sessions shall be assessed; (2) upon pain that every one of them shall forfeit twenty shillings for every month, which they shall fail therein.

3

Brother Juan de Escalona,
Report to the Viceroy of Mexico on Conditions at Santa Fe, 1601

The connection between church and state in Spanish America is made clear in the extraordinary *Report* of Franciscan Brother Juan de Escalona, to the Viceroy of Mexico, in 1601. This is the report of a Catholic religious leader to the chief civil authority of his region—a report not about religious matters so much as about civil misconduct. The *Report* dates from 1601, the same year as the *Statute of Charitable Uses* and half a dozen years before the first permanent British settlement in North America at Jamestown, Virginia. This fact reminds us that much of the territory that was eventually incorporated into the United States had already been claimed from its native inhabitants and been placed under the government of European Catholics before the Protestant British established themselves on the continent.

FRANCISCAN BROTHER JUAN DE ESCALONA

Report to the Viceroy Regarding Spanish Rule in New Mexico

October 1, 1601

Would that I could have spoken to your lordship in person and have given you more directly the information that now I must of necessity put down in writing, lest I be an unfaithful servant of the Lord. I can-

Reprinted with some excisions from George P. Hammond and Agapito Rey, *Don Juan de Onate, Colonizer of New Mexico, 1595–1628* (Albuquerque: University of New Mexico Press, 1953), by permission of the publisher.

not help the situation as much in this I say as by a personal conference and I would have preferred that someone else should make this report. As prelate and protector, however, sent to this land to prevent evil and to seek what is good for God's children, I must inform your lordship of what is and has been transpiring here, for although reports and communications have been sent from here about matters in this land, they do not tell the actual truth about what has been going on since the arrival of Governor Don Juan de Oñate in this province. I shall tell about these matters, not because I wish to meddle in the affairs of others, but because, as prelate, I am under obligation, by informing his majesty and your lordship, to seek a remedy for the difficulties and obstacles that prevent the preaching of the gospel and the conversion of these souls.

The first and foremost difficulty, from which have sprung all the evil and the ruin of this land, is the fact that this conquest was entrusted to a man of such limited resources as Don Juan de Oñate. The result was that soon after he entered the land, his people began to perpetrate many offenses against the natives and to plunder their pueblos of the corn they had gathered for their own sustenance; here corn is God, for they have nothing else with which to support themselves.

Because of this situation and because the Spaniard asked the natives for blankets as tribute, even before teaching them the meaning of God, the Indians began to get restless, abandon their pueblos, and take to the mountains.

The governor did not want to sow a community plot to feed his people, although we friars urged him to do so, and the Indians agreed to it so that they would not be deprived of their food. This effort was all of no avail, and now the Indians have to provide everything. As a result, all the corn they had saved for years past has been consumed, and not a kernel is left over for them. The whole land has thus been reduced to such need that the Indians drop dead from starvation wherever they live; and they eat dirt and charcoal ground up with some seeds and a little corn in order to sustain life. Any Spaniard who gets his fill of tortillas here feels as if he has obtained a grant of nobility.

Your lordship must not believe that the Indians part willingly with their corn, or the blankets with which they cover themselves; on the contrary, this extortion is done by threats and force of arms, the soldiers burning some of the houses and killing the Indians. This was the cause of the Acoma war, as I have clearly established after questioning friars, captains, and soldiers. And the war which was recently waged against the Jumanas started the same way. In these conflicts, more than eight hundred men, women, and children were killed, and three pueblos burned. Their supplies of food were also burned, and this at a time when there was such great need. . . .

In addition to the aforesaid, all of the provisions which the governor and his men took along on this new expedition they took from the

Indians. I was to have gone on this journey, but on observing the great outrages against the Indians and the wars waged against them without rhyme or reason, I did not dare to accompany the governor; instead I sent two friars to go with him. This expedition would have been impossible if the Indians had not furnished him with the provisions and supplies needed, and if I, in the name of his majesty, had not provided him with sixty mules, six carts, and two negroes that your lordship had given us to come to this land. My reason for giving this assistance, even though your lordship had ordered just the opposite, was that the said exploration could not have been undertaken without it, nor could the gospel have been preached to these people; and this was important, especially when we were already at the borders of their lands and the church and his majesty had sent us for this purpose. Furthermore, if this expedition had not been made, all the soldiers would have run away, for all are here against their will, owing to the great privations they endure. To protect his majesty's interests, the governor assumed responsibility for the damages caused by his people and gave me three honorable men with property in New Spain as guarantors. The soldiers and captains provided the rest of the arms and horses, as he had nothing of his own. For lack of these he left here some servants whom he could not take along.

I have told all this to make it clear that the governor does not have the resources to carry out the discovery of these lands. I do not hesitate to say that even if he were to stay here for twenty thousand years, he could never discover what there is to be discovered in this land, unless his majesty should aid him or take over the whole project. Moreover, the governor has oppressed his people so that they are all discontented and anxious to get away, both on account of the sterility of the land and of his harsh conduct toward them.

I do not hesitate to say that his majesty could have discovered this land with fifty well-armed Christian men, giving them the necessary things for this purpose, and that what these fifty men might discover could be placed under the royal crown and the conquest effected in a Christian manner without outraging or killing these poor Indians, who think that we are all evil and that the king who sent us here is ineffective and a tyrant. By so doing we would satisfy the wishes of our mother church, which, not without long consideration and forethought and illuminated by the Holy Spirit, entrusted these conquests and the conversions of souls to the kings of Castile, our lords, acknowledging in them the means, Christianity, and holiness for an undertaking as heroic as is that of winning souls for God.

Because of these matters (and others that I am not telling), we cannot preach the gospel now, for it is despised by these people on account of our great offenses and the harm we have done them. At the same time it is not desirable to abandon this land, either for the service of God or the conscience of his majesty since many souls have already been baptized. Besides, this place where we are now established is a good stepping stone and site from which to explore this whole land. From the City of Mexico to this place we have traveled four hundred leagues, always northward; and from here we can go to the South sea, to the east, or continue northward. If this land should be abandoned, it could not be occupied again without the expenditure of a very large sum of money.

Eager to bring good tidings to his majesty, some people have given free rein to their pens, telling of things which do not exist in this land, making provinces out of pueblos (they called Taos and Santa Domingo provinces). Similarly, they describe the other pueblos as provinces, even though the largest will not contain more than two or three hundred people. The entire land discovered thus far does not contain twenty thousand Indians, and all is disorganized, for they have no rulers to govern them. They are, however, the best infidel people that I have seen; they govern themselves in an orderly manner through natural law.

If his majesty should want to maintain this land without a large expenditure from his royal treasury, he could distribute these pueblos among the married men who are here and who have spent their resources in this expedition and now find themselves very poor; he could also help them with some succor from Mexico for a time, until the land quiets down and the Indians are converted. This would enable the settlers to get along, and this great region could be discovered little by litttle. Otherwise it will be impossible to live here or remain in this land, for it is very sterile and cold and the Spaniards face the prospect of going about naked like the Indians.

We have promising reports that to the south and northwest there are large settlements and good land; and we might even reach a place where the ships that come from China to reconnoiter the coast of California would be able to aid us here and establish commerce with New Spain, which would be a great help. No silver has been found in this land thus far. This I believe was ordained by God so that the Spaniards, instead of remaining here, would go forward for the good that will come to those souls by their conversion. We have reports of this land of Topia—that it extends directly northwest and that it is rich in silver, the Indians wearing articles of silver in their ears and bracelets on their wrists.

May your lordship permit the Carmelite friars, or those of any other order acceptable to your lordship, to come to help us in this godly work; there are many languages here and we are few and unable to attend to everything. All that your lordship gave us is here for the use of everyone, and it will not be necessary to spend more of his majesty's funds, except some for food and clothing which have been used up in the course of time. In case no other friars or priests are sent, I believe it would be best if the barefooted friars or friars from Spain were allowed to come.

All the Indians here are newly arrived from the interior; they say that there are many people farther on and that, because there was no room for all there, they moved away in search of a place where they might live and till the soil. If this undertaking is to prosper, it would be well if your lordship at the outset would order that these Indians be gathered into congregations and be taught the Spanish language, as it was done in Peru. By so doing we could get along with fewer ministers. The natives are anxious to learn Spanish; and by establishing schools for the children, it could easily be accomplished. . . .

4

John Winthrop, *A Model of Christian Charity,* 1630

The first English settlers in Massachusetts were the Pilgrims, who arrived at Plymouth in 1620. Ten years later a larger and better-equipped band of Puritans, under the leadership of John Winthrop, an attorney and country gentleman, landed at Boston. Winthrop preached his famous sermon, calling on his associates to provide the world with *A Model of Christian Charity,* at the outset of the venture, before the Puritans reached North American soil.

A Model of Christian Charity is notable for its emphasis on hierarchy, interdependence, and "covenant" or freely concluded agreement. Winthrop begins with a discussion of the proper relations between rich and poor. He goes on to argue that "law of nature" and the "law of grace" both require that assistance be offered to those in need—and that aid should be offered on the basis of brotherly love, not as an obligation or privilege of the great toward the poor.

After developing the notion that "all true Christians are of one body in Christ," and are as fully tied to one another as are the parts of the body, Winthrop asserts that the Puritans have formed themselves into a unified Christian body "by mutual consent," and have entered into a covenant with one another and with God. Hence they had voluntarily agreed to work together to create in New England a society so perfect "that men shall say of succeeding plantations: 'The Lord make it like that of New England' . . . for we shall be as a city upon a hill."

Winthrop's sermon became one of the most quoted documents in American history, not least because it provides a model exhortation from a leader to those launching any great enterprise.

JOHN WINTHROP

A Modell of Christian Charity

1630

God Almighty in his most holy and wise providence
hath so disposed of the condition of mankind, as in
all times some must be rich some poor, some high
and eminent in power and dignity, others mean and
in subjection.

The reason hereof:

First, to hold conformity with the rest of His works, being delighted to show forth the glory of His wisdom in the variety and difference of the creatures and the glory of His power, in ordering all these
differences for the preservation and good of the whole, and the glory
of His greatness: that as it is the glory of princes to have many officers,
so this great King will have many stewards, counting Himself more
honored in dispensing His gifts to man by man than if He did it by His
own immediate hand.

Secondly, that He might have the more occasion to manifest the
work of His spirit: first, upon the wicked in moderating and restraining
them, so that the rich and mighty should not eat up the poor, nor the
poor and despised rise up against their superiors and shake off their
yoke; secondly, in the regenerate, in exercising His graces in them—as
in the great ones, their love, mercy, gentleness, temperance, etc., in the
poor and inferior sort, their faith, patience, obedience, etc.

Thirdly, that every man might have need of other, and from hence
they might be all knit more nearly together in the bond of brotherly
affection. From hence it appears plainly that no man is made more honorable than another or more wealthy, etc., out of any particular and
singular respect to himself, but for the glory of his creator and the common good of the creature man. Therefore God still reserves the property
of these gifts to Himself. . . . He claims their service as His due: "Honor
the Lord with thy riches."

All men being thus (by divine providence) ranked into two sorts,
rich and poor, under the first are comprehended all such as are able to
live comfortably by their own means duly improved, and all others are
poor. . . .

There are two rules whereby we are to walk, one towards another:

justice and mercy. . . . [S]ometimes there may be an occasion of show-ing mercy to a rich man in some sudden danger of distress, and also doing of mere justice to a poor man in regard to some particular con-tract.

There is likewise a double law by which we are regulated in our conversation, one towards another: . . . the law of nature and the law of grace, or the moral law or the law of the Gospel. . . .

By the first of these laws [the moral law], man, as he was enabled so, [is] commanded to love his neighbor as himself; upon this ground stand all the precepts of the moral law, which concerns our dealings with men. To apply this to the works of mercy, this law requires two things: first, that every man afford his help to another in every want or distress; secondly, that he perform this out of the same affection which makes him careful of his own good according to that of our savior: "Whatsoever you would that men should do to you." This was practiced by Abraham and Lot in entertaining the angels and the old man of Gibea. . . .

The law of the Gospel propounds likewise a difference of seasons and occasions. There is a time when a Christian must sell all and give to the poor as they did in the Apostles' times; there is a time also when a Christian, though they give not all yet, must give beyond their ability, as they of Macedonia. Likewise, community of perils calls for extraordi-nary liberality, and so does community in some special service for the church. Lastly, when there is no other means whereby our Christian brother may be relieved in this distress, we must help him beyond our ability, rather than tempt God in putting him upon help by miraculous or extraordinary means.

> This duty of mercy is exercised in the kinds, Giving, Lending, and Forgiving.
>
> Question: What rule shall a man observe in giving in respect of the measure?
>
> Answer: If the time and occasion be extraordinary he is to give out of his abundance—let him lay aside, as God has blessed him. If the time and occasion be extraordinary he must be ruled by them; taking this with all that then a man cannot likely do too much especially, if he may leave himself and his family under probable means of comfortable subsistance.

> Objection: A man must lay up for posterity, the fathers lay up for posterity and children, and he is worse than an infidel that provide not for his own.
>
> Answer: For the first, it is plain, that it being spoken by way of comparison it must be meant of the ordinary and usual course

of fathers and cannot extend to times and occasions extraordinary; for . . . it is without question, that he is worse then an infidel who through his own sloth and voluptuousness shall neglect to provide for his family.

Objection: The wise men's eyes are in his head (saith Salomon) and foresee the plague, therefore we must forecast and lay up against evil times when he or his may strand in need of all he can gather.

Answer: This very argument Salomon uses to persuade to liberality. Ecclesiastes: "cast thy bread upon the waters etc.: for your knowest not what evil may come upon the land." Luke 16: "make you friends of the riches of iniquity."

You will ask how this shall be? Very well. For first he that gives to the poor lends to the lord, and he will repay him even in this life an life an hundred fold to him or his. The righteous is ever merciful and lends, and his seed enjoy the blessing. And besides we know what advantage it will be to us in the day of account, when many such witnesses shall stand forth for us to witness the improvement of our talent. And I would know of those who plead so much for laying up for time to come, whether they hold that to be Gospel— Matthew: 16.19. "Lay not up for yourselves treasures upon earth etc." If they acknowledge it to what extent will they allow it? If only to those primitive times, let them consider the reason whereupon our Savior grounds it. The first is that they are subject to the moths, the rust, the thief. Secondly, they will steal away the heart, where the treasure is there will the heart be also. . . .

Question: What rule must we observe in lending?

Answer: You must observe whether your brother has present or probable, or possible means of repaying them, if there be none of these, you must give him according to his necessity, rather than lend him as he requires; if he has present means of repaying you, you are to look at him, not as an Act of mercy, but by way of Commerce, wherein you are to walk by the rule of Justice, but if his means of repaying you be only probable or possible then is he an object of your mercy you must lend him, though there be danger of losing it. . . .

Qustion: What rule must we observe in forgiving?

Answer: Whether you did lend by way of Commerce or in mercy. If he have nothing to pay you must forgive him (except in cause where you have a surety or a lawfull pleadge). Every seventh year the Creditor was to quit that he lent to his brother if he were poor. . . . In all these and like cases Christ was a general rule, Matthew 7:22: "Whatsoever you would that men should do to you do you the same to them also."

Question: What rule must we observe and walk by in cause of community of peril?

Answer: The same as before, but with more enlargement towards others and less respect towards ourselves, and our own right. Hence it was that in the primitive Church they sold all, had all things in Common, neither did any man say that that which he possessed was his own.

The definition which the Scripture gives us of love is that Love is the bond of perfection. First, it is a bond, or ligament. Secondly, it makes the work perfect. There is no body but consists of parts and that which knits these parts together gives the body its perfection, because it makes each part so contiguous to other as thereby they do mutually participate with each other, both in strength and infirmity in pleasure and pain, to instance in the most perfect of all bodies, Christ and his church make one body. So this definition is right: Love is the bond of perfection.

From hence we may frame these conclusions.
1. First, all true Christians are of one body in Christ. You are the body of Christ and members of your part.
2. The ligaments of this body which knit together are love.
3. No body can be perfect which wants its proper ligaments.
4. All the parts of this body being thus united are made so contiguous in a special relation as they must needs partake of each others' strength and infirmity, joy and sorrow, weal and woe. If one member suffers all suffer with it, if one be in honor, all rejoice with it.
5. This sensibleness and sympathy of each other's conditions will necessarily infuse into each part a native desire and endeavor, to strengthen, defend, preserve, and comfort the other.

If any shall object that it is not possible that love should be bred or upheld without hope of requital, it is granted but that is not our cause, for this love is always under reward: it never gives, but it always receives with advantage.

Firstly, . . . among the members of the same body, love and affection are reciprocal in a most equal and sweet kind of commerce.

Secondly, in regard of the pleasure and content that the exercise of love carries with it, as we may see: in the natural body the mouth is at the pains to receive and mince the food which serves for the nourishment of all the other parts of the body, yet it has no cause to complain; for, First, the other parts send back by secret passages a due proportion of the same nourishment in a better form for the strengthening and comforting the mouth; Secondly, the labor of the mouth is accompanied with such pleasure and content as far exceeds the pains it takes: so is it in all the labor of love, among Christians, the party loving, reaps love again as was shewed before, which the soul covets more than all the wealth in the world.

[Thirdly], nothing yields more pleasure and content to the soul then when it finds that which it may love fervently, for to love and live beloved is the soul's paradise, both here and in heaven: In the State of Wedlock there be many comforts to bear out the troubles of that Condition; but let such as have tried the most, say if there be any sweetness in that Condition comparable to the exercise of mutual love.

From the former Considerations arises these Conclusions.

1. First, this love among Christians is a real thing not imaginary.
2. This love is as absolutely necessary to the being of the body of Christ, as the sinewes and other ligaments of a natural body are to the being of the body.
3. This love is a divine spiritual nature, free, active, strong, couragious, permanent, under valuing all things beneath its proper object, and of all the graces that makes us nearer to resemble the virtues of our heavenly father.
4. It rests in the love and welfare of its beloved, for the full and certain knowledge of these truths concerning the nature, use, and excellency of this grace, that which the holy ghost has left recorded may give full satisfaction which is needful for every true member of this lovely body of the Lord Jesus, to work upon their hearts, by prayer, meditation, continual exercise at least of the special power of this grace, till Christ be formed in them and they in him all in each other knit together by this bond of love.

It rests now to make some application of this discourse by the present design which gave the occasion of writing of it. Herein are four things to be propounded: first the persons, secondly, the work, thirdly, the end, fourthly the means.

1. For the persons, we are a company professing ourselves fellow members of Christ, in which respect only, though we were absent from each other many miles, and had our employments as far distant, yet we ought to account ourselves knit together by this bond of love, and live in the exercise of it, if we would have comfort of our being in Christ.

2. For the work we have in hands, it is by mutual consent, through a special overruling providence and a more than an ordinary approbation of the churches of Christ, to seek out a place of cohabitation and consortship, under a due form of government both civil and ecclesiastical. In such cases as this, the care of the public must oversway all private respects by which not only conscience but mere civil policy does bind us; for it is a true rule that particular estates cannot subsist in the ruin of the public.

3. The end is to improve our lives to do more service to the Lord, the comfort and increase of the body of Christ whereof we are members, that ourselves and posterity may be the better preserved from the common corruptions of this evil world, to serve the Lord and work out our salvation under the power and purity of His holy ordinances.

4. For the means whereby this must be effected, they are two-fold:

> Conformity with the work and end we aim at, these we see are extraordinary, therefore we must not content ourselves with usual, ordinary means: whatsoever we did or ought to have done when we lived in England, the same must we do and more all so where we go . . . we must love one another with a pure heart; fervently we must bear one anothers burthens, we must not look only on our own things, but also on the things of our brethren,

> Neither must we think that the lord will bear with such failings at our hands as he does from those among whom we have lived, and that for three Reasons.

>> i. In regard of the more near bond of marriage, between him and us, wherein he has taken us to be his after a most strict and peculiar manner which will make him the more jealous of our love and obedience so he tells the people of Israel, you only have I know of all the families of the earth therefore will I punish you for your transgressions.

>> ii. Because the lord will be sanctified in them that come near him. We know that there were many that corrupted the service of the Lord, some setting up altars before his own, others offering both strange fire and strange sacrifices also; yet there came no fire from heaven, or other sudden Judgement upon them as did upon Nadab and Abihu who yet we may think did not sin presumptuously.

>> iii. When God gives a special Commission he looks to

have it strictly observed in every Article, when he gave Saul a Commission to destroy Amaleck he failed in one of the least, and that upon a fair pretence, it lost him the kingdom, which should have been his reward, if he had observed his Commission.

Thus stands the cause between God and us: we are entered into covenant with Him for this work; we have taken out a commission, the Lord hath given us leave to draw our own articles. We have professed to enterprise these actions upon these and these ends; we have hereupon besought Him of favor and blessing.

Now if the Lord shall please to hear us and bring us in peace to the place we desire, then hath He ratified this convenant and sealed our Commission, and will expect a strict performance of the articles contained in it.

But if we shall neglect the observation of these articles which are the ends we have propounded, and dissembling with our God, shall fall to embrance this present world and prosecute our carnal intentions, seeking great things for ourselves and our posterity, the Lord will surely break out in wrath against us, be revenged of such a perjured people, and make us know the price of the breach of such a convenant.

Now the only way to avoid this shipwreck and to provide for our posterity is to follow the counsel of Micah: to do justly, to love mercy, to walk humbly with our God. For this end, we must be knit together in this work as one man. We must entertain each other in brotherly affection; we must be willing to abridge ourselves of our superfluities, for the supply of others' necessities; we must uphold a familiar commerce together in all meekness, gentleness, patience and liberality. We must delight in each other, make others' conditions our own, rejoice together, mourn together, labor and suffer together: always having before our eyes our commission and community in the work, our community as members of the same body.

So shall we keep the unity of the spirit in the bond of peace, the Lord will be our God and delight to dewell among us, as His own people, and will command a blessing upon us in all our Ways, so that we shall see much more of His wisdom, power, goodness, and truth than formerly we have been acquainted with. We shall find that the God of Israel is among us, when ten of us shall be able to resist a thousand of our enemies, when He shall make us a praise and glory, that men shall say of succeeding plantations: "The Lord make it like that of New England."

For we must consider that we shall be as a city upon a hill, the eyes of all people are upon us. So that if we shall deal falsely with our God in this work we have undertaken, and so cause Him to withdraw

His present help from us, we shall be made a story and a by-word through the world: we shall open the mouths of enemies to speak evil of the ways of God and all professors for God's sake; we shall shame the faces of many of God's worthy servants, and cause their prayers to be turned into curses upon us, till we be consumed out of the good land whither we are going.

And to shut up this discourse with that exhortation of Moses, that faithful servant of the Lord, in his last farewell to Israel (Deut. 30): Beloved, there is now set before us life and good, death and evil, in that we are commanded this day to love the Lord our God, and to love one another, to walk in His ways and to keep His commandments and His ordinance and His laws and the articles of our covenant with Him, that we may live and be multiplied, and that the Lord our God may bless us in the land whither we go to possess it: but if our hearts shall turn away so that we will not obey, but shall be seduced and worship . . . other gods, our pleasures and profits, and serve them, it is propounded unto us this day, we shall surely perish out of the good land whither we pass over this vast sea to possess it.

Therefore let us choose life,
that we, and our seed,
may live; by obeying his
voice, and cleaving to him,
or he is our life, and
our prosperity.

Written
On Boarde the Arrabella,
On the Atlantic Ocean.
By the Honorable JOHN Winthrop Esquire.
In his passage, (with the great Company of Religious people, of
which Christian Tribes he was the Brave Leader and famous
Governor;) from the Island of Great Brittaine, to New England
in the North America. Anno 1630.

Virginia General Assembly,
Laws Regulating Religion, 1642

Virginia, the site of the first British settlement in the area that would become the United States, was from the beginning governed in religious and social matters by the established Church of England. At least this was the case in theory. In practice, many Virginians were always reluctant to accept the authority and the taxes that the Church of England demanded as its due. Early colonial officials made many formal efforts to impose order and to secure revenues and authority for the church, as this excerpt from the colony's 1642 legislature indicates.

VIRGINIA GENERAL ASSEMBLY

Laws Regulating Religion

1642

That for the Preservation of Purity & Unity of Doctrine & Discipline in the Church, & the right Administration of the Sacraments, no ministers be admitted to officiate in this Country but such as shall produce to the Governor a Testimonial that he hath receiv'd his Ordination from some Bishop in England, & shall then subscribe to be conformable to the Orders & Constitutions of the Church of England & the Laws there establish'd, upon which the Governor is hereby requested to induct the sd minister into any parish, that shall make Presentation of him; And if any other person pretending himself a minister, shall contrary to this Act presume to teach or preach publickly or privately, the Governor & Council are hereby desir'd and impowered to suspend & silence the Person so offending, & upon his obstinate persistence, to compell him to depart the Country with the first Convenience as it hath been formerly provided by the 77th Act made at James City the 2d March, 1642.

That for the making & proportioning of the Levys & Assessments, for building & repairing the Churches & Chappels, Provision for the poor, maintenance of the ministers & each other necessary Uses, & for the more orderly managing all parochial Affairs; Be it enacted that 12 of the most able men of each parish be by the major part of the said parish chose to be a Vestry out of which number the minister & Vestry to make choice of two Church Wardens yearly, & in Case of the Death of any Vestryman or his departure out of the parish, that the said Minister and Vestry make Choice of another to supply his room; And be it further enacted, that none shall be admitted to be of the Vestry, that doth not take the oaths of Allegiance & Supremacy to His Majesty, & subscribe to be conformable to the Doctrine & Discipline of the Church of England.

6

Hugh Peter and Thomas Weld,
New England's First Fruits, 1643

The New England Puritans lost no time in establishing a college to educate ministers for their congregations. Six years after arriving in Boston they launched Harvard College across the Charles River at Cambridge. The college survived its first years, and by 1643 two Puritan leaders, Hugh Peter and Thomas Weld, had prepared (for use in London) what is probably the first fund-raising appeal for an American institution.

In the course of making the case for contributions, Peter and Weld emphasized two facts: Harvard College received significant financial support from the colonial government, and it insisted on Puritan religious orthodoxy from its pupils. Peter and Weld thus sought to assure English Puritans that their contributions would be matched by significant tax monies—from a government elected only by men who held full membership in the Puritan churches. They assured potential donors that the college, backed up by the Puritan oligarchy that controlled Massachusetts, would hold its students to Puritan values.

Puritan investment in Harvard College paid significant dividends. By 1660, when there were 135 college-trained ministers in Massachusetts (about one for every 400 persons in the colony), 116 had attended Harvard.

HUGH PETER AND THOMAS WELD

New England's First Fruits

1643

After God had carried us safe to New England, and we had builded our houses, provided necessaries for our livelihood, reared convenient places for God's worship, and settled the civil government, one of the next things we longed for and looked after was to advance learning and perpetuate it to prosperity, dreading to leave an illiterate ministry to the churches when our present ministers shall lie in the dust. And as we were thinking and consulting how to effect this great work, it pleased God to stir up the heart of one Mr. Harvard (a godly gentleman and a lover of learning, there living amongst us) to give the one half of his estate (it being in all about £1700) towards the erecting of a college, and all his library. After him, another gave £300, others after them cast in more, and the public hand of the state added the rest. The college was, by common consent, appointed to be at Cambridge (a place very pleasant and accommodate) and is called (according to the name of the first founder) Harvard College.

The edifice is very fair and comely within and without, having in it a spacious hall (where they daily meet at common lectures, exercises), and a large library with some books to it, the gifts of divers of our friends, their chambers and studies also fitted for and possessed by the students, and all other rooms of office necessary and convenient, with all needful offices thereto belonging. And by the side of the College, a fair grammar school, for the training up of young scholars and fitting of them for academical learning, that still as they are judged ripe they may be recieved into the College. Of this school, Master Corlet is the master, who hath very well approved himself for his abilities, dexterity and painfulness, in teaching and education of the youth under him.

Over the College is Master Dunster placed as president, a learned, conscionable and industrious man, who hath so trained up his pupils in the tongues and arts, and so seasoned them with the principals of divinity and Christianity, that we have to our great comfort (and in truth, beyond our hopes) beheld their progress in learning and godliness also. The former of these hath appeared in their public declamations in Latin and Greek, and disputations logical and philosophical, which they have been wont (besides their ordinary exercises in the College hall), in the audience of the magistrates, ministers and other scholars, for the probation of their growth in learning, upon set days, constantly every month, to make and uphold. The latter hath been manifested in sundry of them by the savory breathings of their spirits in godly conversation, insomuch that we are confident, if these early blossoms may be cherished and warmed with the influence of the friends of learning and lovers of this pious work, they will, by the help of God, come to happy maturity in a short time.

Over the College are twelve overseers chosen by the General Court: six of them are of the magistrates, the other six of the ministers, who are to promote the best good of it, and (having a power of influence into all persons in it) are to see that every one be diligent and proficient in his proper place.

Rules and precepts that are observed in the College:

1. When any scholar is able to understand Tullius (Cicero) or such like classical Latin author extempore, and make and speak true Latin in verse and prose, *suo ut aiunt marte* ("to stand, as they say, on his own feet"), and decline perfectly the paradigms of nouns and verbs in the Greek tongue, let him then, and not before, be capable of admission into the College.

2. Let every student be plainly instructed and earnestly pressed to consider well: the main end of his life and studies is "to know God and Jesus Christ, which is eternal life" (John 17.3), and therefore to lay Christ in the bottom, as the only foundation of all sound knowledge and learning.

And seeing the Lord only giveth wisdom, let everyone seriously set himself by prayer in secret to seek it of Him. (Prov. 2.3).

3. Everyone shall so exercise himself in reading the scriptures twice a day that he shall be ready to give such an account of his proficiency therein, both in theoretical observations of the language and logic, and in practical and spiritual truths, as his tudor shall require, according to his ability: seeing "the entrance of the word giveth light; it giveth understanding unto the simple" (Psal. 119. 130).

4. That they, eschewing all profanation of God's name, attributes, word, ordinances and times of worship, do study with good conscience carefully to retain God and the love of His truth in their minds. Else let them know that (notwithstanding their learning) God may give them up "to strong delusions" (II Thess. 2. 11, 12), and in the end "to a reprobate" (Rom. 1. 28).

5. That they studiously redeem the time, observe the general hours appointed for all the students, and the special hours for their own classes; and then diligently attend the lectures, without disturbance by word or gesture. And if in anything they doubt, they shall inquire as of their fellows, so (in case of "non-satisfaction") modestly of their tutors.

6. None shall, under any pretense whatsoever, frequent the company and society of such men as lead an unfit and dissolute life.

Nor shall any, without his tutor's leave or (in his absense) the call of parents or guardians, go abroad to other towns.

7. Every scholar shall be present in his tutor's chamber at the seventh hour in the morning, immediately after the sound of the bell, at his opening the scripture and prayer; so also at the fifth hour at night, and then give account of his own private reading (as aforesaid in particular the third), and constantly attend lectures in the hall at the hours appointed. But if any (without the necessary impediment) shall absent himself from prayer or lectures, he shall be liable to admonition, if he offend above once a week.

8. If any scholar shall be found to transgress any of the laws of God or the school, after twice admonition, he shall be liable, if not *adultus*, to correction; if *adultus*, his name shall be given up to the overseers of the College, that he may be admonished at the public monthly act.

Claude Jean Allouz, S.J., *Account of the Ceremony Proclaiming New France,* 1671

France, like Spain a Catholic country, also laid claim to much of North America. This eyewitness account, by the Jesuit Father Claude Jean Allouz, provides a vivid description of the ceremony proclaiming French control of the area north of the Great Lakes. The fact that the ceremony was at least as much a religious as a civil or military ceremony demonstrates the way French authorities, like their British and Spanish counterparts, intertwined religious and civil government in their American colony during the 1600s.

FATHER CLAUDE JEAN ALLOUZ

Ceremony Laying Claim to New France in the Name of Christianity and the King of France

June 4, 1671

After wintering on the Lake of the Hurons, Monsieur de saint Lusson repaired to sainte Marie du Sault early in May of this year, sixteen hundred and seventy-one . . . for the purpose of the establishment of Christianity here, by aiding [Jesuit] missions, and to cause the name and the sovereignty of ourt invincible Monarch to be acknowledged by even the least known and the most remote Nations.

First, he summoned the surrounding tribes living within a radius of a hundred leagues, and even more; and they responded through their Ambassadors, to the number of fourteen Nations.

After making all necessary preparations for the successful issue of the whole undertaking to the honor of France, he began, on June fourth of the same year, with the most solemn ceremony ever observed in these regions. For, when all had assembled in a great public council, and a height had been chosen well adapted to his purpose—overlooking, as it did, the Village of the people of the Sault,—he caused the Cross to be planted there, and then the King's standard to be raised, with all the pomp that he could devise.

The Cross was publicly blessed, with all the ceremonies of the Church, by the Superior of these Missions; and then, when it had been raised from the ground for the purpose of planting it, the *Vexilla* was sung. Many Frenchmen there present at the time joined in this hymn, to the wonder arnd delight of the assembled Savages; while the whole company was filled with a common joy at sight of this glorious standard of JESUS CHRIST, which seemed to have been raised so high only to rule over the hearts of all these poor peoples.

Then the French Escutcheon, fixed to a cedar pole, was also erected, above the Cross; while the *Exaudiat* was sung, and prayer for his Majesty's Sacred person was offered in that faraway corner of the world. After this, Monsieur de Saint Lusson, observing all the forms customary on such occasions, took possession of those regions, while the air resounded with repeated shouts of "Long live the King!" and with the discharge of musketry, to the delight and astonishment of all those peoples, who had never seen anything of the kind.

After this confused uproar of voices and muskets had ceased, perfect silence was imposed upon the whole assemblage; and Father Claude Allouez began to Eulogize the King, in order to make all those Nations understand what sort of a man he was whose standard they beheld, and to whose sovereignty they were that day submitting. Being well versed in their tongue and in their ways, he was so successful in adapting himself to their comprehension as to give them such an opinion of our incomparable Monarch's greatness; that they have no words with which to express their thoughts upon the subject.

"Here is an excellent matter brought to your attention, my brothers," said he to them, "a great and important matter, which is the cause of this council. Cast your eyes upon the Cross raised so high above your heads: there it was that JESUS CHRIST, the Son of God, making himself man for the love of men, was pleased to be fastened and to die, in atonement to his Eternal Father for our sins. He is the master of our lives, of Heaven, of Earth, and of Hell. Of him I have always spoken to you, and his name and word I have borne into all these countries. But look likewise at that other post, to which are affixed the armorial bearings of the great Captain of France whom we call King. He lives beyond the sea; he is the Captain of the greatest Captains, and has not his equal in the world. All the Captains you have ever seen, or of whom you have ever heard, are mere children compared with him. He is like a great tree, and they, only like little plants that we tread under foot in walking. . . . ."

The Father added much more of this sort. . . .

Following this speech, Monsieur de Saint Lusson took the word, and stated to them in martial and eloquent language the reasons for which he had summoned them,—and especially that he was sent to take possession of that region, receive them under the protection of the great King whose Panegyric they had just heard; and to form thenceforth but one land of their territories and ours. The whole ceremony was closed with a fine bonfire, which was lighted toward evening, and around which the *Te Deum* was sung to thank God, on behalf of those poor peoples, who were now the subjects of so great and powerful a monarch.

TWO

Colonial Reality: Religious Diversity

Colonial reality presented serious difficulties to those who sought to implement the theory of an established church. Nearly all colonists agreed—at least until the fifty years that preceded the Revolution—that the one true religion ought to be established by law. But the colonists did not agree among themselves as to the nature of the one true religion. Difficulties arose almost from the beginning in Massachusetts, where by as early as 1638 both Anne Hutchinson and Roger Williams were banished for failure to conform to Puritan orthodoxy. New York's Dutch authorities found themselves in conflict over the idea of tolerating Quakers by the 1650s. The English settlement of Virginia began at Jamestown in 1607, but sixty years later Virginians were still failing to provide adequate support to their Anglican churches even though these theoretically enjoyed the advantages of establishment. By 1686, William Penn had even secured a charter for Pennsylvania on the basis of a promise to tolerate Protestant sects of all kinds.

Great Britain had its own violent conflicts over religion—conflicts that began with Henry VIII, included the beheading of both Mary and Charles II, and extended to a twenty-year Civil War. In Britain these conflicts came to an end with the "Glorious Revolution" of 1688. Even as it moved toward a policy of an established church and "toleration" for others at home, however, the British government moved to increase its control over public life in America, in part by imposing the Church of England throughout the colonies. The Puritans lost their ability to dominate government in Massachusetts and Connecticut, although large majorities favored what came to be called the Congregationalist denomination, and in New England Congregationalists continued to enjoy the support of colony- and town-approved tax revenues and other marks of authority. Yet many New Englanders had become Baptists by the early 1700s. And despite bitter local protests, British authorities attracted significant numbers to the Church of England. By 1710 Puritan leaders like Cotton Mather were urging their congregations to establish the kingdom of God on earth through the voluntary actions of congregations and reform societies rather than through the instruments of government—which they could no longer control. Mather would have preferred an established Puritan church, but his *Essays to Do Good* provided the first American handbook on the organization of a strenuous religious life through individual congregations and voluntary societies.

British authorities did successfully establish the Church of England in New York, despite the determined opposition of Presbyterians and Dutch Reformed, and in Virginia. They made some effort in New Jersey, the Carolinas, and elsewhere. But in these colonies historical circumstance forced the Anglicans to tolerate Dutch Reformed, Presbyterian, Baptist, Quaker, and even a few Jewish congregations as well. Colonial charters had given special privileges—although not a monopoly of popular belief—to Quakers in Pennsylvania and to Catholics in Maryland. Because the colonies sought to attract immigrants but made it difficult for newcomers from distinct religious backgrounds to obtain aid in emergencies, they allowed minority groups—Scotsmen in Massachusetts, Jews in New York and Charleston, Presbyterians in the Carolina back country—to support their own mutual-benefit social service organizations as well as their own religious congregations. By the 1720s or 1730s religious diversity had become so pronounced a fact of life in New York City and Philadelphia that nonsectarian entrepreneurs like Benjamin Franklin (born in Mather's Boston and a founder of the Free Library Company of Philadelphia and the University of Pennsylvania) were emerging as the most effective institution-builders of their time.

8

Inhabitants of Flushing, Long Island,
Remonstrance against the Law against Quakers,
1657

The Dutch West India Company brought the first settlers to New Netherland in 1623. Although the colony never grew very prosperous, the Dutch held it until they turned over their North American claims to the British in 1664. New Netherland was always above all a commercial venture. But here as elsewhere in the 1600s the church was closely connected to the state. In the 1650s Quakers sought to settle in New Netherland. Dutch settlers in Flushing, on Long Island, welcomed them. But the Dutch government and the Reformed Church in the Netherlands refused, on religious grounds, to allow Flushing to accept the Quakers. In their remonstrance, the settlers of Flushing asserted that it was "the glory of the outward State of Holland" that it accepted "Jews, Turks and Egyptians, as they are considered the sons of Adam." By the same logic, the settlers insisted, The Netherlands should extend "love, peace and liberty . . . to all in Christ Jesus," including the Quakers. The Dutch government, the States General, rejected their appeal.

THE INHABITANTS OF FLUSHING, L.I.

Remonstrance against the Law against Quakers and Subsequent Proceedings by the Dutch Government

1657

Right Honorable. You have been pleased to send up unto us a certain Prohibition or Command, that we should not receive or entertain any of these people called Quakers, because they are supposed to be by some seducers of the people;

For our part we cannot condemn them in this case, neither can we stretch out our hands against them to punish, banish or persecute them, for out of Christ, God is a consuming fire, and it is a fearful thing to fall into the hands of the living God; we desire therefore in this case not to judge lest we be judged, neither to Condemn, lest we be Condemned, but rather let every man stand and fall to his own.

Master we are bound by the Law to do good unto all men, especially to those of the Household of faith; and though for the present we seem to be unsensible of the law and the Lawgiver; yet when death and the Law assault us: if we have (not) our advocate to seek, who shall plead for us in this case of Conscience betwixt God and our own souls; the powers of this world can neither attack us neither excuse us, for if God justify who can Condemn, and if God Condemn there is none can justify; and for those Jealousies and suspicions which somehow [think] of them that they are destructive unto Magistracy and Ministry that cannot be; for the Magistrate hath the Sword in his hand and the Minister hath the Sword in his hand as witness those two great examples which all Magistrates and Ministers are to follow Moses and Christ; whom God raised up Maintained and defended against all the Enemies both of flesh and spirit, and therefore that which is of God will stand, and that which is of man will (come) to nothing: and as the Lord hath taught Moses, or the Civil power, to give an outward liberty in the State by the law written in his heart designed (for) the good of all and can truly judge who is good and who is evil, who is true and who is false, and can pass definitive sentence of life or (death) against that man which rises up against the fundamental law of the States General, so (he) hath made his Ministers a savior of life unto life and a savior of death unto death.

The law of love, peace and liberty in the states [of the Netherlands] extending to Jews, Turks and Egyptians, as they are considered the sons of Adam, which is the glory of the outward State of Holland; so love, peace and liberty extending to all in Christ Jesus, condemns hatred, war and bondage; and because our Savior saith it is impossible but that offense will come, but woe be unto him by whom they Commeth, our desire is not to offend one of his little ones in whatsoever form, name or title he appears in, whether Presbyterian, Independent, Baptist, or Quaker; but shall be glad to see anything of God in any of them: desiring to do unto all men as we desire all men should do unto us, which is the true law both of Church and State; for our Savior saith this is the Law and the Prophets;

Therefore if any of these said persons come in love to us, we cannot in Conscience lay violent hands upon them, but give them free Egresse into our Town and houses as God shall persuade our Consciences; and in this we are true subjects both of the Church and

State; for we are bound by the law of God and man to do good unto all men, and evil to no man; and this is according to the Patent and Charter of our Town given unto us in the name of the States General which we are not willing to infringe and violate but shall hold to our patent and shall remain your Humble Subjects the inhabitants of Flushing; written the 27th of December in the Year 1657 by me

Edward Heart, Clericus

Tobias Feake

The Marke of William Noble

William Thorne, Sr.

The Marke of William Thorne, Jr.

9

Roger Greene, *Virginia's Cure*, 1662

The laws that established the Church of England divided the entire country into parishes, and required the residents of each parish to pay taxes for the support of the parish church and its rector. It was the rector's task not only to provide religious services, but also to tend to the sick and to those "in distress." Representatives of the Church of England expected to find these laws enforced in the American colonies. For the most part they were not enforced. In 1649 there were still just six Anglican ministers in Virginia, only one for every 3239 people. The author of the following pamphlet, perhaps Roger Greene, described the very limited role that religion actually played in early Virginia. Greene then went on to propose a charitable scheme that would enable British authorities and donors to provide a more adequate number of Anglican ministers for Virginia.

ROGER GREENE (?)

Virginia's Cure

1662

To shew the unhappy State of the Church in Virginia, and the true remedy of it, I shall first give a brief Description of the Manner of our Peoples scatter'd Habitations there; next shew the sad unhappy consequences of such their scatter'd Living both in reference to themselves and the poor Heathen that are about them, and by the way briefly set down the cause of scattering their Habitations, then proceed to propound the Remedy, and means of procuring it; next assert the Benefits of it in reference both to themselves and the Heathen; set down the cause why this Remedy hath not been hitherto compassed: and lastly, till it can be procured, give directions for the present supply of their Churches.

That part of Virginia which hath at present craved your Lordship's Assistance to preserve the Christian Religion, and to promote the Building Gods Church among them, by supplying them with sufficient Ministers of the Gospel, is bounded on the North by the great River Potomac, on the South by the River Chawan, including also the Land inhabited on the East side of the Chesapeake Bay, called Accomack, and contains above half as much Land as England; it is divided into several Counties, and those Counties contain in all about Fifty Parishes, the Families whereof are dispersedly and scatteringly seated upon the sides of Rivers; some of which running very far into the Country, bear the English Plantations above a hundred Miles, and being very broad, cause the Inhabitants of either side to be listed in several Parishes.

Every such Parish is extended many Miles in length upon the River's side and usually not above a mile in Breadth backward from the River, which is the common stated breadth of every Plantation belonging to each Particular Proprietor, of which Plantations, some extend themselves half a mile, some a mile, some two miles, some three miles, and upward upon the sides of those Rivers, many of them are parted from each other by small Rivers and Creeks, which small Rivers and Creeks are seated after the manner of the great Rivers. The Families of such Parishes being seated after this manner, at such distances from each other, many of them are very remote from the House of God, though placed in the middest of them.

Many Parishes as yet want both Churches and Gleabes, and I think not above a fifth part of them are supplyed with Ministers, where there are Ministers the People meet together Weekly, but once upon the Lords day, and sometimes not at all, being hindered by Extremities of Wind and Weather; and [many] of the more remote Families being discouraged, by the length or tediousness of the way, through extremities of heat in Summer, frost and Snow in Winter, and tempestuous weather in both, do seldom repair thither.

By which brief Description of their manner of seating themselves in that Wildernesse, Your Lordship may easily apprehend that their very manner of Planting themselves, hath caused them hitherto to rob God in a great measure of that publick Worship and Service, which as a Homage due to his great name, he requires to be constantly paid to him, at the times appointed for it, in the publick Congregations of his people in his House of Prayer. . . .

But though this be the saddest Consequence of their dispersed manner of Planting themselves (for what Misery can be greater than to live under the Curse of God?) yet this hath a very sad Train of Attendants which are likewise consequences of their scatter'd Planting. For, hence is the great want of Christian Neighbourhood, or brotherly admonition, of holy Examples of religious Persons, of the Comfort of theirs, and their Ministers' Administrations in Sickness, and Distress, of the Benefit of Christian and Civil Conference and Commerce.

And hence it is, that the most faithfull and vigilant Pastors, assisted by the most careful Church-wardens, cannot possibly take notice of the vices that reign in their families, of the spiritual defects in their Conversations, or if they have notice of them, provide Spiritual Remedies in their public Ministery. . . . [I]f they should spend time in visiting their remote and far distant habitations, they would have little or none left for their necessary Studies, and to provide necessary spiritual food for the rest of their Flocks.

And hence it is that through the licentious lives of many of them, the Christian Religion is like still to be dishonored, and the Name of God to be blasphemed among the Heathen, who are near them, and oft among them, and consequently their Conversion hindered.

Lastly, their almost general want of Schools, for the education of their Children, is another consequence of their scattered planting, of most sad consideration, most of all bewailed of Parents there, and therefore the arguments drawn from thence, most likely to prevail with them cheerfuly to embrace the Remedy. This want of Schools, as it renders a very numerous generation of Christians' Children born in Virginia (who naturally are of beautiful and comely Persons, and generally of more ingenious Spirits then these in England) unserviceable for any great Employments either in Church or State, so likewise it obstructs the hopefullest way they have, for the Conversion of the Heathen, which is, by winning the Heathen to bring in their Children to be taught and instructed in our Schools, together with the Children of Christians.

. . . I shall humbly in obedience to your Lordship's command endeavour to contribute towards the compassing this Remedy by propounding,

1. That your Lordship would be pleased to acquaint the King with the necessity of promoting the building of Towns in each County of Virginia, upon the consideration of the fore-mentioned sad Consequences of their present Manner of living there.

2. That your Lordship upon the foregoing consideration, be pleased to move the pitiful, and charitable heart of His Gracious majesty (considering the Poverty and needs of Virginia) for a Collection to be made in all the Churches of his three Kingdoms (there being considerable numbers of each Kingdom) for the promoting of a work of so great Charity to the Service of many thousands of his Loyal Subjects, their Children, and the Generations after them, and of numberless poor Heathen, and that the Ministers of each Congregation be enjoyned with more than ordinary care, and pains to stir up the people to a free and liberal Contribution towards it; or if this way be not thought sufficient, then some other way be taken to do it.

3. That the way of dispensing such collections for sending Workmen over for the building of Towns and Schools, and the assistance the persons that shall inhabit them shall contribute towards them may be determin'd here, by the advice of Virginia's present or late Honourable Govenours if in London; and whom they shall make choice of for their assistants (who have formerly lived in Virginia); and that the King (if he shall approve what is so determined) may be humbly Petitioned to authorize it by his special Command, lest what is duly ordered here, be perverted there.

Fourthly, That those Planters who have such a considerable number Servants, as may be judged may enable them for it, if they be not willing (for I have heard some express their willingness and some their aversenesse) may by His Majesty's Authority be enjoyned, to contribute the Assistance that shall be thought meet for them, to build themselves houses in the Towns nearest to them, and to inhabit them, for they having horses enough in that Country, may be convenienced, as their occasions require, to visit their Plantations. And the Masters who shall inhabit the Towns, having Families of Servants upon remote Plantations, may be ordered to take care, that upon Saturday's Afternoon (when by the Custome of Virginia, Servants are freed from their ordinary labour) their Servants (except one or two, left by turns to secure their Plantations) may repair to their Houses in the Towns, and there remain with their Masters, until the public worship and Service of the Lords Day be ended.

Fifthly, That for a continual supply of able Ministers for their Churches after a set term of years, Your Lordship would please to endeavour the procuring an Act of Parliament, whereby a certain number of Fellowships, as they happen to be next proportionably vacant in both the Universities, may bear the name of Virginia Fellowships, so long as the Needs of that Church shall require it; and none be admitted to them, but such as shall engage by promise to hold them seven years and no longer; and at the expiration of those seven years, transport themselves to Virginia, and serve that Church in the Office of the Ministery seven years more (the Church there providing for them) which being expired, they shall be left to their own Liberty to return or not: and if they perform not the Conditions of their Admittance, then to be uncapable of any Preferment.

These things being procured, I think Virginia will be in the most probable way (that her present condition can admit) of being cured of the forementioned evils of her scatter'd Planting.

10

William Penn, *The Great Case of Liberty of Conscience*, 1670

Like other Quakers in the England of his day, William Penn believed that God had not yet fully revealed Truth, and that new truths were from time to time made clear through the "Inner Light." The Inner Light, Quakers believed, enabled each individual to seek and understand the will of God without the intervention of priests or traditional sacred texts.

In his *Great Case of Liberty of Conscience,* written from his cell in London's Newgate Prison, Penn argued that God alone could judge the correctness of a person's religious beliefs and practices. Any human "imposition, restraint, and persecution" of a person for acting on his or her religious beliefs was an invasion of "the divine prerogative." Unlike Anglicans, Puritans, and Presbyterians, Penn and other Quakers distinguished sharply between "wholly independent" meetings for religious purposes and secular activities. With this distinction firmly in mind, Penn also rejected the idea, shared by Anglicans and Puritans, that religious uniformity was essential to civil order.

In 1681, William Penn won the chance to put his ideas into practice in the new colony of Pennsylvania. Penn's willingness to accept people from a wide range of religious traditions (he did *not* welcome Catholics) quickly became well known, and from the beginning Pennsylvania atttracted a very diverse array of settlers, including many from Germany. One of Penn's supporters wrote in 1697 that the colony's Quakers were already forced to take into account the desires of its Dutch, Swede, Finnish, and other settlers "not of our persuasion: Baptist, Independent, Presbyterian, or Church of England." These were soon joined by Mennonites, Moravians, and members of many other Protestant sects from German-speaking lands.

WILLIAM PENN

The Great Case of Liberty of Conscience

(EXCERPTS)

1670

The great case of Liberty of Conscience, so often debated and defended (however dissatisfactorily to such as have so little conscience as to persecute for it) is once more brought to public view, by a late act against dissenters . . . that we all hoped the wisdom of our rulers had long since laid aside, as what was fitter to be passed into an act of perpetual oblivion. The kingdoms are alarmed at this procedure, and thousands greatly at a stand, wondering what should be the meaning of such hasty resolutions, that seem as fatal as they were unexpected. Some ask what wrong they have done? others, what peace they have broken? and all, what plots they have formed to predjudice the present government, or occasions given to hatch new jealousies of them and their proceedings? being not conscious to themselves of guilt in any such respect.

For mine own part, I publicly confess myself to be a very hearty dissenter from the established worship of these nations, as believing Protestants to have much degenerated from their first principles, and as owning the poor despised Quakers, in life and doctrine, to have espoused the cause of God, and to be the undoubted followers of Jesus Christ, in his most holy, straight, and narrow way, that leads to the eternal rest. In all which I know no treason, nor any principle that would urge me to a thought injurious to the civil peace. . . .

Sad it is, when men have so far stupified their understandings with the strong doses of their private interest, as to become insensible of the public's. Certainly such an over-fondness for self, or that strong inclination to raise themselves in the ruin of what does not so much oppose them, as that they will believe so . . . is a malignant enemy to that tranquility, which all dissenting parties seem to believe would be the consequence of a toleration.

In short we say, there can be but two ends in persecution; the one to satisfy (which none can ever do) the insatiable appetites of a decimating clergy (whose best arguments are fines and imprisonments); and the other as thinking therein they do God good service: but it is so hateful a thing upon any account, that we shall make it appear, by this ensuing discourse, to be a declared enemy to God, religion, and the good of human society.

First, By liberty of conscience, we understand not only a mere liberty of the mind, in believing or disbelieving this or that principle or doctrine; but 'the exercise of ourselves in a visible way of worship, upon our believing it to be indispensably required at our hands, that if we neglect it for fear or favor of any mortal man, we sin, and incur divine wrath.' Yet we would be so understood to extend and justify the lawfulness of our so meeting to worship God, as not to contrive, or abet any contrivance destructive of the government and laws of the land, tending to matters of an external nature, directly or indirectly; but so far only as it may refer to religious matters, and a life to come, and consequently wholly independent of the secular affairs of this, wherein we are supposed to transgress.

Secondly, By imposition, restraint, and persecution, we do not only mean the strict requiring of us to believe this to be true, or that to be false; and upon refusal to incur the penalties enacted in such cases; but by those terms we mean thus much, "any coercive let or hinderance to us, from meeting together to perform those religious exercises which are according to our faith and persuasion."

For proof of the aforesaid terms thus given, we singly state the question thus;

Whether imposition, restraint, and persecution, upon persons for exercising such a liberty of conscience as is before expressed, and so circumstantiated, be not to impeach the honor of God, the meekness of the Christian religion, the authority of Scripture, the privilege of nature, the principles of common reason, the well being of government, and apprehensions of the greatest personages of former and latter ages?

First, Then we say, that imposition, restraint, and persecution, for matters relating to conscience, directly invade the divine prerogative, and divest the Almighty of a due, proper to none besides himself. And this we prove by these five particulars:

First, If we do allow the honor of our creation due to God only, and that no other besides himself has endowed us with those excellent gifts of understanding, reason, judgement, and faith, and consequently that he is the object as well as the author, both of our faith, worship, and service; then whosoever shall interpose their authority to enact faith and worship (whose alone property it is to do it) or to restrain us from what we are persuaded is our indespensible duty, they evidently usurp authority, and invade his incommunicable right of government over conscience: for "The inspiration of the Almighty gives understanding: and faith is the gift of God," says the divine writ.

Secondly, Such magisterial determinations carry an evident claim to that infalliability, which Protestants have been hitherto so jealous of owning, that, to avoid the Papists, they have denied it to all but God himself.

Either they have forsook their old plea; or if not, we desire to know when, and where, they were invested with that divine excellency; and whether imposition, restraint, and persecution, were ever deemed important by God the fruits of his spirit. However, that itself was not sufficient; for unless it appear as well to us that they have it, as to them who have it, we cannot believe it upon any convincing evidence, but by tradition only; an anti-protestant way of believing.

Thirdly, It enthrones man as king over conscience, the alone just claim and privilege of his Creator; whose thoughts are not as men's thoughts, but has reserved to himself that empire from all the Caesars on earth: for if men, in reference to souls and bodies, things appertaining to this and the other world, shall be subject to their fellow-creatures, what follows, but that Caesar (however he got it) has all, God's share, and his own too? and being lord of both, both are Caesar's, and not God's.

Fourthly, It defeats God's work of grace, and the investigation operation of his eternal spirit, (which can alone beget faith, and is only to be obeyed, in and about religion and worship) attributes men's conformity to outward force, and corporal punishments. A faith subject to as many revolutions as the powers that enact it.

Fifthly and lastly, Such persons assume the judgement of the great tribunal unto themselves: for to whomsoever men are imposedly or restrictively subject and accountable in matters of faith, worship and conscience; in them alone must the power of judgement reside: but it is equally true that God shall judge all by Jesus Christ; and that no man is so accountable to his fellow-creatures, as to be imposed upon, restrained, or persecuted for any matter of conscience whatever.

Thus, and in many more particulars, are men accustomed to intrench upon divine property, to gratify particular interests in the world; and (at best) through a misguided apprehension to imagine "they do God good service," that where they cannot give faith, they will use force; which kind of sacrifice is nothing less unreasonable than the other is abominable: God will not give his honor to another; and to him only, that searches the heart and tries the reins, it is our duty to ascribe the gifts of understanding and faith, without which none can please God.

11

Cotton Mather, *Bonifacius: Essays to Do Good,* 1710

In England the Glorious Revolution of 1688–89 and the Toleration Act of 1689 ended the violent religious conflicts of the English Civil War and the Restoration period, brought the effective government of William and Mary to the throne, and ushered in a long period of peace and stability in English politics. The result, for the American colonies, was a redoubling of British efforts that had begun in the 1660s to impose order and control from London.

For New England, this meant an end to the ability of Puritan Congregationalists to maintain the control of government and of the law courts that they had enjoyed since 1620. In Massachusetts and Connecticut clergymen strongly opposed the imposition of British control and the introduction of the Church of England and of toleration for religious dissenters. By the early 1700s, however, they were forced to accept the fact that they would not be allowed—as Winthrop had urged in the *Model of Christian Charity*—to control all religious activity by force of law, or to use the law to enforce their own religious notions of correct behavior, in social and economic as well as in religious matters, on all members of the community.

Cotton Mather, the descendant of some of the most influential Puritans of the founding generation, became one of the most influential Massachusetts Puritans of his generation. He had personally to cope with the consequences of the Salem witch trials—and he also played a courageous and pioneering role in the development of vaccination against small pox. Like his fellow Puritan ministers, Mather had to come to terms with the loss of political power by the clergy.

In his *Essays to Do Good,* Mather described the many ways in which Puritan women and men and their ministers could seek to establish Christian virtue on earth even though they had lost control of the government. Drawing explicitly on Jewish practices, Mather argued that Christians should act through their religious congregations, through exertions of "neighborliness," and through voluntary associations, to "do good." In these ways, he argued, private individuals and groups could aid the poor, the orphans, and the widows. They could see to it that children were educated. They could also influence and correct the bad behavior of their neighbors. Mather devoted several pages to the "opportunities to do good, with which God, who gives power to get wealth, has favored and obliged and enriched them." He closed with a brief discussion of "reforming societies" which in 1710 had "begun to grow somewhat into fashion."

For one hundred years, Mather's *Essays to Do Good* remained one of the most widely read and influential essays in America. To some, Mather is the original bluenose Puritan, the philosopher of the "Nosey Parkerism" that makes life in gossipy small towns impossible for those of independent mind. To others, Mather's *Essays* provide a blueprint for the responsible, caring community. In many ways his *Bonifacius* is the founding document of the American nonprofit organization.

COTTON MATHER

Bonifacius: Essays to Do Good

(EXCERPTS)

1710

Neighbors! you stand related unto one another. And you should be full of devices that all the neighbors may have cause to be glad of your being in the neighborhood. We read: "The righteous is more excellent than his neighbor." But we shall scarce own him so, except he be more excellent as a neighbor. He must excel in the duties of good neighborhood. Let that man be better than his neighbor who labors to be a better neighbor, to do most good unto his neighbor.

And here first: the poor people that lie wounded must have wine and oil poured into their wounds. It was a charming stroke in the character which a modern prince had given to him: "To be in distress is to deserve his favor." O good neighbor, put on that princely, that more than royal quality! See who in the neighborhood may deserve thy favor. We are told: "This is pure religion and undefiled" (a jewel that neither is counterfeit nor has any flaws in it), "to visit the fatherless and widows in their affliction." The orphans and widows, and so all the children of affliction in the neighborhood, must be visited and relieved with all agreeable kindness.

Neighbors be concerned that the orphans and widows in your neighborhood may be well provided for. They meet with grievous difficulties, with unknown temptations. While their next relatives were yet living, they were, perhaps, but meanly provided for. What must they now be in their more solitary condition? Their condition should be considered, and the result of the consideration should be: "I delivered the orphan that had no helper, and I caused the heart of the widow to sing for joy."

By consequence, all the afflicted in the neighborhood are to be thought upon. Sirs, would it be too much for you at least once in a week to think: "What neighbor is reduced into a pinching and painful poverty? Or in any degree impoverished with heavy losses?" Think: "What neighbor is languishing with sickness, especially if sick with sore maladies and of some continuance?" Think: "What neighbor is heartbroken with sad bereavements, bereaved of desirable relatives?" And think: "What neighbor has a soul buffeted and hurried with violent assaults of the wicked one?" But then think: "What shall be done for such neighbors?"

First: you will pity them. The evangelical precept is: "Have compassion one of another; be pitiful." It was of old, and ever will be, the just expectation: "To him that is afflicted, pity should be shown." And let our pity to them flame out in our prayer for them. It were a very lovely practice for you, in the daily prayer of your closet every evening, to think: "What miserable object have I seen today that I may do well now to mention for the mercies of the Lord?"

But this is not all. 'Tis possible, 'tis probable, you may do well to visit them: and when you visit them, comfort them. Carry them some good word which may raise a gladness in an heart stooping with heaviness.

And lastly: give them all the assistances that may answer their occasions. Assist them with advice to them, assist them with address to others for them. And if it be needful, bestow your alms upon them: "Deal thy bread to the hungry; bring to thy house the poor that are cast out, when thou seest the naked, cover him." At least Nazianzen's charity, I pray: "If you have nothing else to bestow upon the miserable, bestow a tear or two upon their miseries." This little is better than nothing. . . .

In moving for the devices of good neighborhood, a principal motion which I have to make is that you consult the spiritual interests of your neighborhood as well as the temporal. Be concerned lest the deceitfulness of sin undo any of the neighbors. If there be any idle persons among them, I beseech you, cure them of their idleness. Don't nourish 'em and harden 'em in that, but find employment for them. Find 'em work; set 'em to work; keep 'em to work. Then, as much of your other bounty to them as you please.

If any children in the neighborhood are under no education don't allow 'em to continue so. Let care be taken that they may be better educated, and be taught to read, and be taught their catechism and the truths and ways of their only savior.

Once more: if any in the neighborhood are taking to bad courses, lovingly and faithfully admonish them. If any in the neighborhood are enemies to their own welfare or families, prudently dispense your admonitions unto them. If there are any prayerless families, never leave off entreating and exhorting of them till you have persuaded them to set up the worship of God. If there be any service of God or of His people to which anyone may need to be excited, give him a tender excitation. Whatever snare you see anyone in, be so kind as to tell him of his danger to be ensnared, and save him from it. By putting of good books into the hands of your neighbors, and gaining of them a promise to read the books, who can tell what good you may do unto them. It is possible you may in this way, with ingenuity and with efficacy, administer those reproofs which you may owe unto such neighbors as are to be reproved for their miscarriages. The books will balk nothing that is to be said on the subjects that you would have the neighbors advised upon.

Finally: if there be any base houses, which threaten to debauch and poison and confound the neighborhood, let your charity to your neighbors make you do all you can for the suppression of them.

That my proposal to do good in the neighborhood and as a neighbor may be more fully formed and followed, I will conclude it with minding you that a world of self-denial is to be exercised in the execution of it. You must be armed against selfishness, all selfish and squinting intentions in your generous resolutions.

You shall see how my demands will grow upon you. First: you must not think of making the good you do a pouring of water into a pump to draw out something for yourselves. This might be the meaning of our savior's direction: "Lend, hoping for nothing again." To lend a thing, properly is to hope that we shall receive it again. But this probably refers to the . . . collation usual among the ancients, whereof we find many monuments and mentions in antiquity. If any man by burnings or shipwrecks or other disasters had lost his estate, his friends did use to lend him considerable sums of money, to be repaid not at a certain day but when he should find himself able to repay it without inconvenience. Now, they were so cunning that they would rarely lend upon such disasters unto any but such as they had hope would recover out of their present impoverishment, and not only repay them their money but also requite their kindness, if ever there should be need of it. The thing required by our savior is: "Do good unto such as you are never like to be the better for."

But then, there is yet an higher thing to be demanded. That is: "Do good unto those neighbors who have done hurt unto you." So says our savior: "Love your enemies; bless them that curse you; do good to them

that hate you, and pray for them which despitefully use you and persecute you." Yea, if an injury have been done you, improve it as a provocation to do a benefit unto him who did the injury. Time is noble! It will
bring marvelous consolations!

Another method might make you even with your forward neighbors: This will set you above them all. It were nobly done if, in the close
of the day when you are alone before the Lord, you make a particular
prayer for the pardon and prosperity of any person from whom you
may have suffered any abuse in the day. And it would be nobly done if,
at last combing over the catalogue of such as have been abusive to you,
you may be able to say (the only intention that can justify your doing
anything like to keeping a catalogue of them): "There is not one of these
but I have done him, or watched to do him, a kindness." Among the
Jews themselves there were the Hasideans, one of whose institutions it
was to make this daily prayer unto God: "Forgive all who trouble and
harass us." Christians—go beyond them! Yea, Justin Martyr tells us, in
primitive times they did so: "Praying for their enemies."

But I won't stop here. There is yet an higher thing to be demanded.
That is: do good unto those neighbors who will speak ill of you after you
have done it. So says our savior: "Ye shall be the children of the highest:
he is kind unto the unthankful and unto the evil." You will every day
find, I can tell you, monsters of ingratitude. Yea, if you distinguish any
person with doing for him something more than you have done for
others, it will be well if that very person do not at some time or other
hurt you wonderfully. Oh! the wisdom of divine providence in ordering
this thing! Sirs, it is that you may do good on a divine principle: good
merely for the sake of good! "Lord, increase our faith!"

And God forbid that a Christian faith should not come up to a
Jewish! There is a memorable passage in the Jewish records. There was
a gentleman of whose bounty many people every day received reliefs
and succors. One day he asked: "Well, what do our people say today?"
They told him: "Why, the people partook of your kindnesses and services, and then they blessed you very fervently." "Did they so?" said he,
"Then I shall have no great reward for this day." Another day he asked:
"Well, and what say our people now?" They told him: "Alas, good sir,
the people enjoyed your kindnesses today, and when all was done, they
did nothing but rail at you." "Indeed," said he, "Now for this day I am
sure that God will give me a good and great reward."

Though vile constructions and harsh invectives be never so much
the present reward of doing the best offices for the neighborhood, yet,
my dear Boniface, be victorious over all discouragements. "Thy work
shall be well rewarded," saith the Lord.

If your opportunities to do good reach no further, yet I will offer
you a consolation, which one has elegantly thus expressed: "He that

praises God only on a ten-stringed instrument, with his authority extending but unto his face and his example but unto his neighborhood, may have as thankful an heart here, and as high a place in the celestial choir hereafter, as the greatest monarch that praiseth God upon a ten-thousand-stringed instrument, upon the loudsounding organ having as many millions of pipes as there be people under him."

Would it be amiss for you, to have always lying by you, a list of the poor in your neighborhood, or of those whose calamities may call for the assistances of the neighborhood? Such a list would often furnish you, with matter for a useful conversation, when you are talking with your friends, whom you may provoke to love and good works.

I will go on to say; be glad of opportunities to do good in your neighborhood: yea, look out for them, lay hold on them, with a rapturous assiduity. Be sorry for all the bad circumstances of any neighbor, that bespeak your doing of good unto him. Yet, be glad, if any one tell you of them. Thank him who tells you as having therein done you a very great civility. Let him know, that he could not by anything have more gratified you. Any civility that you can show, by lending, by watching, by . . . all the methods of courtesy; show it; and be glad you can show it. Show it, and give a pleasant countenance, in the showing of it. Let your wisdom cause your face always to shine; look, not with a cloudy but a serene and shining face, upon your neighbors; and shed the rays of your courtesy upon them, with such affability, that they may see they are welcome to all you can do for them. Yea, stay not until you are told of opportunities to do good. Enquire after them; let the enquiry be solicitous, be unwearied. The incomparable pleasure, is worth an enquiry.

How can we leave the offices of good neighborhood, without interposing a proposal, to animate and regulate private meetings of religious people, for the exercises of religion? It is very certain, that where such private meetings under a good conduct, have been kept alive, the Christians which have composed them, have like so many coals of the altar kept one another alive, and kept up a lively Christianity in the neighborhood. Such societies have been tried and strong engines, to uphold the power of godliness. The throwing up of such societies, has been accomplished with a visible decay of godliness; the less love to them, the less there has been of, the kingdom of God.

The rules observed by some, associated families, may be offered on this occasion with some advantage. They will tell us what good may be done by such societies in a neighborhood. It is proposed, that about a dozen families, more or less, of a vicinity, agree to meet (the men and their wives) at each others houses, once in a fortnight, or a month, at such a time as may be agreed upon, and spend a convenient quantity of time together, in the exercises of religion.

I will get me unto the rich men, . . . and will speak unto them:
for they will know the ways to do good, and will think, what they shall
be able to say, when they come into the judgement of their God. An
English person of quality, quoting that passage, *The Desire of Man is his
Kindness,* invited me to read it, the only desireable thing in a man is his
goodness. How happy would the world be if every person of quality
would come into this persuasion! It is an article in my commission;
charge them that are rich in this world, that they do good, that they be
rich in good works, ready to distribute, willing to communicate. In pur-
suance thereof, I will put rich men in mind of the opportunities to do
good, which with the God, who gives power to get wealth, has favored
and obliged and enriched them. It was an account, and a very good one
it was, that has been sometimes given of a good man; the wealth of this
world, he knew no good in it, but the doing of good with it. Yea, those
men who have had very little goodness in them, yet in describing, the
manners of the age, in which they have had perhaps themselves too
deep a share, have seen cause to subscribe and publish this prime dictate
of reason; we are never the better for anything, barely for the propriety
sake; but it is the application of it, that gives everything its value.

Whoever buries his talent, breaks a sacred trust, and cozens those
that stand in need on it. Sirs, you cannot but acknowledge, that it is the
sovereign God, who has bestowed upon you, the riches which distinguish you. A devil himself, when he saw a rich man, could not but make
this acknowledgement unto the God of heaven, "Thou hast blessed the
work of his hands, and his substance is increased in the land." It is also
a thing, whereof it is to be hoped, you are not unappreciative, that the
riches in your possession are some of the talents, whereof you must give
an account unto the glorious Lord, who has betrusted you therewithal:
and that you will give up your account with grief, and not with joy, if it
must be found, that all your estates have been laid out, only to gratify
the appetites of the flesh, and little or nothing of them consecrated unto
the service of God, and of His kingdom in the world. We read of the
servants assigned unto the priests of old, unto you they are given as a
gift for the world. It is what is to be said of all our estates. What God
gives us, is not given us for ourselves, but for the Lord. . . .

Indeed there is hardly any professor of Christianity, so *vicious*, but
he will own, that all of his estate is to be used in honest uses; and part of
it, in pious uses. If any plead their poverty, to excuse them, and exempt
them, from doing anything this way, O poor widow with thy two mites,
eternized in the history of the gospel, thou shalt rise up in the jugement
with that generation, and shalt condemn them. And let them also know,
that they take a course, to condemn and confine themselves unto eternal poverty.

But the main question is, about the quota parts; how much of man's income is to be devoted unto pious uses? And now, let it not seem a hard saying, if I say unto you, that a tenth part is the least that you can bring under a more solemn dedicaton unto the Lord; for whom indeed, after some sort, we are to lay out our all. A farthing less, would make an enlightened and considerate Christian, suspicious, of his coming under the danger of a sacriledge. By the pious uses for which your tenth are thus challenged, I do not intend only the maintenance of the evangelical ministry, but also the relief of the miserable whom our merciful Savior has made the receivers of His rents, and all that is to be more directly done, for the preserving and promoting of piety in the world. Since there is a part of every man's revenues due to the glorious Lord, and such pious uses, it is not fit that the determination of what part, it must be, should be left unto such hearts as ours. My friend thou hast, it may be, too high an opinion of thy own wisdom and goodness, if nothing but thy own carnal heart, shall determine still when, and what, thy revenues are to do, for Him, whom thou art ready to forget, when He has filled thee. But if the Lord Himself, to whom thou art but a steward, has fixed any part of our usual revenues, for Himself, as it is most reasonable that He should have the fixing of it, certainly a tenth will be found the least that He has called for.

I will add in a consideration, wherein, methinks, common humanity should be sensible of a provocation. Let rich men who are not rich towards God, especially such as have no children of their own, to make the heirs of their hoarded riches, consider the vile ingratitude, which with the forks that come after them, will treat them, withal. Sirs, they will hardly allow you a tombstone; and, wallowing in the wealth which you have left, (but they complain, that you left it no sooner unto them) they will only play upon your memory, squib upon your husbandry, ridicule all your parsimony! How much more wisdom, would it be, for you to do good with your estates while you live; and at your death do that, which may embalm your name to posterity in this world, and be for your advantage in that which you are going unto! That your souls may dwell in all ease and good of the paradisian reflections, at the time, when others inherit what you leave unto them.

I only now annex the complement of one to his friend, upon his accession to an estate; much good may it do you; that is, much good may you do with it.

I hope, we are now ready for proposals. We shall set ourselves, to devise liberal things.

Gentlemen, it is of old said, *"res est sacra miser."* To relieve the necessities of the poor this is a thing acceptable to the compassionate God; who has given to you, what He might have given to them; and has given it unto you that you might have the honor and pleasure to impart it unto them: and who has told you, "he that has pity on the poor, lends unto the Lord." The more you consider the command and image of a glorious Christ in what you do this way, the more assurance you have, that in the day of God, you shall find joyfully hear Him saying, "You have done it unto me!" And the more humble, silent, reserved modesty you express, concealing even from the left hand what is done with the right, the more you are assured of, "a great reward in the heavenly world." Such liberal men it is observed, are usually long-lived men. *Fructus liberat arborem.* And at last, they pass from this unto everlasting life.

When you dispense your alms, unto the poor, who know, what it is to pray, you may oblige them to pray for you by name every day. Tis an excellent thing to have, the blessing of them that have been ready to perish, thus coming upon you. Behold, a surprising sense in which you may be, praying always. You are so, even while you are sleeping, if those whom you have obliged are thus praying for you! And now, look for the accomplishment of that word; blessed is he that considers the poor; the Lord will preserve him and keep him alive; and he shall be blessed on earth.

Very often your alms are dispersed among such as very much need admonitions of piety to accompany them. Can't you contrive, to intermix a spiritual charity, with your temporal? Perhaps you may discourse with them about the state of their souls, and obtain from them, which you now have a singular advantage to do, some declared relations to do what they ought to do. Or else you may convey little books unto them, which certainly they will promise to read, when you thus bespeak their doing so.

Charity to the souls of men, is undoubtedly the highest and the noblest charity, and of the greatest consequence. To furnish the poor with Catechisms, and Bibles, is to do an unknown deal of good unto them: to publish and scatter books of piety, and to put into the hands of mankind such treatises of divinity as may have a tendency to make them wiser or better; no man knows what good he does in doing such things!

He that supports the office of the evangelical ministry, supports good work; and performs one; yea, at the second hand performs what is done by the skillful, faithful, painful minister, and that is many a one. The encouraged servant of the Lord, will do the more good, for your assistances, tis done for a glorious Christ, what you have done for him; and in consideration of the glorious gospel preached by him. And you shall receive a prophet's reward! Luther said, "*Si quid scholasties confors, Deo ipsi contulisti.* (Tis more sensibly so, when the scholars are become godly and useful preachers.)"

Landlords, it is worth your considering, whether you may not in your leases, insert some clauses, that may serve the kingdom of God.

You are His tenents, in those very freeholds, where you are landlords to other men! Oblige your tenents to worship God in their families.

To take a poor child, especially an orphan, left in poverty, and bestow an education upon it, especially if it be a liberal education, is an admirable, and a complicated charity; yea, it may draw on a long train of good, and interest you in all the good that shall be done by those whom you have educated.

Hence also what is done for schools, and for colleges, and for hospitals, is done for a general good. The endowing of these, or the maintaining of them, is, at once to do good unto many.

But alas, how much of the silver and gold in the world, is buried in hands, where it is little better than conveyed back to the mines from whence it came? Or employed unto as little purpose, as what arrives at Indostan, where a large part of the silver and gold of the world, is after a circulation carried as unto a fatal center, and by the moguls lodged in subterraneous caves, never to see the light any more. . . .

Sometimes there may be got ready for the press, elaborate composures, of great bulk, and greater worth, by which the best interests of knowledge and virtue, may be considerably served in the world; they lie like the impotent man at the pool of Bethesda; and they are like to lie, till God inspire some wealthy persons, to subscribe nobly for their publication, and by this generous application of their wealth to bring them abroad! The names of such noble benefactors to mankind, ought to live, as long as the works themselves; where the works do any good, what these have done towards the publishing of them, ought to be told for a memorial of them.

Tis an observation of the incomparable Boyl, "That as to religious books in general, it has been observed, that those penned by laymen, and especially gentlemen, have been better entertained, and more effectual than those of Ecclesiasticles." We all know, his own were so. It is no rare thing for men of quality, to accomplish themselves in languages and sciences, until they have been prodigies of literature. Their libraries too, have been stupendous collections; approaching towards Vatican or Bodlesan dimensions. An English gentleman has been sometimes the most accomplished thing in the whole world. How many of these . . . have been benefactors to mankind by their incomparable writings? It were mightily to be wished, that rich men, and persons of an elevated condition, would qualify themselves, for the use of the pen, as well as the sword; and by their pen deserve to have it said of them, they have written excellent things.

I will address you, with one proposal more. Tis, that you would wisely choose a friend of shining abilities, of hearty affections, and of excellent piety: a minister of such a character, if it may be. And entreat him, yea, oblige him, to study for you, and suggest to you, opportunities to do good: make him, as I may say, your monitor. Let him advise you from time to time, what good you may do. Cause him to see, that he never gratifies you more, than by his advice upon this intention. If a David have a seer to do such a good office for him, and to be on the look out for to find out what good he may do, what services may be done for the temple of God in the world.

I will conclude with saying, you must come forth to any public service whereof you may be capable, when you are called unto it. Honest Seans has a pungent pasage; "The world applauds the politic retiredness of those that bury their parts and gifts, in an obscure privacy, though both from God and man, they have a fair call to public employment; but the terrible censure of these men by Christ at the last day, will discover them to be the arrantest fools, that ever were upon the face of the earth." The fault of not employing one's parts for the public, one calls, "A great sacrilege in the temple of the God of nature."

Reforming societies, or societies for the suppression of disorders, have begun to grow somewhat into fashion; and it is one of the best omens that the world has upon it. Behold, how great a matter a little of this heavenly fire may kindle! Five or six gentlemen in London, began with a heroic resolution, and association, to encounter the torrent of wickedness, which was carrying all before it in the nation. More were soon added unto them; and though they met with great opposition, from wicked spirits, and these incarnate as well as invisible, and some in high places too, yet they proceeded with a most honorable and invincible courage. Their success, if not proportionable to their courage, yet was so far from contemptible. In the punishments inflicted on them who transgressed the laws of good morality, there were soon offered many thousands of sacrafices, unto the holiness of God. Hundreds of houses which were chambers of hell, and the scandals of earth, were soon extinguished. There was a remarkable check soon given to raging profanity; and the Lord's day was not openly and horribly profaned as formerly. And among other essays to do good, they scattered thousands of good books, that had a tendency to reform the evil manners of the people. It was not long before this excellent example was followed in other parts of the British empire.

12

William Livingston, *Argument against Anglican Control of King's College* (Columbia), 1753

For several decades after the Glorious Revolution British authorities worked to expand British influence in the American colonies. Colleges sponsored by the crown and run by the Church of England—like the colleges of Oxford and Cambridge in England—provided a means to influence young men who were on their way to leading positions in the colonies. In this sense both the College of William and Mary (chartered in 1693 although not opened until nearly 25 years later) in Williamsburg, Virginia, and King's College in New York (founded in 1754 and renamed Columbia after the Revolution) were designed to serve as instruments of British influence.

But New York City's people practiced many religions—or none. As early as 1686 Governor Dongan stated that New York City contained Dutch Calvinists, French Calvinists, Dutch Lutherans, and ordinary Quakers as well as Anglicans, and, in addition, "Singing Quakers, Ranting Quakers, Sabbatarians; Antisabbatarians; Some Anabaptists some Independants; some Jews; in short [of] all sorts of opinions there are some, and the most part [of the people have no opinions] at all."

In 1754 members of the Church of England were still a minority, outnumbered in the city by Presbyterians and Dutch Reformed. William Livingston, a Presbyterian who worked closely in politics with many Dutch New Yorkers, objected to the British plan to give the Church of England control over Kings College. Livingston denied the very idea that the Church of England was legitimately established in New York. New York's legislature had never voted for it, he pointed out—and New Yorkers had never paid the church taxes or established the church courts called for by English law. They should not, he concluded, be forced to change their practices by accepting an Anglican college.

Rejecting Livingston's argument, British authorities did establish King's College as an Anglican institution. But the new college grew slowly. It had hardly reached a sustainable size before the Stamp Act Crisis of 1765 launched the events that led to the Revolution. For Livingston and many other New Yorkers, the battle over King's College served almost as a rehearsal for the Revolution.

WILLIAM LIVINGSTON

Against Anglican Control
of King's College

1753

They who assert, that the Church of England is established in this province, never, that I have heard of, pretended that it owes its Establishment to any provincial law of our own making. Nor, indeed, is there the least ground for such a supposition. The Acts that establish a Ministry in this, and in three other counties, do not affect the whole colony, and therefore can by no means, be urged in support of a general Establishment. Nor that they originally designed to establish the Episcopalians in preference or to the exclusion of any other Protestants in those counties to which they are limited.

Absurd as the proposition is, that the Establishment of the Church of England is equally binding here as in England; so agreeable thereto, the Arguments they adduce are the following:

> First, That as we are an English Colony the constitutional laws of our mother country, antecedent to a Legislature of our own, are binding upon us; and therefore, at the planting of this Colony, the English religious establishment immediately took place.

> Secondly, That the Act which established the Episcopal Church in Great Britain, previous to the union of England and Scotland, extends to and equally affects all the Colonies.

These are the only Arguments that can be offered with the least plausibility, and if they are shown to be inconclusive the position is disproven, and the arguments of consequence must be impertinent and groundless.

I shall begin with an Examination of the First: and here it must be confessed for undoubted law, that every new Colony, 'till it has a Legislature of its own, is in general subject to the laws of the country from which it originally sprang. But that all of them without distinction, are to be supposed binding upon such planters, is neither agreeable to law nor reason. The laws which they carry with them, and to which they are subject, are such as are absolutely necessary to answer the original intention of our entering into a state of society. Such as are requisite in their New-Colony state, for the advancement of their and the general prosperity; such, without which they will neither be protected in their Lives, Liberty nor Property: And the true reason of their being considered even subject to such laws, arises from the absolute necessity of their being under some kind of government . . . and [it is the government and] laws of their mother country, with which alone they can be supposed to be acquainted.

Even at this day we extend every general Act of Parliament which we think reasonable and fit for us, though it was neither designed to be a law upon us, nor has words to include us, and has even been enacted long since we had a legislature of our own. This is a practice we have introduced for our conveniency; but that the English laws, so far as I have distinguished them, should be binding upon us, antecedent to our having a Legislature of our own, is of absolute unavoidable necessity.

But no such necessity, can be pretended in favour of the introduction of any religious Establishment whatsoever; because, it is evident that different societies do exist with different ecclesiastical laws, or which is sufficient to my purpose, without such as the English Establishments; and that civil society, as it is antecedent to any ecclesiastical Establishments, is in its nature unconnected with them, independent of them, and all social Happiness compleatly attainable without them.

Secondly, To suppose all the laws of England, without distinction, obligatory upon every new Colony at its implantation, is absurd, and would effectually prevent the Subjects from undertaking so hazardous an adventure. Upon such a supposition, a thousand laws will be introduced, inconsistent with the state of a new country, and destructive of the planters. To use the words of the present Attorney General, Sir Dudley Ryder, "It would be acting the part of an unskilful physician, who should prescribe the same dose to every patient, without distinguishing the variety of distempers and constitutions."

According to this doctrine, we are subject to the payment of tythes, ought to have a spiritual court, and impoverished as the first settlers of the province must have been, they were yet liable to the payment of the [church] tax. And had this been the sense of our rulers, and their conduct conformable thereto, scarce ever would our Colonies have appeared in their present flourishing condition; especially if it be considered, that the first settlers of most of them, sought an exemption in these American wilds, from the [religious] establishment to which they were subject at home.

13

Charles Woodmason, *Journal of the Carolina Backcountry,* 1767–68

British authorities sought to use the Church of England to advance British interests throughout their American colonies. One of their chief instruments for this purpose was the Society for the Propagation of the Gospel in Foreign Parts, which supported missionaries and mission churches until they could attract enough parishoners to become self sufficient.

Puritan New Englanders resented the attentions of the Society's missionaries, as Jonathan Mayhew made clear in his *Observations* on its "character and conduct" in 1763, just two years before the Stamp Act crisis. Mayhew argued that the Society sent Anglican missions and schools not to backwoods districts that were in great need of religion, but to "the oldest, most populous, and richest towns" in New England. Using funds contributed in England rather than by Anglicans in New England, they "set up altar against altar," and sought "to encourage and increase small disaffected parties in our towns." The result, Mayhew argued, was that the society actually sought to weaken New England's churches and to use religious influence to advance the political purposes of the British government. The numbers supported his argument: in 1761 the Society for the Propagation of the Gospel was supporting, in

New England	about 30
New York	16
New Jersey	10
Pennsylvania	9
N. Carolina	5
S. Carolina	5
Georgia	1
Bahama Islands	1
Barbados	2

Mayhew concluded: "It does not appear from the abstracts, that the society have any missionaries at all in the other W. India Islands, where, as is commonly reported, there is hardly any show of public worship kept up, of any kind; and where there are so many thousands of Negro slaves in total ignorance of Christianity."

One of the missionaries the Society did send to the South, Charles Woodmason, recorded his experiences in the Carolinas during the years immediately after the Stamp Act crisis in remarkably pungent English.

Woodmason expected that his colonial parishoners would tax themselves in order to provide him with the sort of church, manse, servants, and income he thought appropriate to his station. Carolinians—many of whom were Presbyterians who rejected his ministry altogether—refused to act as he wished. Woodmason reacted with shock, alarm, self-pity, and an extraordinarily vivid (and violently and no doubt unfair anti-Presbyterian) account of life in the Carolina backcountry on the eve of the American Revolution.

CHARLES WOODMASON

Journal of the Carolina Backcountry

(EXCERPTS)

1767–68

Thus you have the travels of a minister in the wild woods of America, destitute often of the very necessaries of life, sometimes starved, often famished, exposed to the burning sun and scorching sands. Obliged to fight his way thro' banditti, profligates, reprobates, and the lowest vilest scum of mankind on the one hand, and of the numerous sectaries pregnant in these countries, on the other. With few friends and fewer assistants, and surmounting difficulties, and braving dangers, that ev'ry clergyman that ever entered this province shrinked even at the thoughts. Which none, not even the meanest of the Scotch clergy that have been sent here, would undertake, and for which he subjected himself to the laughter of fools and ridicule of the licentious for undertaking. . . .

No other clergyman of the Church of England from the sea to the mountains, on the north side of Santee River to the province line. Num-

Excerpts from Richard James Hooker, ed., *The Carolina Backcountry on the Eve of the Revolution: The Journal and Other Writings of Charles Woodmason, Anglican Itinerant* (Chapel Hill: Published for the Institute of Early American History and Culture at Williamburg, Va., by the University of North Carolina Press, 1953). Reprinted by permission.

ber of miles rode this year (all perform'd by one horse), 3185. May say, full four thousand Miles.

Observe that not above 2 or 3 out of any family can attend divine service at one time, thro' want of horses and saddles; otherwise each congregation would be doubled. They therefore come by turns.

Congregations rais'd, and attended occasionally. 1767 auditors more or less.

Great Swamp of Santee	Cheraws, on Pedee River
St. Marks Church	Anson Court House, North Carolina
High Hills of Santee	Camp Creek, and Cedar Creek
Rafting Creek	Beaver Creek, White Oak &c
Pine Tree Hill (The Centre)	Dutchmans Creek
Granny Quarter Creek	Rocky Creek, Wateree Creek &c
Hanging Rock Creek	Fishing Creek
Little Lynchs Creek, Flat Creek	Waxaws
Great Lynch's Creek (2 Places)	Sandy River (near Broad River)
Thompsons Creek (2 Places)	

Could all these congregations be regularly attended ev'ry Sunday... say treble the number would attend. But it would employ 20 Ministers....

These congregations being settled, their children baptiz'd, and the people rouz'd from their insensibility, a new system of things, and an entire alteration in the minds of individuals, seem'd to take place from this period.

I will waive all Political Matters . . . and proceed in my Journal just to set down facts, and occurences respecting my self and the state of religion in this country.

The fatigue and pain, the toil and expense I have sustain'd in these peregrinations are beyond description. Few beside me could have borne them. The Task deterr'd ev'ry one. None to be found to enter on it.

I now proceed in my Journal for the second year. (but forgot to note, that on the 20th November) I was at Beaver Creek where gave sermon to a body of about 2000 arm'd persons, of the populace call'd Regulators and it was happiness for many that I went there as I sav'd many homes from being burnt and stopped the outrages of the mob. No lives were lost nor blood spilt.

September 6, 1767: Officiated at Pine Tree Hill. On the 6th went up to
    Fishing Creek and returned to Pine Tree. 40 miles; 40 miles.

The 13th Gave Sermon at Rafting Creek, the 20th at Little Lynch's Creek.
    The 21 at Grannys Quarter. 36 [miles]; 40 [miles]

The 28th at Beaver Creek. Next day in my way up fell into an ambus-
    cade of the horse theives who lay in wait for me. They carried me

to their gang, who received me with great civility, and promis'd to restore the horses they had stollen. Desir'd I would give them a sermon which I promis'd to do as next Monday. By this detainer great part of the Congregation dispers'd, imagining, that I was sick and could not come. 33 [miles]

On Monday I went to the rendezvous according to promise. But the Militia having notice, took to arms intending to surprise the rogues. As they have spies ev'ry where, they had early intelligence, and moved off leaving their wives, whores and children. So I gave sermon to the Militia instead of the banditti. 20 miles, 33 miles.

October 3d, Officiated at Pine Tree. During sermon the rogues beset several houses and robbed them, stripping both houses and all in them of ev'ry thing they could carry off. The congregation after sermon took to arms and pursu'd them and at 15 Miles end came up with them at 25 Mile Creek, and fir'd on them. One man was wounded whom his companions carried off. They recover'd several horses, and much goods.

October 10, officiated at Rafting Creek, 17th Lynchs Creek, 19th at Grannys Quarters, 20th Rocky Mount, 26th Beaver Creek from whence I was conducted over the Wateree River (across the wild woods where had never before been) to Little River, where I officiated the 31st to about 300 Persons. 18 [miles]; 18 [miles]; 60 [miles]; 64 [miles]; 24 [miles]; 3o [miles] Here a large Body of People met me. I baptized several adults, and of them 3 or 4 Quakers, who conform'd to the Church. 36 [miles]

Returned to Pine Tree and preach'd there the 1st being All Saints but the Presbyterians disliked the service and sermon of the day saying it was Popish &c.

I assembled them on the 5th in the Meeting House, where came the magistrates, elders, &c and several of the principal Quakers. The day's service and sermon (being of Popery) gave satisfaction.

27th: This the first Sermon ever preached on this day in this Province out of Charlestown.

On the 8th preached at Rafting Creek.

9th at the Hills.

15th. Lynchs Creek.

16th Grannys Quarter.

22d Rocky Mount.

24 Dutchmans Creek and on the

26th at Little River. 50 [miles]; 60 [miles]; 45 [miles]; 63 [miles]

December 1767: The 6th at Pine Tree.

8th at Grannys Quarter.

The 13th at Rafting Creek;

the 17th the weather so wet and cold could not journey, so officiated at

Pine Tree; the 20th at Great Lynchs Creek. 32 [miles]; 36 [miles]; 30 [miles].

The Church Warden below came up, and with some other serious Christians accompanied me to Little Lynch's Creek, where had a very religious congregation of 70 persons had 15 or 16 communicants. In afternoon rode 5 Miles to another congregation and gave service to them, spending the evening in singing psalms and hymns. 30 [miles]; 5 [miles]

This day we had another specimen of the envy malice and temper of the Presbyterians. They gave away 2 barrels of whisky to the populace to make drink, and for to disturb the service for this being the 1st time that the communion was ever celebrated in this wild remote part of the world, it gave a great alarm, and caus'd them much pain and vexation. The company got drunk by 10 o'th Clock and we could hear them firing, hooping, and hallowing like Indians. Some few came before the communion was finish'd and were very noisy, and could I have found out the individuals, would have punish'd them. 837 [total miles]

They took another step to interrupt the service of the day. The Captain of the Corps of Militia on this creek being a Presbyterian, order'd the company to appear as this day under arms to muster. The [Anglican] Church people refus'd. He threatn'd to fire. They defy'd him: And had he attempted it, a battle would certainly have ensu'd in the muster field between the Church folks and Presbyterians, and blood been spilt. His apprehension of danger to his person made him defer it till the 26th.

Some of the New Lights and Baptists would have communicated as to day, but I did not approve it, till I knew them better, had some proofs of their sincerity, and could judge whether motives of curiosity, not religion, prompted them.

Cross'd the country, and the Wateree River to Rocky Mount; was in great danger of my life, the Stream being so rapid that it carried away the boat down the river and stove us on the rocks. We threw the horses over, and they swam to shore and we were taken out by canoos that came off. I was quite spent with toil and sweat. Wet to the skin, and all my linen and baggage soak'd in water. 25 [miles]; 862 [total miles]

December 27. Officiated at Rocky Mount. Had but a small congregation and 5 Communicants; the name of the Holy Sacrament frightened them all away. Returned with the Church Warden down the country. 33 [miles]

1768, January 1: Preached at Granny Quarter Creek to a mix'd multitude of people from various quarters but no bringing of this tribe into any order. They are the lowest pack of wretches my eyes ever saw, or that I have met with in these woods. As wild as the very deer. No making of them sit still during service, but they will be in and out, forward and backward the whole time (women especially) as bees to and fro to their hives. All this must be borne with at the beginning of things. Nor can be mended till churches are built, and the country reduc'd to some form. How would the polite people of London stare, to see the females (many very pretty) come to service in their shifts.

14

Benjamin Franklin, *Autobiography: Recollections of Institution-Building, 1771–84*

Benjamin Franklin was born in Boston in 1706. His father was a soap- and candle-maker who had migrated from England's Oxfordshire in 1683; his mother was the daughter of a Nantucket miller, teacher, Indian interpreter, versifier, and defender of Baptists and Quakers against Puritan intolerance. Benjamin's early love of reading led his father to try to educate him for the clergy. The family's poverty quickly proved too severe to support that project, however, and at age twelve young Ben was apprenticed to his brother, a printer.

Eighteenth-century printers often filled their newspapers with their own writings. Benjamin Franklin began this practice at age sixteen, with a series of essays published under the pen-name of "Mrs. Silence Dogood," ostensibly the widow of a rural clergyman. The pen-name revealed Franklin's purpose: in the spirit of Daniel Defoe's *Essay on Projects* to satirize—but also to honor and promote—Cotton Mather's *Bonifacius: Essays to Do Good.*

In 1722 Franklin moved from Puritan Boston to a Philadelphia that was dominated by Quakers but that, more than any other city in the American colonies, tolerated people of all religions. Arriving in Philadelphia with "a Dutch dollar, and about a shilling in copper," Franklin set about building his fortune. He gained work as a printer and within twenty years had become the most important publisher in the colonies. Through his own shop in Philadelphia he produced Pennsylvania's official documents as well as newspapers and *Poor Richard's Almanac.* Through firms he owned in partnership with others he did similar business in New York, Charleston, and Antigua.

Franklin also made a remarkable career as a civic leader. A newcomer to Philadelphia, lacking inherited wealth or family connections in the city, he rose to prominence by organizing cooperative action among what he called the "middling people." His most notable success came through his effort to promote the creation of a "voluntary association" for the defense of the colony during a period of British war with France. A voluntary militia was necessary because the Quakers who then controlled the Pennsylvania legislature refused to abandon their pacifist commitments even in the face of war. Many Quaker leaders did, however, acknowledge that the colony must defend itself, and they indirectly fostered Franklin's rise. By the 1750s he was leading in the affairs not only of Pennsylvania but of all of British North America.

Within Philadelphia itself, Franklin won credit for promoting the Free Library Company, the Philadelphia Hospital, and the University of Pennsylvania. Unlike their counterparts in the other colonies, these institutions were independent from both church and state—though they did secure subsidies from the municipal or provincial goverment. Franklin persuaded people of diverse religious and national backgrounds to come together for a common purpose. Each institution was designed to encourage and support individual efforts at self-improvement. Franklin successfully argued that private institutions, supported by private contributions, government subsidies, and fees, would advance civic public purposes and at the same time support the self-help efforts of individuals.

Benjamin Franklin wrote his *Autobiography* for his own family in two episodes in 1771 and in 1784. This selection includes his statements on voluntary associations in colonial Philadelphia.

BENJAMIN FRANKLIN

Autobiography

EXCERPTS

1771, 1784

[I]n [about 1727] I had form'd most of my ingenious acquaintance into a club of mutual improvement, which we called the JUNTO; we met on Friday evenings. The rules that I drew up required that every member, in turn, should produce one or more queries on any point of Morals, Politics, or Natural Philosophy, to be discuss'd by the company; and once in three months produce and read an essay of his own writing, on any subject he pleased. Our debates were to be under the direction of a president, and to be conducted in the sincere spirit of inquiry after truth, without fondness for dispute, or desire of victory; and, to prevent warmth, all expression of positiveness in opinions, or direct contradiction, were after some time made contraband, and prohibited under small pecuniary penalties.

The first members were Joseph Breintnal, a copyer of deeds for the scriveners, a good-natured, friendly, middleag'd man, a great lover of poetry, reading all he could meet with, and writing some that was tolerable; very ingenious in many little Nicknackeries, and of a sensible conversation.

Thomas Godfrey, a self-taught mathematician, great in his way, and afterwards inventor of what is now called Hadley's Quadrant. But he knew little out of his way, and was not a pleasing companion; as, like most great mathematicians I have met with, he expected universal precision in everything said, or was for ever denying or distinguishing upon trifles, to the disturbance of all conversation. He soon left us.

Nicholas Scull, a surveyor, afterwards surveyor-general, who lov'd books, and sometimes made a few verses.

William Parsons, bred a shoemaker, but, loving reading, had acquir'd a considerable share of mathematics, which he first studied with a view to astrology, that he afterward laught at it. He also became surveryor-general.

William Maugridge, a joiner, a most exquisite mechanic, and a solid, sensible man.

Hugh Meredith, Stephen Potts, and George Webb I have characterized before.

Robert Grace, a young gentleman of some fortune. . . .

About this time, our club meeting, not at a tavern, but in a little room of Mr Grace's, set apart for that purpose, a proposition was make by me, that, since our books were often referr'd to in our disquisitions upon the queries, it might be convenient to us to have them altogether where we met, that upon occasion they might be consulted; and by thus clubbing our books to a common library, we should, while we lik'd to keep them together, have each of us the advantage of using the books of all the other members, which would be nearly as beneficial as if each owned the whole. It was lik'd and agreed to, and we fill'd one end of the room with such books as we could best spare. The number was not so great as we expected; and tho' they had been of great use, yet some inconveniences occurring for want of due care of them, the collection, after about a year, was separated, and each took his books home again.

And now I set on foot my first project of a public nature, that for a subscription library. I drew up the proposals, got them put into form by our great scrivener, Brockden, and, by the help of my friends in the Junto, procured fifty subscribers of forty shillings each to begin with, and ten shillings a year for fifty years, the term our company was to continue. We afterwards obtain'd a charter, the company being increased to one hundred: this was the mother of all the North American subscription libraries, now so numerous. It is become a great thing itself, and continually increasing. These libraries have improved the general conversation of the Americans, made the common tradesmen and farmers as intelligent as most gentlemen from other countries, and perhaps have contributed in some degree to the stand so generally made throughout the colonies in defence of their privileges.

. . . .

Our club, the Junto, was found so useful, and afforded such satisfaction to the members, that several were desirous of introducing their friends, which could not well be done without exceeding what we had settled as a convenient number, viz., twelve. We had from the beginning made it a rule to keep our institution a secret, which was pretty well observ'd; the intention was to avoid applications of improper persons for admittance, some of whom, perhaps, we might find it difficult to refuse. I was one of those who were against any addition to our number, but, instead of it, made in writing a proposal, that every member separately should endeavor to form a subordinate club, with the same rules respecting queries, etc., and without informing them of the connection with the Junto. The advantages proposed were, the improvement of so many more young citizens by the use of our institutions; our better acquaintance with the general sentiments of the inhabitants on any occasion, as the Junto member might propose what queries we should desire, and was to report to the Junto what pass'd in his separate club; the promotion of our particular interests in business by more extensive recommendation, and the increase of our influence in public affairs, and our power of doing good by spreading thro' the several clubs the sentiments of the Junto.

The project was approv'd, and every member undertook to form his club, but they did not all succeed. Five or six only were compleated, which were called by different names, as the Vine, the Union, the Band, etc. They were useful to themselves, and afforded us a good deal of amusement, information, and instruction, besides answering, in some considerable degree, our views of influencing the public opinion on particular occasions, of which I shall give some instances in course of time as they happened.

My first promotion was my being chosen, in 1736, clerk of the General Assembly. The choice was made that year without opposition; but the year following, when I was again propos'd (the choice, like that of the member, being annual), a new member made a long speech against me, in order to favor some other candidate. I was, however, chosen, which was the more agreeable to me, as, besides the pay for the immediate service as clerk, the place gave me a better opportunity of keeping up an interest among the members, which secur'd to me the business of printing the votes, laws, paper money, and other occasional jobs for the public, that, on the whole, were very profitable. . . .

I began now to turn my thoughts a little to public affairs, beginning, however, with small matters. The city watch was one of the first things that I conceiv'd to want regulation. It was managed by the constables of the respective wards in turn; the constable warned a number of housekeepers to attend him for the night. Those who chose never to attend, paid him six shillings a year to be excus'd, which was suppos'd to be for hiring substitutes, but was, in reality, much more than was necessary for that purpose, and made the constableship a place of profit; and the constable, for a little drink, often got such ragamuffins about him as a watch, that respectable housekeepers did not choose to mix with. Walking the rounds, too, was often neglected, and most of the nights spent in tippling. I thereupon wrote a paper to be read more particularly on the inequality of this six-shilling tax of the constables, respecting the circumstances of those who paid it, since a poor widow housekeeper, all whose property to be guarded by the watch did not perhaps exceed the value of fifty pounds, paid as much as the wealthiest merchant, who had thousands of pounds' worth of goods in his stores.

On the whole, I proposed as a more effectual watch, the hiring of proper men to serve constantly in that business; and as a more equitable way of supporting the charge, the levying a tax that should be proportioned to the property. This idea, being approv'd by the Junto, was communicated to the other clubs, but as arising in each of them; and though the plan was not immediately carried into execution, yet, by preparing the minds of people for the change, it paved the way for the law obtained a few years after, when the members of our clubs were grown into more influence.

About this time I wrote a paper (first to be read in the Junto, but it was afterward publish'd) on the different accidents and carelessnesses by which houses were set on fire, with cautions against them, and means proposed of avoiding them. This was much spoken of as a useful piece, and gave rise to a project, which soon followed it, of forming a company for the more ready extinguishing of fires, and mutual assistance in removing and securing of goods when in danger. Associates in this scheme were presently found, amounting to thirty. Our articles of agreement oblig'd every member to keep always in good order, and fit for use, a certain number of baskets (for packing and transporting of goods), which were to be brought to every fire; and we agreed to meet once a month and spend a social evening together, in discoursing and communicating such ideas as occurred to us upon the subject of fires, as might be useful in our conduct on such occasions.

The utility of this institution soon appeared, and many more desiring to be admitted than we thought convenient for one company, they were advised to form another, which was accordingly done; and this went on, one new company being formed after another, till they became so numerous as to include most of the inhabitants who were men of property; and now, at the time of my writing this, tho' upward of fifty years since its establishment, that which I first formed, called the Union Fire Company, still subsists and flourishes, tho' the first members are all deceas'd but myself and one, who is older by a year than I am. The small fines that have been paid by members for absence at the monthly meetings have been apply'd to the purchase of fire-engines, ladders, fire-hooks, and other useful implements for each company, so that I question whether there is a city in the world better provided with the means of putting a stop to beginning conflagrations; and, in fact, since these institutions, the city has never lost by fire more than one or two houses at a time, and the flames have often been extinguished before the house in which they began has been half consumed.

In 1739 arrived among us from Ireland the Reverend Mr Whitefield, who had made himself remarkable there as an itinerant preacher. He was first permitted to preach in some of our churches; but the clergy, taking a dislike to him, soon refus'd him their pulpits, and he was oblig'd to preach in the fields. The multitudes of all sects and denominations that attended his sermons were enormous, and it was matter of speculation to me, who was one of the number, to observe the extraordinary influence of his oratory on his hearers, and how much they admir'd and respected him, notwithstanding his common abuse of them, by assuring them they were naturally half beasts and half devils. It was wonderful to see the change soon made in the manners of our inhabitants. From being all the world were growing religious, so that one could not walk thro' the town in an evening without hearing psalms sung in different familes of every street.

And it being found inconvenient to assemble in the open air, subject to its inclemencies, the building of a house to meet in was no sooner propos'd, and persons appointed to receive contributions, but sufficient sums were soon receiv'd to procure the ground and erect the building, which was one hundred feet long and seventy broad, about the size of Westminster Hall; and the work was carried on with such spirit as to be finished in a much shorter time than could have been expected. Both house and ground were vested in trustees, expressly for the use of any preacher of any religious persuasion who might desire to say something to the people at Philadelphia; the design in building not being to accommodate any particular sect, but the inhabitants in general; so that even if the Mufti of Constantinople were to send a missionary to preach Mohammedanism to us, he would find a pulpit at his service.

Mr Whitefield, in leaving us, went preaching all the way thro' the colonies to Georgia. The settlement of that province had lately been begun, but, instead of being made with hardy, industrious husband-man, accustomed to labor, the only people fit for such an enterprise, it was with families of broken shop-keepers and other insolvent debtors, many of indolent and idle habits, taken out of the jails, who, being set down in the woods, unqualified for clearing land, and unable to endure the hardships of a new settlement, perished in numbers, leaving many helpless children unprovided for. The sight of their miserable situation inspir'd the benevolent heart of Mr Whitefield with the idea of building an Orphan House there, in which they might be supported and edu-cated. Returning northward, he preach'd up this charity, and made large collections, for his eloquence had a wonderful power over the hearts and purses of his hearers, of which I myself was an instance.

I did not disapprove of the design, but, as Georgia was then desti-tute of materials and workmen, and it was proposed to send them from Philadelphia at a great expense, I thought it would have been better to have built the house here, and brought the children to it. This I advis'd; but he was resolute in his first project, rejected my counsel, and I there-for refus'd to contribute. I happened soon after to attend one of his sermons, in the course of which I perceived he intended to finish with a collection, and I silently resolved he should get nothing from me. I had in my pocket a handful of copper money, three or four silver dollars, and five pistoles in gold. As he proceeded I began to soften, and con-cluded to give the coppers. Another stroke of his oratory make me asham'd of that, and determined me to give the silver; and he finish'd so admirably, that I empty'd my pocket wholly into the collector's dish, gold and all. At this sermon there was also one of our club, who, being of my sentiments respecting the building in Georgia, and suspecting a collection might be intended, had, by way of precaution, emptied his pockets before he came from home. Towards the conclusion of the dis-course, however, he felt a strong desire to give, and apply'd to a neigh-bor, who stood near him, to borrow some money for the purpose. The application was unfortunately [made] to perhaps the only man in the company who had the firmness not to be affected by the preacher. His answer was, *"At any other time, Friend Hopkinson, I would lend to thee freely; but not now, for thee seems to be out of thy right senses."*

Some of Mr Whitefield's enemies affected to suppose that he would apply these collections to his own private emolument; but I, who was intimately acquainted with him (being employed in printing his Sermons and Journals, etc.), never had the least suspicion of his integrity.

. . . .

I had, on the whole, abundant reason to be satisfied with my being established in Pennsylvania. There were, however, two things that I regretted, there being no provision for defense, nor for a compleat education of youth; no militia, nor any college. I therefore, in 1743, drew up a proposal for establishing an academy; and at that time, thinking the Reverend Mr Peter, who was out of employ, a fit person to superintend such an institution, I communicated the project to him; but he, having more profitable views in the service of the proprietaries [the Penn family and other Proprietors of Pennsylvania], which succeeded, declin'd the undertaking; and, not knowing another at that time suitable for such a trust, I let the scheme lie a while dormant. I succeeded better the next year, in 1744, in proposing and establishing a Philosophical Society. The paper I wrote for that purpose will be found among my writings, when collected.

. . . .

With respect to defense, Spain having been several years at war against Great Britain, and being at length join'd by France, which brought us into great danger; and the labored and long-continued endeavor of our governor, Thomas, to prevail with our Quaker Assembly to pass a militia law, and make other provisions for the security of the province, having proved abortive, I determined to try what might be done by a voluntary association of the people. To promote this, I first wrote and published a pamphlet, entitled *Plain Truth*, in which I stated our defenceless situation in strong lights, with the necessity of union and discipline for our defense, and promis'd to propose in a few days an association, to be generally signed for that purpose. The pamphlet had a sudden and surprising efect. I was call'd upon for the instrument of association, and having settled the draft of it with a few friends, I appointed a meeting of the citizens in the large building before mentioned. The house was pretty full; I had prepared a number of printed copies, and provided pens and ink dispers'd all over the room I harangued them a little on the subject, read the paper, and explained it, and then distributed the copies which were eagerly signed, not the least objection being made.

When the company separated, and the papers were collected, we found above twelve hundred hands; and, other copies being dispersed in the country, the subscribers amounted at length to upward of ten thousand. These all furnished themselves as soon as they could with arms, formed themselves into companies and regiments, chose their own officers, and met every week to be instructed in the manual exercise, and other parts of military discipline. The women, by subscriptions among themselves, provided silk colors, which they presented to the companies, painted with different devices and mottoes, which I supplied.

The officers of the companies composing the Philadelphia regiment, being met, chose me for their colonel, but, conceiving myself unfit, I declin'd that station, and recommended Mr Lawrence, a fine person, and a man of influence, who was accordingly appointed. I then propos'd a lottery to defray the expense of building a battery below the town, and furnishing it with cannon. It filled expeditiously, and the battery was soon erected, the merlons being fram'd of logs and fill'd with earth. We bought some old cannon from Boston, but, these not being sufficient, we wrote to England for more, soliciting, at the same time, our proprietaries for some assistance, tho' without much expectation of obtaining it.

Meanwhile, Colonel Lawrence, William Allen, Abram Taylor, Esqr., and myself were sent to New York by the associators, commissioned to borrow some cannon of Governor Clinton. He at first refus'd us peremptorily; but at dinner with his council, where there was great drinking of Madeira wine, as the custom of that place then was, he softened by degrees, and said he would lend us six. After a few more bumpers he advanc'd to ten; and at length he very good-naturedly conceded eighteen. They were fine cannon, eighteen-pounders, with their carriages, which we soon transported and mounted on our battery, where the associators kept a nightly guard while the war lasted, and among the rest I regularly took my turn of duty there as a common soldier.

My activity in these operations was agreeable to the governor and council; they took me into confidence, and I was consulted by them in every measure wherein their concurrence was thought useful to the association. Calling in the aid of religion, I propos'd to them the proclaiming a fast, to promote reformation, and implore the blessing of Heaven on our undertaking. They embrac'd the motion; but, as it was the first fast ever thought of in the province, the secretary had no precedent from which to draw the proclamation. My education in New England, where a fast is proclaimed every year, was here of some advantage: I drew it in the accustomed stile, it was translated into German, printed in both languages, and divulg'd thro' the province. This gave the clergy of the different sects an opportunity of influencing their congregations to join in the association, and it would probably have been general among all but Quakers if the peace had not soon intervened.

It was thought by some of my friends that, by my activity in these affairs, I should offend that sect, and thereby lose my interest in the Assembly of the province, where they formed a great majority. A young gentleman who had likewise some friends in the House, and wished to succeed me as their clerk, acquainted me that it was decided to displace me at the next election; and he, therefore, in good will, advis'd me to resign, as more consistent with my honor than being turn'd out. My answer to him was, that I had read or heard of some public man who made it a rule never to ask for an office, and never to refuse one when offer'd to him. "I approve," says I, "of his rule, and will practice it with a small addition; I shall never ask, never refuse; nor ever resign an office. If they will have my office of clerk to dispose of to another, they shall take it from me. I will not, by giving it up, lose my right of some time or other making reprisals on my adversaries." I heard, however, no more of this; I was chosen again unanimously as usual at the next election. Possibly, as they dislik'd my late intimacy with the members of council, who had join'd the governors in all the disputes about military preparation, with which the House had long been harass'd, they might have been pleas'd if I would voluntarily have left them; but they did not care to displace me on account merely of my zeal for the association, and they could not well give another reason.

Indeed I had some cause to believe that the defense of the country was not disagreeable to any of them, provided they were not requir'd to assist in it. And I found that a much greater number of them that I could have imagined, tho' against offensive war, were clearly for the defensive. Many pamphlets *pro and con* were publish'd on the subject, and some by good Quakers, in favor of defense, which I believe convinc'd most of their younger people.

A transaction in our fire company gave me some insight into their prevailing sentiments. It had been propos'd that we should encourage the scheme for building a battery by laying out the present stock, then about sixty pounds, in tickets of the lottery. By our rules, no money could be dispos'd of till the next meeting after the proposal. The company consisted of thirty members, of which twenty-two were Quakers, and eight only of other persuasions. We eight punctually attended the meeting; but, tho' we thought that some of the Quakers would join us, we were by no means sure of a majority. Only one Quaker, Mr James Morris, appear'd to oppose the measure. He expressed much sorrow that it had ever been propos'd, as he said *Friends* were all against it, and it would create such discord as might break up the company. We told him that we saw no reason for that; we were the minority, and if *Friends* were against the measure, and outvoted us, we must and should, agreeably to the usage of all societies, submit. When the hour for business arriv'd it was mov'd to put the vote; he allow'd we might then do it by the rules, but, as he could assure that a number of members intended to be present for the purpose of opposing it, it would be but candid to allow a little time for their appearing.

While we were disputing this, a waiter came to tell me two gentlemen below desir'd to speak with me. I went down, and found they were two of our Quaker members. They told me there were eight of them assembled at a tavern just by; that they were determined to come and vote with us if there should be occasion, which they hop'd would not be the case, and desir'd we would not call for their assistance if we could do without it, as their voting for such a measure might embroil them with their elders and friends. Being thus secure of a majority, I went up, and after a little seeming hesitation, agreed to a delay of another hour. This Mr Morris allow'd to be extreamly fair. Not one of his opposing friends appear'd, at which he express'd a great surprise; and, at the expiration of the hour, we carr'd the resolution eight to one; and as, of the twenty-two Quakers, eight were ready vote with us, and thirteen, by their absence manifested that they were not inclin'd to oppose the measure, I afterward estimated the proportion of Quakers sincerely against defense as one to twenty-one only; for these were all regular members of that society, and in good reputation among them, and had due notice of what was propos'd at that meeting. . . .

Peace being concluded, and the association business therefor at an end, I turn'd my thoughts again to the affair of establishing an academy. The first step I took was to associate in the design a number of active friends, of whom the Junto furnished a good part; the next was to write and publish a pamphlet, entitled *Proposals Relating to the Education of Youth in Pennsylvania*. This I distributed among the inhabitants gratis; and as soon as I could suppose their minds a little prepared by the persual of it, I set on foot a subscription for opening and supporting an academy; it was to be paid in quotas yearly for five years; by so dividing it, I judg'd the subscription might be larger, and I believed it was so, amounting to no less, if I remember right, than five thousand pounds.

In the introduction to these proposals, I stated their publication, not as an act of mine, but of some *publick-spirited gentlemen,* avoiding as much as I could, according to my usual rule, the presenting myself to the publick as the author of any scheme for their benefit.

The subscribers, to carry the project into immediate execution, chose out of their number twenty-four trustees, and appointed Mr Francis, then attorney-general, and myself to draw up constitutions for the government of the academy; which being done and signed, a house was hired, masters engag'd, and the schools opened, I think, in that same year, 1749. . . .

The trustees of the Academy, after a while, were incorporated by a charter from the Governor; their funds were increas'd by contributions in Britain and grants of land from the proprietaries, to which the Assembly has since made considerable addition; and thus was established the present University of Philadelphia. I have been continued one of its trustees from the beginning, now near forty years, and have had the very great plesure of seeing a number of the youth who have receiv'd their education in it, distinguished by their improv'd abilities, serviceable in public stations, and ornaments to their country. . . .

. . . .

In 1751, Dr Thomas Bond, a particular friend of mine, conceived the idea of establishing a hospital in Philadelphia (a very beneficent design, which has been ascrib'd to me, but was originally his), for the reception and cure of poor sick persons, whether inhabitants of the province or strangers. He was zealous and active in endeavoring to procure subscriptions for it, but the proposal being a novelty in America, and at first not well understood, he met with but small success.

At length he came to me with the compliment that he found there was no such thing as carrying a public-spirited project through without my being concern'd in it. "For," says he, "I am often ask'd by those to whom I propose subscribing, Have you consulted Franklin upon this business? And what does he think of it? And when I tell them that I have not (supposing it rather out of your line), they do not subscribe, but say they will consider of it." I enquired into the nature and probable utility of his scheme, and receiving from him a very satisfactory explanation, I not only subscribed to it myself, but engag'd heartily in the design of procuring subscriptions from others. Previously, however, to the solicitation, I endeavored to prepare the minds of the people by writing on the subject in the newspapers, which was my usual custom in such cases, but which he had omitted.

The subscriptions afterwards were more free and generous; but, beginning to flag, I saw they would be insufficient without some assistance from the Assembly, and therefore propos'd to petition for it, which was done. The country members did not at first relish the project; they objected that it could only be serviceable to the city, and therefore the citizens alone should be at the expense of it; and they doubted whether the citizens themselves generally approv'd of it. My allegation on the contrary, that it met with such approbation as to leave no doubt of our being able to raise two thousand pounds by voluntary donations, they considered as a most extravagant supposition, and utterly impossible.

On this I form'd my plan; and, asking leave to bring in a bill for incorporating the contributors according to the prayer of their petition, and granting them a blank sum of money, which leave was obtained chiefly on the consideration that the House could throw the bill out if they did not like it, I drew it so as to make the important clause a conditional one, viz., "And be it enacted, by the authority aforesaid, that when the said contributors shall have met and chosen their managers and treasurer, *and shall have raised by their contributions a capital stock of* _____ *value* (the yearly interest of which is to be applied to the accommodating of the sick poor in the said hospital, free of charge for diet, attendance, advice, and medicines), and *shall make the same appear to the satisfaction of the speaker of the Assembly for the time being,* that *then* it shall and may be lawful for the said speaker, and he is hereby required, to sign an order on the provincial treasurer for the payment of two thousand pounds, in two yearly payments, to the treasurer of the said hospital, to be applied to the founding, building, and finishing of the same."

The condition carried the bill through; for the members, who had oppos'd the grant, and now conceiv'd they might have the credit of being charitable without the expence, agreed to its passage; and then, in soliciting subscriptions among the people, we urg'd the conditional promise of the law as an additional motive to give, since every man's donation would be doubled; thus the clause work'd both ways. The subscriptions accordingly soon exceeded the requisite sum, and we claim'd and receiv'd the public gift, which enabled us to carry the design into execution. A convenient and handsome building was soon erected; the institution has by constant experience been found useful, and flourishes to this day; and I do not remember any of my political manoeuvres, the success of which gave me at the time more pleasure, or wherin, after thinking of it, I more easily excus'd myself for having made some use of cunning.

It was about this time that another projector, the Rev. Gilbert Tennent, came to me with a request that I would assist him in procuring a subscription for erecting a new meeting-house. It was to be for the use of a congregation he had gathered among the Presbyterians, who were originally disciples of Mr Whitefield. Unwilling to make myself disagreeable to my fellow-citizens by too frequently soliciting their contribution, I absolutely refus'd. He then desired I would furnish him with a list of the names of persons I knew by experience to be generous and public-spirited. I thought it would be unbecoming in me, after their kind compliance with my solicitations, to mark them out to be worried by other beggars, and therfore refus'd also to give such a list. He then desir'd I would at least give him my advice. "That I will readily do," said I; "and, in the first place, I advise you to apply to all those whom you know will give something; next, to those whom you are uncertain whether they will give any thing or not, and show them the list of those who have given; and, lastly, do not neglect those who you are sure will give nothing, for in some of them you may be mistaken." He laugh'd and thank'd me, and said he would take my advice. He did so, for he ask'd *everybody;*

and he obtain'd a much larger sum than he expected, with which he erected the capacious and very elegant meeting-house that stands in Arch-street.

Our city, tho' laid out with a beautiful regularity, the streets large, strait, and crossing each other at right angles, had the disgrace of suffering those streets to remain long unpav'd, and in wet weather the wheels of heavy carriages plough'd them into a quagmire, so that it was difficult to cross them; and in dry weather the dust was offensive. I had liv'd near what was call'd the Jersey Market, and saw with pain the inhabitants wading in mud while purchasing their provisions. A strip of ground down the middle of that market was at length pav'd with brick, so that, being once in the market, they had firm footing, but were often over shoes in dirt to get there. By talking and writing on the subject, I was at length instrumental in getting the street pav'd with stone between the market and the brick'd foot-pavement, that was on each side next the houses. This, for some time, gave an easy access to the market dry-shod; but, the rest of the street not being pav'd, whenever a carriage came out of the mud upon this pavement, it shook off and left its dirt upon it, and it was soon cover'd with mire, which was not remov'd, the city as yet having no scavengers.

After some inquiry, I found a poor, industrious man, who was willing to undertake keeping the pavement clean, by sweeping it twice a week, carrying off the dirt from before all the neighbors' doors for the sum of sixpence per month, to be paid by each house. I then wrote and printed a paper setting forth the advantage to the neighborhood that might be obtain'd by this small expense; the greater ease in keeping our houses clean, so much dirt not being brought in by people's feet; the benefit to the shops by more custom, etc., etc., as buyers could more easily get at them; and by not having, in windy weather, the dust blown in upon their goods, etc., etc. I sent one of these papers to each house, and in a day or two went round to see who would subscribe an agreement to pay these sixpences; it was unanimously sign'd, and for a time well executed. All the inhabitants of the city were delighted with the cleanliness of the pavement that surrounded the market, it being a convenience to all, and this rais'd a general desire to have all the streets paved, and made the people more willing to submit to a tax for that purpose.

After some time I drew a bill for paving the city, and brought it into the Assembly. It was just before I went to England, in 1757, and did not pass till I was gone, and then with an alteration in the mode of assessment, which I thought not for the better, but with an additional provision for lighting as well as paving the streets, which was a great improvement. It was by [a] private person, the late Mr John Clifton, . . . giving a sample of the utility of lamps, by placing one at his door, that the people were first impress'd with the idea of enlighting all the city. The honor of this public benefit has also been ascrib'd to me, but it belongs truly to that gentleman. I did but follow his example, and have only some merit to claim respecting the form of our lamps, as differing from the globe lamps we were at first supply'd with from London. Those we found inconvenient in these respects: they admitted no air below; the smoke, therefore, did not readily go out above, but circulated in the globe, lodg'd on its inside, and soon obstructed the light they were intended to afford; giving, besides, the daily trouble of wiping them clean; and an accidental stroke on one of them would demolish it, and render it totally useless. I therefore suggested the composing of four flat panes, with a long funnel above to draw up the smoke, and crevices admitting air below, to facilitate the ascent of the smoke; by this means they were kept clean, and did not grow dark in a few hours, as the London lamps do, but continu'd bright till morning, and an accidental stroke would generally break but a single pane, easily repair'd. . . .

THE AMERICAN REVOLUTION

Sources of the Nonprofit Sector

THREE

To the Constitution: Limited Government and Disestablishment

Americans of the Revolutionary generation established a political culture and a set of political institutions—defined above all in the Constitution's separation of powers (legislative, executive, judicial), its checks and balances, and its federalism—that resisted both governmental action and taxes. The principles of limited government and low taxes also shaped most of the early state governments—though with important exceptions, especially in Massachusetts, Connecticut, New York, and Pennsylvania. Nineteenth-century American governments did play important roles in the regulation and promotion of the economy, but more significantly through a legal system that guaranteed the rights of property and encouraged entrepreneurs, and through the creation of a vast, unified continent-wide market, than through subsidies or the direct provision of services by government agencies. Local governments—especially in cities and in the northeast and upper midwest—did raise and spend significant funds on education, the relief of poverty, and public health. From a Constitutional point of view local governments are simply corporations that are the creatures of their states, so it can well be said that early New York, Pennsylvania, Maryland, and other states played governing roles, through their municipal governments, that were quite active. But until the twentieth century neither the federal nor the state governments developed the capacity to provide much in the way of education, health care, or social service. Almost no one thought that government in the United States should serve as a patron of the arts in any way except as the builder of capitol buildings, courthouses, and city halls, and—perhaps—of waterworks, bridges, and streets and parks.

British writers like John Trenchard and Thomas Gordon, who wrote as "Cato" in the 1720s, published arguments against taxes and strong government that influenced many American revolutionaries. During the debate over the constitution, James Madison argued, in his famous essay *Federalist No. 10* (1787), that the constitution would preserve American liberties because it established a representative form of government for a vast territory that embraced a large and diverse array of organized interests. Madison did not use the term voluntary association, but his argument that many small interests would check one another provided the basis for a political theory that makes voluntary associations central to American politics.

Americans of the Revolutionary generation dealt with the reality of religious diversity by agreeing to separate church and state, launching a process that took nearly fifty years. The process began with the debate over the Virginia Statute of Religious Freedom of 1786 and the Northwest Ordinance of 1787, which called "for extending the fundamental principles of civil and religious liberty, which form the basis whereupon these republics, their laws and constitutions are erected." The First Amendment to the Constitution, adopted in 1791, established the principle of separation of church and state at the federal level. Revolutionary-era leaders ranging from James Madison and Thomas Jefferson to Isaac Backus, the Massachusetts Baptist, argued that questions of religious belief should also be left out of government in the states as well as in the federal administration. Following the logic of this decision, they also agreed that governments should not use tax funds to support churches. This last idea led to protracted conflicts over the use of glebe lands granted by the British government for the support of Anglican churches in Virginia, and was not implemented in Connecticut until 1817, or in Massachusetts until as late as 1833.

The full story of the debates over the U.S. constitution and the development of American political ideas is of course far more complex than these few selections can possibly suggest. The framers of the Constitution knew from their own experience that they could not anticipate all the challenges that might face their new nation, so they opened the Constitution with a preamble stating that its purposes were, in part, to "insure domestic Tranquility," "to promote the general Welfare," and "to secure the blessings of Liberty." These are very broad purposes, which American leaders and voters have interpreted in widely varying ways over the years. Article I, Section 8, which enumerates the powers assigned to Congress, also contains many clauses that can reasonably be interpreted to allow for the exercise of very broad powers by the federal government. It states that Congress is "to provide for . . . the general Welfare of the United States," "to regulate Commerce with foreign nations, and among the several States"; and "to make all laws which shall be necessary and proper for carrying into Execution the foregoing Powers, and all other Powers vested by this Constitution in the Government of the United States."

Over the years, Congress has provided for many activities under the General Welfare, Commerce, and Necessary and Proper clauses of the Constitution. But in view of the continuing consensus that the federal government's role should be limited except in times of national emergency, Congress has usually arranged for federally supported services to be offered not by federal agencies, but by the states (through state universities, for example, or state-chartered local governments and special-purpose districts), or by private, nonprofit organizations including private colleges and universities, private, nonprofit hospitals, pre-schools, private community development organizations, and other organizations that have come to make up the nonprofit sector.

The Constitution also stated, in Article IV, Section 4, that "The United States shall guarantee to every State in this Union a Republican Form of Government," leaving it to the future to define what, exactly, a Republic was to be. The Fifth Amendment added that "No person shall . . . be deprived of life, liberty, or property, without due process of law" and that "nor shall private property be taken for public use, without just compensation." As we will see, the Supreme Court later ruled that these clauses could be applied to corporations as well as to individuals. The fifth Amendment did not prevent slavery; it was not until after the Civil War, in December, 1865, that the Thirteenth Amendment was added: "Neither slavery nor involuntary servitude, except as a punishment for a crime whereof the party shall have been duly convicted, shall exist within the United States, or any place subject to their jurisdiction." The Fourteenth Amendment gave Congress additional powers to intervene in state legislation, adding the language that "No state shall make or enforce any law which shall abridge the privileges of immunities of citizens of the United States; nor shall any State deprive any person of life, liberty, or property, without due process of law; nor deny to any person within its jurisdiction the equal protection of the laws." Again, the Supreme Court later ruled that these phrases applied to corporations, including nonprofit corporations, as well as to individuals.

15

John Trenchard and Thomas Gordon, *Cato's Letters: Arguments against a Strong Central Government,* 1720

The American Revolution led to the creation of a new government that lacked the ability of the British or other European governments to take decisive action or to raise substantial funds through taxation. Such leaders of the Revolution as Ben Franklin, Alexander Hamilton, and—in some of his moods, as for example in his advocacy of state support for the University of Virginia—Thomas Jefferson favored an active role for both state and national government and the levying of sufficient taxes to enable government to act. But for at least one hundred and fifty years after the Revolution (with the brief exception of the Civil War), a majority of the Americans who were able to take part in elections (white men only until 1920, few African Americans in the South until after the 1960s) viewed with skepticism nearly every effort to impose taxes and expand the services offered by government—unless they could see a direct and immediate benefit to themselves.

An important source of the American opposition to strong government lay in the writings of England's "Real Whigs" or "Country Party." The Real Whigs opposed the effective efforts of Sir Robert Walpole, the first powerful Prime Minister of Great Britain, to increase the powers and raise the revenues of the British government in the early decades of the eighteenth century. Defending what they conceived to be the interests of honest country landowners against Walpole's Parliament and the Royal Court, the Real Whigs insisted that honest citizens wished only to be left alone to work in peace and to enjoy the fruits of their labors. A legitimate government would protect their modest desires. Walpole's government, they argued, had become corrupt in the sense that it had allowed private interests to prevail over public virtue. Sure signs of corruption in government, according to the Real Whigs, included an increase in taxes, an expansion of the public debt, the use of tax money to purchase the support of legislators or to grant pensions and contracts to the influential or well-connected, the use of tax money to pay for lavish ceremonies at court and spectacular entertainments for the public, the undertaking of foreign adventures, and the creation of a large standing army.

The American revolutionaries were deeply influenced by the Real

Whigs. Many of them viewed a work entitled *Cato's Letters: Essays on Liberty, Civil and Religious,* by John Trenchard and Thomas Gordon, as a classic statement of political principle. An essay from *Cato's Letters* demonstrates its criticism of strong government and its warnings against every sort of government action from an over-development of the military to government sponsorship for the arts.

JOHN TRENCHARD AND THOMAS GORDON

Cato's Letters, No. 17

Saturday, Februry 18, 1720

What Measures are actually taken by wicked and desperate Ministers to ruin and enslave their Country.

S I R ,

As under the best Princes, and the best Servants to Princes alone, it is safe to speak what is true of the worst; so, according to my former Promise to the Publick, I shall take the Advantage of our excellent King's most gentle Government, and the virtuous Administration of an uncorrupt Ministry, to warn Mankind against the Mischiefs which may hereafter be dreaded from corrupt ones. It is too true, that every Country in the World has sometimes groaned under that heavy Misfortune, and our own as much as any; though I cannot allow it to be true, what Monsieur de Witt has long since observed, that the English Court has always been the most thievish Court in Europe.

Few Men have been desperate enough to attack openly, and barefaced, the Liberties of a free People. Such avowed Conspirators can rarely succeed: The Attempt would destroy itself. Even when the Enterprize is begun and visible, the End must be hid, or denied. It is the Business and Policy of Traytors, so to disguise their Treason with plausible Names, and so to recommend it with popular and bewitching Colours, that they themselves shall be adored, while their Work is detested, and yet carried on by those that detest it.

Thus one Nation has been surrendered to another under the fair Name of mutual Alliance: The Fortresses of a Nation have been given up, or attempted to be given up, under the frugal Notion of saving Charges to a Nation; and Commonwealths have been trepanned into Slavery, by Troops raised or increased to defend them from Slavery.

It may therefore be of Service to the World, to shew what Measures have been taken to corrupt Ministers, in some of our neighbouring Countries, to ruin and enslave the People over whom they presided; to shew by what Steps and Gradations of Mischief Nations have been undone, and consequently what methods may be hereafter taken to undo others: And this Subject I rather choose, because my Countrymen may be the more sensible of, and know how to value the inestimable Blessing of living under the best Prince, and the best established Government in the Universe, where we have none of these Things to fear.

Such Traitors will probably endeavour first to get their Prince into their Possession, and, like Sejanus, shut him up in a little Island, or perhaps make him a Prisoner in his Court; whilst, with full Range, they devour his Dominions, and plunder his Subjects. When he is thus secluded from the Access of his Friends, and the Knowledge of his Affairs, he must be content with such Misrepresentations as they shall find expedient to give him. False Cases will be stated, to justify wicked Counsel; wicked Counsel will be given, to procure unjust Orders. He will be made to mistake his Foes for his Friends, his Friends for his Foes; and to believe that his Affairs are in the highest Prosperity, when they are in the greatest Distress; and that publick Matters go on in the greatest Harmony, when they are in the utmost Confusion.

THE USES OF PUBLIC PROJECTS, WARS, PENSIONS

They will be ever contriving and forming wicked and dangerous Projects, to make the People poor, and themselves rich; well knowing that Dominion follows Property; that where there are Wealth and Power, there will be always Crowds of servile Dependents; and that, on the contrary, Poverty dejects the Mind, fashions it to Slavery, and renders it unequal to any generous Undertaking, and incapable of opposing any bold Usurpation.

They will squander away the publick Money in wanton Presents to Minions, and their Creatures of Pleasure or of Burthen, or in Pensions to mercenary and worthless Men and Women, for vile Ends and traiterous Purposes.

They will engage their Country in ridiculous, expensive, fantastical Wars, to keep the Minds of Men in continual Hurry and Agitation, and under constant Fears and Alarms; and, by such Means, deprive them both of Leisure and Inclination to look into publick Miscarriages. Men, on the contrary, will, instead of such Inspection, be disposed to fall into all Measures offered, seemingly, for their Defence, and will agree to every wild Demand made by those who are betraying them.

When they have served their Ends by such Wars, or have other Motives to make Peace, they will have no View to the publick Interest;

but will often, to procure such Peace, deliver up the Strong-Holds of their Country, or its Colonies for Trade, to open Enemies, suspected Friends, or dangerous Neighbours, that they may not be interrupted in their domestick Designs.

PARTIES AND PATRONAGE

They will create Parties in the Commonwealth, or keep them up where they already are; and, by playing them by Turns upon each other, will rule both. By making the Guelfs afraid of the Ghibelines, and these afraid of the Guelfs, they will make themselves the Mediums and Balance between the two Factions; and both Factions, in their Turns, the Props of their Authority, and the Instruments of their Designs.

They will not suffer any Men, who have once tasted of Authority, though personally their Enemies, and whose Posts they enjoy, to be called to an Account for past Crimes, though ever so enormous. They will make no such Precedents for their own Punishment; nor censure Treason, which they intend to commit. On the contrary, they will form new Conspiracies, and invent new Fences for their own Impunity and Protection; and endeavour to engage such numbers in their Guilt, as to set themselves above all Fear of Punishment.

They will prefer worthless and wicked Men, and not suffer a Man of Knowledge or Honesty to come near them, or enjoy a Post under them. They will disgrace Men of Virtue, and ridicule Virtue itself, and laugh at Publick Spirit. They will put Men into Employments, without any Regard to the Qualifications for those Employments, or indeed to any Qualifications at all, but as they contribute to their Designs, and shew a stupid Alacrity to do what they are bid. They must be either Fools or Beggars; either void of Capacity to discover their Intrigues, or of Credit and Inclination to disappoint them.

PUBLIC ENTERTAINMENTS

They will promote Luxury, Idleness, and Expence, and a general Depravation of Manners, by their own Example, as well as by Connivance and publick Encouragement. This will not only divert Mens Thoughts from examining their Behaviour and Politicks, but likewise let them loose from all the Restraints of private and publick Virtue. From Immorality and Excesses they will fall into Necessity; and from thence into a servile Dependence upon Power.

In order to do this, they will bring into Fashion Gaming, Drunkenness, Gluttony, and profuse and costly Dress. They will debauch their Country with foreign Vices, and foreign Instruments of vicious Pleasures; and will contrive and encourage publick Revels, nightly Disguises, and debauched Mummeries.

They will, by all practicable Means of Oppression, provoke the People to Disaffection; and then make that Disaffection an Argument for new Oppression, for not trusting them any further, and for keeping up Troops; and, in fine, for depriving them of Liberties and Privileges, to which they are entitled by their Birth, and the Laws of their Country.

GOVERNMENT CONTRACTS AND GRANTS

If such Measures should ever be taken in any free Country, where the People choose Deputies to represent them, then they will endeavour to bribe the Electors in the Choice of their Representatives, and so to get a Council of their own Creatures; and where they cannot succeed with the Electors, they will endeavour to corrupt the Deputies after they are chosen, with the Money given for the publick Defence; and to draw into the Perpetration of their Crimes those very Men, from whom the betrayed People expect the Redress of their Grievances, and the Punishment of those Crimes. And when they have thus made the Representatives of the People afraid of the People, and the People afraid of their Representatives; then they will endeavour to persuade those Deputies to seize the Government to themselves, and not to trust their Principals any longer with the Power of resenting their Treachery and Ill-Usage, and of sending honester and wiser Men in their room.

But if the Constitution should be so stubbornly framed, that it will still preserve itself and the People's Liberties, in spite of all villainous Contrivances to destroy both; then must the Constitution itself be attacked and broken, because it will not bend. There must be an Endeavour, under some Pretence of publick Good, to alter a Balance of the Government, and to get it into the sole Power of their Creatures, and of such who will have constantly an Interest distinct from that of the Body of the People.

But if all these Schemes for the Ruin of the Publick, and their own Impunity, should fail them; and the worthy Patriots of a free Country should prove obstinate in Defense of their Country, and resolve to call its Betrayers to a strict Account; there is then but one thing left for such Traytors to do; namely, to veer about, and, by joining with the Enemy of their Prince and Country, complete their Treason.

I have somewhere read of a Favourite and First Minister to a neighbouring Prince, long since dead, who played his Part so well, that, though he had, by his evil Counsels, raised a Rebellion, and a Contest for the Crown; yet he preserved himself a Resource, whoever got the better: If his old Master succeeded, then this Achitophel, by the Help of a baffled Rebellion, ever favourable to Princes, had the Glory of fixing his Master in absolute Power: But, as his brave Rival got the Day, Achitophel had the Merit of betraying his old Master to plead; and was accordingly taken into Favour.

Happy therefore, thrice happy, are we, who can be unconcerned Spectators of the Miseries which the greatest Part of Europe is reduced to suffer, having lost their Liberties by the Intrigues and Wickedness of those whom they trusted; whilst we continue in full Enjoyment of ours, and can be in no Danger of losing them, while we have so excellent a King, assisted and obeyed by so wise a Parliament.

16

Isaac Backus, *Argument against Taxes for Religious Purposes in Massachusetts,* 1774

Colonial Massachusetts required every property-owner to pay a tax for the support of the town church, its minister, and its school. During the American Revolution Baptists like Isaac Backus protested that this law forced them to support the religious activities of Congregationalists, whose views they had rejected. At a time when most of Massachusetts was protesting taxes imposed upon the colonies by a British Parliament in which no colonist had a vote, Backus argued, it was impossible to understand how the Massachusetts legislature could force Baptists to pay for the support of Congregationalist churches.

It would be wrong, however, to conclude that Backus was an all-out advocate of the separation of church and state. Even as he protested against the religious tax he accepted the idea that the colonial (and later the state) government should declare special fast days, and like his Congregationalist colleagues he preached sermons on topics for which the legislature declared fasts. After the Revolution Backus also supported the idea that the national government should take action to assure the purity of Christianity: in 1790 he joined other New England ministers in urging Congress to "take such measures as the Constitution may permit, that no edition of the Bible, or its translation, may be published in America, without its being carefully inspected, and certified to be free from error."[1]

---

1. Quoted in Jon Butler, *Awash in a Sea of Faith: Christianizing the American People* [Cambridge: Harvard University Press, 1990], p. 261.

ISAAC BACKUS

Protest against Taxes for the Established Churches in Massachusetts

December 2, 1774

Honored Gentlemen:

At a time when all America are alarmed at the open and violent attempts that have been made against their liberties, it affords great cause of joy and thankfulness, to see the colonies so happily united to defend their rights; and particularly that their late Continental Congress have been directed into measures so wise and salutary for obtaining relief and securing our future liberties and who have wisely extended their regards to the rights and freedom of the poor Africans. Since then the law of equity has prevailed so far, we hope that it will move this honorable assembly to have a just regard to their English neighbors and brethren at home.

It seems that the two main rights which all America are contending for at this day, are not to be taxed where they are not represented, and to have their causes tried by unbiased judges. And the Baptist churches in this province as heartily unite with their countrymen in this cause, as any denomination in the land; and are as ready to exert all their abilities to defend it. Yet only because they have thought it to be their duty to claim an equal title to these rights with their neighbors, they have repeatedly been accused of evil attempts against the general welfare of the colony; therefore, we have thought it expedient to lay a brief statement of the case before this assembly. . . .

Massachusetts legislators never were empowered to lay any taxes but what were of a civil and worldly nature; and to impose religious taxes is as much out of their jurisdiction, as it can be for Britain to tax America; yet how much of this has been done in this province. Indeed, many try to elude the force of this reasoning by saying that the taxes which our rulers impose for the support of ministers, are of a civil nature. But it is certain that they call themselves ministers of Christ; and the taxes now referred to are to support them under that name; and they either are such, or else they deceive the people. If they are Christ's ministers, he has made laws enough to support them; if they are not, where are the rulers who will dare to compel people to maintain men who call themselves Christ's ministers when they are not? Those who ministered about holy things and at God's altar in the Jewish church, partook of and lived upon the things which were freely offered there; Even so hath the Lord ordained that they who preach the Gospel, should live of the Gospel. And such communications are called sacrifices to God more than once in the New Testament. And why may not civil rulers appoint and enforce with the sword, any other sacrifice as well as this. . . .

Must we be blamed for not lying still, and thus let our countrymen trample upon our rights, and deny us that very liberty that they are ready to take up arms to defend for themselves? You profess to exempt us from taxes to your worship, and yet tax us every year. Great complaints have been made about a tax which the British Parliament laid upon paper; but you require a paper tax of us annually.

That which has made the greatest noise, is a tax of three pence a pound upon tea: but your law of last June laid a tax of the same sum every year upon the Baptists in each parish, as they would expect to defend themselves against a greater one. And only because the Baptists in Middleboro' have refused to pay that little tax, we hear that the first parish in said town have this fall voted to lay a greater tax upon us. All America are alarmed at the tea tax; though, if they please, they can avoid it by not buying the tea; but we have no such liberty. We must either pay the little tax, or else your people appear even in this time of extremity, determined to lay the great one upon us.

But these lines are to let you know, that we are determined not to pay either of them; not only upon your principle of not being taxed where we are not represented, but also because we dare not render that homage to any earthly power, which I and many of my brethren are fully convinced belongs only to God. We cannot give in the certificates you require, without implicitly allowing to men that authority which we believe in our consciences belongs only to God. Here, therefore, we claim charter rights, liberty of conscience. And if any still deny it to us, they must answer it to Him who has said, "With what measure ye mete, it shall be measured to you again."

If any ask what we would have, we answer: Only allow us freely to enjoy the religious liberty that they do in Boston, and we ask no more.

We remain hearty friends to our country, and ready to do all in our power for its general welfare.

ISAAC BACKUS, Agent for the Baptist Churches in this Province.
By advice of their Committee. Boston, Dec. 2, 1774.

17

Thomas Jefferson, *Virginia Act Establishing Religious Freedom*, 1786

The Revolutionary War ended with the military defeat of the British in 1783. As they turned to govern themselves, the victorious Americans in most colonies had to consider the position of the established church. In Virginia, the Church of England had been supported by taxes and by glebe lands granted by the crown; and Baptists had endured a "Great Persecution" in which they had been punished with jail and public whippings between 1768 and 1774. Meanwhile, Presbyterians had grown numerous in the Valley of Virginia. After the Revolution, Virginia disestablished the Anglican Church and engaged in a long debate as to the disposition of its glebe lands. In 1786 it enacted a law, drafted by Thomas Jefferson, protecting religious freedom. Jefferson's law allowed complete religious freedom, and prevented the state from giving any advantage of a material or civil character to any religious group.

THOMAS JEFFERSON

Virginia Act Establishing Religious Freedom

January 16, 1786

I. WHEREAS Almighty God hath created the mind free;

that all attempts to influence it by temporal punishments or burthens, by civil incapacitations, tend only to beg habits of hypocrisy and meanness, and are a departure from the plan of the Holy author of our religion, who being Lord both of body and mind, yet chose not to propagate it by coercions on either, as was in his Almighty power to do;

that the impious presumption of legislators and rulers, civil as well as ecclesiastical, who being themselves but fallible and uninspired men, have assumed dominion over the faith of others, setting their own opinions and modes of thinking as the only true and infallible, and as such endeavouring to impose them on others, hath established and maintained false religions over the greatest part of the world, and through all time;

that to compel a man to furnish contributions of money for the propagation of opinions which he disbelieve is sinful and tyrannical;

that even the forcing him to support this or that teacher of his own religious persuasion, is depriving him of the comfortable liberty of giving his contributions to the particular pastor whose morals he would make his pattern, and whose powers be feels most persuasive to righteousness, and his withdrawing from the ministry those temporary rewards, which proceeding from an approbation of their personal conduct, are an additional incitement to earnest and unremitting labours for the instruction of mankind;

that our civil rights have no dependence on our religious opinion any more than our opinions in physics or geometry;

that therefore the proscribing any citizen as unworthy the public confidence by laying upon him an incapacity of being called to offices of trust and emolument, unless he profess or renounce this or that religious opinion, is depriving him injuriously of those privileges and advantages to which in common with his fellow-citizen he has a natural right,

that it tends only to corrupt the principles of that religion it is meant to encourage, by bribing with a monopoly of worldly honours and emoluments, those who will externally profess and conform to it; that though indeed these are criminals who do not withstand such temption, yet neither are those innocent lay the bait in their way;

that to suffer the civil magistrate to intrude his powers in the field of opinion, and to restrain the profession or propagation of principles on supposition of their ill tendency, is a dangerous fallacy, which at once destroys all religious liberty, because he being of course judge of that tendency will make his opinions the rule of judgment, and approve or condemn the sentiments of others only as they square with or differ from his own;

that it is time enough for the rightful purposes of civil government, for its officers to interfere when principles break out into overt acts against peace and good order;

and finally, that truth is great and will prevail if left to herself, that she is the proper and sufficient antagonist to error, and has nothing to fear from the conflict, unless by human interposition disarmed of her natural weapons, free argument and debate, errors ceasing to be dangerous when it is permitted freely to contradict them.

II. BE IT ENACTED BY THE GENERAL ASSEMBLY, that no man shall be compelled to frequent or support any religious worship, place or ministry whatsoever, nor shall be enforced, restrained, molested, or burdened in his body or goods, nor shall otherwise suffer on account of his religious opinions or belief; but that all men shall be free to profess, and by argument to maintain, their opinion in matters of religion, and that the same shall in no wise diminish, enlarge or affect their civil capacities.

III. And though we well know that this assembly, elected by the people for the ordinary purposes of legislation only, have no power to restrain the acts of succeeding assemblies, constituted with powers equal to our own, and that therefore to declare this act to be irrevocable would be of no effect in law; yet as we are free to declare, and do declare, that the rights hereby asserted are of the natural rights of mankind, and that if any act shall hereafter be passed to repeal the present, or to narrow its operation, such act will be an infringement of natural right.

18

James Madison, *The Federalist, No. 10,* 1787

During the Revolutionary War, the United States was governed under the Articles of Confederation, which provided for a very weak central government—one that was, for example, unable to levy taxes and was limited to asking the states to tax themselves to cover federal expenses. This arrangement did not work very well. During the Revolutionary War, for example, the army was always short of funds, so that at Valley Forge Washington could not afford to provide tents and food for his soldiers and had to allow his troops to disperse to their homes. The Constitutional Convention of 1787 proposed a stronger, more centralized federal government. Opponents argued that a strong national government could be used to oppress the states and individual citizens. In the *Federalist Papers,* James Madison, Alexander Hamilton, and John Jay laid out the arguments for the stronger federal government of the Constitution. Madison's *The Federalist, No. 10,* the most famous of these papers, argued that Americans did not need to fear that the federal government would oppress them.

Ideally, Madison began, all members of a nation would share a common understanding of "the permanent and aggregate interests of the community." In reality, however, every nation contained "factions," which might be majorities as well as minorities, who were "united . . . by some common impulse of passion, or of interest." In meeting the challenge of controlling the dangerous effects of faction, Madison argued, the United States had the advantage of large size and great economic and social diversity, which made it difficult for any one interest or faction to dominate.

The Constitution, Madison insisted, created a *republic,* governed through elected representatives, rather than a *direct democracy,* governed by the votes of all citizens gathered in a general assembly. And "as each representative will be chosen by a greater number of citizens in the large than in the small republic, it will be more difficult for unworthy candidates" to win election by "vicious arts." Altogether, *Federalist No. 10* is the great statement of the value, in the American Republic, of the "greater variety of parties" and organized interests.

JAMES MADISON

The Federalist, No. 10

1787

To the People of the State of New York:

AMONG the numerous advantages promised by a well constructed Union, none deserve to be more accurately developed than its tendency to break and control the violence of faction. The friend of popular governments never finds himself so much alarmed for their character and fate, as when he contemplates their propensity to this dangerous vice. He will not fail, therefore, to set a due value on any plan which, without violating the principles to which he is attached, provides a proper cure for it.

The instability, injustice, and confusion introduced into the public councils, have, in truth, been the mortal diseases under which popular governments have ever here perished; as they continue to be the favorite and fruitful topics from which the adversaries to liberty derive their most specious declamations.

The valuable improvements made by the American constitutions on the popular models, both ancient and modern, cannot certainly be too much admired; but it would be an unwarrantable partiality, to contend that they have as effectually obviated the danger on this side, as was wished and expected. Complaints are everywhere heard from our most considerate and virtuous citizens, equally the friends of public and private faith, and of public and personal liberty, that our governments are too unstable, that the public good is disregarded in the conflicts of rival parties, and that measures are too often decided, not according to the rules of justice and the rights of the minor party, but by the superior force of an interested and overbearing majority.

However anxiously we may wish that these complaints had no foundation, the evidence of known facts will not permit us to deny that they are in some degree true. It will be found, indeed, on a candid review of our situation, that some of the distresses under which we labor have been erroneously charged on the operation of our governments; but it will be found, at the same time, that other causes will not alone account for many of our heaviest misfortunes; and, particularly, for that prevailing and increasing distrust of public engagements,, and alarm for private rights, which are echoed from one end of the continent to the other. These must be chiefly, if not wholly, effects of the unsteadiness and injustice with which a factious spirit has tainted our public administrations.

By a faction, I understand a number of citizens, whether amounting to a majority or minority of the whole, who are united and actuated by some common impulse of passion, or of interest, adverse to the rights of other citizens, or to the permanent and aggregate interests of the community.

There are two methods of curing the mischiefs of faction: the one, by removing its causes; the other, by controlling its effects.

There are again two methods of removing the cause of faction: the one, by destroying the liberty which is essential to its existence; the other, by giving to every citizen the same opinions, the same passions, and the same interests.

It could never be more truly said than of the first remedy, that it was worse than the disease. Liberty is to faction what air is to fire, an aliment without which instantly expires. But it could not be less folly to abolish liberty, which is essential to political life, because it nourishes faction, than it would be to wish the annihilation of air, which is essential to animal life, because it imparts to fire its destructive agency.

The second expedient is as impracticable as the first would be unwise. As long as the reason of man continues fallible, and he is at liberty to exercise it, different opinions will be formed. As long as the connection subsists between his reason and his self-love, his opinions and his passions will have a reciprocal influence on each other and the former will be objects to which the latter will attach themselves.

The diversity in the faculties of men from which the rights of property originate, is not an insuperable obstacle to a uniformity of interests. The protection of these faculties is the first object of government. From the protection of different and unequal faculties of acquiring property, the possession of different degrees and kinds of property immediately results;. and from the influence of these on the sentiments and views of the respective proprietors, ensues a division of the society into different interests and parties.

The latent causes of faction are thus sown in the nature of man; and we see them everywhere brought in different degrees of activity, according to the different circumstances of civil society. A zeal for different opinion concerning religion, concerning government, and many other points, as well of speculation as of practice; an attachment to different leaders ambitiously contending for pre-eminence and power; or to persons of other descriptions whose fortunes have been interesting to the human passions, have, in turn, divided mankind into parties, inflamed them with mutual animosity, and rendered them much more disposed to vex and oppress each other than to co-operate for their common good.

So strong is this propensity of mankind to fall into mutual animosities, that where no substantial occasion presents itself, the most frivolous and fanciful distinctions have been sufficient to kindle their unfriendly passions and excite their most violent conflicts. But the most common and durable source of factions has been the various and unequal distribution of property. Those who hold and those who are without property have ever formed distinct interests in society. Those who are creditors, and those who are debtors, fall under a like discrimination. A landed interest, a manufacturing interest, a mercantile interest, a moneyed interest, with many lesser interests, grow up of necessity in civilized nations, and divide them into different classes, actuated by different sentiments and views. The regulation of these various and interfering interests forms the principal task of modern legislation, and involves the spirit of party and faction in the necessary and ordinary operations of the government.

No man is allowed to be a judge in his own cause, because his interest would certainly bias his judgment, and, not improbably, corrupt his integrity. With equal, nay with greater reason a body of men are unfit to be both judges and parties at the same time; yet what are many of the most important acts of legislation, but so many judicial determinations, not indeed concerning the rights of single persons, but concerning the rights of large bodies of citizens? And what are the different classes of legislators but advocates and parties to the causes which they determine? Is a law proposed concerning private debts? It is a question to which the creditors are parties on one side and the debtors on the other. Justice ought to hold the balance between them. Yet the parties are, and must, be, themselves the judges; and the most numerous party, or, in other words, the most powerful faction must be expected to prevail.

Shall domestic manufactures be encouraged, and in what degree, by restrictions on foreign manufactures? are questions which would be differently decided by the landed and the manufacturing classes, and probably by neither with a sole regard to justice and the public good. The apportionment of taxes on the various descriptions of property is an act which seems to require the most exact impartiality; yet there is, perhaps, no legislative act in which greater opportunity and temptation are given to a predominant party to trample on the rules of justice. Every shilling with which they overburden the inferior number, is a shilling saved to their own pockets.

It is in vain to say that enlightened statesmen will be able to adjust these clashing interests, and render them all subservient to the public good. Enlightened statesmen will not always be at the helm. Nor, in many cases, can such an adjustment be made at all without taking into view indirect and remote considerations, which will rarely prevail over the immediate interest which one party may find in disregarding the rights of another or the good of the whole.

The inference to which we are brought is, that the *causes* of faction cannot be removed, and that relief is only to be sought in the means of controlling its *effects*.

If a faction consists of less than a majority, relief is supplied by the republican principle, which enables the majority to defeat its sinister views by regular vote. It may clog the administration, it may convulse the society; but it will be unable to execute and mask its violence under the forms of the Constitution.

When a majority is included in a faction, the form of popular government, on the other hand, enables it to sacrifice to its ruling passion or interest both the public good and the rights of other citizens. To secure the public good and private rights against the danger of such a faction, and at the same time to preserve the spirit and the form of popular government, is then the great object to which our inquiries are directed. Let me add that it is the great desideratum by which this form of government can be rescued from the opprobrium under which it has so long labored, and be recommended to the esteem and adoption of mankind.

By what means is this object attainable? Evidently by one of two only. Either the existence of the same passion or interest in a majority at the same time must be prevented, or the majority, having such coexistent passion or interest, must be rendered, by their number and local situation, unable to concert and carry into effect schemes of oppression. If the impulse and the opportunity be suffered to coincide, we well know that neither moral nor religious motives can be relied on as an adequate control. They are not found to be such on the injustice and violence of individuals, and lose their efficacy in proportion to the number combined together, that is, in proportion as their efficacy becomes needful.

From this view of the subject it may be concluded that a pure democracy, by which I mean a society consisting of a small number of citizens, who assemble and administer the government in person, can admit of no cure for the mischiefs of faction. A common passion or interest will, in almost every case, be felt by a majority of the whole; a communication and concert result from the form of government itself; and there is nothing to check the inducements to sacrifice the weaker party or an obnoxious individual. Hence it is that such democracies have ever been spectacles of turbulence and contention; have ever been found incompatible with personal security or the rights of property; and have in general been as short in their lives as they have been violent in their deaths. Theoretic politicians, who have patronized this species of government, have erroneously supposed that by reducing mankind to a perfect equality in their political rights, they would, at the same time, be perfectly equalized and assimilated in their possessions, their opinions, and their passions.

A republic, by which I mean a government in which the scheme of representation takes place, opens a different prospect, and promises the cure for which we are seeking. Let us examine the points in which it varies from pure democracy, and we shall comprehend both the nature of the cure and the efficacy which it must derive from the Union.

The two great points of difference between a democracy and a republic are: first, the delegation of the government, in the latter, to a small number of citizens elected by the rest; secondly, the greater number of citizens, and greater sphere of country, over which the latter may be extended.

The effect of the first difference is, on the one hand, to, refine and enlarge the public views, by passing them through the medium of a chosen body of citizens, whose wisdom may best discern the true interest of their country, and whose patriotism and love of justice will be least likely to sacrifice it to temporary or partial considerations. Under such a regulation, it may well happen that the public voice, pronounced by the representatives of the people, will be more consonant to the public good than if pronounced by the people themselves, convened for the purpose. On the other hand, the effect may be inverted. Men of factious tempers, of local prejudices, or of sinister designs, may, by intrigue, by corruption, or by other means, first obtain the suffrages, and then betray the interests, of the people. The question resulting is, whether small or extensive republics are more favorable to the election of proper guardians of the public weal; and it is clearly decided in favor of the latter by two obvious considerations:

In the first place, it is to be remarked that, however small the republic may be, the representatives must be raised to a certain number, in order to guard against the cabals of a few; and that, however large it may be, they must be limited to a certain number, in order to guard against the confusion of a multitude. Hence, the number of representatives in the two cases not being in proportion to that of the two constituents, and being proportionally greater in the small republic, it follows that, if the proportion of fit characters be not less in the large than in the small republic, the former will present a greater option, and consequently a greater probability of a fit choice.

In the next place, as each representative will be chosen by a greater number of citizens in the large than in the small republic, it will be more difficult for unworthy candidates to practise with success the vicious arts by which elections are too often carried; and the suffrages of the people being more free, will be more likely to centre in men who possess the most attractive merit and the most diffusive and established characters.

It must be confessed that in this, as in most other cases, there is a mean, on both sides of which inconveniences will be found to lie. By enlarging too much the number of electors, you render the representative too little acquainted with all their local circumstances and lesser interests; as by reducing it too much, you render him unduly attached to these, and too little fit to comprehend and pursue great and national objects. The federal Constitution forms a happy combination in this respect; the great and aggregate interests being referred to the national, the local and particular to the State legislatures.

The other point of difference is, the greater number of citizens and extent of territory which may be brought within the compass of republican than of democratic government; and it is this circumstance principally which renders factious combinations less to be dreaded in the former than in the latter. The smaller the society, the fewer probably will be the distinct parties and interests composing it; the fewer the distinct parties and interests, the more frequently will a majority be found of the same party; and the smaller the number of individuals composing a majority, and the smaller the compass within which they are placed, the more easily will they concert and execute their plans of oppression. Extend the sphere, and you take in a greater variety of parties and interests; you make it less probable that a majority of the whole will have a common motive to invade the rights of other citizens; or if such a common motive exists, it will be more difficult for all who feel it to discover their own strength, and to act in unison with each other. Besides other impediments, it may be remarked that, where there is a consciousness of unjust or dishonorable purposes, communication is always checked by distrust in proportion to the number whose concurrence is necessary.

Hence, it clearly appears, that the same advantage which a republic has over a democracy, in controlling the effects of faction, is enjoyed by a large over a small republic,—is enjoyed by the Union over the States composing it. Does the advantage consist in the substitution of representatives whose enlightened views and virtuous sentiments render them superior to local prejudices and to schemes of injustice? It will not be denied that the representation of the Union will be most likely to possess these requisite endowments. Does it consist in the greater security afforded by a greater variety of parties, against the event of any one party being able to outnumber and oppress the rest? In an equal degree does the increase variety of parties comprised within the Union, increase this security? Does it, in fine, consist in the greater obstacles opposed to the concert and accomplishment of the secret wishes of an unjust and interested majority? Here, again, the extent of the Union gives it the most palpable advantage.

The influence of factious leaders may kindle a flame within their particular States, but will be unable to spread a general conflagration through the other States. A religious sect may degenerate into a political faction in part of the Confederacy; but the variety of sects dispersed over the entire face of it must secure the national councils against any danger from that source. A rage for paper money, for an abolition of debts, for an equal division of property, or for any other improper or wicked project, will be less apt to pervade the whole body of the Union than a particular member of it; in the same proportion as such a malady is more likely to taint a particular county or district, than an entire State.

In the extent and proper structure of the Union, therefore, we behold a republican remedy for the diseases most incident to republican government. And according to the degree of pleasure and pride we feel in being republicans, ought to be our zeal in cherishing the spirit and supporting the character of Federalists.

PUBLIUS

19

The *Constitution of the United States,* excerpts, 1789, and *The First and Tenth Amendments,* 1791

As Madison was to argue in *Federalist No. 10,* an essay advocating its adoption, the Constitution of the United States was carefully designed to make it difficult for the federal government to act. It separated the legislative, executive, and judicial powers. It established a federal relationship that reserved some powers of government to the individual states. It set up a complex series of checks and balances between the House of Representatives (elected on a two-year cycle) and the Senate (elected on staggered six-year cycles), between Congress and the President (elected on a four-year cycle), and between the Congress and the President, which together passed and accepted legislation, and the Supreme Court, which soon asserted its right to the judicial review of legislation. The Constitution required that all money bills originate in the House of Representatives, whose members, being subject to frequent election from small districts, were correctly expected to be inclined to keep taxes low: but it also required that the Senate be allowed to amend money bills subject to House agreement, and that the President sign them.

Heeding the argument of Real Whigs like Trenchard and Gordon that a corrupt ruler might use titles and honors to buy the support of influential citizens or legislators, the Constitution denied the federal government the power to confer titles of nobility. It also denied the federal government the power to impose any test of religious belief on those who wished to hold federal offices.

All of these provisions reduced the role of the national government in American society, and indeed made it difficult for the federal government to act. Compared to the more comprehensive governments of Europe and Asia, the Constitution left American society with a national government unlikely to win authority to do many things. Because most state governments adopted constitutions that closely resembled the federal constitution, they were similarly limited in their ability to act.

The First Amendment to the Constitution, with its guarantees of freedom of religion, speech, assembly, press, and petition, created the possibility that Americans might act to fill through private organziations some of the void left by their restricted government. And the Tenth Amendment seemed to limit the possibility that the federal government would fill gaps left by the states

The Constitution of the United States

(EXCERPTS)

1789, 1791

Article I, Section 7

All Bills for raising Revenue shall originate in the House of Representives; but the Senate may propose or concur with Amendments as on other Bills.

Every Bill which shall have passed the House of Representatives and the Senate, shall, before it becomes a Law, be presented to the President of the United States; If he approve he shall sign it, but if not he shall return it, with his Objections to that House in which it shall have originated, who shall enter the Objections at large on their Journal, and proceed to reconsider it. If after such reconsideration two thirds of that House shall agree to pass the bill, it shall be sent, together with the Objections, to the other House, by which it shall likewise be reconsidered, and if approved by two thirds of that House it shall become a Law.

Article I, Section 9

. . . No title of nobility shall be granted by the United States: And no person holding any Office of Profit or Trust under them, shall, without the Consent of the Congress, accept any present, Emolument, Office, or Title, of any kind whatever, from any King, Prince, or foreign State.

Article I, Section 10

No State shall . . . grant any title of nobility.

Article VI

. . . no religious Test shall ever be required as a Qualification to any Office or public Trust under the United States.

The First Amendment

Congress shall make no law respecting an establishment of religion, or prohibiting the free exercise thereof; or abridging the freedom of speech, or of the press; or the right of people peacably to asssemble, and to petition the government for redress of grievances.

The Tenth Amendment

The powers not delegated to the United States by the Constitution, nor prohibited by it to the States, are reserved to the States respectively, or to the people.

FOUR

Voluntarism under the Constitution

In most parts of the world at the beginning of the nineteenth century—in Asia as well as throughout Europe and the European colonies of South America—tax-supported religious institutions, government agencies, and wealthy noble landowners or merchant groups sponsored nearly all religious, education, health care, social service, and public arts activity. Once they had made it difficult for their governments to levy taxes, to take vigorous action, or to grant wealth and power to a favored few, and once they had disestablished their churches, Americans had to find alternative ways to provide these services.

To maintain their religious activities, Americans built on the colonial traditions of Baptist, Presbyterian, Quaker, and other dissenting congregations. By the 1830s they had all—even the formerly established Puritan Congregationalists like those in Connecticut's "standing order" led by Lyman Beecher—developed the voluntary, congregation-based Protestant religious denominations that are to this day characteristic components of the American scene.

After the Revolution Americans transferred primary responsibility for the care of the poor from the parishes of an established church to the secular governments of their counties or towns. During the colonial period a few schools, academies, colleges, and hospitals had secured charters from the British crown, or operated without any charter at all. Most of the very oldest chartered organizations in Massachusetts were mutual benefit societies created by non-Congregationalist outsiders, including Scots Presbyterians (before 1684), Irish Presbyterians (1737), and members of the Church of England (1824), who did not belong to the congregations that cared for their own. A few civic and mutual benefit associations, notably fire companies, libraries, and Masonic lodges like those Franklin had promoted in Philadelphia, also dated from late colonial times. On the eve of the Revolution in 1760, historian Richard D. Brown estimates, there were two hundred forty seven Protestant Congregations in Massachusetts, but only twenty-five other organized voluntary societies (including three Masonic lodges).

After the Revolution state governments (not the federal government) succeeded the British government as charterers and supervisors of such institutions. As the established church lost ground and as Americans were swept up in waves of civic enthusiasm and religious fervor, the people of Massachusetts launched many new churches, an average of more than ten churches every year from 1790 to 1820, and twenty-five each year during the 1820s, nearly tripling the total number of organized congregations in the state. But the people of Massachusetts created new schools and charitable societies even more rapidly: the thirty-five schools of 1790 increased to 418 by 1830. These institutions required property in order to do their jobs, and so those who organized them sought the legal protections and continuity offered by corporate charters. Across the United States the numbers of chartered institutions increased rapidly, as academies, libraries, and lyceums, and soon clinics, foundling homes, orphanages, homes for unwed mothers, and homes for the handicapped and the elderly, joined the few colleges, hospitals, and mutual-benefit associations that dated from colonial times. Richard D. Brown notes that a handbook for organizers of lyceums and schools appeared as early as 1829. Only for-profit corporations increased more rapidly than schools in these years: where just nine for-profit corporations had been organized in Massachusetts by 1790, there were nearly 500 by 1830.

The few eleemosynary (nonprofit) and profit-seeking corporations that predated the revolution had held British charters. What were their powers to be under the American Constitution? Americans disagreed. Thomas Jefferson doubted that corporations of any sort should have the power to govern themselves: they should, he thought, be subject to the continuing control of state legislatures. Large numbers of Jefferson's political associates, especially in the South, agreed with him. But many of

Jefferson's contemporaries disagreed: like Daniel Webster and U.S. Supreme Court Justice Joseph Story, they saw corporations as essential to American liberty. After a period of great uncertainty, the United States Supreme Court settled the question with its decision in the *Dartmouth College Case* (1817). Under that decision, once a state had granted a corporate charter it had to leave the corporation's affairs in the hands of its directors or trustees, except that it did retain general police powers. Most states passed general incorporation laws in the next two or three decades, so that it was no longer necessary to obtain a special legislative act for each new corporation.

Even as most states made it easier to create nonprofit corporations, state and local governments shaped these private institutions in many ways. They exempted them from the property tax, at a time when, in the absence of sales and income taxes, the property tax was by far the most important source of government revenue. State and local governments often granted them land, and sometimes provided them with buildings. State governments regulated nonprofits' ability to create endowments; Massachusetts, Connecticut, and Ohio encouraged endowments while New York, Virginia, and most southern states discouraged them. Local and state governments also contracted with nonprofits for many services, from caring for foundlings, orphans, and indigent elderly women to the provision of secondary education to "town scholars." By 1830 Americans were using both nonprofit organizations and profit-seeking corporations for a wide array of purposes, and many American commentators were discussing their advantages and disadvantages.

Alexis de Tocqueville arrived in the United States just as the early use of nonprofit corporations was reaching its early peak. Tocqueville talked with the leaders of many nonprofits and with the lawyers, clergymen, and journalists who set them up and wrote about them, and his great book, *Democracy in America,* reflected Americans' own understanding of their new institutions. As Tocqueville emphasized, American nonprofits served political as well as social purposes.

20

Lyman Beecher, *Autobiographical Statement on the 1818 Disestablishment of the "Standing Order" in Connecticut*, 1864

In the 1860s Lyman Beecher, a distinguished Congregationalist minister and the father of Harriet Beecher Stowe, agreed to work with his children to create an autobiography for his grandchildren. Among the personal and family stories included in Beecher's *Autobiography* is this account of the political fight that led to the disestablishment of the Congregationalist "Standing Order" of government officials, landowners and merchants, and ministers that had dominated Connecticut from its settlement in the early 1600s.

Beecher wrote as a member of the Standing Order, one who was proud of its services to "morals" and "piety" and who took for granted the superiority of the Federalist Party that it supported in American politics. He viewed the "democracy"—the Democratic Party of Thomas Jefferson—as a minority, less capable and less fit for leadership, and he scorned the Federalists and Episcopalians who finally decided to abandon establishment. Beecher dismissed members of other Protestant denominations as "dissidents," members of "minor sects," an inappropriately "ambitious minority."

In the end, however, Beecher came to view disestablishment as *"the best thing that ever happened"* because it freed the Congregationalists from the burden of tailoring their statements and actions to political realities, allowed them to advocate the religious and moral causes they deemed most important, and forced them to take vigorous action, through revivals, fundraising campaigns, and other means, to obtain the material support they needed.

LYMAN BEECHER

Autobiography

ON THE END OF THE CONGREGATIONALIST STANDING ORDER IN CONNECTICUT

1864

The efforts we made to execute the laws and secure a reformation of morals reached the men of piety, and waked up the energies of the whole state, so far as the members of our churches, and the intelligent and moral portion of our congregations were concerned. These, however, proved to be a minority of the suffrage of the state.

Originally all were obliged to support the standing order. Every body paid without kicking. I remember once Uncle Stephen Benton, a cross-grained sort of man, for some reason or other refused to pay, and they levied on his heifer and sold her.

When, however, other denominations began to rise, and complained of their consciences, the laws were modified. There never was a more noble regard to the rights of conscience than was shown in Connecticut. Never was there a body of men that held the whole power that yielded to the rights of conscience more honorably.

The habit of legislation from the beginning had been to favor Congregational order and provide for it. Congregationalism was the established religion. All others were dissenters, and complained of favoritism. The ambitious minority early began to make use of the minor sects on ground of invidious distinctions, thus making them restive. So the democracy, as it rose, included nearly all the minor sects, besides the Sabbath-breakers, rum-selling tippling folk, infidels, and ruff-scuff generally, and made a dead set at us of the standing order.

It was a long time, however, before they could accomplish any thing, so small were the sects and so united the Federal phalanx. After defeat upon defeat, and while other state delegations in Congress divided, ours, for twenty years a unit, Pierrepont Edwards, a leader of the Democrats, exclaimed, "As well attempt to revolutionize the kingdom of heaven as the State of Connecticut!"

But throwing Treadwell over in 1811 broke the charm and divided the [Federalist] party; persons of third-rate ability, on our side, who wanted to be somebody, deserted; all the infidels in the state had long been leading on that side; the minor sects had swollen, and complained of having to get a certificate to pay their tax where they liked; our efforts to enforce reformation of morals by law made us unpopular; they attacked the clergy unceasingly, and myself in particular, in season and out of season, with all sorts of misrepresentation, ridicule, and abuse; and finally, the Episcopalians, who had always been staunch Federalists, were disappointed of an appropriation for the Bishop's Fund, which they asked for, and went over to the Democrats.[1] That overset us. They slung us out like a stone from a sling. . . .

It was a time of great depression and suffering. It was the worst attack I ever met in my life. . . . I worked as hard as mortal man could, and at the same time preached for revivals with all my might, and with success, till at last, what with domestic afflictions and all, my health and spirits began to fail. It was as dark a day as ever I saw. The odium thrown upon the ministry was inconceivable. The injury done to the cause of Christ, as we then supposed, was irreparable.

For several days I suffered what no tongue can tell *for the best thing that ever happened to the State of Connecticut.* It cut the churches loose from dependence on state support. It threw them wholly on their own resources and on God.[2]

They say ministers have lost their influence; the fact is, they have gained. By voluntary efforts, societies, missions, and revivals, they exert a deeper influence than ever they could by queues, and shoe-buckles, and cocked hats and gold-headed canes. . . .[3]

---

1. It finally began to be whispered that some one of the denominations called Dissenters must be conciliated, or the Federal party would be overborne at last by the concerted action of those who were opposed to the Congregational form of religion. When the charter of the Phoenix Bank was asked for, it was therefore suggested that the $50,000 bonus which was to be sequestered from its large capital for public uses should be divided between Yale College and the Bishop's Fund, and petitions were circulated to that effect among the people. Some of the Federalists thought it desirable to conciliate the Episcopalians, who now numbered some of the first men in the state.

"The bank was chartered, and $20,000 of the bonus was bestowed upon Yale College; but, from some cause, the Bishop's Fund did not get the portion anticipated for it by its friends. This was a severe disappointment to the denomination interested in that fund. The Episcopalians now arrayed themselves against the party in power with all the appliances that they could bring to bear upon an opponent."— G. H. Hollister, *The History of Connecticut from the First Settlement of the Colony to the Adoption of the Present Constitution* (Hartford, 1855), ii, p. 515.

2. The most remarkable exhibition of most of these peculiarities is to be found in the history of Connecticut during the period of Dr. Beecher's Litchfield ministry; and one of the most remarkable phases of his whole career is that in which we see him, on the one hand, making Herculean efforts to uphold the system of Church and State, and, on the other, lavishing almost superhuman energies in laying the foundations of the voluntary system. His favorite comparison for the old standing order was a ship. Its fate reminds us of Paul's description: "And falling into a place where two seas met, they ran the ship aground; and the fore part stuck fast, but the hinder part was broken with the violence of the waves. But the centurion commanded that they which could swim should cast themselves first into the sea and get to land; and the rest, some on boards, and some on broken pieces of the ship; and so it came to pass that they escaped all safe to land."

It was not very long after my return from Salem when the tide began to turn. For years we of the standing order had been the scoff and by-word of politicians, sectarians, and infidels, and had held our tongues; but now the Lord began to pour out his Spirit.

Brother Hawes, then recently settled at Hartford, sent two of his deacons to ask me to come and help him in a revival. I remember, when I saw them and heard their errand, I turned round and said, "Now, wife, it is my turn. Now I will speak." I went to Hartford, and the Spirit of God was there. I spent about three weeks in the work. Preached all the while; it was a powerful revival. I was gone two Sabbaths, getting home on Saturday.

Revivals now began to pervade the state. The ministers were united, and had been consulting and praying. Political revolution had cut them off from former sources of support, and caused them to look to God. Then there came such a time of revival as never before in the state.

I remember how we all used to feel before the revolution happened. Our people thought they should be destroyed if the law should be taken away from under them. They did not think any thing about God—did not seem to. And the fact is, we all felt that our children would scatter like partridges if the tax law was lost. We saw it coming. In Goshen they raised a fund. In Litchfield the people bid off the pews, and so it has been ever since.

But the effect, when it did come, was just the reverse of the expectation. When the storm burst upon us, indeed, we thought we were dead for a while. But we found we were not dead. Our fears had magnified the danger. We were thrown on God and on ourselves, and this created that moral coercion which makes men work. Before we had

---

3. "The great aim of the Christian Church in its relation to the present life is not only to renew the individual man, but also to reform human society. That it may do this it needs full and free scope. The Protestantism of the Old World is still fettered by the union of the Church with the State. Only in the United States of America has the experiment been tried of applying Christianity directly to man and to society without the intervention of the state.

"Accordingly the history of the Church in this country is difficult to grasp in its principles and bearings. Some of the peculiarities of this history are the following: 1. It is not the history of the conversion of a new people, but of the transplantation of old races already Christianized to a new theatre comparatively untrámmeled by institutions and traditions. 2. Independence of the civil power. 3. The voluntary principle applied to the support of religious institutions. 4. Moral and ecclesiastical, but not civil power, the means of retaining the members of any communion. 5. Development of the Christian system in its practical and moral aspects rather than in its theoretical and theological. 6. Stricter discipline in the churches than is practicable when Church and State are one. 7. Increase of the churches, to a considerable extent, through revivals of religion rather than by the natural growth of the children in an establishment. 8. Excessive multiplication of sects, and divisions on questions of moral reform." —H. B. Smith, D.D., *Tables of Church History*.

been standing on what our fathers had done, but now we were obliged to develop all our energy.

On the other hand, the other denominations lost all the advantage they had had before, so that the very thing in which the enemy said, "Raze it—raze it to the foundations," laid the corner-stone of our prosperity to all generations. The law compelling every man to pay somewhere was repealed. The consequence unexpectedly was, first, that the occasion of animosity between us and the minor sects was removed, and infidels could no more make capital with them against us, and they then began themselves to feel the dangers of infidelity, and to react against it, and this laid the basis of co-operation and union of spirit.

And, besides, that tax law had for more than twenty years really worked to weaken us and strengthen them. All the stones that shelled off and rolled down from our eminence lodged in their swamp. Whenever a man grew disaffected, he went off and paid his rates with the minor sects; but on the repeal of the law there was no such temptation. Take this revolution through, it was one of the most desperate battles ever fought in the United States. It was the last struggle of the separation of Church and State.

21

The Dartmouth College Case: Daniel Webster, *Argument before the U.S. Supreme Court,* 1818; Chief Justice John Marshall, *Decision,* and Joseph Story, *Concurring Opinion,* 1819

The Reverend Eleazar Wheelock obtained a royal charter for Dartmouth College in 1769, just a few years before the American Revolution. Supported by New Hampshire and Vermont as well as by private donors and by tuition payments from its students, Dartmouth fared quite well as a small Christian liberal arts college devoted to educating young men and Indians for the ministry. In 1816 a new Democratic majority gained control of New Hampshire's government, and decided to assert the view that because the state had succeeded the King as the grantor of charters, and because Dartmouth accepted students from the public at large, the college remained under the direct control of the state. New Hampshire's Democratic government went on to insist that the state needed practical schools of agriculture and engineering more than it needed a liberal arts college for would-be ministers. Thus the state legislature passed, and the governor signed and sought to enforce, a law expanding Dartmouth's board to include several public officials and directing the college to add the desired new schools.

Dartmouth's trustees rejected these changes and went to court to defend their right to control the college. In 1818 the matter went to the U.S. Supreme Court, where Daniel Webster, a Dartmouth graduate and one of the most highly regarded attorneys of his generation, argued the college's case. Webster made a very strong case for the powers of trustees, and closed his argument with a striking emotional appeal. In its 1819 Decision, The Court agreed with nearly all of Webster's arguments.

This case is important for several things. It demonstrates that Americans were already thinking in terms of what we now call the "nonprofit sector": Webster's *Argument,* Chief Justice John Marshall's *Opinion,* and Associate Justice Joseph Story's *Concurring Opinion* all used the term "eleemosynary" where we would today use the term "nonprofit" to apply to private charitable organizations that provide services to a general public, including hospitals, old age homes, and orphanages as well as schools and colleges. The *Dartmouth College Case* established the legal rights of such private organizations and their trustees to manage their own affairs without constant and detailed interference by legislatures. The case also shows how American lawyers and courts relied on English law and English law writers.

John Marshall of Virginia, Chief Justice of the U.S. Supreme Court, delivered the majority opinion in the *Dartmouth College Case*. In supporting the Dartmouth trustees' claim to independence from the legislature, Marshall emphasized his view that a corporate charter was a contract between the government that granted it and the incorporators who held positions on its board. Like all contracts, under the Tenth Section of Article One of the U.S. Constitution, he held, the contract that established a corporation could be changed only if all parties to the original contract (or their successors) agreed. Although Marshall's opinion did more to establish the powers of private business corporations and to limit the freedom of action of elected legislatures than to define the powers of private charities, it did explicitly apply to charitable corporations.

In his concurring opinion, Associate Justice of the U.S. Supreme Court Joseph Story of Massachusetts emphasized British common law traditions regarding the nature of charitable or "eleemosynary" corporations and of the powers, including the "visitatorial power," of their donors and boards.

Although Webster carried the day in the *Dartmouth College Case*, those who shared Jefferson's opposition to corporations remained very influential in New York and in much of the South and West. They made it more difficult to obtain corporate charters in many states, and when they could they limited corporate powers and forced them to accept state supervision. Nevertheless, the trend toward greater use of corporate powers was general.

DANIEL WEBSTER

Argument in the Dartmouth College Case

(EXCERPTS)

1818

INTRODUCTION: THE DONOR'S INTENT AND THE LEGISLATURE'S POWERS

The Charter of 1769 created & established a corporation, to consist of twelve persons & no more, to be called the Trustees of Dartmouth College. The preamble to the Charter recites that it is granted on the application & request of the Revd. Eleazar Wheelock. That Dr. Wheelock about the year 1754, established a charity school, at his own expense, & on his own estate & plantation; That for several years, thro' the assistance of well disposed persons in America at his solicitation he clothed, maintained & educated a number of the native Indians, & employed them afterwards as missionaries and schoolmasters; That he had requested [certain] Gentlemen to be Trustees; And inasmuch as a number of the proprietors of lands in New Hampshire, in consideration that the school might be enlarged & improved to promote learning among the English, & to supply ministers to the people of the Province, had promised large tracts of land, provided the school should be established in that Province. Upon this recital, & in consideration of the laudable original design of Dr. Wheelock, & willing that the best means of education be established in New Hampshire for the benefit of the Province, the King grants the Charter, by the advice of his Provincial Council.

Legislative bodies sometimes deem themselves the exclusive representatives & agents of the people, & are inclined to exercise, not only such powers as are granted to them, but all such other powers as they do not find granted to other departments. The Legislature of New Hampshire [was] not competent to pass the Acts in question, & to make them binding because these Acts are not the exercise of a power properly Legislative. Their object is to take away from one, rights, property, & franchises, & to grant them to another.

CHARITABLE AND OTHER CORPORATIONS

By the Law of England, the power to create Corporations is part of the Royal prerogative. By the revolution this power may be considered as having devolved on the Legislature of the State. It has accordingly been exercised by the legislature. But the king cannot abolish a corporation, or new model it, or alter its powers or organization without its assent.

There are divers sorts of corporations; and it may be safely admitted that the Legislature has more power over some than over others. Some corporations are for government & political arrangement, such for example as Cities, Counties, & the Towns in New England. These may be changed & modified, as public convenience may require, due regard always being had to the rights of property. Other civil corporations are for the advancement of trade & business, such as Banks, Insurance Companies, & the like. The corporation in question is not a civil, although it is a *lay* [and thus not a *religious]* corporation. It is an *eleemosynary* corporation. It is a private Charity. The legal signification of a *Charity* is derived chiefly from the Statute of Charitable Uses. Colleges are enumerated, as Charities in that Statute.

RIGHTS OF TRUSTEES

In New England, & perhaps throughout the United States, eleemosynary corporations have generally been founded by incorporating Governors or trustees, & vesting in them the right of visitation. The numerous academies (as at Exeter & Andover) in New England were established substantially in the same manner. They held their property by the same tenure, & no other. Nor has Harvard College any surer title than Dartmouth College. It may, today, have more friends; but, tomorrow it may have more enemies. Its legal rights are the same. So also of Yale College; and indeed of all the others.

The *privilege* of being a member of a corporation, under a lawful grant, and of exercising the rights & powers of such member, is such a privilege, liberty, or franchise, as has been the object of legal protection & the subject of a legal interest from the time of Magna Charta to the present moment. It cannot be necessary to say much in refutation of the idea, that there cannot be a legal interest or ownership in any thing which does not yield a pecuniary profit; as if the law regard no rights but the rights of money, & of visible, tangible property. Of what nature are all rights of suffrage? No elector has a particular personal interest, but each has a legal right, to be exercised at his own discretion, & it cannot be taken away from him. The exercise of this right of suffrage directly & very materially affects the public, much more so than the exercise of the privileges of a trustee of this college. Consequences of the utmost magnitude may sometimes depend on the exercise of the right of suffrage by one or a few electors. Nobody was ever yet heard to contend, that on that account the public might take away the right or impair it.

Under this Charter property was legally vested in the trustees. It was to be possessed by them for the use of such as were described in the Charter. These acts take this property out of their hands & give it to others, & authorise those others to hold it for new uses. The Legislature cannot do this. They cannot rob the legal holders, nor disappoint the will of the donors. Some years ago the Messrs. Phillips endowed Exeter Academy. They gave $80–100,000 to be administered in promoting learning & piety, & they gave stated & declared uses. The Legislature granted a Charter with all necessary powers to answer the donors' purposes. The donors had the right to make this gift, & the Legislature had the right to grant the Charter. But can they now seize the property, at pleasure, & grant it to others? Such would be, in effect, acts of confiscation. That all property, of which the use may be beneficial to the public, belongs therefore to the public is quite a new doctrine. It has no precedent, & is supported by no known principle.

Lord Hardwicke says, in so many words, "The Charter of the Crown cannot make a Charity more or less public, but only more permanent than it would otherwith be." The granting of the corporation is but making the trust perpetual, & does not alter the nature of the Charity. The very object sought in obtaining such Charters, & in giving property to such a corporation, is to make it private property; & to clothe it with it the security & inviolability of private property. The intent is, that there shall be a legal private ownership, & that the legal owners shall maintain & protect the property, for the benefit of those, for whose use it was designed. Whoever appointed a Legislature to administer his Charity? Or whoever heard before, that a gift to a College, a Hospital, or an asylum, was in reality nothing but a gift to the State?

That the power of electing & appointing the officers of this College, is not only a right of the Trustees as a corporation, generally, and in the aggregate, but that each individual Trustee has his own individual franchise in such right of election & appointment is the language of all the authorities. Lord Holt says, "it is agreeable to reason, & the rules of law, that a franchise should be vested in the corportation aggregate, & yet the benefit of it to redound to the particular members, & to be enjoyed by them In their private capacity. Where the Privilege of election is used by particular persons; *it is a particular right vested in every particular man."*

RIGHTS OF EMPLOYEES

It is also to be considered that the President & Professors of this College have rights to be affected by these Acts. Their interest is similar to that of Fellows in the English Colleges; because they derive their livings, wholly or in part from the founder's bounty. They have freeholds, in their offices; subject only to be removed, by the Trustees, as Visitors, for good cause.

Nothing could have been less expected, in this age, than that there should have been an attempt by acts of the Legislature to take away these College livings, the inadequate, but the only support of literary men, who have devoted their lives to the instruction of youth. They are a most deserving class of men; scholars, who have consented to forego the advantages of professional & public life, & to devote themselves to science & literature & the instruction of youth in the quiet retreats of academic life. Whether to dispossess & oust them; to do all this, not by the power of their legal visitors, but by act of the Legislature; & to do it without forfeiture, and without fault; whether all this be not, in the highest degree, an indefensible & arbitrary proceeding, is a question, of which there would seem to be but one side, fit for a lawyer, or a scholar, to espouse.

INDEPENDENCE OF THE COLLEGE

Under the government and protection of the general laws of the land, these institutions have always been found safe, as well as useful. They go on, with the progress of society, accomodating themselves easily, without sudden change or violence, to the alterations which take place in its condition, & in the knowledge, the habits & the pursuits of men. The English Colleges were founded in Catholic ages. Their Religion was reformed, with the general reformation of the Nation, & they are suited perfectly well to the purpose of educating the Protestant youth of Modern times. Dartmouth college was established under a Charter granted by the Provincial Government; but a better Constitution for a College or one more adapted to the Condition of things under the present Government, in all material respects, could not now be framed. Nothing in it was found to need alteration at the Revolution. The wise men of that day saw in it one of the best hopes of future times, & commended it, as it was, with parental care, to the protection & guardianship of the Government of the States. A Charter of more liberal sentiments, of wiser provisions, drawn with more care, or in a better spirit, could not be expected at any time or from any source. The College neded no change in its organization or Government. That which it did need was the kindness, the patronage, the bounty of the Legislature; not a mock elevation into the character of a University, without the solid benefit of a shilling's donation to sustain the Character; not the swelling & empty *Institutes* & authority of establishing *other Colleges*. This empty pageantry was but division of the scanty endowment & limited means of this unobtrusive but useful & growing seminary.

CONCLUSION

The case before the Court is not of ordinary importance, nor of every day occurrence. It affects not this College only, but every College, & all the Literary institutions of the Country. They have flourished, hitherto, & have become in a high degree respectable & useful to the Community. They have all a common principle of existence, the inviolability of their Charters. It will be a dangerous, a most dangerous experiment, to hold these institutions subject to the rise & fall of popular parties, & the fluctuations of political opinions. If the franchise may be at any time taken away, or impaired, the property also may be taken away, or its use perverted. Benefactors will have no certainty of effecting the object of their bounty, literary men will be deterred from devoting themselves to the service of such institutions, from the precarious title of their offices. Colleges & halls will be deserted by all better spirits, & become a theatre for the contention of politics. Party & faction will be cherished, in the places consecrated to piety & to learning. These consequences are neither remote nor possible only. They are certain & immediate.

This, Sir, is my case! It is the case not merely of that humble institution, it is the case of every college in our Land! It is more! It is the case of every eleemosynary institution throughout our country—of all those great charities founded by the piety of our ancestors to alleviate human misery, and scatter blessings along the pathway of life! It is more! It is, in some sense, the case of every man among us who has property of which he may be stripped, for the question is simple this, "Shall our State Legislature be allowed to take *that which is not their own,* to turn it from its original use, and apply it to such ends and purposes as they in their discretion shall see fit!"

Sir, you may destroy this little institution; it is weak, it is in your hands! I know it is one of the lesser lights in the literary horizon of our country. You may put it out! But if you do so, you must carry through your work! You must extinguish, one after another, all those great lights of science which for more than a century have thrown their radiance over our land! It is, Sir, as I have said, a small college. And yet *there are those who love it!* Sir, I know not how others may feel, but for myself, when I see my *Alma Mater* surrounded, like Caesar in the senate house, by those who are reiterating stab upon stab, I would not for this right hand have her to say to me, *"Et tu quoque, mi fili!"* ("and you too, my son!")

CHIEF JUSTICE JOHN MARSHALL

The Dartmouth College Case

MAJORITY OPINION OF THE U.S. SUPREME COURT

(EXCERPTS)

1819

. . . It can require no argument to prove, that the circumstances of this case constitute a contract. An application is made to the crown for a charter to incorporate a religious and literary institution. In the application, it is stated, that large contributions have been made for the object, which will be conferred on the corporation, as soon as it shall be created. The charter is granted, and on its faith the property is conveyed. Surely, in this transaction every ingredient of a complete and legitimate contract is to be found.

. . . .

The parties in this case differ less on general principles, less on the true construction of the constitution in the abstract, than on the application of those principles to this case, and on the true construction of the charter of 1769. This is the point on which the cause essentially depends. If the act of incorporation be a grant of political power, if it create a civil institution, to be employed in the administration of the government, or if the funds of the college be public property, or if the state of New Hampshire, as a government, be alone interested in its transactions, the subject is one in which the legislature of the state may act according to its own judgment, unrestrained by any limitation of its power imposed by the constitution of the United States.

But if this be a private eleemosynary institution, endowed with a capacity to take property, for objects unconnected with government, whose funds are bestowed by individuals, on the faith of the charter; if the donors have stipulated for the future disposition and management of those funds, in the manner prescribed by themselves; there may be more difficulty in the case, although neither the persons who have made these stipulations, nor those for whose benefit they were made, should be parties to the cause.

Those who are no longer interested in the property, may yet retain such an interest in the preservation of their own arrangements, as to have a right to insist, that those arrangements shall be held sacred. Or, if they have themselves disappeared, it becomes a subject of serious and anxious inquiry, whether those whom they have legally empowered to represent them for ever, may not assert all the rights which they possessed, while in being; whether, if they be without personal representatives, who may feel injured by a violation of the compact, the trustees be not so completely their representatives, in the eye of the law, as to stand in their place, not only as respects the government of the college, but also as respects the maintenance of the college charter. It becomes then the duty of the court, most seriously to examine this charter, and to ascertain its true character. . . .

It is then an eleemosynary, and so far as respects its funds, a private corporation. Do its objects stamp on it a different character? Are the trustees and professors public officers, invested with any portion of political power, partaking in any degree in the administration of civil government, and performing duties which flow from the sovereign authority?

That education is an object of national concern, and a proper subject of legislation, all admit. That there may be an institution, founded by government, and placed entirely under its immediate control, the officers of which would be public officers, amenable exclusively to government, none will deny. But is Dartmouth College such an institution? Is education altogether in the hands of government? Does every teacher of youth become a public officer, and do donations for the purpose of education necessarily become public property, so far that the will of the legislature, not the will of the donor, becomes the law of the donation?

These questions are of serious moment to society, and deserve to be well considered. Doctor Wheelock, as the keeper of his charity-school, instructing the Indians in the art of reading, and in our holy religion; sustaining them at his own expense, and on the voluntary contributions of the charitable, could scarcely be considered as a public officer, exercising any portion of those duties which belong to government; nor could the legislature have supposed, that his private funds, or those given by others, were subject to legislative management, because they were applied to the purposes of education. When, afterwards, his school was enlarged, and the liberal contributions made in England, and in America, enabled him to extend his care to the education of the youth of his own country, no change was wrought in his own character, or in the nature of his duties. Had he employed assistant-tutors with the funds contributed by others, or had the trustees in England established a school, with Dr. Wheelock at its head, and paid salaries to him and his assistants, they would still have been private tutors; and the fact, that they were employed in the education of youth, could not have converted them into public officers, concerned in the administration of public duties, or have given the legislature a right to interfere in the management of the fund. The trustees, in whose care that fund was placed by the contributors, would have been permitted to execute their trust, uncontrolled by legislative authority.

Whence, then, can be derived the idea, that Dartmouth College has become a public institution, and its trustees public officers, exercising powers conferred by the public for public objects? Not from the source whence its funds were drawn; for its foundation is purely private and eleemosynary—not from the application of those funds; for money may be given for education, and the persons receiving it do not, by being employed in the education of youth, become members of the civil government. Is it from the act of incorporation? Let this subject be considered.

A corporation is an artificial being, invisible, intangible, and existing only in contemplation of law. Being the mere creature of law, it possesses only those properties which the charter of its creation confers upon it, either expressly, or as incidental to its very existence. These are such as are supposed best calculated to effect the object for which it was created. Among the most important are immortality, and, if the expression may be allowed, individuality; properties, by which a perpetual succession of many persons are considered as the same, and may act as a single individual. They enable a corporation to manage its own affairs,and to hold property, without the perplexing intricacies, the hazardous and endless necessity, of perpetual conveyances for the purpose of transmitting it from hand to hand. It is chiefly for the purpose of clothing bodies of men, in succession, with these qualities and capacities, that corporations were invented, and are in use. By these means, a perpetual succession of individuals are capable of acting for the promotion of the particular object, like one immortal being.

But this being does not share in the civil government of the country, unless that be the purpose for which it was created. Its immortality no more confers on it political power, or a political character, than immortality would confer such power or character on a natural person. It is no more a state instrument, than a natural person exercising the same powers would be.

If, then, a natural person, employed by individuals in the education of youth, or for the government of a seminary in which youth is educated, would not become a public officer, or be considered as a member of the civil government, how is it, that this artificial being, created by law, for the purpose of being employed by the same individuals, for the same purposes, should become a part of the civil government of the country?

Is it because its existence, its capacities, its powers, are given by law?

Because the government has given it the power to take and to hold property, in a particular form, and for particular purposes, has the government a consequent right substantially to change that form, or to vary the purposes to which the property is to be applied? This principle has never been asserted or recognised, and is supported by no authority. Can it derive aid from reason? The objects for which a corporation is created are universally such as the government wishes to promote. They are deemed beneficial to the country; and this benefit consitutes the consideration, and in most cases, the sole consideration of the grant.

In most eleemosynary institutions, the object would be difficult, perhaps unattainable, without the aid of a charter of incorporation. Charitable or public-spirited individuals, desirous of making permanent appropriations for charitable or other useful purposes, find it impossible to effect their design securely and certainly, without an incorporating act. They apply to the government, state their beneficent object, and offer to advance the money necessary for its accomplishment, provided the government will confer on the instrument which is to execute their designs the capacity to execute them. The proposition is considered and approved. The benefit to the public is considered as an ample compensation for the faculty it confers, and the corporation is created.

If the advantages to the public constitute a full compensation for the faculty it gives, there can be no reason for exacting a further compensation, by claiming a right to exercise over this artificial being, a power which changes its nature, and touches the fund, for the security and application of which it was created. There can be no reason for implying in a charter, given for a valuable consideration, a power which is not only not expressed, but is in direct contradiction to its express stipulations.

From the fact, then, that a charter of incorporation has been granted, nothing can be inferred, which changes the character of the institution, or transfers to the government any new power over it.

The character of civil institutions does not grow out of their incorporation, but out of the manner in which they are formed, and the objects for which they are created. The right to change them is not founded on their being incorporated, but on their being the instruments of government, created for its purposes. The same institutions, created for the same objects, though not incorporated, would be public institutions, and, of course, be controllable by the legislature. The incorporating act neither gives nor prevents this control.

Neither, in reason, can the incorporating act change the character of a private eleemosynary institution.

We are next led to the inquiry, for whose benefit the property given to Dartmouth College was secured?

. . . .

Contracts, the parties to which have a vested beneficial interest, and those only, it has been said, are the objects about which the constitution is solicitous, and to which its protection is extended. The court has bestowed on this argument the most deliberate consideration, and the result will be stated. Dr. Wheelock, acting for himself, and for those who, at his solicitation, had made contributions to his school, applied for this charter, as the instrument which should enable him, and them, to perpetuate their beneficent intention. It was granted. An artificial, immortal being, was created by the crown, capable of receiving and distributing for ever, according to the will of the donors, the donations which should be made to it. On this being, the contributions which had been collected were immediately bestowed. These gifts were made, not indeed to make a profit for the donors, or their posterity, but for something, in their opinion, of inestimable value; for something which they deemed a full equivalent for the money with which it was purchased. The consideration for which they stipulated, is the perpetual application of the fund to its object, in the mode prescribed by themselves.

Their descendants may take no interest in the preservation of this consideration. But in this respect their descendants are not their representatives; they are represented by the corporation. The corporation is the assignee of their rights, stands in their place, and distributes their bounty, as they would themselves have distributed it, had they been immortal. So, with respect to the students who are to derive learning from this source; the corporation is a trustee for them also. Their potential rights, which, taken distributively, are imperceptible, amount collectively to a most important interest. These are, in the aggregate, to be exercised, asserted and protected, by the corporation. They were as completely out of the donors, at the instant of their being vested in the corporation, and as incapable of being asserted by the students, as at present.

It is, then, a contract within the letter of the constitution, and within its spirit also, unless the fact, that the property is invested by the donors in trustees, for the promotion of religion and education, for the benefit of persons who are perpetually changing, though the objects remain the same, shall create a particular exception, taking this case out of the prohibition contained in the constitution. . . .

. . . .

Almost all eleemosynary corporations, those which are created for the promotion of religion, of charity or of education, are of the same character. The law of this case is the law of all. In every literary or charitable institution, unless the objects of the bounty be themselves incorporated, the whole legal interest is in trustees, and can be asserted only by them. The donors, or claimants of the bounty, if they can appear in court at all, can appear only to complain of the trustees. In all other situations, they are identified with, and personated by, the trustees; and their rights are to be defended and maintained by them.

Religion, charity and education are, in the law of England, legatees or donees, capable of receiving bequests or donations in this form. They appear in court, and claim or defend by the corporation. Are they of so little estimation in the United States, that contracts for their benefit must be excluded from the protection of words, which in their natural import include them? Or do such contracts so necessarily require new modelling by the authority of the legislature, that the ordinary rules of construction must be disregarded, in order to leave them exposed to legislative alteration?

All feel, that these objects are not deemed unimportant in the United States. . . .

These eleemosynary institutions do not fill the place, which would otherwise be occupied by government, but that which would otherwise remain vacant. They are complete acquisitions to literature. They are donations to education; donations, which any government must be disposed rather to encourage than to discountenance. It requires no very critical examination of the human mind, to enable us to determine, that one great inducement to these gifts is the conviction felt by the giver, that the disposition he makes of them is immutable.

It is probable, that no man ever was, and that no man ever will be, the founder of a college, believing at the time, that an act of incorporation constitutes no security for the institution; believing, that it is immediately to be deemed a public institution, whose funds are to be governed and applied, not by the will of the donor, but by the will of the legislature. All such gifts are made in the pleasing, perhaps, delusive hope, that the charity will flow for ever in the channel which the givers have marked out for it.

If every man finds in his own bosom strong evidence of the universality of this sentiment, there can be but little reason to imagine, that the framers of our constitution were strangers to it, and that, feeling the necessity and policy of giving permanence and security to contracts, of withdrawing them from the influence of legislative bodies, whose fluctuating policy, and repeated interferences, produced the most perplexing and injurious embarrassments, they still deemed it necessary to leave these contracts subject to those interferences. The motives for such an exception must be very powerful, to justify the construction which makes it.

. . . .

We next proceed to the inquiry, whether its obligation has been impaired by those acts of the legislature of New Hampshire, to which the special verdict refers?

. . . On the effect of this law, two opinions cannot be entertained. . . . The whole power of governing the college is transferred from trustees, appointed according to the will of the founder, expressed in the charter, to the executive of New Hampshire. The management and application of the funds of this eleemosynary institution, which are placed by the donors in the hands of trustees named in the charter, and empowered to perpetuate themselves, are placed by this act under the control of the government of the state. The will of the state is substituted for the will of the donors, in every essential operation of the college.

This is not an immaterial change. The founders of the college contracted, not merely for the perpetual application of the funds which they gave, to the objects for which those funds were given; they contracted also, to secure that application by the constitution of the corporation. They contracted for a system, which should, so far as human foresight can provide, retain for ever the government of the literary institution they had formed, in the hands of persons approved by themselves. This system is totally changed. The charter of 1769 exists no longer. It is re-organized; and re-organized in such a manner, as to convert a literary institution, moulded according to the will of its founders, and placed under the control of private literary men, into a machine entirely subservient to the will of government.

This may be for the advantage of this college in particular, and may be for the advantage of literature in general; but it is not according to the will of the donors, and is subversive of that contract, on the faith of which their property was given. In the view which has been taken of this interesting case, the court has confined itself to the rights possessed by the trustees, as the assignees and representatives of the donors and founders, for the benefit of religion and literature.

[T]he court [is] . . . of opinion, on general principles, that in these private eleemosynary institutions, the body corporate, as possessing the whole legal and equitable interest, and completely representing the donors, for the purpose of executing the trust, has rights which are protected by the constitution. It results from this opinion, that the acts of the legislature of New Hampshire, which are stated in the special verdict found in this cause, are repugnant to the constitution of the United States; and that the judgment on this special verdict ought to have been for the plaintiffs. The judgment of the state court must, therefore, be reversed.

ASSOCIATE SUPREME COURT JUSTICE JOSEPH STORY

Concurring Opinion in The Dartmouth College Case

(EXCERPTS)

1819

This is a cause of great importance, and as the very learned discussions, as well here, as in the state court, show, of no inconsiderable difficulty.

It will be necessary, . . . before we proceed . . . , to institute an inquiry into the nature, rights and duties of aggregate corporations, at common law; that we may apply the principles, drawn from this source, to the exposition of this charter, which was granted emphatically with reference to that law. An aggregate corporation, at common law, is a collection of individuals, united into one collective body, under a special name, and possessing certain immunities, privileges and capacities, in its collective character, which do not belong to the natural persons composing it. Among other things, it possesses the capacity of perpetual succession, and of acting by the collected vote or will of its component members, and of suing and being sued in all things touching its corporate rights and duties. It is, in short, an artificial person, existing in contemplation of law, and endowed with certain powers and franchises which, though they must be exercised through the medium of its natural members, are yet considered as subsisting in the corporation itself, as distinctly as if it were a real personage. Hence, such a corporation may sue and be sued by its own members, and may contract with them in the same manner, as with any strangers.

A great variety of these corporations exist, in every country governed by the common law; in some of which, the corporate existence is perpetuated by new elections, made from time to time; and in others, by a continual accession of new members, without any corporate act. Some of these corporations are, from the particular purposes to which they are devoted, denominated spiritual, and some lay; and the latter are again divided into civil and eleemosynary corporations. . . . Eleemosynary corporations are such as are constituted for the perpetual distribution of the free-alms and bounty of the founder, in such manner as he has directed; and in this class, are ranked hospitals for the relief of poor and impotent persons, and colleges for the promotion of learning and piety, and the support of persons engaged in literary pursuits.

Another division of corporations is into public and private. Public corporations are generally esteemed such as exist for public political purposes only, such as towns, cities, parishes and counties; and in many repects, they are so, although they involve some private interests; but strictly speaking, public corporations are such only as are founded by the government, for public purposes, where the whole interests belong also to the government. If, therefore, the foundation be private, though under the charter of the government, the corporation is private, however extensive the uses may be to which it is devoted, either by the bounty of the founder, or the nature and objects of the institution. . . .

This reasoning applies in its full force to eleemosynary corporations. An hospital, founded by a private benefactor, is, in point of law, a private corporation, although dedicated by its charter to general charity. So, a college, founded and endowed in the same manner, although, being for the promotion of learning and piety, it may extend its charity to scholars from every class in the community, and thus acquire the character of a public institution. This is the unequivocal doctrine of the authorities; and cannot be shaken but by undermining the most solid foundations of the common law.

. . . .

When the corporation is said, [by counsel for the State of New Hampshire] at the bar, to be public, it is not merely meant, that the whole community may be the proper objects of the bounty, but that the government have the sole right, as trustees of the public interests, to regulate, control and direct the corporation, and its funds and its franchises, at its own good will and pleasure. Now, such an authority does not exist in the government, except where the corporation, is in the strictest sense, public; that is, where its whole interests and franchises are the exclusive property and domain of the government itself. If it had been otherwise, courts of law would have been spared many laborious adjudications in respect to eleemosynary corporations, and the visitatorial powers over them, from the time of Lord HOLT down to the present day.

Nay, more, private trustees for charitable purposes would have been liable to have the property confided to their care taken away from them, without any assent or default on their part, and the administration submitted, not to the control of law and equity, but to the arbitrary discretion of the government. Yet who ever thought before, that the munificent gifts of private donors for general charity became instantaneously the property of the government; and that the trustees appointed by the donors, whether corporate or unincorporated, might be compelled to yield up their rights to whomsoever the government might appoint to administer them? If we were to establish such a principle, it would extinguish all future eleemosynary endowments; and we should find as little of public policy, as we now find of law to sustain it.

An eleemosynary corporation, then, upon a private foundation, being a private corporation, it is next to be considered, what is deemed a foundation, and who is the founder. This cannot be stated with more brevity and exactness, than in the language of the elegant commentator upon the laws of England:

> The founder of all corporations (says Sir William Blackstone), in the strictest and original sense, is the king alone, for he only can incorporate a society; and in civil corporations, such as mayor, commonalty, &c., where there are no possessions or endowments given to the body, there is no other founder but the king; but in eleemosynary foundations, such as colleges and hospitals, where there is an endowment of lands, the law distinguishes and makes two species of foundation, the one *fundatio incipiens,* or the incorporation, in which sense the king is the general founder of all colleges and hospitals; the other *fundatio perficiens,* or the donation of it, in which sense, the first gift of the revenues is the foundation, and he who gives them is, in the law, the founder; and it is in this last sense, we generally call a man the founder of a college or hospital.

To all eleemosynary corporations, a visitatorial power attaches, as a necessary incident; for these corporations being composed of individuals, subject to human infirmities, are liable, as well as private persons, to deviate from the end of their institution. The law, therefore, has provided, that there shall somewhere exist a power to visit, inquire into, and correct all irregularities and abuses in such corporations, and to compel the original purposes of the charity to be faithfully fulfilled. . . .

And of common right, by the donation, the founder and his heirs are the legal visitors, unless the founder has appointed and assigned another person to be visitor. For the founder may, if he please, at the time of the endowment, part with his visitatorial power, and the person to whom it is assigned will, in that case, possess it in exclusion of the founder's heirs.

This visitatorial power is, therefore, an hereditament founded in property, and valuable, in intendment of law; and stands upon the maxim, that he who gives his property, has a right to regulate it in future. It includes also the legal right of patronage, for as Lord HOLT justly observes, "patronage and visitation are necessary consequents one upon another."

No technical terms are necessary to assign or vest the visitatorial power; it is sufficient if, from the nature of the duties to be performed by particular persons, under the charter, it can be inferred, that the founder meant to part with it in their favor; and he may divide it among various persons, or subject it to any modifications or control, by the fundamental statutes of the corporation. But where the appointment is given in general terms, the whole power vests in the appointee.

. . . .

When a private eleemosynary corporation is thus created, by the charter of the crown, it is subject to no other control on the part of the crown, than what is expressly or implicitly reserved by the charter itself. . . .

But an eleemosynary, like every other corporation, is subject to the general law of the land. It may forfeit its corporate franchises, by misuser or non-user of them. It is subject to the controlling authority of its legal visitor, who, unless restrained by the terms of the charter, may amend and repeal its statutes, remove its officers, correct abuses, and generally superintend the management of the trusts. Where, indeed, the visitatorial power is vested in the trustees of the charity, in virtue of their incorporation, there can be no amotion of them from their corporate capacity. But they are not, therefore, placed beyond the reach of the law. As managers of the revenues of the corporation, they are subject to the general superintending power of the court of chancery, not as itself possessing a visitatorial power, or a right to control the charity, but as possessing a general jurisdiction, in all cases of an abuse of trust, to redress grievances and suppress frauds.

And where a corporation is a mere trustee of a charity, a court of equity will go yet further; and though it cannot appoint or remove a corporator, it will, yet, in a case of gross fraud, or abuse of trust, take away the trust from the corporation, and vest it in other hands. Thus much it has been thought proper to premise respecting the nature, rights, and duties of eleemosynary corporations, growing out of the common law. . . .

. . . .

The corporators are not mere agents, but have vested rights, in their character, as corporators. The right to be a freeman of a corporation, is a valuable temporal right. It is a right of voting and acting in the corporate concerns, which the law recognises and enforces, and for a violation of which it provides a remedy. It is founded on the same basis as the right of voting in public elections; it is as sacred a right; and whatever might have been the prevalence of former doubts, since the time of Lord HOLT, such right has always been deemed a valuable franchise or privilege.

This reasoning, which has been thus far urged, applies with full force to the case of Dartmouth College. The franchises granted by the charter were vested in the trustees, in their corporate character. The lands and other property, subsequently acquired, were held by them in the same manner. They were the private demesnes of the corporation, held by it, not, as the argument supposes, for the use and benefit of the people of New Hampshire, but, as the charter itself declares, "for the use of Dartmouth College." . . .

The principal objections having been thus answered, satisfactorily, at least, to my own mind, it remains only to declare, that my opinion, after the most mature deliberation is, that the charter of Dartmouth College, granted in 1769, is a contract within the purview of the constitutional prohibition. . . .

In my judgment, it is perfectly clear, that any act of a legislature which takes away any powers or franchises vested by its charter in a private corporation, or its corporate officers, or which restrains or controls the legitimate exercise of them, or transfers them to other persons, without its assent, is a violation of the obligations of that charter. If the legislature mean to claim such an authority, it must be reserved in the grant. The charter of Dartmouth College contains no such reservation; and I am, therefore, bound to declare, that the acts of the legislature of New Hampshire, now in question, do impair the obligations of that charter, and are, consequently, unconstitutional and void.

In pronouncing this judgment, it has not for one moment escaped me, how delicate, difficult and ungracious is the task devolved upon us. The predicament in which this court stands in relation to the nation at large, is full of perplexities and embarrassments. It is called to decide on causes between citizens of different states, between a state and its citizens, and between different states. It stands, therefore in the midst of jealousies and rivalries of conflicting parties, with the most momentous interests confided to its care. Under such circumstances, it never can have a motive to do more than its duty; and I trust, it will always be found to possess firmness enough to do that. Under these impressions, I have pondered on the case before us with the most anxious deliberation. I entertain great respect for the legislature, whose acts are in question. I entertain no less respect for the enlightened tribunal whose decision we are called upon to review. In the examination, I have endeavored to keep my steps *super antiquas vias* of the law, under the guidance of authority and principle. It is not for judges to listen to the voice of persuasive eloquence, or popular appeal. We have nothing to do, but to pronounce the law as we find it; and having done this, our justification must be left to the impartial judgment of our country.

22

Alexis de Tocqueville, *Political Associations in the United States,* 1835, and *Of the Use Which Americans Make of Public Associations in Civil Society,* 1840

Alexis de Tocqueville traveled from France to the United States in 1830 to prepare an official report on America's new-model prisons and asylums, which some French leaders believed to be the most effective and humane in the world. In addition to studying America's asylums, Tocqueville became fascinated by American political life. A member of a family from the minor aristocracy that had survived the French Revolution, Tocqueville had political ambitions that were handicapped, in post-revolutionary France, by his aristocratic family background. He saw the United States as a working democracy that might foreshadow the political opportunities and problems that lay before France as it moved toward democracy. Traveling widely through the United States, Tocqueville discussed American democracy with everyone he met, from illiterate deckhands to eminent statesmen.

In preparing his great book, *Democracy in America,* Tocqueville drew heavily on the writings of many Americans who had devoted great effort to comprehend their own country: in many ways, his work offers a brilliant summary of Americans' analysis of their own society. Tocqueville found especially interesting the fact that Americans voluntarily joined together to do things that, in Europe, were done by great landed aristocrats, by the established, tax-supported Church, or by the State. *Democracy in America* contains two striking essays on voluntary associations: one on their role in American politics, the other on their role in "civil society." Each of these essays contains striking descriptions of American associations at work.

ALEXIS DE TOCQUEVILLE

Political Associations in the United States

FROM *DEMOCRACY IN AMERICA*

1834

In no country in the world has the principle of association been more successfully used or applied to a greater multitude of objects than in America. Besides the permanent associations which are established by law under the names of townships, cities, and counties, a vast number of others are formed and maintained by the agency of private individuals.

The citizen of the United States is taught from infancy to rely upon his own exertions in order to resist the evils and the difficulties of life; he looks upon the social authority with an eye of mistrust and anxiety, and he claims its assistance only when he is unable to do without it. This habit may be traced even in the schools, where the children in their games are wont to submit to rules which they have themselves established, and to punish misdemeanors which they have themselves defined. The same spirit pervades every act of social life. If a stoppage occurs in a thoroughfare and the circulation of vehicles is hindered, the neighbors immediately form themselves into a deliberative body; and this extemporaneous assembly gives rise to an executive power which remedies the inconvenience before anybody has thought of recurring to a pre-existing authority superior to that of the persons immediately concerned. If some public pleasure is concerned, an association is formed to give more splendor and regularity to the entertainment. Societies are formed to resist evils that are exclusively of a moral nature, as to diminish the vice of intemperance. In the United States associations are established to promote the public safety, commerce, industry, morality, and religion. There is no end which the human will despairs of attaining through the combined power of individuals united into a society.

I shall have occasion hereafter to show the effects of association in civil life; I confine myself for the present to the political world. When once the right of association is recognized, the citizens may use it in different ways.

An association consists simply in the public assent which a number of individuals give to certain doctrines and in the engagement which they contract to promote in a certain manner the spread of those doc-

trines. The right of associating in this fashion almost merges with freedom of the press, but societies thus formed possess more authority than
the press. When an opinion is represented by a society, it necessarily
assumes a more exact and explicit form. It numbers its partisans and
engages them in its cause; they, on the other hand, become acquainted
with one another, and their zeal is increased by their number. An association unites into one channel the efforts of divergent minds and urges
them vigorously towards the one end which it clearly points out.

The second degree in the exercise of the right of association is the
power of meeting. When an association is allowed to establish centers of
action at certain important points in the country, its activity is increased
and its influence extended. Men have the opportunity of seeing one
another; means of execution are combined; and opinions are maintained
with a warmth and energy that written language can never attain.

Lastly, in the exercise of the right of political association there is a
third degree: the partisans of an opinion may unite in electoral bodies
and choose delegates to represent them in a central assembly. This is,
properly speaking, the application of the representative system to a party.

Thus, in the first instance, a society is formed between individuals
professing the same opinion, and the tie that keeps it together is of a
purely intellectual nature. In the second case, small assemblies are
formed, which represent only a fraction of the party. Lastly, in the third
case, they constitute, as it were, a separate nation in the midst of the
nation, a government within the government. Their delegates, like the
real delegates of the majority, represent the whole collective force of
their party, and like them, also, have an appearance of nationality and
all the moral power that results from it. It is true that they have not the
right, like the others, of making the laws; but they have the power of
attacking those which are in force and of drawing up beforehand those
which ought to be enacted.

If, among a people who are imperfectly accustomed to the exercise
of freedom, or are exposed to violent political passions, by the side of
the majority which makes the laws is placed a minority which only
deliberates and gets laws ready for adoption, I cannot but believe that
public tranquillity would there incur very great risks. There is doubtless
a wide difference between proving that one law is in itself better than
another and proving that the former ought to be substituted for the
latter. But the imagination of the multitude is very apt to overlook this
difference, which is so apparent to the minds of thinking men. It sometimes happens that a nation is divided into two nearly equal parties,
each of which affects to represent the majority. If, near the directing
power, another power is established which exercises almost as much
moral authority as the former, we are not to believe that it will long be
content to speak without acting; or that it will always be restrained by

the abstract consideration that associations are meant to direct opinions, but not to enforce them, to suggest but not to make the laws.

The more I consider the independence of the press in its principal consequences, the more am I convinced that in the modern world it is the chief and, so to speak, the constitutive element of liberty. A nation that is determined to remain free is therefore right in demanding, at any price, the exercise of this independence. But the *unlimited* liberty of political association cannot be entirely assimilated to the liberty of the press. The one is at the same time less necessary and more dangerous than the other. A nation may confine it within certain limits without forfeiting any part of its self-directing power; and it may sometimes be obliged to do so in order to maintain its own authority.

In America the liberty of association for political purposes is unlimited. An example will show in the clearest light to what an extent this privilege is tolerated.

The question of a tariff or free trade has much agitated the minds of Americans. The tariff was not only a subject of debate as a matter of opinion, but it affected some great material interests of the states. The North attributed a portion of its prosperity, and the South nearly all its sufferings, to this system. For a long time the tariff was the sole source of the political animosities that agitated the Union.

In 1831, when the dispute was raging with the greatest violence, a private citizen of Massachusetts proposed, by means of the newspapers, to all the enemies of the tariff to send delegates to Philadelphia in order to consult together upon the best means of restoring freedom of trade. This proposal circulated in a few days, by the power of the press, from Maine to New Orleans. The opponents of the tariff adopted it with enthusiasm; meetings were held in all quarters, and delegates were appointed. The majority of these delegates were well known, and some of them had earned a considerable degree of celebrity. South Carolina alone, which afterwards took up arms in the same cause, sent sixty-three delegates. On the lst of October 1831 this assembly, which, according to the American custom, had taken the name of a Convention, met at Philadelphia; it consisted of more than two hundred members. Its debates were public, and they at once assumed a legislative character; the extent of the powers of Congress, the theories of free trade, and the different provisions of the tariff were discussed. At the end of ten days the Convention broke up, having drawn up an address to the American people in which it declared: (1) that Congress had not the right of making a tariff, and that the existing tariff was unconstitutional; (2) that the prohibition of free trade was prejudicial to the interests of any nation, and to those of the American people especially.

It must be acknowledged that the unrestrained liberty of political association has not hitherto produced in the United States the fatal results that might perhaps be expected from it elsewhere. The right of association was imported from England, and it has always existed in America; the exercise of this privilege is now incorporated with the manners and customs of the people. At the present time the liberty of association has become a necessary guarantee against the tyranny of the majority. In the United States, as soon as a party has become dominant, all public authority passes into its hands; its private supporters occupy all the offices and have all the force of the administration at their disposal. As the most distinguished members of the opposite party cannot surmount the barrier that excludes them from power, they must establish themselves outside of it and oppose the whole moral authority of the minority to the physical power that domineers over it. Thus a dangerous expedient is used to obviate a still more formidable danger.

The omnipotence of the majority appears to me to be so full of peril to the American republics that the dangerous means used to bridle it seem to be more advantageous than prejudicial. And here I will express an opinion that may remind the reader of what I said when speaking of the freedom of townships. There are no countries in which associations are more needed to prevent the despotism of faction or the arbitrary power of a prince than those which are democratically constituted. In aristocratic nations the body of the nobles and the wealthy are in themselves natural associations which check the abuses of power. In countries where such associations do not exist, if private individuals cannot create an artificial and temporary substitute for them I can see no permanent protection against the most galling tyranny; and a great people may be oppressed with impunity by a small faction or by a single individual.

The meeting of a great political convention (for there are conventions of all kinds), which may frequently become a necessary measure, is always a serious occurrence, even in America, and one that judicious patriots cannot regard without alarm. This was very perceptible in the Convention of 1831, at which all the most distinguished members strove to moderate its language and to restrain its objects within certain limits. It is probable that this Convention exercised a great influence on the minds of the malcontents and prepared them for the open revolt against the commercial laws of the Union that took place in 1832.

It cannot be denied that the unrestrained liberty of association for political purposes is the privilege which a people is longest in learning how to exercise. If it does not throw the nation into anarchy, it perpetually augments the chances of that calamity. On one point, however, this perilous liberty offers a security against dangers of another kind; in countries where associations are free, *secret* societies are unknown. In America there are factions, but no conspiracies.

DIFFERENT WAYS in which the right of association is understood in Europe and in the United States— Different use which is made of it.

The most natural privilege of man, next to the right of acting for himself, is that of combining his exertions with those of his fellow creatures and of acting in common with them. The right of association therefore appears to me almost as inalienable in its nature, as the right of personal liberty. No legislator can attack it without impairing the foundations of society. Nevertheless, if the liberty of association is only a source of advantage and prosperity to some nations, it may be perverted or carried to excess by others, and from an element of life may be changed into a cause of destruction. A comparison of the different methods that associations pursue in those countries in which liberty is well understood and in those where liberty degenerates into license may be useful both to governments and to parties.

Most Europeans look upon association as a weapon which is to be hastily fashioned and immediately tried in the conflict. A society is formed for discussion, but the idea of impending action prevails in the minds of all those who constitute it. It is, in fact, an army; and the time given to speech serves to reckon up the strength and to animate the courage of the host, after which they march against the enemy. To the persons who compose it, resources which lie within the bounds of law may suggest themselves as means of success, but never as the only means.

Such, however, is not the manner in which the right of association is understood in the United States. In America the citizens who form the minority associate in order, first, to show their numerical strength and so to diminish the moral power of the majority; and, secondly, to stimulate competition and thus to discover those arguments that are most fitted to act upon the majority; for they always entertain hopes of drawing over the majority to their own side, and then controlling the supreme power in its name. Political associations in the United States are therefore peaceable in their intentions and strictly legal in the means which they employ; and they assert with perfect truth that they aim at success only by lawful expedients.

The difference that exists in this respect between Americans and Europeans depends on several causes. In Europe there are parties which differ so much from the majority that they can never hope to acquire its support, and yet they think they are strong enough in themselves to contend against it. When a party of this kind forms an association, its object is not to convince, but to fight. In America the individuals who hold opinions much opposed to those of the majority can do nothing against it, and all other parties hope to win it over to their own principles. The exercise of the right of association becomes dangerous, then, in proportion as great parties find themselves wholly unable to acquire the majority. In a country like the United States, in which the differences of opinion are mere differences of hue, the right of association may remain unrestrained without evil consequences. Our inexperience of liberty leads us to regard the liberty of association only as a right of attacking the government. The first notion that presents itself to a party, as well as to an individual, when it has acquired a consciousness of its own strength is that of violence; the notion of persuasion arises at a later period, and is derived from experience. The English, who are divided into parties which differ essentially from each other, rarely abuse the right of association because they have long been accustomed to exercise it. In France, the passion for war is so intense that there is no undertaking so mad, or so injurious to the welfare of the state, that a man does not consider himself honored in defending it at the risk of his life.

But perhaps the most powerful of the causes that tend to mitigate the violence of political associations in the United States is universal suffrage. In countries in which universal suffrage exists, the majority is never doubtful, because neither party can reasonably pretend to represent that portion of the community which has not voted. The associations know as well as the nation at large that they do not represent the majority. This results, indeed, from the very fact of their existence; for if they did represent the preponderating power, they would change the law instead of soliciting its reform. The consequence of this is that the moral influence of the government which they attack is much increased, and their own power is much enfeebled.

In Europe there are few associations which do not affect to represent the majority, or which do not believe that they represent it. This conviction or this pretension tends to augment their force amazingly and contributes no less legalize their measures. Violence may seem to be excusable in defense of the cause of oppressed right. Thus it is, in the vast complication of human laws, that extreme liberty some times corrects the abuses of liberty, and that extreme democracy obviates the dangers of democracy. In Europe associations consider themselves, in some degree, as the legislative and executive council of the people, who are unable to speak for themselves; moved by this belief, they act and they command. In America, where they represent in the eyes of all only a minority of the nation, they argue and petition.

The means that associations in Europe employ are in accordance with the end which they propose to obtain. As the principal aim of these bodies is to act and not to debate, to fight rather than to convince, they are naturally led to adopt an organization which is not civic and peaceable, but partakes of the habits and maxims of military life. They also centralize the direction of their forces as much as possible and entrust the power of the whole party to a small number of leaders.

The members of these associations respond to a watch word, like soldiers on duty; they profess the doctrine of passive obedience; say, rather, that in uniting together they at once abjure the exercise of their own judgment and free will; and the tyrannical control that these societies exercise is often far more insupportable than the authority possessed over society by the government which they attack. Their moral force is much diminished by these proceedings, and they lose the sacred character which always attaches to struggle of the oppressed against their oppressors. He who in given cases consents to obey his fellows with servility and who submits his will and even his thoughts to their control, how can he pretend that he wishes to be free?

The Americans have also established a government in their associations, but it is invariably borrowed from the forms of the civil administration. The independence of each individual is recognized; as in society, all the members advance at the same time towards the same end, but they are not all obliged to follow the same track. No one abjures the exercise of his reason and free will, but everyone exerts that reason and will to promote a common undertaking.

ALEXIS DE TOCQUEVILLE

Of the Use which the Americans Make of Public Associations in Civil Life

FROM *DEMOCRACY IN AMERICA*

1840

I do not propose to speak of those political associations by the aid of which men endeavor to defend themselves against the despotic action of a majority or against the aggressions of regal power. That subject I have already treated. If each citizen did not learn, in proportion as he individually becomes more feeble and consequently more incapable of preserving his freedom single-handed, to combine with his fellow citizens for the purpose of defending it, it is clear that tyranny would unavoidably increase together with equality.

Only those associations that are formed in civil life without reference to political objects are here referred to. The political associations that exist in the United States are only a single feature in the midst of the immense assemblage of associations in that country. Americans of all ages, all conditions, and all dispositions constantly form associations. They have not only commercial and manufacturing companies, in which all take part, but associations of a thousand other kinds, religious, moral, serious, futile, general or restricted, enormous or diminutive. The Americans make associations to give entertainments, to found seminaries, to build inns, to construct churches, to diffuse books, to send missionaries to the antipodes; in this manner they found hospitals, prisons, and schools. If it is proposed to inculcate some truth or to foster some feeling by the encouragement of a great example, they form a society. Wherever at the head of some new undertaking you see the government in France, or a man of rank in England, in the United States you will be sure to find an association.

I met with several kinds of associations in America which I confess I had no previous notion; and I have often admired the extreme skill with which the inhabitants of the United States succeed in proposing a common object for the exertions of a great many men and inducing them voluntarily to pursue it.

I have since traveled over England, from which the Americans have taken some of their laws and many of their customs; and it seemed to me that the principle of association was by no means so constantly or adroitly used in that country. The English often perform great things singly, whereas the Americans form associations for the smallest undertakings. It is evident that the former people consider association as a powerful means of action, but the latter seem to regard it as the only means they have of acting.

Thus the most democratic country on the face of the earth is that in which men have, in our time, carried to the highest perfection the art of pursuing in common the object of their common desires and have applied this new science to the greatest number of purposes. Is this the result of accident, or is there in reality any necessary connection between the principle of association and that of equality?

Aristocratic communities always contain, among a multitude of persons who by themselves are powerless, a small number of powerful and wealthy citizens, each of whom can achieve great undertakings single-handed. In aristocratic societies men do not need to combine in order to act, because they are strongly held together. Every wealthy and powerful citizen constitutes the head of a permanent and compulsory association, composed of all those who are dependent upon him or whom he makes subservient to the execution of his designs.

Among democratic nations, on the contrary, all the citizens are independent and feeble; they can do hardly anything by themselves, and none of them can oblige his fellow men to lend him their assistance. They all, therefore, become powerless if they do not learn voluntarily to help one another. If men living in democratic countries had no right and no inclination to associate for political purposes, their independence would be in great jeopardy, but they might long preserve their wealth and their cultivation: whereas if they never acquired the habit of form-ing associations in ordinary life, civilization itself would be endangered. A people among whom individuals lost the power of achieving great things single-handed, without acquiring the means of producing them by united exertions, would soon relapse into barbarism.

Unhappily, the same social condition that renders associations so necessary to democratic nations renders their formation more difficult among those nations than among all others. When several members of an aristocracy agree to combine, they easily succeed in doing so; as each of them brings great strength to the partnership, the number of its mem-bers may be very limited; and when the members of an assocation are limited in number, they may easily become mutually acquainted, un-derstand each other, and establish fixed regulations. The same opportu-nities do not occur among democratic nations, where the associated members must always be very numerous for their association to have any power.

I am aware that many of my countrymen are not in the least em-barrassed by this difficulty. They contend that the more enfeebled and incompetent the citizens become, the more able and active the govern-ment ought to be rendered in order that society at large may execute what individuals can no longer accomplish. They believe this answers the whole difficulty, but I think they are mistaken.

A government might perform the part of some of the largest Ameri-can companies, and several states, members of the Union, have already attempted it; but what political power could ever carry on the vast mul-titude of lesser undertakings which the American citizens perform ev-ery day, with the assistance of the principle of association? It is easy to foresee that the time is drawing near when man will be less and less able to produce, by himself alone, the commonest necessaries of life. The task of the governing power will therefore perpetually increase, and its very efforts will extend it every day. The more it stands in the place of associations, the more will individuals, losing the notion of combining together, require its assistance: these are causes and effects that unceas-ingly create each other. Will the administration of the country ultimately assume the management of all the manufactures which no single citizen is able to carry on? And if a time at length arrives when, in consequence of the extreme subdivision of landed property, the soil is split into an infinite number of parcels, so that it can be cultivated only by compa-nies of tillers, will it be necessary that the head of the government should leave the helm of state to follow the plow? The morals and the intelligence of a democratic people would be as much endangered as its business and manufactures if the government ever wholly usurped the place of private companies.

Feelings and opinions are recruited, the heart is enlarged, and the human mind is developed only by the reciprocal influence of men upon one another. I have shown that these influences are almost null in democratic countries; they must therefore be artificially created, and this can only be accomplished by associations.

When the members of an aristocratic community adopt a new opinion or conceive a new sentiment, they give it a station, as it were, beside themselves, upon the lofty platform where they stand; and opinions or sentiments so conspicuous to the eyes of the multitude are easily introduced into the minds or hearts of all around. In democratic countries the governing power alone is naturally in a condition to act in this manner, but it is easy to see that its action is always inadequate, and often dangerous. A government can no more be competent to keep alive and to renew the circulation of opinions and feelings among a great people than to manage all the speculations of productive industry. No sooner does a government attempt to go beyond its political sphere and to enter upon this new track than it exercises, even unintentionally, an insupportable tyranny; for a government can only dictate strict rules, the opinions which it favors are rigidly enforced, and it is never easy to discriminate between its advice and its commands. Worse still will be the case if the government really believes itself interested in preventing all circulation of ideas; it will then stand motionless and oppressed by the heaviness of voluntary torpor. Governments, therefore, should not be the only active powers; associations ought, in democratic nations, to stand in lieu of those powerful private individuals whom the equality of conditions has swept away.

As soon as several of the inhabitants of the United States have taken up an opinion or a feeling which they wish to promote in the world, they look out for mutual assistance; and as soon as they have found one another out, they combine. From that moment they are no longer isolated men, but a power seen from afar, whose actions serve for an example and whose language is listened to. The first time I heard in the United States that a hundred thousand men had bound themselves publicly to abstain from spirituous liquors, it appeared to me more like a joke than a serious engagement, and I did not at once perceive why these temperate citizens could not content themselves with drinking water by their own firesides. I at last understood that these hundred thousand Americans, alarmed by the progress of drunkenness around them, had made up their minds to patronize temperance. They acted in just the same way as a man of high rank who should dress very plainly in order to inspire the humbler orders with a contempt of luxury. It is probable that if these hundred thousand men had lived in France, each of them would singly have memorialized the government to watch the public houses all over the kingdom. Nothing, in my opinion, is more deserving of our attention than the intellectual and moral associations of America. The political and industrial associations of that country strike us forcibly; but the others elude our observation, or if we discover them, we understand them imperfectly because we have hardly ever seen anything of the kind. It must be acknowledged, however, that they are as necessary to the American people as the former, and perhaps more so. In democratic countries the science of association is the mother of science; the progress of all the rest depends upon the progress it has made.

Among the laws that rule human societies there is one which seems to be more precise and clear than all others. If men are to remain civilized or to become so, the art of associating together must grow and improve in the same ratio in which the equality of conditions is increased.

USES OF
NONPROFIT
ORGANIZATIONS

FIVE

Varieties of Religious Nonprofits

For Robert Baird, who represented American Presbyterians to Europe and who wrote *The Voluntary Principle in American Christianity* (1840)—and for most other American Protestants— the "rise of voluntary religion" was the great cause of the nineteenth century. Voluntary religion, as they saw it, manifested itself in nonprofit educational and human-service organizations as well as in churches. In their eyes, the struggle to spread the Protestant faith and works was the great American drama, a drama filled with tension and crisis but destined for triumphal success.

Not everyone agreed at the time. Evangelical Protestants strongly objected to Catholicism and opposed the growth of the Catholic Church in the United States. They also objected vigorously to deists and Unitarians, and they rejected the Masons' emphasis on tolerance. Many recent historians have argued that most nonprofits sponsored by nineteenth-century evangelicals served purposes that were narrowly bigoted. Sometimes, these historians have added, the evangelicals' nonprofits hypocritically advanced the selfish interests of the wealthy men who served on their boards. As Peter Dobkin Hall makes clear in his sophisticated study of Yale University, one of the most successful of the early nonprofit corporations, the story is not a simple one.

The abolitionist movement was one of the notable achievements of nineteenth-century American voluntarism, but voluntary religion had mixed implications for African Americans. Many slaves embraced Christianity, and like other Americans they sought to create their own churches. But Christian slaves met the determined opposition of their masters, most of whom also objected to missionary work intended for the slaves' benefit. Free African Americans did establish their own churches, charities, and self-help societies, but they were also hampered by severe restrictions on their political and legal rights in the "free" states. And the ministers employed by voluntary congregations in the south lacked the autonomy that might have enabled the leaders of an established church to criticize the nature or existence of slavery—as the Franciscans and Jesuits criticized the actions of Spanish conquistadors.

Voluntary religion also shaped the actions of non-Protestant religious groups in nineteenth-century America. Jewish congregations found it relatively easy to fit into America's voluntary institutional framework. Catholics, Lutherans, and others whose ideal was a comprehensive hierarchy established by government and supported by taxes had to develop new arrangements. The Catholic effort to adapt to the voluntary institutional framework of the United States produced an extended debate, which is beyond the scope of this Reader. The key question had to do with the question of "trusteeship," the role within the Catholic Church of the lay people who—in the absence of government support for religious activity—purchased land, built churches, and voluntarily raised funds for priests and members of the religious orders. Once Catholics had settled the trusteeship question, however, they found that the nonprofit framework accommodated Catholic schools, orphanages, and hospitals, just as well as it accommodated Protestant institutions.

23

Organized Activity among Slaves: Henry Bibb, *The Suppression of Religion among Slaves*, 1849, and Daniel A. Payne, *Account of Slave Preachers*, 1839

The voluntary associations of early America stood in basic contradiction to America's involuntary slavery. One of the fundamental facts about American history is that most African Americans encountered violent resistance to their efforts to do good to others through the organizations that were so important to so many of their white fellow-countrymen. Thousands of Africans had, of course, already arrived in the American colonies in the 1600s: by the early nineteenth century they were as "American" as any of the settlers whose ancestors had come from Europe. The Africans made many contributions to American culture; and they brought and developed their own ways of extending aid to others. They received, of course, many influences in turn. Many of them adopted the Christian faith. Free African Americans, like the whites who often excluded them in the north as well as in the south, formed their own churches, mutual-benefit societies, and benevolent associations. Slaves sought to do the same, despite the oppressive hostility of their owners and other whites.

Henry Bibb, born and raised a slave, later became a Methodist preacher. In a talk designed for white audiences, he described the measures taken by white "patrols" to prevent "a poor white girl" from maintaining a Sunday School for slaves in 1833. Six years later Daniel Payne, a white man who had lived for a quarter century in the slave south, described the actions of white "patrols" in suppressing the religious activities of slaves who, despite their own condition, organized to preach to African slaves and to white farmers alike.

HENRY BIBB

The Suppression of Religion
among Slaves

1849

In 1833, I had some very serious religious impressions, and there was quite a number of slaves in that neighborhood, who felt very desirous to be taught to read the Bible. There was a Miss Davis, a poor white girl, who offered to teach a Sabbath School for the slaves, notwithstanding public opinion and the law was opposed to it. Books were furnished and she commenced the school; but the news soon got to our owners that she was teaching us to read. This caused quite an excitement in the neighborhood. Patrols were appointed to go and break it up the next Sabbath. They were determined that we should not have a Sabbath School in operation. For slaves this was called an incendiary movement.

The Sabbath is not regarded by a large number of the slaves as a day of rest. They have no schools to go to; no moral nor religious instruction at all in many localities where there are hundreds of slaves. Hence they resort to some kind of amusement. Those who make no profession of religion, resort to the woods in large numbers on that day to gamble, fight, get drunk and break the Sabbath. This is often encouraged by slaveholders. When they wish to have a little sport of that kind, they go among the slaves and give them whiskey, to see them dance, "pat juber," sing and play on the banjo. Then get them to wrestling, fighting, jumping, running foot races, and butting each other like sheep. This is urged on by giving them whiskey; making bets on them; laying chips on one slave's head, and daring another to tip it off with his hand; and if he tipped it off, it would be called an insult, and cause a fight. Before fighting, the parties choose their seconds to stand by them while fighting; a ring or a circle is formed to fight in, and no one is allowed to enter the ring while they are fighting, but their seconds and the white gentlemen. They are not allowed to fight a duel, nor to use weapons of any kind. The blows are made by kicking, knocking, and butting with their heads; they grab each other by their ears, and jam their heads together like sheep. If they are likely to hurt each other very bad, their masters would rap them with their walking canes, and make them stop. After fighting, they make friends, shake hands, and take a dram together, and there is no more of it.

But this is all principally for want of moral instruction. This is where they have no Sabbath Schools; no one to read the Bible to them; no one to preach the gospel who is competent to expound the Scriptures, except slaveholders. And the slaves, with but few exceptions, have no confidence at all in their preaching, because they preach a pro-slavery doctrine. They say, "Servants be obedient to your masters; and he that knoweth his master's will and doeth it not, shall be beaten with many stripes"; means that God will send them to hell, if they disobey their masters. This kind of preaching has driven thousands into infidelity. They view themselves as suffering unjustly under the lash, without friends, without protection of law or gospel, and the green-eyed monster tyranny staring them in the face.

They know that they are destined to die in that wretched condition, unless they are delivered by the arm of Omnipotence. And they cannot believe or trust in such a religion, as above named.

DANIEL A. PAYNE

Slaves as Preachers

1839

I am opposed to slavery, not because it enslaves the black man, but because it enslaves man. And were all the slaveholders in this land men of color, and the slaves white men, I would be as thorough and uncompromising an abolitionist as I now am; for whatever and whenever I may see a being in the form of a man, enslaved by his fellow man, without respect to his complexion, I shall lift up my voice to plead his cause, against all the claims of his proud oppressors and I shall do it not merely from the sympathy which man feels towards suffering man, but because God, the living God, whom I dare not disobey, has commanded me to open my mouth for the dumb, and to plead the cause of the oppressed. . . .

The very moment that a man conceives the diabolic design of enslaving his brother's body, that very moment does he also conceive the still more heinous design of fettering his will, for well does he know that in order to make his dominion supreme over the body, he must fetter the living spring of all its motions. Hence, the first lesson the slave is taught is to yield his will unreservedly and exclusively to the dictates of his master.

And if a slave desire to educate himself or his children, in obedience to the dictates of reason, or the laws of God, he does not, he cannot do it without the consent of his master. Does reason and circumstances and the Bible command a slave to preach the gospel to his brethren Slavery arises, and with a frown, an oath and a whip, fetters or obstructs the holy volition of his soul!

I knew a pious slave in Charleston, who was a licensed exhorter in the Methodist Episcopal Church; this good man was in the habit of spending his Saturday nights on the surrounding plantations, preaching to the slaves. One night, as usual, he got into a canoe, sailed upon James' Island. While in the very act of preaching the unsearchable riches of Christ to dying men, the patrols seized him and whipped him in the most cruel manner, and compelled him to promise that he would never return to preach again to those slaves.

In the year 1834, several colored brethren, who were also exhorters in the Methodist Episcopal Church commenced preaching to several destitute White families, who gained a subsistence by cultivating some poor lands about three or four miles from Charleston. The first Sunday I was present; the house was nearly filled with these poor white farmers. The master of the house was awakened to a sense of his lost condition and during the following week he was converted. On the third Sunday from the day he was convinced of sin he died in the triumphs of faith, and went to heaven. On the fourth Sunday from the time the dear brethren began to preach, the patrols scented their track, and put them to chase. Thus, an end was put to their labors. Their willing souls were fettered, and the poor whites constrained to go without the preaching of the gospel.

In a word, it is in view of man's moral agency that God commands him to shun vice, and practice virtue. But what female slave can do this? I lived 24 years in the midst of slavery, and never knew but six female slaves who were reputedly virtuous! What profit is to the female slave that she is disposed to be virtuous? Her will, like her body, is not her own; they are both at the pleasure of her master; and he brands them at his will. So it subverts the moral government of God.

24

Robert Baird, *The Voluntary Principle in American Christianity,* 1844

European Protestants—especially Calvinists who belonged to the established, tax-supported churches of Presbyterian Scotland, Reformed Holland, the Lutheran states of Germany and Scandinavia, and Calvinist Geneva—doubted that the Protestant faith could thrive in an America that had disestablished the church and denied it the power to tax. Mid-nineteenth century American Protestants hastened to defend themselves. Several Americans wrote ambitious books designed to show that far from fading away in the wake of disestablishment, Protestantism had flourished as a voluntary religion in America. They argued that Lyman Beecher had been right, and that disestablishment "was the best thing that had ever happened!" Typically written from the point of view of an evangelical New England Calvinist rather than of a southern Baptist, Methodist, or Episcopalian, these books celebrated the rise and triumph of voluntary religion, both in the United States itself and then, through a vast and energetic American-led missionary movement, around the world.

Robert Baird, an American Presbyterian who served as a missionary to Catholics in Europe, established the pattern for these evangelical rise-and-triumph of America and of the Protestant faith histories in his *Religion in the United States of America,* first published in England in 1843. For Baird, one of the chief evidences of the success of evangelical Protestantism in the United States was the creation of the many private, Protestant-sponsored schools, colleges, social service agencies, and clinics that constituted by far the largest share of nonprofits in nineteenth-century America.

Baird's assertion that Protestant-sponsored voluntary societies ran most nineteenth-century American schools and social service agencies was correct. He did exaggerate the degree to which these agencies provided schooling for all, and he failed to acknowledge that much of the money they used to care for the poor was in fact tax money, provided through local governments.

ROBERT BAIRD

The Voluntary Principle in American Religion and American Life

(EXCERPTS)

1844

Here I close these brief notices of the home missions of the chief evangelical churches in the United States. They will give the reader some idea of the mode in which new and feeble congregations are aided by the older and stronger, until able to maintain the institutions of religion themselves. The societies which we have passed under review in these four chapters, support, in all, above 1600 ministers of the gospel, in new, and as yet, feeble churches and flocks. Year after year many of these cease to require assistance, and then others are taken up in their turn. Be it remembered that the work has been systematically prosecuted for no long course of time. Twenty years ago, in fact, the most powerful and extensive of these societies did not exist; others were but commencing their operations. It is an enterprise with respect to which the churches have as yet but partially developed their energies and resources; still, they have accomplished enough to demonstrate how much may be done by the voluntary principle towards the calling into existence of churches and congregations in the settlements rapidly forming, whether in the new or the old States.

INFLUENCE OF THE VOLUNTARY PRINCIPLE ON EDUCATION: PRIMARY SCHOOLS

We have seen how the voluntary principle operates in America in relation to the building of churches, and also the support of ministers of the gospel in the new settlements forming every year, more or less, in all quarters. We now come to consider its influence on education. Hundreds of ministers, it will be perceived, are required to meet the demands of the rapidly augmenting population. Where are these to come from? Besides, in a country where the right of suffrage is almost universal, and where so much of the order, peace, and happiness, that are the true objects of all good government, depend on officers chosen in the most direct manner from among themselves, these must be instructed before they can become intelligent, virtuous, and capable citizens. Ignorance is incompatible with the acquisition or preservation of any freedom worth possessing; and, above all, such a republic as that of the United States must depend for its very existence on the wide diffusion of sound knowledge and religious principles among all classes of the people. Let us, therefore, trace the bearings of the voluntary principle upon education, in all its forms, among the various ranks of society in the United States. We shall begin with primary schools. . . .

The right of giving instruction is, in the United States, universal. Even where there is an all-pervading system of public schools, any number of families may join together, and employ any teacher for their children that they may prefer. Nor has that teacher to procure any license or "brevet of instruction" before entering on the duties of his office. His employers are the sole judges of his capacity, and should he prove inefficient the remedy is in their own bands. The teachers employed by the State pass an examination before a proper committee. In all the States where there is a legal provision for primary schools, there is a yearly report from each to a committee of the township, from which again there is a report to a county committee, and that, in its turn, sends a report to the secretary or school commissioner of the state.

In most cases, a pious and judicious teacher, if he will only confine himself to the great doctrines and precepts of the gospel, in which all who hold the fundamental truths of the Bible are agreed, can easily give as much religious instruction as he chooses. Where the teacher himself is not decidedly religious, much religious instruction cannot be expected; nor should any but religious teachers attempt to give anything more than general moral instruction, and make the scholars read portions of the scriptures, and of other good books.

The Bible is very generally used as a reading book in our primary schools, though in some places, as at St. Louis, the Roman Catholics have succeeded in excluding it, and they have been struggling to do the same in New York, where they will, probably, sooner or later succeed. In so far as relates to public schools, I see no other course but that of leaving it to the people themselves; the majority deciding and leaving the minority the alternative of supporting a school of their own. This will generally be done by Christians rather than give up the Bible.

SECONDARY SCHOOLS

But, if primary schools in the United States owe much to religion, grammar schools and academies, which may be called secondary institutions, owe still more.

In 1647, not many years after the settlement of the Puritans in New England, we find the colony of Massachusetts Bay making a legal provision, not only for primary, but for secondary schools also. . . . Such was the origin of the grammar schools of New England, and now they are so numerous that not only has almost every county one, but many of the more populous and wealthy possess several.

Not only so; all the other States have incorporated academies and grammar schools in very considerable numbers. Some, by a single act, have made an appropriation for the establishment of one such institution in every county within their jurisdiction. Thus in Pennsylvania, many years ago, 2000 dollars were granted for the erection of a building for a grammar school, at the seat of justice for each county, and a board of trustees, with power to fill up vacancies as they might occur in their numbers, was appointed for each.

In no case, however, does a State endow such an institution. A grant is made at the outset for the edifice that may be required; in most cases this is all that is done by the state, after which the institution has to depend upon the fees paid by the scholars for the support of the master or masters employed. In some instances, as in that of the State of New York, the grammar school has a yearly subsidy from the state, in which case there is usually some condition attached to the grant, such as gratis instruction to a certain number of poor lads, or of youths intending to become teachers of primary schools. But in most, even of the cases in which they have been aided by the state, these institutions have not only been privately commenced and carried to a certain point, previous to such assistance, but owe much more afterwards to the spontaneous support of their friends.

Indeed, in all parts of the country, grammar schools, and some of these the very best, may be found which owe their existence purely to individual or associated efforts. Such is the "Burr Seminary," in the town of Manchester, and state of Vermont, which originated in a legacy of 10,000 dollars, left by a gentleman of the name of Joseph Burr,[1] for the education of poor and pious young men for the ministry. By the terms of his will, in case of an equal sum being raised by the citizens of the place for the erection of suitable building, the purchase of apparatus, library, &c., then his legacy of $10,000 might be invested as a perma-

---

1. Mr. Burr had been for many years a resident at Manchester, in Vermont. By patient industry and upright dealings he acquired a fortune estimated at 150,000 dollars at the time of his death. A large part of this sum he bequeathed to the American Bible Society, Board of Commissioners for foreign missions, Home Missionary Society, and Education Society, besides endowing a professorship in one college, and contributing largely to the same object in another. And in addition to all this, by the above bequest of 10,000 dollars he founded the seminary that bears his name.

nent fund, the interest of which was to be applied to paying for the education of such young men as he should designate. This was done even beyond the extent required by the testator. A large and commodious edifice was erected, containing rooms for the recitation of lessons, lectures, library, philosophical apparatus &c. The school was opened on the 15th of May, 1833, and the number of scholars for the first term was 146; many of whom were pious youths, devoting themselves to study with view to the ministry. The institution still flourishes under the instructions of excellent men, and being situated in a secluded and moral village in the midst of the Green mountains, where living is cheap, it is attended by choice youths, some thirty or forty of whom are educated gratuitously. Such, again, is "Philips' Academy," at Andover in Massachusetts, about twenty miles north of Boston. Founded in 1778, by the joint liberality of two brothers, the Hon. Samuel Philips, of Andover, and the Hon. John Philips, of Exeter, New Hampshire; it, two years afterwards, received a charter of incorporation from the state. The fund supplied by these two brothers was afterwards augmented by the bequest of a third, the Hon. William Philips, of Boston. This academy, which is one of the best endowed in the United States, has been truly a blessing to the cause of religion and learning. By the terms prescribed by its pious founders, it is open to all youth of good character, but they have placed it under the control of Protestants, and the religious instruction given must be orthodox in the true sense of the word. Instructions are required to be given in the English, Latin, and Greek languages; in writing, arithmetic, and music; in the art of speaking; also in practical geometry, logic, and any other of the liberal arts, sciences, or languages, as opportunity and ability may from time to time admit, and the trustees shall direct. As the education of suitable young men for the ministry, was a leading consideration with the founders, so has the institution been in this respect abundantly blessed.

COLLEGES AND UNIVERSITIES

In almost all instances, the colleges in the United States have been founded by religious men. The common sense in establishing them is as follows. A company is organised, a subscription list opened, and certain men of influence in the neighbourhood consent to act as trustees. A charter is then asked from the legislature of the State within which the protected institution is to be placed, and a grant in aid of the funds at the same time solicited. The charter is obtained, and with it a few thousand dollars perhaps, by way of assistance. What else is required for the purchase of a site, erecting buildings, providing a library, apparatus, &c., &c., must be made up by those interested in the project. Thus have vast sums been raised, particularly during the last twenty years, for founding colleges in all parts of the country, but particularly in the west. A great proportion of these sums have been subscribed by persons in the neighbourhood, and more directly interested in the success of the undertakings subscribed for; but in many cases, money to a large amount has been obtained from the churches along the Atlantic coast.

SUNDAY SCHOOLS

Measures were taken in 1823 for the forming of a national society which should extend the benefit of Sunday schools to all parts of the country; and, accordingly, the American Sunday School Union was instituted—an association composed of excellent men of all evangelical denominations, and in which therefore no particular denomination is represented as such. It has now been diffusing its blessings for above eighteen years. The board of managers is composed of intelligent and zealous laymen of the various evangelical denominations, the greater part residing in Philadelphia and its vicinity, as that is the centre of the society's operations.

Its grand object is twofold;—to promote the establishment of Sunday schools where required, and to prepare and publish suitable books, some to be employed as manuals in the schools, and others for libraries intended to furnish the children with suitable reading at home. In both departments much good has been done. In the former, Sunday school missionaries, commonly ministers of the gospel and sometimes capable laymen, have been employed in visiting almost all parts of the country. They hold public meetings in every district or neighbourhood where they have any prospect of success, endeavour to interest the people in the subject, and to establish a school. Time and care are required for such a work. The nature of a Sunday school must be well explained; fit persons must be engaged as teachers, these must have their duties pointed out to them, and the motives that ought to prompt them to undertake the office presented and enforced; and money must be collected for the purchase of books.

In 1830, the society resolved to establish a Sunday school in every neighbourhood that was without any, throughout the western States or valley of the Mississippi, wherever practicable. Three years thereafter it adopted a like resolution with respect to the southern states. Both, but particularly the former of these resolutions, called forth much effort. Large sums were collected, and a great many schools were established. Every year since its commencement the society has employed many of the above missionaries; in some years as many as twenty, thirty, forty, and even fifty such. These traverse the country throughout its vast extent, resuscitate decaying schools, establish new ones, and encourage all.

INFLUENCE OF THE VOLUNTARY PRINCIPLE ON THE BENEFICENT INSTITUTIONS OF THE COUNTRY

Nor is the voluntary principle less operative in the formation and support of beneficent institutions than of associations for attacking and vanquishing existing evils. But these present too wide a field to be fully gone over in this work, besides that they do not come properly within its scope. I shall therefore glance only at a few points, showing how the voluntary principle operates in this direction for the furtherance of the gospel.

In efforts to relieve the temporal wants and sufferings of mankind, as well as in all other good undertakings, Christians, and those, too, with few exceptions, evangelical Christians, almost invariably take the lead. Whenever there is a call for the vigorous exercise of benevolence, proceeding from whatever cause, Christians immediately go to work, and endeavour to meet the exigency by their own exertions if possible; but should the nature and extent of the relief required properly demand cooperation on the part of municipal and state authorities, they bring the case before these authorities, and invoke their aid. It naturally follows that when this is given, it should be applied through the bands of those who were the first to stir in the matter; and this wisely too, since who can be supposed so fit to administer the charities of the civil government as those who have first had the heart to make sacrifices for the same object themselves? Such alone are likely to have the experience that in such affairs is necessary.

All this I might illustrate by adducing many instances were it necessary. In this chapter, however, I shall notice a few, and take these collectively. There is not a city or large town, I may say, hardly a village, in all the country, which has not its voluntary associations of good men and women for the relief of poverty, especially where its sufferings are aggravated by disease. These efforts, in countless instances, may not be extensive, only because there is no extensive call for their being made. Created by circumstances, when these disappear, the associations also cease to exist. But where the sufferings to be relieved are perpetually recurring, as well as too extensive to be overtaken by individual effort, these benevolent associations become permanent. Their objects are accomplished, in most instances, by the unaided exertions of the benevolent who voluntarily associate for the purpose; but if these prove insufficient, municipal or state assistance is sought, and never sought in vain. Accordingly, the stranger who visits the United States will find hospitals for the sick, alms-houses for the poor, and dispensaries for furnishing the indigent with medicines gratuitously, in all the large cities where they are required.[2] There is a legal provision in all the States for the poor, not such, however, as to do away with the necessity of individual or associated effort to meet extraordinary cases of want, especially when it comes on suddenly, and in the train of disease. The rapid and wide-spreading attacks of epidemics may demand, and will assuredly find benevolent individuals ready to associate themselves for meeting such exigencies, before the measures provided by law can be brought to bear upon them.[3]

It is with great pleasure that I have to state that the gospel finds admittance into the establishments for the relief of poverty and disease, which have been created and maintained by the municipal and state authorities; and that I have never heard of any case in which the directors have opposed obstacles to the endeavours of judicious Christians to make known to the inmates the blessings of religion. Prudent and zealous Christians, both ministers and laymen, are allowed to visit, and ministers to preach to the occupants of such establishments; and in several of our cities, one or more excellent ministers of the gospel are employed to preach in them as well as in the prisons. With rare exceptions they are in the hands of Protestants, though Romish priests are no where forbidden to enter and teach all who desire their ministrations.

Of all the beneficent institutions of our large cities, there is none more interesting than those intended for the benefit of children. Orphan asylums, well established and properly conducted, are to be found in every city of any consideration throughout the Union. Nor are these asylums for white children only, they are also for the coloured. Indeed, it cannot be said with truth that the poor and the sick of the African race, in our cities and large towns, are less cared for than those of the

---

2. The manner of providing for the poor differs greatly in different States. In the west, where there is but little extreme poverty, the inhabitants of each township look after their poor in such a way, as best suits them. Money is raised, and by a "commissioner of the poor" appropriated to the support of such as need it. Those who have families live in houses hired for them; single persons board with others who are willing to take them for the stipulated sum. In the Atlantic States, where there are more poor who need assistance, the same course is pursued in many cases. In others, "poor-houses" are erected in such counties as choose to have such establishments, and to these the townships send their quota of paupers, and pay for their board, clothing, &c. In the cities on the sea-board, the municipal authorities make abundant provision for the poor who need aid; and a great proportion of whom are foreigners.

3. There were many illustrations of the expensive nature of individual and associated charity during the prevalence of the cholera. In all our large cities, associations, comprising the very best Christians in them, were formed with the utmost promptitude, and zealously sustained as long as needed. I saw myself, having often attended their meetings, an association of Christian ladies formed in Philadelphia, as soon as the pestilence commenced its ravages in that city. They took a house, converted it into an hospital, gathered into it all the children whom the plague had orphanised, both white and black, whom they could find, and day after day, and week after week, washed, dressed, and took care of those children with their own hands, and defrayed all the expenses of the establishment. Two of the children died of the cholera in their arms! These ladies belonged, many of them, to some of the first families in that city in point of respectability.

white race. Nor are those children only who have lost both parents thus provided for. In some of our cities, asylums are in the course of being provided for what are called *half-orphans*--that is, who have still one parent or both, but are not supported by them. I may state it, however, as a fact of which I am perfectly certain, that there is not a single found-ling hospital in the United States.

In some of our cities we have admirable institutions, called *houses of refuge* for neglected children, and such as are encouraged by their parents to live a vagabond life, or are disposed of themselves to lead such a life. In these establishments they not only receive the elements of a good English education, but are instructed also in the mechanical arts; and with these religious instruction is faithfully and successfully com-bined. All of these institutions were commenced, and are carried on by the voluntary efforts of Christians, though they have been greatly as-sisted by appropriations in their favour, in the shape of endowments or annuities from the state governments.[4]

Nor are the aged poor neglected. Asylums for widows are to be met with in all our large towns, where they are in fact most needed; and old and infirm men are also provided for.

At the same time, that charity which seeketh not her own, but the good of all others, no matter what may have been their character or what their crimes, has not forgotten those unfortunate females who have been the victims of the faithlessness of men. Magdalene asylums have been founded in all our chief cities, especially on the seaboard, where they are most needed, and have been the means of doing much good. It is only to be regretted that this branch of Christian kindness and effort has not been far more extensively prosecuted. Nevertheless, there are many hearts that are interested in it; and in the institutions which they have erected, the glorious gospel of him who said to the penitent woman in Simon's house, "Thy faith hath saved thee; go in peace," is not only preached, but also received into hearts which the Spirit of God has touched and broken.

---

4. One of the best conducted of these establishments is at Philadelphia. It stands a little out of the city, occupies a beautiful site, and has a number of acres of ground at-tached to it. There are here usually between 100 and 200 youth of both sexes, who occupy different apartments, and are under the care of excellent teachers. The magis-trates of the city have the power to send vagrant, idle, and neglected children to it. Very many youth have left this institution greatly benefitted by their residence in it. It has fallen to the lot of the writer to preach often to its inmates, and never has he seen a more affecting sight. If a man wishes to learn the value of the parental relation, and the bless-ings which flow from a faithful fulfilment of its duties, let him visit such an institution, and inquire into the history of each youth whom it contains. The "Farm Schools" for orphans and for neglected children, in the neighbourhoods of Boston and New York, are excellent, and have been the means of doing much good.

CONCLUSION: ON THE VOLUNTARY SYSTEM

We here close our notice of the developments of the voluntary principle in the United States. . . . If it is thought that I have dealt too much in details, I can only say that these seemed necessary for obvious reasons. There being no longer a union of church and state in any part of the country, so that religion must depend, under God, for its temporal support wholly upon the voluntary principle, it seemed of consequence to show how vigorously, and how extensively, that principle has brought gospel influences to bear in every direction upon the objects within its legitimate sphere. In doing this, I have aimed at answering a multitude of questions proposed to me during, my residence in Europe.

Thus I have shown how, and by what means, funds are raised for the erection of church edifices, for the support of pastors, and for providing destitute places with the preaching of the gospel—this last involving the whole subject of our home missionary efforts. And as ministers must be provided for the settlements forming apace in the West, as well as for the constantly increasing population to be found in the villages, towns, and cities of the East, I entered somewhat at length into the subject of education, from the primary schools up to the theological seminaries and faculties.

It was next of importance to show how the press is made subservient to the cause of the gospel and the extension of the kingdom of God— then, how the voluntary principle can grapple with existing evils in society, such as intemperance, Sabbath breaking, slavery, and war, by means of diverse associations formed for their repression or removal. And, finally, I have reviewed my country's beneficent and humane institutions, and shown how much the voluntary principle has had to do with their origin and progress.

The reader who has had the patience to follow me thus far, must have been struck with the vast versatility, if I may so speak, of this great principle. Not an exigency occurs in which its application is called for, but forthwith those who have the heart, the hand, and the purse to meet the case, combine their efforts. Thus the principle seems to extend itself in every direction with an all-powerful influence. Adapting itself to every variety of circumstances, it acts wherever the gospel is to be preached, wherever vice is to be attacked, and wherever suffering humanity has to be relieved.[5]

---

5. There is one field on which the voluntary principle is accomplishing perhaps greater triumphs, and diffusing as happy an influence as on any other, but which I have not yet noticed. I refer to that presented by the numerous manufacturing establishments which have been springing up during the last five and twenty years in the middle and northern States. Large factories in the old world are proverbial for ignorance and vice. But if a man would like to see religion flourishing in manufacturing towns and among

Nor is this principle less beneficial to those whom it enlists in the various enterprises of Christian philanthropy, than to those who are the express objects of these enterprises. The very activity, energy, and self-reliance which it calls forth, is a great blessing to the individual who exercises these qualities, as well as to those for whose behoof they are put forth, and to the community at large. Men are so constituted as to derive happiness from the cultivation of an independent, energetic, and benevolent spirit, in being "co-workers for God" in promoting his glory, and the true welfare of their fellow-men.

We now take leave of this part of our work, to enter on that for which all that has hitherto been said must be considered as preparatory—I mean the direct work of bringing men to the knowledge and possession of salvation.

"operatives," let him visit some of those towns in New England in which cotton, woollen, or other factories have grown up, and where hundreds, in some instances thousands, of men and women are collected together under circumstances in which they are apt to exercise a most corrupting influence on one another. Let him there observe the pains taken by bands of devoted Christians, pastors, and members of their flocks, to gather these into Bible classes and Sunday schools, to induce them to attend church, to provide libraries of good books for them, to open public lectures on scientific and general as well as religious subjects; above all, let him mark the earnestness with which faithful ministers preach the gospel to them, and the assiduity with which they watch for their souls, and he will percieve how much may be done, even under very unfavorable circumstances, for saving men's souls from ruin. I have never visited more virtuous communities than I have seen in some of those villages, or any in which the gospel triumphed more signally over all obstacles.

No manufacturing town in the United States has grown up more rapidly than Lowell, near the Merrimac river, about thirty miles north-west of Boston. It was but a small village not many years ago, and in 1827 had only 3500 inhabitants. But in 1840 these had increased to 20,000. As it derives great advantages for cotton, woollen, and other factories, from the vast water power it possesses, several companies have built large mills, and employ a great number of people, mostly young women above fifteen years of age, who have been led to leave other parts of New England by the inducement of higher wages than they could command at home. This is an object with some, in order that they may help their poor parents; with others, that they may prosecute their education, and with a third and numerous class, who being betrothed to young men in their native districts, come to earn for themselves a little "outfit" for the married life. Let us see what opportunities of religious instruction are presented to these young persons.

In 1840 there were fifteen or sixteen churches in Lowell, in the Sunday schools attached to ten of which there were 4936 scholars and forty-three teachers, in all 5369. About three-fourths of the scholars are girls, a large proportion of whom are above fifteen years of age. More than 500 became hopefully pious in 1839, yet that year was not more remarkable than others in regard to religion. Including the Sunday schools attached to the other five or six churches, the number of scholars and teachers for 1840 considerably exceeded 6000, and nearly equalled a third of the population. Nearly 1000 of the factory girls had funds in the savings banks, amounting in all to 100,000 dollars. A decided taste for reading prevails amongst them. When in Lowell in the summer of 1841, I found that two monthly magazines of handsome appearance were publishing there. One of these was the *"Operatives' Magazine,"* and the other the *"Lowell Offering."* Both were of octavo form, the one containing sixteen pages, the other thirty-two. Both displayed very considerable talent, and the *Offering* was filled with original articles, written solely by the female operatives.

25

Peter Dobkin Hall, *Institutions, Autonomy, and National Networks,* 1982

By several measures Connecticut's "Standing Order"—the elite of Congregationalist lay and clerical religious leaders, local and state government officials, and property-owners—lost authority early in the nineteenth century. Its Congregational churches lost the support of state and local taxes. The Federalist Party, which most propertied Connecticut citizens had favored, declined, finding itself unable to win a national election after 1796 and at an increasing disadvantage even within Connecticut and other New England states. Many leaders of the Standing Order feared not only that they and their families were losing power, but that American society as a whole was falling into moral and social decay and disorder.

Historian Peter Hall argues that leaders of Connecticut's Standing Order, and their counterparts among Boston's Brahmins as well, sought to reestablish order and regain authority by revising and reinvigorating a set of private, nonprofit organizations, with Yale and Harvard colleges at the center, and by inventing new institutions, such as the academy and the lyceum. The process, as he describes it, was a complex one that evolved over several decades. "By the 1850s," Hall argues, "the movement which had begun as a religiously based evangelical counteroffensive to the ideas of Thomas Jefferson and the French Revolution had cast a very wide net over the nation as a whole." Hall may well exaggerate the impact of what he also calls the "evangelical united front" in the South, the Southwest, and the West. But his interpretation stands as one of the most challenging and influential approaches to the role of nonprofit organizations in the history of nineteenth-century America, and it has many implications for the present. Hall's account is of particular interest to nonprofit managers for its close attention to some of the earliest and most effective college fund-raising drives.

PETER DOBKIN HALL

Institutions, Autonomy, and National Networks

(EXCERPTS)

1982

... The Standing Order, in retreat from political power after 1800, had only two organizational bases from which to proceed in its effort to re-establish order and authority: institutions of religion and institutions of education. Although religion was threatened by post-Revolutionary toleration acts that permitted dissident sects to operate freely and by Jeffersonian efforts to disestablish churches, the Federalist faith in the utility of religion as a means of providing the moral core viewed as essential to democracy and to civic virtue remained unimpaired. Indeed, because the corporate status of the churches was, unlike their formal establishment, unchallenged by the Jeffersonians, the Standing Order was able to proceed through religious organizations to launch a concerted effort to extend its influence beyond the realm of politics. This effort took the form of what one historian has called the "evangelical united front."

The "united front" involved more than mere evangelism, although religious revivalism, in the form of the Second Great Awakening, provided the fuel for the "evangelical machinery," the network of organizations that the Federalist sponsors of the revival proceeded to erect. This machinery, through the education societies, provided funds for the hundreds of young men who were moved by the revival to forsake their plows and workshops, and enabled them to attend college, where they were to be trained as ministers and teachers. (Actually, some of them became merchants, physicians and lawyers.) Following graduation, many were placed in strategic positions as teachers and preachers in new settlements in the West and South through the domestic missionary societies. And their contact with the "mother country" of New En-

Excerpted from chapter 8 of Hall, *The Organization of American Culture, 1700–1900: Private Institutions, Elites, and the Origins of American Nationality* (New York: New York University Press, 1982). Reprinted by permission.

gland was maintained through a wide assortment of religious newspapers, and through eastern-based temperance, Bible, tract, and Sunday-school societies. Because of the peculiarly expansive and implicitly political character of these organizations, and because their spread was closely tied to the migration of New Englanders to the South and West, their impact was not confined to religion.

As [historian] Paul Johnson points out in his study of the Second Great Awakening in Rochester, New York, the basic support for the revival of religion came from transplanted New Englanders and was closely tied to their efforts to wrest economic control of the city away from the older political and local elite. As such, evangelical religion came to be closely tied in some places to the nationalist political party, the Whigs, to the anti-Masonic movement, and to a broad range of social reform efforts including, ultimately, abolitionism and support for the Republican Party. Most importantly, however, the machinery of the evangelical united front resulted in the establishment of distinctive privately supported and controlled corporate institutions, usually staffed by New Englanders, as the cultural core of the new settlements. These institutions, when combined with the unusual acquisitiveness and high level of economic success among New Englanders wherever they went, ensured that New Englanders, even if vastly outnumbered, as was the case in southern Illinois, Indiana, Kentucky, and in the South itself, managed to set the tone of the local culture. Thus, for example, young men as diverse as the sons of the First Families of Virginia who poured into Harvard, Princeton, and Yale after 1810, and the young and gawky Abraham Lincoln in rural Illinois, looked to New England, New Englanders, and New England-institutional patterns of corporate voluntarism as models for emulation.

Even when political differences over such issues as slavery and the tariff began to separate Northerners and Southerners into different national political factions, the common institutional core, the disposition to organize activity through private corporations and the recognition of a moral core that made possible effective individual and collective action, remained intact.

The Jeffersonians had no organizations comparable to those created by the Federalists. To be sure, the Jeffersonian political enterprise was set up along bureaucratic lines. But its impact went little further than politics. For in specifically separating political authority from economic, intellectual, and religious authority, and in concentrating their efforts in the realm of politics, the Jeffersonians had cut themselves off from a major source of influence. In the end, by the 1830s, this would have serious effects. For the religious dissidents who had supported the party because of its stand on religious toleration would move away from the secular and anti-clerical elements in the Democratic party and find common cause with the moral reformers and their national organizational machinery. Thus, even when Jacksonians and non–New Englanders were predominant numerically and consistently able to outvote their conservative opponents, New Englanders were able to exert their influence in other more important and less easily perceptible ways.

The institutions on which Americans in the new republic centered their attention as they looked for alternatives to politics as a source of order and authority were the school and the college. This concern with education, which was shared by both Jeffersonians and Federalists, stemmed from their common heritage of Protestant Christianity, which emphasized the importance of the believer's direct access to the Word, and from their common grounding in the political thought of the Enlightenment, which stressed the importance of an educated electorate in a Republic. If the Federalists and the Jeffersonians agreed on the importance of education, they differed violently on the kinds of institutions through which it should be carried out and on the forms of pedagogy, curriculum, and discipline appropriate to educational institutions in a new republic.

The Jeffersonians favored publicly and locally controlled schools and colleges and, because they believed in the immanence of truth and the preeminence of man's rational faculties, advocated systems of pedagogy that emphasized the practical and utilitarian over abstract morality, and systems of discipline in which students exercised control over one another. Jeffersonian education in its purest form was based on the educational thought of the French Enlightenment. . . .

As actually implemented, however, Jeffersonian education in the local schools took the form of a curriculum of "basics" and a system of discipline based on the Lancastrian model in which "one master instructed a number of older pupils, who, in turn, taught younger ones carefully prescribed lessons. Discipline was strict, based often on shame and the use of humiliating punishments. Competition among students was keenly promoted." . . .

The Federalist response to the educational challenges of the early republic, especially as they lost control of the political system and, hence, of public education, was to form their own schools, private incorporated academies, in which pedagogy, curriculum, and discipline reflected their distinctive views of education and the roles they envisioned for individuals in the world of democratic capitalism.

The most influential of the Federalist educational reformers was Timothy Dwight. Born to a wealthy mercantile family in western Massachusetts, Dwight was the grandson of Jonathan Edwards, the leader of the Great Awakening. He graduated from Yale in 1769. A tutor there until the outbreak of the Revolution, in 1776, he joined the army as a chaplain, serving until his father's death two years later forced him

to return to Northampton to care for his mother and his younger brothers and sisters. After four years as a farmer, schoolmaster, and politician
(he served two terms in the General Court), Dwight was called to the
pulpit of the Congregational church at Greenfield (now Southport), Connecticut. Here he began his work as an educational reformer, work that
he would later carry on to Yale. . . .

2. YALE AS A NATIONAL INSTITUTION

. . . by 1828, Yale was in a very different situation than it was when
Dwight assumed the presidency in 1795. By 1828, the church had been
disestablished, and the college no longer received any public support. It
subsisted on tuitions and fees and a meagre income from its small endowment. One of the objects that the faculty had in mind in drafting the
Yale Report was attracting private support, and two years later it would
initiate its first fund drive among alumni and friends scattered across
the country. Yale was, moreover, in a highly competitive situation. It no
longer had a monopoly on higher education in Connecticut: Trinity had
received a charter in 1823, and Wesleyan would be granted one by 1831.
Improved transportation and the founding of new schools placed it in
competition not only with older schools like Harvard, Brown, Princeton,
and Columbia, but also with colleges like Williams, Middlebury, Colby,
Amherst, and Bowdoin. It was therefore imperative, in the minds of
Yale's professors, to make the college's philosophy of education and the
advantages that flowed from it as explicit as possible. . . .

But Yale's significance as a national institution went well beyond
its ability to attract students from outside Connecticut. Just as important
was its role, and the role of its graduates, in promoting the establishment of private schools and colleges in the West and South. While the
expansive tendency was already evident in the mid-eighteenth century,
when Yale graduates were instrumental in establishing Dartmouth,
Princeton, and Columbia, it became even more evident after 1790, when
Yale graduates acted as the dominant figures in establishing, governing,
and teaching at Williams, Middlebury, and Trinity in New England, New
York University, Hamilton, the United States Military Academy (West
Point), Rutgers, and Lafayette in the middle states; Kenyon, Western
Reserve, Transylvania, Oberlin, and the universities of Illinois, Wiscon-
sin, Michigan, Missouri, and California, in the West; and the United
States Naval Academy, St. John's, The College of Charleston, and the
universities of Maryland, Missouri, North Carolina, South Carolina,
Georgia, Louisiana, Alabama, and Mississippi in the South. Yale, of
course, was not alone in this enterprise of collegiate imperialism; it was
assisted in this task by Princeton and Dartmouth, the officers of which
shared in the political, pedagogical, and theological outlooks of Timothy
Dwight and Jeremiah Day, and were their allies in the evangelical united

front. And Dwight's doctrines were carried out into the lower schools by men like Henry Barnard, William Woodbridge, and early promoters of the professionalization of teaching.

3. THE CENTUM MILIA FUND AND THE ORIGINS OF A NATIONAL ALUMNI CONSTITUENCY

There can be no doubting that Dwight, Day, and their Federalist and Congregationalist friends would have preferred that Yale, while attracting students from all over the country, should remain in their own hands. They had good reasons to believe that New England was, if not the hub of the universe, then certainly the hub of culture and civic virtue. But having lost control of Connecticut politics and, thereby, state support, the college was placed in a difficult situation. For without the support of the state and the established church, the college could not carry out its public mission unaided.

No sooner had the citizens of Connecticut voted in the party of ecclesiastical disestablishment than Yale made its first moves to create a private basis of financial support. The Tolerationist victory came in the September elections of 1817; by March of 1818, the college issued its first general appeal for funds:

> BEING insufficient to found and support Professorships, and en-
> large the Library, to the extent which the advanced state of science
> demands, many respectable citizens, in different parts of the State,
> friends of the College, have advised that an appeal be made to the
> liberality of the public, in aid of the Institution—And the President
> and Fellows having concurred in the proposition, the undersigned
> a Committee, appointed to carry the same into effect, cherish the
> hope that, when the wants of the College are known, the public
> will not suffer its interests to languish.

The simple broadside was signed by a committee consisting of three members of the faculty, one lawyer, and three New Haven merchants who were largely interested in the government of the College. The appeal did not generate much attention. 1818 was a year not only of political crisis, but also of financial depression. Further, the College's understated appeal was unlikely to stimulate the interest either of non-Congregationalists, who had turned their backs on Yale, or of Yale's Congregationalist partisans. For the college did not state its case with any particular urgency.

The officers of the college reacted to the failure of their plea for funds by proceeding along two lines. First, they came to recognize that if they were to be successful, they could not simply appeal to the public. Rather, it was clearly necessary to appeal to that segment of the public which sympathized with the school's political and sectarian goals. Secondly, they became aware, probably by casting an eye at Harvard's rapidly increasing endowment, that the college's funds, once acquired, could yield considerably more as investments in commerce than as investments in land and mortgages.

The appeal of 1818 was, within four years, revised as a much more sectarian document. The college needed, it stated, not only new dormitories, but also a new chapel. It was also necessary, given the impulses unleashed by the Second Great Awakening, to ensure that the services of Yale remained available to the pious but impoverished young men of New England. This appeal was somewhat more successful: between 1821 and 1825, Yale took in almost $75,000 in donations, most of them to support the Dwight Professorship of Sacred Theology. Religion was not the only sentiment on which the officers of the college played in seeking a more stable economic foundation. Both local pride and the American fascination with science were the banners waved in 1825, when Benjamin Silliman wanted to raise $20,000 for the purchase of a collection of minerals deemed vital to the continued study of geology at Yale. . . .

In July [1831], while [fundraiser Wyllys] Warner began privately gathering contributions in Connecticut and western New York, Professor Goodrich composed and sent out a "circular letter" announcing the agreed-on plan of action:

> I wish now to mention a subject of deep interest to every friend of Yale College. It has been obvious for years that their venerable institution cannot long continue to discharge her duties to the public without efficient pecuniary patronage. While Cambridge [Harvard College] has an income of $25,000 a year from permanent funds that of Yale College is scarcely $2500. While Cambridge with a library of from thirty or forty thousand volumes expends $1000 a year on the purchase of books, Yale College with a library of only nine thousand volumes can with difficulty appropriate $400 a year to this important object. . . .
>
> Under the circumstances some spirited friends of the College at the south have proposed the plan of making one great and final effort on the broad scale of our whole country to raise $100,000 by subscription, and to place the institution *at once* on a safe and honorable foundation. Extensive consultations have been held with friends of the College on the subject and the result has been universal approbation of the plan. A full conviction that it can be accomplished and a tender of large subscription on condition that the business can be taken up on a broad scale. Members of a number of classes which have graduated within the last ten years have expressed their fullest confidence that $2500 or $3000 would be contributed as a donation by their respective classes. It is thought that one quarter of the sum might be raised by the classes which had graduated since 1820. Some individuals who are earning their

subsistence by the instruction of schools have voluntarily tendered subscriptions of $100 if such a plan should be adopted. The senior class for the present year have already resolved to take the lead. A general meeting of the alumni on this subject will be held on the day before commencement, Tuesday, September 13, at four o'clock p.m. It will probably be the fullest ever assembled. A representation will be present from New Orleans and other remote places.

As Goodrich's circular suggests, the spring discussions between Day, Warner, and others interested in the welfare of Yale must have been wide-ranging. They appear to have recognized that Yale's importance as a national institution was not merely a rhetorical assertion. It was a reality that had to be dealt with. With students drawn from all over the country and graduates nationally dispersed, the college had to make its raising effort on the "broad scale" of the whole country. Further, the leaders appear to have recognized the significance of class organization as a basis for soliciting funds. Students and alumni did not, they realized, relate to Yale as an abstraction. They related to it as a set of concrete ties of friendship, kinship, and common experiences in a class context (a very Dwightian notion).

Of course, they did not abandon hope of Yale's traditional constituencies, as Wyllys Warner's travels during the late spring and summer 1831 show. He paid as much attention to non-alumnus village nabobs in backcountry Connecticut as he did to wealthy alumni and prominent Congregationalists in New York. Efforts were even made to prod the college's friends in the legislature to renewed action in favor of Yale. What comes through most clearly from Warner's almost daily reports to President Day is the importance of personal contact between agents of the college and potential benefactors, combined with emphatic assertions of Yale's national importance. . . .

The great meeting of the friends and alumni of Yale on the question of the proposed fund drive in September of 1831 was a resounding success, and a remarkable testament both to Wyllys Warner's talents as organizer and to Yale's national character. Chairing the meeting was James Kent, the leading judicial intellect of New York State, a graduate of the class of 1781. Also there was Stephen Van Rensselaer, the immensely rich Patroon of Albany, a former Lieutenant-Governor and Member of Congress from New York. With him were his three sons, all recent Yale alumni. The meeting not only acclaimed the need for a nation-wide fund drive, but also repeated in the strongest terms the college's importance as a national institution:

> the state of society is greatly changed. The standard of education is very greatly elevated among all classes, and in all the departments of learning. The comforts of life are multiplied. The inventions in the arts, and the changes in the habits of the community are num-

berless, and have imposed upon Colleges the necessity of a somewhat more liberal system of expenditure. The early plan of conducting the affairs of Yale College, in respect to the conveniences of living and study, and especially to the course of instruction, would at the present day be deemed unworthy of the Institution, and would doubtless result in its ultimate ruin. Neither institutions nor men can long remain stationary in our country, without sustaining a loss of rank and character; and Yale College, aware of this fact, has pushed onward, striving to keep pace with the progress of society; and in doing this, she is rapidly exhausting her powers. Without more aid therefore, she must soon come to a final stand. Nor should it be forgotten, that Yale College has had, for many years, a greater number of students than any American College. But she has no warrant that such will be the case in the future—certainly she has not, if deprived of her character, or which is the same thing, the means of preserving it. Other Colleges are springing up in every quarter of the country, and in this fact, all should change. In these circumstances however, if Yale fails to maintain her rank as a primary Institution, her students are reduced and her last resources are gone.

But Yale was doing more than trying to part rich men from their money by appealing to their desire to maintain Yale as an institution of national importance. In a period in which Harvard was being increasingly criticized as a seminary for the rich and an enemy of democracy, Yale was willing to make a surprisingly Jacksonian assertion:

The College is also in want of funds for the relief of necessitous students. Individuals of this class, have not unfrequently risen to the highest stations of influence and authority in the nation; the welfare of our republic requires, that such men be educated. Other Colleges very generally offer education to them at a reduced price. Yale must therefore do the same, both to promote the interest of the community and to secure her own prosperity.

The final results of the 1832 fund drive were gratifying: $108,733 was pledged to Yale. Most importantly, especially for the future direction of the college, a number of interesting trends became apparent that spelled a clear departure from traditional bases of support. First, the alumni constituency emerged as the most significant contributing group; over sixty percent of the subscriptions came from graduates. Secondly, while Connecticut subscribers donated the largest amount of the total, subscriptions from outside Connecticut constituted almost half (44 percent) of the total fund. Thirdly, and perhaps most important of all, the largest average subscriptions came from out-of-state alumni. While the pledge from Connecticut was $146, the average pledge from New

York was $385, and from Massachusetts, $220. Not only were subscriptions from out-of-state alumni higher on the average than those gathered in Connecticut, but out-of-state alumni participated on a much higher basis.

The significance of the out-of-state alumni as the emerging primary constituency of the college must have been greeted by Yale's officers with a certain amount of ambivalence. On the one hand it supported their contention that Yale was an institution of national significance. On the other hand, it contained an implicit threat to the school's ability to remain a citadel of Connecticut-dominated Congregationalism and Federalism (which, by the 1830s, had become Whiggery). The officers of the College were not unmindful of the threat. In the course of his travels Wyllys Warner more than once found himself in situations in which potential donors balked at supporting an institution over which they could not exert any significant influence. In New York, for example, in conversing with the Reverend Gardiner Spring, a leading clergyman and a graduate of the class of 1805, the following scene ensued:

> I have seen Doctor Spring, find him more alarmed at the Theology of Yale than ever—he says he will not oppose me, but I fear his negative influence. He is much pleased with your sermon, expresses a high regard for the Academical Department, but fears it must be swept away with the tide of censure. The fact that Doctor Taylor does not reply to Dr. Wood leads him, and he says, others to believe that Dr. Taylor intends to keep his views to himself and propagate them silently through his students.

And religion was not the only ground on which potential donors reined in their impulses to support Yale. Warner arrived in Washington, D.C., in mid-February of 1832, during the great debate on the "Tariff of Abominations," a strong protective tariff that would have favored New England manufacturers over southern planters. Here Warner found that, because of feelings over the bill, doors that had been open to Yale, like that of John Calhoun, who had given one hundred dollars for the Dwight Professorship some years before, were now closed. He wrote despairingly to President Day, who tried to assure him:

> South Carolina is chafed with the hearings of the tariff upon her interests; and if she finds no relief from the measures of the present session, I think she will not be very ready to send money to the north. You are, however, in a better position than I am, to form an opinion of our prospects in that quarter. If the south does not help us, we must be ready for a resolute charge upon the cities, and upon Connecticut.

Although the subscription was successfully accomplished without assistance from the South, Warner's reports about political and religious differences between the alumni and the officers of the College, coupled with Yale's obvious dependence on the good will of out-of-state alumni, must have been disquieting. When the college next attempted to raise funds, in 1854, it proceeded much less indiscriminately than it had two before, confining its appeals to a small number of wealthy Connecticut and New York alumni. The time would come, however, when the college would have to face the uncomfortable fact that an institution which drew both its students and its financial support from persons outside of Connecticut would have to concede the alumni some degree of control.

Yale's resistance to the involvement of alumni and other laymen in its governance was atypical of the other agencies of the evangelical united front. The colleges founded by Yale graduates, most notably Princeton, and Williams, included sympathetic laymen on their governing boards from their inception. The reasons for this inclusiveness were diverse. In part, it stemmed from a recognition of the position that tight clerical control had aroused against Yale from the 1740s on. In part, it was a product of the distinctively New Light origins of the newer colleges, particularly the fact that New Light and organization were much more predicated on voluntarism than on Old Light coercion. Certainly the fact that the newer institutions were not state-supported played a role, for it meant that, from the beginning, they would have to seek financial assistance from wealthy laymen. Indeed, some, like Williams, went so far as to nominate as men like H. Van Schaak, "in the hope and expectation, as he had no children, that he would bestow a portion of his property on the college."

But it was seldom necessary to take on men like Van Schaak, merely because they were wealthy and might leave bequests in favor of the college (as Van Schaak, in fact, did not). For there were plenty of laymen who were willing to contribute their money and their energies to colleges and related enterprises. Even before the mounting of the united front, in the mid-eighteenth century when the New Lights were still doing battle with theological conservatives, the founders of Princeton found their advantage to include as trustees such powerful laymen as William Smith, Attorney General of New York, Peter Van Brugh Livingston, a New York political leader and Treasurer of the State, and Edward Shippen, scion of a prominent Philadelphia family and an important Pennsylvania jurist. And even Yale had made significant concessions to the laity through the Act of Union of 1792, permitting broad informal influence, especially in governing the College's financial affairs.

Beyond the realm of the colleges, in the tract, moral, temperance, missionary, and education societies, the influence of laymen was deci-

sive. Such enterprises simply could not be carried out on a narrow clerical basis. And although clergymen like Lyman Beecher took the lead in
establishing the organizations and in articulating their purposes, laymen like the Tappans, Gerrit Smith, Richard Varick, and the Van
Rensselaers in New York; and the Hubbards, Evarts, and Greenes in
Boston provided the basic financial and administrative support for the
enterprise. Yale's effort in the Centum Milia Fund merely underlined
what was already obvious by the late 1820s to most participants in the
evangelical united front: that the effort of national redemption the restoration of order, authority, and virtue in the republic, could not rest on
narrow sectarian and geographical bases. The aristocracy of virtue would
have to be inclusive if it hoped to be effective.

4. ALUMNI, STUDENT SOCIETIES, AND THE DEVELOPMENT OF NATIONAL NETWORKS

. . . The increasing diversity of students' geographical and economic
backgrounds heightened the importance of the student societies as a
part of the college experience. By the 1820s, when the student society
movement began to be a distinctive characteristic of the colleges, over
half of the students at Yale, Princeton, Williams, Amherst, and the other
centers of the evangelical united front had been born outside the states
in which the colleges were situated. More and more students came from
the South and the Middle and Far West. And fewer and fewer of these
students were expecting to follow their fathers' careers, to enter family
businesses, or to pursue careers in the places where they had been born.
For students cut off from traditional sources of values and control, excluded from the communities and kin-based support systems available
to earlier generations, the college experience as a whole and, in particular, the process of mutual socialization fostered by the student societies
assumed inordinate importance. For the college and the friendships
formed in college became the basis of community continuity that had
largely ceased to exist in society itself. . . .

    College administrators favored the formation of student societies.
Not only did men like Dwight and Day encourage the activities at Yale of
the older eighteenth-century societies—Linonia, Brother-in-Unity, and
Phi Beta Kappa—they also promoted new ones. The Moral Society at
Yale was viewed by Dwight as particularly useful in combating infidelity
and misbehavior among students. And under Day the Calliope, the Benevolent, and the Society of Alumni were formed. The pace of student
organization increased in the 1820s, as the increasingly diverse student
bodies strove to enunciate common values and to articulate a viable
sense of community, and as the colleges themselves came to recognize
the utility of such organizations in maintaining ties between alumni that

were useful in fundraising efforts. In this period, student societies changed in character. . . . By the mid-1830s, many student societies had ceased to be merely local affairs and were, like Alpha Delta Phi, organized on a national basis and meeting in annual conventions. For those not fortunate enough to be selected by the societies and fraternities, and for the purpose of tying the interests of society men to those of the institutions as a whole, the graduating classes themselves became formal organizations by the 1840s, electing officers, publishing regular class books, holding reunions, and gathering funds.

By the mid-nineteenth century, Yale and the other evangelical institutions had become, through the student societies, the hubs of extensive networks of graduates who maintained regular communication with one another. This worked not only to the advantage of the colleges—twenty of the thirty-eight organizers of the Yale fund drive of of 1871 were society men—but to the mutual advantage of the graduates, who came to regard collegiate affiliation and society membership as important indicators of character and trustworthiness and, hence, credit-worthiness and employability. . . .

Because the enterprise of character education was centered in the colleges, and because the society system and the organization of alumni into a functioning communication network on a national scale stemmed from the colleges, character, the possession of certain traits of personality in which individuals were rendered peculiarly trustworthy by their willingness to subordinate personal ambition to higher purposes, came to be associated with the credentials issued by the colleges. The possession of a degree and membership in certain student societies came to signify more than the mastery of a body of knowledge; it was a credential of a more general kind of trustworthiness and breadth of purpose which, as the nineteenth-century economy and its political and social activities became more diverse and tumultuous, assumed particular importance, both in the view of the college men themselves and, by the end of the Civil War, in the eyes of society itself.

But it would be a grave error to suggest that the significance of character education and national networks was restricted to a nationally dispersed group of a few thousand college graduates. Its real significance lay in the extent to which the college influence permeated every community in the country. Through the evangelical institutions, college graduates dominated the pulpits and taught in the common schools of the West and South; college men set the tone of professional life, not only by their polished manners, but by their ability to draw on the resources of the great world beyond their localities for capital, clientage, and knowledge. It was no accident that young men like Abraham Lincoln found their inspiration, and their access to the best law books, in transplanted New Englanders and graduates of New England schools who practiced in the rural counties of southern Illinois. For who else at the time participated systematically in a larger world, maintaining communication with persons beyond the locality?

Not only did the colleges reach out to the masses through evangelism, moral reform, and the schools, they also did so through such enterprises as the lyceums and other mutual improvement and education societies which were first developed in New England and later spread across the nation with the migration of New England's population. Originally proposed by Josiah Holbrook in an article in the *American Journal of Education,* a publication begun by Yale graduates Henry Barnard and William Woodbridge, the lyceum became a national network that brought to rural communities in and beyond New England the wisdom of such men as Bronson Alcott, Lyman Beecher, Orestes Bronson, George William Curtis, Ralph Waldo Emerson, Oliver Wendell Holmes, Theodore Parker, Wendell Phillips, and many others. The lyceum, the mechanics' libraries, the temperance societies, and the Young Men's Christian Associations were in many ways organizational parallels to the college networks. And their parallelism was not accidental, for college men played important roles both in their formation and in determining through journalism, through speakers' bureaus, and through financial support, the direction of their interests.

By the 1850s, the movement which had begun as a religiously based evangelical counteroffensive to the ideas of Thomas Jefferson and the French Revolution had cast a very wide net over the nation as a whole. It had undergone important changes, becoming secularized and geographically and denominationally particularistic. Politically, from the standpoint of its founders, it had failed, or so it appeared as the nation moved inexorably towards civil war. The hope of the Dwights and the Lyman Beechers had been for a much more rapid and direct influence— "When all the colleges are under our control it will establish sentiments and influence, so that we can manage the civil government as we please."

The Federalist Party had failed. The Whig Party had been still-born. And the reintegration of cultural, economic and political authority seemed either a lost cause, or a goal whose achievement lay far in the future. To others, however, especially those for whom the discontinuity of moral and political authority seemed most intolerable, the coming national crisis, which they exerted themselves to bring on through antislavery agitation, seemed a great opportunity to carry the war of words and institutions into the political arena. And among these were not only clergymen, merchants, professionals and others who participated in collegiate networks, but also, and perhaps more importantly, obscure men, men like John Brown and Abraham Lincoln, who had been profoundly influenced by the cultural activities of the evangelical united front and its agents.

26

Jay P. Dolan, *Social Catholicism*, 1975

With his book *The Immigrant Church* Jay Dolan shifted the attention of many Catholic historians from religious doctrine to the realistic examination of human institutions. Earlier historians of Catholic institutions in the United States had emphasized the beliefs and intentions of religious leaders. Important questions of Catholic religious doctrine *were,* in fact, at stake as Catholics worked to adapt their traditionally hierarchical, centrally directed institutions to the voluntary basis offered by American law in the wake of the *Dartmouth College Case.* For several decades, Catholics engaged in the "trusteeship controversy," debating among themselves the relationship between the lay trustees who purchased land and voluntarily provided funds for Catholic churches, schools, and hospitals, and the priests and bishops who provided religious services. Historians have yet to integrate this trusteeship controversy into the general history of America's nonprofit sector.

Writing in the wake of John F. Kennedy's presidency and of the changes in Catholic life associated with Vatican II, Jay Dolan felt free to move beyond the doctrinal issues raised by the trusteeship controversy to produce a clear account of struggles over social policy and ethnic ambition. His book takes readers into the complicated and sometimes contentious and contradictory world of New York's nineteenth-century Irish, German, and French Catholics. New York's Catholics had to contend with many intolerant, anti-foreigner, anti-Catholic, "nativist" Protestants, and with a society that welcomed their labor but not their religion. They also had to cope with the difficult material realities of life in a rapidly growing city that offered many jobs but also offered strenuous competition and expensive, overcrowded, and often unhealthy housing, in a time when no one had a good understanding of the principles of public health.

As Dolan shows, Catholic immigrants—like their Protestant neighbors and forerunners—brought specific ideas about social life and charity with them from Europe, and did their best to hold on to their traditions as they sought to make a life in the United States. Although it was not exactly his intention to contribute to the history of the nonprofit sector, Dolan clearly demonstrated that immigrant (and native-born) Catholics used nonprofit organizations for purposes that were just as active and varied as those of nineteenth-century Evangelical Protestants.

JAY P. DOLAN

Social Catholicism

1975

In the ante-bellum period the spirit of reform was in the air. Americans were challenging traditional institutions of society; and such issues as abolition, prison reform, the role of women, public education, and evangelical theology made up the galaxy of reforms that absorbed people's energies. At mid-century Catholics were alienated from these movements of reform and looked upon them with a great deal of suspicion. They appeared to be only American versions of Red republicanism, communism, or socialism, and the strong Protestant tone of many reform movements only made them more suspect. The nativist crusade reinforced these suspicions, and the church remained aloof from the arena of reform; in adopting this position it demonstrated how alienated it was from the rest of American society. This did not mean that Catholics ignored social problems, but it did indicate that the problems and their solutions would be defined in terms of the Catholic tradition, not in terms of the American reform movement.

Catholics defined social reform in a very traditional and conservative manner: it was basically carrying out the corporal works of mercy and was directed toward the poor, the hungry, and the homeless. It was a crusade of charity and not one of social change. The emphasis was on bettering the lot of the individual, with the guiding principle always being the salvation of one's soul. The goal was to make the situation of the oppressed more humane, a stepping stone to salvation, not a stumbling block.

This view of social reform was rooted in Catholic theology and was judged by Catholics to be antithetical to reform movements abroad in America. "Social evils which afflict mankind are the result of Adam's sin," one priest wrote, and "all reform, properly understood, begins with a return to religion and the Church." Orestes Brownson further developed the Catholic position:

Selected from chapter 7 of Dolan, *The Immigrant Church: New York's Irish and German Catholics, 1815–1865* (Baltimore: The Johns Hopkins University Press, 1975), pp. 195–229. Reprinted by permission of the publisher.

> The Church teaches us to rely on moral power, the grace of God, and individual conscience. She demands the intervention of government only in the material order, for the maintenance or vindication of justice; what lies entirely in the moral or spiritual order, she regards as no proper object of governmental suppression. So of great moral and philanthropic objects. She does not call upon the government to enact them, and make it a legal offense to neglect them. Hence, she leaves the care of the poor, the provision for orphans, emancipation of slaves and similar good works, to the charity of the faithful, without calling upon the government to exact them as a matter of justice.

In his opinion the American reform movement led to either despotism or anarchy; charity on the individual level was the only true avenue of reform. Society was a static, stratified social system, and man could not alter it. The charity of Catholics thus was able to adapt itself to capitalism as readily as it had to feudalism. This conservative view of society and social reform was the tradition that immigrants brought with them to the United States.

Irish immigrants came from a land where poverty, unemployment, and hunger were every day occurrences; the peasant was idealized and not disparaged. Confronted with such widespread suffering, the response of the church was, in the words of one priest to his hungry flock, "to have confidence in God" A priest could comfort a dying man with the assurance that "when one has had as little happiness as you have had in this world, and when one has known how to profit by its miseries, one has nothing to fear in the next." The Irish peasant was sustained by a religion that was little concerned with social reform, and by keeping his sights on the world beyond, he could find solace in the hardships of the earthly kingdom. Poverty, self-denial, and resignation to God's will were Christian ideals aptly suited for a peasant society, and Irish clergy were trained to reinforce this world view.

German immigrants brought with them a similar tradition. During the first half of the century Catholics in Germany evidenced little concern for social questions. As in Ireland, the principal task of the church was to renew Catholic life in a changing social order. Political questions were paramount. Social problems were accepted as part of the divine plan, and no one could change the law of God. Unlike in Ireland, Catholicism in Germany eventually acquired a social awareness through the reform movement spearheaded by the bishop of Mainz, Emmanuel von Ketteler. But as late as 1869 von Ketteler was able to describe the German clergy as having little interest in the fate of the working classes "because they are ignorant of the existence and the impact of the dangers which lurk in these threatening social conditions, because they have failed to size up the character and the breadth of the social question, finally because they have no conception of possible remedies." This was the prevailing tradition that clergy and laity brought with them to the United States, and it influenced the social thought of American Catholics until late in the nineteenth century.

The church's opposition to American reform movements underlined the foreignness of Catholics. Nativist attacks emphasized this aspect of Catholicism, and Catholics were forced to counterattack such charges by demonstrating their compatibility with the American system. This was the principal social issue confronting Catholics in the antebellum period, and the debate against Protestants and nativists left little time to examine the church's attitude toward the presence of human suffering in the New World. In fact, why should one question the hallowed tradition of Christian charity that had worked so well in the past? American Protestants were moving along the same traditional path, and Catholics had little time or little reason to question its validity. What worked in the old country was sure to work in America, since it was God's plan to have rich and poor live together so that one could practice almsgiving and the other patience and resignation.

Few people dared to question this divine order. Archbishop Hughes emphasized this perception of society to a Baltimore audience:

> To every class and condition [the church] assigned its own peculiar range of Christian obligations: To sovereigns and legislators, those of justice and mercy in the enactment and execution of laws. To the rich, moderation in enjoyment and liberality toward the poor. To the poor, patience under their trials and affection toward their wealthier brethren. Toward all, the common obligation of loving one another, not in work, but in deed.

God had permitted poverty, and the church was the protector of the poor; they were representatives of Christ, and Catholics were reminded that "to extend a generous and charitable hand to a fellow creature in distress is one of the most exalting and noble acts of man."

This interpretation of society was echoed in the pulpit, the lecture hall, and the press. The salvation of one's soul was the highest law, and "as for the rest, though you should be reduced to the lowest condition; though you should be stripped of all your worldly possessions, all this is nothing if you arrive at length at the happy term of salvation." For Father Jeremiah Cummings, a distinguished New York priest, who lectured on the topic of social reform, social reform was synonymous with spiritual reform, and only the Catholic church could achieve the necessary social reform, since it gave men supernatural powers and a supernatural motive. The press also reinforced this attitude. The *Catholic World* was a progressive publication, alert to the social problems of urban life, but its outlook was very traditional: Christianity was the foundation of society; without religion, society was doomed to failure. The journal urged Catholics to give more attention to the city's poor through "practical benevolence" (in this context "practical benevolence" meant almsgiving and establishing institutions for the sick and the poor). The practice of good works, long a Christian tradition, still remained the fundamental approach to human suffering for nineteenth-century Catholics. If they exercised such charity, poverty, in the words of John Hughes, "would never have existed at all."

Catholic fiction also idealized poverty and faithful resignation to God's will. Anna Dorsey wrote *The Oriental Pearl* in 1848 to prove that "confidence in the mercy and wisdom of God is the best preservative from temptation and despair."Following the fortunes of three German Catholic immigrants in the United States, the author emphasized the benevolent providence of God and the need to accept His holy will. "There are troubles our Good Lord permits to follow us," the father told his daughter, "so that our faith may be tried," and as long as the poor immigrant has his religion, nothing else matters because "a poor man's religion is a mine of inestimable wealth." One of the more popular Catholic novels was *Willy Burke; or, The Irish Orphan in America,* written by Mary Sadlier in 1850. Like most Catholic fiction at that time, it was a moralistic exhortation written to support the Catholic religion in Protestant America. Willy Burke gained success by keeping his mind fixed on God and remaining faithful to his religion. As long as he had trials to bear, he could not forget God; and trusting in Him was the way to sustain the sufferings of this world.

Catholics could emerge from poverty through hard work and fidelity to God. Such attitudes merited their reward in heaven as well as on earth.

. . . .

Other Catholic novelists, writing for both German and Irish readers, reiterated this theme of a moral life meriting material rewards. The main characters in these novels were often poor Catholics, but poverty was scarcely a hindrance to leading a good moral life. It was a way of life imitative of Jesus, who had "led a most holy life, in poverty and suffering"; his followers could expect no less, and they were continually reminded of how difficult it was for a rich man to enter heaven. For the poor the key to success was to persevere in one state in life, trust in God, and possibly reap a tangible reward for living a good life.

Readers used in Catholic schools further reinforced the ideal of resigning oneself to God's will and to one's position in society. Tales depicted the heroic resignation of early Christian martyrs and other saints. Additional stories repeated this theme to the degree that acceptance of

God's will became the singular trademark of the faithful Christian. Children were exhorted to be "completely resigned to God's will in all things." A songbook summed up this theme in the following manner: "The blessing sent to win my love, O Lord, I freely take, the trial sent my faith to prove, I bear for thy dear sake."

Such were the ideals presented to Catholic immigrants. They reiterated the tradition of the old country and never sought to challenge the economic system. A faithful Catholic was told to accept his condition in life as part of God's will, and his focus was to be a world different from the one in which he lived. Such an attitude fostered a brand of religion that was socially complacent and unquestioning but such a conceptualization of man's place in society did not remain isolated in the realm of ideas. What Catholics did reflected what the church taught, and the parish was the principal location where such ideals were put into practice.

A central figure in the social apostolate of the parish was the priest. Father Varela, pastor of Transfiguration, came to New York with the reputation of one "exclusively dedicated to the good of others." While in New York, he lived up to this reputation. He visited the sick and poor at all hours of the day. His labors took him to quarantined ships; and during the cholera epidemic of 1832 it was said that he "lived in the hospitals." Soon stories began to circulate about his unselfish work with the poor and sick. Tales recounted how he gave his clothes, his watch, and even his bedding to the poor who often gathered outside his window to receive such gifts. His friends gave him a watch to replace one that he had given away, but in a few days it was gone; later it was found in the hands of a poor parishioner ready to pawn it. While visiting the sick he often gave away the clothes on his back. When he ran out of clothes, he would call upon his friends to replenish his supply. People claimed that he gave away everything he owned.

Another priest in the parish gained a similar reputation. Father Alexander Mupiatti worked at Transfiguration for only five years, but when he died in 1846, large crowds followed his body to the cemetery, and in later years people remembered him as a saint. An historical epitaph noted that "his day was divided between the confessional and the bedside of the sick . . . and all flocked to him for advice and direction."

The Redemptorist priests carried on the charitable apostolate in the German neighborhood. They visited the sick and administered the sacraments to the dying; in addition to their parochial responsibilities, they also cared for German Catholics housed in the city's public asylums on Blackwell's Island. For a time they also ministered to the needs of German children in the asylum located on Randall's Island. Unlike Varela, however, no priest in Redeemer parish gained exceptional notoriety for working with the poor. Several of them died from illnesses contracted while visiting the sick, but such unselfish service appeared to be commonplace among the Redemptorists.

The individual efforts of the clergy illustrated the traditional approach of Catholic benevolence. Religion was the one avenue of reform in society, and charity was the key to such reform. Accepting poverty as a given condition of human existence, they desired to reduce the level of suffering by visiting the sick, comforting the dying, and clothing the naked. This concern for one's neighbor was also organized and channeled into parish societies, which provided an outlet for the charity of parishioners, in the hope of improving the lot of the poor.

Transfiguration Church had charitable organizations for both men and women. The Ladies Society of Charity was the principal female organization, and as the name suggests, they sought to realize the gospel ideal by performing good works. Their main task was to buy clothing for the poor and provide work for the unemployed in the making of clothes. In one year they distributed over 350 garments to poor parishioners. Women in the parish also organized annual fairs for the benefit of the poor.

The principal organization for men was the St. Vincent de Paul Society, whose goal was "the exercise of charity in many ways, but chiefly, to visit poor families, to minister to their physical wants as far as means will admit and to give such counsel for their spiritual good as circumstances may require and to look after male orphans when they shall have left the asylum." It was first introduced into New York in 1846, and by 1864 twenty parishes, including Transfiguration, had Vincent de Paul societies. Even though active membership in each parish numbered less than fifty men, many more supported the society's work. The principal boast of their annual reports was the number of visitations made to relieve the financial and spiritual distress of the poor. Founded in France and imported to the United States, the St. Vincent de Paul Society was the principal Catholic benevolent organization. The press praised its work, and the hierarchy urged its formation in every parish. As an outlet for charity, it enabled laymen to practice the works of mercy; as a conservative expression of social Catholicism, it sought to alleviate the suffering of the poor rather than to prevent it.

Most Holy Redeemer did not have a Vincent de Paul conference until later in the century, but the parish did have its own version of social Catholicism. The most widespread form of this apostolate was the parochial relief verein. These vereins were parish-centered organizations which sought to relieve poor and sick members of the society through financial assistance.

The one significant difference between the Irish and German social apostolates was in their attitudes toward the temperance movement.

Although German Catholics did not support the temperance movement in New York, they did not come out in favor of intemperance. Mission sermons portrayed its evil consequences, and good German Catholics were told to avoid the disruptive environment of rowdy taverns. At the same time, however, they were called on to support the good taverns and *Biergartens* of Little Germany. A recommended spot, owned by a German Catholic, was located directly opposite the church on Third Street. The newspaper commented on the good quality of the clientele and claimed that they "were always a sober group, mostly people from the community, orderly people"; it was a place "where one can have a good glass of beer or wine and also carry on a Christian discourse." Germans regarded beer "as healthy and nourishing," and unlike the Irish press, German newspapers always printed advertisements for beer and wine, as well as for German Biergartens. Among the Irish, however, temperance became a holy crusade.

For Irish Catholics a principal cause of poverty was intemperance. A standard sermon in the parish mission concerned drunkenness; preachers were advised to denounce it in every sermon, but its evil effects demanded that "a special and a most powerful sermon be given on this vice." The spiritual ruin caused by intemperance received special emphasis, since it led to eternal damnation. Equally significant were the social consequences of drunkenness. As a vice it inevitably was denounced as a source of misery and poverty for the family. The preacher claimed that poverty could not exist if temperance and industry prevailed; for the virtuous man material success was possible in this life, but intemperance closed off this possibility. Thus, as a virtue temperance became a means of improving one's position in life. John Hughes pointed out this connection by emphasizing that in those parishes where temperance associations existed . . . "prosperity had been the reward of industry and as a matter of course, more of the comforts of life are enjoyed." With the promise of such material and spiritual blessings, it was not surprising that the temperance movement gained support among Catholics.

Father Varela and Transfiguration parish spearheaded the temperance movement among New York Catholics. In 1840 Varela founded the New York Catholic Temperance Association, and within a year it numbered five thousand members. Evening meetings, which took place in the church, opened with a talk extolling the spiritual and material benefits of a temperate life. At the conclusion of the talk as many as two hundred to four hundred people came forward to take the pledge. The movement continued to spread to other parishes in the city and reached a peak in 1849 with the arrival of the Irish temperance crusader Father Theobald Mathew. While he was in New York, he gave the pledge to more than twenty thousand people. After Mathew's departure the temperance movement lost momentum in the city. Transfiguration and other city parishes continued the crusade, but in an area notorious for its many drinking establishments, whose residents enjoyed the friendship and refreshment offered in the neighborhood pub, the movement met with relatively little success.

Another dimension to the Catholic benevolent apostolate was the organization of charitable institutions. Institutional child care was one aspect of the reform movement in the United States, and Catholics responded to this humanitarian impulse by establishing homes for orphans. The public health movement was making progress in the face of increasing demands, and Catholics characteristically organized their own hospitals. An increasing amount of specialization in welfare work developed at this time, and general indiscriminate care gave way to more specialized treatment. The Catholic response was especially evident in the care of young single women living in the city. The piety that fostered this development did not differ from that which inspired individual Catholics to alleviate the suffering of their neighbors. The only difference was that personal piety was now institutionalized and its efforts extended beyond the narrow confines of the parish. Yet, there was an ingredient in this citywide apostolate that was not so visible in the parish-centered version of social Christianity. Basic to the foundation of these charitable institutions was the fear of Protestant proselytizing; the fear was not unfounded, and as Protestant New Yorkers expanded their benevolent apostolate, Catholics were forced to react in kind or suffer the loss of many coreligionists to Protestant denominations. Another motivating impulse was less reactionary and more typically American. Catholic New Yorkers had a dim view of urban life. Immigrants came to the United States with lurid images of city life fixed in their minds. As one Irish priest put it, "better one meal a day of potatoes and salt in Ireland than face the sin and horror of American city life." To protect young men and women from such "sin and horror" as well as from the missionary zeal of Protestants, the church established a substantial network of charitable institutions throughout the city.

Increasing immigration and periodic epidemics underlined the need for better health facilities in New York City. As early as 1834 Bishop Dubois emphasized the need for a Catholic hospital that would "afford our poor emigrants, particularly from Ireland, the necessary relief, attendance in sickness and spiritual comfort, amidst the disease of a climate new to them." The Protestant atmosphere of public institutions increasingly dramatized this need. Priests were not allowed to visit Catholic patients, and when they did, their anti-Protestant bias often made them unwelcome. In a pastoral letter in 1847, Bishop Hughes attacked the adverse religious atmosphere that Catholics encountered in public hospitals and urged the establishment of a Catholic hospital to care for his immigrant flock. Two years later St. Vincent's Hospital opened in New York under the direction of the Sisters of Charity.

The Sisters of Charity had gained a favorable reputation for their work with the sick poor. Their unselfish service during the cholera epidemic of 1832 captured the attention of many New Yorkers, and in the 1849 epidemic the sisters again achieved public acclaim. During the cholera years "admiration of the Sisters was general and unqualified; their benevolence was of a practical sort, their lives not idled away in the convent's living tomb." The superintendent of a New York hospital described them as a "noble band of women" and sought their services when cholera struck again in 1866. Such singular devotion made the Sisters of Charity a good choice for undertaking the institutional care of Catholics.

In 1849 St. Vincent's had room for thirty patients; by 1861 expanded facilities made room for 150. In comparison with public institutions this was a very limited capacity, and Catholics necessarily frequented other hospitals, where discrimination was gradually disappearing. Though the hospital was open to all New York Catholics, it had one drawback. The English-speaking sisters could not communicate satisfactorily with German Catholics, and as expected, the Germans founded their own hospital.

The language problem was only one reason for the organization in 1865 of St. Francis Hospital on the Lower East Side. As was true in the case of St. Vincent's, the fear of Protestant proselytization exerted a decisive influence, even as late as 1865. In the minds of German Catholics it was "a fact, universally known and felt, that the sick and infirm of the Congregation of the Church of Most Holy Redeemer were not satisfactorily well cared for in the public hospitals not only on account of their language but still more on account of their religion since in those institutions they were surrounded by Infidels, Apostates and even around enemies of religion, circumstances which rendered those institutions anything but desirable for a Catholic who wished to prepare for eternity."

Although the impulse for the establishment of St. Francis Hospital originated in Redeemer parish, it served German Catholics throughout the city and gained their financial support. The German Sisters of the Poor of St. Francis were in charge of the hospital, and within a few years after its foundation they began to care for people of all nationalities and religions. Like St. Vincent's, it was a modest response to the needs of an urban community, but it did illustrate the style of social Catholicism at mid-century.

Another aspect of Catholic benevolence was institutions for the care of a special group of individuals—young single women. Like the hospital, these institutions cared for females from all parishes; the dangers of urban life were a more motivating impulse than fears of Protestant proselytization. Priests did advise single girls to avoid romantic links with Protestant boys, since difference in religion was a source of great unhappiness and a drawback to love and would ultimately raise problems in their children's education. Survival handbooks for Catholic women portrayed the Protestant Bible as an evil book; and if the only employment they could find was with Protestant families, the young ladies were to insist that time be allowed for Sunday Mass. But in addition to this customary anti-Protestant counsel, the city was singled out as a particularly degenerate locale for young immigrant girls. In the opinion of John Hughes, New York needed a special home where "the virtue and innocence of destitute females of good character might be shielded from the snares and dangers to which their destitution exposes them in a wealthy and corrupt metropolis like New York." His successor, John McCloskey, did not think much differently, describing New York as a "vast, and alas, wicked city." It was this ideology that fostered the foundation of special institutions for young women whose aim was to make urban life as virtuous an experience as possible.

Through the personal efforts of John Hughes the Irish Sisters of Mercy came to New York in 1846. In Ireland they had acquired a favorable reputation for their work with "poor women of good character." Hughes wanted them to continue this apostolate in New York, and in 1849 they founded a House of Mercy for the care of recently arrived immigrant girls. This was their special apostolate: their goal was to teach the girls domestic trades and to find them work in the city. As an employment agency the House of Mercy was quite effective, providing jobs for over eight thousand girls within five years after it opened. The irony was that the sisters had founded the home to protect young women from the dangers of city life, but in the end they sent them forth trained to work in an urban economy. The hope was that the religious formation acquired in the House of Mercy would adequately equip the young women in their struggle with the city devil.

Some girls were not as successful as others in warding off the evils of city life. To respond to the needs of these delinquent females a group of Catholic women sought to establish a special institution. John Hughes approved their plan, though with some hesitation, and the House of the Good Shepherd opened in 1857. The program of reform of the Sisters of the Good Shepherd centered on religion, education, and work. Like the Sisters of Mercy, the Sisters of the Good Shepherd trained the girls in domestic trades needed in the city; spiritually they sought to strengthen the young women so that they could lead a virtuous life in a locale described by one priest as "the Sodom of Atlantic cities."

The negative attitude of Catholics toward the city was shared by most Americans. Underlying this mentality was the idealization of rural life. In the face of increasing urbanization, Americans sought to cling to the pastoral ideals of the recent past. The hallowed traditions of rural origins and a country environment received increased emphasis during this period of transformation. The country was portrayed as a garden of innocence and virtue, while the city remained a den of sin and corruption. Guidebooks for immigrant Catholics reinforced this mentality. They instructed Irish newcomers to settle on the rural frontier, where work was better; there a man could preside over his own homestead and watch his "family grow up prosperous and industrious removed from the pestilential examples and practices of city life." Irish authors idealized the image of the "simple innocent countryman" and extolled the frontier as a place where the immigrant could enjoy "not merely a home, but comfort and independence."

. . . .

Yet coupled with this idyllic prose was a strain of urban boosterism. As a church leader in the city, John Hughes could not gloss over its attributes. For the archbishop the city was a cultural center where immigrants could enjoy the "comparative comforts of a temporary home." In his opinion, New York was a center of education that supported "colleges, seminaries, convents, schools, altogether ranging from the highest education to the very humblest elements of learning." Such a pro-urban attitude was more evident, though more indirect, in his analysis of rural life. Hughes realistically assessed farm life as one which was beset with "discomforts [and] afflictions": "mental and religious evils were frequently the result of rude Western life"; hidden behind the romance of the frontier were hardships "which were untold and could not be foreseen—hardships which were not to be found in a map." . . .

Other New York Catholics illustrated the same ambivalence. . . . Like their Protestant contemporaries, Catholics sought to make country boys and girls out of city youth.

Through the initiative of Catholic laymen and with the approval of the bishop, the Roman Catholic Orphan Asylum was founded in 1817. At that time there was only one other orphanage in New York. The asylum began in simple surroundings on the outskirts of the city, and by the end of the first year, twenty-eight children lived together in an old wooden shanty cared for by three Sisters of Charity. With the growth in population and disruption of family life through sickness, desertion, and death, the need for child care increased. A second orphanage for children of one surviving parent, half-orphans, opened in 1830 to meet these needs. By 1845 the two orphanages were caring for 350 boys and girls. With the passage of time the orphanage expanded its facilities. In 1859 close to eight hundred children lived in the institution, and the number exceeded one thousand during the Civil War, due to the death of many "Catholic fathers, brothers, and guardians in the field of battle."

Catholics throughout the city supported the orphanage, and children from every parish were able to find refuge within its walls; but the parishes that supported the asylum and the people who guided its operations belonged to the predominantly Irish community. As was true in the area of hospital work, ethnic groups sought to establish their own orphanages to meet their particular needs.

In the case of the Germans, once again it was Redeemer parish that provided the necessary impulse to found a benevolent institution for German Catholics. The cholera epidemic of 1849 had left many children homeless or without one parent. The priests of the parish temporarily remedied the situation by placing the children in homes of parishioners. Eventually plans were made to establish a permanent home near the Church of St. Alphonsus: the orphanage opened in 1850 with twenty-three children in residence. Five years later it closed, and the children went to live with German families in New York and Rochester. In 1858 the pastor of the parish reorganized the orphanage, sought financial support for it among the German Catholic community, and reopened the institution in February 1859 in the Yorkville section of the city. The new building had a capacity of 200, and by 1870, 160 boys and girls were living there under the supervision of the School Sisters of Notre Dame.

Parishioners of the French Catholic church opened an orphanage in 1858 which, compared with other homes, sheltered very few children, only sixty girls and twenty-five boys in 1867. The small number of orphans reflected the size of the French community, but the French exhibited the same ethnic consciousness as German and Irish immigrants.

The motivating force behind the organization of these asylums certainly included a genuine desire to care for deprived children. Institutional child care was one aspect of reform in antebellum America, and Catholics were not immune to this humanitarian spirit. In fact, increased interest on the part of Protestants in child care impelled Catholics to respond in like manner. With the expansion of Protestant benevolent enterprises and with public welfare institutions still unfriendly to foreign papists, Catholics in New York and elsewhere feared that many children would be lost to the church. The result was the development of a widespread system of child care centered in most of the principal cities of the nation.

In addition to the twofold impulse of charity and self-protection, the myth of the pastoral ideal exercised considerable influence on the child care enterprise. The moral superiority of the country was quite evident in the practice of "binding out" city children to the country, which was a general pattern among reformers and which quite naturally became part of the program of the Roman Catholic Orphan Asylum. The practice of moving children from the institution to a home was present from the very beginning, but such a practice did not always mean that the child was sent to live on a farm in the West. On the contrary, children were often placed in homes in the city to learn a trade useful in the urban economy. Gradually, however, the pattern shifted, and more emphasis was placed on binding out children to the country, preferably to a farm. It is difficult to pinpoint exactly when the shift occurred, but certainly by 1858 the Catholic Orphan Asylum was actively encouraging the removal of city boys and girls to the country. The change in emphasis was due not only to an increasing sense of rural superiority but also to the enthusiastic support given to this practice by the Children's Aid Society. C. Loring Brace had founded the society in 1853, and his success among the city youth not only posed a threat to Catholics but also suggested a way to deal with the problem of homeless children. . . .

To secure rural homes for city children advertisements were carried in the Catholic press, and circulars were sent to priests on the frontier asking their assistance in placing city youth in their parishes. The asylum insisted that the applicants be Catholic and that they tend to the religious practice of the child. In addition to this requirement, the authorities added the statement that "applications from farmers, whether for boys or girls, will have preference over all others." The superiority of country life could not have been more clearly implied.

Another benevolent institution founded during the episcopacy of John Hughes was the Catholic Protectory, officially known as The Society for the Protection of Destitute Roman Catholic Children in the City of New York. Organized in 1863 under the impetus of Catholic laymen, principally Levi Silliman Ives, the Protectory sought to rehabilitate delinquent and neglected children, especially Irish youth. A principal motive behind its establishment was the large number of Catholics among the city's vagrant population and the success of Protestant missionaries in drawing these children away from the church. More specifically the Catholic Protectory was a countermovement to the Children's Aid Society and its practice of transporting vagrant youth to the country.

The rural ideal was very evident in the operation of the Protectory. Early in its history two directors of the society made a grand tour of the West to select a suitable site for a rural settlement, after which they submitted a report to the managers of the Protectory recommending several available locations. No further action was taken, however, and the project was dropped. A further indication of the influence of the pastoral ideal was the purchase in 1865 of 114 acres of farmland in the

Bronx. The site was to be the new location of the Protectory, since the managers "were convinced that proper care of the children demanded a site outside the city." The Bronx property was transformed into a rural training center where young city boys learned the skills of farming. The plan to make farm boys out of city youth continued throughout the century, but it never achieved its anticipated success. Levi Silliman Ives had quickly recognized the weakness of the project: it was simply too difficult to keep city boys on the farm after they had seen the bright lights of the city. Some boys did learn farming skills, while others mastered trades useful in the city, but the rural training program was eventually abandoned as a failure.

. . . .

The emphasis on the moral superiority of rural life and the antiurban bias of Catholics reinforced their social conservatism. Since the city was portrayed as basically evil with few if any redeeming qualities, reformers tended to ignore the possibility of changing it; rather, they sought to reform the individual even if this meant removing him from the city. They accepted the poverty and disorganization present in the city as a natural state of existence and did not dare to challenge what God had ordered. Resigned to His will, they endeavored to ameliorate the condition of the less fortunate through a parochial and citywide benevolent enterprise. It was only later in the century that Catholics, along with Protestants, began to question the social order and challenge the hallowed tradition of laissez-faire economics. Only then did they shift their focus from the individual to the environment and look upon poverty more from an economic point of view than from a moralistic perspective.

Thus, during the middle decades of the century Catholics continued to follow the traditional paths of benevolence. Hospitals, orphanages, and charitable societies had long been a trademark of the church, and what developed in the United States did not differ dramatically from the past. As was true with the Protestant enterprise, American Catholic philanthropy had its roots in Europe, and the church reconstructed a pattern of benevolence that scarcely differed from the practice of the old country. . . .

27

Arthur A. Goren, *The Jewish Tradition of Community,* 1970

American Jews also made extensive use of nonprofit organizations in the nineteenth century. The nonprofit form allowed Jewish communities to create schools, hospitals, and social service organizations to serve their co-religionists during a period (which extended in its most extreme form from the 1880s to the 1940s) when Jews were denied equal access to most private institutions in the United States. In meeting the need created by American anti-semitism as well as by the desire of many Jews to maintain a degree of autonomy, the Jewish community was able to draw not only on the American First Amendment and Constitutional law, but also on traditions and practices developed by Jewish communities in Europe.

Historian Arthur Goren's *New York Jews and the Quest for Community: The Kehillah Experiment* tells the story of the sustained effort to create a comprehensive agency capable of representing New York City's large, varied, and rapidly growing Jewish population in the face of the hostility and slurs offered by many non-Jewish New Yorkers. The immediate provocation for the effort to create a kehillah was the slanderously untrue statement of the city's police chief that Jews committed far more than their share of the city's crimes. Ultimately, the kehillah failed because no single organization was able to satisfy a majority of the city's exceedingly diverse Jews, who spoke not only English, but also German, Hungarian, Rumanian, Polish, Russian, Serbo-Croat, Yiddish, and other languages; who practiced many different varieties of Judaism (or no religion at all); who divided politically between the Republicans and the Democrats as well as among the Zionists, Austrian Monarchists, and Socialists; and who numbered among themselves craftsmen, small manufacturers, shopkeepers, professionals, journalists, and wealthy investors.

Goren opens his book with a pointed and provocative discussion of the implications of East European traditions for the New York Jews who sought to establish the kehillah.

ARTHUR A. GOREN

New York Jews and the Quest for Community

1970

New York's Jews were well endowed for the task of community-building. From Europe they brought, in addition to the economic and social skills of an urban people, a monumental experience as a minority. For a millennium and more they had accommodated themselves to the sovereign powers and majority cultures of the countries of their dispersion.

The interplay of historical development and public law set the terms of the encounter. Christendom's pervasive hostility toward the Jews, the corporate status assigned to them by medieval society, and then the marginal position they occupied as subjects of the rising national state, isolated and repressed them as a group. Viewed, however, through the prism of their religious inheritance, segregation had assured the integrity of the congregation and subjection had been interpreted as a token of divine election. The communal thrust of rabbinic Judaism—its faith in collective redemption, the emphasis it gave to the study of the sacred law and to charitable works equipped generations of European Jewry with an acute sense of common fate and group discipline and with a unifying intellectual tradition.

These elements complemented one another and shaped the Jewish communal order. Rulers interested in the Jews for fiscal and financial reasons permitted them a measure of authority in arranging their communal life; governments thereby held the community accountable for the obligations of the individual. They granted Jews the right to self-taxation, limited juridical autonomy, and a free hand in the internal administration of the community. The leadership—lay and rabbinical—used this secular power to reinforce a body of religious precepts which, in its own right, claimed authority over the private and public life of the Jew.

In Poland during the early seventeenth century, Jewish commu-

From "The Traditions of Community," chapter 1 of Goren's *New York Jews and the Quest for Community: The Kehillah Experiment, 1908–1922* (New York: Columbia University Press, 1970). Reprinted by permission of the author and Columbia University Press.

nal settlement reached its zenith. In size and density of population, it constituted the heartland of European Jewry. The key role the Jews played in Polish life in part accounts for this development. In a sharply divided and backward society of landlords and peasants, the Jews supplied needed services as entrepreneurs, tradesmen, and artisans. Communities expanded, achieved a modicum of stability and well-being and, in the process, enlarged and refined their authority. With the establishment of a network of regional and national councils and courts, Polish Jewry exercised a high degree of minority self-government. This golden age of kehillah, moreover, coincided with the flowering of rabbinic Judaism. The erudition of its interpreters, the fame of its academies, and its diffusion through the folk culture bore witness to this fact. The ascendancy of rabbinic Judaism further solidified the kehillah.

The two million Jews who immigrated to the United States in the thirty years before World War I came from this center. A substantial number still subscribed to a communal tradition whose core reached back to Polish Jewry's creative age of kehillah. Indeed, for those who, like the founders of the New York kehillah, were seeking to check the dissolution of community life, the kehillah heritage suggested continuity, the model for and chief determinant in reviving the community.

What, then, was the shape and quality of the kehillah polity both in its classic form and as it was modified by later and harsher times?

Structurally, the seventeenth-century Polish kehillah combined, in its quintessence, a strong executive body and a wide-ranging network of voluntary associations. Elected elders, drawn from the wealthy and learned classes, operated within the well-defined bounds of communal regulations. Paid officials assisted them: the town rabbi, rabbinical judges, teachers, administrators, clerks, and inspectors. Meanwhile, the associations, products of individual initiative, enabled large numbers of the middle strata to participate in the life of the community.

The associations tended to specialize in given areas of public endeavor. They addressed themselves most frequently to such causes as: interring the dead, ministering to the sick, and supporting particular welfare services (i.e., care of orphans, loans to the distressed, free education to needy children, and maintenance of a hostelry for paupers and wayfarers). Other societies—adult education circles, in essence, dedicated their efforts to the study of Bible or Talmud. In addition, artisans established guilds to protect their craft interests, while the upkeep and management of the synagogue offered another range of opportunities for societal activity. Beside its interest, however, each society responded to the general needs of its own membership. Social and religious activities and mutual aid provisions reinforced the associations and gave them a fraternal character. Yet despite their broad scope and wide latitude, they remained under the close supervision of the kehillah council. The latter certified the individual regulatory codes, granted permission to solicit funds, mediated internal disputes, and on occasion participated in the selection of association functionaries. Organizing a new body—the establishment of an additional synagogue, for example—required the council's approval.

The kehillah's elders devoted considerable time to civic and economic problems. The Jewish quarter required municipal services, and the kehillah administration either supplied them or negotiated for them with the town's officials. In economic matters, the general welfare of the community provided the justification for intervention. The council established guidelines for the Jewish merchant in his dealings with the outside world. Within the community, it supervised the market, determined rights of domicile, imposed rent controls, and sought to prevent cutthroat competition. Individual insolvency, after all, imposed added burdens upon a kehillah facing the fiscal claims of church, town, nobles, and king, in addition to its own administrative needs.

In the middle of the seventeenth century, the Jewish settlement in Eastern Europe entered its long, dark age of tribulation. Oppression from without pauperized the group and, in moments of convulsion, threatened its physical survival. Spiritual upheavals shook the besieged community from within.

First came the disintegration of the Polish state: a century and a half of disorder and anarchy, of invasions and pillage. For the Jews, the period brought decimation, flight, or—at best—a perilous existence which imposed upon the community immense tasks of defense and reconstruction. The kehillah regime buckled under the ordeal: economic calamity reduced its fiscal resources; exorbitant new taxes and extortionist practices drove it toward bankruptcy. The wealthy elders, themselves hard-pressed and no longer swayed by the moral constraints of an earlier age, frequently shifted the burden to an already impoverished and desperate commonalty. Aggressive leaders seized communal power and used it for self-aggrandizement. These developments affected the entire fabric of kehillah life. Standards of education and of rabbinical leadership declined, and class antagonism damaged group solidarity.

Hasidism, the pietistic movement of religious revival, constituted a disruptive force of another kind. Its emphasis on personal spontaneity rather than fixed practice, on faith rather than knowledge, on the prophetically inspired rather than the rabbinically ordained, challenged the rational and legalistic nature of the classic communal tradition. Indeed, the sect (which by the turn of the nineteenth century dominated the greater part of East European Jewry) either bypassed the existing kehillah or absorbed its institutions. This process was in large measure effected by the charismatic figure of the saddik, the Hasidic leader who, invested with divine grace, became the infallible guide of his flock. He dispensed charity, arbitrated disputes, trained disciples, and exalted public worship with his presence. For the zealots, faith in the saddik and attendance at his court replaced, in part, the institutions of the established community.

In the course of the first half of the nineteenth century, forces operated to restore a measure of equilibrium. The bitter controversies between the followers of hasidism and rabbinic Judaism subsided. Areas of influence became fixed, and numerous hasidic circles moderated their positions. One could speak again of a homogeneous religious culture, though a culture of variegated styles and nuances. Regionalism, past feuds, the decline of kehillah authority, and doctrinal particularism had left their marks. (In a later period, in the new centers of immigrant settlement like New York, these muted and substantively minor disparities contributed to the disorganization of normative Judaism.) Nevertheless, external conditions had in the meantime strengthened Orthodoxy and community.

These conditions became manifest following Poland's final dismemberment as a sovereign state. East European Jewry then found itself divided between three absolutist monarchies: Prussia (in possession of Posen's Jews); Austria (holding the much larger Galician community); and Russia (ruling the remaining and greatest part of Polish Jewry). All three governments subscribed to the notion that the Jews represented an alien, harmful, and benighted element. They prepared Draconian "rehabilitation" programs to purge the group of its "antisocial ways" and prepare it for "fusion" with the native population. (Fusion, hopefully, would lead to conversion.) Consequently, the Jewish communities, confronted by centralized, bureaucratic powers, brutal in their methods and bent upon reordering if not eliminating Jewish life, responded by closing ranks and treating external innovations and influences as stratagems and heresies.

The most oppressive and persistent practitioner of assimilation-by-duress was czarist Russia. Convinced that the Jewish communal establishment was a major impediment to its program's success, the regime circumscribed communal autonomy. In 1844 it abolished kehillah self-government altogether. As this "reform" program and its long-standing discriminatory practices required an administrative apparatus, the government converted part of the old kehillah administration into a municipal bureau of Jewish affairs.

This policy tried the inner unity of the local community. Jewish notables, for example, were charged with enforcing the notorious conscription laws of Nicholas I even after the annulment of communal autonomy. Whenever the government's demands for recruits were unfilled—the term of military service was twenty-five years—juveniles as young as twelve were forcibly enlisted to meet the quotas. The system of exemptions placed nearly the entire burden of supplying conscripts upon the poorer classes. In another instance, kehillah worthies, acting as tax farmers and aides, continued to administer the burdensome and hated *korobka*, a sales tax levied primarily on meat. Instituted originally to meet the community's needs, the fund was placed under municipal control when kehillah self-government was abolished. The municipality now used the income to finance the government's Jewish program—so repugnant to the group—and to reduce the fiscal debt of the old kehillah establishment. Only then were appropriations made to the religious and welfare agencies of the community. Under such conditions, enmity for the Jewish "autocrats" and aversion for any supervisory authority crystallized into a formidable opposition. It was reinforced, in the last two decades of the nineteenth century, by secular Jewish movements which challenged Orthodoxy's communal hegemony by appealing to the disaffected intelligentsia and the lower strata of traditionalist society.

These movements, radical and nationalist in outlook, represented one response to the calamities of the 1880s and 1890s (the great migration westward constituted another). For the Jews who had embraced modernism, the events of those decades proved to be a shattering experience. Not only did the pogroms of 1881, and others which followed periodically, underscore once again the deep-seated antipathy the common people harbored for the Jews: they also indicated government collusion. Perhaps most depressing of all, they laid bare the apathy and even enmity of Russian intellectuals to the plight of the Jews. Russified Jews and *maskilim* (the latter had imbibed their "enlightenment" in Hebrew translation) were thus disabused of certain cherished notions: that the regime would reward those who had disengaged themselves from Orthodoxy in favor of Westernization; and that a progressive front, in which "enlightened" Jews were welcome, was laying the groundwork for a more tolerant and equitable society.

Economic factors widened the crisis. The increasing pace of industrialization, well underway by the 1870s, was playing havoc with the small artisans and petty tradesmen of the Pale. Now came expulsion from townlet and countryside, additional occupational restrictions, and the consequences of rapid, internal migration to the new industrial centers. The Orthodox had nothing to offer dislocated intellectuals and depressed proletarians except the traditional services of the Jewish community. The cosmopolitans and nationalists, identifiable as socialists and Zionists, proposed secular redemption.

By 1900, these socialists and Zionists—to mention the two main camps of what would shortly become an ideological patchwork of factions, splits, and alliances—had developed full-grown organizations. The economic, political, and cultural programs they offered were carried on, for the most part outside the kehillah framework. The Zionists created fund-raising machinery, superintended agricultural settlements in Palestine, participated in political work through the World Zionist Congress, and inspired a prolific publicistic literature in Hebrew. The Jewish Labor Bund organized strikes and strike funds, cooperated with the general socialist parties, and operated underground cells which preached class consciousness, revolution and, incidentally, promoted popular Yiddish culture.

Secular causes unsettled Jewish institutional life and on occasion disrupted it altogether. Nevertheless, the old communal order remained, at least outwardly, a viable one. The largest part of East European Jewry continued to hold to traditional ways. In fact many may well have identified with their kehillah at the same time that they enlisted in a secular movement. Nor were all regions or settlements equally affected by the new intellectual currents and economic changes. Finally, the kehillah tradition was a flexible one. When the kehillah's governing body was formally abolished the group substituted other communal devices. The voluntary associations grew in importance, and sometimes a particularly strong one would, in effect, direct the affairs of the entire community. There were cases of kehillah rabbis or powerful laymen who enjoyed the prestige or wealth to establish an unofficial hegemony over the community, just as there were instances of welfare agency functionaries directing public affairs. In one section of Greater Russia—Congress Poland—the congregational councils created by the government soon appropriated to themselves the more extensive functions of the old kehillah.

The great immigration to America during the three decades which preceded World War I brought, then, both uprooted kehillah men and earnest party workers. It brought, too, a multitude of tractable, pragmatic townspeople. Yet all did possess a single broad culture—the Yiddish-speaking culture of Eastern Europe, all had suffered from czarist oppression, and all now shared the common lot of the newcomer. In brief: the preconditions existed for a reconstruction of community or for its fragmentation.

The East European Jews (Russian Jews as they were generally called) who settled in New York City found a Jewish community in existence dominated by a group strikingly different in its cultural background, social standing, and communal outlook. Americanized and prosperous, it stemmed largely from the German-speaking areas of central Europe. By 1900, thirty years separated the colony from its own last wave of immigrating countrymen, though a trickle continued to come.

Predominantly native-born by then, it was intent on casting Jewish life into a liberal, denominational mold, a task begun by the immigrant generation.

Old World origins prepared the way for the new communal outlook. The Jewish communities the older settlers left behind in the 1830s to 1850s were small, scattered, and located for the most part in the rural areas of southern and western Germany. Unlike the East European kehillahs, they boasted neither an abundant nor distinguished leadership. The folk who emigrated from these communities possessed hardly more than a perfunctory knowledge of the tradition. Moreover, the Enlightenment ideals of the eighteenth century and the political turmoils of the early nineteenth century corroded a religious-ethnic constancy that had been present until then. Immigration, in turn, nullified the formal constraints of community, permitted unhampered experimentation, and loosened group ties.

The Jewish arrivals of the middle decades of the nineteenth century also belonged to the great stream of German immigration. Despite prejudice and religious differences, they were drawn to the German cultural milieu. In their own Jewish circles and in German-American societies they cultivated the language, literature, and music of the fatherland. Until the crisis of World War I, Jews remained receptive to German intellectual currents and sympathetic to Germany's political ambitions. Nor were these ties merely emotional. In the cities, they lived in German neighborhoods or close by and drew upon a common language to build their business and professional clientele. Thus a double ethnicity operated which further diluted group solidarity.

By 1900 a remarkable number of German Jews and their sons had won distinguished places in the economic and civic life of New York. Founders of the great department stores like the Straus, Stern, and Bloomingdale families, financiers like Jacob H. Schiff and Isaac N. Seligman, and corporation lawyers like Louis Marshall and Edward Lauterbach used their fortunes and prestige to champion civic reform movements, support philanthropic work, and wield political influence. For these notables Jewish matters comprised only one of their many interests, an interest, however, which was too important to be left to others.

Their Jewish affiliation manifested itself in two ways: membership in a Reform temple (by 1900 nearly all the prominent German-Jewish congregations were Reform); and sponsorship of Jewish welfare institutions. The first represented, to no small degree, an expression of middle-class propriety. The emphasis on prestigious externals bears this out: elaborate temple construction and the engagement of distinguished and well-paid rabbis contrasted sharply with an indifferent attendance at services and the paltry religious training offered the young. But membership in a temple was also an affirmation of Jewish identity, though in a manner intended to encourage integration in the wider community. Thus Reform Judaism inveighed against the "insularity" and "obscurantism" of the Orthodox regimen: the ancient ordinances were anachronistic and irrational; the notion of an exiled people awaiting redemption was false, if not dangerous. Probably with the Orthodox, Yiddish-speaking immigrants in mind, Kaufmann Kohler, minister of New York's Temple Beth El, asserted:

> Judaism must drop its orientalism, and become truly American in
> spirit and form. . . . It will not do to offer our prayers in a tongue
> which only few scholars nowadays understand. We cannot afford
> any longer to pray for a return to Jerusalem. It is a blasphemy and
> lie upon the lips of every American Jew.

Reform congregations conducted themselves as members of a religious denomination, in tone and form modeled upon liberal Protestantism. But Reform did all this, at least in theory, in the name of the authentic teachings of Judaism. Reform ministers exhorted their congregants to do good works and live uprightly. These were universal ideals, and conventional aphorisms, which bound good men of all faiths and placed preacher and congregation in the American mainstream.

More than any other institution, Temple Emanuel represented the older community's conception of the ultimate achievement of Judaism in America. When it moved to its new building on Fifth Avenue and Forty-third Street, the [New York] *Times* hailed the congregation as "the first to stand forward before the world and proclaim the dominion of reason over blind and bigoted faith." In the 1900s, its membership, celebrated for its wealth and public service, elected boards of trustees which regularly included banker James Seligman as president; Louis Stern, of department-store fame; Emanuel Lehman, a senior partner in the Lehman Brothers brokerage firm; Daniel Guggenheim, head of the American Smelting and Refining Corporation; and Louis Marshall (in 1916, Marshall succeeded Seligman as president). For the immigrants of the lower East Side, Emanuel and its Jews personified "uptown"—the territory of the wealthy and the Americanized. Their own "downtown" domain formed the other camp of a polarized New York Jewry.

Philanthropy provided a useful, less problematical, and more congenial way of expressing one's Jewish ties. Patrician practice, moreover, commended it. These sentiments combined with a persistent sense of collective accountability for the group's dependents. The result was the creation, in the half century before 1900, of a number of large, efficient, and worthy institutions: general relief agencies, hospitals, old-age homes, orphan asylums, vocational training schools, and settlement houses. Prominent members of the community not only contributed handsomely to their support and attended the ceremonial gatherings, but they also served actively as directors. Mayer Lehman "consciously walked the wards" of Mount Sinai Hospital and "kept a vigilant eye on nurses and doctors." Jacob Schiff, for thirty-five years president of the Montefiore Home for Chronic Invalids, spent each Sunday morning at the home and knew all but the transient patients personally. In a similar fashion, Isidor Straus and Judge Samuel Greenbaum were identified with the Educational Alliance; Morris Loeb, son of Solomon Loeb, a founder of Kuhn, Loeb and Company investment bankers, with the Hebrew Technical Institute; and George Blumenthal, senior partner of the banking house of Lazard Freres, with Mount Sinai Hospital.

These welfare establishments, like the temples, were staunchly autonomous. A coterie of sponsors closely controlled each institution, a majority of whom opposed all efforts at collaboration. Beginning in 1895, agencies coordinating fund-raising activities (the charity federation movement) had proven their worth in a number of cities. In New York, however, more than twenty years elapsed before the opposition of the larger institutions was completely overcome. Nevertheless, an informal liaison existed among the leaders of philanthropy. They belonged to the same German-Jewish social clubs and temples and met one another at meetings of the boards of directors of their philanthropies. Ties of marriage among the children of the elite further strengthened the group. The older settlement, moreover, had its dominant figure—Jacob Schiff, head of Kuhn, Loeb and Company.

By the early years of the 1900s, Schiff had won his fame as a railroad organizer who had challenged J. P. Morgan, an international banker who refused loans to czarist Russia, and a power in the Republican Party and counselor to its leaders. His munificence toward a wide range of educational institutions and civic causes enhanced his influence. Morris D. Waldman, a young social worker at the time, recalled Schiff's standing in the Jewish community:

> His appearance at a board meeting invariably caused a quiet stir and a sudden hush in conversation in deference not merely to his great wealth . . . but rather because of an aristocratic quality in his personality that palpably, yet subtly, distinguished him and, in a manner, separated him from them.

Schiff's warm attachment to Jewish learning and tradition, his own religious education in the Orthodox community of Frankfurt-am-Main, and a lineage that included rabbinical scholars and communal leaders, added a further dimension to his stature in the eyes of the Russian Jews. Schiff was the foremost figure of both communities.

Uptown's charities reflected the receptivity of the established leadership to the social currents of the time no less than did its temples.

Scientific philanthropy, with its condemnation of "open-handed but indiscriminate alms-giving," its insistence on the thorough investigation of the needy applicant, and its sociological view of poverty, also affected Jewish welfare work. The attention paid to administrative efficiency, the professionalization of welfare services, and the growing support of "preventive social work" (broadly based social reform) these were other features borrowed from the general field of philanthropy.

In practice this progressive stance generated conflicting institutional policies. Some uptown philanthropists encouraged the communal, self-help endeavors of the affected public (i.e., downtown's Russian Jews). They assisted such immigrant-supported bodies as the Hebrew Sheltering and Immigrant Aid Society and the Hebrew Free Loan Society. They permitted the United Hebrew Charities to experiment with local participation in the management of specially organized district offices. The same line of thought led some uptown leaders to endorse the aims of the Jewish labor movement. However, there were also those who stressed other nuances of progressive social work philosophy. They condemned the inefficiency of duplicating organizations and the substandard services provided by the small and unprofessional immigrant bodies. Such establishments, these uptown critics claimed, merely perpetuated ghetto self-segregation and the concomitant vices of radicalism and Orthodoxy by handing the tutelage of the immigrants to the immigrants themselves.

Both approaches represented, in fact, different expedients for achieving the identical goal: creating social controls to assure the efficient and unobtrusive integration of the newcomers. What the Americanized leadership would have to learn, however—and the kehillah episode was part of this education—was that its frame of reference for dealing with downtown was unsuitable. The size of the immigrant settlement, its store of communal experience, its proud intelligentsia and independent temper of mind, severely limited the efficacy of uptown philanthropy and its oligarchic system.

In less than a generation the East European migration had produced a demographic and communal upheaval. It had transformed a fairly homogeneous community into a vast, volatile, and multifarious public. In 1880, Jews of German stock formed the majority of Greater New York's Jewish population of 85,000. Twenty years later they made up about a fifth of the city's half million Jews. By 1914, when the Jewish population had risen to 1,335,000, the German Jewish stock represented some 10 percent of the total. For seven of the eleven years which preceded the outbreak of World War I, over 100,000 Jews arrived annually from Eastern Europe. Those who remained in New York—and they may have been as many as 70 percent of the arrivals—poured into the

Jewish immigrant districts of the city and most of all into the lower East Side, the preeminent Jewish quarter. In 1910, that area reached a peak of 542,061 inhabitants.

By that time, the Jewish quarter had become, in a number of respects, a self-contained enclave. In the economic realm, the clothing industry bulked large as the single major source of employment for the immigrant Jews. The minute division of labor (which permitted the semiskilled and the unskilled to enter the industry), the proximity of the shops to the Jewish quarter (in 1900, 79.8 percent of the industry was located below Fourteenth Street), and their ethnic homogeneity, turned the needle trades into the most accessible field of employment. Workers were typically employed in small factory units or in the "outside shops" where contractors and subcontractors processed the cut garments received from the manufacturer. In 1913, the 16,552 factories in New York City's clothing industry employed an average of 18.8 workers per factory. In the important men's tailoring branch, however, 78 percent of the shops averaged five employees each. Though the contractor frequently fared no better than his worker, and the small manufacturer waged a relentless struggle to survive in a highly competitive industry, the apparel trades beckoned to the immigrant with ambitions to become an independent entrepreneur. As early as the 1890s, the industry began to pass from the hands of the German-Jewish manufacturer to those of the Russian Jew, a process which paralleled the rise of the contractor and the small manufacturer.

This "Jewish economy" included other principal areas of activity. Branches of the food-processing industry—like baking and the slaughtering and dressing of meat—were "Jewish industries" due to the ritual requirements of kashruth. Cigar-making and the building trades also drew high concentrations of Russian-Jewish labor. In addition, a host of Yiddish-speaking professionals, merchants, and petty tradesmen made their living in the Jewish quarter. In 1907, one scholar estimates, 200 physicians, 115 pharmacists, and 175 dentists served downtown's Jews. The most densely populated Assembly District of the lower East Side, the Eighth, in 1899, numbered among its businesses: 140 groceries, 131 butcher shops, 62 candy stores, and 36 bakeries. Isaac M. Rubinow, physician, economist, and statistician wrote in 1905 of the recent growth of "Russian Jewish fortunes in New York," many of which ranged between $25,000 and $200,000. "Almost every newly arrived Russian-Jewish laborer comes into contact with a Russian-Jewish employer, almost every Russian-Jewish tenement dweller must pay his exorbitant rent to a Russian-Jewish landlord."

The Jewish trade union movement, which these laborers created, occupied an ambivalent position in the communal life of the quarter. Its most notable figures considered the Jewish East Side as one sector of the world struggle with capitalism. Most of the movement's leadership had broken with the traditional community in Europe and embraced the revolutionary doctrines of Russian radicalism. It now applied the idiom of class war and of anticlericalism to Jewish communal life. Jewish workers, the rhetoric went, had nothing in common with uptown philanthropists, who used charity and Americanization to silence social protest; nor could immigrant workers properly enter the conventional life of the Jewish quarter. Synagogues and lodges, the leadership declared, were irrelevant, wasteful, and a plaything for those seeking prestige and power. They were dominated by the class enemy—the very bosses against whom the unions struck with such passion. Moreover, the respected place accorded Zionism provided further indication of the gulf separating socialist and community. Nationalistic pipe-dreaming, they charged, flouted the cosmopolitan ideal and turned the heads of the Jewish public from the vital issue. To a considerable extent, then, the labor movement formed a community unto itself. By the early years of the 1900s it had created, in addition to its trade unions, a fraternal order (the Arbeiter Ring), an influential press (the Yiddish daily, the *Forward,* was the outstanding example), and a political platform (the downtown Socialist Party).

Despite its cosmopolitanism and class-war vocabulary, the Jewish labor movement did not secede from the ethnic community. Language, a common past, present domicile, and group interests tied it to the larger public. The *Forward* differed little with its three competing dailies, one radical-nationalist and two Orthodox, in condemning manifestations of anti-Semitism, efforts to restrict immigration and czarist ruthlessness. In its eagerness to increase its circulation, the *Forward* appealed to a broad ethnic public, and in succeeding, it played a major role in encouraging Yiddish letters. Moreover, the tactics of the Jewish labor movement presumed the existence of a bedrock of ethnic unity. When the trade unions called their strikes, they appealed for assistance to the good will of the entire community, a call which touched upon traditional charitable instincts. The unions, furthermore, accepted the mediation offered by uptown Jews in settling with the downtown manufacturers. Finally, as in the European kehillah, an indeterminate, but probably a considerable, number participated in the institutional life of both communities.

Ethnic attachments, then, operated even upon those who considered them harmful and passed. Indeed, the most pervasive force in the institutional life of the quarter was the *landsmanshaft,* the society of townsmen. In a census of Jewish organizations conducted in 1917, of 3,600 enumerated, 1,000 called themselves by the name of some locality in Eastern Europe. The glut of small associations bearing the town and regional names of emigration mirrored the poignant but parochial loyalties of the newcomers. Nostalgia for the town only recently left behind was coupled with a desire to assist newly arrived old neighbors.

These town loyalties reflected, as well, sectional variations of some moment. Galicians, Lithuanians, Ukrainians, Poles, and Rumanians spoke Yiddish with different dialects and diverged from one another in minor matters of ritual and religious emphasis. Though the distinctions carried little substantive importance, they were nevertheless meaningful. In the initial adjustment to the shock of loneliness (even in a Yiddish-speaking quarter), the newcomers sought out the remnant of town and region.

The vast majority of the 326 permanent congregations which existed on the lower East Side in 1907 were *landsmanshaft* synagogues (by 1917 an additional 96 had been founded). Writing about them in 1905, Louis Lipsky described the downtown synagogues as "really institutional churches." They were actually microcosms, as far as conditions permitted, of the old kehillahs. Synagogues sponsored associations which owned burial plots or provided small funds for the needy or supported religious schools. If affluent enough the congregation supported a rabbi. Invariably he came from the old town or region.

The *landsmanshaft* principle carried well beyond the synagogue. The mutual aid societies, which provided sick and death benefits, were essentially associations of fellow townsmen. When these groups affiliated with a national fraternal order they generally retained their *landsmanshaft* identity and not even the socialist Arbeiter Ring significantly altered the pattern. The *landsmanshaft* motif also appeared in the economic life of the ghetto. The contractor or clothing manufacturer recruiting his workers from among the arrivals from the old town was a well-known feature of the industry. Whole branches of the apparel trades were identified with particular towns of Eastern Europe.

The Americanized Jews observed this downtown world and were appalled at the jangle of provincial loyalties, religious "medievalism," and strident radicalism. To nativists, its bizarreness personified the menace posed by the new breed of immigrants. Since the American public failed at times to discriminate between old-stock American Jews and new, the conspicuousness of the ghetto threatened the established settlement. Willy-nilly, the latter was becoming the upper stratum of the former. However, alongside the aversion for the immigrants as outlandish and perhaps unassimilable, there also existed pity for the victims of oppression. A number of uptowners went further and indicated their admiration for the dynamism of the ghetto. (Sympathetic gentile journalists, like Hutchins Hapgood and Lincoln Steffens, may have taught them this.) The immigrant's thirst for education was a byword. Progressives praised his political independence. Even the older generation's affecting loyalty to the tradition found its sympathetic observers. Thus ambivalence marked uptown's relationship to the Russian Jew: imperiousness coincided with compassion, disdain with engagement.

The deterioration of conditions in Russia beginning in 1903, exemplified by the Kishinev pogrom, produced wide discussion of the need for more formal communal coordination. The precipitous rise in immigration, political activity in support of the Jews in Russia, and the raising of large funds on their behalf, dominated the interests of the Jewish public. Different elements of the community came together in ad hoc committees, protest meetings, and joint enterprises. A climate of mutual concern softened, for the moment, intergroup animosities. It led also to the creation in 1906 of a national body, the American Jewish Committee (AJC), among whose founders were the leaders of New York's German-Jewish group: Jacob Schiff, Oscar Straus, and Louis Marshall.

The negotiations and the public debate which accompanied them underscored both the durability of the elitist-populist, uptown-downtown syndrome, and the recognition of the need for a regulatory body. Only when the more liberal element among the notables—represented by Marshall, who favored a limited representative structure—retreated and agreed that the organization be established on a self-appointed basis and as a self-perpetuating body was a split avoided. The prestige and wisdom of its membership, men like Adolph Kraus and Oscar Straus held, was its mandate to act on behalf of American Jewry. In the press, the alternative proposal of a Jewish congress was debated. Indeed, the fear that others would create a popularly led body and preempt the field served as a major consideration in the establishment of the AJC. The leadership of the AJC was, nevertheless, sensitive to the cry of plutocracy levied against it. Marshall, in particular, continued to press for an arrangement which would broaden the base of the AJC and tie it to local constituencies.

The quest for new institutional forms and strategies affected different sectors of the New York community itself. In 1907, the Council for Jewish Communal Institutions was established. It consisted of eleven of the largest philanthropic agencies in the city, ten of whom belonged to the uptown community. The Council acted merely as an advisory body to consider the "mutual betterment in methods and economies of administration." In the event of conditions arising "not recognizable by existing organizations," it undertook to recommend "ways and means" of dealing with the situation. Despite its very limited powers, the Council did represent a departure of sorts from institutional isolationism. The years between 1903 and 1908 witnessed, furthermore, the organization of three federations of *landsmanshaftn:* the Rumanian, Galician, and Russian-Polish groups. During this period, the Federation of Jewish Organizations was founded as well. It drew its support from the downtown community and operated primarily as a lobby group fighting immigration restriction.

There were also signs just before 1903 that uptown Jews were prepared to employ new approaches in dealing with the immigrant community. In 1901, Jacob Schiff, his son-in-law, Felix M. Warburg, Daniel Guggenheim, and Louis Marshall, among others, undertook to sponsor the reorganization of the Jewish Theological Seminary. The institution, it was hoped, would attract young Russian Jews and prepare them to be rabbis, faithful to the tradition yet leaders in the Americanization of the immigrant. Solomon Schechter—theologian and reader of rabbinics at Cambridge—was invited to head the Seminary and attract the young scholars deserting East Side Orthodoxy. In 1902, Louis Marshall experimented with a Yiddish newspaper in an effort to encourage a "responsible" press. Even the Educational Alliance, the German Jews' foremost Americanizing agency on the East Side, softened its antipathy to Yiddish culture about this time in an attempt to reach its constituents more effectively.

A mediating force of another sort was the cultural Zionists. They called for the unification of the community as a desirable end in itself. As nationalists, they considered the preservation of the Jewish collectivity a value transcending in importance all particularistic conceptions of Judaism. This approach endowed them with a latitudinarianism which enabled them to treat sympathetically with the full range of groups and movements. Judah Magnes, associate rabbi of Temple Emanuel and secretary of the Federation of American Zionists, best articulated this stand. Another forceful exponent of this approach was Israel Friedlaender, a professor of biblical literature at the Jewish Theological Seminary.

Apathy for the ethnic heritage so pervasive among the children of the immigrants deeply distressed both men. The group's survival, they held, depended upon a cultural revival. In this analysis, they were deeply moved by the views of Ahad Ha'am, the Russian Zionist, Hebraist, and publicist. Abad Ha'am placed his version of Zionism in apposition to Theodor Herzl's political construction. For the Herzlians, anti-Semitism constituted the central problem to be confronted, and a Jewish state was the one honorable solution. The Ahad Ha'amists placed the cultural predicament of the Jews at the heart of the debate. Assimilation loomed as the great danger. This description, to Magnes' and Friedlaender's minds, fit the American situation. Ahad Ha'am's nationalistic emphasis on the Hebrew language as preserver of the Jewish people and its spiritual values, and his concept of a Palestine center which would assist the Diaspora in its educational and cultural tasks, seemed relevant indeed. Only so inspired and so aided, Magnes and Friedlaender believed, would the forces arise to combat the cultural impoverishment of the community and assure its continuity.

Thus before the actual proposal was made to create a unified and democratic communal polity, trends and attitudes were current which lent themselves to this end. Uptown Jews were seeking better ways to stem the social disorganization and expedite the integration of the immigrants. The kehillah could be presented to them as a progressive philanthropic device or as a necessary cooption to their councils of downtown's responsible leadership. The immigrant Jews were bewildered by the communal anarchy and by the ineffectualness of their own traditional institutions. They would respond to the prospect of order, recognition, and financial assistance. Overburdened communal elders from all camps, observing the rising curve of immigration, would be receptive to a plea for a rational division of labor. Finally, a group of young intellectuals—influenced by Jewish national ideas and American progressive notions—were prepared to use these trends and communal developments in a grand experiment which would be meaningful for the Jewish group and American society at large.

The catalyst which brought these interests together in the fall of 1908 originated in a statement by a high city official that the crime rate among immigrant Jews far exceeded that of other groups. For the uptown leaders, the statistic, though exaggerated, confirmed their long-standing criticism of the East Side: delinquency was rising, a grim indication of the presence of moral dissolution. Sensitive downtown Jewry read the statement as bald anti-Semitism, a blot upon their name. The incident produced a virulent debate within the community over the course of Jewish communal life and prepared the ground for the emergence of the kehillah movement.

SIX

Nonprofit Organizations as Alternative Power Structures

The nonprofit form that enabled a variety of religious faith traditions to create their own religious, educational, and social service organizations in the United States also made it possible for people who were excluded from active participation in political life to construct alternative power structures for themselves. Women constituted the largest such group until the 20th Amendment to the U.S. Constitution, which went into effect in 1920, granted them the vote. African American men had the constitutional right to vote if they were free even before abolition, but in practice nearly all African Americans were excluded from the electorate until the Reconstruction period after the Civil War. Then in the 1890s and early 1900s African American men were driven from nearly all the voting booths of the South, first at gunpoint later and more permanently through such devices as the poll tax, which could take a large portion of a poor southern farmer's annual cash income. The poll tax and other devices also excluded many poor whites from the southern electorate through the first two-thirds of the twentieth century. Despite their lack of the vote, women, African Americans, and others who were disfranchised or otherwise excluded from politics often found ways, through the creation of nonprofit organizations, to participate actively in American civic life.

The fact that the nonprofit organizational form made it possible to create alternative power structures did not make it easy to do so, nor did it grant equal rights to the disenfranchised. The nonprofit form is a legal structure, designed to protect rights to property and to the control of policy: those who understand and can afford legal skill make the best use of nonprofits. African Americans who could not vote were always at a severe disadvantage when they had to defend the property owned by their nonprofit organizations in courts led by elected judges. The nonprofit form allows people to support causes that appeal to them through donations or the purchase of services, but it does not provide anyone with the needed funds. Governments have always supported many American nonprofits, and democratic governments respond to voters, not to nonvoters. Moreover, important disadvantaged groups were severely limited in their use of nonprofit organizations until the middle of the twentieth century; American courts long limited the rights of labor unions, for example, on the theory that under certain circumstances they represented conspiracies in restraint of trade.

In recent years historians of American women have greatly increased our understanding of the roles of nonprofit organizations as "parallel power structures," the phrase Kathleen McCarthy uses for the title of her essay. Many have contributed to this line of work. Suzanne Lebsock's study of *The Free Women of Petersburg* is notable for its demonstration of women's ability to obtain corporate charters and to receive the authority to carry out government purposes, such as the control of orphans, long before the advent of women's suffrage. Other important contributions include Carol Smith-Rosenberg's study of women in big-city charities, *Religion and the Rise of the American City* (1970), and Nancy Hewitt's examination of *Women's Activism and Social Change: Rochester, New York, 1856–1872* (1984). Lori Ginsberg emphasizes the importance of the financial and other resources of upper-class women in *Women and the Work of Benevolence: Morality and Politics in the Northeastern United States, 1820–1885* (1990). Anne Firor Scott provides an excellent survey of these and many other studies in *Natural Allies: Women's Associations in American History* (1992).

The great W. E. B. Du Bois anticipated the view that nonprofit organizations could provide alternative power structures in his brilliant and courageous essay on *Cooperation among Negro Americans* (1907), extensive portions of which are excerpted below. In many ways the African American organizations that Du Bois described were very similar to those created by immigrant ethnic groups in the nineteenth and early twentieth centuries. There were great similarities between the groups of African American church, school, and social service organizations described by Du Bois and his sources, and those created by immigrant and ethnic communities.

The fact that Americans use nonprofits to promote a wide variety of independent religious activities and to create alternative power structures should not obscure the fact that American governments have always used nonprofit corporations to advance mainstream and official purposes as well. New York State, for example, authorized New York Hospital to provide the public benefit of hospital care with public funds but a private board through much of the nineteenth century. New York also used the private Public School Society to provide free education to poor children in New York City until the mid-1840s. Later in the nineteenth century, New York created the private Metropolitan Museum of Art and American Museum of Natural History to operate institutions erected with tax dollars on city land. New York and most other states also delegated to private societies such delicate tasks as the housing of foundlings and orphans, the placing of children for adoption, the protection of animals and children, and the discouragement of vice. During the Civil War, Abraham Lincoln found that the private United States Sanitary Commission, using funds raised largely by women's groups as well as government payments, was best able to provide sanitary and hospital services to the Union armies. Clearly, nonprofit organizations have always provided structures for official, established power as well as alternative structures for insurgents.

28

Suzanne Lebsock, *Women Together: Organizations in Antebellum Petersburg, Virginia,* 1984

Suzanne Lebsock's pioneering book, *The Free Women of Petersburg,* takes the reader into the long-unexplored world of women's lives in small southern towns before the Civil War. Previous historians had doubted that it was possible to find the records needed to reconstruct this world: because women changed their names at marriage, and while married could not own or control property in their own names, they usually went unmentioned in property tax records; local records of marriages, births, and deaths are often incomplete or missing; and women were rarely mentioned in nineteenth-century newspapers. When they do appear in public records women often appear as "Mrs. John Jones" rather than as "Anna Smith Jones," making it difficult to trace individuals over time. Through extraordinarily imaginative and patient research, Lebsock demonstrated that it is possible to overcome these problems. She found extensive records of women's lives, especially in wills, letters, family genealogies, and the papers of women's associations and churches.

Lebsock's chapter on "Women Together: Organizations," shows that despite their lack of direct control over most family property and the need to work within a male-dominated legal system, women were able to create associations capable of meeting some of their most pressing needs and concerns. By reviewing the entire set of provisions for Petersburg's poor and unfortunate, Lebsock supports her general argument that women had, in effect, their own culture, values and practices that differed from men's by emphasizing the care of those who needed assistance and the equal treatment of boys and girls.

The creators of Petersburg's orphan asylum, Lebsock also shows, were some of Virginia's best-educated and best-connected white women; one of their leaders was the sister of U.S. Supreme Court Chief Justice John Marshall. These women demonstrated a special concern for the protection of white girls whose lack of family support put them in danger of sexual exploitation. For reasons that the historical record seems to have left unexplained, these women did not extend their concern to African American girls who suffered a similar plight.

SUZANNE LEBSOCK

Women Together: Organizations

1984

When Eliza Spencer died in 1800, Petersburg lost one of its most notable women of affairs. The town lost a curiously representative character as well, for in her last will, Spencer captured a critical shift in the public roles of Petersburg's women. Parts of her will crackled with the crusty independence of the prosperous eighteenth-century widow. In a bold hand, Spencer directed that any ambiguities be settled by her executors and not by litigation: "Let no lawyer nor Doctor," she insisted, "have a shilling of what I leave." But in providing for the education of the poorest of her nieces and nephews, Spencer struck the altruistic keynote for the women of the century to come:

> My heart clings and cleaves to the poor while young. O help the young, push them forward, pray do, a shilling to the young is far better than a pound to the old. How many is [in] want all their lives for want of a friend to assist them while young. O my friends when I am gone remem[ber] the young, push them forward with what little I leave and I hope God Almighty will Help both you and them with his choisest blessings both hear and hear after.

A few years later, the white women of Spencer's class made her plea the basis for collective action in the public sphere. The landmark was the official incorporation of the Female Orphan Asylum in 1813; then and thereafter women made it their particular business to organize on behalf of charity and the church. This was something new. Earlier, on the few occasions when Petersburg women attempted to exert some public influence, they did so as individual proprietors. Women could not vote or hold office, but they did have the right to petition the Virginia legislature, and beginning in the 1780s, taxpaying widows joined men in the exercise of that right. Eliza Spencer herself signed several petitions, one (granted) to make a single corporation of the town's three settlements, another (not granted) to dissolve that corporation, and a

---

Selected from chapter 7 of Lebsock, *The Free Women of Petersburg: Status and Culture in a Southern Town, 1784–1860* (New York: W. W. Norton, Inc., 1984). Reprinted by permission.

third to build a new tobacco warehouse (granted, and the warehouse was built on Spencer's land).

In the new century, women taxpayers continued to sign the occasional petitions in which they had some immediate interest. But the more prominent form of public activity by far was organization, initially for the benefit of the female poor and subsequently for the spread of the gospel. Such organizations were mushrooming all over the country, of course, and historians have rightly identified them as essential to the changing status and developing consciousness of nineteenth-century women. To what ends they were essential, however, is the subject of some controversy, a controversy that is part of the larger argument over the value of women's separate "sphere." Most scholars would agree that the growth of organized benevolence brought women a number of short-term benefits—an area for activity outside the home, a heightened sense of personal usefulness, a deeper appreciation of the needs and abilities of other women, and a chance to develop leadership and organizing skills and to participate in democratic decision making. The debate centers on what all of this had to do with the origins of organized feminism and the growth of feminist consciousness. It has been contended on the one hand that the women's rights movement was a direct outgrowth of organized benevolence. It can also be argued that organized benevolence inhibited the development of feminism, first by perpetuating the image of woman as possessed of a special mission (as opposed to equal capacities) and second by encouraging women to engage in projects that gave them the semblance but not the substance of power. The compromise position is that benevolent activity helped women to become conscious of themselves as a group, a necessary precondition for feminist protest, though not in itself a sufficient cause.

Different as these conclusions are from one another, their defenders in fact share considerable ground. . . . [They] leave us with no very clear idea of how much gender really mattered in the proliferation of voluntary associations that characterized the first half of the nineteenth century.

Local records can help, and in several ways. Petersburg's records, first of all, make it abundantly clear that there were indeed women's organizations in the antebellum South, a fact that has generally escaped the notice of historians of southern culture. Second, it takes immersion in local detail to arrive at sufficiently refined answers to the questions of why organizations were created and how they served their members. The local approach, moreover, makes a manageable task of keeping tabs on the organizational lives of men, and this introduces all kinds of new analytic possibilities, clarifying some issues while complicating others. One fairly simple question, the question of whether voluntary associations provided more opportunities for women than for men, begets a fairly simple answer: Men had it better, especially in the white lower classes. Comparison of the organizational lives of women and men also makes it possible to clarify the boundaries of a distinct women's culture. The concept of a women's culture may well be the most important concept introduced by historians of women to date, but it remains rather fuzzily defined. We need to know to what degree the organizational lives of men and women were in fact separate from each other; we need to know, even more urgently, whether women's collective behavior in fact differed from that of men. The evidence from Petersburg suggests that there was indeed an identifiable women's culture and that its public manifestations were special contributions in the realms of religion and social welfare.

However, and here come the complications, while comparison of male and female organizations highlights the separation of the sexes, it also reveals the development of new forms of togetherness. In the 1850s, for example, after decades in which poor relief had been left to the women, men adopted the cause as their own. There were convergences in organizational structure as well; after several decades in which single-sex societies were the rule, the 1850s witnessed the rise of mixed associations in which the women usually assumed auxiliary roles. The 1840s and 1850s also brought new forms of ritual submission, as women were increasingly identified by their husbands' names (Mary Smith became Mrs. John Smith) and as females were decisively denied the privilege of public speech.

However these developments may be interpreted, they make one point clear: "Woman's sphere" was never a fixed space. True enough, the nineteenth century's basic ideology of male and female spheres was already ossified by 1820; women were endlessly told that they belonged in the home while their men braved the crueler worlds of commerce, politics, and war. But this left a considerable quantity of social space unaccounted for. Rigid as nineteenth-century Americans were in defining sex roles, with voluntary associations they left themselves room for invention, maneuver, and experimentation. The results were intriguing.

The women who organized the asylum in Petersburg behaved as though the need for an orphanage for girls was self-evident. If in the beginning they found it necessary to plead their case before the townspeople, none of their propaganda was preserved. The fragments that have survived reveal a no-nonsense approach to institution building that might have won an approving smile from Eliza Spencer. The scheme was evidently hatched in the winter of 1811–1812. By March 1812, the women had collected enough subscriptions and contributions to open a school, if not to operate a full-fledged caretaking institution, and the leaders called a meeting "for the purpose of making the necessary arrangements for immediately putting the SCHOOL into operation. . . . " Within the week the subscribers met, unanimously passed "such laws as were deemed necessary for the government of the Society and the School," and elected officers and directors. No sooner were the directors elected than they hired a matron to supervise the school. It was in a subdued, we-told-you-so style that the women then appealed for further support from the people of Petersburg:

> There is now no doubt but the institution will be carried into effect, and it is hoped that those who have not yet contributed, under an impression that the plan could not succeed, will now, that the prospect of success is so flattering, come forward, and by their patronage, aid and assist in more fully accomplishing the designs and wishes, not only of the Society, but also of the whole community.

The subscribers were confident that they had launched a laudable project; the point was to persuade potential donors that they were quite capable of following through on their good intentions.

Contributors had every reason to hold out for some promise of success, for Petersburg's one previous experiment in quasi-public education had been a disappointment. The Petersburg Academy was chartered in 1794. Nearly two decades later, the academy had yet to be built. The women of the orphan asylum probably had the phantom academy in mind when they petitioned the general assembly for legal incorporation late in 1812: " . . . the fate of other Institutions of a similar description," they explained, "has taught your petitioners that such compacts however ardently entered into, in the moment of enthusiasm, will decline, and finally perish as that enthusiasm abates, unless protected by an Act of Incorporation which will enable the Society to bind and punish refractory members." A steady income was essential. With an eye to relatively long-term commitments, the society had already determined that membership was to be for a five-year period; but without incorporation, there was no sure means of seeing to it that members fulfilled their pledges. When inspiration gave way to routine, the association might need power to take its delinquent subscribers to court. Control over their own membership was evidently the petitioners' first concern, but they wanted other powers as well, powers to control both their financial assets and the girls in their care. In concise paragraphs that were markedly free of the deference that informed most petitions of the time, the subscribers asked for power to hold and convey property and for the right to participate in litigation. (Standing in court was necessary not only for suing recalcitrant subscribers, but was also an essential condition for engaging in property transactions.) And they wanted a free hand with the children themselves. They requested power to manage any inheritance an orphan might bring with her; the society, in other words, intended to act as a corporate legal guardian, looking after the girl's estate until she was old enough to manage it herself. A legal guardian, however, controlled only the child's property and not her person. To meet all contingencies, the petitioners asked "that they may be vested with the authority of controuling in every respect, the Orphan Female Children, whom they may take under their protection, until they shall respectively attain their lawfull ages."

The women did not get everything they asked for. They were indeed duly incorporated by the general assembly in January 1813, but the statute made no reference to control of the orphans. The legislators probably decided that the existing law of apprenticeship would suffice. Just two years earlier the legislature had empowered the local authorities to apprentice destitute children to institutions; under the law of apprenticeship, the asylum managers exercised day-to-day authority over the child until she turned eighteen, but the local court retained power to revoke the apprenticeship if the child was mistreated. On all other counts, the "Act for incorporating the female association for providing a female orphan asylum in the town of Petersburg" gave the petitioners what they wanted. The powers to make laws, elect officers, deal in property, and appear in court were the standard provisions of acts of incorporation, but for women they took on special significance. Here the wives among them assumed rights that they were ordinarily denied by law. In concert with one another, the petitioners opened a large loophole in the common-law doctrine of civil death for married women.

Within a year of the association's incorporation, the orphanage was in full operation. In 1814, the society rented a house on High Street, and that summer the court ordered that "such Orphans as may be under their care" be bound out from time to time as the directors stipulated. The asylum itself was intended to harbor and instruct only the younger girls, while those old enough to be apprenticed were placed with selected families or with women in the skilled needle trades. No other evidence on the early program of the asylum exists, but the court's order made one thing clear: The elected officials had transferred their lawful responsibility for one group of Petersburg's poor—"the most helpless and interesting of the community," in the women's words—to the organized women. It was a small slice of public authority, but it was public authority nonetheless.

The question remains: Why the asylum? A pioneering article painted early women's charity as the offspring of the churches, one of many Christian outreach efforts inspired by revival-style religion. But this will not do for Petersburg. The town retained its reputation for god-lessness until a revival finally took hold in 1821–22; certainly none of Petersburg's struggling little congregations showed any signs of mission-ary or benevolent zeal before 1822. For Petersburg, it makes more sense to begin where the founders did, by looking at the condition of the poor.

Poverty was becoming more widespread in the early nineteenth century, and the most vulnerable poor people of all were orphaned girls. In some other time, this might not have evoked an organized response. At this time, however, wealthier women had both the leisure and the need to organize. The leisure, of course, came from their positions of privilege in the same economy that made throwaways of the orphaned daughters of the poor. The need seems to have sprung from education. The founders had some education, enough to create ambitions that nei-ther domestic nor social routines could satisfy. To them, learning was precious. Poor girls, meanwhile, had no access at all to formal schooling, and that must have made their plight seem all the more desolate.

Petersburg's women spelled out their explanation of the need for an asylum in the preamble to their 1812 petition to the legislature: " . . . your petitioners," they wrote,

> deeply impressed with the forlorn and helpless Situation of poor
> Orphan female Children, in the town of Petersburg, left entirely
> destitute of the means wherewith to support, and educate them-
> selves; and aware of the many incalculable benefits to be derived to
> them, from moral and usefull education, in whatever situations in
> life they may in future be placed—and deprecating the many evils,
> almost too sure to come upon them, if left to struggle through this
> life, without good precept and example, have associated themselves
> together, with the view and wish to snatch from ignorance and ruin,
> as many of that class of children, as the funds to be raised from their
> association will admit. . . .

The petitioners had cause for concern. Ignorance, sexual abuse, destitu-tion, prostitution—these were the standard elements of female debase-ment. None of these was new, but a close search of the local records suggests that all of them may have been growing more serious. In the eighteenth century, as in this century, poverty was prima-rily a woman's problem, and all the signs for Petersburg indicate that the problem was getting worse. While there is no direct, numerical evidence for the period after 1797, when the town clerk ceased report-ing allocations to impoverished individuals, the numbers for the 1790s suggest increasing economic distress among women. From 1789 to 1793, the substantial majority of the town's adult poor were women (18/28), even though females were but 37 percent of the town's free white population. Between 1794 and 1797, the proportion of the poor who were female grew to 80 percent (35/44). There is no reason to believe the trend was reversed as time went on. From 1790 to 1810, Petersburg's total population doubled, but the number of persons who owned taxable property increased by only 11 percent. Of course, not everyone who paid no tax could be classified as poor, but the fastest growing segment of the population was clearly the lower class. The most spectacular growth rate was that of the free blacks, who more than tripled their numbers during the two decades. All in all, Petersburg's population was becoming younger, more female, blacker, and, even among the white men, poorer.

It seems probable that the relief supplied by the local officials was not keeping pace with the need. For the orphaned daughters of the poor, the court was instructed to provide both maintenance and a skill through apprenticeship, but the apprenticeship system was apparently on the decline. For one thing, some children were very likely neglected altogether as the town grew and the poor consequently decreased in visibility. While the number of female children had probably increased some two and a half times since 1790, the number of orphaned girls bound out by the court was not much greater in the first decade of the nineteenth century than it had been in the last decade of the eighteenth. It may also have been the case that some of the girls who were apprenticed were regarded as cheap labor, emerging from their indenture at eighteen with few skills and without prospects; the overseers of the poor, in any case, do not appear to have exercised ongoing supervision of the treatment of apprentices. Finally, for half orphans the system was discriminatory. Poor boys whose fathers had died were customarily taken from their mothers and bound to skilled craftsmen. Girls in a like situation were usually kept with their mothers and took their chances with what they could learn at home. While there was perhaps much to be said for keeping families together, the daughters stood to inherit their mothers' dependent status.

They also stood to inherit their mothers' ignorance, this in a time when the education of young women was assuming new importance. As Linda K. Kerber has shown, stock in female education was going up. Educational reformers argued that a republic could not survive unless its citizens were virtuous and that its citizens would not be virtuous unless they were properly instructed from an early age. Mothers, therefore, played a pivotal role, and they could not play it well unless they themselves were well educated; some went so far as to claim that the fate of the nation hinged on the education of its mothers. While educational theorists debated what sort of schooling would best accomplish the desired object, Petersburg provided no public schooling of any kind.

This was a hardship for poor children of both sexes, but for the girls the deprivation was greater; girls were less likely than their brothers to achieve a degree of literacy through apprenticeship.

The founders of the asylum no doubt saw all this as the fast path to prostitution, a particularly worrisome development given the fact that the public authorities made next to no effort to regulate sexual behavior. The grand jury rode roughshod on unlicensed purveyors of liquor and made periodic forays against gamblers. The single case "relative to keeping a Bawdy House & House of bad fame," however, was dismissed. The criminal docket, meanwhile, had been free of rape accusations since Andrew Edwards had been found not guilty of beating and raping Fanny Gibson back in 1791. That same year two men had been summoned on charges of fathering bastard children; one further case—dismissed—in 1807 was the only paternity suit in recent memory. A girl without family evidently could not look to the judicial system for protection or redress. The asylum could offer her physical shelter in the short run and moral instruction and a trade for the longer haul, all preventive measures in a town where no punitive ones were in sight.

Orphaned girls, in short, were sexually endangered, intellectually disadvantaged, and economically vulnerable—more so than orphaned boys. In our own time, the word "asylum" calls up images of psychosis and gloom. In the early nineteenth century, it meant only a place of safety. This is what the founders of Petersburg's Female Orphan Asylum meant to provide.

What was in it for the founders themselves? Obviously, in organizing and sustaining the asylum, they made a place for themselves beyond their homes, engaging in work of community-wide significance. The magnitude of this departure should not be missed. While founding an orphanage for girls may seem unremarkable to us, it is important to remember that any such organizing on the part of women was unprecedented; before the asylum, organized, public life was entirely in the hands of men: the legislature, the court, the vestry, the militia. The founding of the asylum was an act of assertiveness that needs to be accounted for.

The best guess is that education made the difference; the founding of the asylum marked the coming of age of Petersburg's first generation of educated women. How they acquired their learning is not quite clear. It was probably acquired at home, from their brothers' tutors and from indulgent parents, and continued afterward by reading and conversation. Their achievement was most evident in their letters; they wrote with verve, with humor sometimes, and with command of the language. Education may also have propelled them toward a wider sphere of usefulness. The domestic routine, much as the women were committed to it, made little use of their schooling. The social routine, much as they may have enjoyed it, was unsuited to their seriousness of purpose. Founding the asylum was a partial solution.

In the forefront were women of formidable personality and considerable learning. Jane Taylor was one of them. Taylor makes her appearance in local histories partly by virtue of blood; Chief Justice John Marshall was her brother, and her husband, George Keith Taylor, was Petersburg's leading attorney and one of Virginia's outstanding legislators. But she was an outstanding character in her own right, "a lady of genius and information," a visiting minister wrote of her in 1828. In asylum-founding days, she had a reputation for being downright intimidating. "Often before I had the pleasure of knowing this lady I had heard of her," Mary Cumming wrote. "I was told she was extremely lively, witty, and sensible, keen in her remarks, and will have her laugh no matter at whose expense." Cumming happily found the reality less frightening than the reputation: "I thought I should feel rather afraid of her, but my opinion changed the first time she came to see me, I found her lively, cheerful, and agreeable . . . " Within three years of the founding of the asylum, George Keith Taylor was dead, and despite the fact that she had a handsome income and three young daughters, Jane Taylor would embark on a long and distinguished, at times controversial, teaching career.

Then there was Mildred Walker Campbell. As with Taylor, Campbell's teaching career began only after death claimed her husband; in the 1840s, she was the one female instructor in the Petersburg Classical Institute, a prestigious academy for boys. In 1812, she and her husband, an ordained minister turned bookseller, were the town trendsetters in literary taste. "Mr. Campbell," an elderly citizen reminisced in 1868, "was not more esteemed for learning and scholarship than was his accomplished lady." The author went on to recall an incident of some fifty years before when two attorneys got into a wrangle over a point of grammar: ". . . Mrs. C. was selected as umpire, being, as was agreed on all hands, to be better qualified than any other person in the place to decide." So impressive was Mildred Campbell's intelligence that her friend Edmund Ruffin found it necessary to exempt her from her gender: "Her mind is masculine," Ruffin wrote, "& of superior order."

It may have been the broadening effect of education that led the asylum's founders to concern themselves with events taking place outside their homes; they did, in any case, feel free to express political opinions. To an immigrant like Mary Cumming, women's interest in politics was remarkable. "Men, women, and children are all politicians in this country, politics is the general topic of conversation among the gentlemen and even of the ladies of this place. Some of the females of my acquaintance," she added, "are most violent democrats."

In 1812, meanwhile, Campbell, Taylor, Cumming, and their friends were deeply enmeshed in conventionally feminine tasks, or so it appears from the surviving evidence on the asylum's founders. Forty-six women signed the incorporation petition of 1812. For forty-one of them, some information on family and income is available, and the profile that emerges bears a striking resemblance to the classic profile of the American volunteer; the founders of the asylum were for the most part young, educated mothers of the upper middle class. Conspicuously absent from the petition were the signatures of Petersburg's female entrepreneurs. The one exception was Elizabeth Goodwyn, whose husband had died just a few months before, leaving her his inn and the administration of his estate. There was only one other widow among the subscribers. The great majority (32) were married, and almost all of the married women were rearing young children. Of the seven single women, six were young and would soon marry. None of the unmarried women headed households of their own. Most lived with their parents, and the one permanent spinster kept house for her brother.

Financially, most of the subscribers were comfortable. The men who headed their households were mostly merchants who engaged in the unspecialized commerce of the day, and there were several professionals as well. While their relative wealth is difficult to determine with any precision, thirty of these men appeared on the 1810 tax list, nine of them in the top tenth of Petersburg taxpayers and twenty-five in the top third. All but one were slaveholders, and all but four kept one or more adult female slaves to do household chores. A few of the men were struggling financially, but like bookseller John Wilson Campbell, their relative poverty was offset by the prestige they won as members of the local intellectual elite.

If we may draw from the numbers and from imagination a portrait of the typical subscriber, her story reads something like this: She was in her early thirties and the mother of three young children; she had lost another child in its infancy; she was a white, native Virginian, raised and educated on a plantation in the country; marriage had brought her to the city some ten years before; marriage had also brought her relative financial comfort and leisure, at least to the extent that her slaves could look after household and children when she was away; whatever marriage had meant in the beginning—the new experience of town life, of running a household, of sexuality, of childbirth, the excitement and trauma had since worn into something more like routine; in short, she was in a position to be getting restless.

Still, it would not be fair to see in the founding of the asylum a simple flight from domesticity. Education may well have been responsible for the women fixing their visions beyond the confines of their own households, but it was probably motherhood—the passionate concern for the shape of the world their children would grow up in that moved them to action. Education and maternity together, one suspects, were powerful fuel for volunteer activity, and probably remained so well into this century. Moreover, in any probe of the relations between the domestic world that women inhabited and the public roles they created, one should guard against seeing in the nineteenth century problems that became acute only in the twentieth. It has become customary to portray the upper middle-class housewife as a person beset by feelings of boredom, uselessness, and isolation. Whatever the justice of this description for the present, it only half applies, at most, to the early nineteenth century. Boredom there may have been, and there was undoubtedly a desire to feel useful beyond one's own household. Isolation, however, is a relatively recent addition. In early Petersburg, as in much of the rest of the country, women of the upper middle class were engaged in a dense network of relationships with other women.

The network was based on kinship, neighborhood, and common experience, and from it grew the asylum. The list of subscribers is a genealogist's delight, for at least half the subscribers were related to some other subscriber. There were three sets of mothers and daughters, four of aunts and nieces, and five of sisters, as well as more distant connections. But the network went beyond kin groups and expanded to take in newcomers, as Mary Cumming discovered when she arrived a young bride from the north of Ireland in 1811. "I have had a great many visitors since I wrote last," she told her sister, "Indeed, the ladies are remarkably kind and attentive to me, I never met with more pleasing people. I have got several little presents sent me by them, knowing I was a young beginner." The women who formed Cumming's welcoming committee—Clara Colquhoun, Mary Haxall, Sarah Freeland, Mary Read Anderson, Ann Robinson, Mary Moore—all knew one another, and all of them soon became promoters of the orphan asylum.

Polite calls, however, did not constitute the essence of the women's community. The stronger bonds were those that grew from mutual support in times of childbirth, sickness, and mourning. Again Mary Cumming is the witness. In the fall of 1812, both Mary and her husband William were helpless with fever, a disease that had already taken the life of their infant daughter. "I do not know what I should have done during my illness if it had not been for Mrs. Freeland," Mary wrote. "I never experienced so much kindness and attention from any stranger as I have done from her at the time poor William and I were so much distressed that we could do nothing. She came here, ordered everything to be done that was necessary, and indeed appeared more like a kind relation than an acquaintance." Sarah Freeland and her fifteen-year-old daughter Agnes were soon Mary Cumming's intimate friends, and they were on hand again when her second daughter was stillborn. "As usual,

my good and kind friend, Mrs. Freeland, has paid me the greatest attention of late. She was with me when I was confined, and for a week after
she stayed day and night, nursed me as if I was her own daughter, my
dear Agnes was my housekeeper. Never, never shall I forget what I owe
to that family."

The asylum was an affirmation of women's role as friend in need;
the founding of the orphanage was not so much a rejection of woman's
sphere as it was an attempt to give institutional form and public importance to its most positive features. Women valued and protected other
women. Organization in turn reinforced the women's network. Given
who her friends were, it was no surprise that Mary Cumming was drawn
into the work of the asylum, but she herself seemed proud. "William
says I shall soon be a *great character* in this country." The asylum was a
channel for ambition, and that is where organization went tradition one
better.

For the upper-middle-class women of Petersburg, there was nothing quite comparable to the asylum to give focus to that special combination of sisterhood and ambition, and that helps explain why the
women launched the institution so rapidly, took it so seriously, and sustained it so loyally through the decades. Once established, the organization clearly heightened the women's sense of their own significance; the
most prominent symptom of this was the development of an active mode
of fundraising. In the beginning, the founders of the asylum collected
dues from the membership but otherwise relied on men to raise their
money for them. Local poet Martha Ann Davis made the point in "A
PIECE In behalf of the Orphans Under the protection of the FEMALE
ORPHAN ASYLUM":

>And there stands a brother, whose trembling emotions
>Evince he ne'er turn'd from humanity's woes;
>He flies to the Orphans, he vows to befriend them,
>And on the Asylum donations bestows.

In public fundraising events, only men took the stage. Clergymen
preached charity sermons, and for theatre-lovers there were benefit
comedies and farces performed by the Thespian Society, a company of
local male amateurs. These sources were not abandoned as time went
on, but beginning in the 1820s, the women took over most of the
fundraising, discovering in the process their capacity to raise large sums
of money. The first "fair" was held in 1829, a four-day sale of all kinds of
handcrafted goods. "As we were all novices in the business, it has given
us a good deal of trouble," wrote one of the managers. The trials of
inexperience made success all the sweeter, however, and Mary L.
Simpson reported the good news: "Why they cleared about Two thousand Dollars!!!" "We are informed," echoed a newspaper, "that the nett

profits amount to about Two Thousand Dollars." Thereafter, periodic fairs and feasts testified to the women's commitment to an active and visible style of raising money.

The asylum itself, meanwhile, remained true to its origins in an intimate female network; in this there were both limitations and virtues. The asylum remained small. With only fifteen or at the outside twenty girls in residence, the institution could not have made much impact on the overall condition of the white poor. As for free blacks, the asylum had no impact at all, for the programs were for whites only. (No one ever said that blacks were to be excluded, but the few white girls bound out by the court after 1813 were all bound to the asylum while the black girls were bound to individuals as before.) It may never have occurred to the organizers that it might be any other way. Petersburg's free black population had been growing fast, and by 1810, free blacks and slaves together outnumbered the whites four to three. Conscious or not, the decision to exclude black children may have been triggered by fear of contamination, an impulse to confine illiteracy, poverty, and sexual deviance to the other side of the color line. The prevailing assumption, in any case, was that for black women poverty was almost inevitable and licentiousness natural. It is not clear whether the organizing women of Petersburg believed this. It is clear that they failed to challenge it, that there was no personal identification strong enough to cut through or transcend racial barriers.

Personalism had its virtues, however, for the asylum never sank to severe regimentation or mere custodial care. Officers and members of the society maintained ongoing, personal relationships with the orphans. They made demands: "[I] heard Mary Price say her Collect [a religious statement]; which she did, only tolerably," one volunteer informed another in 1842; "I gave her another, with strict injunctions, to get it with more care, as I would write you . . . about it." They searched out promising apprenticeship opportunities: "The Ladies have instructed Mrs. Damish to write Miss Benteen, to look out a suitable situation for Margaret Tucker, while she is in Baltimore: one in a Mantua Makers, or Milliners establishment, if to be procured." And some of them remained personally involved for decades. Mary L. Simpson became active in the asylum's work in the 1820s. In the 1850s, she was as concerned as ever. "I am delighted to hear of the good condition of our Orphan Asylum," she wrote from England in 1858, "& pray daily for its encreased prosperity." Simpson was abroad for weeks, and every letter home contained inquiries about the asylum's welfare.

As time went on, Petersburg's women undertook a number of other poor-relief efforts. In the 1830s, a House of Industry was established, probably to give work relief to poor women; in 1847, a second female orphan asylum was founded; and throughout the antebellum period, women's societies organized poor-relief endeavors within the churches. Because these activities are so sparsely documented, it is difficult to assess the women's total contribution. When the behavior of the women is contrasted with the behavior of men of the same class, however, even the feeblest of the women's efforts take on greater significance.

Until the 1850s, the men's collective response to the plight of the poor was typified by neglect, delay, and tightfistedness. Voluntary associations seem to have interested them not at all. An obligation to establish a charity school was foisted on them in 1812 by the will of David Anderson, merchant and town chamberlain, who left the bulk of his estate for "the education of Poor Boys and Girls (white Children). . . ." The town eventually placed an imposing marker over Anderson's grave "to mark their gratitude for his beneficence," but in the beginning there was something less than enthusiasm; "inactivity and slowth" were the words chosen by a local editor. Anderson's executors first attempted to have the will voided. That failing, they went forward, but the Anderson Seminary was not established until 1821, nine years after David Anderson's will was first admitted to probate. The school was organized on the Lancasterian plan, a system much in vogue at the time for its efficiency. In 1823, the *Republican* reported that 165 students were learning their three Rs under the supervision of just one instructor.

The town government, meanwhile, could have given lessons to Ebenezer Scrooge. The panic of 1819 and the depression that surrounded it touched off a crisis in local government's relationship to its poor, and in Petersburg the official response was to get tough. From 1820 to 1823, the bill for poor relief averaged more than five thousand dollars a year, a sum triple or quadruple the normal expense. Radical cuts were called for. In 1823, the outdoor relief system was abolished; only persons who would go to live in the poorhouse were eligible for assistance. In 1824, it was ordered "that the Poorhouse establishment of this town be hereafter also considered & used as a Workhouse." These two moves set the policy for the remainder of the antebellum period and together created the standard irony of nineteenth-century poor relief: Inmates of the poorhouse were expected to work for their keep, but so dreary was the prospect of life in the poorhouse that only the very desperate—people who could not work to begin with—would let themselves be taken there. This problem did not go unnoticed by the Overseers of the Poor. In 1830, they reported that most of the twenty-seven paupers in residence were "wholly unable to perform any duty" due to old age and illness. The town was undaunted, however, and in the late 1830s, on the promise that in the future only a "small pittance" would be needed for the support of the poor, it invested several thousand dollars in transforming the poorhouse property into a working farm.

The farm never did meet the expectations of its promoters (it was operated largely by hired slave labor), but its establishment apparently satisfied taxpayers that all due efforts had been made to put the poor to work. The real saving came from the continued refusal to assist "out paupers," poor people who would not live in the poorhouse. This was effective from the start. In 1825, just two years after the policy's adoption (and with some help from a partially revived economy), the total expenditure for the relief of the poor was only one-third what it had been in 1823. Even as late as the middle 1850s, despite substantial population growth, annual spending for the poor did not come close to the amounts spent in the crisis years of the early 1820s.

How people got by is a mystery. Those most likely to find charity outside the poorhouse were Petersburg's most venerable poor—aging, respectable, white widows. "Kind Sir," one of them wrote to her pastor, "If you have any Wood please Send me Some, as I have not one whole Stick in the House." Most of the churches seem to have offered occasional aid, in cash or in kind, to their impoverished members, and fraternal associations also played some role in taking care of their own. The Petersburg Benevolent Mechanic Association, an organization of white artisans and manufacturers, was founded in 1825, in part to look after distressed widows and orphans. In the 1840s and 1850s, the mechanics made reasonably regular cash payments to six widows of deceased members; ". . . we have never let a deserving application pass unheeded," they claimed.

For the less respectable poor, sources of charity were even fewer. The town government's refusal to expand or alter its poor-relief system seems particularly hardnosed given the growth of the new industrial working class free blacks in the tobacco factories and whites in the cotton mills. By the late 1830s, hundreds of factory workers lost their jobs whenever financial panic struck. "The Manufacturers here are discharging all the free negroes," a Petersburg retailer reported in 1837, "and the number is said to be between 1200 and 2000." Another crisis in 1842 generated the same sort of dismal news. "The pressure of the times here is great and I believe increasing—but the suffering of the poor is much more to be deplored—There are many families now without the means of subsistence since some of the factories have stopped work." How people got by, to repeat, is a mystery.

Until 1858, voluntary, organized charity was the exclusive province of women. Women were also the mainstays of the churches and of church-related organizations. In all parts of the country, the majority of church members were female, and in Petersburg the pattern held good. Membership statistics can be recovered from the records of five of

Petersburg's white, Protestant churches. The proportion of members who were female ranged from a low of 65 percent to a high of over 80 percent.

The appeal of the churches was enormous, and historians have done much to account for it. Through religious activity women found personal identity and a sense of order and larger purpose in life, at the same time that they found community, the chance to associate with like-minded, serious Christians. While religion could, of course, do the same for men, men had access to alternative sources of identity and community and were therefore less likely to turn to the churches. Religion also spoke to the particular needs of women as a subordinate group. It gave them psychological distance from male authority, and it offered a respectable space in which women could indulge in new kinds of assertion, from the quiet self-absorption of writing in a devotional diary to the assumption of visible leadership roles in benevolent organizations.

The evidence from Petersburg confirms all of this and underscores the importance of still another bond between women and their churches, the economic bond. The standard cluster of women's benevolent organizations in any given white Protestant church included at least one mission society, a cent or mite society, an education society, and a Dorcas society for relief of the poor, and women taught in the Sunday schools as well. With the exception of the Sunday schools, the main activity of all of these groups was to raise and redistribute money. As time went on, moreover, congregations—white, black, Protestant, and Catholic— became increasingly dependent on the proceeds of women's fundraising events to pay for the construction and maintenance of church buildings. The economic bonds tugged both ways; some women needed the churches as much as the churches needed the women. Church membership was the one means by which a woman, on her own initiative, could buy into a kind of social security system. In exchange for years of faithful giving and service, an elderly communicant could turn to her congregation for rent money, food, fuel, and medicine. Women who were still in a position to contribute, meanwhile, found satisfaction in working for the cause. Religious benevolence diminished the status gap between middle-class women and men by providing the women with opportunities to engage in productive, income-generating labor. For some women, organized benevolence was a career in itself.

The growth of religious activism among the women of Petersburg cannot be mapped with anything approaching accuracy; the women themselves worked quietly, and the written records left by men usually ignored women's societies altogether. We do know that organized benevolence preceded the revivals. Petersburg's first Sunday school was established in 1817. No one knows who organized it, but it was staffed by "the ladies." Two years later, sixteen Presbyterian women banded together to form the town's first mission society, and by 1821, a Dorcas society had gathered to aid the poor. Then came the revival. In 1822, Methodists and Presbyterians together succeeded in stirring up Petersburg's first dramatic religious awakening. William S. Simpson (Anglican) found the shrieking and groaning "quite appalling." Samuel Mordecai (Jewish) retained a certain dry detachment: "The town is half deserted and the remaining half so pious that I hear of nothing but preaching and Conversion—One of the religious characters is doing penance in jail for forgery . . . but faith will wipe away these trifling stains." To Methodist insider William W. Bennett, however, the revival launched "the era of a great moral revolution in Petersburg."

Bennett claimed too much, but after 1822 there were indeed new indications that a substantial segment of the townspeople supported sterner standards of public moral behavior. When J. L. Roqueta brought his Grand Moving Theatre to town in the summer of 1823, he tendered his assurances: "Any ladies and gentlemen, of different sects of religion, may with propriety visit this theatre, as it contains nothing offensive to the feelings of moral people." The following summer, the common hall outlawed daylight skinnydipping in the river and passed ordinances requiring artisans and storekeepers to close on Sundays. Predictably enough, the revival also gave a boost to organized benevolence, as it generated scores of new church members, greater enthusiasm, and deeper concern for the remaining unchurched. In 1822, women of the Presbyterian church established the Education Society to raise money for the training of impoverished young candidates for the ministry. Year in and year out, it was Petersburg's most impressive benevolent association. New organizations proliferated with renewed revivals in 1827 and the early 1830s. By 1833, the list of Presbyterian women's organizations included a Young Ladies' Missionary Society, a Married Ladies' Missionary Society, a Tract Distribution Society, a Dorcas Society, and an Education Society. Presbyterian women also contributed to an interdenominational Female Bible Society.

We will never know just how many of these organizations were begun, how active they were, or how long they survived. What is certain is that they made a great deal of money. The most commonplace means of raising funds was the "ladies' fair," and this was ordinarily a major undertaking. Most fairs ran for only three or four days, but since the women made by hand most of what they sold, the preparations could take months. The organizers also mobilized their country cousins when they could. In 1860, for example, the daughter of a Methodist minister passed word to her brother: "If the ladies about your neighborhood are not very busy, I wish you would get them to fix me up some little things for the fair." Susan Catharine Bott, directress and prime mover of the Education Society, sent the raw materials out first and asked for help later:

> I am induced by Yr former obliging readiness, to worke for the Ed. Society to request yr assistance in helping us to prepare for our annual meeting. . . . I have therefore taken the liberty of sending to you some Bobinett and Hop for the purpose of working infant Caps, also Scarlet Merino Cloth which I will thank you or your sisters to make up in Emery Strawberries such as was made at your House some years ago. . . . It will afford me pleasure if I can give you patterns to aid you in Yr labor of Love.

After all the months of stitching and crafting, the fair itself brought an intense burst of activity. The organizers of most fairs put on at least one public dinner—sometimes there were daily lunches and dinners— and they arranged for concerts and other kinds of entertainment as well. The prize for originality went to the Ladies' Benevolent Society of the High Street Presbyterian Church, whose 1843 fair featured a lecture on electricity, "in addition to which, the Electrical Shock will be administered to as many of the audience as may desire it."

The main attraction for customers, meantime, was the opportunity for social interaction. Ronald G. Walters has aptly characterized the fairs staged by northern abolitionists as rituals of community. Although fairs were profitable, Walters suggests, their more important function was to reinforce commitment to the movement.

In Petersburg, the process was not so straightfoward, not for most of the men, anyway. It may well have been that fairs gave men the chance to show their good intentions while stopping short of thorough commitment. By spending money at a fair, one could contribute to religious causes without undergoing the public act of submission that was required for church membership. In any event, fairs certainly encouraged interaction of the boy-meets-girl variety, as sales of some items (and returns—boy buys and then returns the item; girl keeps the money) were converted into rituals of flirtation and courtship. Ann T. Davis described a particularly lucrative series of transactions at a Methodist fair of 1860:

> Alice undertook to sell a boquet for me the other night, and she got for it $2.01. She at first sold it for 50. cts, and it was given back to her; she sold it the second time for the same price, and it was again given to her; she afterward met with a spry old widower, who seemed to be much taken with her, he told her that he would give her for it all the money he had left in his purse, which amounted to

$1.01. The next morning she handed back the boquet with the money. Several of the girls have resold their boquets, and made from $1. to $1.25 cts, and then brought back the flowers.

Note that Ann Davis, who was a married woman with grown children, was not in the business of selling bouquets. What was on sale here was youthful charm. The system must have been excruciating for the most bashful of the young saleswomen, but it was undeniably profitable. In 1859, the one year for which a number of totals happen to be available, the women of the Gillfield Church (black Baptist) made $328, the women of the Market Street Methodist Church made $750, the women of Grace Episcopal Church made $1,160, and the women of the Catholic church made $1,200. [At this time an unskilled laborer might expect to make $200 a year.]

Ann Davis's close accounting of the flower sales suggests that for the organizers, the profits were at least as important as the rituals, something to be expected from women who were generally isolated from the experience of making money in a purely commercial context. For middle-class women as a group, the material significance of organized religious benevolence was that it blunted the impact of the economic forces that separated women's experience from that of men in the nineteenth century. For some time now, historians of women, particularly those who see the early nineteenth century as a time when women's status deteriorated, have emphasized the process by which economic modernization increased the status gap between men and women: Production moved out of the home; men moved with it and earned money; and women were left at home, unproductive and earning nothing. . . . we still have much to learn about the nature, timing, and meaning of this process. For the present, be it noted that religious benevolence did something to soften and obscure its force. The preparation of goods for a fair was in fact productive labor, and the sale of those goods did in fact yield a cash return. For most of those involved, the work was part-time and seasonal, but there were also those who worked overtime all of the time, women who made a career of religious benevolence.

In Petersburg, the outstanding example was Susan C. Bott, "a woman of admirable & rare qualities," as Edmund Ruffin put it. "I had an uncommon degree of respect for her," mused Anna Campbell, and in this her contemporaries were agreed. After Bott's death in 1853, her sister church women placed a headstone over her grave "as a tribute of affection and a memorial of her eminent piety," and the Presbyterian press in Philadelphia published her life story. A veteran of the founding of the Female Orphan Asylum and a charter member of the Female Missionary Society, Bott was active in organized benevolence from its beginnings. After she found herself widowed and nearly impoverished in 1824, she intensified her commitment, assuming leadership of the Presbyterian Education Society. From then on, Susan Bott never let up. She organized fairs, she found outlets for private sales in other cities, and she dedicated every spare minute to fashioning some salable article. Under her direction, the Education Society raised close to seven thousand dollars. When she died in 1853, so legend had it, sewing for the Education Society fell from her hands.

How much the women had to say about how their money was spent is an open question. Control over allocation of funds varied enormously from one organization to another. Some societies exercised minute supervision over spending; this was most commonly the case when the stakes were small and the organization unaffiliated with any regional or national network. The Dorcas Society of the First Baptist Church (Washington Street), for example, had an annual budget of less than seventy-five dollars, funds derived from membership dues of twelve and a half cents a month. The minutes of a meeting of 1856 reveal the care with which each appropriation was made:

> The subject of disbursements coming next in order, the ladies were unanimously agreed, after deliberating; that the sum of 5.00, should be sent to Mrs. Holloway as a donation; but in view of Mrs. Hughes low state of health, and Mrs. Wells' frequent and violent attacks of illness, a regular appropriation shall be made monthly for their benefit on and after Nov 1st; of 1.50 to Mrs. Hughes and 1.50 to Mrs. Wells towards the payment of their rents.

Education societies, on the other hand, were generally auxiliaries to centralized boards in charge of ministerial training, and the women who raised the money locally lost control of it almost as fast as they made it. It had not always been that way. When Petersburg's Presbyterian women first organized their Education Society in 1822, they allotted money directly to ministerial candidates of their own choosing. In time, however (it is not clear exactly when), the Education Society threw in with the growing bureaucracy of benevolence, sending its earnings to a central Board of Education.

For all its probable efficiency, the auxiliary system increased the distance between contributors and recipients, and this aggravated a problem inherent in Christian outreach efforts: It became all the more difficult for contributors to see the results of their labors. The numbers of clergymen trained, of new congregations gathered, and of Bibles and tracts distributed all could be added up and pored over, but the fundamental object of evangelism, the salvation of souls, remained stubbornly intangible. In the 1840s and 1850s, the women of Petersburg's churches made a decisive turn in the direction of the local, the specific, and the literally concrete, as they committed the greater part of their fundraising skills to the construction of new buildings for their own congregations.

The founding of Grace Episcopal Church provides a remarkably neat illustration of the inward turn. In 1840, the women of St. Paul's Church, Petersburg's only Episcopal congregation, proposed that the vestry hire a fulltime missionary to work among the people of Petersburg's cotton mill district. As the women offered to pay the missionary's salary, the vestry had no cause for hesitation, and before the end of 1841, Reverend Churchill Jones Gibson had accepted the new post and begun his work. He met with a mixed reception. Forty or fifty children attended his Sunday school, but hardly any grownups would come to hear him preach. "As to my labors at the Factories," Gibson reflected, "I am sometimes disposed to be encouraged & at others to think that I am quite useless." With his middle-class sponsors, however, Gibson was an instant success, and a campaign was soon initiated to establish a second Episcopal church in Petersburg with Gibson as its pastor. The deed was done quickly; Grace Episcopal Church was consecrated in February 1843. Thereafter the women of Grace Church devoted their fundraising efforts to paying for the construction and repair of buildings.

So, for that matter, did the women of St. Paul's and most of the other churches. To anyone who sees attempts to reach the unchurched as a critical Christian endeavor, the new concentration on buildings represents retreat and decline; investing in buildings—and there were some very fine buildings—was part of the larger process by which southern Protestantism made itself respectable. And yet there was an assertive quality to the women's participation. This was explicit in the case of Petersburg's oldest black Baptist church, the Gillfield Baptist Church. Late in 1858, all the constituent societies of the church were asked to turn over the contents of their treasuries so that lumber could be purchased for a new building. The church's main women's organization, the Good Samaritan Sisters, refused. The next month the Sisters made their report, but still released no funds. "We the sisters that hold the money thought it right to give you the Church an answer the money we hold was gotten up to enlarge or rebuild and when the Building is in progress we will come up with our mite." Six months later, the women relinquished several hundred dollars, making good on the promise that the church would see the Sisters' money when the Sisters saw some progress on the church. Even when the women had very little to say about when and how construction funds were spent, there was an implicit assertiveness in their involvement in the building of a church. Every new building was a visible monument to the labor and values of women.

To see in benevolent activity motives and rewards of a material sort is not to disparage the quality of the women's piety. For Susan C. Bott, money and labor were of no value except as they advanced the cause of Christ, and if she was atypical in the exclusiveness of her preoccupation with the faith, she nonetheless symbolized a set of priorities that was most often found among women. The women's investments of money and time in benevolent causes cannot be compared precisely with those of men, but a count of gifts to church and charity by will reveals a clear difference between the sexes. With deathbed giving, family came first; very few testators of either sex left legacies to anyone but kin and close friends. Still, the women were twice as likely as the men to allot parts of their estates to churches, benevolent societies, and the relief of the poor.

There was indeed an identifiable women's culture in Petersburg, and some of its components went hand-in-glove with nineteenth-century stereotypes. Women did inhabit a separate sphere, as they were told they must; except for attendance at church services, the organizational lives of women were almost entirely segregated from those of men. And through their organizational activities, women confirmed what the nineteenth century chose to believe of them: Woman was first in piety and benevolence. Life and ideology were remarkably well matched.

Men, of course, continued their dominion in commerce and politics, and, as Barbara Welter has pointed out, this was not a separate-but-equal arrangement. The ladies were permitted to amuse themselves with benevolent enterprises precisely because American men, by and large, did not think religion and charity mattered very much. There are a number of ways to read this division of labor. One is to accept the judgment of nineteenth-century men as to what (and who) mattered; women's activities, for all the high-flying rhetoric, were second best. It is also possible to reverse the judgment of nineteenth-century men, as many women must have done at the time. Where was the riveting significance, after all, in managing a shoestore or in campaigning for the Whig who was nearly indistinguishable from the Democrat?

A third approach emerges from the recognition that living with separate spheres was not as comfortable as it looked. The creation of separate spheres was a temporary and uneasy solution to the continuing problem of how to distribute tasks and spaces under new conditions, and like most solutions, it brought problems of its own. Interestingly enough, the main problem was not so much that women thought they had been given too little, but rather that men thought they had conceded too much. The 1850s brought an intriguing sequence of convergences and trade-offs.

. . . .

A final evaluation of the overall progress of women's organizations up to 1860 hinges, as do so many questions of progress and decline, on our point of reference. If we compare women's options in the 1850s with those available to them at the beginning of the century, there is no question that their organizational lives had grown immeasurably richer. If we compare women's options to those available to men, the women consistently come up short. In every decade, men had access to organizations that were closed to women. There were long-standing fraternal associations like the Masons; there were shorter-lived debating clubs; there were two mechanics' organizations; there were several single-sex temperance societies; and there were political parties, fire companies, and the militia. These last two were particularly important (and so were political parties after 1851, when propertiless white men got the vote) in that they engaged white men of the working class. For working-class white women, there appear to have been no formal organizations at all.

Comparing the organizational opportunities open to women with those open to men makes it clearer than ever that women's place was indeed mainly in the home. Once again, the cult of true womanhood turns out to be a closer description of social reality than we might like.

29

Kathleen D. McCarthy
Parallel Power Structures:
Women and the Voluntary Sphere, 1990

Kathleen D. McCarthy, Director of the Center for the Study of Philanthropy at the Graduate Center of the City University of New York, is a leader in recent scholarly study of philanthropy. Her essay, "Parallel Power Structures: Women and the Voluntary Sphere," serves as the introduction to a collection of essays on *Women, Philanthropy, and Power* that she edited in 1990. In this essay, she reviews a great deal of recent historical scholarship to demonstrate that, over the course of American history, women have used nonprofit organizations to develop important social institutions, to advance many kinds of social reform, and to bring about political reform, and that women have also used their donations "to leverage new opportunities and careers" for women.

KATHLEEN D. MCCARTHY

Parallel Power Structures

WOMEN AND THE VOLUNTARY SPHERE

1990

The enduring caricature of Lady Bountiful has served to stigmatize women's philanthropy, often trivializing its presence on the American scene. Nonetheless, the legacy of the women who participated in charitable and philanthropic movements is impressive, ranging from the creation of new institutions and professions to Constitutional reform.

From McCarthy, *Lady Bountiful Revisited: Women, Philanthropy, and Power* (New Brunswick: Rutgers, The State University, 1990), pp. 1–31. Reprinted by permission of the author and Rutgers University Press.

Women have traditionally used these activities to wield power in societies intent upon rendering them powerless. Unlike men, who enjoyed a host of political, commercial, and social options in their pursuit of meaningful careers, women most often turned to nonprofit institutions and reform associations as their primary points of access to public roles. In the process, they forged parallel power structures to those used by men, creating a growing array of opportunities for their sisters and themselves.

This essay provides an overview of five distinctive aspects of women's efforts within the voluntary sphere. The first section, on institutional development, examines the efforts of women and men in providing organizational responses to public needs, ranging from charitable to cultural endeavors. The section on social movements focuses on the impact of women's reform initiatives, both among the constituencies they sought to aid and among themselves. The analysis of the ways in which women used nongovernmental organizations to effect political reform considers the ways in which prevailing political ideologies have shaped women's choices and campaigns. The section on donations centers on the ways in which women have used their contributions to leverage new opportunities and careers. The final section seeks to place American trends within the context of comparable practices in selected countries overseas. In each, the common denominator is power, and the ways in which women have used their charitable, social, and political movements to recast the contours of their public sphere.

INSTITUTIONAL DEVELOPMENT

In 1797 a band of New York women gathered together to form a new institution. Their mission was well defined, their goal direct. As they explained, because no other charitable resources existed to succor that "large class of sufferers who have peculiar claims on the public beneficence, poor widows with small children," they had elected to do it themselves. Although the Society for the Relief of Poor Widows with Small Children (SRPWC) was one of the first female relief organizations founded in the United States, the members of the newly formed board had a clear idea of what they wanted to do, and how to it. Prospective clients were to be visited in their homes, and women of dubious moral character winnowed from their more deserving counterparts. "Immorality," the board members firmly resolved, "excludes from the patronage of the Society." For those who qualified, relief would be given in the form of "necessaries," rather than cash, except by special dispensation of the board. The funds for these beneficences were to be culled in two ways: through $3 annual subscriptions from members and contributions from solicitous males who, although barred from membership, were assured that their donations would be entered "with peculiar pleasure on the list of Benefactors."

Gifts of "necessaries," would, of course, come heavily interlarded with sisterly advice. The managers vowed to find schools for the children who indirectly came under their care, and work for their impecunious mothers. The board members had particularly strong views about the proper disposition of the children, noting their intention to withhold aid from any applicant "who refuses to put out at service to trades, such of her Children as are fit; and to place the younger ones of a proper age, at a Charity School." Despite the stern tone of their warning, these women envisioned forming personal relationships with those they sought to serve; transferring applicants from one manager to another was roundly discouraged!

As in the case of many early charities, their attitude evokes an ambivalent response. While the board members' notions about other people's children seem unduly intrusive to the modern observer, their courage and commitment were undeniable. New York was an extremely unhealthy place during the society's infancy. In 1798 and 1799, the city was racked by yellow fever epidemics. Those who could, fled to the countryside. Yet several of the society's board members tarried in the city to minister to their wards, "at risk of their lives," proffering consolation, food, advice, and medicine to those in need. Whether the current epidemic was yellow fever, whooping cough, scarlet fever, or smallpox, these women persisted in their rounds, visiting the homes of the widows they had chosen to aid.

In part, their actions were inspired by empathy. "WIDOW is a word of sorrow in the best of circumstances: but a widow, left poor, destitute, friendless, surrounded with a number of small Children shivering with cold, pale with want . . . her situation is neither to be described nor conceived!" In an era of jarringly high death rates, the founders must have readily identified with the fate of the women they sought to aid. But they were not entirely swayed by images of blameless suffering, for—as they pointed out—the artisan class had a bad habit of living "not only plentifully, but luxuriously" and "our poor widows have been partners in the evil, and now sustain the whole of the punishment." The society's task, as they saw it, was to help these hapless women to "learn oeconomy [sic] from adversity," and set them on the road to self-support. Toward this end, much of their available cash was invested in fabric—nearly three thousand yards of it were purchased within the first three years—and distributed to the widows as a means of enabling them to sew their way to financial security. Each woman helped off charity was celebrated as a victory, not only for the society, but as a testimonial to the "industry and frugality" of the widows themselves.

Their businesslike approach was echoed in the society's organizational form as well. Lack of previous experience notwithstanding, these women were obviously adept at promoting their cause. Within the first year more than two hundred annual subscribers had been secured, and over $1,000 in donations culled from members and sympathetic men.

They were also extremely clear about their collective prerogatives. Granted in 1802, the society's formal act of incorporation limited participation to women. Subscribers were duly anointed "a Body Corporate' and legally empowered to "have perpetual succession, be in law capable of suing and being sued, defending and being defended, in all courts and places . . . and shall also . . . be capable in law of purchasing, holding, and conveying any estate, real or personal, for the use of the said Corporation, *Provided,* that such estate shall never exceed in value Fifty Thousand Dollars, nor be applied to any other purposes than the charitable one for which this Incorporation is formed." Just in case, however, the state deemed it prudent to add that members' husbands would be exempted for "any loss occasioned by the neglect or malfeasance of his wife." Only if the man himself pilfered the funds would his estate be liable for repayment. Nonetheless, in an era when Married Women's Property Acts were still far in the future, this must have provided a fairly heady measure of responsibility.

The SRPWC highlighted a host of themes that came to typify female philanthropy. It was devised to aid a narrowly defined constituency, women and children, as were the majority of charities founded by women in the nineteenth century. It blended a significant degree of personal commitment and labor by the participants with small-scale fund raising and modest donations. It placed a strong emphasis on securing the means of self-support for other women. "Personalism" was also a factor: the board members identified with their charges and sought to establish ongoing relationships and programs tailored to individual needs. And, in their corporate state, participation expanded the board members' legal options, enabling them to own and alienate property, go to court, and superintend the futures of those they sought to aid. It gave them an enhanced public role, and a toehold in public policymaking processes.

Yet these were only minor gains in comparison to the range of options available to men. Philanthropy was just one of many routes to public stature open to men in the decades after the Revolution. Even within the philanthropic sphere, male alternatives were more varied, and the avenues for participation more complex. During the first half of the nineteenth century, most women entered charitable work via the church. First, the community would define a need, such as sheltering orphans, and then the task of institutional development would be turned over to interdenominational boards of directresses culled from local congregations. Although American religion became "feminized" in the aftermath of the Revolution, men also used their churches as conduits into a welter of social and charitable reforms, including Bible and tract societies and temperance work. Civic obligations played a role in drawing men into the charitable arena. So did affinity groups: history buffs, fledgling connoisseurs, and burgeoning literati coalesced into inward-turning cliques for self-improvement and cultural uplift. Their efforts were often bolstered by civic motives, since cities with cultural amenities had a competitive edge in the rough and tumble game of urban rivalry. Professional considerations were another lure. Doctors, for example, often founded and served in dispensaries and hospitals, which provided opportunities to hone their skills on impoverished patients.

Benevolent Ladies operated in a more constricted sphere. Cultural institutions are a case in point. Organizations for the promotion of the fine arts, such as the American Art-Union or the Pennsylvania Academy of Fine Arts, often traced their origins to subtle webs of masculine relationships that wedded business, professional, and cultural aims in extraordinary ways. Male artists and their patrons often traveled together, they promoted each others' professional wares among their acquaintances and peers, they dined together and occasionally translated these social relationships into more formal men's clubs such as the Century Association. Women were excluded from these social, professional, and institutional roles for a variety of reasons. Many of these early ventures were begun as joint stock companies, relying on heavy infusions of cash from their members to keep them afloat during times of economic duress. Women's organizations tended to subsist on small amounts of cash backed by substantial contributions of personal labor. But while domestic skills could handily run an asylum, they were superfluous in cultural institutions where the standard bill of fare included signing contracts for exhibitions, managing the transportation of valuable consignments, and devising legal mechanisms such as joint stock companies to keep the institution solvent. Denied control of their own funds by the common law doctrine of *femme couverte*, matrons also lacked the requisite business experience to run a cultural venture.

Nor did they have the necessary public sanctions to comfortably promote public cultural ventures. The justification for women's participation in antebellum charities and reform crusades was primarily domestic. Under the banner of religion, the ideology of Republican Motherhood, and the cult of domesticity, women broadened their range of maternal responsibilities beyond the home to encompass the needs of dependents and the dispossessed. When causes strayed toward more secular aims, their claims to moral authority became more tenuous. In many quarters bluestockings were greeted with a degree of public derision that few Benevolent Ladies would have comfortably borne. Conversely, those who stayed within their duly appointed sphere were rewarded with opportunities to carve out "invisible careers" that paralleled the more public roles of their brothers, spouses, and sires.

In the process, Benevolent Ladies formed "an identifiable women's culture" centered on charities, nourished by "a special combination of sisterhood and ambition," and reinforced by a "dense network of relationships with other women . . . based on kinship, neighborhood, and common experiences" rooted in "mutual support in times of childbearing, sickness and mourning."

As the American frontier extended toward the Pacific, these networks stretched across the nation. For women shorn of family and friends by the westward exodus, charitable ventures provided new communities, new support networks, and new challenges. By the 1920s, the gender-segregated initiatives that were borne of these relationships had lost much of their appeal. But in the nineteenth century, women's culture and women's charities played a central role in many women's lives.

2   SOCIAL REFORM

Mark Twain once quipped that "nothing so needs reforming as other people's habits," and women proved no more able to resist the lure of social reform than men. Nancy Hewitt's carefully detailed analysis of women's activism and social change in antebellum Rochester delineates the differing venues of women's philanthropic domain. Reform groups, which were often more radical than those devoted to straightforward charitable work, sought to remedy social ills through noninstitutional means. Rooted in an eager faith in human perfectibility, these groups ultimately helped to reshape their proponents lives as well, carving out new interpretations of gender, geography, and class.

The role of Female Moral Reform Societies has been particularly well researched. Antebellum urbanization engendered a panoply of social ills in its wake, not the least of which was a burgeoning trade in prostitution. Sexual misconduct proved to be a particularly compelling cause for women reformers for a number of reasons. Prostitution posed a constant threat to the sanctity of the family, and significant health risks as well, since venereal diseases were still incurable and wayward husbands could easily pass infections picked up in the bordello to their innocent wives. Moreover, the presence of brothels served as a constant reminder of the limits of wifely influence within the home. They also represented a religious affront, since prostitution was clearly a sin, as well as a repudiation of emerging middle-class values and familial norms.

Poverty, immigration, and broken homes swelled the ranks of urban prostitutes in the decades before the Civil War, trends dutifully charted by social observers such as John McDowall, a former divinity student who published two popular exposés of prostitution in New York: *The Magdalen Report* and *Magdalen Facts*, which alleged that a legion of ten thousand "malevolent and cruel" harlots were plying the city's streets. Galvanized by his findings, a group of women formed a Magdalen Society in 1832, which was followed by the Female Moral Reform Society two years later. Unable to contain their enthusiasm, the founders vowed to clone auxiliaries in every city and village in the United States. As of 1836 they had crafted sixty-six new chapters; by 1840, the number had risen to over five hundred. This vast empire was held together not only by sisterly spirit and collective indignation, but also through its national publication entitled *The Advocate for Moral Reform*, which claimed over sixteen thousand readers at its peak. Begun as a mechanism for combating vice, the society soon evolved into a weapon in women's attack on the double standard. To bolster their campaign, its members began to publish the names of brothel patrons in their columns, storming local bordellos in search of converts as well as erring males. Their research helped to illuminate the causes of feminine poverty as well, giving yet another slant to women's charitable concerns.

The moral reform movement produced a windfall of changes that reached well beyond its stated aims. Although prostitution continued to flourish, the society's efforts helped to reshape Victorian notions about feminine demeanor and sexual mores. Revolutionary theorists justified women's dependent political status with arguments steeped in ill-concealed misogyny. By their reasoning, women were immodest, easily corrupted, and hopelessly vain. They needed the firm hand of patriarchal guidance to keep their passions in check and curb the threat of their presence within the nascent Republic. The moral reform societies' exposés substantially recast these notions by highlighting the themes of female victimization and masculine sexual excess. In the process, they provided a key crucible in which Victorian mores and notions of women's moral superiority were promulgated and cast. To quote Nancy Cott, "the language of moral reform evoked women's power: power to revenge, power to control and reform." It also helped to alter the social geography of the city. As Christine Stansell notes in her book, *City of Women*, prior to the 1830s, few respectable women dared to venture into New York's business district, much less commercial establishments such as restaurants, unaccompanied by a man. The Moral Reform Society gave them new license to go where they pleased, even into "the most powerfully tabooed spots for women in the entire city," the oblique demimonde of "male sexual terrain."

Antebellum reform associations helped to recast the boundaries of class as well as gender. In Stansell's words, evangelical moral reform groups "served as a nexus of social identity, an impulse toward self definition, a need to avow publicly one's own class aspirations which led people to seek each other out across a range of incomes and occupations, differentiating themselves from the classes above and below them."

These differences revealed themselves in widely divergent attitudes about hygiene, privacy, and childrearing practices. Benevolent Ladies and social activists alike were often repulsed by the conditions that greeted them on entering the homes of the poor. At a time when middle-class families were becoming increasingly insular and privatized, working-class families were spilling onto the streets. Stansell does a particularly good job of outlining these cultural conflicts, as middle-class reformers sought to "domesticate" the women of the slums. In effect, these encounters embodied a clash of cultures in which volunteers evinced little sympathy for the noisy sociability, the earthy courtship practices, and the lenient childrearing methods of their impoverished peers. . . . Whether these programs helped their intended charges, or simply evoked new sources of friction between the classes, remains open to debate. Ross outlines not only the psychological dimensions of "the good mother/bad mother" debates, but also some of the results. As she explains, many infant welfare organizations ended by merely harassing the working-class mothers they sought to aid, rather than helping to secure needed clothing and food. In policymaking terms, then, the London-based groups had a decidedly negative effect.

Their legacies are more clearly etched within the lives of the volunteers themselves. Under the rubric of religion and maternal solicitude, women used their reform organizations as they used their charities, to expand the parameters of their influence and reshape public discourse on the content and meaning of their lives.

3   POLITICAL REFORM

Voluntary associations played a crucial political role as well. While men exercised the option of effecting social change through partisan politics, "women carried out social policy through voluntary action." The long campaign for women's enfranchisement serves as an ideal laboratory for tracing the political implications of feminine philanthropy in the United States.

Despite their ostensibly nonpolitical status, voluntary associations have historically provided one of the primary mechanisms for that most fundamental and far-reaching aspect of political change, Constitutional reform. Indeed, these institutions draw their legitimacy from the Constitution itself. Under the provisions of the First Amendment, citizens are guaranteed not only freedom of religion, speech, and the press, but also of "the right of the people peaceably to assemble, and to petition the government for a redress of grievances." In effect, voluntary associations play an indispensable political role in this society by providing ongoing mechanisms for peaceful, gradualist change.

Women's participation in more direct forms of political action was far more limited. Ironically, American women were not specifically disfranchised by the architects of the new republic; they were simply ignored. They are neither mentioned specifically in the Constitution, nor in the Federalist Papers that cadenced the nationalist debates. Indeed, the latter documents contain only one reference to women's role, warning of the dangers posed by the political intrigues of courtesans and the mistresses of public figures. This silence masked a welter of social and political concerns, one of the most important of which was women's subservient status under common law. Under the doctrine of femme couverte, wives (and this was an era in which most women married) forfeited control of their estates, their possessions, and their future wages to their spouses upon marriage. Since the authors of the Constitution believed that political rights stemmed from property ownership, the ability of the majority of the nation's women to make independent political judgments apart from the influence of their spouses was therefore politically suspect. Technically "covered" by their husbands' legal identity, they were doomed to political invisibility as well.

Added to this were philosophical arguments that held that while men were ostensibly rational beings, women were closer to nature, more governed by their emotions, and therefore better suited to nurturing, maternal roles. The upshot of all of this was that while men's public, political roles were justified by their supposed ability to make informed, rational decisions, women's political roles were cast in a more domestic idiom under the guise of Republican Motherhood. Rather than voting, their task was to preserve the Republic by rearing successive generations of responsible, enlightened citizens.

The tension between the egalitarian rhetoric in which the Revolution and the Constitution were forged, and the domestic, maternal justification for women's political role was to have profound implications for the strategies adopted by women's voluntary associations in their quest for political power. While the champions of suffrage rights for black males forwarded their claims under the banner of social and political justice, women adopted a different rationale. Rather than demanding change in the name of simple justice, equity, or egalitarian norms, they made their greatest impact when they cast their arguments in the idiom of hearth and home.

The history of the suffrage movement underscores the difficulties inherent in sustaining this approach. The relationship of feminism and the suffrage campaign to the abolitionist movement is well known. Female abolitionists made significant contributions to the movement's success, garnering contributions, circulating petitions, addressing audiences, and opening their homes as way stations on the underground railroad. In the process, the abolitionist movement served as a training ground for leading feminists, including such pioneers as Elizabeth Cady Stanton and her colleague, Susan B. Anthony. Yet despite their contributions, women were ultimately asked to set aside their feminist agenda, including the demand for equal suffrage, in order to ensure passage of the Fifteenth Amendment giving black males the right to vote.

This in turn raises intriguing questions about how a radical fringe movement within a movement—the feminist quest for feminist gains, including the right to vote—succeeded in becoming a mainstream crusade by the opening decades of the twentieth century. Hewitt's book on women's groups in Rochester, New York, does an especially effective job of underscoring the distinctions that separated the constituents of various types of causes. While the wives of Rochester's social and commercial leaders created charities, evangelical perfectionists turned their attention to moral reform crusades to curb the excesses of liquor and vice. The more radical elements who espoused abolitionism and women's rights stood at the fringes of the local commercial circles, and as such had the least to lose by advocating the sweeping social, legal, and economic reforms and fundamental political changes that their campaigns entailed.

Indeed, the image of the defiantly bloomer-clad feminist of the mid-nineteenth century contrasts sharply with her Progressive-era counterparts, who ran the gamut from committed ideologues chaining themselves to the White House gates, to moderate reformers and settlement workers such as Jane Addams, to socialists and middleclass clubwomen from the hinterland, and sedate society matrons such as Louisine Havemeyer and Mrs. Potter Palmer. The changing rhetoric of the women's movement provides an important clue to the emergence of this complex coalition. Reduced to its simplest terms, it is possible to trace at least three differing, yet increasingly inclusive rationales for promoting the female franchise between 1878, when the suffrage amendment was first introduced in Congress, and 1919 when it was finally passed.

The fiery rhetoric of an Elizabeth Cady Stanton was uncompromisingly egalitarian. Her Declaration at the Seneca Falls Convention of 1848 borrowed liberally from the sentiments of Thomas Jefferson, declaring that "we hold these truths to be self-evident: that all men and women are created equal." A straightforward approach, but one that was fraught with problems, since it directly challenged the notion of separate spheres embodied in the ideologies of Republican Motherhood and the cult of domesticity, which were used by many women as the basis for their participation in charities and social reform. As a result, early equal rights advocates faced social ostracism for their unladylike behavior, public ridicule for attempting to invade masculine terrain, and censure from other women activists who were working along different ideological lines. None of this was a particularly appealing prospect, and taken together it undoubtedly deterred many Benevolent Ladies and moral reformers from embracing more radical demands for suffrage and equal rights during the antebellum years.

The movement's appeal was broadened during the Gilded Age through the spread of the Women's Christian Temperance Union (WCTU). Under the able stewardship of Frances Willard, the movement blossomed into a national grass-roots crusade. And, by equating temperance, and eventually suffrage as well, with "home protection," Willard broadened the ranks of American feminism by arguing that women needed the vote to protect their families from the evils of liquor. Unfortunately, the temperance movement ultimately proved an insufficient vehicle for rallying national support for suffrage reform. Cautioned by the threat of an antifeminist backlash from the liquor interests, suffrage leaders developed a wary alliance with the WCTU, which faltered with Willard's passing.

Yet by the 1910s a more inclusive rationale had begun to emerge. The notion of "municipal housekeeping" was promoted by a range of women's voluntary associations and clubs, casting the cause of suffrage in more broadly etched, still more democratic terms. As Addams explained, the political system was merely an extension of the home. Women, as mothers, needed the vote to maintain the quality of the educational system, to ensure that their cities were clean, their children's milk unadulterated, and vice curbed, so that their families would have healthy environments in which to live, prosper, and grow.

Municipal housekeeping provided the common denominator that united women of various persuasions. It was a brilliant strategy, because it coupled the demand for equal rights with domestic imagery, countering antifeminist arguments that predicted that female suffrage would undermine the home. It was a special moment in history, one that has not been repeated since. Neither the Equal Rights Amendment, which was first introduced in 1923 (an even longer period of gestation than the suffrage amendment); nor more recent pro-life/pro-choice campaigns have managed to unite both sides of women's political role. As a result, they have failed to build the broadly based coalitions that lie at the heart of Constitutional reform.

Once the vote was secured, women continued to draw upon their voluntary networks to enrich and consolidate their political gains. It was a symbiotic alliance. Participation in settlements and female centered social reform movements during the Progressive era provided the necessary credentials used by many women to enter governmental careers, particularly in agencies catering to the needs of women and children. It also forged a platform for their campaigns, and provided a continuing source of new ideas. As Susan Ware points out in her study, *Beyond Suffrage: Women in the New Deal,* "women in government turned to their friends in voluntary associations for expert technical help and to obtain broader public support for specific proposals." In the process, voluntary associations continued to exercise political power in a variety of new fields, enabling women to bolster their public presence in new ways.

4   CONTRIBUTIONS AND CAREERS

While women's voluntary associations campaigned for wide-ranging political reforms, women's donations provided yet another arena for the exercise of feminine power. Prior to the passage of married women's property acts in the mid-nineteenth century, women made their greatest contributions through fund-raising campaigns rather than individual gifts. While men raised funds through individual solicitation among their colleagues and friends, antebellum women turned their attention to charity fairs and bazaars.

As in the case of asylum work, these efforts drew upon domestic skills, as women busily painted, baked, knitted, and sewed the articles to be sold. These small-scale efforts generated public recognition and a modicum of power within the larger community. They also helped to bolster women's roles within a variety of institutions. Congregations became increasingly dependent on women's fund-raising skills, which also fueled the fires of revivalism. According to one historian, women's groups "ultimately built the infrastructure and financed the operations of the revival ministry," including Charles Grandison Finney's first sweep through the fertile soil of the Burned Over District in upstate New York. As they became more adept in these roles, a surprising variety of organizations attempted to tap their skills, providing an entree into abolitionist work and even a marginal role in some of country's more haughty cultural institutions.

The importance of women's fund-raising skills has continued down to the present, constituting an enduring element of their "invisible careers" within the voluntary sphere. This in turn gradually opened new arenas for the exercise of feminine talents. In the Gilded Age, for example, some wealthy matrons became cultural impresarios, opening their mansions to theatrical performances and musical events for carefully selected audiences of their friends. Fees were charged, and the proceeds given to charity. At a time when women still played a negligible role in most major urban cultural institutions, wealthy dowagers such as Mrs. George Pullman succeeded in attracting renowned singers, pianists, and other musicians to their homes for private performances under the rubric of charity.

The role of women as individual donors is harder to trace, and raises many intriguing questions. How widespread was female giving prior to the passage of married women's property laws? Who were their favored recipients? For example, only one woman was recorded among the twenty-eight major donors ($5,000 or more) to Harvard University between 1800 and 1850—Mrs. Sarah Jackson, who made a donation to the Divinity School. Similarly, only one gift of $5,000 or more was given by a woman in Chicago before the Civil War. Like Mrs. Jackson, Chicagoan Eliza Garrett donated a valuable parcel of land to help found a theological seminary in her husband's memory. Were most of their donations invested in religious causes, or did women underwrite other areas as well?

Marital status is another interesting consideration. Were the majority of antebellum women donors single, widowed, or were they wives? At this point the findings are fragmentary, but interesting. Suzanne Lebsock found in her study, *The Free Women of Petersburg*, that women were two times as likely as men to bequeath part of their estates to churches, benevolent societies, or poor relief, although admittedly the percentage of women who made these gifts was extremely low (6.7 percent of the wills examined). F. K. Prochaska posits a similar pattern among Victorian Englishwomen, whom he deems "much more likely than men to leave a large portion of their assets to philanthropy." According to Prochaska's book, widows and single women were particularly generous. Basing his study on a sample of wills probated in the 1840s and 1860s, he concludes that women donated "vast sums," particularly to religious causes.

One of the most important contributions of women's giving and voluntarism was their role in opening a growing array of female careers. From the outset, groups such as the SRPWC evinced a keen interest in promoting female self-support. The development of asylums created new employment opportunities for women, as did groups such as the New York Female Moral Reform Society, which hired only female staff as a matter of policy.

Interest in creating new careers for respectable middle-class women accelerated after the Civil War. Wartime casualties deprived many women of suitable mates, generating fresh concerns for their economic well-being. At the same time, the increasing secularization of feminine philanthropy provided a host of novel ideas for new careers. Some of these, such as nursing, were directly linked to wartime exigencies. Others were born of the women's club movement, new charitable techniques, and emerging social needs. Social work, settlement work, and the medical profession were all opened to women in large measure because of the power of feminine philanthropy.

Health proved to be an area of particular interest to women donors. In Chicago, for example, female donors gave over $700,000 in gifts of $5,000 or more to local women's and children's hospitals and nursing schools in the 1870s and 1880s. More traditional charities such as asylums also fared quite well, netting an almost equal amount (although the figure was distorted by Clarissa Peck's $625,000 bequest to the Home for Incurables). Cultural endeavors lagged far behind, recording a scant $18,000 in major gifts during these years.

This in turn underscores the point that although women began to move beyond religious charities in the decades after the Civil War, they continued to concentrate their giving in traditional areas of feminine concern: health, education, and social work. As the figures from Chicago suggest, health was a particularly popular cause. Many women were undoubtedly drawn to the task of educating female doctors after suffering at the hands of male physicians. Institutions such as the New England Hospital for Women and Children (1862) were heavily dependent on feminine support. Designed to provide advanced clinical training for women doctors, the hospital also assured patients that they would have recourse to qualified feminine medical care. The institution was nurtured during its infancy by a flurry of timely bequests from local women, as well as a series of benefits sponsored by women's groups. As Mary Roth Walsh explains, the director's "dependence on the women's movement was total: she needed female supporters to help finance her education, to raise money, to promote the hospital, to help administer it, to serve as patients, and—probably most critically—to proffer their friendship in critical times."

The extent to which women's friendships promoted institutional development has yet to be fully explored. In some instances, however, alliances between prominent feminists and wealthy female supporters were crucial determinants in individual careers. For example, M. Carey Thomas, the strong-minded president of Bryn Mawr, was appointed to that position after her friend and longtime companion, railroad heiress Mary Garrett, offered the college $10,000 per annum to underwrite Thomas's salary. Hull-House, too, had its financial angel in the form of Mary Rozet Smith, a relationship explored in Kathryn Kish Sklar's essay, "Who Funded Hull House?" Although the exact nature of Mary Smith's relationship to Jane Addams may never be fully determined, her role in financially backing Addams's career was undeniably important. As Sklar points out, other wealthy Chicago matrons such as Louise deKoven Bowen also provided financial backing as well as moral support. Interestingly, she finds far lower levels of support from men, including celebrated philanthropists of Julius Rosenwald's ilk. By concentrating on Addams's financial backers, Sklar's essay helps to add a new dimension to our understanding of women's networks and their role in shaping the careers of women who successfully assumed pioneering roles in new fields.

Margaret Rossiter's study, *Women Scientists in America,* addresses this issue in a more general way in her discussion of the impact of "creative philanthropy" in opening scientific careers to women. The most famous example of this leveraging technique was Mary Garrett's offer to give Johns Hopkins University $60,000 if the institution would require baccalaureate degrees for admission to its medical school and admit women on an equal footing with men. The offer was finally accepted after she considerably upped the ante, donating the $307,000 needed to top off the school's $500,000 fund-raising campaign.

Occasionally, this technique backfired. In 1865, for example, a group of women in Boston and New York raised $50,000 to endow scholarships for women in leading medical schools. When their offers were repeatedly rebuffed, they used the money instead to enlarge Dr. Elizabeth Blackwell's infirmary in New York. Cornell University was induced to open its undergraduate courses to women in return for a $25,000 gift, but the University of Michigan managed to sidestep a similar offer. According to the stipulations surrounding Dr. Elizabeth Bates's $133,000 bequest, the university was to develop professorships of gynecology and pediatrics and to train women medical students on a par with men, including allowing them access to clinical instruction. Instead, the university used the money to bolster its obstetrics department and build a new wing for the children's hospital, ignoring Bates's other injunctions. Despite these lapses, some women were keenly sensitive to the reforming potential of large gifts. In the words of Dr. Mary Putnam Jacobi, "it is astonishing how many invincible objections on the score of feasibility, modesty, propriety, and prejudice melt away before the charmed touch of a few thousand dollars."

It was a dictum that men had followed for a long time. Throughout the nineteenth and early twentieth centuries, women's gifts tended to be smaller and more targeted than men's. There were occasionally differences in form as well. Foundations are a case in point. Although single-purpose charitable trusts trace their genesis into the mists of antiquity, the modern foundation is of fairly recent vintage. Born at the turn of the century, these institutions were highly flexible, funded in perpetuity, rooted in professional expertise, national and international in scope, and designed to centralize individual giving in the same way that the rise of the corporation had systematized the nation's business affairs. Not surprisingly, this form was pioneered by some of the country's richest and most famous (or infamous, depending on one's point of view) entrepreneurs—men such as Andrew Carnegie and John D. Rockefeller.

Women proved far less likely to create major foundations. One exception was the Russell Sage Foundation. Founded by Olivia Sage in 1907, the Sage Foundation was at first heavily staffed by women and played a pioneering role in promoting the professionalization of social work. Later, it increasingly passed to male managers, and the social work programs were gradually supplanted by other kinds of research. By the turn of the century the scale and power of science were rapidly evolving beyond the influence of many women philanthropists, becoming the province of "professionals, millionaires, and soon, the big foundations, which few women ever penetrated." Whether women shied away from foundation development because of an enduring inclination toward "personalism," or whether their financial and legal advisers warned them away remains to be explored. Equally intriguing are questions about the kinds of foundations they did create, and how their impact differed from that of the "big foundations" funded, managed, and staffed by men. . . .

CONCLUSIONS

Women traditionally used their gifts of time and money within the American context to create parallel power structures outside the domestic, commercial, and political spheres dominated by men. . . .

For nonpoliticized American women, giving and voluntarism have provided ongoing sources of recruitment, socialization, training, and advancement into public roles. For disfranchised groups such as women and minorities, philanthropic activities have provided the means for leveraging political and even Constitutional change. In effect, the charities and voluntary associations that women created functioned precisely as the Founding Fathers intended, providing ongoing mechanisms for achieving peaceful, gradualist, and often fundamental political change.

They have also provided the crucibles in which women have reshaped public policies and popular attitudes about gender, class, domesticity, and race. Female philanthropy has served, and continues to serve, as the means through which American women—once legally invisible and without the vote, and still denied Constitutional assurances that their "equal rights under the law will not be denied or abridged on account of sex"—have made a lasting imprint on social and institutional reforms, professionalization, legislation, and even on the Constitution itself. The differing approaches fostered by ethnic and minority groups, doners and volunteers, as well as the ways in which their achievements may have been replicated in other cultures is just beginning to be understood.

30

W. E. B. Du Bois, *Economic Cooperation among Negro Americans*, excerpts, 1907

For African Americans, the first decade of the twentieth century was a desperately discouraging time. The southern states were still mired in the appalling poverty of the debt-peonage system that had succeeded slavery as a means of exploiting African American labor. Using such devices as the arbitrary "literacy test" (from which whites were exempted by the "grandfather clause" because their ancestors had had the right to vote), the poll tax (which most poor people, white as well as black, could not afford in the almost cashless rural economies of the South), and the white-voters-only primary, white southern leaders completed the effort they had begun in the 1880s to exclude the freedmen (as well as many poor whites) from politics. White-dominated school boards in the South routinely refused to appropriate funds for African American children whose schools received, on average, about 10 cents for every dollar spent on white children. And the white-controlled southern law enforcement and court system simply ignored the surge of lynchings through which white supremacists made it clear that they would brutalize any African American who refused to subordinate himself to whites.

It was in this context that the great African American scholar and political leader W. E. B. Du Bois put together his report on *Cooperation among Negro Americans.* Du Bois, who had been raised in Massachusetts and received his doctorate from Harvard and who had written an impressive study of the *Philadelphia Negro*, prepared the report not long after his arrival at Atlanta University. Under the circumstances it was not surprising that he (and his many informants) emphasized the efforts of African Americans to help themselves. Nor was it surprising that he began by referring to the sometimes violent revolts through which American slaves had sought to work together to set themselves free. In view of the fact that African Americans faced severe disadvantages when they sought to defend their property rights in the courts, one of the most impressive parts of Du Bois's report is its account of the growth of the African American religious publishers in Nashville.

Du Bois also describes the way that African Americans (usually by themselves, occasionally with the help of white northern philanthropists and volunteers) created schools, clinics, and social-service centers in connection with their churches. These African American religious/school/ social centers closely resembled the parish churches, schools and social centers built by Catholic immigrants in the industrial cities of the North. Altogether, African American self-help efforts as Du Bois described them closely paralleled the self-help efforts of white immigrants and white northerners as they created burial and sickness societies, labor unions, mutual savings and mortgage banks and credit unions, and mutual insurance companies in these same years. Thus his account of African American institution-building can also serve as an account of the ways most Americans of limited means used nonprofit organizations in the years between the Civil War and World War II.

W. E. B. DU BOIS

Co-operation among Negro Americans

1907

INTRODUCTION: COOPERATION FOR REVOLT, EMANCIPATION, FLIGHT, AND ADVANCEMENT

A sketch of co-operation among the Negro Americans begins naturally with the Negro church. The vast power of the priest in the African state was not fully overcome by slavery and transportation; it still remained on the plantation. The Negro priest, therefore, early became an important figure and found his function as the interpreter of the supernatural, the comforter of the sorrowing, and the one who expressed rudely but picturesquely the longing, disappointment and resentment of a stolen people.

From such beginnings rose and spread with marvellous rapidity the Negro church in America, the first distinctively Negro American social institution. It was not at first by any means a Christian church, but rather an adaptation of those heathen rites which we roughly designate by the term Obi worship or Voodooism. Association and missionary effort soon gave these rites a veneer of Christianity and gradually after two centuries the church became Christian with a Calvinistic creed and

Excerpted from W. E. B. Du Bois, *Cooperation among Negro Americans* (Atlanta: Atlanta University Press, 1907).

with many of the old customs still clinging to the services. It is this historic fact, that the Negro church of today bases itself on one of the few
surviving social institutions of the African Fatherland, that accounts for
its extraordinary growth and vitality. We must remember that in the
United States today there is a church organization for every sixty Negro
families. This institution therefore naturally assumed many functions
which the other harshly suppressed social organs had to surrender, and
especially the church became the center of economic activity as well as
of amusement, education and social intercourse.

It was in the church, too, or rather the organization that went by
the name of church, that many of the insurrections among the slaves
from the sixteenth century down had their origin; we must find in these
insurrections the beginning of co-operation which eventually ended in
the peaceful economic co-operation. A full list of these insurrections it is
impossible to make, but if we take the larger and more significant ones
they will show us the trend. The chief Negro insurrections are as follows:

> Revolt of the Maroons, Jamaica.
> Uprising in Danish Islands.
> New York, 1712.
> Cato of Stono, South Carolina, 1734.
> New York, 1741.
> San Domingo, 1791.
> Gabriel, Virginia, 1800.
> Vesey, South Carolina, 1822.
> Nat Turner, Virginia, 1831.

Both Vesey and Turner were preachers and used the church as a center
of their plots; Gabriel and Cato may have been preachers, although this
is not known.

These insurrections fall into three categories: unorganized outbursts
of fury, as in the Danish Islands and in early Carolina; military organizations, as in the case of the Maroons; movements of small knots of conspirators, as in New York in 1712 and 1741; and carefully planned efforts
at widespread co-operation for freedom, as in the case of San Domingo,
and the uprisings under Cato, Gabriel, Vesey and Turner. It was these
latter that in most cases grew out of the church organizations.

It was the fact that the Negro church thus loaned itself to insurrection and plot that led to its partial suppression and careful oversight in
the latter part of the seventeenth and again in the eighteenth and early
nineteenth centuries. Nevertheless there arose out of the church in the
latter part of the eighteenth and early in the nineteenth centuries the

beneficial society, a small and usually clandestine organization for bury-ing the dead; this development usually took place in cities.

From the beneficial society arose naturally after emancipation the other co-operative movements: secret societies (which may date back even beyond the church in some way, although there is no tangible proof of this), and cemeteries which began to be bought and arranged for very early in the history of the church. The same sort of movement that started the cemeteries brought the hospital in the latter part of the nineteenth century, and from the secret societies came the homes and orphanages. Out of the beneficial society also developed late in the nine-teenth century the first attempts at co-operative business, and still later the insurance societies, out of which came the banks in the last ten years.

THE UNDERGROUND RAILROAD

Meantime, however, the spirit of insurrection and revolt had found out-let earlier than by this slower development.

There was early discovered an easier method of attaining freedom than by insurrection and that was by flight to the free states. In the West Indies this safety valve was wanting and the result was San Domingo. In America freedom cleared a refuge for slaves as follows:

Vermont, 1779.
Massachusetts, 1780.
Pennsylvania, 1780.
New Hampshire, 1783.
Connecticut, 1784.
Rhode Island, 1784.
Northwest Territory, 1787.
New York, 1799,
New Jersey, 1804.

Consequently we find that the spirit of revolt which tried to co-operate by means of insurrection led to widespread organization for the rescue of fugitive slaves among Negroes themselves, and developed before the war in the North and during and after the war in the South, into various co-operative efforts toward economic emancipation and land-buying. Gradually these efforts led to co-operative business, build-ing and loan associations and trade unions. On the other hand, the Underground Railroad led directly to various efforts at migration, espe-cially to Canada, and in some cases to Africa. These migrations in our day have led to certain Negro towns and settlements; and finally from the efforts at migration began the various conventions of Negroes which have endeavored to organize them into one national body, and give them a group consciousness. Let us now notice in detail certain of these steps toward co-operation. We have already spoken of insurrections and can now take up the Underground Railroad and the co-operative efforts during emancipation, and the various schemes of migration. . . .

From the beginning of the nineteenth century slaves began to escape in considerable numbers from the region south of Mason and Dixon's line and the Ohio to the North. Even here, however, they were not safe from the fugitive slave laws, and soon after 1812 the Negro soldiers and sailors discovered a surer refuge in Canada and the tide set thither. Gradually between 1830 and 1850 there were signs of definite concerted co-operation to assist fugitives which came to be known as the Underground Railroad. The organization is best known from the side of the white abolitionists who aided and sheltered the fugitives and furnished them means.

But it must not be forgotten that back of these helpers must have lain a more or less conscious co-operation and organization on the part of the colored people. In the first place, the running away of slaves was too systematic to be accidental; without doubt there was widespread knowledge of paths and places and times for going. Constant communication between the land of freedom and the slave states must be kept up by persons going and coming, and there can be no doubt but that the Negro organization back of the Underground Railroad was widespread and very effective. Redpath, writing just before the war, says: "In the Canadian provinces there are thousands of fugitive slaves; these are the picked men of the Southern states, many of them are intelligent and rich and all of them are deadly enemies of the South; . . . They should leave home well prepared with certain knowledge of localities to which they intend to move; money enough to pay their passage and enable them to begin life in their new homes with prospect of ultimate success. . . ."

MIGRATION TO KANSAS AND THE NORTH

On the Northern side both Negroes and whites organized immigration aid societies. Some of them simply spent money furnished by others. Others were more extensive organizations. In Indianapolis, for instance:

> On Wednesday evening, December 3, 1879, a meeting was held in the lecture room of the Second Baptist Church to organize a relief society to care for the colored emigrants, as we learned that some of them were on their way here from North Carolina, and that they would arrive here destitute. After the preliminary organization of

the meeting, the object of the same being stated, on motion. It was voted that a society be organized tonight for the purpose of helping and caring for those people when they arrive here, similar to and in co-operation with the relief society which was organized at the A. M. E. Church, November 24. . . .

Two similar societies worked in St. Louis:

The colored men of this city, who have been active in the organization of the . . . society to assist the colored immigrants from the South in finding local habitation in the rich and growing West, have just perfected that organization, with . . . as president, secretary, treasurer and directors. These names include some of the leading colored men of the place and an advisory board, to be composed of some of the most public-spirited and benevolent of our citizens, and these are a guaranty to all who know them of perfect good faith, integrity and trustworthiness in the distribution of such funds as may be contributed to them for the purposes indicated.

The result of [the] great movement [to Kansas] was thus reported . . . [in] February, 1880, [by] John M. Brown, Esq., general superintendent of the Freedmen's Relief Association, [in] an interesting report . . . , from which the following extract is taken:

The great exodus of the colored people from the South began about the first of February, 1879. By the first of April 1,300 refugees had gathered around Wyandotte, Kans. Many of them were in a suffering condition.

It was then that the Kansas Relief Association came into existence for the purpose of helping the most needy among the refugees from the Southern states. Up to date about 60,000 refugees have come to the state of Kansas to live. Nearly 40,000 of them were in a destitute condition when they arrived, and have been helped by our association. We have received to date $68,000 for the relief of the refugees. About 5,000 of those who have come to Kansas have gone to other states to live, leaving about 55,000 yet in Kansas. About 30,000 of that number have settled in the country, some of them on lands of their own or rented lands; others have hired out to the farmers, leaving about 25,000 in and around the different cities and towns of Kansas. . . .

THE CHURCH

The Christian Church did but little . . . until the establishment of the Society for the Propagation of the Gospel in Foreign Parts in 1701; this society and the rising Methodists and Baptists rapidly brought the body of slaves into nominal communion with the Christian Church. No sooner, however, did they appear in the Church than discrimination began to be practiced which the free Negroes of the North refused to accept. They, therefore, withdrew into the African Methodist and Zion Methodist Churches. The Baptists even among the slaves early had their separate churches, and these churches in the North began to federate about 1836. In 1871 the Methodist Church, South, set aside their colored members into the Colored Methodist Episcopal Church, and the other Southern churches drove their members into the other colored churches. The remaining Northern denominations regained their Negro members, but organized them for the most part into separate congregations.

Practically, then, the seven-eighths of the whole Negro population is included in its own self-sustaining, self-governing church bodies. . . . Consequently a study of economic co-operation among Negroes must begin with the Church group. The most compact and powerful of the Negro churches is the African Methodist Episcopal Church whose membership has grown as follows. . . .

The African Methodists had but a few posts in slave territory outside of Maryland and Delaware. William Paul Quinn, the pioneer of the West, blazed a path from Pittsburg to St. Louis, including Louisville, Ky. Good, substantial buildings were erected on slave territory at St. Louis, Louisville and New Orleans, La., in the early 50's.

In the wake of the army the banner of African Methodism was firmly planted under the leadership of Chaplains Turner and Hunter in the East and Southeast, followed by Carr and others in South Carolina. . . .

The history of the Publication Department [of the African Methodist Episcopal Church began with the 1817 publication of] the First Book of Discipline . . . by Richard Allen [which] contained the articles of religion, government of the church, confession of faith, ritual, etc. A Hymn Book, for the use of the church, was compiled and published. Aside from this and the publishing of the Conference Minutes, but little was accomplished until the year 1841, when in the New York Conference a resolution was made that a magazine be published monthly; but for the want of proper funds could only be published quarterly. This gave promise of some considerable success for nearly eight years.

In 1848 the General Conference elected Rev. A. R. Green general book steward and authorized him to purchase a newspaper called the *Mystery*, edited by Martin R. Delany, and to change its name to the *Christian Herald*, also to move the Book Concern from Philadelphia to Pittsburg; which he did and continued the publication of the paper until the General Conference in 1852. The name of the paper was then changed to the *Christian Recorder.*

This paper was looked upon by the slaveholders of the South and pro-slavery people of the North as a very dangerous document or sheet, and was watched with a critical eye. It could not be circulated in the slave-holding states by neighbors nor ministers nor members. Hence its circulation was proscribed until the breaking out of the war in 1860, when through the aid of the Christian Commission it did valuable service to the freedmen throughout the South. It followed the army, went into the hovels of the freedmen and also the hospital, placed in the hands of soldiers, speaking cheer and comfort to the law-abiding and liberty-loving slave whose manacles were about to fall off. . . .

The Department of Church Extension of the African Methodist Episcopal Church was organized in 1892 by the Annual Conference at Philadelphia. . . . It was the intention that one dollar from or for each member of the church should cover all the expenses of the general connection for missionary and educational work, the support of bishops, general officers, superannuated preachers, and help the Conferences to help the widows of deceased preachers, and assisting in making up the support of pastors on poor fields. "In one year," the church reported, "we have secured through the efforts of our resident bishop $50,000 of church property in South Africa alone, while word from one of our presiding elders in Liberia to the secretary of Church Extension is, 'We are pushing into the interior; stand by us. . . .'"

The next largest Negro church is that of the Baptists. The growth in numbers of this sect is not accurately known. They are primarily small disassociated groups of worshippers whose economic activities were small, except in large cities, until the individual groups united into associations. The first of these associations was formed in Ohio in 1836, followed by another in Illinois in 1838. . . .

The most remarkable department of the Baptist Church is the National Baptist Publication Board. . . . This organization is so unique that a careful history is necessary. The proposition to establish a publishing house was adopted at the Savannah Convention in 1893. In 1894 at Montgomery, Ala., the question was again discussed, but many obstacles were found in the way. Rev. R. H. Boyd of San Antonio, Texas, offered a set of resolutions [which were adopted], setting forth that this publishing committee, board, or concern should proceed at once to the publication of Sunday School literature, consisting of the International Lessons in either newspaper, magazine or pamphlet form for the benefit of their own schools.

On the 15th of December, 1896, Rev. R. H. Boyd, secretary and manager, opened his office in Nashville, Tenn., and secured copies of the electrotype plates from the Sunday Schools of the Southern Baptist Convention and employed the Brandon Printing Company, the University Printing Press of Nashville, Tenn., to publish for him ten thousand copies of the Advanced Quarterly, ten thousand Intermediate Quarterlies, ten thousand Primary Quarterlies and two thousand copies of the Teachers' Monthly, thus launching the long-talked of Negro Publishing Concern. At the next meeting of the National Baptist Convention in Boston, Mass., Secretary Boyd reported having sent out during the year 700,000 copies of the periodicals, together with song books, Bibles and other religious literature.

The Publishing Board is an incorporated publishing institution, incorporated in 1898, under the special provision granted by the legislature of Tennessee, with headquarters at Nashville, domiciled in the Publishing House, 523 Second Avenue, North, or on the corner of Second avenue and Locust street. This Publishing board owns or holds in trust for the National Baptist Convention three lots with four brick buildings thereon. Besides this it rents or leases two other brick buildings. These make up the domicile of the Publishing Board, and is known as the National Baptist Publishing House.

All the work of the Publishing Board is operated under the supervision of a general secretary, assisted by a local Board of management, consisting of nine members. These nine members hold monthly meetings, the second Tuesday in each month. In these meetings they hear and pass upon the reports, recommendations, etc., of the general secretary, and up to this time make quarterly reports to the Executive Committee of the Home Mission Board located at Little Rock, Ark. In this way the Home Mission Board has been a kind of clearing house through which this local committee of management, better known and styled as Board of Directors of the National Baptist Publishing Board, could clear itself and make its reports. . . .

Besides the circulation of . . . 9,000,000 copies of Sunday school periodicals annually among the 15,000 Negro Baptist Sunday schools, [it sends] out 170,617 religious circulars, 178,559 religious tracts and booklets. . . . "Take a glance at the dividends arising from the sale of thousands of song books, Bibles and other standard religious books that are being sold and distributed by the thousands throughout the length and breadth of this country, and some faint idea can be had of the magnitude of the work that is being performed by this National Baptist Publishing Board" [wrote a representative], "starting ten years ago from nothing—nothing but faith in God and the justice of its cause, going forth as a great giant strengthened with new wine to battle against the opposition that is hurled against the Bible, the Christian religion and the true Baptist doctrine. . . . "

The Baptists were the first Negro missionaries. From Georgia, where he preached the gospel in 1777, during the Revolution, George Lisle, a Negro Baptist, went to Jamaica in 1783. He preached the gospel to his own race of people at the race course and in his own hired house or room. He gathered a church of four and supported himself by his own labor. He spread the gospel among bond and free on neighboring plantations and to distant parts of the island, personally and by his own converts, so that in about seven years he had baptized 500 believers.

Rev. Lot Carey, who was a slave in Richmond, Va., purchased his freedom in 1813, raised $700 for missions in Africa, and was the first missionary from America to Africa. From the days of Lisle and Carey the Negro Baptists of America have been prosecuting missionary work in the West India Islands and in Africa. They have four general organizations of their own through which they are doing missionary work in this and in other lands, besides many Negro churches contribute to both Home and Foreign Missions through the missionary organizations of their white Baptist brethren. . . .

SCHOOLS

The early interest of the Negroes in education and their willingness to work and pay for it is attested to in many ways. In Philadelphia in 1796 we have the following minutes:

> To the Teachers of the African School for Free Instruction of the Black People: We, the Trustees of the African Methodist Episcopal Church, called Bethel, . . . being convened on matters of importance relative to the education of the people of color, are desirous of a First Day school being held in our meeting house in such manner that it shall not interfere with the time of our meeting or worship. There has been a school kept in said meeting house last summer which was orderly attended by about sixty scholars, under the care of Thomas Miller, deceased, and having seen the good effects of the said school, are anxious to have a permanent school kept in the said house—so long as it may be convenient or agreeable. Signed by order of the Board of Trustees, Richard Allen, March, 1796.
>
> We, the overseers and teachers of the First Day school, being present, it was then concluded that a night school be opened for the further utility of the people of color, and a solemnity attending, it was unanimously agreed that an orderly night school should commence in the next month, beginning at the sixth hour on the first or second day in the said month. And it is fully agreed that no disorderly person be admitted into said school.

In the city of Washington it was announced in 1818 that

A School, founded by an association of free people of color of the
city of Washington, called the Resolute Beneficial Society, situated
near the Eastern Public School and the dwelling of Mrs. Tenwick, is
now open for the reception of children of free people of color and
others, that ladies or gentlemen may think proper to send to be
instructed in reading, writing, arithmetic, English grammar or other,
branches of education apposite to their capacities, by a steady,
active and experienced teacher, whose attention is wholly devoted
to the purposes described. It is presumed that free colored families
will embrace the advantages thus presented to them, either by subscribing to the funds of the society or by sending their children to
the school. An improvement of the intellect and morals of colored
youth being the object of this institution, the patronage of benevolent ladies and gentlemen, by donation or subscription, is humbly
solicited in aid of the fund, the demands thereon being heavy and
the means at present much too limited. For the satisfaction of the
public, the constitution and articles of association are printed and
published, and to avoid disagreeable occurrences no writings are to
be done by the teacher for a slave, neither directly nor indirectly, to
serve the purpose of a slave on any account whatever. Further
particulars may be known by applying to any of the undersigned
officers. . . .

In Ohio a hard fight was made for schools. In earlier times a few
Negroes attended the public schools. . . . Whatever privileges they may
have enjoyed in the schools were cut off in 1829 by a law passed that
year that "the attendance of black or mulatto persons be specifically
prohibited, but all taxes assessed upon the property of colored persons
for school purposes should be appropriated to their instruction and for
no other purpose." The prohibition was vigorously enforced, but the
second clause was practically a dead letter. . . . In Cincinnati as early as
1820 a few earnest colored men, desiring to give their children the
benefit of a school, raised by subscription a small sum of money, hired a
teacher, rented a room and opened a school; but with such uncertain
and limited funds it was possible to continue the school for only a few
weeks, and it was finally closed altogether. This experiment was continued from time to time during the next ten years in Cincinnati. In September, 1832, a small Sunday school was gathered, which in three years
numbered 125 scholars. In their zeal for improvement, a lyceum also
was organized, where three times a week practical talks were given on
different literary and scientific subjects, and often an attendance of 300
would gather for instruction. A circulating library of 100 volumes was
also collected, but owing to the inability of so many to read and write, it
was of little use save for its value as an inspiration. In March, 1832, an
effort was again made for a school. A suitable room was rented from a
colored man and a teacher secured. The clamor of the adults to gain

admittance became so great that night schools were opened for two evenings a week, the number of teachers necessary being obtained from Lane Theological Seminary from among the young men preparing for the ministry. This school soon assumed such proportions that three additional schools were demanded and organized, one exclusively for girls, where instruction in sewing was made especially prominent. . . .

Some few schools for Negroes existed here and there in the South before the war. In the District of Columbia, as already mentioned, no less than fifteen different schools were conducted here mainly at the expense of the colored people between 1800 and 1861. In Maryland, St. Frances Academy for colored girls was founded by the Roman Catholics in 1829. The convent originated with the French Dominican refugees, who came to Baltimore during the uprising in the West Indies. The sisters were colored. Another school, established in 1835, gave instruction to free colored children. In North Carolina there were 13 before 1835 several schools maintained by the free Negroes. They had usually white teachers. After 1835 the few clandestine schools were taught by Negroes. In Charleston, S. C., there was a school for Negroes opened in 1844, which lasted some ten years. It was taught by a Negro and was for free Negroes only, although some slaves who hired their time managed to send their children there.

Free Negroes in Georgia used to send children to Charleston for education. They returned and opened clandestine schools in Georgia. In Savannah a French Negro, Julian Froumontaine, from San Domingo, conducted a free Negro school openly from 1819 to 1829, and secretly for some time after. Schools were stopped nearly everywhere after 1830 and as slavery became more and more a commercial venture all attempts at Negro education was given up. . . .

To the Negro slave, freedom meant schools first of all. Consequently, schools immediately sprang up after emancipation. [For example, in] Georgia, in December, 1865, the colored people of Savannah, within a few days after the entrance of Sherman's army, opened a number of schools, having an enrollment of 500 pupils and contributed $1,000 for the support of teachers. Two of the largest of these were in Bryant's Slave Mart. In January, 1866, the Negroes of Georgia organized the Georgia Educational Association, whose object was to induce the freedmen to establish and support schools in their own counties and neighborhoods. In 1867, 191 day schools and 45 night schools were reported as existing. Of these, 96 were reported either wholly or in part supported by the freedmen, who also owned 57 of the school buildings.

General [O. O.] Howard's first Freedmen's Bureau report says:

> Schools were taken in charge by the Bureau, and in some
> States carried on wholly-in connection with local efforts-by use of a

refugees' and freedmen's fund, which had been collected from various sources. Teachers came under the general direction of the assistant commissioners, and protection through the department commanders was given to all engaged in the work.

[The inspector of schools testified] . . . As showing the desire for education among the freedmen, we give the following fact: When the collection of a general tax for colored schools was suspended in Louisiana by military order, the consternation of the colored population was intense. Petitions began to pour in. I saw one from the plantations across the river, at least thirty feet in length, representing 10,000 Negroes. It was affecting to examine it and note the names and marks (X) of such a long list of parents, ignorant themselves, but begging that their children might be educated; promising that from beneath their present burdens and out of their extreme poverty, they would pay for it. . . .

The report of the [Freedmen's] Bureau for 1869 which summed up the work, said:

[N]ot more than one-tenth of the children of freedmen are attending school. Their parents are not yet able to defray the expenses of education. They are already doing something, probably more in proportion to their means, than any other class. During the last year it is estimated that they have raised, and expended for the construction of school houses and the support of the teachers not less than two hundred thousand dollars ($200,000). They have shown a willingness to help, and as they prosper and acquire property, they will assume a larger share of the burden, either by voluntary contributions or by the payment of taxes for the support of schools.

The freedmen assist in the support of their schools to the extent of their ability. As their condition is improved, their willingness to contribute for education, as they always have for religious interests, exhibits itself in the largely augmented amount paid for the support of schools. Forty-four thousand three hundred and eighty-six pupils paid $106,866.19 for tuition.—This is by far the largest aggregate sum we have yet had the privilege of reporting; while many thousands of dollars were expended for board and salaries of teachers, and for construction of school houses, of which we received no report, the actual amount of which would greatly increase the above sum. . . .

Today the efforts of Negroes to encourage education take three forms: Church schools; Aid to private schools; Aid to public schools. . . .

[T]here [is] . . . a fairly widespread system of supplementing the public school funds. No data of these schools are available, but the following instance in Virginia is instructive: Mr. T. C. Walker personally supervised the collection of $1,685 from the people [of eleven Virginia counties] by which 77 schools had their terms prolonged from one to two months, and permanent improvements were made to the amount of $400. . . .

The visitor of the General Educational Board makes this report:

In the rural districts it is the Negro who must lengthen the term and provide better [school]houses. Often it is necessary for him to build the house, while the school authorities pay for the teacher. Sometimes rent is received from these buildings, but more often, particularly in the far South, none is received. Accomac county, in Virginia, for instance, owns scarcely one-third of the school houses in use in the county. At convenient points throughout the county, however, Negroes have purchased land and erected in most cases a church, a hall for secret society purposes, and a schoolhouse. In some places the hall serves as a school house. So closely are these schools and churches associated that nearly every school is known by the name of the church near it. First Baptist, Ebenezer, etc., are the names commonly applied to the schools. The property is usually owned by the entire Negro community. This condition is common in the South. Such a contribution to Negro education is so closely associated with public education that it frequently escapes notice.

The way most in vogue at present for supplementing public education in the South, among whites especially, is through local taxation, together with the consolidation of schools. North Carolina is doubtless in the front in this educational revival in the South. Here they have built, on an average, a school house a day for the last two years. This movement, however, has affected the Negro but little as the Superintendent of Public Instruction informed me. The Negro is hardly in a position now to benefit by political methods. He is not consulted nor always included, in communities even where local taxation is adopted by the whites. He does not, of course, under such circumstances pay the local tax. He generally uses another method for raising many in the interest of his schools. Here, as in many other phases of Negro life, the church is the agency employed. Through religious denominations the Negro is doing most toward supplementing his elementary public education. This sometimes results in undue multiplicity of schools, but there are not wanting instances where communities, regardless of the various religious faiths, unite in the support of a single school. . . .

The Americus Institute, situated in the very heart of the black belt of Georgia, represents even better the possibilities of the Negroes along the line of self-help. In its present organization this school is only seven years old. Prior to that, however, an effort had been made to establish a school there, but owing to the dishonesty of a white man employed as agent the people sustained a loss of $1,000 in cash and eleven acres of land, besides another loss of

$275 stolen by a dishonest clerk of the association. Nevertheless, in seven years Mr. M. W. Reddick, the principal, has built up a school with property worth $7,000. This has practically all come through the small contributions of the Negroes themselves. He collects from the neighborhood, through various Baptist organizations, churches and individuals, about $1,000 yearly. Mr. Reddick and his teachers go out to the various churches to collect the monthly contributions. Thus the school and the idea of education are kept in the minds of the people, who are being educated to habits of giving and to a feeling of ownership and pride in their local institutions. . . .

BENEFICIAL AND INSURANCE SOCIETIES

Out of the churches sprang two different lines of economic co-operation: 1. Schools; 2. Burial Societies. From the burial societies developed sickness and death insurance, on the one hand, and cemeteries, homes and orphanages, on the other. From the insurance societies came banks and co-operative business. . . .

No complete account of Negro beneficial societies is possible, so large is their number and so wide their ramification. Nor can any hard and fast line between them and industrial insurance societies be drawn save in membership and extent of business. These societies are also difficult to separate from secret societies; many have more or less ritual work, and like regular secret societies do much fraternal insurance business.

An account of the secret and beneficial societies in several towns of various sizes and in different localities will give some idea of the distribution of these organizations. . . . There is probably no city in the land where there are as many societies among the colored people as in Baltimore, and several of the large societies which have spread far and wide, north and south, had their origin here. Nearly all of the societies are beneficial, but they may be divided in general into two classes, those beneficial merely and those with secret features. In order to help one another in sickness and provide for decent burial, through a system of small but regular payments, beneficial societies were formed among little groups of acquaintances or fellow laborers. In Baltimore they date back to 1820, and were afterwards specially exempted from the state laws forbidding meetings of colored people. Twenty-five, at least, had been formed before the war; from 1865 to 1870, seventeen or more were formed; since 1870, twenty or more have been added, several as late as 1884 and 1885. The number of members vary from a dozen to over 100.

In 1884 was held a meeting of many connected with these societies to arouse a more general interest in the work, and very interesting reports were presented. For 117 of them gave an aggregate membership of over 2,100. Nearly 1,400 members had been buried, over $45,000 having been given tn funeral expenses; $126,000 had been given as sick dues; $27,000 had been paid widows by some thirty of the societies; over $10,700 had been given towards house rent; and over $10,700 had been paid for incidental expenses. Yet there had been paid back to the members of many of the societies, from unexpended balances, as dividends, a total of over $40,000; and there remained in the banks, to the credit of the societies, over $21,400, and in the treasurers' hands a cash balance amounting to some $1,400. Five had small sums invested besides, and one the goodly sum of $5,642. The total amount of money handled by all had been nearly $290,000.

These societies vary somewhat in details. The usual fees from members are 60 cents a month; the usual benefits are $4 a week for a number of weeks, and then reduced sums, in sickness, and $4,000 for death benefit. Some pay as long as sickness lasts. Some give widow's dues according to need. One, for example, the Friendly Beneficial Society, organized chiefly by the members of a Baptist church, some fifteen years ago, with the usual fees and benefits, carries a standing fund of about $1,000, and the yearly fees of the members have paid the current expenses of from $300 to $500, and has usually allowed an annual dividend of $5 to each. The Colored Barbers' Society, over fifty years old, gives $80 at the death of a member. Three societies, originally very large, have been gotten up in the last twenty years, by one colored woman, whose name one of them bears.

A few of these beneficial societies have disbanded; a few have changed to secret societies. Very few of them have been badly managed, although unincorporated and without any public oversight, and everybody seems to speak well of them and of their work.

Secret societies among the colored people are now very numerous. Many important ones date back to before the war. The colored Masons and Independent Order of Odd Fellows are entirely independent of the whites in Baltimore, the colored men having been obliged from the state of public feeling in the United States in the old days to get a charter from the white brethren in England. In 1884 there were nearly 600 colored Masons in Baltimore; now there are probably 700. Of the Independent Order of Odd Fellows, fifty lodges of the seventy-seven working ones, giving a membership of over 2,300. The fifty lodges had, during the past two years, aided their sick, buried eighty-three brothers and relieved seventy-seven widows and orphans, at a total expenditure of over $13,000. The order held real estate worth $18,500 and had over $10,000 in cash.

Of the secret societies in Baltimore, the most influential are the Samaritans, the Nazarites, the Galilean Fishermen and the Wise Men. The first two were instituted some years before the war. The first has spread from Baltimore, during the forty years of its existence, to a number of states; but a third of all the lodges and nearly a third of all the members are in Maryland (1890). About one-half of the order are women, Daughters of Samaria, and they meet by themselves in their own lodges. There are now in Maryland fifty-eight lodges, with a membership of 1,925.

The order of Galilean Fishermen, of men and women together, was begun in Baltimore in 1856, by a handful of earnest workers; it was legally incorporated in 1869. The order has become influential. It is said to number over 5,000 in Maryland.

The order of the Seven Wise Men is a more recent order. There are many more of the same secret, beneficial nature, but these are the largest.

NONPROFIT STRUCTURES FOR THE TWENTIETH CENTURY

SEVEN

Science, Profession-alism, Foundations, Federations

Large, national, secular nonprofit organizations assumed a prominent place in the American nonprofit world early in the twentieth century. Between 1900 and 1920 a highly influential group of foundations, research univer-sities, and social service federations—all of which espoused a nonsectar-ian and "scientific" outlook—appeared on the American scene. Nine-teenth-century nonprofits, which continued to operate, were small, even domestic in scale, and were closely associated with religious groups. Even the larger private colleges, hospitals, and museums that had accumulated substantial physical assets were still governed by self-contained boards whose members shared clearly defined religious and cultural outlooks. Many of the American communities that nonprofits served, however, had become large and diverse. In 1900 the five boroughs of New York City contained well over 3 million people; Chicago's population had passed 1.5 million, Philadelphia's, 1 million; and many communities had more than 250,000. After 1900, moreover, medicine and other professions that persuasively advanced the claims of science gained overwhelming prestige in the provision of most health care, educational, and even human services. Small, sectarian organizations could not excel in the new environment.

Municipal and county governments and local school districts had always provided most of the funds needed for elementary education and for the care of the poor, the elderly, and the sick. That pattern continued into the twentieth century, as local and state governments accepted responsibility for new services ranging from sanitary water and sewer systems to high schools and expanded state colleges. After 1900, however, the very large foundations that Andrew Carnegie, John D. Rockefeller, and others created out of their industrial wealth played a key role in the transition to large-scale scientific institutions. Applying to their giving the systematic, methodical thinking that had helped them gain vast fortunes, Carnegie and Rockefeller articulated explicit philosophies of giving, philosophies that emphasized what Rockefeller called a "wholesale," broad and institution-shaping approach, rather than "retail" giving to individuals and small agencies. Early managers of the national foundations played key parts in the development of the national policy "think tank," city planning, social work, public health, the modern medical school, the research university, standardized college admissions tests, the high school curriculum for "college-bound" students. Where European and Asian nations used national governments to develop similar institutions and standards, as historians Stanley N. Katz and Barry D. Karl have shown, the highly decentralized government of the United States left the field to new, national, nonsectarian, foundations that celebrated "objective" science.

American nonprofits also transformed their relationships with small donors and with those who pay for their services: in effect, they applied the principles of mass marketing to the field. By the beginning of the twentieth century fundraisers had learned that narrowly defined Protestant evangelical causes did not appeal to the rapidly increasing numbers of potential donors in the great industrial cities who were devout Catholics or who belonged to other religious traditions. Nonprofit leaders responded with the nonsectarian federation, the "community chest," and the community foundation, first in Cleveland by 1914, then throughout the midwest, much of the northeast, and the far west. In another break with the religious, amateur, voluntary basis of so many nineteenth-century nonprofits, the new nonsectarian federations emphasized their commitment to the provision of service—medical care, education, job training, family counseling—by highly educated professionals, at the highest possible up-to-date, scientifically determined, national standard.

The new federations succeeded, with the critical assistance of corporate payroll offices, in attracting significant new flows of funds for their member agencies. The first federations were local community chests, but their new formula had national implications, as the March of Dimes demonstrated in the 1930s and 1940s. The hospital officials who created what became the Blue Cross movement (also in the midwest) during the same years applied a similar formula as they successfully sought to persuade ordinary salary- and wage-earners to "prepay" for hospital care. Together, the new national foundations and the largely local federations seemed, during the 1920s, to bring corporate leaders and ordinary citizens together into what historian Ellis Hawley has described as the "Associational State," a national government based on voluntary cooperation among private interests.

National foundations and nonsectarian federations helped to transform health care, human services, and higher education—and indeed the entire nonprofit sector—in the first third of the twentieth century. They emphasized scientific progress, efficiency, and universality, but they did not please everyone. Deeply committed evangelical Protestants (and, less prominently, some Catholic and Jewish leaders as well) objected to the abandonment of a religious basis for human service. Labor leaders objected that the massive exploitation of workers, not the genius of a few industrialists, created the fortunes that made possible the great foundations: hence, they insisted, any power assumed by foundation leaders was illegitimate. More profoundly but less noted at the time was the fact that where women had played central roles in the religiously based human service and health care nonprofits of the nineteenth century, men dominated the new enterprises of science and professionalism from the 1920s through the 1970s.

31

Debate over Government Subsidies:
Amos G. Warner, *Argument against*
Public Subsidies to Private Charities, 1908;
Everett P. Wheeler, *The Unofficial*
Government of Cities, 1900

Amos G. Warner's *American Charities* went through many editions, serving for nearly 50 years as the essential text on charities and their administration in the United States. In editions published around the turn of the century Warner included an extensive description and critique of the widespread practice by which municipal (and county) governments provided funds to private orphanages and other charitable institutions, most of which were sponsored by religious bodies. In his critique, Warner explicitly rejected the arguments in favor of public support for private agencies advanced by Everett P. Wheeler.

Warner designed his account of public subsidies to private charitable agencies not in the spirit of impartial research, but as part of his powerful argument against such subsidies. Although his account is very extensive, it is not a complete description of the subsidies that nineteenth and early twentieth-century governments provided to private agencies. In particular, Warner failed to discuss the important role of *county* subsidies, of food and fuel as well as building and operating funds, to orphanages, hospitals, sanitoria, and homes for the elderly.

Warner sought above all to persuade his readers that public funds should not go to private agencies. He asserted that only governments—preferably state governments—were sufficiently powerful and accountable to create comprehensive, effective, fair, efficient, up-to-date services. He made five main arguments against government subsidies to private agencies:

> Because private institutions provide care that the public views as better and more respectable than the care offered by public asylums, irresponsible parents and children are more likely to place their dependents in private institutions. Thus public subsidies "promote pauperism by disguising it."

Because virtually all private institutions are sponsored by religious groups, subsidies to charities are necessarily subsidies to religion, in violation of the First Amendment and of good political sense: moreover, any democratic government that subsidizes one religious agency must subsidize many others, so that the multiplication of agencies and the inefficient duplication of services is the inevitable result. Moreover, a government that provides public subsidies to private charities sets a precedent for public subsidies to private and parochial schools.

Private agencies pull resources from and thus displace efficient, comprehensive public systems of social care.

Because private agencies are sponsored by religious groups, legislators cannot exercise their critical judgement in voting on subsidies. Once established, public subsidies introduce religious issues into politics, create powerful vested interests, and make it difficult to achieve political or programmatic reform.

Public subsidies displace private benevolence; public subsidies allow charitable agencies to become dependent on and deferential to the government officals who control the flow of funds, thus encouraging agency managers to distort programs to maximize subsidy payments.

A New York City lawyer and civic leader who often represented Catholic institutions, Everett P. Wheeler offered a remarkable overview of the role of nonprofit organizations in his city at the beginning of the twentieth century in this article published in the *Atlantic Monthly.*

Wheeler began with a reference to the contemporary movement to reform city governments in the United States. In fact, he pointed out, Americans were already working to solve many problems through the "unofficial governments" of nonprofit organizations. "Private corporations, chartered by the legislature, but receiving no pecuniary aid from the state, do in fact discharge a very considerable and important part of the functions which by charter are devolved upon officials," Wheeler wrote. His examples included the vigilantes who provided private police services (of a fashion) in early San Francisco, as well as the Society for the Prevention of Cruelty to Animals; its successor, the Society for the Prevention of Cruelty to Children; and Anthony Comstock's anti-birth control, anti-abortion Society for the Suppression of Vice.

Wheeler acknowledged in passing that these law enforcement societies did in fact receive public support, in the form of rent-free office space in courthouses. Orphanages, of course, received very significant funds from state and municipal governments. Wheeler's defense of municipal subsidies for such charities was perhaps his strongest motivation for writing this striking essay on nonprofits as a sort of "unofficial government" for American cities.

AMOS G. WARNER

Argument against Public Subsidies to Private Charities

1908

When contributions are hard to get, when fairs and balls no longer net large sums, and when endowments are slow to come, the managers of private charities frequently turn to the public authorities and ask for a contribution from the public revenues. On the other hand, when State legislatures see the annual appropriation bills increasing too rapidly, and when they see existing public institutions made political spoils, and the administration wasteful and inefficient, they are apt to approve of giving a subsidy to some private institution, instead of providing for more public buildings and more public officials.

This problem of granting or of not granting public subsidies to private charitable corporations is analogous to the problem of public *versus* sectarian schools on the one hand, and of governmental control of private business corporations on the other—allied to both but identical with neither. It is related to the school question not only because the care of dependent and delinquent children by sectarian institutions involves their education in the faith of a particular sect, but because there is reason to believe that the subsidizing of sectarian charities has been resorted to with the conscious purpose of evading the laws that forbid public aid to sectarian schools. It is related to the problem of governmental control of private corporations not only by the fact that the legal questions involved are frequently the same, but by the fact that the methods used by eleemosynary corporations to secure public subsidies are often not unlike those used by money-making corporations to secure legislative favors.

The States most largely committed to the subsidy or contract system are shown in Table 1. It is seen from this table that Pennsylvania, New York, California, and the District of Columbia give the largest amounts in subsidies to private charitable institutions. A review of the

---

Excerpts from chapter 17 of Warner's *American Charities* (New York: 1908).

Table 1:
Subsidies to Private Charities, 1901*

States Granting Largest Amounts	State Subsidies Granted	Other State Aid	Local Subsidies Granted	Other Local Aid, Amount Not Reported
Vermont	$54,000		$2,000	Yes
Connecticut	101,750	Yes	24,500	Probably
New York	235,000		3,410,000	
Pennsylvania	6,700,000		153,500	Large
Maryland	96,000		185,000	
District of Columbia	. . .		200,000	
North Carolina	35,000		6,200	
California	410,000		. . .	Probably

*Condensed from Fetter's table, *Am. Jour. of Soc.*, vol. vii., 1901, No. 8, p. 868.

facts regarding State aid in these localities will serve as a basis for the discussion of the advantages and dangers of the system.

On Feb. 2, 1893, while the Senate of the United States was sitting as town council for the city of Washington, a member moved to amend the appropriation bill by inserting a proviso that almshouse initiates or other paupers and destitute persons who might be a charge upon the public should be turned over to any private institution that would contract to provide for them at 10 per cent less than they were then costing the District. Senator Call, who introduced the amendment, explained that it was in lieu of one which had been rejected at the previous session of Congress, whereby he had sought to have $40,000 of public money given to the Little Sisters of the Poor, to enable them to build an addition to their Home for the Aged. He defended the original proposal on the ground that this sisterhood cared for the aged poor better and more cheaply than the almshouse, and that the existence of their institution had saved to the taxpayers of the District in the last twenty years a sum believed to be not less than $300,000. It was not a novel plea; for Congress had already appropriated, since 1874, $55,000 to aid the Home for the Aged of the Little Sisters of the Poor; and each year the District appropriation bill had included subsidies for a large number of private charitable institutions, some of them avowedly under sectarian management. How far the tendency to grant public subsidies to private charities had gone in the District of Columbia is in some sort indicated by Table 2.

From this table it will be seen that the amount given for maintenance to private charitable institutions at the beginning of the period was a little less than one-third of the whole amount, while at the close of the period it is a little less than one-half. The most surprising fact, however, is that the District had given to private institutions nearly twice

Table 2
Public Subsidies to Charities in the District of Columbia
1880-1892

	Number of Institutions		Appropriation for Maintenance		
	1880	1892	1880	1892	Increase
Public	7	8	$78,048.82	$110,475.05	160%
Private	8	28	46,500.00	117,630.00	253%
Totals			$124,548.82	$237,105.50	

	Appropriations 13 Years, 1880-1892		
	Construction	Maintenance	Construction and Maintenance
Public	$155,130.70	$1,296,125.95	$1,351,256.65
Private	300,812.53	840,940.00	1,141,752.53
Totals	$455,943.23	$2,137,065.95	$2,493,009.18

as much money to be used in acquiring real estate and erecting buildings as it had granted to its civil public institutions. Were we to deduct a sum of $66,900 charged to the workhouse, a purely correctional branch of the so-called Washington Asylum, it would appear that more than three-fourths of the money appropriated for permanent improvements in charitable institutions was given to private corporations. . . .

The tendency of public subsidies to increase rapidly—although usually granted in the first place on the ground of economy—and of subsidized charities to multiply at the expense of public institutions, is illustrated by the experience of Pennsylvania. Table 3 shows the appropriations to both classes of institutions for a period of fifty-five years.

Under the Pennsylvania system, subsidies are voted in lump sums for "maintenance" and "buildings," but the buildings when erected do not belong to the State but to private boards on which the State is not represented. Moreover, the amounts given have no relation to the number of persons cared for, nor to the amount of private subscriptions received. Private giving is thus discouraged, and the development of private charities is determined by the subsidies obtainable rather than by the needs of the community. With charitable budgets approaching five million dollars in 1905, Pennsylvania, an old and rich State, was enlarging her accommodations for the insane with cheap, temporary one-story buildings, had no separate provision for epileptics, and no adequate provision for the feeble-minded. This neglect of State dependents is a far greater evil than the political log-rolling and favoritism which inevitably accompany the appropriation of such large sums to private interests.

The best-known and most frequently quoted example of the policy of subsidies to private charities is that of New York City. In 1894, and

Table 3
Appropriations to Public and Private Charities
in Pennsylvania, 1850-1905

Year	Public Charities		Private Charities		All Charities	
	Appropria-tions	No. of Institu-tions	Subsidies	No. of Institu-tions	Total Appro-priations	Total Institu-tions
1850	$69,000	3	$66,000	4	$135,000	7
1855	59,000	4	56,000	5	115,000	9
1860	139,000	4	116,000	6	255,000	10
1865	123,000	4	227,000	26	350,000	30
1870	222.000	5	173,000	10	395,000	15
1875*	413,000	8	275,000	13	688,000	21
1880	458,000	8	171,000	8	629,000	16
1885	650,000	11	378,000	22	1,028,000	33
1890	755,000	9	822,000	52	1,577,000	61
1895	1,097,000	15	1,248,000	95	2,345,000	110
1900	1,430,000	15	1,149,000	129	2,579,000	196
1905	2,336,000	20	2,328,000	176	4,664,000	196

*Boyle, "Fifty Years," etc. (pamphlet), 1905; table reprinted in *Charities*, vol. xii., 1905, p. 561.

again in 1899, the [private, state-chartered] State Charities Aid Association made a thorough analysis of the finances of children's institutions especially, and in 1899 made a number of recommendations regarding the subsidy policy to the Comptroller of the city. In 1894, 23 institutions were receiving $1,625,994 from the city for the care of 15,331 children; that is, they received 69 per cent of the total cost of maintenance in subsidies. In the decade 1885–1894, from 6 to 13 institutions received a total sum of $631,040 in *excess of the cost of maintenance*. Of these, two received in 1894 alone a total grant of more than $250,000 each. In some cases, the care of dependent children might be thus said to have become a profitable business.

The report made to the Comptroller in 1899 includes the information in Table 4.

The adoption of a system of investigation by the Department of Public Charities and of per capita payment had an immediate effect upon the amounts appropriated. In 1903 the amount voted for children's institutions constituted only 52 per cent of the total cost of maintenance. A rule that acceptance by the Department is for one year only has further decreased the number of dependent children; and in spite of rapid increase of population, New York City has now fewer dependent children than it had ten years ago. . . .

Table 4
Subsidies to Institutions in New York City, 1899*

Institutions by Classes	Number	Amount Received
Children's Institutions	51	$1,665,723
Infants' and Foundling Asylums	7	551,050
Maternity Hospitals	12	54,823
Hospitals	60	271,550
Dispensaries	33	37,904
Reformatories for Women	6	40,604
General Relief Societies	22	19,251
Homes for the Aged	15	20,796
Corporate Schools, Mandatory	28	205,000
Institutions for Defective Children	15	206,197
Miscellaneous	33	170,724
All Institutions	282	$3,249,624

*New York State Charities Aid Society, Publication No. 78, 1899, p.5.

California has a system of subsidies for dependent children similar
to that of New York, except that the per capita payments are exclusively
from the State treasury, and there is no official investigation or control
of admissions. The law provides that every institution in the State conducted for the care of orphan, half-orphan, or abandoned children, shall
receive from the State treasury the sum of $100 for each orphan, $5 per
year for each half-orphan or abandoned child under 14. The institution,
in order to qualify for this subsidy, need only have been in operation
one year with 20 inmates. In 1883 foundlings were added to the list at
the rate of $12 per month until 18 months old. As a result of this sys-
tem, the number of dependent children has been increasing since 1890
more than twice as fast as the population of the State (see Table 5). . . .

The growth and persistence of the subsidy system, particularly in
caring for dependent children, is closely connected with the desire of
different churches to control their education in morals and religion. Of
all orphanages and children's homes in the United States, 45 per cent
are under ecclesiastical control, and a considerable percentage of those
nominally non-sectarian are, in fact, strongly under sectarian influence.
That there is no general recognized definition of the word "sectarian" is
noteworthy. There are few institutions that will admit its applicability to
themselves, and there are few to which it is not applied by some one.
Many institutions having no trace of sectarianism in charter, constitution, or by-laws are yet administered in the interests of a sect. A willingness to admit beneficiaries of all denominations is frequently less an
evidence of non-sectarianism than of a tendency to make proselytes.

Table 5
The Subsidy Contract System in California
1900–1907

Six Months Ending	Number of Dependent Children		Amount Paid by State		Total Amount Paid by State Each Half Year
	Asylums	Counties	Asylums	Counties	
June 30, 1900	5494	2185	$178,542.27	$46,276.16	$224,818.43
Dec. 31, 1900	5684	2287	180,713.38	48,492.34	229,205.72
June 30, 1901	5525	2428	181,676.73	53,186.54	234,863.27
Dec. 31, 1901	5397	2435	177,972.10	54,013.06	231,985.16
June 30, 1902	5519	2327	183,224.67	51,097.52	234,322.19
Dec. 31, 1902	5837	2565	185,967.29	60,376.01	246,343.30
June 30, 1903	5883	2410	187,268.78	56,043.04	232,542.34
June 30, 1904	5336	2051	175,157.07	44,861.04	220,018.11
Dec. 31, 1904	5370	2182	166,450.84	50,466.84	216,917.68
June 30, 1905	5215	2238	169,903.69	53,464.82	223,447.49
Dec. 31, 1906	5189	2127	164,438.49	53,777.25	218,215.74
June 30, 1907	5047	2057	161,718.46	52,428.07	214,146.53

Much might be said in favor of the idea that all private institutions are sectarian, when not in a religious then in a medical or social sense. Public aid to a hospital may help to build up a medical school or a school of medicine just as surely as aid to in infant asylum may be used to build up a church, and social rivalries may stimulate people in pushing charities just as much as interdenominational competition.

In States where a constitutional limitation forbids the voting of public money to "sectarian" institutions, members of the Protestant denominations often seek to have this clause so interpreted as to exclude the institutions officered by the Roman Catholic orders, while charitable enterprises in which they are themselves interested are nominally unsectarian. The Catholics not infrequently try to evade the constitutional limitation by disingenuous subterfuges; and the Protestants, with characteristic shortsightedness, encourage such a course by their own eagerness to secure public money for the private institutions in which they are themselves interested.

The fact that there is a clear-cut distinction between public and private charities, but none between sectarian and nonsectarian charities, is one that those who oppose public aid to sectarian schools would do well to recognize. Protestants are willing to tease legislators for public money on behalf of a hospital or an orphan asylum in which they are interested, urging that it is "doing good," and that it is preventing crime and pauperism, and so saving money to the taxpayers. They do not see or will not acknowledge the same could be said of a parochial school, and that the claim which they set up that their own institution is "nonsectarian" is equivocal and unfair, and one which in practice the courts have never been able to make definite.

A tendency could hardly have gone as far as that of granting public subsidies to private charities, unless there were many considerations either apparent or real of great force in its favor. As favoring this policy, the consideration which is first and foremost in the minds of "practical" people is the matter of economy. Especially where the number of dependents in a given class is small, it is cheaper to hire them cared for than to establish an institution for them. This is the reason that in most small towns a private hospital is subsidized instead of one being erected at public expense; but, when we find a great city like Brooklyn depending entirely on subsidized hospitals for the care of its sick poor, this argument is inapplicable. Economy, however, may result from other causes, as when the private institutions are administered by religious orders, the members of which receive no pay except their support. In almost every branch of philanthropic work Roman Catholic institutions can underbid competitors, so to speak, because of the great organizations of teachers and nurses and administrators whose gratuitous services they can command; and if the State is to sublet its relief on the contract system, it is hard to see why those who can bid low should not get the contracts.

In reformatory institutions, those under private management have an economic advantage over those managed by public officials in that the former are able to keep the inmates busy at remunerative employment with less opposition from trade organizations. A public reformatory for girls that should keep its inmates busy with work from a great shirt factory would be sure to be attacked on the ground of its competing with poor sewing women; but such employment in private institutions, even those receiving public subsidies, is quite common. Even in institutions not officered by members of a religious order, the salaries are apt to be lower and all the items of expense to be more closely scrutinized than in a public institution. Add to all this the fact that frequently private contributors aid in the support of a private institution, and we see how great may be its advantage on the side of economy. To the real economies of this method of operation should be added the apparent economies when a private institution is willing to make a very low bid, to make great temporary sacrifices, in order to get the subsidy system introduced—in order to establish connections between itself and the public treasury. "At first," said a United States senator, speaking of the charities of the District of Columbia, "at first they thrust in only the nose of the camel."

Secondly, it is urged that private institutions, especially those for dependent and delinquent children, have a better effect upon the inmates than can public institutions. For one thing, dogmatic religious instruction can be given. For another, the spirit of self-sacrifice that pervades a private institution has a good effect upon the inmates, and is contrasted with the cold and officialized administration of the public institutions. Connected with this, as also with the matter of economy, is the fact that boards of trustees and of lady managers and visitors give freely of their time and energy and sympathy in aid of private undertakings.

Thirdly, it is urged that, by subsidizing private institutions, we free them from the blight of partisan politics and the spoils system. The miserable political jobbery connected with so many almshouses and insane asylums and other public institutions is pointed out, and it seems necessary to shield as many as possible of the state's dependents from similar evils.

A fourth consideration is, that by means of subsidies we aid the poor without attaching to them the stigma of pauperism. A home for the aged is more respectable than an almshouse, and a private protectory or industrial school is supposed not to discredit the inmates as much as a public reform school.

But this consideration brings us to a turning-point, for it is urged against such subsidies as well as in favor of them. It is said that private institutions receiving public money promote pauperism by disguising it. Children who would support aged parents rather than allow them to go to the almshouse desert them promptly when some provision is made for them that is ostensibly more honorable. An illustration is afforded by the case of an abandoned woman who supported her mother for years rather than permit her to go to the poorhouse, but who was trying all the while to get her admitted to a "private" home for the aged. Parents unload their children upon the community more recklessly when they know that such children will be provided for in private orphan asylums or protectories, where the religious training that they prefer will be given them.

And thus we reach the first great objection to granting public subsidies to private charities. While it may be cheaper to provide thus for each dependent during a year, yet the number of dependents increases so rapidly that eventually the charge upon the public is greater than if the alternative policy were pursued. The results are most astounding, where, as in the case of dependent children in California, the managers of each institution are free to admit children and have them charged to the community. When the present law was being debated in the California Senate, it was estimated that the cost could never exceed $30,000 a year, yet since then, according to Professor Frank A. Fetter,

> It has reached nearly a half a million annually, has almost killed any efforts to place the children in family homes, has in a large measure demoralized many families whose children are thus supported, and has noted unfavorably upon the spirit and motive of many of the charitable societies themselves.

In New York City in 1894 there was 1 dependent child to each 117 of the population as compared with 1 to 206 in London, and 1 to 856 in Boston. In 1904, with the modified and greatly improved contract subsidy system, the burden of New York remains far in excess of that of States having other systems. Where public officials alone have the right to commit dependents to the subsidized institutions, a check is put upon reckless admissions. But even under this system there is danger that many will be charged to the public who would never have sought admission to a public institution.

In Illinois the constitution forbids public grants to sectarian institutions; but a law was framed providing that a county court might adjudge a girl to be dependent, commit her to an industrial school, and that school should then be entitled to receive $10 a month for her "tuition, care, and maintenance," besides an allowance for clothing. After the passage of this act the Chicago Industrial School for Girls was incorporated. Of the nine incorporators and directors, seven were officers and managers of the House of the Good Shepherd; and all the girls committed under the act to the Chicago Industrial School for Girls were placed either in the House of the Good Shepherd or in St. Joseph's Orphan Asylum. Questioning as to the legality of such an arrangement brought the matter into court; and during the trial it transpired that about seventy-three girls who were committed to the Chicago Industrial School for Girls by the county court were already in the House of the Good Shepherd and St. Joseph's Orphan Asylum at the time of such commitments. "In other words, being already inmates of the institutions, they were taken to the county court and adjudged to be dependent girls, and at once returned to those institutions, and thereafter the county was charged with $10 per month for tuition for each of them, and $15 or $20 or $25 for clothing for each of them." The courts at first decided that the Chicago Industrial School was a "sectarian" institution, and the payment of the money therefore illegal; but the institution later found a way to evade the constitutional limitations. This is a very good example of the unsubstantial nature of the barrier which such a constitutional limitation forms.

In the second place, the argument from economy, in support of the subsidy system, is negatived by the fact that under this system there must be so many duplicate institutions. In Maryland, for instance, there are two reformatories for boys within a mile of each other, and two for girls, both in Baltimore. Catholics manage one pair of institutions, and private Protestant corporations the other. In Baltimore alone there are thirty orphanages and homes for children under private, generally sectarian, management, two-thirds of which received subsidies in 1903.

Many charitable institutions have been established less from brotherly love than from a quarrel in the board of managers in an older institution. This, together with the influence of individual ambitions, has led especially to the establishment of a great number of medical charities. When the public begins to grant such favors, it is hard to draw a line. As a United States senator once said, in speaking of the situation in the District [of Columbia]:

> The very fact that Congress makes these appropriations has caused, to a great degree, the multiplication of the organizations. A few people getting together who are desirous of doing charitable work, or who have discovered some special need, or who are dissatisfied with some feature of some existing institution, instead of adding to or modifying such an institution, will start a new one, because they can appeal directly to Congress for the money necessary to begin it, and can base their claim on the ground that they are just as good as some other association already on the list.

Again, the subsidy system proves extravagant in that it tends to dry up the sources of private benevolence. Individual contributors dislike to have their mites lost in the abundance of a public appropriation. Almost without exception those institutions that have received public aid the longest and the most constantly receive least from private contributors. In looking up the history of a considerable number of institutions, it was found that, after the public became a contributor, private contributions fell off from year to year, not only relatively but absolutely, and in some cases ceased altogether.

Even where the contract subsidy system exists, it operates to keep the dependent in the institution unnecessarily long, and is therefore uneconomical. In 1894 of 8,000 dependent children about whom the facts were ascertained, 23 per cent had been held as public charges from five to fourteen years. When the placing-out of a child or the discharge of an inmate actually involves the loss of $75 to $110 per year, the managers will naturally hesitate.

It has been pointed out by Professor Fetter that under this system it is impossible to unify and systematize the public charities; hospital appliances will be duplicated, beds will be empty in the public hospitals while private institutions are receiving pay for public patients; and maternity hospitals will be multiplied for the sake of clinical and teaching purposes without reference to the public need.

A third reason for objecting to the subsidies we are considering is, that when voting upon them the legislator must resist special pressure. He has not a clear-cut issue of a given service to be rendered, balanced by a given expenditure, but it becomes partly a question of offending or favoring some sect or nationality. The contention that the subsidy system takes the charitable institutions out of politics is not supported by experience. On the contrary, it drags them into politics in a new and unfortunate way—in a way that is found in practice to give great scope to logrolling and kindred expedients. Some who will not do anything else for a charitable institution are willing to bully a legislator on its behalf. Most of the lobbyists are sincere even to fanaticism, but their view of the situation is terribly one-sided. It had come to pass that when the District of Columbia appropriation bill was under consideration, and in the haste of the last days of the session, the Congressional committee rooms would be full of the representatives of the various charities, both men and women, intent upon getting the largest share possible. There was neither time, nor ability, nor opportunity on the part of the committee to come to any intelligent conclusion. Often those applicants most skilled or most personally attractive were most successful, and sometimes the committees were obliged to average their gifts. After such a policy has been entered upon, it cannot be altered without injury to great vested interests, and without giving offense to large and powerful constituencies.

One of the most unfortunate results of subsidizing private charities is that the patrons and friends of those charities are set in opposition to general measures of social reform. Professor Fetter quotes the well-known fact that the establishment of State Boards of Charities has been almost invariably opposed by subsidized charities. In California, during more than a decade of agitation which was required to establish a State Board of Charities, it was opposed by the subsidized orphan asylums for fear their subsidies might be curtailed. Moreover, under the subsidy system the trustees and friends of these institutions must beg favors from political leaders. In Pennsylvania this fund has become a great corruption fund and the philanthropy which shares in the spoils must necessarily be silent.

This brings us to a fifth reason for objecting to the granting of public subsidies to private charities. It frequently does positive harm to a charitable institution, and sometimes wholly destroys its usefulness. A private institution that receives no public money is not only freer in all its operations, and more highly valued by those who sustain and manage it, but its beneficiaries feel differently toward their benefactors. When visiting one subsidized institution the request was made that nothing should be said before the inmates that would inform them that the institution received any public money. One could understand the wish, and presume that the inmates would work more faithfully, be more grateful for favors received, and finally "turn out better," because they were kept in ignorance of the fact. Yet we may doubt the possibility or propriety of thus using public money, and at the same time, trying to conceal the fact of doing so. By no hocus-pocus of subsidy-granting can we make taxation do the work of self-sacrifice.

In most instances States and municipalities have entered upon this policy of subsidizing private charities without deciding to do so, and even without perceiving that a decision was called for. Each request for a subsidy has been treated as a matter of administrative detail, involving no principle, and not significant as a precedent. The resultant system is about as businesslike as though a city should try to get its streets paved by announcing that any regularly incorporated association that should have a given number of square yards of street—location, time, and method to he decided by itself—should receive a given amount from the public treasury. It is as though private associations were allowed to do paving at their own discretion, and then, on coming to the legislature and teasing with sufficient skill and pertinacity, they should be given subsidies on the general theory that they were "doing good" and rendering "public service."

In its old form of payments in gross amounts, the subsidy system must and will be abolished; and even the contract subsidy system at its best must be carefully regulated. First, on behalf of the poor as well as the taxpayers, the government must provide for the thorough inspection of subsidized institutions, and the systematic auditing of their accounts. This work cannot be done by grand juries, or legislative committees, or *ex-officio* inspectors, who may from time to time thrust their inexperienced noses into matters which they know nothing about. The work of inspection must be done by some thoroughly experienced and otherwise suitable administrative officer, who is definitely responsible for the thoroughness of his work. Second, the State must keep in the hands of its own officials the right of deciding what persons shall be admitted to the benefits for which it pays, and how long each person may continue to receive those benefits. If it pays for beds in its hospital, one of its own officials should have entire control of admitting and discharging the patients cared for. This is necessary in order that "there may be some gauge of indigency, and some assurance that the gauge will be used." Third, subsidies should only be granted on the principle of specific payment for specific work. When any one of these three conditions is lacking, the policy of subsidy-granting is necessarily pernicious.

The opinion of nearly all charity experts is unanimously against it; Professor Fetter, after a thorough discussion of the results in the States which have employed it for a period of years, concluded:

The logic of the situation demands the abolition of the policy of charity subsidies. It is a medieval device. Formerly the line between the action of the state and that of private and ecclesiastical corporations was dim. Public functions were exercised by many guilds, societies, and church corporations, but the modern State has gradually overtaken these functions. As a matter of expediency there is abundant reason to carry this change to its logical end in the complete separation of public taxation from private, charity. . . . The subsidy method is not a policy, it is an accident. The strongest argument in its favor are merely negative—that it should be kept because we have it. . . . Nowhere is there any effective sentiment favorable to the extension of subsidies . . . in fact, the advocates of subsidies are entirely on the defensive. Within the last few years they have distinctly lost ground in the older States.

All that can be said against subsidies in general can be said against this form of subsidies, and more: because here we have to deal with religious, medical, and social sectarianism, and because we are giving over the defenseless to the care of the irresponsible. As a transition policy for growing communities, or for new and developing varieties of benevolent work, it may possibly have had its place; but it should not now be entered upon inadvertently, for while all its advantages and economics are greatest at the beginning, its disadvantages and dangers constantly increase as time goes on. Those who would entirely avoid establishing any precedent whatever for the voting of public money to private schools can take properly but one course, a consistent opposition to any and all public subsidies to private charities.

EVERETT P. WHEELER

The Unofficial Government of Cities

1900

There is probably no subject to which, during the last few years, the attention of the public-spirited Americans has been more carefully directed than that of municipal government. It is admitted that the government of great cities in the United States is in many respects un-

Everett P. Wheeler, "The Unofficial Government of Cities," *Atlantic Monthly* 86 (1900), pp. 370–76.

satisfactory. This result is attributed partly to the defective machinery provided by law, and partly to defects in administration. The real cause of the evils which all deplore appears to be this; The American people with their characteristic conservatism, have adhered to forms of government which were suited well enough to the conditions existing seventy-five years ago. Then our population was more homogeneous, the distinction between rich and poor less marked, the relations of the different members of society were more intimate; and consequently, individual citizens were able to, and did in fact, cooperate more effectively to administer the government of cities as they had done that of their towns. Moreover, many subjects, which have since come to be recognized as a proper or even necessary part of municipal administration, were then left entirely to individual direction and control; so that organizations which were suited well enough to the simpler requirements of the social conditions of that time might well have proved inadequate to the more difficult task which is now required of city governments, even if the other obstacles alluded to had not multiplied.

It is no part of my purpose to underrate the evils to which I have referred, but I desire to point out some of the ways in which they have been mitigated or obviated altogether.

One of the characteristics of the Anglo-Saxon race is its indisposition to consider theoretical objections, and its willingness to adopt methods which for the time being are convenient and adequate, even though they may be subject to many such objections. In no respect is this more manifest than in the means which have been adopted for dealing with these admitted evils of municipal administration. Individual citizens, without sharing in the official administration of the city government or holding offices mentioned in its charter, in many cases discharge duties which are now recognized as being incumbent upon any intelligent government of a great civilized city; and that, too, in cases relating both to criminal and to civil administration. Very little attention, apparently, has been paid to this amelioration of conditions which has been produced by the voluntary action of public-spirited citizens. Experience shows that when a person lose his sight his sense of touch becomes more delicate; if he loses a hand, the other hand becomes more dexterous, and supplies, as far as may be, the deficiency. In like manner, individuals have stepped in and performed voluntarily the duties that, theoretically and in the ideal city, would be performed by the officials of the local government.

It would seem that nothing could be more distinctively the function of public officials than the enforcement of the laws. This duty is devolved by the charter of all cities upon certain officers mentioned therein. Yet in practice, private corporations, chartered by the legislature, but receiving no pecuniary aid from the state, do in fact discharge a very considerable and important part of the functions which by charter are devolved upon officials. Among the oldest and the most notable instances are the Societies for the Prevention of Cruelty to Animals, which are to be found in all our important cities. The New York association was incorporated in 1866, "to enforce all laws which then were or might thereafter be enacted for the protection of animals, and to secure by lawful means the arrest and conviction of all persons found violating such laws." This parent society (which is indeed designated as the "American Society for the Prevention of Cruelty to Animals") has authority, under its charter, "to provide effective means for the prevention of cruelty to animals throughout the United States." But in practice, as stated in its last report, the organization and influence of the American society soon led to the establishment of local societies in all parts of the union, and in other countries on the American continent and elsewhere. The number of local societies incorporated in the United States is now 209, and in other American nations eleven societies have been established and incorporated since 1866, making a total of 220. To quote again from its last report:

> The officers of the society are clothed with ample police powers. They wear a distinctive uniform, and patrol the street by day and by night. They have full power to arrest and prosecute offenders against the laws relating to animals. In addition to the uniformed-police, the society has nearly two hundred special agents in different parts of the state, clothed with the same authority, and engaged in enforcing the laws for the prevention of cruelty. In the boroughs of Manhattan and Brooklyn, the society has ambulances for the removal of injured, sick, and disabled animals; appliances for the rescue of drowning animals and animals which have fallen into excavations; and a patrol wagon which carries with it the necessary apparatus and medicines for rendering aid to injured animals in the streets.

Yet this society, which thus aids essentially in the performance of some of the recognized functions of municipal government, "receives no appropriations from the city or state, and is dependent upon voluntary donations and bequests."

A similar Society for the Prevention of Cruelty to Children was incorporated in 1875. A Society for the Prevention of Vice has since been incorporated in New York, which is charged with the enforcement of other laws of the state which, theoretically, should be enforced by the district attorney and his subordinates, and by the police.

Indeed, to such an extent are these societies recognized as an unofficial but actual part of the city goverrment that in the Criminal Court House one of them has an office, in which an officer, employed by it, is regularly stationed, who has come to be considered as really a part of the municipal organization.

On the civil side of municipal administration, a still more notable development of this unofficial government is to be noted. This is more marked in some cities than in others. For example, in the city of New York, the entire duty of providing public circulating libraries is performed by private corporations, chartered under state laws for that purpose. These are under the supervision of the regents of the university, and receive aid from the city, pursuant to a general law of the state. But their officers are not selected by the city authorities. In Boston, however, the Public Library is managed by the municipal authorities. In Washington the Library is under the control of Congress. It would be unreasonable to say that either method is practically better than the other.

One great fault of constitution and charter makers is to assume that a method which is advantageous in one locality is necessarily the best for another. It might as well be said that because a suit of clothes fits one man, it must therefore fit every other. This Procrustean method of compelling the sleeper to fit the bed was laughed at long ago by the Greeks, and ought to be the subject of ridicule in every intelligent community.

The New York system has two distinct advantages. In the first place, it tends to encourage private liberality. The entire plant of the public libraries in that city, including the buildings which they occupy and most of the books which they use, has been furnished without expense to the city, by private benefactions.

Again, in a polyglot city like New York or Chicago, the tendency of the foreigners who come there is to form colonies in particular localities. In New York City, for example, the Italians are mostly in one quarter, the Bohemians in another, the Chinese in another, the colored people in still another. In Buffalo the Poles occupy a separate district. Each neighborhood has its distinctive requirements, and intelligent librarians in each district, administering a library founded for the requirements of that locality, are far more likely to meet the special needs of that neighborhood than public functionaries appointed by a central authority, necessarily chosen under general rules and without adequate attention to individual needs.

The provision of museums of art and natural history, zoology and similar subjects has also come to be recognized as an appropriate function of a city. Such museums exist in many large cities, and are supported to a great degree at public expense. Yet experience in this country has shown that these museums are more intelligently conducted by private corporations chartered by the legislature, and under the management of public-spirited and art-loving citizens, than they would be if directed by committees of the board of aldermen. The truth is (and no intelligent reforms can be accomplished in municipal government without the recognition of this truth) that the official government of our large cities is democratic, founded upon universal suffrage. Each voter likes to feel that there is somebody in the city government who represents him. This is the reason why the democracy has clung so persistently to the district system of electing members of one branch, at least, of the city council. The alderman is alderman of the district. He represents his constituents, not merely in his functions as a member of a municipal legislature, but in all his relations with the constituted authorities. It is very well that it should be so, and that voters should feel that there is some official personage to whom they can directly appeal, and who does distinctly represent the people of his district.

It is equally natural that these voters should elect a representative of their own kind. The fact that a man is very much wiser and better educated than the majority in his district is rather a disqualification for this kind of representation. On the other hand, the voters are intelligent enough to know that the representative they elect for their particular district is not necessarily qualified to discharge all the duties that might theoretically be intrusted to the municipal legislature. To devolve general legislative functions upon a municipal council elected on the district system is one of the absurdities of theoretical charter-makers, and a blunder into which no one should fall who had studied the subject of municipal government intelligently and practically, and is not misled by the ordinary vice of charter-makers, who want to turn out a pretty piece of work, all shining with the last gloss of the most recent theory.

Another very important function of municipal government is the administration of public charities. In all cities there are hospitals and asylums which are supported at the expense of the public, and managed by officials who are either elected by the people or appointed by those who are so elected. It must be said that in the administration of these charities something is lacking of that personal tenderness and thoughtful care which ought, if possible, to attend ministrations to the sick, to the insane, and especially to young children. The mortality among infants in public institutions in the city of New York, for example, is certainly greater than it is in the best private institutions. How this may be in other cities I have no means of knowing. But it is almost inevitable that the causes which have produced these results in one city should, to some extent at least, produce similar results in others.

These deficiencies in public charities are to a large degree supplied by private institutions. Any one who is at all familiar with the feeling of the plain people must be aware that, as a rule, they are more willing to be sent, in case of sickness, to a hospital managed by a private corporation than to one managed by the public. Yet a vigorous agitation to abolish all public aid to private charities has been lately set on foot by many well-meaning citizens, who, it seems to me, look at the subject too exclusively from a theoretical standpoint. On the other hand, as the super-

visor of Catholic charities in New York has very well put that side of the
question, the "private" institutions give the use of their grounds, buildings, and equipments to the public without charge, and in addition do
the work cheaper than it could be done in public institutions. Mr.
Kinkead then takes as an instance the work of the New York Foundling
Asylum, and puts the case for this institution so clearly that it is worth
quoting as an admirable illustration of the point under consideration:

> The public wards of this institution are paid for by the city
> only while they are in the institution or being nursed at its expense.
> At the age of three or four years, or even younger, these children
> are placed in good permanent family homes, where for at least
> twelve or fifteen years longer they are under the supervision of the
> institution; and the institution receives no compensation for this
> long after-care. It costs an average of $1000 for each group of about
> fifty children sent to homes in the West, and for the supervision of
> those already placed. Several of these trips are made during the
> year, yet the institution is not reimbursed for its outlay. Thus the
> city has been relieved, during thirty years, of the care and mainte-
> nance of thousands of children for whom it could not have pro-
> vided in the same manner without maintaining a force of officials
> at great expense in other states,—a thing evidently impracticable.

The argument against the continuance of this unofficial system is
based largely upon abuses that have grown up in its administration.
These abuses do undoubtedly exist, and ought to be prevented. No private institution should claim exemption from the most rigorous public
inspection. Its accounts and its management should at all times be open
to the examination of the public authorities. Because it is an unofficial
part of the government of the city, it should not therefore claim to be
free from public control. But such control is equally necessary for public
institutions, in which similar and even greater abuses have frequently
been discovered. It is trite to say that the possibility of abuse is no argument against the existence of a system. The question always for the
lawmaker to determine is, not whether abuse is possible, but whether,
on the whole, under existing conditions, one system is more likely to
produce satisfactory results than the other. It is quite possible that, in
the future development of municipal government, some of the functions that are now discharged by unofficial agencies may be performed
by public officials; and this change will come when the public is ready
for it, and when the administration of the municipality so improves that
the change will be desirable. For example, it is not more than twenty-
years since many residents of the city of New York paid private persons
to clean the streets in front of their houses more frequently and more
efficiently than the city was prepared to do it, and employed a private

watchman to patrol the street in which they lived, because patrol duty was not done efficiently by the public police. So great an improvement has taken place in the management of the streetcleaning department and of the police department that these private agencies have gone out of use.

There is another branch of the unofficial government of the cities that deserves consideration, but which has had an entirely different origin from those already referred to. In all large cities, political leaders, holding no municipal office, perform a very important part in the selection by the public officials of their subordinates. These leaders very frequently determine that one proposed public improvement shall be undertaken, and another postponed or rejected. It is to them, as well as to the public officials that persons having dealings with the city government go in order to get business done to their satisfaction. A great deal of invective has been bestowed on these "bosses," as they are commonly called, and certainly there is no occasion to enter upon a defense of their acts. Yet candor compels the admission that in some cases these political leaders give very intelligent directions, which are distinctly beneficial to the public, and that in many respects public business is better done through their influence than it would be without it. The great point on which good citizens should insist is, that these political leaders should perform their functions with more regard to the public interest. The machinery of party government, from which municipalities have not yet been freed, gives to citizens some opportunity of punishing the selfish actions of political leaders, and of securing for legitimate public uses at least the larger part of the money raised by public taxation. But the indiscriminate abuse of political leaders tends to dishearten the average man, and to quench his purpose to better the administration of the city in which he lives. It is in the public interest to give even the devil his due, and to perceive that during one campaign a political leader may be sincere in his expressed desire to elect honest and capable candidates, even though at another election his influence has been thrown in the opposite scale.

The wise reformer should be an opportunist. He should "sow beside all waters," and "mitigate where he cannot cure."

The explanation of the facts to which attention has thus been drawn is this; in large cities the function of a pure democracy has been indeed to give to the humblest citizen a right to vote, and by means of his vote to protect, according to his choice, his personal liberty and individual rights. But these democracies, as yet, have not proved themselves equal to the task of administering, even to their own satisfaction, the complicated functions of municipal goverment. It is by the consent of the people, their chosen representatives, that all the associations before referred to have been incorporated, for the discharge of functions which might very well been performed by public officers elected or appointed for that specific purpose, had these proved adequate to the task. These associations have actually become a part of the *de facto* government of our cities. They constitute an essential part of it. Functions recognized by all thinking men as essential to the completeness of municipal government are performed solely by them. It is of great importance that the actual situation should be appreciated, and that these associations should realize the responsibility of their position, and should be satisfied with the duties they perform, though unsalaried and noncompensated in any way out of the public treasury, are just as necessary a part of the administration of the city and of the state as if they were specified in the charter and paid by the public.

It is interesting to notice that, centuries ago, the same conditions, in wealthy and prosperous cities, produced the same results. The free cities of Italy, during the Middle Ages, while their government continued democratic, were the abodes of wealth, the homes of literature and art, the centers of thriving commerce and manufactures. Their organization was as complicated as ours, and their democratic governments proved as inadequate as ours to discharge all the complex municipal functions that were devolved upon them. To use the language of Armstrong in the *Life of Lorenzo de' Medici:*

> As the function of government became more extensive, its constitutional forms proved inadequate. The predominant feature was the fear of a strong executive, the elimination or emasculation of ability by division of authority, by rapid rotation in office, by an intricate tangle of checks and councils, by the substitution of lot for selection, by the denial of military power. Thus it was that when vigor and experience, secrecy and rapidity, were needed, they must be sought outside the official government. This is the secret of all Florentine history until the republic became a principality. This, therefore, was the secret of that unofficial organization the "Parte Guelfa," which, when the conflict with the Ghibellines was closed, still continued to control the state, possessing large independent resources and a highly organized executive.
>
> For a time the Guelph party was so powerful in the affairs of the city that it may almost be said to have exercised an *imperium in imperio*. They have their own captains, who were the mouthpiece and the executor of the party. . . . As their power increased, the pride of party leaders waxed apace, and their insolence toward the reminder of the citizens became almost intolerable. They were feared more than the signoria, and the decisions of their court appear to have been more respected than those of any other body of men in the Commonwealth. . . . The party was composed largely of the ancient nobility, who in this guise continued for a long period to be among the leaders of the city.

No doubt the condition thus described by the historian was largely due to the party feuds in these mediaeval republics, which were even more fierce than those which prevail in modern cities. These feuds exercised an important and sometimes a disastrous influence upon the administration of the government. Their parties were organized as thoroughly as our own. The description which Hallam gave of the condition of Milan was true of other cities, and is equally true, in substance though not in form, of New York and Chicago:

> Milan had for a considerable time been agitated by civil dissensions between the nobility and inferior citizens. These parties were pretty equally balanced, and their success was consequently alternate. Each had its own podesta, as a party leader, distinct from the legitimate magistrate of the city.

The American word "boss" is a very good vernacular translation of the Italian word ["podesta"] mentioned by Hallam. The existing facts in municipal history, when compared with the past, show plainly enough that history repeats itself, and that the same conditions in human life and character produce similar results in successive epochs.

The Anglo-Saxon race has usually been indifferent to the logical construction of its government, provided its practical results were satisfactory or even tolerable, and has consistently utilized legal forms for purposes very different from those for which they were originally intended. We need not be apprehensive that these ancillary associations upon which so many important duties have been devolved by law will be deprived of power, if they use it well. Notwithstanding all the imperfections in the government of American cities, we may rationally hope that if public spirit continues to be vigorous enough to maintain these various associations in active life, and they use fearlessly and well the powers given them by their charters, the aggregate result of municipal administration will become more and more satisfactory. The development may be slow and uneven, but it will be continuous.

32

David Rosner, *Business at the Bedside: Health Care in Brooklyn, 1890–1915,* 1979

Whatever their field, nearly all nineteenth-century nonprofits remained small, even domestic in scale. Large size came with the twentieth century. In this classic essay, historian David Rosner explains why hospitals grew large after about 1890. He also explains why hospital care came to be offered in different ways *within* the hospital, according to each patient's ability to pay.

DAVID ROSNER

Business at the Bedside

HEALTH CARE IN BROOKLYN, 1890–1915

1979

Most of us recognize that patients are assigned space in the hospital in accordance with special medical needs. But it is also true that patients are assigned beds according to ability to pay, insurance coverage, and source of referral. Private and semiprivate rooms and small wards are as much a characteristic of contemporary hospitals as are the medical, surgical, and specialty services.

The separation of patients according to economic class and other social factors has a long history. In nineteenth-century America, for instance, wealthier clients generally received care at home or in private doctors' offices; working-class and indigent patients often received care

From Susan Reverby and David Rosner, eds., *Health Care in America: Essays in Social History* (Philadelphia: Temple University Press, 1979), pp. 117–31. Reprinted by permission of the author and Temple University Press.

through the out-patient department of hospitals, local dispensaries, workers' associations (lodges), or the charity hospital. While distinctions in service for the rich and the poor have always existed in the American health system as a whole, the incorporation of differing services within the hospital is a relatively recent phenomenon.

Before the turn of the century most non-municipal institutions were charitable in nature and served a primarily working-class population. In that sense, the nineteenth-century hospital was a "one-class" facility. While separate institutions existed for women, blacks, and distinct immigrant groups, internally they were organized in a relatively uniform way. Patients were housed in wards with few distinctions based upon the patient's ability to pay. Services were provided at the expense of philanthropists and hospital trustees. As Morris Vogel has illustrated, the nineteenth-century facility served primarily social, rather than medical needs for working class and/or destitute persons. By the early 1900s a change occurred in the organization of hospital services in charity institutions. During that period the more modern voluntary hospital system arose. This development entailed a dramatic reorganization of the physical space and administrative hierarchy of the hospital. First, the development of class-specific services was a prominent feature of the physical restructuring of the facilities. As trustees sought private patients and their fees, private and semi-private rooms and wards began to displace public and charity wards. Second, as trustees sought to make their institutions more amenable to paying patients, private physicians were admitted to the institutions in the hope that they would bring their patients with them. Ironically, the authority of lay trustees declined as physicians began to exert greater control over the day-to-day services provided their private patients. Third, the care of the charity patient, originally the function of these facilities, was increasingly seen as an inconvenience. In New York the municipal and later the state governments were called upon to bear a larger portion of the financial responsibilities for poor patients in voluntary institutions. This [essay] will examine some of the economic pressures that forced trustees in Brooklyn's Progressive Era hospitals to abandon their older, traditional functions as stewards to the poor and to allow their facilities to undergo profound, and at times disruptive, change.

The decline in the charity functions of philanthropic institutions resulted in part from the severe economic crisis that affected many facilities in the wake of the depression of the 1890s. This depression hit Brooklyn's institutions during a period when costs for health care were rapidly rising. In general, institutions in need of money turned to the paying patient as the most likely source. The provision of hospital care ceased to be an act of charity and became a commodity to be bought and sold by those who could afford it.

The move away from charity to pay services was rationalized as part of the larger Progressive Era movements toward order, efficiency, and bureaucracy. However, the hospitals of the period also exemplify changes that do not fit neatly into any historiographical package. The application of business principles to charity hospitals had a different result: other reform movements led to greater emphasis on corporate responsibility, while changes in hospital finance placed the burden on individuals.

I

In the early years of the twentieth century a prominent Brooklyn businessman, Abraham Abraham, became deeply involved in the formation of the Jewish Hospital of Brooklyn. This hospital, Abraham stated, would avoid some of the chronic problems that plagued many of the city's charitable institutions; it would be so organized that it would "not run in debt." Abraham, owner of Abraham and Straus, the city's largest department store, noted that a hospital was not very different from other large enterprises. He believed that "charitable institutions, however laudable and worthy, should be conducted on sound business principles."

Abraham's concern for the development of "business principles" in charity institutions was spurred by a mounting crisis in hospital financing. During the depression years of the 1890s, many of Brooklyn's charity institutions had found their costs rising at the very time that their incomes from philanthropy were shrinking. As economic conditions worsened, working-class patients increasingly demanded hospital service. Ever larger numbers of patients found themselves in need of the traditional services that hospitals provided—shelter and food. As demand increased, so too did the costs of running the facilities. At Brooklyn Hospital, for instance, hospital utilization nearly doubled during the depression years, growing from just over 1,200 patients in 1895 to nearly 2,300 by 1899. At Brooklyn Maternity Hospital the secretary noted a similar dramatic increase. "When the necessity for relief [is great], the greater will the demand be upon all charitable institutions for that relief." Others noted that the "times have been hard . . . but it is hard to turn away appeals for aid [from patients]." Even in relatively good times, the use of the hospital by those who needed non-medical services and aid was common. "The coming of Spring always brings remarkable recoveries to some of our most stubborn cases," sarcastically noted one hospital surgeon.

At the very time that patient demand was rising, hospital trustees were faced with another challenge to the financial security of their institutions: costs for medical supplies were growing. As bacteriological practices began to be felt in terms of higher standards of general cleanliness, sterile surroundings, and aseptic surgery, a slow growth in costs for medical supplies and maintenance resulted. During the period, for instance, the use of rubber gloves, sterile bandages, supplies, and equipment became a standard part of hospital expense. At Brooklyn Hospital the average cost for a day of care rose from $.89 in 1890 to $2.78 by 1915.

These two factors, rising patient demand and increasing costs for medical supplies, had a significant impact upon many hospitals. But the ultimate crisis in finance was a result of the fact that philanthropists could no longer make donations large enough to rescue the hospitals from their plight. In the earlier years of the nineteenth century philanthropists could be counted on to cover deficits that were chronic features in most nineteenth-century charity facilities. Many hospitals, in fact, used small but manageable deficits as part of their appeals for funds. A deficit was seen as an indication of the worth of the institution, just as modest want was seen as proof of the worthiness of one of the hospital's inmates. Philanthropists were more willing to give to an institution that had a small end-of-the-year deficit.

The depression forced philanthropists to reassess this long-standing practice. Hospital deficits were now growing larger every year. Furthermore, the trustees and philanthropists themselves were feeling the pinch of this long and severe depression. They were less willing and able to part with their money than they had been in the past.

In sum, charity was proving an inadequate means of supporting the hospitals. Trustees and managers alike remarked that there was a "tendency of charitable bequests to diminish" and that this was "a matter of great concern." One trustee noted that when the "Financial depression struck this land, we were obliged to struggle on as best as we could." The president of Brooklyn Hospital reported in 1895 that the hospital's financial condition was poor. "On the financial side," he remarked, "we have not been able to meet our expenses." The president of one of Brooklyn's oldest specialty facilities summed up the crisis that plagued many institutions during the depression years: "Not only are the demands upon the hospital greater and the expenses consistently increasing, but the sources of revenue from individual subscription are diminishing."

The economic crunch that hit Brooklyn's hospitals served as a warning to the trustees of some institutions and as a death blow to others. During the 1890s, for instance, no fewer than five of Brooklyn's largest hospitals closed their doors. One trustee noted that Memorial Hospital "had an uphill and hopeless struggle. . . . Disaster after disaster overtook them until burdened with debt, [it] . . . had to succumb." When the Williamsburg Hospital in a large working-class neighborhood closed in the early 1900s, the trustees were deeply in debt and could not gather the necessary funds. Homeopathic Hospital struggled through the depression and was taken over by the city, $70,000 in debt. By 1899 one of the prominent hospitals reported that it owed $27,000 to various banks and that a substantial portion of its endowment had been spent.

By the early years of the twentieth century, the general crisis in hospital finance had become so widely recognized that a "Conference on Hospital Needs and Hospital Finances" was called for by administrators and the Charity Organization Society. In the announcement for the meeting the sponsors noted that "heavy annual deficits are the rule rather than the exception" in most of the city's hospitals.

In New York and Brooklyn alike, trustees and superintendents recognized that the charity system was breaking down. A few wealthy benefactors and local annual subscription drives were an inadequate means of financing the city's private institutions. Hospital administrators and trustees were faced with the necessity of finding alternative sources of financial support. As Mr. Abraham pointed out in his own inimitable way, "in reading over the reports of [Brooklyn's] charitable (institutions) they all ring . . . the one 'leit motif' and the one refrain: appeal upon appeal to the public to help pay off large mortgages and other indebtedness." A new means of financing charitable institutions was clearly needed. During the early 1900s, in the wake of a severe depression, trustees in many facilities began to look toward pay patients as a new source of income and as a means of forestalling the collapse of their facilities.

II

The traditional financial bases of most Brooklyn hospitals had been the benevolence of wealthy trustees, patrons, churchgoers, and other private individuals. They participated in hospital work for many reasons: partly from a sense of noblesse oblige, in order to gain or maintain recognition as community leaders, or because of their interest in social control and cultural hegemony. The objects of their benevolence had uniformly been the poor and working class of the city.

But by the early 1900s it was clear that there were good economic reasons for reluctant trustees to abandon their uniform objective of servicing the poor. Scientific medicine was changing the character of the old charity facilities, wealthier patients seemed ready to utilize the hospital, and poorer persons were a severe drain on the resources of many facilities. Hospital income could be increased significantly if, first, patients could be convinced to pay for their care and, second, if a greater number of wealthier clients could be attracted to the facility.

Most trustees still maintained that charity was the proper justification for the hospital. But, increasingly, "free" or "charity" patients were seen as a growing burden to financially pressed trustees.

Some trustees felt that the number of poor persons admitted should be limited, while others felt that more extreme measures were necessary. Some actually refused care to those who could not pay. Especially during the depression, trustees learned that limiting the number of working-class patients who needed "free" care was the only means open to them to cut costs. "Early last winter, it became apparent that something must be done to procure immediate pecuniary relief," one hospital president remarked. "A cruel fact stated us in the face. . . . We had been rolling up a debt. . . . After careful study, our advisors decided that . . . we should limit the number of inmates." At a small Williamsburg facility, trustees reluctantly observed that there was a "limit to our resources."

During bad times it was clear that no facility could not accommodate everyone. But this practice of excluding poorer patients was carried on past the immediate depression years and became an axiom of hospital administration during the early twentieth century. At the Brooklyn hospital, for instance, the trustees began to see the paying patient as an important source of income and the free patient as all increasingly expendable burden. "Further space in the wards must be prepared for the [pay] service if we wish to further increase our income from this source," the vice-president of the board of trustees declared in 1899. By 1902 the trustee "decided to shut out part of the charity patients [in order to] keep expenditures down." The hospital, the president remarked, had previously "attempted to do more charity work than it could afford." In 1892 only 12 percent of this hospital's income came directly from the patient. By 1905 nearly 45 percent was derived from patient payments.

Although changes in hospital organization and administration had begun earlier in the nineteenth century, the depression of the 1890s greatly accelerated them. Specifically, the deficits made the businessman's cry for efficiency, bureaucracy, and business practices more convincing to hospital boards. The deficits also undermined the charity orientation of many trustees. Furthermore, the crisis led to the hospitals' new dependence on physicians who claimed they could supply them with a new class of patients who could *pay* for care. This meant that new amenities and services would have to be provided in order to attract doctors and their patients. Advanced technology services that were of interest to practitioners were introduced. Private rooms, wards, doctoring, and nursing had to be provided for wealthier clients. In quick succession hospital boards voted to expand their visiting and attending staffs. Brooklyn Hospital increased the number of associated physicians from fewer than a dozen in 1890 to nearly sixty by 1915. At Methodist the number rose from about fifteen to fifty-five during the same period."

The introduction of private physicians into the charity hospital had a profound and longlasting effect on the organization of these facilities. First, trustees had traditionally seen the hospital as their private responsibility and the arrival of large numbers of physicians meant a new challenge to their authority as benefactors and stewards to the poor. Second, the physicians had a substantial impact on the underlying purpose of these institutions. Hospitals became more clearly defined as places for medical treatment rather than shelters for the poor and homeless.

While doctors changed the tone of the wards, businessmen on the boards changed the tenor of board meetings. Like Abraham Abraham at the Jewish Hospital, businessmen gained a new importance at other institutions as well. The president of the board at the small Bushwick Hospital announced that H. C. Bohack, who had recently opened a chain of food stores, had joined the board. As the president saw it, "the business interests of the hospital could not more effectively be safeguarded" than by directly involving such men. At Brooklyn Hospital, Charles Pratt became president of the board. Pratt, whose family had founded the oil refineries in Greenpoint and who managed John D. Rockefeller's East Coast refineries, made substantial changes at this institution as well.

The direct effects of the involvement of all of these individuals was ambiguous. But they certainly did bring a business point of view to challenge the norms of the hospital boards. Managers and trustees, who ascribed to older paternalist ideologies, found themselves hard put to defend their roles as financial stewards when they themselves had no solution to the chronic financial crises. Older ideals began to be played down and newer business ones placed in their stead. Some trustees were often put in a quandary, denying that the facility had changed into a business. The president of one hospital cried out that his facility was "a work of mercy . . . not a business." Another declared in 1907 that "we are not in hospital work to make money."

At the end of the Progressive Era one prominent surgeon commented on a paper about a Brooklyn hospital published in the *Bulletin of the Taylor Society,* the society dedicated to scientific management. The paper sought to apply principles of scientific management to the organization of the hospital. In commenting on the paper, Ernest Codman, a Boston surgeon concerned with the rationalization of the hospital, observed that "charitable hospitals have become businesses and are . . . wolves in sheep's clothing." Clearly the older charitable impetus for hospital work was waning as the financial crunch hit many facilities.

Charity clients were a burden. As one trustee pointed out, "Additional income must be had, and that can come only from pay patients."

III

The turn away from charity affected the working-class patients in two ways. First, trustees sometimes converted "free" wards into pay wards or rooms. This took away space previously available for indigent patients. Second, trustees more often began to charge working-class patients for services that were previously provided free. Different levels of services were devised for those willing to pay. Also, existing ethnic and other social distinctions functioned to convince those who would afford it not to use a "lower grade" of service. This divided different working-class groups into separate quarters and perpetuated existing divisions within this class. Moreover, the poorest of the patients, those unable to pay anything for their care, were increasingly seen as the *source* of the financial problems of the hospital rather than the *victims* of the crisis in hospital finance. The "fruitful cause for the annual deficiency in the hospitals," remarked one hospital manager in New York, "is the large number of free patients." If the former objects of charity did not pay for their care, then they were now defined as the problem. "If hospital patients had more honor and pride, I do not think there would be any large deficiency," he concluded. Instead of seeing the poorer patients as needy and consequently deserving of care, hospital administrators viewed neediness as a moral failing of the patient.

If hospitals now charged only wealthier clients for their care while maintaining services to working-class patients, the practical effect of this reorientation toward the paying patient might not have been terribly important. This was not the case, however. In Brooklyn there was no ready and willing group of middle class patients eager to use charity facilities long associated with the most degrading type of care; only special services and new accommodations could attract the middle class. The small, financially unstable facilities of Brooklyn could hardly afford to build additional wings and services. Consequently, space for free patients was often converted into space for pay patients and, more often than not, formerly charity patients were required to pay for their care. At Brooklyn Hospital, for instance, the number of "free" patients grew from about 1,000 to 1,600 during the depression years and immediately following but then dropped dramatically from 1,600 in 1900 to 1,200 in 1903. As noted earlier, it was 1900 when the hospital trustees announced that beds in the charity ward would be converted into pay beds in order to increase income. At the same point the number of paying patients began to grow dramatically, rising from just over 200 in 1899 to 1,400 by 1911. The number of private room patients, never a large number in any particular year, remained relatively small throughout the period. In 1895, 16.3 percent of all patient days were used for pay-ward patients. By 1905 this category had grown to 44.5 percent.

While the change in hospital space usage was dramatic, the change in the class of the hospital patient was not. This leads to the conclusion that the pay wards were primarily filled by the same class of patients that previously used the free hospital space. In Brooklyn Hospital, for example, white-collar workers accounted for 13 percent of the patients in 1892 and grew slowly to 21 percent by 1902. The bulk of the patients were still working class—only now they had to pay for their care. On the one hand, it was "obvious that there can be no very great increase in income from [pay patients] unless the accommodations . . . are increased at the expense of space alloted now to those [who] . . . cannot pay at all." On the other hand, charging the same group of patients who had previously used the facility for free accomplished much the same thing. At Brooklyn Hospital this appeared to be what was done. The trustees periodically transformed charity wards into pay wards when income was needed.

The internal organization of many facilities was also greatly affected by the change from charity to pay. Hospitals throughout Brooklyn began to assign bed space to patients according to social and economic criteria rather than medical need. Within the context of the growing acceptance of patient payment as a legitimate source of hospital revenue, it became mandatory for hospital managers to make services distinctly different for the charity and paying patients in order to convince patients that, if they could afford to, they should use the paying service. The source of referral, whether the social service and business office or the private practitioner, gave some basis for differentiating between those able to pay and those who were indigent. But the offering of different services provided a surer means of selecting out patients. The right to a private physician, smaller wards or private rooms, and better food were immediately seen as prerogatives of the pay service. In contrast, charity patients were provided with care that was determined by the administration rather than by a private physician. Private patients were serviced in entirely different quarters. Some called for separate facilities for the rich and the poor. *The Journal of the American Medical Association* pointed out that the "absolute segregation of charity patients from pay patients" was necessary if the wealthier patient was to be convinced to pay for his or her care. "Those who really have no means will perforce go to the genuine charity hospitals, while few of those who have any income will sink their pride so far as to enter an institution patronized by none but the destitute. . . . When the only alternative is a pay hospital where none are treated free, the deed is done. So long as rich and poor are treated under one roof, the well-to-do will not scruple at getting free treatment [since] no stigma attaches to residence in an institution where many pay their way." Separation of services along class lines was necessary to guarantee that clients would, if able, pay for their treatment.

The transformation of the structure and organization of the hospital preceded the introduction of wealthier clients. In many facilities private rooms and pay wards remained empty until after World War I. But in the interim many working-class patients were refused entrance, charged for services previously provided free, and made to feel that the hospital was no longer concerned with their well-being. Some poorer patients were able to scrape together the necessary cash and enter the new "pay" wards. Others were forced to seek care in the growing system of public institutions. Still others were taken into the voluntary institutions only when payment from the city coffers was guaranteed.

The relationship between the charity hospitals and the city government had a long history, dating back to the 1840s. At that time the city of Brooklyn issued lump-sum payments to charity facilities so that these institutions would care for poor persons who were deemed to be proper recipients of the city's protection. But in the early 1900s this flat-grant system of payments was transformed into per capita, per diem payment schemes based upon a means test of all patients. The means test and new grant system further accelerated the administrators' plan to exclude those whose expenses were not covered.

It would be naive to conclude that trustees consciously reorganized hospital services along social class lines. Rather, such actions to develop class-distinct services were an outgrowth of a complex process of financial, intellectual, and social changes that had little to do with the trustees and superintendents themselves. Once patients were accepted as a reasonable source of income, the selling of health services—through private rooms, wards, private nursing, doctors, and special amenities—swiftly arose. Most trustees, in fact, had little or no understanding of how profoundly their institutions would change once patients were turned to its a source of income. In fact, the trustees' own declining authority was further threatened by the very practitioners whom they needed to save the hospital. These practitioners brought with them a growing expertise and professional authority that would quickly allow them to bypass the trustees in influence. The decisions of trustees to change the base of their financial support had a deleterious effect on their own position as well.

By the end of the Progressive Era the modern outlines of an internally fragmented hospital system were apparent in many of Brooklyn's facilities. Not only were physicians much more prominent, and not only were their interests reflected in an increasingly complex medical organization, but the hospital itself was now split between public and private services. In 1916 the Brooklyn Hospital distributed a brochure with an illustration of the hospital on its cover. Engraved across the roof of one of the two wings of the hospital was the word *"PUBLIC."* Across the roof of the other was the word *"PRIVATE."* Between them stood the administration building that kept two worlds of medicine far apart.

33

Frederick T. Gates, *Address on the Tenth Anniversary of the Rockefeller Institute,* 1911

As John D. Rockefeller's chief philanthropic advisor, Frederick T. Gates had a major impact on the development of the nonprofit sector in twentieth-century America. Born in 1853 and educated as a Baptist minister, Gates came to work for Rockefeller after a successful career both in the church and in business. The founding director of the Rockefeller Institute for Medical Research, Gates also headed the General Education Board of the Rockefeller Foundation.

As a philanthropist, Rockefeller began by supporting the religious activities characteristic of nineteenth-century America. He first became interested in the University of Chicago as a seminary for Baptist ministers for the western states, and in his early years he made important contributions to Baptist missions. But by the end of the nineteenth century Rockefeller's philanthropy was becoming notable for its support of scientific research and for the development of professions that were based on science rather than on religious claims to moral superiority.

In his address on the tenth anniversary of the Rockefeller Institute, Gates offered a striking rationale for this redirection of large charitable donations from religious purposes to scientific research. Scientific research, Gates argued, was itself a form of religious activity. Scientific medical research was "as universal in its scope as the love of God . . . and as beneficial in its purpose. . . ." He went on to compare medical researchers, in effect, to theologians, and to suggest that Simon Flexner, the scientific director of the Rockefeller Institute, was a "D.D."—a doctor of divinity. God, Gates asserted, was allowing Flexner and his fellow scientists to open "up the mysterious depths of His Being." Even more, Gates believed that scientific researchers were engaged in theological and social research as well, that they would find "new moral laws and new social laws, new definitions of what is right and wrong in our relations with each other." This basic belief shaped much of the activity of the Rockefeller, Carnegie, and several other great national foundations for over fifty years.

FREDERICK T. GATES

Address on the Tenth Anniversary of the Rockefeller Institute

1911

... It is to me the greatest honor and privilege of my life, indeed, the greatest significance of my life, if it have any significance at all, to have been connected, even though in a subordinate and external way, with the history of this Institute, to have been a sort of hewer of wood and drawer of water to this modern temple of Jehovah, and particularly to you, who are the life of the Institute itself, and to Dr. Flexner, your presiding genius. I say it has been the greatest privilege of my life; but I ought to make one exception. My eldest son, the apple of my eye, is on the staff of Dr. Meltzer, and is thus permitted to work along with you in your high vocation. That interior service of my son I regard as of far higher dignity than any external service such as mine.

Some years ago, as I was walking down Broadway one morning, I had the good fortune to have as companion the President Emeritus of [Harvard] the oldest and, in some ways, the greatest of our American universities, made greatest in those ways by him; a man full of years, as you know, with a breast laden with wisdom, an author of distinction, a patriot, a statesman, a man who for nearly eighty years has been pondering the great problems of humanity and of human life. We happened to be talking about the Institute, and I ventured to confess to him that to me this Institute was the most interesting thing in the world. Nothing, said I, is to me as exciting, so fascinating as the work that the Institute is doing. Dr. Eliot stopped, turned to me, and said, in the fullness of his wisdom and experience: "I myself feel precisely so. The Rockefeller Institute is to me the most interesting thing in this world."

That, gentlemen, was significant. Of course Dr. Eliot could know little, if anything, of the technique of your work. Certainly it was not the technique that interested him; it was those great underlying general considerations, which give peculiar greatness and value to your work, and which make an irresistible appeal to a layman, even though he can know nothing of the technicalities of your daily studies. If I have any claim at all on your attention tonight, I have wondered if it might not be found in opening up to you, who are professional men, technicians, the heart of a layman for a little, about your great vocation. Why is it, for illustration, that the founder of this Institute, who is a layman, has done this great thing? The doing of it was not suggested to him by any technician nor by any professional man. The thought itself originated in the heart of a layman, and it has been throughout supported and enlarged by laymen—laymen who think it the most interesting possible theme for study and thought and for the play of imagination. Why is it so?

It is so for one thing, if one stops to think about it just a moment, because the values of research are universal values. Picture in your thought for a moment this round globe on which we live. Trace its hemispheres and its continents. They are all limited and bounded by their shores, and they are inhabited by nations which have their own fixed boundaries, and their separate speech, and their unique histories. The nations have their racial antagonisms and their peculiar ideals and their distinctive literatures. There is very little indeed in the world that is universal, common to us all. Authors, the greatest of them, can speak in a single language only and are little heard in other tongues. Statesmen and generals are confined in their influence to single nations, the empire of kings is limited. But here is an institution or in this medical research is a work whose value touches the life of every man that lives. Think of that! Is there not something within us, an instinct of humanity, which cannot be fenced in by the boundaries of a merely national patriotism, a sympathy which transcends national boundaries and which finds complete expression only when it identities us with all humanity? Who has not felt the throbbing of desire to be useful to the whole wide world? Here at least is a work for all humanity, which fully satisfies and fills that glorious aspiration.

I do not exaggerate. This work is as universal in its values as the atmosphere which surrounds the globe and presses down with fifteen pounds of weight on every square inch of it, a work whose values go to the palace of the rich and the hovel of the poor, a work alike for the babe in the cradle and for tottering age, a work which penetrates everywhere. The discoveries of this Institute have already reached the depths of Africa with their healing ministrations. You announce a discovery here. Before night your discovery will be flashed around the world. In thirty days it will be in every medical college on earth. In sixty days it will be at the bedsides of the best hospitals, and from those hospitals it will work its way to every sick room in the world that is visited by a competent physician. Universal diffusion may sometimes take years, but with the progress of civilization and the deeper wearing of present grooves, diffusion will come more rapidly. So your work in the scope of its values is as universal as the love of God.

I say as universal in its scope as the love of God. I add, and as beneficial in its purpose. Mere universality would not, of course, be of itself very significant. Disease, too, is universal. But this is a healing ministration, to prevent or destroy disease. It is rescue from disease, and so it is the most intimate, the most precious, the superlative interest of every man that lives. It touches his health, his life, and the lives of his most dearly beloved. It does not affect the mere externals of life, the appointments, the circumstances, the business, the accomplishments of life. Your vocation goes to the foundations of life itself. It deals with the innermost heart of every man that lives. It deals with his life and its well being. For what is health? Health is happiness; health itself is happiness. God has so made us in His beneficence that man when he is in perfect health, with all his functions working perfectly and in harmony, cannot but be happy in the mere exercise of the functions of abounding health. Look at a child, in the exuberance of its health. It has no great thoughts. It can read no great books. It has no mighty enterprise to fill its life and inflame its imagination. It cannot be thrilled with eloquence, with art, or with music. It is just healthy, and being in perfect health it is radiantly happy in the unconscious exercises of its beneficent functions.

So the values of medical research are the most universal values on earth, and they are the most intimate and important values to every human being that lives. Why, then, should it not be the most interesting thing in the world to us and to all men?

And then think of its permanency as well! You work not for today, but for ever; not for this generation, but for every generation of humanity that shall come after you. Thus your work is multiplied by infinity. Has it not often occurred to us that after all science is about the only thing that is destined to live forever in this world? Humanity in its progress, moving forward majestically from age to age, carries with it, nevertheless, just as little useless baggage as is possible. The generations as they succeed each other take from the past and hand on to the future only the things that are proven to be permanently useful. The useless thing is thrown into the limbo of oblivion and left behind, whether it be the history of kings or empires, whether it be literatures or inventions, philosophies or religions—all go as soon as they are proved to be useless. But there is one thing that humanity has always got to live with, and that is old Nature and her laws in this world. Whatever you learn about nature and her forces and prove and incorporate into your science will be carried forward, though all else be forgotten. Humanity, as I said, must always live in this world with her forces and their reactions on mankind. These forces are not going to change. Humanity cannot afford to leave your work behind, whatever else it leaves behind. Humanity must carry it forward, and it will. What you do can never be lost.

I hesitate to speak of another thing that makes this Institute highly interesting to me, because you will say that this, at least, is a more personal idiosyncrasy. You will say that it is a reminiscence of the days when I was a minister, interested in theology. You will smile if I say to you that I often think of this Institute as a theological seminary, presided over by the Rev. Simon Flexner, D.D. (Laughter and applause) But I tell you, friends, if there be over us all the Sum of All, and that Sum conscious—a Conscious, Intelligent Being, and that Being has any favorites on this little planet, I must believe that those favorites are made up of that ever enlarging group of men and women who are most intimately and in very truth studying him and his ways with man. That is your work. To you He is whispering His secrets. To you He is opening up the mysterious depths of His Being. There have been times when as I looked through your microscopes, I have been stricken with speechless awe. I felt that I was gazing with unhallowed eyes into the secret places of the Most High. I say if God looks down on this world and has any favorites, it must be the men who are studying Him, who are working every day, with limited intelligence and in the darkness—for clouds and darkness are round about Him—and feeling their way into His heart.

You smiled just now when I spoke of our honored guest as the Rev. Simon Flexner, D.D. Why did you smile? Friends, it was only because your ideas of religion are the traditional and ecclesiastical ideas of the past, but I am now talking about the religion, not of the past, but of the future, and I tell you that as this medical research goes on you will find out and promulgate as an unforeseen by-product of your work new moral laws and new social laws, new definitions of what is right and wrong in our relations with each other. You will educate the human conscience in new directions and new duties. You will make it sensitive to new distinctions. You will teach nobler conceptions of our social relations and of the God who is over us all. You may be doing work here far more important than you dream for the ethics and the religion of the future. Theology is already being reconstructed in the light of science, in the light of what you and others are doing in research, and that reconstruction is one of the most important of the services which scientific research is performing for humanity.

These, then, are some of the ways in which a layman looks at your work. What I have said thus far applies to all medical research; but let me now speak a word in conclusion more particularly of our own Institute. I have the advantage of some of you. You look over yonder at those splendid buildings—soon to be more splendid and more numerous—and think of them as forming the Institute. They and the workers there, which are in fact the Institute, limit your conceptions of it. But I had the good fortune to be in at an earlier day. I am acquainted with what I may call the prenatal history of the Institute, when there were no buildings and when none of you had ever seen each other or dreamed of being here. I remember the time when the Institute existed simply as a dream in the minds of Mr. Rockefeller and his staff, unknown to all the world outside of his office. (Turning to the Chairman) I am talking too long, am I not?

TOASTMASTER: No, no; go on, Mr. Gates.

MR. GATES (continuing): Then let me tell you just a word about that. We did not know anything of any of you. We had never heard of Dr. Flexner. I, at least, had never heard of Dr. [William H.] Welch, [reforming dean of the Johns Hopkins University School of Medicine and founding Chair of the Board of the Rockefeller Institute]. We knew very little indeed about medicine, but some few things, after all, we did know for certain. Down there at the office we had read Dr. [William] Osler's "Principles and Practice of Medicine." We did have a dim idea as to what it meant, for we had read it with a medical dictionary at our side. We did intelligently and clearly see that there was a tremendous need of medical research. We knew that Pasteur had put forth and established the germ theory of disease. We knew that at that time some half dozen or dozen of the disease germs had been isolated. We knew that there were one or two specifics, and we also knew that there were sixty or seventy more diseases that were certainly germ diseases of which the germs had not been yet even discovered. We knew that they must be discovered; we knew that specifics must be found for them all.

As we reflected upon the situation our horizon enlarged. It dawned upon us with tremendous power that Pasteur had discovered a new hemisphere, that he was a new Columbus, and that as certainly as Columbus he had opened up nothing less than a new era for the whole human race. We saw that the duty of thoughtful and intelligent men was fully to explore and open up that continent which Pasteur had discovered. That is what we saw. It did not take much imagination to see that, and we could guess a good deal, too, even with our lay minds. We could guess that that continent had great river systems, and if exploration could only discover the mouths of those rivers science could work her way along up these rivers, finding tributary rivers and rivulets and rills, forming the controlling, the fundamental principles of the science of medicine, and that we could through these rivers and their tributaries probably explore considerable areas of country, with its fauna and its flora. We could easily guess that there would be found great continental divides, with their lofty mountain ranges, like the Alleghenies and the Rockies, and that these mountain ranges would have passes that human curiosity would thread, or that the great ranges would ultimately be tunneled, with immense labor and cost. We knew also that the old continent, the old world of medicine, was after all very little known, that until very late times little accurate scientific exploration had been done in any department of medicine. Or, turning directly to the human body, we then knew that there was a very considerable number of rooms in this wondrous palace in which we live, into which the healing hand of the surgeon had never yet been admitted, rooms which had never been unlocked to the human eye, and we dared even to guess that Carrels and Meltzers and others might arise who would open up the human system to surgery in its every room.

And now to carry forward my figure. Just as after Columbus had discovered the new continent, all the more civilized and enterprising nations began to send exploring expeditions thither, so we thought that all the nations, and particularly America, should fit out ships and send out exploring expeditions into this new continent of medicine and into the old one as well. As so we fitted out our ship and put Captain Flexner on board (laughter).

But I want to say here for your comfort, or more likely for your amusement, that we did not cherish any extravagant dreams. I want to assure you that not only did we think, but we actually said—s-a-i-d, said—to each other that very likely this Institute would never discover a single important medical fact. I say that we said it to each other, out loud; in fact, we wrote it down. But we also said that even if we knew for certain that our enterprise would never add anything to medical knowledge, we would nevertheless do this thing. Why? In the first place, because we believed that the mere announcement of the establishment of this Institute, the bringing together of the faculty, the conducting of the work, would call public attention to the importance of research, and that very likely many thoughtful men of wealth would think it a good thing for them to start out in the same line on their own account, and that as a result there would probably be added to the various medical schools of the country departments of investigation and research, suitably endowed; and that a good many families of wealth, having had grievous experience with some particular mysterious or fatal trouble, would endow research for that particular disease. We foresaw that much and foresaw, as we all now know, quite truly. Ten years have passed, and already there are many departments of research, many great and splendid funds for research. They are springing up on every side. Our conclusion was correct, that if our particular baby never amounted to anything we might reasonably count on many others, and that among them all there would be great discoveries, and medical science would be notably advanced.

We were right about that, but we never dreamed in the highest flights of our imagination of the brilliant results which you have attained. We never dreamed that within ten years would be gathered here a group of men who would have discovered fundamental medical facts hitherto unguessed, that would form a galaxy of fixed stars in the firmament forever. Never did we dream it. But such is now the fact. We have lived to see men coming here practically unknown and rising in this brief time to imperishable fame; renown as imperishable as the stars. Their names will be associated with the history of medicine as long as medical history is written. We have lived to see the time when kings and emperors, great societies and foreign institutions, have vied with each other to honor themselves by honoring you. If you had made only one of the many important discoveries that are credited to the Institute, I can say to you from the founder tonight and from the men who have been associated with him, that he would feel and all would feel abundantly repaid for every dollar of money and every moment of thought that has ever been put into this institution, though it were never to achieve anything else.

I cannot forbear a brief mention of a great moral value that medical research is conferring. The time was—we can all remember it—when medicine was under such difficulties and in such darkness that the enthusiastic young men who committed themselves to medicine pretty soon found themselves, too many of them, in one of two categories, either confirmed pessimist, disappointed and chagrined, or else mere reckless pill slingers for money. This Institute and others like it have conferred dignity and glory upon medicine. They have awakened the medical profession to a proud and healthy consciousness of the dignity of their vocation. They have created or are creating out of the chaos of the past a true science of medicine. They are giving to every physician a new sense of pride and dignity in his calling. They are making him realize that his life is devoted to a great science, that he himself may be and ought to be an observer, a close and reverent student at the bedside of the sick, that it is possible for him to heal, and that he has a great and worthy function in life. The elevation of the medical profession, the high character of the young men who are now being drawn into it because it is becoming a science, the dignity that this work of research is giving to the medical profession—that, of itself, if research had nothing else to offer, would be a most worthy result.

I conclude with a single word, but for that word I have said all the other words. That word is this: The spirit of this great Institute, the inspiration of it, the directing force of it, that spirit which, more than any other single agency, has wrought these great and beneficent results, is and embodied spirit. It has a local habitation and a name, and that name is Simon Flexner.

We are met together primarily to speak of the honored guest of the evening, but I am sure you will join with me and sympathize with my feeling if I preface what I say with an appreciative word of the founder. It has been my privilege for more than twenty years to be associated with the founder personally, in some of those years very intimately associated; and those years of intimate personal relationship have wrought in me an ever increasing appreciation and reverence for the greatness of his character and the nobility of his aims. He is not given to display of any kind, least of all to exploiting of himself, but, ladies and gentlemen, Mr. Rockefeller is a very great man. He has not one only, but many great titles to distinction, and that world wide. He has broken several world records; they are not likely to be broken again. If he were placed in a group of say twenty of the greatest men of affairs of today, he would be the most modest, retiring, and deferential man of them all, but before these giants had been with him for long, the most self-confident, self-assertive of them would be coming to him in private for his counsel. He has done many things which entitle him to the reverence and gratitude of the generation in which he lives, and that reverence and that gratitude, I am glad to say, is beginning to be shown in increasing volume. But he is one of the few great men, I am persuaded, whose fame will increase with the years instead of diminishing. His renown will be greater in future generations than it is in this, as the world in retrospect comes to know the value of his services. Among may titles to the gratitude of posterity, I count his worthiest title, the title that will carry his name widest ever the earth and deepest into the future, to be the founding of this Institute for Medical Research.

34

David C. Hammack, *Community Foundations: The Delicate Question of Purpose,* 1989

The Tax Reform Act of 1969 required the U.S. Department of the Treasury to develop new guidelines for tax-exempt organizations. When completed in 1975, these guidelines conferred new advantages on "public charities" that received substantial support through annual donations. These advantages—including a reduced level of federal regulation and exemption from certain fees—were not available to family and private foundations that owed their existence to large initial gifts from individuals or families, nor were they available to company foundations that depended on annual gifts from a single corporation or group of corporations. But the "public charity" advantages did apply to *community foundations,* a special form of foundation that accepts gifts from many donors and provides grants for the benefit of a specific community. The Tax Reform Act of 1969 thus had the effect, intended or not, of encouraging the growth of community foundations. Several large private foundations—notably the Mott and Kellogg foundations and the Lilly Endowment—decided to encourage the further development of community foundations in the 1970s and 1980s. One result was a comprehensive book, subtitled "Community Leadership by Community Foundations," edited by Richard Magat. The following essay was written to provide a historical analysis of the growth of community foundations in the United States from their origin at the time of World War I to the 1980s.

DAVID C. HAMMACK

Community Foundations: The Delicate Question of Purpose

1989

Frederick H. Goff's often-quoted rationale for the community foundation—that it is "an agency for making philanthropy more effective and for cutting off as much as is harmful of the dead past from the living present and the unborn future"—has an eminently sensible ring. As a careful student of the movement noted in 1961, Goff's "concept involved a partnership of expertness between the banks and citizen leaders," with bank trust departments managing the funds and "a committee of citizens selected by representative community leaders as being well versed in community needs and services" supervising the distribution of income and, where appropriate, principal and holding the power, "if literal compliance with the donor's instructions became impossible, impracticable, unnecessary, or undesirable, so to amend the specifications for the use of funds that the donor's intent could still be carried out effectively."

But on second thought, a community foundation seems a strange sort of institution. It differs in two striking respects from other philanthropic organizations that create endowments—such organizations as churches, schools, libraries, hospitals, museums, orchestras, and dance companies. By intent and definition, a community foundation has no single, fixed, active purpose. Nor are its leaders definitely to be drawn from a particular segment of the community: by intent, the archetypal distribution committee consists of people chosen for their knowledge of "community needs and services," not for their leadership in any particular religious group or profession or for their acceptability to previous members of the committee. Classically too, the members of a distribution committee are selected not by donors or their acquaintances, but by people who hold key posts in the courts and in such private institutions as chambers of commerce and universities, people whose

Hammack, "Community Foundations: The Delicate Question of Purpose," from Richard Magat, ed., *An Agile Servant: Community Leadership by Community Foundations* (New York: The Foundation Center, 1989), pp. 23–50. Reprinted by permission.

qualifications and characteristics are certain to change from time to time. To put the point baldly, those who commit unrestricted funds to a community foundation agree to support purposes they cannot know, purposes that are certain to be changed in ways they cannot anticipate by a group of people whose identities and commitments are also certain to change. It was this very arrangement that Goff described as an instrument "for cutting off . . . the dead past from the living present."

Since contributors to community foundations are very much alive when they make their donations or write their wills, they must have reason to believe that the foundation's purposes will, in fact, be purposes they approve. To judge from the ups and downs of 75 years of history, potential contributors have accepted the community foundation rationale much more readily at some times and places than at others. As a result, community foundations have expanded (if we measure their size in total assets, valued in constant dollars) with particular vigor in the Midwest and the Northeast in two distinct periods: the 1920s and the 1950s and 1960s.

More recently, community foundations have shown considerable vigor in the 1980s, both in their original regions and also in parts of the West and the South (see Table 1). Looking back, we can identify clear purposes and the social conditions that account for community foundation growth. Perhaps we can also discern some of the leading purposes that are guiding the community foundation movement at present.

Figure 1
Community Foundation Assets: Average Annual Growth Rate for Periods of Varying Length, 1921–1987

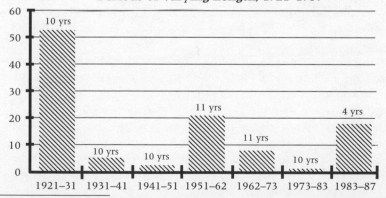

Sources: *Community Trusts in the United States and Canada,* issued by the Trust Company Division, American Bankers Association, 1931. Frank D. Loomis, *Community Trusts of America, 1914–1950* (Chicago: National Committee on Foundations and Trusts for Community Welfare, 1950). *Community Foundations in the United States and Canada, 1914–1961,* prepared by Wilmer Shields Rich (New York: National Council on Community Foundations, Inc., 1961).

Table 1
Community Foundation Assets, 1921–1987

Year	Current assets ($ million)	Assets in 1967 ($ million)	Period growth rate in 1967 (%)	Average Annual growth rate in period (%)	Assets of NY, Chicago, Boston, San Francisco, Marin, & Cleveland, as % all assets
1921	7	13	-	-	76
1931	37	81	523	52	58
1941	54	122	51	5	42
1951	110	141	16	2	45
1962	425	469	233	21	45
1973	1,200	902	92	8	48
1983	2,800	966	9	1	50
1987	4,719	1,675	73	18	44

Sources: *Community Trusts in the United States and Canada*, issued by the Trust Company Division, American Bankers Association 1931; Frank D. Loomis, *Community Trusts of America*, 1914-1950 (Chicago: National Committee on Foundations and Trusts for Community Welfare, 1950); *Community Foundations in the United States and Canada, 1914-1961*, prepared by Wilmer Shields Rich (New York: National Council on Community Foundations, Inc., 1961); Frederick Bartenstein III, and Charles W. Ingler, "Community Foundations Growth Analysis," unpublished working document, The Dayton Foundation, June 1985; Joanne Scanlan, Council on Foundations, 1989.

ORIGINS OF THE COMMUNITY FOUNDATION

A clue to the success of the community foundation movement in the 1920s can be found in the circumstances of the creation of the pioneer community foundation in Cleveland, Ohio, in 1914. The Cleveland Foundation was only one of several new organizations that provided a new framework for philanthropic and nonprofit activity between 1903 and 1919. Nineteenth-century philanthropy generally involved small organizations affiliated with particular religious groups; in nearly every case, these organizations were personally controlled by small numbers of wealthy sponsors. Twentieth-century philanthropy increasingly distinguished religious from secular purposes; provided greater scope for professional control of medical, educational, and social services; and developed funding and coordinating agencies that served the metropolitan community as a whole. Cleveland took the lead in this national transformation of the charitable framework.

The critical first step in the creation of Cleveland's new philanthropic framework was a decision on the part of Protestant leaders to separate religion from most charitable activity, and to establish a new organization, the Federated Churches of Greater Cleveland (1911; now the Interchurch Council of Greater Cleveland) to coordinate fundraising and specifically religious charitable activities for most Protestant denominations. The Jewish Community Federation, established in 1903, provided a partial example for the Federated Churches; the Catholic Charities Corporation, dating in preliminary form to 1910, formally organized in 1919, followed.

Once the separate religious associations were in place, the Cleveland Chamber of Commerce took the lead in creating a new Federation for Charity and Philanthropy (1913). Designed to evaluate and monitor the nonreligious activities of charities in the metropolitan area and to conduct annual community chest-type drives to raise operating funds for them, the Federation for Charity and Philanthropy emphasized professionalism and businesslike management rather than religious commitment. In effect, the charity federation played the role of a private government, carrying out both the annual fundraising and supervisory functions now carried out by United Way, and the planning and coordination functions of many welfare councils. To the distress of those who believed that "any system of charity which ignores the transforming power which the Gospel brings to the needy ones is false"—but to the relief of Catholics and Jews who also wished to participate in community-wide charitable activities—the federation's leaders emphasized secular virtues: businesslike efficiency and professional expertise.

The Cleveland Foundation fit very well into the new governing framework for private charity. As defined by Goff, president of the Cleveland Trust Company, it was to be a private, nonsectarian organization with public purposes. In keeping with the defining purpose of flexibility, and with the new emphasis on interfaith cooperation based on a separation of charitable work from religious work, the funds were also to be used "for such other charitable purposes as will best make for the mental, moral, and physical improvement of the inhabitants of the City of Cleveland as now or hereafter constituted, regardless of race, color or creed."

Goff was determined that his new organization should serve two special purposes. One had to do with the kinds of funds involved: the community foundation was to accumulate and manage permanent charitable endowments, rather than to raise annual operating funds. The community foundation's second distinctive purpose had to do with leadership. The great new foundations—Russell Sage Foundation (1907), Carnegie Corporation (1911), Rockefeller Foundation (1913)—sought to understand the causes of human misfortune and social dysfunction through scientific, medical, and social research. Having identified the causes, the great foundations intended to lead—to find and promote, among both private and public agencies, new social policies that would put the results of disciplined inquiry into effect.

Goff himself had been an attorney for John D. Rockefeller and he had read the account of *Seven Great Foundations* by Leonard C. Ayres of the Russell Sage Foundation; he fully understood the ways in which a foundation might play a leading part in defining needs.

To assure that the Cleveland Foundation would indeed carry out its public purposes and contribute effectively to the new coordination of philanthropy, Goff acceded to the suggestions of a Cleveland journalist—and of his own wife—and worked out a way to secure public representation on what would later be known as the distribution committee. This would consist of five people, two selected by the Cleveland Trust Company, and one each chosen by the mayor of Cleveland, the senior judge of the United States District Court, and the senior probate judge of Cuyahoga County.

Having defined most of the legal and institutional arrangements that would characterize community foundations, Goff moved quickly to make the Cleveland Foundation creditable to the public and attractive to donors by arranging for several ambitious "surveys." Using Cleveland Trust Company funds and his own, he brought to Cleveland as survey director Allen T. Burns, who had for five years directed the effort of a local civic committee to carry out the recommendations of the Russell Sage Foundation's famous Pittsburgh Survey, a study of living and working conditions in the steel district. Under Burns and, later, Raymond Moley, a Western Reserve University political science professor who would go on to become a member of Franklin D. Roosevelt's brain trust, the Cleveland Foundation sponsored a remarkable series of studies of relief agencies, public schools, recreation, and criminal justice. Conducted with the cooperation of such other agencies as the charity federation, the public school system, and the bar association, these studies were carried out by such nationally distinguished experts as Sherman C. Kingsley, director of the Elizabeth McCormick Memorial Fund of Chicago; Leonard C. Ayres, head of the Russell Sage Foundation's Education Department; and Harvard law professors Roscoe Pound and Felix Frankfurter.

The "fundamental purpose" of the surveys, as Moley put it, was "to make the public want certain conditions changed." Change itself, he added, would come when "democratic institutions," both private and public, "be they schools or settlement houses or courts," recognized that the public demanded it.

TRUST COMPANIES AND CHAMBERS OF COMMERCE: INITIAL SUCCESS IN THE MIDWEST AND NORTHEAST, 1915–1935

The community foundation spread quickly from its Cleveland origin in the years between 1914 and 1929. Two regions proved most receptive:

the Midwest, where community foundations fit effectively into the civic culture, and the Northeast, where nonprofit organizations already played such important roles. Trust companies, which at the time provided valued investment management and advising services to many people who held large estates, took the lead in promoting community foundations everywhere; to assist them, the Trust Division of the American Bankers Association established in 1920 a Committee on Community Trusts.

Community foundations fit particularly well into the civic culture of many cities in the greater midwestern region that reaches from Buffalo to Minneapolis to St. Louis, and whose influence extends south to Dallas and Atlanta and west to Denver. In the years between 1900 and 1929 this culture found vigorous expression in the activities of chambers of commerce. As in Cleveland, many chambers of commerce in this region took the lead in setting up both federated fundraising campaigns and community foundations, thus subordinating social agencies to a central community chest. Historian Peter Dobkin Hall has shown that, by 1922, there were active community foundations and charitable federations in many midwestern cities, and nowhere else in the United States.

Community foundations in many midwestern cities also emulated Cleveland's example by sponsoring forthright surveys, as they were called, of disputed social problems. In Chicago, Norman Wait Harris and his son, Albert Wadsworth Harris, of the Harris Trust and Savings Bank, set up a community trust in 1915, underwrote its early expenses, and endowed it with their own funds. To attract attention and support, they launched a systematic study of "Americanization Services in Chicago," a matter of great controversy at the time. This study gained a good deal of local attention and led, between 1918 and 1922, to surveys of other contemporary problems, ranging from housing for young working women, to prenatal care, to the deplorable conditions in the Cook County Jail. In 1930 the Buffalo Foundation still maintained a Bureau of Studies and Social Statistics. Similarly, the Dayton Foundation was, in 1930, devoting much of its income of just over $16,000 to "Research in Civic Affairs" through the Dayton Research Foundation and the Community Chest.

In the Northeast, Connecticut and New York revised their laws in the mid-1920s to encourage community foundations, and these states, together with Massachusetts, proved fertile ground for the new institution. But here the appeal had less to do with a comprehensive restructuring of philanthropic activity. In many northeastern cities, as William P. Gest, chairman of the board of the Fidelity-Philadelphia Trust Company put it in 1927, the community foundation was seen simply as "the mechanical side of individual philanthropy . . . a mechanism of conservation and distribution of charitable funds."

For its first three decades the New York Community Trust provided the most striking example of the "mechanical" quality that Gest emphasized, a quality that might more accurately be described as that of a utility or common carrier providing efficient service to many donors but eschewing a leading role in the general reorganization of philanthropy. Although the New York Community Trust hired Frederick Goff's special assistant, Ralph Hayes, as its first director in 1923, it put its emphasis on the accumulation of distinct funds devoted to a specific purpose—on the creation of what it called "a community of funds, a community of trusts"—and it did not limit itself to funds designed to serve the New York region. One of the first funds that Hayes and his distribution committee attracted, the Moritz and Charlotte Warburg Memorial Fund, was established as early as 1925 to provide scholarships at the Hebrew University in Jerusalem. In 1931, the New York Community Trust accepted its first donor-advised fund, $50,000 from William S. Barstow, who determined himself how the fund's income was to be spent each year until his death more than ten years later. The New York Community trust also influenced many other community foundations, and further developed the community foundation idea as a utility, by adopting from the start the Multiple Trust Plan arrangement, first employed in Indianapolis, of inviting several banks to serve as trustees.

The northeastern community foundations also eschewed the midwestern practice of conducting independent surveys of social and civic problems. In Hartford, Connecticut, for example, the distribution committee formally decided "that it should *not* act in a research or demonstration capacity, but should appropriate funds to already established institutions," enabling them to conduct research or provide services they could not otherwise afford.

As they gathered large resources, however, many of the northeastern foundations found themselves in the thick of debates over the policies that controlled both government and private agencies. The Hartford Foundation supported surveys carried out by the Council of Social Agencies. And by 1930 the Permanent Charity Fund of Boston was appropriating over $200,000 to 117 different private organizations, and taking pride in the leverage it was able to wield over their operating procedures. "One of the most valuable results" of its work, it reported to the American Bankers Association, "has been the strengthening of the trend toward closer association and cooperation between the charitable organizations of Boston and its vicinity." Each of the organizations to which the Fund contributed was required to "consider itself in relation to the whole work of the community, and to adopt a uniform accounting system."

Despite regional differences, community foundations throughout

Table 2
Community Trusts with Assets Greater than $100,000 in 1930 by Region and Date of Origin

| Region/City | Year formed | Assets ($1,000) | | | |
		1930	1949	1960	1987
Midwest					
Cleveland, OH	1914	3,000	11,100	26,000	459,051
Chicago, IL	1915	5,100	10,800	31,000	278,024
Detroit, MI	1915	200	300	600	*
Milwaukee,Wl	1915	700	300	1,100	61,737
Minneapolis, MN	1915	200	1,900	4,600	106,322
Indianapolis, IN	1916	1,900	3,200	8,100	44,712
Youngstown, OH	1918	700	800	2,200	32,396
Dayton, OH	1921	300	300	700	20,532
Grand Rapids, MI	1922	100	400	4,100	38,334
Northeast					
Boston, MA	1915	4,800	8,700	36,600	194,375
Cambridge, MA	1916	200	400	600	2,826
Williamsport, MA	1916	200	700	1,100	16,881
Philadelphia, PA	1918	600	1,500	3,800	60,865
Buffalo, NY	1920	1,000	1,600	4,800	24,001
New York, NY	1920	8,700	18,700	30,100	545,076
Hartford, CT	1925	100	1,700	11,600	133,393
New Haven, CT	1927	100	1,700	9,000	73,510
South					
Winston-Salem, NC	1919	400	3,700	9,700	42,165
Tulsa, OK	1919	100	20	200	1,024
West					
Los Angeles, CA	1915	300	4,300	8,700	69,961
Denver, CO	1925	1,000	200	-	19,021
Canada					
Winnipeg, Manitoba	1921	2.3	3.0	5.2	NA

*Defunct after 1985; assets of about $1 million turned over to the Community Foundation of Southeastern Michigan.

the United States attracted funds from two groups of donors: well-known business leaders and obscure citizens who identified with the community. Established business leaders played a key role in starting the foundations, defining their purposes, and lending them credibility. Some, like Goff in Cleveland, the Harris family in Chicago, John H. Patterson of Dayton's National Cash Register Corporation, and James Longley of

the Boston Safe Deposit and Trust Co., provided significant initial endowments to foundations they started. Others, like the Warburgs in New
York and "Wheat King" James A. Patten of Chicago, sought both to use
a community foundation's facilities and to lend support to a local institution.

These established leaders sought to define a sense of community: a
considerable number of obscure citizens responded with contributions
and bequests. One of the first was Alphonse P. Pettis, who had made a
small fortune through investments in Indianapolis. He heard about the
Indianapolis Foundation many years later, during his retirement on the
French Riviera, and he left it an entirely unexpected $300,000 for the
benefit of a city in which he had never lived. Every community foundation also received modest contributions: in the 1930s the Hartford Foundation for Public Giving received a typical legacy of this sort, $13,220
from Clara M. Goodman, a public school teacher.

To judge from the paucity of references in the literature, however,
smaller contributions were never sufficiently numerous to give community foundations the resounding vote of public approval and support
that their leaders might have wished. As Loomis of the Chicago Community Trust observed in 1949, the "glowing expectancy of large and
easy money which seems to have animated many of the early Community Trusts [was] seldom realized. Three or four of the early Trusts were
fortunate in having substantial funds turned over to them for administration soon after they were organized." But, he added, "most of the
Community Trusts which have achieved any success at all soon found
they would have to settle down to hard work, to diligent, patient, intelligent promotion of the community trust idea on its own merits."

POSTWAR GROWTH: COMMUNITY FOUNDATIONS AND COMMUNITY CHESTS, 1945–1965

The Great Depression brought the community foundation movement
nearly to a halt. The "Crash" reduced many fortunes, and the economic
uncertainty that followed may well have discouraged wealthy people
from parting with their money. But the depression also reduced confidence in the banks. In 1933, the terrible year of the "bank holiday," the
Committee on Community Trusts of the Trust Division of the American
Bankers Association ceased to function. Banks appeared to be less secure, and bankers were no longer so self-assured and respected as leaders of civic and charitable affairs. Popular sentiment, and perhaps the
sentiment of some people wealthy enough to contribute to community
foundations, saw many private organizations as failures and shifted in
favor of action by government. As Wilmer Shields Rich pointed out, "by
far the outstanding characteristic of these . . . years was the lapse into

inactivity of a number of community foundations," including those of Louisville, New Orleans, Cincinnati, Houston, Washington, D.C., and Spokane, as well as many in smaller cities. At least 91 community foundations had been started between 1914 and 1939; only 66 remained in operation in 1949, and only 35 controlled the $200,000 in assets needed to earn, at 5 percent, the minimum of $10,000 to pay for a full-time staff person and an office.

The community foundation movement did revive after World War II but when it did so, it was directed not by banks and trust companies, but by "leaders in community planning." The name of the new umbrella organization for the movement, the National Committee on Foundations and Trusts for Community Welfare, reflected the change. The new promoters often preferred the charitable corporation form (already adopted, largely for tax purposes, in Boston and several other cities) rather than the bank trust agreement; and in some cases they also broke with earlier practice by making their boards self-perpetuating. They also preferred the multiple trustee plan, so as to give all banks providing trust services a reason to encourage donors. The corporate form placed general control in the hands of a citizen committee, subordinating the trust functions carried out by banks.

Postwar community foundation leaders also emphasized a version of the purpose stressed before 1929, the creation of a strengthened framework for private charity, a framework responsive to business and professional leadership and independent of government. More specifically several spokesmen insisted that their main purpose was to strengthen the local Community Chest. The community chest movement that had developed in middle-sized and large cities in the Midwest, West, and parts of the South in the 1920s had not been ready for the challenge of the depression, and in many places community chests were only weakly established by the late 1940s. After the war, community chest advocates sought to take advantage of revived patriotic and community feeling to put more community chests on a stable footing.

In the West and the South, postwar community chest promoters sought to cope with new problems, and to respond to new opportunities created by rapid urbanization during the war. Everywhere, the leaders of private social welfare organizations were looking for ways to cope with uncertainties about the scope of continuing federal and state activity in the social welfare field. Everywhere, too, private social welfare, medical, and related organizations were pressed to respond to the new situation presented by the historic labor agreements that settled the great strikes of the postwar years. Under these agreements, the company unions and corporate welfare plans provided by many manufacturing and some retail corporations, and some of the welfare activities historically provided by independent unions, were ended. Workers in manufacturing won a very large increase in fringe benefits and vacation time: henceforth they would be able to pay for more medical services, able to make more use of recreational facilities—and more able to contribute to community chest campaigns. In many manufacturing centers, community chests would be called on to support the diagnostic, rehabilitative, and recreational services formerly provided by corporate welfare programs. Everywhere, they would need new resources—often capital resources for new buildings and equipment—to support new activities and to persuade old agencies to accept new missions or consolidations. Community foundations promised the community chest movement stability legitimacy, and access to a significant source of capital.

The statement of purpose for the community foundation movement offered in 1950 by Edward L. Ryerson, who had been the founding president of the Community Fund of Chicago (a limited community chest organized to coordinate private fundraising during the depression), makes sense in this context. "Community planning for health and welfare, in recent years, has been largely the work of local community chests and councils, and it has been restricted largely to current financing of current needs," Ryerson wrote. "Community planning for social welfare will never be well-rounded or comprehensive until it includes planning for capital gifts and bequests. These are likely to affect the character, the stability and the adaptability of many of our community services over long periods of time."

Accounts of many community foundations in the 1940s and 1950s emphasize their support of community chests. According to Loomis, those in "Boston, Buffalo and Chicago . . . had an important part in the development of the local Council of Social Agencies and the local Community Chest." The relationship was reversed in Dallas, Colorado Springs, Norfolk, Newark, Syracuse, New Britain, Bridgeport, Flint, Fort Wayne, Columbus, and Madison, where Community Chest leaders took the initiative in starting or reviving community foundations.

The fullest analysis of community foundation giving patterns in the 1950s concluded that more than half of their grants were going for the operating expenses of social agencies. In 1953 the Indianapolis Foundation played a major role in financing a $2-million building for the United Fund and 35 member agencies. And according to one historian, "in its early days, most of [the New Haven Foundation's] income went almost automatically to established agencies . . . the Community Chest regularly received a large contribution." Between 1931 and 1947 the Cleveland Foundation made an annual grant from the Coulby Fund to the community chest.

The close alliance between community foundations and community chests was by no means universal. The San Francisco Foundation, for example, took the position from the time of its creation in 1949 that it would not contribute to federated fundraising campaigns. Like the Philadelphia and Pittsburgh foundations, it took the view that if it made such contributions it would be "abandoning its responsibility to make the best possible distribution of the undesignated funds at its disposal." These community foundations promoted themselves as custodians of capital funds for the changing capital needs of their communities, not for operating needs of ongoing organizations.

Everywhere, contributions to community foundations may well have been stimulated by more general factors. Notable among these was surely the general revival of national pride stimulated by the American experience in World War II. Characterized by the "we've got to do this together" spirit that had removed some of the barriers between Protestants, Catholics, and Jews during the war, this new national pride encouraged a more inclusive sense of community and may well have been behind an increase in the number of smaller contributions to community foundations. There was also a spillover sense of local community pride, especially in towns—in the West and the South as well as in the Midwest and the Northeast—where many people had been deeply engaged in the war effort. And there was the strong postwar suspicion of government and a growing commitment to voluntarism, exemplified by the fringe-benefit clauses of the new labor contracts and the concomitant development of Blue Cross rather than a national health service.

Whatever the explanation, community foundations did grow vigorously in assets between 1945 and 1965. Despite scattered new interest in the South and the West, the Midwest and the Northeast continued not only to sustain the largest number of established community foundations, but to produce the largest numbers of new ones. The result, by 1960, was the general adoption in the larger and wealthier cities of the United States outside the South, of the community chest and the community foundation as central elements in the framework of private agencies for the control of community life.

COMMUNITY FOUNDATIONS SINCE THE MID-1960S: NEW COMMUNITIES, NEW PURPOSES

After expanding vigorously from the end of World War II to the mid-1960s, the total assets of community foundations, measured in constant dollars, failed to grow much at all for 15 years. Why? And why have those assets grown again—at nearly the pace of the postwar years—in the 1980s? The answers seem to have to do with . . . abrupt changes in the sense of community . . . —and with changing notions of community foundation purposes.

In the mid-1960s several of the largest community foundations played a direct part in challenging the sense of community that had prevailed since World War II. Much of that sense was expressed in what now reads as a very dated statement of the qualities to be desired in a community foundation director. This statement, by the leader of a large community trust in the late 1940s, was intended as advice for the use of community foundation boards across the country. Implicitly, it also described the nature of the community such a director would serve.

"The community trust executive," the statement began, "should preferably be a man (although one of us was a woman who in time became a great social leader in her community) who is a *college graduate* and who is 'native' to the community to be served." It went on to explain each of the desired qualities. "Men," it noted, "have better entree . . . in the numerous areas in which the community trust executive works—such as the banking and legal professions, the courts, the universities, and the social agencies." College training was necessary, "because he will eventually have to turn to the university for help." And the executive should be "'native' to the community in the sense that he is well-acquainted, well known, and believes in its heritage, present and future." Jews had played important roles in community foundations in Connecticut, New York, San Francisco, and elsewhere; nevertheless, the statement was couched in the language of Protestant discourse: "Since a community trust exists to improve the community, the director must have an abiding faith in it."

Chicago's Frank Loomis added that while "mere professionalism" was to be avoided, a "community trust executive must have an aptitude for welfare work, a 'feel' for it . . . ability to understand and appreciate [and evaluate] the teachers, the preachers, the nurses and physicians, the social workers." Loomis expected these criteria to be applied by trustees selected without regard to "political, partisan, or sectarian considerations." Trustees should be "men and women highly respected for their character, intelligence, and good judgement . . . in community welfare work"; they would ordinarily include former "presidents or vice presidents of the Community Chest, or chairmen of its Budget Committee, or . . . of the Welfare Council or of one of the large private charities." The trustees, in turn, would be selected by such public officials as the mayor, a judge of the United States District Court, and the judge of a probate court; and by such "semi-public" officials as "the president of a local college or university, the president of the Welfare Council or Community Chest, the president of the Chamber of Commerce or the Bar Association."

The civil rights and women's movements challenged the racial, gender, class, and religious-group assumptions that defined the sense of community for Loomis and other community foundation leaders in the late 1940s. Remarkably, executives and boards at several of the larger, firmly established community foundations quickly "got the message" and changed direction.

These community foundations were able to change because they were large and well-established in four ways: they had significant unrestricted endowments, independence (of a kind never available to a community chest or a welfare council) from both donors and grantees, professional and imaginative staffs, and strong leadership from their boards. They were also strongly encouraged by the Ford Foundation, especially by Public Affairs Program director Paul Ylvisaker. Ylvisaker was seeking ways "to move out of safe and sane hospital, university and similar do-nothing grants . . . to begin getting after the more gutsy urban problems." He thought that perhaps "Ford block grants to local foundations [could] . . . address the tough problems . . . get other philanthropists involved . . . and gain the large-scale leverage necessary for getting this country to wake up to social change."

The Kansas City Association of Trusts and Foundations (organized in 1949 to manage four separate trust funds; reorganized as the Kansas City Community Foundation in 1986) enjoyed all the advantages that permitted a sharp change, and it was perhaps the first to move in the new direction. With assets of about $12 million in 1961, a forceful director, Homer C. Wadsworth, and a $1.25 million grant from Ylvisaker's Ford program, the Kansas City organization moved boldly, about 1960, into "community-action style philanthropy," some of which involved work with the public schools, even as it also pressed separate initiatives to reorganize health care and increase opportunities for higher education.

In Cleveland, a Ford Foundation evaluator would later write, such key business and civic leaders as Kent Smith and Harold Clark had become "dissatisfied with the course of philanthropy," and in particular with the Cleveland Foundation. In their view the oldest community foundation had become "embedded in a routine pattern of responding to unimaginative requests from a standard fist of institutional grantees . . . a pattern that was . . . less and less responsive to the real and changing needs of the Cleveland community." Encouraged by the availability of the very considerable assets of the newly available Hanna Trust and by conversations with Ylvisaker and Henry Heald, then president of the Ford Foundation, Smith and Clark developed a plan to shake things up. As journalist Diana Tittle reconstructs it, their plan called for a new "Greater Cleveland Associated Foundation," to be sponsored by, but somewhat separate from, the Cleveland Foundation and four other local foundations, and to be financed and endorsed by the

Ford Foundation. The purposes assigned to the Associated Foundation harkened back to the Cleveland Foundation's early surveys and anticipated the work that several other community foundations would undertake in the later 1960s and the 1970s:

- to encourage research on and solutions of community social welfare problems . . . ;
- to establish priorities for community action thereon;
- to make grants for research, pilot, experimental and other projects toward the solutions of such problems;
- to make professional staff services available for . . . trusts and foundations . . . operating . . . under difficult circumstances, without professional aid.

Dolph Norton, a young public administration professor whom Kent Smith and Case Institute of Technology president T. Keith Glennan had brought to Cleveland to work in what proved to be an unsuccessful campaign to secure metropolitan-area government, became the head of the new Associated Foundation. Deeply concerned that "the metropolis has no regularized democratic procedures for choosing its goals and bringing the community's resources to bear in achieving them," Norton thought the foundation might, in part, play the role of a regional government.

In practice, Norton and Smith used the Greater Cleveland Associated Foundation to bring the region's business leaders into contact—for the first time—with leaders of the black community, and to provide leadership and resources for aggressive efforts to confront segregated and inadequate public education and employment opportunities, juvenile delinquency, and other intractable urban problems. Several years later Norton also successfully encouraged the Ford Foundation to support a voter registration program in Cleveland's black neighborhoods (part of a national voter registration effort by the Ford Foundation, this action drew severe criticism and restrictive legislation in Congress). When votes from those neighborhoods helped elect Carl Stokes, the city's first black mayor, in 1967, the Greater Cleveland Associated Foundation underwrote Stokes's effort to develop a program. The foundation provided a one-year grant of $68,000 to enable him to employ a public relations consultant. It also worked, with varying degrees of success, to encourage diverse business, neighborhood, and institutional groups to define economic and physical redevelopment plans for the City.

The more active community foundation programs pioneered in Kansas City and Cleveland soon found counterparts elsewhere. Bruce Newman, who went on from an internship at the Greater Cleveland Associated Foundation to become director of the Chicago Community Trust, later asserted that Dolph Norton had "opened up the very closed world" of the community foundation by getting "out in the community, talking with people." Quite independently, John R. May of the San Francisco Foundation was also "out in the community" in the mid-1960s. By the early 1970s, May later recalled, "an overwhelming proportion" of San Francisco Foundation grants were going "to support efforts to try to equalize opportunity in every way."

At the other end of the country between 1961 and 1964 the Permanent Charity Fund of Boston (now the Boston Foundation) invested over $500,000 in Action for Boston Community Development, which later became the city's official antipoverty agency and related efforts. In San Francisco and Boston, as in Kansas City and Cleveland, community foundations were pursuing a new purpose, that of enlarging the sense of public—and government—responsibility.

The new sense of community at these and other foundations was soon reflected in staff policies as well. When Dolph Norton left the Cleveland Foundation in 1973, Barbara Rawson, his administrative assistant, became the foundation's acting director— one of the first women to hold such a post. By the mid-1980s black administrators held important positions in several community foundations. Two of them, one man and one woman, head two of the largest—those in Cleveland and Boston. In her first annual report, Boston's Anna Faith Jones announced a $10 million, five-year commitment to "a new assault on poverty."

FEDERAL REGULATION AND METROPOLITAN REGIONS: COMMUNITY FOUNDATIONS SINCE 1969

The new community purposes advanced by the more active community foundations—and by the Ford Foundation and several major private foundations—after 1960 provoked criticism as well as praise, and some of the criticism contributed to the stagnation in asset growth between about 1965 and 1980 shown in Table 1. (The failure of the stock market to keep pace with inflation during these same years—and the deflating effect of inflation on the value of bonds—also accounted for some of the asset stagnation.) Some potential donors certainly rejected the newly inclusive definitions of community advanced by the Cleveland, Boston, Kansas City, San Francisco, and other community foundations. Less affluent whites, members of European ethnic groups and of labor unions, and Catholics perceived, not incorrectly, that they were only marginal to community-building activities that emphasized relations between blacks (or women) and business leaders: they added protests of their own.

Several congressmen responded to these and other currents by challenging the Ford Foundation's support for voter registration drives in black communities and the efforts of many foundations, including

several community foundations, to develop and promote new policies
to address poverty and inequality. Wright Patman and other congressional critics also objected to the self-dealing and other abuses of many
family foundations. These concerns led to the passage of the Tax Reform
Act of 1969, with extensive new provisions for foundations of all kinds.
Although the Act treated community foundations relatively well its
passage failed to settle many questions. Treasury officials found the entire foundation field baffling, and they did not issue the rules and regulations required by the Act until 1976. There followed a period of
negotiation and adjustment as Norman A. Sugarman and other community foundation leaders worked to modify the new rules. . . . It is not
surprising that donations to community foundations lagged during this
period of uncertainty.

When the new federal tax rules were established in late 1976, community foundations emerged with significant new advantages. . . . These
regulations encouraged the wealthy to give to community foundations,
with their more accountable boards and often more adequate professional staffs, rather than to set up private family foundations. Under the
tax code, community foundations offered greater deductions to donors,
were burdened with fewer limitations on their operations, and, after a
few years of additional negotiations, were relieved of the excise tax
placed on other foundations. Several large national foundations moved
to reinforce the new federal encouragement of community foundations.
Four community foundation missions, singled out by the Charles Stewart
Mott Foundation, impressed these national foundations:

- Developing a permanent, unrestricted endowment.
- Responding to emerging, changing community needs.
- Providing a vehicle and a service for donors with varied interests.
- Serving as resource, broker, and catalyst in the community.

These are the general agenda-setting, decision-making functions
Paul Ylvisaker has in mind when he describes community foundations . . . as "private legislatures." They are also the functions pioneered
in Cleveland through surveys and demonstration projects to provide,
through a private organization, a kind of leadership unavailable through
metropolitan government.

The development of community foundations, encouraged by federal government regulations and by national foundations alike, has apparently been effective. Certainly, community leaders in many cities
were impressed by the arguments for community foundations. Businessman Robert H. Levi, for example, became convinced that "you can't
sit back and say a city the size of Baltimore is going to survive as a first-
class city without a community foundation—without that tool to work
with," and joined the board of the Greater Baltimore Foundation. Al-

Figure 2
Community Foundation Asset Growth: 1921–1987

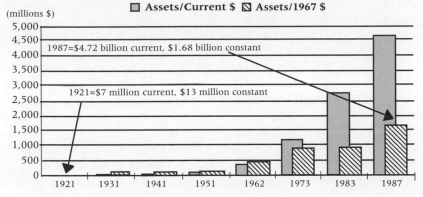

□ Assets/Current $ ◩ Assets/1967 $

(millions $)

1987=$4.72 billion current, $1.68 billion constant

1921=$7 million current, $13 million constant

Figure 3
Community Foundation Asset Growth: 1981–1987

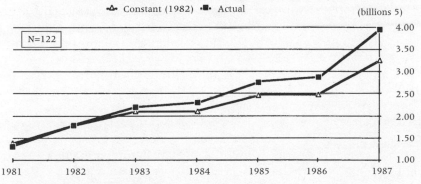

–△– Constant (1982) –■– Actual

(billions 5)

N=122

Source: Council on Foundations
1988 Survey of Community Foundations

Source: Council on Foundations 1988 Survey of Community Foundations.

though most community foundations continued to place the greatest value on the unrestricted endowment, many moved aggressively to attract money that might previously have gone into family foundations by emphasizing "donor-advised funds" and "special interest funds" through which donors (and sometimes their heirs) might continue to influence the use of their money. As Table 1 shows, community foundation assets grew as rapidly in the 1980s as they did in the 1950s.

The newer cities of the South and West have, at last, become large enough and wealthy enough to support effective community foundations. In most of them, donors have been persuaded that community foundations play an essential part among the controlling institutions of private charity. The Midwest and Northeast, however, continue to provide the most fertile ground, established foundations in those regions have continued to grow, new ones have appeared, and community foundation assets per capita remain much higher than in most places in the South and West. As total assets grew the largest community foundations held their own. New York, Cleveland, Chicago, and Boston, joined in the 1970s by San Francisco and in the 1980s by the Marin Community Foundation, created by the Buck Trust, held between 45 and 50 percent of all community foundation assets throughout the period from 1941 on. Finally, and still more striking, is the emergence of multiple community foundations in many metropolitan regions, especially in the already well-developed Midwest and Northeast (see Table 3).

All this points to one last observation: community foundations, like other private—and public—governing organizations in the United States, have become so numerous and diverse that it is impossible to pin them down to particular organizational forms or animating purposes. Community foundations are divided according to size, region, relationship with the local United Way, and local tradition. They also compete with one another, with operating agencies, and in some places with other coordinating organizations like United Way and the Jewish federations for endowment funds, including funds intended to be used in flexible ways.

Similar patterns operate in other spheres of American life, in the public sector as well as among other "private legislatures" and "private governments." Several chambers of commerce operate simultaneously in many large cities: a large, general chamber often dominated by banks and retail firms, large and small; an elite general chamber comprised of the 50 or so largest corporations in a metropolitan region; many neighborhood and suburban chambers serving local retailers; and a variety of industrial and professional associations. Nor is it any easier to draw boundaries around municipal governments: certain Cleveland residents, for example, live within the boundaries of the school district of Shaker Heights, an adjacent suburb; suburban residents pay a Cleveland department for water and sewer services; residents of many municipalities use the trolleys and buses of the Regional Transit Authority and the Metropolitan Parks; and the police employed by the private housekeeping organization for most of the city's cultural institutions, University Circle, Inc., have arrest powers within Cleveland's city limits.

The purposes of community foundations are bound to continue to proliferate. But in the increasingly fragmented context of the great metropolitan regions that now house nearly four-fifths of the American population, well-endowed and effectively led community foundations may be able to shape many social, cultural, and economic development policies. Under Herbert West, president for the last 22 years, the New York Community Trust, for example, took on growing responsibility for community leadership in response to New York City's fiscal, energy, and substance abuse crises, encouraged the development of the Tri-State United Way, and supported the formation of community foundations in three suburban areas. As private organizations with quasi-public boards, strongly public purposes, and expansive territories, community foundations may be particularly well designed for such a role in metropolitan regions where no central city houses a large portion of the total population.

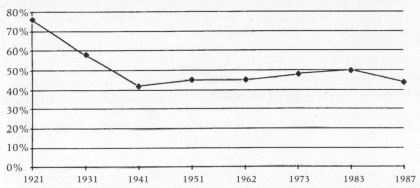

Figure 4
Assets of Six Largest Community Foundations* as % of all Assets

*Boston, Chicago, Cleveland, Marin, New York, San Francisco

Sources: Frederick Bartenstein III and Charles W. Ingler, "Community Foundation Growth Analysis," unpublished working document, The Dayton Foundation, June 1985; Joanne Scanlan, Council on Foundations, 1989.

As they become more important, community foundations will certainly attract more attention. At present, we have only a few impressionistic efforts to evaluate their impact; only three or four community foundations have yet been the subject of extensive histories. Hence this initial overview of their history can only raise some basic questions: To what extent do community foundations attract endowment funds that might otherwise go to individual agencies? What is the effect of reserving a portion of a community's capital for demonstrations, projects, start-up costs of new organizations, rather than making it available for the difficult-to-finance operating expenses of ongoing agencies—particularly universities, museums, and other educational and cultural institutions? Do metropolitan areas with large community foundations have larger numbers of inadequately funded small research and social service organizations? Or do community foundations increase the tendency to encourage small organizations to merge into larger ones? How widespread are the trends toward more professional management and toward boards that are more representative of the entire community? How general is the apparent shift from support for the capital and operating needs of existing social welfare organizations to investment in active antipoverty programs, inner-city or downtown or regional economic development initiatives, and humanities and the arts? The research agenda will lengthen as community foundations grow.

Table 3
Fifty Largest Metropolitan Regions, by Population, 1986, with Selected Community Foundations Size and Rank, 1987

Rank	Region	Population (1,000)	Foundation	Assets ($1000)	Rank	Founding Date
1	NY-NJ-Long Island	17,968	NY Com. Trust)	545,076	1	1923
			(Westchester)	1,520		1975
			(Long Island)			1978
			(Corn. Fdn. NJ)	4,157		1979
			(Plainfield, NJ)	3,603		1920
			(Westfield, NJ)	1,502		1975
	-Connecticut		(Bridgeport, CT)	6,011		1967
			(Berkshire-Taconic Fdn.)			
			(Fairfield, CT)	878		1982
			(Greenwich, CT)	705		1955
			(New Canaan, CT)	1,900		1977
	-New Haven	512	(New Haven, CT)	73,510	13	1928
			(Branford, CT)			1981
			(Guilford, CT)			1975
			(Waterbury, CT)	5,354		1924
			(Meriden, CT)	2,600		1932
2	LA-Anaheim -Riverside	13,075	(California)	69,961	14	1915
			(Riverside)	6,268		1941
			(Pasadena)	3,215		1953
			(Glendale)	1,200		1956
	-Ventura		(Ventura)	103		1987
	-Santa Barbara	339	(Santa Barbara)	31,536	28	1928
3	Chicago-Gary	8,116	(Chicago Com. Trust)	278,024	4	1915
	-Kenosha		(Aurora)	7,162		1948
			(Evanston)	149		1986
			(Oak Pk-Riverforest)			1959

Rank	Region	Population (1,000)	Foundation	Assets ($1000)	Rank	Founding Date
			(Kenosha)			1926
4	SF-Oakland	5,878	(San Francisco)	164,144	6	1948
	-San Jose		(Marin)	448,972	3	1986
			(East Bay)	6,962		1928
			(Peninsula)	14,289	47	1964
			(Santa Clara)	7,160		1954
			(Santa Cruz)	2,119		1982
			(Sonoma)			1986
5	Phila-Wilm	5,833	(Philadelphia)	60,865	19	1918
	-Trenton		(Delaware)	50		1986
6	Detroit	4,601	(SE Mich)	15,081	45	1984
	-Ann Arbor		(Ann Arbor)	2,820		1963
7	Boston	3,705	(Boston)	194,375	5	1915
	-Lowell		(Old Colony)	2,790		1955
			(Cornerstone)			1953
			(Perpetual)	1,788		1932
			(Cambridge)	2,826		1916
	-Nashua, NH		(New Hampshire)	33,830	26	1962
	-Worcester	408	(Worcester)	10,048	61	1975
8	Dallas-Fort Worth	3,655	(Texas)	157,964	7	1953
			(Dallas)	12,344	53	1929
			(Tarrant Cty.)	14,808	46	1980
			(Navarro)	7,053		1938
			(Waxahachie)	450	1970	
9	Houston -Galveston	3,634	(Houston)	–		–
10	Washington, D.C.	3,563	(C.F. of Greater Wash.)	9,253	62	1973
			(N. Virginia)	250		1978
			(Columbia, Md.)	792		1969
11	Miami	2,912	(Dade Cty)	12,182	55	1067
	-Ft. Lauderdale		(Broward Cty.)	996		1984
			(Palm Beach Cty.)	3,309		1972
12	Cleveland-	2,766	(Cleveland)	459,051	2	1914
	Akron-Lorain		(Bratenahl)			
			(Akron)	9,214	63	1955
			(Stark Cty.)	23,371	35	1964
			(Lorain Cty.)	8,395	69	1980
			(Lake Cty.)			1932
	-Canton	400	(Canton)	9,000	64	1963

Rank	Region	Population (1,000)	Foundation	Assets ($1000)	Rank	Founding Date
	-Wooster		(Wayne Cty)	435		
	-Mansfield		(Richland Cty)	15,245	43	1945
13	Atlanta	2,561	(Metro. Atl.)	68,020	15	1951
			(Atlanta Fdn.)	6,416		1921
			(Gwinnett)			1986
14	St. Louis	2,438	(St. Louis)	6,686		1915
15	Pittsburgh	2,316	(Pittsburgh)	108,690	10	1945
16	Minneapolis	2,295	(Minneapolis)	106,322	11	1915
	-St. Paul		(St. Paul)	104,132	12	1940
			(Minnesota)	8,025	72	1949
17	Seattle-Tacoma	2,285	(Seattle)	31,394	29	1946
			(Tacoma)	4,952		1977
			(Stanwood-Camano)	69		1961
			(Spokane)			
18	Baltimore	2,280	(Baltimore)	11,252	58	1972
19	San Diego	2,201	(San Diego)	29,802	31	1975
20	Tampa-St. Petersburg	1,914				
21	Phoenix	1,900	(Arizona)	12,298	54	1978
22	Denver-Boulder	1,847	(Denver Fdn.)	19,021	39	1925
23	Cincinnati, OH-IN-KY	1,690	(Greater Cin.)	61,835	16	1963
			(Hamilton Cty.)	8,386	70	1951
24	Milwaukee	1,552	(Milwaukee Fdn.)	61,737	17	1915
25	Kansas City, MO-KS	1,518	(Greater K.C.)	27,764	32	1978
26	Portland– Vancouver, WA	1,364	(Oregon)	41,151	23	1973
			(Clark City, WA)	1,040		
27	New Orleans	1,334	(Greater New Orleans)	5,151		1924
28	Norfolk-Va. Beach	1,310	(Norfolk)	26,061	33	1950
29	Columbus, OH	1,299	(Columbus)	119,000	9	1943
			(Columbus Youth)			
			(Mt. Vernon)	6,714		1944
			(Licking Cty.)			1956
30	Sacramento	1,291	(Sacramento Reg.)	2,755		1983
31	San Antonio	1,276	(San Antonio Area)	13,696	50	1964
32	Indianapolis	1,213	(Indianapolis)	44,712	21	1916
33	Buffalo-Niagara	1,182	(Buffalo)	24,000	34	1919
34	Providence– Pawtucket	1,108	(Rhode Island)	59,000	20	1916

Rank	Region	Population (1,000)	Foundation	Assets ($1000)	Rank	Founding Date
35	Charlotte–Gastonia	1,065	(Carolinas)	35,753	25	1925
			(Gaston Cty)	2,353		1978
36	Hartford–New Britain	1,044	(Hartford)	133,393	8	1925
			(New Britain)	1,700		1941
38	Oklahoma City	983	(Oklahoma Cty.)	29,900	30	1969
39	Rochester, NY	980	(Rochester Area)	11,351	57	1983
40	Louisville	963	(Louisville)	5,827		1916
41	Memphis	960	(Greater Memphis)	18,339	40	1969
42	Dayton	934	(Dayton)	20,532	38	1921
			(Springfield)	2,500		1948
			(Troy)	9,000	64	1924
43	Nashville	931				
44	Birmingham	911	(Greater Birmingham)	14,017	48	1959
45	Greensboro–Winston-Salem	900	(Fdn. of Gtr. Greensboro)	2,427		1983
			(Winston-Salem)	42,165	22	1919
46	Orlando	898	(Winter Park Corm. Trust)	2,043		1951
47	Jacksonville, FL	853	(Greater Jacksonville)	3,897		1964
48	Albany–Schenectady-Troy	844	(Mohawk-Hudson)	1,028		1968
			(Cooperstown)	50		1960
			(Corning)			1972
49	Honolulu	817	(Hawaii)	8,785	65	1916
50	Richmond–Petersburg	810	(Greater Richmond)	3,515		1968

Sources: *Statistical Abstract of the U.S., 1989;* Council on Foundations.

35

John R. Seeley et al., *Community Chest*, 1957

In the early 1950s many people in Indianapolis, Indiana, became very concerned about the Community Chest effort in their city. Year after year, the Community Chest failed to reach its money-raising goal. Community Chest directors, disappointed with the level of support the local business community seemed to provide, often resigned after only a couple of years in office. Agency directors routinely felt that the chest failed to provide them with the resources they legitimately needed. Business leaders who worked with the chest found themselves growing impatient with the demands of dependent agencies and dissatisfied with the performance of the Chest.

At last Eli Lilly, the most prominent philanthropist in Indianapolis, agreed to fund a special (and very ambitious) study of the Indianapolis Community Chest and its problems. For a full year John Seeley, a distinguished social scientist who had trained at the University of Chicago but who then held a post at the University of Toronto, led a team of researchers in an extraordinarily thorough study of giving and fundraising in Indianapolis.

Eli Lilly and the business leaders who had agreed to bring Seeley to their city may have expected a brief "executive report." Instead, Seeley and his associates produced one of the longest and most detailed community studies anyone ever published. This book contains a penetrating account of the culture of asking and giving in Indianapolis during the 1950s (including a lengthy historical essay on philanthropy and charity in Indianapolis that asks, among many other things, whether "Hoosier" culture is stingy—and concludes that it is not). It also contains a classic analysis of the tensions that seem to be inherent in federated fundraising efforts of any kind.

In the end, Seeley and his associates suggested that the problems encountered by the Community Chest in Indianapolis were not the "fault" of Community Chest leaders or of a particular "culture" in the city. Instead, the problems reflected disagreements that were almost inevitable among people whose situations placed them in very different relations to a fundraising drive. Large donors, for example, naturally wanted not only recognition for their contributions but also the acknowledgement of their leadership that is implied by the willingness of small donors to follow their lead. And large donors tend to identify with the community as a whole and to take a long-term view of its needs. Fundraising professionals, by contrast, often make their careers by leading a series of successively larger campaigns in a series of locales: hence they necessarily took a short-term view and focused on reaching monetary goals as quickly and efficiently as possible.

JOHN R. SEELEY ET AL.

Community Chest

1957

Every social organization has more or less explicit aims and purposes. These purposes, if they are effective, serve to guide policy and action in the short run; and, over the long run, they are in a sense what organizes the organization and gives meaning to membership in it. One "belongs" to an organization to the degree that one shares in its purposes; and the organization "belongs to" its membership (in a different sense) in so far as that membership determines or controls policy, or shares in its determination or control. Thus purpose acts both as the test of fitness in action and as the felt basis for the social or moral solidarity which is the measure, objectively, of the organization's strength, and, subjectively, of its value.

It is patently not necessary for the survival of some organizations that they have only one purpose at a given time—nor that every member make any particular one of its purposes his own. The purpose of an army may be to defeat the enemy, the purpose of a sergeant within it may be to "buck for promotion" by making his the best platoon in the company, and the purpose of a private may be more simply to minimize his discomforts under stated conditions. These things may and do occur without detracting sensibly from the effectiveness of the army: the command organization, with its relatively unbounded control of rewards and punishments, ensures that disparity of purpose among members does not result in unconcerted, disconcerted, or otherwise self-defeating action.

But a "voluntary" fundraising organization is not an army. It is true . . . that it wields considerable powers of punishment and holds out

---

Selected from chapter 5, "Aims and Purposes," Seeley et al., eds., *Community Chest* (Toronto: University of Toronto Press, 1957), pp. 107–66. Reprinted by permission.

considerable possibilities of reward to the "volunteers" and to the "voluntary" givers. These powers, however, compared with those operating in an army, are somewhat attenuated, and a great deal of reliance must be placed on relatively free consent, or, at least, on minimizing active resistance. Under these circumstances, it is of considerable importance that participants of all kinds should have the feeling of sharing in a common purpose (as against, say, feeling either that the program and procedure are meaningless—have no purpose—or that the purposes they have are opposed to the participants' wishes). In the absence of such a consensus about aims, actions are likely to be stultified or mutually self-canceling; and, even where parallel action is "engineered," it is likely to be emptied, for many participants, of satisfaction, let alone the glow of enthusiasm. In so far as an organization like the [Community] Chest is a "voluntary" movement, therefore, it must rely for unity and effectiveness in action, to a considerable degree, on the attractiveness of its purposes—as expressed in word, ceremony, and businesslike action—for those whom it needs to motivate and enthuse.

But the [Community Chest]—together with similar organizations—is not merely a *voluntary* fundraising organization. It is a *mass* voluntary fundraising organization; it views as in its potential donorship everyone living within a given area, or, indeed, everyone whom it could bring under suasion, whether living in the area or not. The statement that it is a mass fundraising organization does not quite mean that it is a *mass* movement, and the distinction is rather important. It is a mass organization only in the sense that it needs contributions of money from everyone—the masses—not that it needs the enthusiastic moral commitment of everyone. On the contrary . . . "success" in money-raising will turn largely on

(1) the enthusiasm of a few leaders,
(2) the "positive support" of a larger number of power-figures,
(3) the willingness to give (as directed or suggested by the power-figures) of the greater part of the employee population,
(4) some small similar willingness in part of the residentially organized "public" and, probably,
(5) no strong, organized or vocal opposition anywhere.

If the structure of the [Community] Chest (or a similar organization) is seen as something like that in the accompanying diagram, then the relevance of purpose to effectiveness increases as we work from the upper right corner ("the outside") in, decreases as we work from the lower left corner (the "inside") out. At the outside, about all that is really needed is the absence of effective opposition or veto. In the inner shells, something only a little short of total commitment is probably necessary and certainly desirable. Disagreement or confusion on any

matters felt fundamental will have progressively greater repercu
on the outside, the nearer the center that confusion or disagreement
occurs or persists.

It will be the contention of this chapter

(1) that the [Community] Chest seems plagued by a number of
conflicts and confusions about its basic role or mission or
purpose,

(2) that these confusions and conflicts are rarely made explicit,

(3) that they can be seen as sources of irritation and mutual frus-
tration between people in the Chest organization,

(4) that concerted action is difficult and inefficient as a consequence of these frustrations, among other things, and

(5) that the removal of these frustrations depends on setting up
appropriate procedures and machinery to deal with them. . . .

Figure 1
Approximate "Structure of Intimacy" of Indianapolis
Community Chest

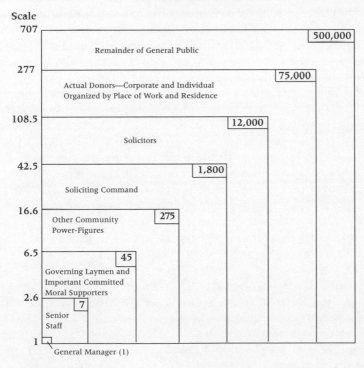

(Scale: The numbers in each square correspond to the area—on a logarithmic scale)

The confusions and contradictions are found not only in opinions regarding what are the primary *objectives* of the organization (a "value" problem) but also in opinions as to what are the *facts of life* in this field (a "fact" problem) and what are and are not acceptable modes of arguing about or *discussing* them (a "logical" problem).

CENTRAL VALUE-CONFLICTS

Business Success versus Community Organization

In a recent [Community Chest] campaign a very prominent layman shocked some part, at least, of the Chest's staff by referring to the Chest as essentially a "collecting agency" (for the social agencies). What was shocking to the staff people was not so much the possibility of a public-relations error in referring to the Chest's function so baldly and unemotionally. Rather they received a genuine moral shock—a sudden feeling of social distance and alienation between those who regard the Chest primarily as a semi-sacred movement in the realm of "community organization" (for which money is, incidentally, needed) and those who regard money-raising as the commonsense and natural heart of the enterprise (for which some community organization is, incidentally, necessary). Persons may be found, probably, in every intermediate position from those who consider the money-raising function nearly all-important to those who consider the community organization nearly all important. For some, the Chest represents almost a venture in brotherhood in which money-raising occurs; for others, it is almost an adventure in motherhood, in which the emotional focus is on the money-extracting process.

These alternate views as to the paramount or primary interest to be served do not represent merely matters of interpretation of what is going on, or more or less devotion to or interest in different elements of a total program. They may not represent purely opposed alternatives, such as, say, the alternative between driving north or driving south; but they do represent substantial opposition, such as, say, driving northeast or driving southeast—one gets east in either case, but not at the same point or near it.

The conflict has a bearing on practical matters. Should the primary criterion of the Chest's success, for instance, be a campaign measure such as "participation," or "gift per donor," or "per capita gift," or should it be a non-campaign measure such as would be reflected in an estimate of the proportion of people that "knew about" the Chest or "were in favor of" the Chest, whether or not they could or did contribute. No one perhaps took seriously any attempt to set one of these as having exclusive priority or value; this was particularly true of those who thought some non-financial measure "really" most important—i.e., no one could be found to say that the education of the community or its organization sentimentally was justifiable if it yielded no money or a net loss. But those who thought that participation was more important as an immediate issue than percapita really felt divided from the others, and were inclined to promote or pursue other policies in practice.

Among those who thought first priority ought to be given to increasing participation were people convinced either that existing givers were giving "enough" (an ethical judgment) or "about as much as they're going to give, anyway" (a judgment of fact or of practicality). On this view, since either no increase should be demanded of the givers or no such demand would be effective, the only possible source of increase is the non-giver, the successful persuasion of whom would then increase participation.

Others among the participation-emphasizers, however, had different practical and ethical reasons to adduce for their preferences. One of the practical arguments, quite credible on its face, ran to the effect that in any giving unit (such as the employees in a factory department) the acts of giving are more interdependent when it comes to the question of *whether* to give at all (which is frequently known to everyone in the unit) than they are when it comes to the alternative question as to *how much* to give (which is frequently not known to most of them). On this view, it is it "easier" to use social interaction to increase participation than it is to use interaction to increase percapita. And what is easiest ought to be done first. Another practical argument rests on an "intuitive" conviction that the ease of getting another giver out of any particular group is in some way related to the number one already has got—so that great attention to participation is justified from the viewpoint of economizing persuasive resources.

In any case, the gulf between the percapita-minded and the participation-minded is less often founded on such practical arguments, and much more frequently on an important difference in general orientation, value-system, or ethical set. For those oriented to participation, the question of the relative ease or difficulty of securing increased participation as against increased percapita is largely irrelevant, since their question is not "What is easy?" but "What is *right?*" or "What is *good?*"

The participation-minded and the percapita-minded are found among both the laymen and the professionals, although their reasons for occupying these positions are somewhat different.

The percapita-minded *professionals* tend to pay attention to the "undergiving" of those who do give; they feel (comparing their city with other cities, or comparing different classes of givers, or contrasting actuality with wish) that

(1) the givers give too little,

(2) that this is "wrong" and should be "righted" and

(3) that the fact that these givers give at all shows recognition of an obligation, which it would take relatively little effort to get discharged on a more appropriate scale.

The percapita-minded *laymen*, on the other hand, tend towards the same conclusion on one of two very different urgings:

(1) a sense of *noblesse oblige* (or, more exactly, *argent oblige*)—a feeling that they and their peers are not giving enough in proportion to their "potential" or

(2) a feeling of "injustice" or unfairness in that, while they give enough, the givers among their peers do not, and that this is urgent for correction.

The lay and professional participation-minded differ similarly. This layman feels that low participation is "bad" either because it is "poor public relations" or because, without the check of "saleability," he considers he has, himself, little or no basis for judging value. It is "poor public relations" because it is "risky to get too far out ahead of the crowd." The second reason means that, probably, "if the crowd won't buy it, it shouldn't be sold," i.e., the unpopular isn't worthy of support. The high premium put on participation is in the first case a measure of safety; in the second a check by the market, as it were, on selling enthusiasm.

The professional, on the other hand, is less likely to feel that his enthusiasm needs check, or that the value of his product needs proof or supporting evidence. He is likely to take his stand on a feeling, a mystique almost, that flows from his high valuation of, and his interpretation of what is involved in, "democracy." The general feeling that, in all matters that concern them, as many people as possible should be "involved"—ideally "all the people"—runs like a thread thick and strong through much of the social-work fabric, and participation in money-giving on a wide scale is just one particular expression of the desire to "get everybody in" so it will be "democratic," i.e., from this viewpoint, right.

Democratic versus Aristocratic Orientation

The discussion of the "business success" versus "community organization" (and percapita versus participation) orientation has brought us to the edge of another distinction or division of view as to aims and purposes: what might be called an "aristocratic" view of the organization as against what might be called a "democratic" view.

The "aristocratic" view takes it for granted that the [Community]

Chest is inevitably, or "ought" to be, an organization of the "best" people for the sake of "those not so favored." If this is the case, or if it ought to be, then the Chest's principal advantage is (or would be) just precisely that it is able to indulge the aristocratic virtues—nobility, generosity, a certain ability to deal largely and openhandedly and to make quick decisions on large events without being unduly sensitive to public relations and general opinion.

The "democratic" view maintains that, on the contrary, an organization like the [Community] Chest "ought to be" essentially an organization of "all the people" or, at the very least, an organization that "represents" all the people.

Again, the differences in view have considerable practical consequences; some effort will be made by the democratic-minded to secure the involvement of "more people" or the "representation" of "more groups," or at least the semblance of the latter. The "aristocratic-minded" may, and some do, feel that the representation of fewer interests would lead to a firmer and more certain policy and one that would involve the relevant few (relevant in terms of power in the community and ability to give or cause giving) more deeply and enthusiastically. They may well feel that too many people are already engaged in decision-making for resultant decisions to be really bold and commanding of effective support.

Some compromise clearly characterizes the Indianapolis Chest as it probably does most Chests. The typical compromise is to extend the nominal governorship of the institution, while effectively concentrating power in "committees" on which the elite or community power-group is disproportionately represented.

The greatest loss in connection with this unresolved and largely unconfronted issue comes, however, not so much, we suspect, from actual struggles to concentrate or disperse power in line with the respective views as it does from a vague uneasiness or distress or feeling of "bad conscience," stemming from the discrepancy between what many feel to be "proper" or ideal and what is actually the case or what may be the only possibility. There is little or no open—as against "off the record"—discussion of what is involved, and particularly little facing of the possibility that for an organization like the Chest an elite or power-group control might be not only inevitable but appropriate. For some others, distress arises less because of the discrepancy in this respect between what the Chest is and what it ought to be and much more because of a felt discrepancy between what it is and what it makes itself out to be. What it makes itself out to be is very various, depending at least on the particular audience addressed and the purpose of the "message." But with sometimes one emphasis, sometimes the other, and, most often, both, it makes itself out either as an organization of the very best people, the leaders of the leaders, or as a "representative" group "no different from you or me," almost in the sense of a random sample of the community population. That the latter version has always or nearly always to be emphasized indicates the feeling either that it ought to be the true one, or that it must be made to appear so.

The preceding discussion brings us face to face with another perennial issue: appearance versus substance.

Appearance versus Substance

A famous recommendation to effective government may be found in Machiavelli's *Discourses:* the Prince, to be "successful," should seem to be honest. A more long-standing recommendation, also embedded in Judeo-Christian culture, is found in the unconditional "Thou shalt not lie."

The choice between (relative) honesty as a goal and the mere appearance of it is not, of course, peculiar to any one human organization. For some, it hardly appears as a problem at all. A vendor in the more high, wide, and handsome days of selling, when even the legal maxim bade the buyer beware, could scarcely feel himself enjoined to any more honesty than made for effective selling (in the short run), which was often not a very great deal. In more recent days, while honesty is said to be the best policy, some allowance is commonly made in practice for something less than "full, frank and free disclosure." The amount of what may be called "permissible dishonesty" will vary from enterprise to enterprise and business to business, though all will permit themselves some leeway.

In many, if not most, human enterprises that fall clearly within *either* the secular field or the sacred field, the weight to be given to honesty as against its semblance is determined with relative ease by the definition of the field within which each falls. . . . [I]ndeed, for most people, the standard of honesty is probably the standard of what is customary.

But, when, on the contrary, a movement is both sufficiently new, so that no tradition has had opportunity to crystallize . . . and also, for some, on the border between sacred and secular, for others an admixture of both, for still others a secular expression of sacred motives and for yet others a secular substitute for sacred functions . . . , it is likely that there will be marked differences of opinion as to what constitutes proper behavior, and marked conflict within and between people as a consequence. Such conflict might be expected to be peculiarly acute in an organization that aims to be at one and the same time the epitome of business—money-getting—and a major focus for the American secular religion of "service."

Unfortunately for simplicity, we cannot attribute the differential concern with honesty (as against enough appearance of it to "get by") to one party or the other, either layman or professional. . . . . A layman sitting temporarily on a budget committee, or critically examining an internal financial statement, will have standards of accuracy very different from those he will have as a campaign chairman. Similarly, the same professional, acting now as general manager now as campaign director, will also have different standards on different occasions, and will feel some strain and consequently exhibit some cynicism.

Each will, generally, also allow himself [or herself] much greater leeway with the facts when . . . addressing a large audience than when . . . addressing a small one. The addressees may otherwise be the same, but large numbers reduce intimacy and therewith, simultaneously, the felt mandate to honesty and the possibility of cross-examination, i.e., the internal and external checks on wish and imagination.

Again, these are matters of immense consequence for policy: some people experience an acute "internal" problem of wear and tear because they feel either that they are driven to act in terms of an ethic they cannot approve, or that they are hampered in their effectiveness by over-scrupulous and unrealistic "social dreamers." But there are also "external" problems arising out of this evidently unresolved conflict between the substance and the seeming of truth. We have seen laymen and professionals, disaffected, alienated, or in some degree demoralized because of the conflict as to standards; we have also heard expression of a cynical "how could it be otherwise?" Thus while there is considerable individual uneasiness, there is no collective policy, explicit in words or implicit from practice.

But this may not be the most important practical problem—though it is not trivial. Another practical problem that arises inescapably when a deception-system is to be adopted is the protection of that system so that the organization does not too patently appear to contradict itself when it speaks at the same time through different members, or at successive times through the same member. This requires superior communication and record-keeping, as every propaganda director knows. It also requires clear distinction between the in-group to whom relative access to truth is permitted and the out-group to whom it is not. Some devices are also needed to prevent detection—an analogue to counter-intelligence in military or political affairs. In the absence of such machinery, experience would indicate some difficulty in maintaining elaborate deceptions (i.e., in effectively deceiving those who are to be deceived) *in the long run.*

Long-Run and Short-Run Emphasis
But this brings us to another type of division within and between people

as we have encountered them. And this difference also characterizes laymen and professionals.

The difference is essentially between those with predominantly short-run preoccupations and those with predominantly long-run ones. If a simile can be permitted that treats the population of potential givers as a "field," the difference lies between those who would "farm the land" and those who would "mine the land," between the "cultivators" and the "exploiters," the "conservators" and the "harvesters." One group tends to think in terms of maximum yield now; the other, in terms of greatest total yield over an indefinitely long life, perhaps extending beyond the present generation.

It is a well-known fact that most of the "leading citizens" associated with a movement such as the Chest will ordinarily regard themselves as more permanent members of the community, while many if not most professionals will recognize that, willing or not, they are relatively transient through it. It is widely believed, upon this ground, that the laymen will incline to the long-run view and the professionals to the short. Again, unfortunately for simplicity, this appears simply not to be the case.

In the first place, the laymen, even the town's "leading citizens," are no longer, in these days of large national firms, so predominantly people whose past is that of their present community or whose future— if they are "successful"—is bound up with the future of any one city. They were born elsewhere, and they expect and frequently hope to be yet elsewhere soon. They are therefore, even though otherwise conservative, under some necessity to follow the mandate "That thou doest, do quickly."

For many other leading laymen, moreover, time presses in the sense that their "period of service" in such organizations as the Chest has to fit into increasingly stringent career requirements. If the "service" is to be useful to the career it must not come too early in it or too late, and this means that whatever is to be done must be done fast; it also means that what is done fast should be "successful," for little credit, relatively, accrues to the businessman in the business world from service in a "failing" organization. For both of these reasons there is considerable pressure on laymen to produce notable results immediately. One would have to add to these complications a third: that under some circumstances leaders who are in one or many senses marginal to the "top top leadership" will be called into positions of most active direction precisely *because* their marginality will permit or encourage them to take steps that are, to say the least, not traditional and therefore, while potentially "successful," not open to the "top top leadership." Such steps are almost inevitably in the direction of improvising relatively startling schemes for relatively short-run ends, with reduced regard for long-run consequences.

On the other side, for the professional, is the erroneous guess that his transience would invariably give him a short-run view. Three factors in his situation, and perhaps a fourth, incline him, however, in the opposite direction:

(1) his professional past
(2) his professional future,
(3) his immediate social relations, and
(4) his (somewhat remoter) relations to other fundraisers.

His past experience and his expectation of a permanent career in fundraising somewhere, give his knowledge some extension by way of information is to what has succeeded and failed elsewhere, and put him under some pressure to develop a personal ethic and a relatively long-run policy for himself. His relative social distance from businessmen and his relative social closeness to social workers incline him perhaps to take a "professional" view of what is involved, and therefore to view it in a longer time-perspective. His association with other fundraisers works probably ambiguously, since the ethics of stewardship seem no more dominantly represented in their gatherings than the ethics of exploit.

In any case, and for whatever reasons, it seems unambiguously clear that both laymen and professionals can be found who have long-run and short-run orientations.

And again it seems clear that no simple resolution of the conflicting claims of present and future can be made-in general, or at any one time-as a permanent solution. What is remarkable, perhaps, is the relative lack of awareness of the problem despite disputes actually based upon it, the absence of a working policy (which nearly every good business has explicitly, and nearly every good farmer implicitly), and the resultant tendency for "policy" in the long run to become, therefore, a succession of short-run adaptations to successive emergencies or crises.

Volunteer and Conscript: Suasion and Pressure
One might suppose that the ideal situation for a [*mass* voluntary fundraising organization] would be one in which enough people would spontaneously send in enough money (preferably for the "right" reasons), often enough and with enough promptness, to make any large effort unnecessary and, therefore, any large organization superfluous.

Since people do not in general so act, it appears that they must be "sold," and in order to sell them, a vast organization of salesmen—"volunteers"—must be recruited, trained, motivated, controlled, and maintained. Ideally, again, even if spontaneous money-giving on a wide scale cannot be had it would be desirable that the army of "volunteer" salesmen or persuaders should be genuinely a volunteer army. It seems obvious that, in practice, this cannot be had either, and there must therefore be a prior process to "persuade" the army of workers who are to "persuade" the much larger population of "givers." "Voluntary gifts" which are not wholly voluntary must thus be collected by "volunteer solicitors" who are not wholly volunteers.

Every voluntary organization, no doubt, would wish to appear to be as voluntary as possible, while desire for "efficiency" tempts it constantly to mobilize all the sanctions—rewards or penalties—it can muster to ensure that "free" choice shall have a foregone outcome. But for every organization this poses at least three problems:

> where shall the actuality be located (how much "pressure" is actually to be used—or is it "proper" to use);
>
> where shall the public image be located ("What is our pitch, here?"); and
>
> how is the discrepancy between the two to be accounted for and thus rendered harmless or even palatable?

For an organization like the Chest (or probably for any [*mass* voluntary fundraising organization]) these problems are peculiarly acute since the need to *seem* ethical—for the sake of efficiency—referred to earlier is conjoined with the need (for many) to *be* ethical—which stems from the Chest's origins and from the meaning the whole operation has for many laymen and professionals involved in it.

The tendency, in practice, is to locate the public representation close to the "voluntary" pole, so that, with rare exceptions, the public image fostered or the private image cherished is very largely one of free men willingly banded together to achieve an object that most or all actively desire. The main difficulties and conflicts, therefore, occur chiefly around where to locate the actual level of coercion; and, to a less degree, how to deal with the gap between appearance and reality. Both difficulties have to do with pressuring the pressurers ("recruitment"), and the pressurers' pressuring the givers ("soliciting").

There are really, two problems in connection with "pressure" that are often sharply felt but only dimly distinguished; these have to do . . . with the amount of pressure applied and with its nature or character. Pressure may be much or little, high or low as to amount; it may also, in its nature, be relevant to the issue at hand or largely irrelevant. Relevant pressure means pressure that really addresses itself to the issues at hand; irrelevant pressure makes use of rewards or sanctions that have little or nothing to do with any natural consequence of the choice, for example, a threat to cease trading with a given individual unless a gift is forthcoming. The accompanying schema may make the various kinds of pressure clear. Among both laymen and professionals can be found those who are willing or eager to use each of these types of pressure, some of them or all of them, according to need or circumstance. A few laymen think that none should be used, and many people "wish" none need be.

Figure 2
Pressure—Amount Applied and Its Character

Kind of Pressure	Degree of Pressure		
	Relatively low		Relatively high
Largely relevant	Type I	→	Type III
	↓		↓
Largely irrelevant	Type II	→	Type IV

Suggestions as to how best to secure results range through all these types of pressure:

Type I: gently (by printed matter and mail) "telling people about the need"

Type II: trying to involve them in games and stunts and mild competition which "people don't like to miss"

Type III: earnest, forceful, face-to-face and heart-to-heart talk about the facts and the moral issues involved

Type IV: publishing a "blacklist" of non-donors or "inadequate" donors, which, hopefully, would "bring a man around" under pressure of threat to his business or livelihood.

The major conflict is, however, between those who would wish to see only Type I pressure employed ("just give people the opportunity to give") and those who favor fairly widespread use of Type IV ("There are always some . . . that are hard to get in").

The division of opinion as to what is legitimate and proper, here, is of course highly correlated with the division between those who think dominantly in financial terms and those who think dominantly in human terms. But the coincidence is not exact, for among those who do think predominantly in terms of human values, many are so deeply impressed with the need of the ultimate beneficiaries (whom they see largely as the poor or disadvantaged) that the end of serving them adequately justifies the use of almost any means; and among some who do think primarily in financial terms here is a realization that, except in the very short run, some bounds on pressure may actually yield more money.

For obvious reasons, there is also some correlation between those who divide on the issue of pressure and those who divide on short-run versus long-run perspective. But again the coincidence is not perfect since more considerations than these enter into a decision as to what kinds of pressure to apply.

Except under rare circumstances, it is probably difficult to find a campaign or an element of a campaign where only Type I pressure is actually used, though there are some situations where indifference to the Chest's "cause," or delicate relations with labor, or ethical principle has maintained such an island or islands. But, in general, pressure both to man the machine and to secure "gifts" tends to be of Type II or III. As fortune fails to smile or, for whatever reason, failures cumulate, there is great temptation to resort to Type IV—especially perhaps, though not exclusively, against those who are neither so big as to be identified with the policy-making group ("one of us") nor so small as to be thought worthy of special protection ("the little giver"). The tendency to and direction of breakdown to higher and more irrelevant pressure are indicated by the arrows in the chart.

There is reason to believe, perhaps, that the cycle of failure could be reversed by a few successes, and that this might make for less pressure, so that those who believe in the present use of high and irrelevant pressures may be neither short-sighted nor unprincipled. Some of these people believe, in fact, that present high pressure will lead to "success," success will permit a lowering of pressure, and with lower pressure a spiral could occur, which would make for greater success, leading to still less pressure—and so on.

Nobody knows, of course, whether this could occur. Everybody, however, is working on some implicit model of "how it works" and on some implicit assumptions of "what is right." With different people, these models of reality and demands for ideality are different, and the policy recommendations that all of them put forth, often with considerable force, are correspondingly incompatible but vested with deep feeling. It is difficult to believe that clarification of what is at issue and subsequent discussion would not eventuate in fruitful, if temporary, compromise and some diminution in intrapersonal and interpersonal tensions.

Charity and Service

One more continuous latent conflict (probably less important than the foregoing) lies between those who think the Chest is or ought to be primarily a "charity" organization and those who think of it primarily as a "community service" organization.

For some, mostly laymen, the whole meaning of the enterprise is that it represents or makes possible the discharge of the impulse or deep desire to help the less fortunate. On humane or religious grounds or both, it is deemed desirable or necessary to give aid, in suitable form and under suitable safeguards, to the disadvantaged; the Chest is intended as the major vehicle for the performance of this privilege or duty.

For others, this is almost the exact antithesis of what they would wish to think of the Chest as being, or what they would wish it to become, in so far as they can at all affect policy. The discharge of the obligation to "clothe the naked, feed the hungry, visit the sick, and comfort the fatherless" they would regard as being sufficiently met by government at various levels: "For that, we pay taxes." The object of a Community Chest should be, they feel, the provision of a better life for all, but most particularly the provision of "services," not for the unfortunate, but for those most worthy or promising, the solid, substantial "backbone of the community" or "promise of America's future."

Few see this as an all-or-none choice between sharply defined alternatives, but many would wish to reduce in fact or play down in publicity the one element or the other in what the Chest "supports." Indeed there are four related sets of preferences, presented in the accompanying diagram, upon which individuals will express preferences, sometimes very strong ones. Those who are attracted to one end of any one scale are usually similarly attracted to the same end of the other scales: indeed one could work out combinations showing polar opposite preferences such as: a character-building agency giving service to young and not-needy boys *versus* a charity agency relieving the needs of old women.

Figure 3
Scale of Preference

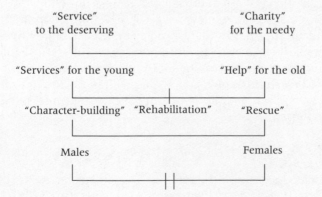

For those who have strong preferences, the Chest is in the perhaps unfortunate position that it and a great many of "its" agencies do not represent in anything like pure form either one type of program or the other. Many agencies incorporated in the Chest's appeal have both a "charitable" function and a "service" one; some agencies incline more heavily one way or the other (e.g., the . . . Mission as against, say, the Boy Scouts), but few, if any, represent pure cases, and the Chest cannot successfully represent itself as fulfilling either the one or the other function.

The solution the Chest finds in practice to the problem of self-representation in this respect is a not very successful attempt to emphasize or mention exclusively now its one aspect, now the other, for different audiences or on different occasions. But at campaign time it is particularly difficult to limit the appropriately biased message to its intended audience; and, on occasion, it is hard to escape appearing to say to one and the same audience that the Chest benefits primarily or exclusively "people like you," and that it is really, primarily, or exclusively intended to care for the "less fortunate."

This problem of representation makes for enough difficulty, but the really tough problems are those of action: what agencies are to be admitted or kept out of the Chest? And, for those admitted, what is to be budget policy towards agencies differentially emphasizing opposite ends of these various dimensions of possibility?

Again in practice this problem tends to be dealt with by a polite sort of log-rolling, which poses this particular agency's budget request presented by these particular laymen or power-groups against that one, for this particular year. Compromises are thus effectively arrived at, but hardly enduring ones, and very often unsatisfactory ones with some residue of bitterness. Complaint is frequently made that laymen are "agency-minded" (i.e., they tend to fight against the whole for the interest of "their particular agency"). The observation is, no doubt, well founded, but the possibility that, underlying these choices of favored agencies, are perhaps deep-seated preferences for different segments of the population or types of work or social relations seems never to have been explored. Perhaps exploration of such differences might make for better, clearer, and more enduring, or, at least, better understood, resolutions or compromises.

HUMAN RELATIONS AND BELIEFS

These unresolved, continuous, latent value-conflicts have direct consequences of the kind suggested in connection with each of them. But, taken as a whole, the situation of unresolved conflict is intimately bound up (both as cause and as consequence) with the prevailing interpersonal relations, with the state of belief as to what the key facts in the field are, and even with some peculiarities in the forms of "logic" employed (and accepted) as convincing argument. One might say that all these are reciprocally related in the following fashion, without implying any opinion as to which is the cause of which (Fig. 4).

Figure 4
Consequences of Latent Value-Conflicts

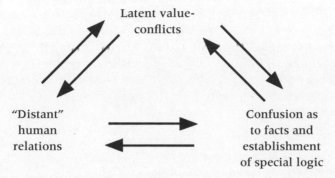

This is not the place to undertake a detailed documentation of these statements. They will be expanded upon later. It will perhaps suffice to say here that our observation indicates that the latent conflicts are both causes and symptoms of what seems a lack of intimacy between the protagonists of various views, especially perhaps, but by no means exclusively, between professionals and laymen.

The lack of "'intimacy" *expresses* also markedly different opinions as to what the facts are. But it also *causes* great difficulty in discovering what is fact, since it is often characteristic in situations of low intimacy for each party to treat as a pawn or counter in the implicit struggle or competition. Thus "a certain amount of selling" or "making the best of the figures" or "putting things in their best light" goes on on all sides, but in different directions. When this goes on long enough, and parties run the risk of being taken in by their own propaganda, and being therefore unable any longer to determine even relatively elementary facts, whether for "home consumption" or the enlightenment of relatively neutral and benign researchers. Lastly, under these circumstances, there tend to develop (and we have observed them in action and document) some peculiar, though evidently accepted, logical forms that still further confuse views of the facts and tend to perpetuate the conflicts about purposes.

The questions that confront any organization like the Chest can, we believe, be put in purely social engineering terms, if it is preferred to avoid discussion in openly ethical ones. The first question is as to the nature or character of the human relations that must obtain if such an organization is (*a*) to be successful, (*b*) to endure, without, presumably, intolerable strains, and (*c*) to retain some acceptable level of "voluntariness," sufficient, for example, to distinguish it from fraud on one side or formal government on the other.

If this question can be settled, at least in terms of working approximations, the level or levels of intimacy required will become obvious, the requirements for the machinery of operation evident, and procedures for getting true and relevant facts, and for solving or resolving value-problems by discussion or compromise, manifest.

There are other and "technical" questions for any [*mass* voluntary fundraising organization]. But solving the technical problems in the absence of solutions for these major non-technical problems is not likely, we think, to lead towards what any party to such an enterprise would regard as full success.

36

David L. Sills, *The March of Dimes: Origins and Prospects,* 1957

In the mid-1950s the March of Dimes faced a crisis brought on by success. Over thirty years of dedicated and imaginative work the March of Dimes had built up an extraordinary national organization. Using such pioneering devices as the "poster child" it focussed the nation's attention on the needs of polio victims. Through hundreds of local chapters it coordinated an annual door-to-door "march" and "Birthday Balls" in honor of President Franklin D. Roosevelt: altogether, these activities raised, through very large numbers of small contributions, unprecedented amounts of money for research and medical care. By the early 1950s the Salk and Sabin vaccines developed—in part with support from the March of Dimes—promised to make it possible to eliminate polio epidemics.

Paradoxically, this success created a big problem for the March of Dimes. If the organization existed for the purpose of reaching the goal of eliminating polio, the organization should, logically, disappear once that goal was reached. But why, leaders of the March of Dimes had to ask, eliminate an organization that had been so difficult to build up and that was so effective?

David L. Sills, one of the leading students of American society at the time, saw that the immediate problem facing the March of Dimes raised questions relevant to our understanding of other voluntary organizations, ranging from the American Heart Association, the American Cancer Society, and the Red Cross, to the YMCA and the Women's Christian Temperance Union.

Sills noted that all organizations, even those that emphasize the importance of active participation by all members, must cope with what Robert Michels called the "iron law of oligarchy:" the tendency of power and authority to move upwards within any organization, with the corresponding consequence that ordinary members of the organization feel less and less connected with it, become apathetic, and cease to give the organization their best efforts. Over the years the March of Dimes had apparently retained an unusually high degree of participation and enthusiasm in its rank-and-file members. Had the March of Dimes really done this, Sills asked, and if so, how? If it had succeeded in mitigating the effects of the iron law of oligarchy, the March of Dimes really was an unusually valuable organization, one that should be encouraged to survive after it had reached its stated goal.

Sills also saw that the March of Dimes crisis raised fundamental questions about the role of voluntary associations in American democracy as a whole. If voluntary associations are as important to American democracy as political theorists like Alexis de Tocqueville have said they are, Sills suggested, it is important not just for their managers but for the nation as a whole that we understand them. How, he asked, did successful organizations manage to change with the times and yet retain their coherence and their effectiveness? Why did some organizations successfully change, why did others fail to change and decline?

DAVID L. SILLS

The March of Dimes

ORIGINS AND PROSPECTS

1957

THE MARCH OF DIMES: A NOTE ON HISTORICAL ORIGINS

The Georgia Warm Springs Foundation was initially a private philanthropy, established by Franklin D. Roosevelt in 1927. In its early years, the treatment center at Georgia Warm Springs was supported financially by Roosevelt himself and by some of his friends. The Depression made large gifts increasingly difficult to obtain, however, and donations declined from a peak of $368,991 in 1929 to $30,331 in 1932. The Georgia Warm Springs Foundation, like much of America, was nearly bankrupt.

The First Mass Fund-Raising
In 1933, two decisions were made which were to have far-reaching consequences for the then unborn National Foundation for Infantile Paralysis. First, in order to raise the necessary funds to replace the old Meriwether Inn—the main building at Warm Springs, and, according to

Selected from Sills, *The Volunteers: Means and Ends in a National Organization* (New York: The Free Press, 1958). Reprinted by permission of The Free Press, a Division of Simon & Schuster.

Roosevelt, "our principal handicap"—a decision was made to abandon an earlier plan to seek large gifts from wealthy Georgians and to embark instead upon a mass fund-raising campaign. As a result, over 60,000 gifts, ranging from a dime to $500, from farm produce to hand-made articles, were contributed by the people of Georgia for the construction of a new building named Georgia Hall. As the anonymous author of a history of Georgia Hall phrased it, this building was "a gift great in itself . . . but greater because it unlocked the door for the future development of a crusade on a nation-wide scale."

The President's Birthday Ball
The second far-reaching decision made by the Georgia Warm Springs Foundation in 1933 was to embark upon a nationwide fund-raising campaign—a decision which was of course an outgrowth of Roosevelt's election to the Presidency the previous November. On Thanksgiving weekend a group of people interested in Georgia Warm Springs met there to discuss fund-raising possibilities. Here is one participant's report of the most important conversation of the weekend:

> Col. Doherty insisted that it should not be a long campaign, that it should be some particular event connected with some particular day, the kind of thing that could be repeated from year-to-year. "Give the people some sort of entertainment, a party, so that it will not be a matter of passing the hat," Col. Doherty said.
> "The President's Birthday!" someone exclaimed, "Why not a President's Birthday Ball?"
> To save me, I can't say now which one of us four men made the suggestion. I just don't remember. We were all so pleased by the idea we paid little attention to who made it.

A few moments later another important decision was made, as the question was discussed as to who—on such short notice—could organize Birthday Balls throughout the country. "I've got it!" said Keith Morgan. "The Postmasters. They just got jobs after ten Republican years. They ought to be glad to do something for the boss."

Keith Morgan was right, and Birthday Balls and similar celebrations were quickly organized in thousands of communities throughout America, many of them by postmasters. This first venture into a nationwide, publicly supported fund-raising campaign turned out to be more successful than anyone had dared hope. Basil O'Connor, for example, had thought "the entire stunt might not even hit the first $100,000" and was "actually shaken" when he learned that the event had been a huge success. For so many Americans turned out on the evening of January 30, 1934—either to honor the President, to help fight infantile paralysis, or just to dance—that $1,016,444 was raised, after expenses.

The unanticipated success of the first President's Birthday Ball confronted the Georgia Warm Springs Foundation with something of a dilemma. Although part of the proceeds could have been used to repay Roosevelt and others for what they had personally advanced to the Foundation, Roosevelt—in accepting the check for the Foundation—vetoed this suggestion, saying that "of course no part of this fund will be used to repay any advances made the Foundation by any of its officers or trustees." Another solution would have been to establish a permanent endowment fund, the proceeds of which would have contributed to the support of Georgia Warm Springs. The Trustees, however, believed that they now had a mandate to launch a nationwide program to combat infantile paralysis, a program envisioned nearly three years before by Roosevelt when he proposed "one vast national crusade against infantile paralysis." Accordingly, the Certificate of Incorporation was amended to extend the territory in which the Georgia Warm Springs Foundation would carry out its activities. Instead of being confined to the states of New York and Georgia, it now became empowered to operate in "the United States of America, its possessions and dependencies, but the operation of the corporation shall not be limited to such territory." Furthermore, the proceeds from the 1934 celebrations were used both to support Georgia Warm Springs and to launch a nationwide program for combating infantile paralysis. In the three subsequent years, 1935 through 1937, the local Committees for the Celebration of the President's Birthday were authorized to retain for use in their own communities 70 per cent of the proceeds from the Birthday Balls—the remaining 30 per cent going, in 1935, to the newly-created President's Birthday Ball Commission for Infantile Paralysis Research, and, in 1936 and 1937, to the Georgia Warm Springs Foundation.

Origins of the Patient Care Program

Local communities made use of their portion of the proceeds from the Birthday Balls in a number of ways, including providing financial assistance to polio patients. The local patient care program thus emerged accidentally, as the result of a "too successful" fund-raising idea. Accordingly, when plans for establishing a new National Foundation for Infantile Paralysis were being made in the latter part of 1937 the planners had to decide not only how to insure continuity to the Georgia Warm Springs Foundation, but also how to convert the already-established fund-raising and patient care programs to the uses of the new organization. President Roosevelt asked Basil O'Connor, who was then Treasurer of the Georgia Warm Springs Foundation, to take charge of the 1938 Birthday Ball, and to decide how the funds should best be utilized. In his reply to the President, O'Connor reviewed the previous Birthday Balls, and said:

Any funds raised from the celebration of your birthday in 1938 are to be administered by the new Foundation. The efforts of that new Foundation are not to be confined to research or after-treatment or any one phase of the disease, but are to attack the problem from every angle and as a whole. With this thought in mind . . . it is unhesitatingly recommended that all funds raised in the communities . . . be sent in their entirety to the committee . . . to be given to the new National Foundation to be administered by it for the good of the cause locally or nationally.

Early in November, 1937, an announcement was made to the press that President Roosevelt had "given his birthday to the new National Foundation for Infantile Paralysis," and the new plan for the centralized administration of the funds was explained. The Foundation was thus launched as a truly national organization with no mention made of local affiliates or branches.

It is easy to say in retrospect that it should have been possible to predict an unfavorable reaction to this announcement that henceforth local communities would retain none of the proceeds of the Birthday Balls. But to Basil O'Connor and his associates, who were entering into the unknown field of a large-scale, publicly supported attack upon a still mysterious disease, it must have seemed perfectly sensible to want to have control over the expenditure of the available funds. In any event, protests did come in from local communities shortly after the announcement was made.

Origins of Local Chapters
The reaction of the national leadership to these protests from the local Committees proved to have far-reaching effects. In a report to the Board of Trustees on November 30, 1938, Basil O'Connor reviewed his reasoning in having previously recommended the centralized control of the Foundation's funds, and noted that a large number of "requests for financial assistance from local communities" had been received. "I think the experience of this last year indicates clearly that the time has now come," his report went on to say, "when the so-called local situation can be properly handled only by the National Foundation taking a certain amount of activity in it, otherwise the localities will be unable to finance their requirements."

Therefore, he recommended that "in each year a certain percentage of the money raised . . . be left in the localities where raised throughout the country on a county basis where practical" and that "the Foundation organize in each county . . . a chapter or unit to administer the funds left in the particular county, the method of organization and the personnel of said chapters or units, and the method of administering its funds to be worked out by the committee of Trustees. . . . "

This plan to establish local chapters was approved by the Trustees, and O'Connor was given approval to appoint a committee of three trustees to prepare a *Manual for Chapters.*

Most of O'Connor's report to the Trustees was included in a radio broadcast he made that same day. But he stressed to the public even more strongly than he had to the Trustees that the plan to establish Chapters was the result of local pressures. "The National Foundation does not seek this," he said, "the local situation requires it."

November, 1938, like the November five years before when the Birthday Balls were first planned, was thus a crucial month in the Foundation's history, since a program of locally-administered assistance to polio patients was established and local organizations were authorized to administer it for the first time.

Most Chapters were initially organized by the local Chairman of the Committee for the Celebration of the President's Birthday, but the Committees as such did not go out of existence. Instead, the newly-formed Chapters were assigned responsibility for the patient care program, and the Committees—which gradually evolved into March of Dimes organizations—remained as the fund-raising units of the Foundation.

This brief historical review has demonstrated that the current structural differences between Chapter and March of Dimes organizations were not explicitly planned, but developed as unanticipated consequences of decisions made in order to solve pressing problems. March of Dimes organizations had their origin in the local Committees for the Celebration of the President's Birthday, which were established in order to raise the funds necessary for the continued existence of the Georgia Warm Springs Foundation; local Chapters were established in order to administer a patient care program which had evolved in an unplanned fashion as a result of the decision to permit the local Committees to retain part of the proceeds from the second and the two subsequent Birthday Balls. Before continuing with the discussion of the Foundation today, however, it is necessary to note the impact of these decisions upon the Volunteer personnel of the Foundation.

Origins of Middle-Class Volunteers

It is virtually impossible to describe accurately the political composition of the early membership of Foundation Chapters, since the only comprehensive records which are available include only the names and the occupations of the people involved. It is known that many of the Committees for the Celebration of the President's Birthday were originally headed, following Keith Morgan's suggestion, by postmasters—who, because of the political appointment system then in effect, were in most cases Democrats—and by local Democratic leaders. In fact, thirty-four Volunteers in thirteen of the thirty-seven Chapters studied intensively

during this research spontaneously mentioned that their Chapter origi-·
nally had had close relationships with the local Democratic Party. Furthermore, the Volunteers interviewed during this research by the
American Institute of Public Opinion were asked specifically to relate
what they knew of the origins of their Chapter: In fifty-nine out of
eighty-five Chapters, one or more Volunteers reported that the original
members had largely been Democrats.

Not all of these original Volunteers were Democrats, however, and
some were even active in Republican Party activities. By and large they
were businessmen, professionals, and persons of *civic* prominence for
one reason or another; in most cases, however, they were not persons
of *social* prominence in the community. When the original Chairman
were asked to organize local Chapters they naturally turned to people
who had worked with them in the past, either on the Birthday Ball or
on some other activity. As a result, the early Chapters included members who were not necessarily active in Democratic Party activities, but
very seldom people of high social status in the community.

The decision to ask postmasters and persons of civic prominence to
head the first Birthday Balls thus had far-reaching consequences for the
Foundation. For it established the tradition that Foundation Volunteers
are recruited from what might be best described as the "functioning" or
"Main Street" segment of the community, rather than from the ranks of
the socially prominent. It is this characteristic of Foundation Volunteers,
rather than Democratic Party affiliation, which has remained most un-
changed with the passing years. As noted earlier, Volunteers—regardless of political affiliation—generally think of themselves as members of
the middle class, and consider the Foundation to be unique among
health and welfare associations because of the middle-class composition
of its personnel.

· · · ·

MAINTAINING MEMBERSHIP INTEREST
IN A VOLUNTARY ASSOCIATION

Discussions of voluntary associations in America characteristically stress
one of three major themes. First, throughout our history participation
in voluntary activity has been regarded as having its origins in the fun-
damentally democratic nature of American society, as being an essential
requirement for the survival of democracy in America, and above all as
being a peculiarly *American* phenomenon.*

A second theme—more frequent in sociological analysis of volun-

---

*The assertion that voluntary associations currently play a unique role in Ameri-
can life cannot, however, be accepted uncritically, since there are many indications that—
particularly with reference to local associations—many societies exhibit a similar

tary associations—attempts to correct this somewhat misleading picture of American life by pointing out that participation in voluntary activities is by no means a universal phenomenon in America. Most such studies have shown that from one-third to one-half of the adult population does not belong to any voluntary associations, and that at best perhaps one-fourth of the population belongs to more than one association. Socio-economic status has uniformly been found to be the major correlate of participation. A large majority of people of higher status belong to voluntary associations and a majority of people of lower status do not.

A third theme which dominates many discussions of voluntary associations concerns the actual character of the participation of the membership. The general finding with respect to participation is that voluntary associations tend to be characterized by an active minority which actually controls the association's affairs and an inactive majority which participates only occasionally in the organization's activities and which in other ways expresses disinterest and apathy. Lord Bryce, for example, who found voluntary associations to be an important component of American democracy, nevertheless recognized the near-universality of minority rule in "all assemblies and groups and organized bodies of men . . . ." More recently, Philip Selznick has described the typical voluntary association in the following terms:

> Most voluntary associations . . . are skeletal in the sense that they are manned by a small core of individuals—the administration, the local sub-leaders, a few faithful meeting-goers—around whom there fluctuates a loosely bound mass of dues-payers. This type of membership has, on the whole, only a very limited relation to the organization; its agreement with it may be of the vaguest sort; it may give little or no time to the organization nor be guided by its pronouncements save, as in unions and professional groups, on very narrow issues; in short, the power implications of membership are minimal.

---

proliferation of voluntary associations. This seems particularly to be the case in the Scandinavian countries, Germany, Austria, and Great Britain. However, not all countries which have a large number of voluntary associations are Western. Rural Japanese society, in particular, is characterized by many voluntary associations. [John F. Embree, *Suye Mura: A Japanese Village* (Chicago: University of Chicago Press, 1939); Arthur F. Raper, Tamie Tsuchiyama, Herbert Passin, and David L. Sills, *The Japanese Village in Transition* (Tokyo: General Headquarters, Supreme Commander for the Allied Powers, 1950); S. N. Eisenstadt, "The Social Conditions of the Development of Voluntary Associations—A Case Study of Israel," in Eliezer Kaplan School of Economics and Social Sciences, *Scripta Hierosolymitana,* Vol. III (Jerusalem: Hebrew University, 1955).] Nor do voluntary associations play an equally important role in all Western countries [on the relative paucity of voluntary associations in France, see Arnold M. Rose, *Theory and Method in the Social Sciences* (Minneapolis: University of Minnesota Press, 1954).]

. . . .

It must be noted at the outset that an active minority and a passive majority may exist in many organizations without interfering in any way with progress toward goals, just as widespread membership participation does not necessarily indicate an adherence to democratic practices. An inactive membership may not interfere with goal achievement particularly in organizations which serve highly specific functions for their members, and which depend for their financial support entirely upon membership dues—an automobile association or a medical payment plan are obvious examples. In organizations of this type, membership apathy may be deplored because of the fact that democratic values are violated, but the organization itself is generally not adversely affected. As long as services for the membership are provided, the inactive majority will generally be satisfied.

In other voluntary associations, on the other hand, membership participation is of crucial importance for the achievement of goals. This is particularly true of those organizations—like the Foundation—which are totally dependent upon their fund-raising campaigns for their financial support, in contrast to organizations which are supported by membership dues. Since the March of Dimes is a fund-raising campaign specifically geared to soliciting small contributions from millions of people, a large and active membership is necessary in order to reach these millions.

The generic problem of maintaining membership interest in voluntary associations must thus be stated in these terms: When authority and functions are delegated *upward* in an association, there is a tendency for the membership to lose interest in participating in the program of the organization, thus permitting an active minority to gain control. Two consequences may result from this process. First, the individuals to whom authority and functions have been delegated may develop interests of their own, and consequently may neglect the initial goals of the organization. Second, if some phase of the organization's program is dependent upon widespread membership participation, this process may make it impossible for the organization to achieve its goals.

In face of this problem, how has the [National] Foundation [for Infantile Paralysis] been able to maintain a sufficiently high level of membership participation to ensure that its operational and fund-raising programs do not suffer from membership apathy? This question cannot of course be fully answered [here]; in fact, this entire volume is in many respects devoted to an examination of this general problem. But a beginning can be made by pointing out various features of the Foundation's formal structure which are related to the problem of membership participation.

The section which follows immediately is devoted to a general description of the Volunteer membership of the Foundation, and particularly to the Volunteers whose experiences are the main subject matter of this study. Following this description, a section is devoted to the major sources of membership apathy which students of large-scale organizations have identified. A final sections describes those features of the Foundation's structure which serve to mitigate the adverse consequences of membership apathy.

The Volunteer Membership of the Foundation

Since the Foundation is a voluntary association, it utilizes Volunteers—individuals who are not remunerated financially for their services—at all levels of the organization. Basil O'Connor, who has been President since the organization was founded, is a Volunteer, as are all members of the Board of Trustees. The medical doctors and research scientists who serve on national advisory committees are Volunteers, as were the 20,000 doctors and 40,000 nurses who administered the Salk vaccine during the 1954 vaccine field trials. Each state has at least one Volunteer Advisor on Women's Activities who helps Chapter women develop year-round programs, and a Volunteer State March of Dimes Chairman who coordinates the activities of county Campaign Directors during the annual fund-raising campaign. Finally, in each county in the United States there are two local units of the national organization. First, a local Chapter—comprised of Volunteer members—is responsible for the infantile paralysis program in the county throughout the year. Second, during the annual March of Dimes each county has a fund-raising organization which is closely related to, but administratively separate from, the Foundation Chapter in the same county. (A few Chapters serve two counties, and a few counties contain more than one Chapter. There are 3,076 counties in the United States; at the time of this research there were 3,073 Chapters in the continental United States, plus Chapters in Alaska, the Canal Zone, Hawaii, Puerto Rico, and the Virgin Islands. In 1956 there were 3,086 Chapters in all.)

A word of explanation is necessary concerning the relationship of these local Chapters to the national organization. It was noted in the Introduction to this study that the Foundation has a corporate-type formal structure; that is, the primary locus of authority within the organization is in the National Headquarters. The *historical* origins of this structure are described [above]; its *legal* basis stems from the fact that the Foundation is a nonprofit membership corporation, established under the laws of the State of New York. The *By-laws* define the membership of the corporation in these terms:

The Membership of the Corporation shall consist of the Board of Trustees of the Corporation, each Trustee automatically becoming a Member upon qualifying as a Trustee and ceasing to be a Member upon ceasing to be a Trustee of the Corporation.

It is readily apparent that this official membership of the Foundation does not constitute the working membership. Although the Board of Trustees is currently comprised of only thirty-eight men, many thousands of Volunteers consider themselves members of the organization. The importance of this legal definition, however, is that it locates the policy-making functions of the organization in one group of people—the Board of Trustees—rather than in the membership generally.

Since the Board of Trustees obviously cannot carry on the activities of the organization by itself, it has authorized the establishment of both a National Headquarters and local Chapters. The legal position of these Chapters in the formal structure is that of *ad hoc* instrumentalities, authorized by the Board of Trustees as a means of accomplishing the objectives for which the organization was established. That is, they are component units of the organization. . . .

A similar—but not identical—situation obtains in other voluntary health associations which have a corporate structure, although for both historical and operational reasons other organizations do not place as much emphasis upon the "unity" of the national office and the component units. The American Cancer Society, for example, is comprised of sixty Chartered Divisions, largely organized along state lines, which are required to incorporate themselves in the state in which they are located. The conditions of incorporation, however, are stipulated by the national organization. The more than 3,000 local Units are component parts of the sixty Divisions, and have a relationship to the Divisions similar in some ways to the Foundation's Chapter-National headquarters relationship. The National Multiple Sclerosis Society, to cite another example of an association with a corporate-type formal structure, permits but does not encourage its Chapters to incorporate, and requires that incorporation be under conditions set by the national office. The actual relationship of its Chapters to the national office appears to be nearly identical to that which prevails in the Foundation.

The Volunteers who belong to local Chapter and March of Dimes organizations constitute, of course, the overwhelming proportion of the Foundation's membership. Accordingly, it is necessary to preface a description of them with a brief statement of the ways in which these Volunteers resemble or differ from the volunteer members of other voluntary associations.

National voluntary health associations of the type represented by the Foundation differ markedly from other types of voluntary associations with respect to the composition and nature of their membership. According to Rose, most voluntary associations are formed when "a small group of people, finding they have a certain interest (or purpose) in common, agree to meet and act together in order to satisfy that interest or achieve that purpose." In the case of many voluntary associations, particularly local health and welfare associations, these people constitute the volunteer membership of the organizations, usually its "board." Since board members are often too busy to devote a great deal of time to the organization, they generally appoint a professional staff to carry out the day-to-day tasks of running the organization. Since the nature of these tasks frequently requires some specialized training, this professional staff is generally composed of people trained in office management, public relations, and social work. Textbooks used in schools of social work, accordingly, generally devote some attention to the related techniques of maintaining good working relationships with volunteer boards and educating the board members in the problems faced by the professional staff. In organizations having this character, volunteers are in effect the employers of the working-level staff.

In addition to board members, another type of volunteer worker is often found in this type of health or welfare association: the part-time volunteer who assists the professional staff in such activities as home visitations, clerical work, speech-making, and fund-raising, but does not necessarily become an official member of the association. Here again, textbooks and other publications written for professional social workers place much emphasis upon the advantages of utilizing volunteer assistance for such purposes. *Adult Leadership,* a magazine devoted entirely to the problems of community organizations, recently devoted an entire issue to a "Workshop on the Volunteer," and defined a volunteer worker as: "The non-paid person who gives time to furthering the purposes of the agency or organization. He or she may be a hospital aide, agency or hospital board member, doorbell ringer in a get-out-the-vote drive, youth group leader, Sunday School teacher."

A standard reference book on voluntary health associations by Selskar Gunn and Philip Platt defines volunteers as follows:

> It was a "volunteer" who, seeing unattended health needs not far from his own doorstep, set out to remedy conditions. A group or society of such volunteers make up the voluntary health agency. The society sooner or later engages a professional worker, who gradually replaces the volunteers in the daily tasks except for the routine direction of boards and committees. in time, and especially in emergencies, such organizations call for help from lay volunteers.

The point cannot be made too strongly that this generic definition of a "volunteer" does not adequately describe the Volunteer members of the Foundation. True, the Foundation's membership contains all the component elements: a Volunteer Board of Trustees which comprises the official membership of the association; a professional staff which carries out many of the day-to-day activities; and a corps of lay Volunteers which assists the professional staff. But when the inter-relationship of these component elements is considered, and when the role played by each is examined, the inadequacy of this definition becomes very apparent. Although the full import of this statement cannot be appreciated until the conclusion of this volume, some understanding can be achieved through a description of the Foundation's Volunteer membership. . . .

Chapter Volunteers

Many—if not most—national organizations consist of a national headquarters, forty-eight or forty-nine state organizations, and local units administratively related to the state organizations. The Foundation, on the other hand, does not have state organizations (each state has a March of Dimes Chairman, but the organization which he directs consists solely of the county March of Dimes organizations throughout the state. Similarly, each state has a "state office," which is the headquarters of the State not an organization of Volunteers). [The March of Dimes Foundation's] organizational structure consists of the national Board of Trustees, the headquarters staff employed by the Board, and the local units. The responsibilities and activities of local Chapters are officially defined as follows:

1. Making sure that no polio patient—man, woman or child—shall go without the best available medical care for lack of funds.
2. Informing the public about the disease, methods of dealing with it, and of the activities and goals of the National Foundation.
3. Raising sufficient funds through the March of Dimes to finance adequately the National Foundation's program of research, professional education, patient care, and polio prevention.

. . . Regardless of the size of a Chapter, the nature of the program is such that major responsibility must be assumed either by the Chairman or by various committees. That is, there are few activities outside of one or two meetings each year—except for the March of Dimes . . .—in which the membership as a whole can take part. Large Chapters may have four or five committees—Finance, Membership, Women's Activities, Public Information, and the like—but in most Chapters only two are needed. The Executive Committee is responsible for general Chapter administration and activities, and the Medical Advisory Committee, composed of such professionals as doctors, health officials, hospital administrators, nurses, and physical therapists, advises the Executive Committee concerning aid for polio patients.

Officially, the Chapter Executive Committee is elected by the Chapter membership at the annual meeting. Since in most Chapters the Executive Committee constitutes the majority of the membership, formal elections are seldom held; a more realistic formulation is that the Executive Committee consists of those members who are informally asked to serve in this capacity for the year ahead. All other committees are appointed by the Chapter Chairman in consultation with the Executive Committee. Chapter Officers—Chairman, Vice-Chairman, Treasurer and Secretary—are elected annually by the Executive Committee from its own membership.

The Volunteer membership of Foundation Chapters thus . . . are for the most part neither "board members" who employ a professional worker to carry out the daily tasks of the organization nor assistants who are called in during emergencies to help out. Of course, in some respects members of the Executive Committee are the equivalent of "board members. . . . " But the central point is that Chapter Volunteers both make decisions and actually perform the day-to-day tasks of their organization. In large cities, of course, this becomes technically impossible, and metropolitan Chapters often engage an Executive Secretary to handle correspondence, keep records, etc. But at the time of this research only 197 Chapters (6 per cent of all Chapters) employed an Executive Secretary, and eighty-three of these were on a part-time basis. By and large, Chapter Volunteers perform the tasks which in many other voluntary associations are performed by professional personnel. . . .

THE FUTURE OF THE FOUNDATION

The analysis of the local program of the [National] Foundation [for Infantile Paralysis] presented [here] has been largely static in nature: it has been concerned with those characteristics of the organization and its membership which have relevance for the continuation of the present program. These characteristics, the analysis has shown, serve to explain the success which the Foundation has had in recruiting Volunteers, in maintaining their active interest in the program, in providing financial assistance to every victim of infantile paralysis who needs it, in raising funds, and in making progress toward the Foundation's ultimate goal of eliminating the threat of epidemic polio. Any analysis of a goal-directed organization, however, cannot be confined to things as they are, since the future state of affairs toward which the organization's activities are oriented is very much a component of the contemporary organization.

It must, in the very nature of the case, inquire into the relationship of present activities to future developments.

The relevance of this statement to the present analysis is rooted in the fact that the Foundation's major goal is by definition a finite one. A fundamental assumption underlying the original establishment of the Foundation was that infantile paralysis was a disease which medical science would eventually be able to bring under control and a major reason for the capacity of the Foundation to maintain through the years its high ratio of goal-related activities has been the very real possibility that the organization's goal would be realized—perhaps within the lifetime of the participants. The recent development of the Salk vaccine, and its rise on a nationwide scale, serve as dramatic evidence that the full achievement of the Foundation's major goal will be realized in the not too distant future. In fact, Dr. Jonas E. Salk, who developed the vaccine, and Dr. Leonard E. Scheele, former Surgeon General of the United States Public Health Service, recently reported to the American Medical Association that by the middle of 1959 paralytic polio should be completely eliminated as a threat to both children and adults.

The imminence of this full achievement of its major goal naturally raises the question of what will happen to the Foundation at that time. Will it simply go out of existence, will it continue on a more limited scale, providing assistance to persons already afflicted by polio, or will it—taking advantage of experience gained in conquering polio—turn its attention to another health or welfare problem? The seriousness of these questions, as they apply to organizations generally, has been noted by a number of students of voluntary associations and social movements. Wendell King, for example, states that "an apparently unanticipated and rarely desired outcome of achieving goals can be the abrupt demolition of the whole organization. Unless additional objectives are devised, the movement lies robbed of its reason for existence." Their relevance to a concrete organization, however, has been only infrequently examined. . . .

The Succession of Goals

In order to achieve a perspective through which to approach the topic of the future of the foundation it is helpful to recall the major conclusions reached by Philip Selznik in his analysis of the relationship between doctrine and action in the Tennessee Valley Authority. Organizations, Selznik notes, develop obligations over a period of time to act in a certain way, obligations which Selznik terms "commitments." He summarizes the importance of these commitments as follows:

> The systematized commitments of an organization define its character. Day-to-day decisions, relevant to the actual problems met in

the translation of policy into action, create precedents, alliances, effective symbols, and personal loyalties which transform the organization from a profane, manipulable instrument into something having a sacred status and thus resistant to treatment simply as a means to some external goal. That is why organizations are often cast aside when new goals are sought. . . . So long as goals are given, and the impulse to act persists, there will be a series of enforced lines of action demanded by the nature of the tools at hand. These commitments may lead to unanticipated consequences resulting in a deflection of original goals. . . .

Although the major focus of this study has been the current membership and activities of the Foundation, rather than the details of its history, sufficient attention has been given to the circumstances surrounding the original emergence of various features of the organization to document . . . that decisions made for the purpose of solving immediate problems often determine the ultimate character of an organization. It has been noted, for example, that the Foundation's almost total dependence upon a fund-raising strategy based upon obtaining small gifts from large numbers of people emerged from two decisions made in the Depression year 1933: to solicit gifts from the people of Georgia in order to finance the construction of a new building at Georgia Warm Springs, and to raise funds nationally by sponsoring President's Birthday Balls; that the characteristically middle-class composition of the Foundation's Volunteer membership may be traced in large part to the decision to ask postmasters, Democrats, and persons of civic prominence generally to organize these Birthday Balls; and that the patient care program is a direct outgrowth of the decision to permit local Committees for the Celebration of the President's Birthday to retain for use in their own communities a portion of the funds raised in 1935. This brief listing of examples suggests the general applicability to the Foundation of this aspect of Selznick's thesis: the Foundation's "character" today is clearly in many respects the result of decisions made with other ends in view.

The second part of Selznick's statement concerns the consequences which may result from the emergence of organizational commitments— goal displacement and the destruction of the organization itself. Sufficient evidence from other studies has been cited throughout this volume to suggest the near-universality of the phenomenon of goal displacement within organizations, and a number of reasons underlying the Foundation's capacity to maintain itself as a goal-oriented organization have been cited. But what of the Foundation's capacity to maintain itself as an organization after its initial goals have been realized, and "new goals are sought"? Will its organizational structure be "cast aside"? It is to a consideration of these questions that the discussion now turns.

Evidence from Other Organizations

It should be noted first of all that Selznick is not alone in asserting the close relationship between organizational goals and organizational survival. Arnold Rose, for example, has stated that the purposes of voluntary associations are limited, and "almost never will an association act for a purpose different from the original one which brought the members together." And the Kluckhohns have observed that "American associations are also a way that an antifeudalistic society chooses to 'get things done.' We form thousands of organizations to accomplish a specific purpose and then dissolve them."

It is not difficult to find illustrations in American history which document the truth of these assertions. For example, two important voluntary associations in our early history, the Sons of Liberty and the Committees of Correspondence, were dissolved when the anti-British purposes for which they were established culminated in the American Revolution and the establishment of the Continental Congress. Sometimes organizations decline long before their goals are achieved, as, for example, the American Anti-Slavery Society, which split through internal dissension and controversy over policy matters some twenty years before the Emancipation Proclamation. And sometimes they are dissolved when their functions are taken over by governmental bodies, as happened to the Public School Society of New York City when the public school system was established.

Dissolution, however, is not the only course of action open to an organization when its purposes are either achieved or become irrelevant because of changes in the social environment; in fact, it is equally easy to find examples of organizations which have remained intact for the purpose of working toward new or sharply modified objectives. Peter Blau has called this process the "succession of goals," which he states is "the reverse of the displacement of goals." He describes the process in these terms:

> The attainment of organizational objectives generates a strain toward finding new objectives. To provide incentives for its members and to justify its existence, an organization has to adopt new goals as its old ones are realized. Unions illustrate this transformation of ends into means. After a union establishes the right of collective bargaining, this original objective becomes a means for the accomplishment of new objectives, such as pensions and seniority rights for workers.

Unions are of course not the only illustration of the tendency of organizations to seek new objectives, nor do organizations necessarily wait until the achievement of their original objectives before they establish new ones. The American Union, to cite one example, was originally established in order to preserve the spirit which characterized the American Expeditionary Force in World War I, but it very soon included in its objectives the protection of the rights of veterans and, particularly among local Posts, the instigation of community service projects. Dartmouth College, to cite another example, was originally founded primarily in order to educate and Christianize the Indians of New England, but it experienced no great difficulty in transforming itself into a general liberal arts college.

Voluntary health and welfare agencies exhibit similar tendencies. The Birth Control Federation, for example, in 1942 adopted the more comprehensive name of the Planned Parenthood Federation of America, and has since that time expanded its objectives to include treatment for infertility, education for marriage, and marriage counseling. The American Social Hygiene Association, which has traditionally concerned itself with combating both prostitution and venereal diseases, has in recent years adjusted to the decline in organized prostitution and the drastic lowering of the incidence of venereal diseases, and has established such new objectives as supporting family life education and preparing high school boys for the social and psychological strains which they will undergo during military service. In fact, thousands of organizations of all kinds have adapted in one way or another to external conditions affecting the relevance of their objectives, but there have been very few systematic analyses of such organizations from this point of view. It is therefore instructive to examine briefly the process of organizational adaptation as it has taken place in four organizations for which relatively complete information is available. Two of these organizations, the Woman's Christian Temperance Union and the Townsend Organization, have failed to adjust themselves to a changed environment, and exist today as fossil remains of their previous life. The other two, the Young Men's Christian Association and the American National Red Cross, have made highly successful adaptations.

The Young Men's Christian Association

Although there have been a number of organizational histories of the Y.M.C.A., Owen Pence's volume, *The Y.M.C.A. and Social Need,* is most useful for an examination of the Y.M.C.A. as an illustration of the process of organizational adaptation. The book is sub-titled, "A Study of Institutional Adaptation"; more specifically, it is an examination of how the goals of the Y.M.C.A. have changed in response to various changes in the social environment, particularly the secularization of American society which has taken place in the past century.

Today the Y.M.C.A. places a great deal of emphasis upon the opportunities for recreation and physical exercise which it offers, but the first Association in London stated that its objective was "to improve the spiritual condition of young men engaged in the drapery and other trades"; the first Association in America, in Boston, expanded its objective to include "the improvement of the spiritual and mental condition of young men"; and the first New York Association included in its objectives the following:

> The object of this Association shall be the improvement of the spiritual, mental, and social condition of young men . . . to bring them under moral and religious influences, by aiding them in the selection of suitable boarding places and employment . . . .

With the passing years, as Pence shows, the Y.M.C.A. has devoted increasing attention to its physical and social goals, and less attention to its original religious and spiritual aims. Thus transition is summarized in these terms:

> In contrast with the conception of earlier years, when the principal concern of the Association was with the securing of individual commitments to the Christian life, the realization has steadily grown in recent years that religious living and interest are so gravely-conditioned by the total social experience that the two cannot be dealt with separately.

And again, in more direct language:

> In time, the Associations began to take their objectives for granted. In their place activity (that is, whatever met and satisfied expressed interests of members), became the real objective.

The Y.M.C.A., therefore, is an example of an organization whose goals have changed not because they were achieved, but rather because of fundamental changes in the social environment in which its activities were carried out. The "spiritual improvement" of young men has come to be regarded as less relevant than it was in the 19th century, and other activities have achieved greater relevance. As a result, the organization's membership has been broadened to include boys, women and non-Protestants; professionally-trained group leaders have often replaced the original laymen who served as volunteer workers; and an increased emphasis has been placed upon the construction of adequate buildings in which to carry out its broadened program.

Today the Y.M.C.A. is a highly successful organization, and it would be presumptuous to suggest that its success bears no relationship to the Christian ideals held by so many of its leaders. In fact, if its original objective had been to provide recreational facilities to "young men engaged in the drapery and other trades," it is highly probable that it would exist today only as some sort of athletic club in London. But the evidence is also quite clear that its success is in large part attributable to the fact that it has had the flexibility, in keeping with its Christian ideals, to redefine its objectives in accordance with the needs of the society which it serves.

The Woman's Christian Temperance Union

The central problem which led Joseph Gusfield to study the W.C.T.U. is the fact that changes in American drinking habits and the increased acceptance of drinking as a part of general social life "have presented the W.C.T.U. with an environment more hostile to the doctrine of total abstinence than was true in the years of the organization's formation and development." In the face of this situation, Gusfield sought both to determine "whether the change in environment has led to changes in the goals and doctrine of the movement" and to explain "changes, or lack of change, in the organization."

In many respects, the Y.M.C.A. and the W.C.T.U. have had similar histories. Both organizations were established at a time when a powerful middle class believed that its mission was to improve the social conditions under which the lower class lived. The Y.M.C.A. sought to improve these conditions by Christianizing and educating young men; the W.C.T.U. believed that working class people could enjoy the benefits of middle class life if they stopped drinking—"drink is the curse of the working classes" was a popular slogan of the 19th Century temperance movement. And both organizations have survived in spite of a sharp decline in the popularity of these theories of humanitarian reform. But they differ greatly in the manner in which they have survived.

As previously indicated, the Y.M.C.A.'s history has been characterized by successive adjustments to its social environment. The W.C.T.U., on the other hand, has not adjusted:

> Today the W.C.T.U. is an organization in retreat. Contrary to the expectations of theories of institutionalization, the movement has not acted to preserve organizational values at the expense of past doctrine.

How has this been possible? As Gusfield shows, the W.C.T.U. has not abandoned its goal of establishing temperance norms, but has instead shifted its attention to a new audience. Originally the organization was composed largely of middle- and upper middle-class women who sought both to dissuade working class people from drinking and to improve their general welfare in other ways; today it is less upper middle-class and more lower middle- and working-class in composition, and its chief target is the drinking habits of middle-class groups. In short, the

W.C.T.U. has elected *not* to change its goals to meet changed conditions, although Gusfield suggests two courses of action it might have taken:

> One possible position would be a reversal of past doctrine and the embracing of a doctrine of moderate drinking. This would be the acceptance of the new standard of the middle classes. Another possibility might be a de-emphasis of temperance aims and a substitution of other aims, such as those of a social welfare nature or an attack on "popular" enemies, such as drug addiction or juvenile delinquency.

Instead, the organization has changed the composition of its membership, limited its goals to the discouragement of middle-class drinking, and shifted its strategy from active campaigning against intemperance to indulging in what Gusfield terms "moral indignation."

. . . .

The American National Red Cross
Like the Y.M.C.A., the Red Cross is a highly successful organization, and for much the same reasons: it has made successive adjustments to changes in its social environment. Its initial objective, as set forth in its first constitution, was "to hold itself in readiness in the event of war or any calamity great enough to be considered national, to inaugurate such practical measures in mitigation of the suffering and for the protection and relief of sick and wounded as may be consistent with the objects of the Association. . . ." The organization was small in its early years, and floods and other disasters, the Spanish-American War, and most importantly, World War I, provided sufficient challenges to its resources to make any expansion of its objectives unnecessary. The end of World War I, however, found a greatly expanded Red Cross without an objective of sufficient scope to maintain the organization. There was a decline in membership interest, and the leaders feared the organization would suffer. Foster Dulles has summarized this crisis in the Red Cross's history in these terms:

> The officers of the Red Cross, discouraged but not dismayed, were determined to find a way out in spite of chapter apathy. There was a natural desire on their part to see the American Red Cross maintain its position and still further broaden its field of usefulness, not only for the sake of whatever contributions could be made toward improving the conditions of American life, *but for the sake of the organization itself.*

This crisis was surmounted by adopting a new program—"the preservation and improvement of the public health"—and the Red Cross had no need to question the adequacy of its objectives until the Depression of the 1930's, when there was disagreement among the leaders concerning the role the organization should play in dispensing unemployment relief. But the most severe test to date of the adequacy of the Red Cross's objectives came at the end of World War II, when again a greatly expanded organization found that its capacity to act outpaced its goals. Furthermore, there now existed a new threat to the organization—the increased intervention of the Government in welfare and relief activities as a result of the responsibilities it had assumed during the Depression and War years. "Clouds are appearing on the disaster relief horizon," wrote one Red Cross disaster worker in 1946. "Government today is rendering a number of services to disaster sufferers that were rendered by Red Cross disaster relief 10, 15, or 20 years ago." This new crisis was summarized by Basil O'Connor, who was then National Chairman of the American Red Cross, at the 1949 annual convention, in a speech entitled "Can the Red Cross Survive?" Dulles summarizes this speech as follows:

> The convention delegates were told that it was not only necessary to re-evaluate the mission of the American Red Cross, but to ask themselves the fundamental question of whether an organization founded in the remote past of the nineteenth century still had any place at all in the vastly altered world of the mid-twentieth century. O'Connor's own answer was strongly affirmative.

It was of course not sufficient to give an affirmative answer to this question; it was necessary as well to establish new objectives and new activities. These were found in "the adoption of a national blood donor program as the core of its peacetime activities apart from disaster relief." In this way the most recent crisis has been met, and the Red Cross has both maintained an active program and obtained adequate volunteer and public support in the postwar years. The decision to embark upon this program was made with full realization of its implications for the organization's survival:

> Apart from meeting a very real need, the national blood program also appeared the best possible thing for the Red Cross to undertake on its own account. Just as health activities had been promoted after the First World War to give the chapters something to do as well as to advance public health, so the new project was expected to provide an outlet for volunteer activity in the new period of peace which would bring together, in one unified undertaking, the varied interests of the volunteer services.

This brief review of the history of four organizations has of necessity mentioned only a few of the major conclusions reached by the authors cited. Nevertheless, it has called attention to the fact that organizations are by no means necessarily "cast aside when new goals are sought" and indicated some of the ways in which organizations have adjusted to changes in their environment and the relevancy of their goals. Furthermore, the histories of these . . . organizations suggest that the fate of an organization after its goals have been either achieved or rendered irrelevant cannot be determined on a priori grounds, but is rather a resultant of a given set of forces. "What," Blau asks, "determines whether displacement of goals or succession of goals predominates in an organization?" Although he admits that this crucial question can be answered only in part, Blau does suggest two determining factors: "structural constraints in the organization" and acceptance on the part of the community. "When the community permits an organization . . . to become established and attain at least some of its first objectives in a relatively short period, it will probably find new fields to conquer in the course of its development." It goes without saying that American society has permitted the [March of Dimes] Foundation to be established and to attain its first objectives; in fact, it has given it more encouragement and support than it has given any comparable organization. Accordingly, in order to pursue the inquiry implied in Blau's formulation of the problem of goal succession, it is necessary to examine what structural constraints might impede the Foundation from seeking new goals.

The Foundation's Structure and the Future

The relevance of the Foundation's corporate-type structure to its capacity to carry out its program has been stated in some detail throughout this volume, and need only be summarized here. Local Chapters, for example, being *ad hoc* instrumentality's of the Board of Trustees, are subject to all rules, regulations and policies of the National Headquarters—a situation which enables National Headquarters, if the need should ever arise, to exert considerable authority over the activities of a local Chapter. The March of Dimes is officially directed by National Headquarters, and local Campaign Directors are appointed by the State Chairman, who is in turn appointed by National Headquarters. Here again, the structural machinery exists through which National Headquarters can exercise control over the activities of local organizations. The patient care program, although financed largely by the 50 per cent of all campaign receipts which is retained in the local community, is dependent, for its effective operation, upon the redistribution of funds by National Headquarters. The research program is entirely under the direction of National Headquarters, and Chapters are specifically prohibited from making grants to support research projects. In short, if National Headquarters (i.e., the Board of Trustees) should decide to embark upon a new program, there is no organizational machinery to stand in the way. The new program would not need to be ratified by local Chapters, and there are no effective sub-groups within the organization which could offer effective resistance to it. The Foundation, in other words, has an organizational structure which would make "the succession of goals" quite feasible.

Volunteers and the Future

The statement that the Foundation's structure would permit "the succession of goals," although true in a legal sense, does not of course acknowledge the fundamental fact that the Foundation is a voluntary association. Its members are free to leave at any time, and no one is obliged to join. For this reason, no program sponsored by National Headquarters could possibly be successful if it did not command the enthusiastic support of Volunteers throughout the county. Witness for example, the ill-fated attempt of National Headquarters in the first year of the Foundation's existence to have full authority over the expenditure of all the funds raised during the March of Dimes. In order to examine the Foundation's future prospects it is therefore necessary to examine the potential support for a new program which exists among the Foundation's Volunteer membership.

The interviews with Volunteers reported in this volume were held after the Salk vaccine had been developed, but immediately prior to the nationwide field trials of the vaccine, and hence before the public announcement on April 12, 1955, that a safe and effective anti-polio vaccine had at last been perfected. Nevertheless, many Volunteers believed at the time of the research that the vaccine would be effective, and some gave evidence that they had given thought to the impact of this development upon the Foundation. A sampling of these future oriented remarks is given below, but the major conclusions concerning potential Volunteer participation in a future program of the Foundation must be drawn not from Volunteer reactions to the development of the Salk vaccine, but rather from Volunteer perceptions of the Foundation as an *innovating* organization.

The fact that voluntary associations, such as the Foundation, which carry on programs extending beyond the immediate interests of their membership serve the function of instituting change in society has been noted by many observers. Arnold Rose, for example, states that "voluntary associations provide a *social mechanism for continually instituting social changes,* so that the United States is a society in flux, constantly seeking (not always successfully, but seeking nevertheless) to solve long-standing problems and to satisfy new needs of groups of citizens as these needs arise." Lipset and his colleagues have recently observed that voluntary associations are "a source of new opinions independent of the state and a means of communicating these new suggestions to a large section of the citizenry."

Speaking from a British perspective, V. L. Allen has commented that "it is perhaps as pace-makers that voluntary organizations have the most important and permanent function to perform in society. . . ." And in reference to the Foundation specifically, Victor Cohn calls it "not just an attack on polio," but "a pattern by which we Americans may be able to help solve many problems." Observations such as these, however, are generally made by outsiders, who are in a position to assess the role played by a voluntary association in broad perspective. It is less frequent that a participant in a voluntary association, involved as he is in day-to-day problems, is able to detect the far-reaching implications of his organization.

Objectively speaking, the Foundation has obviously served as an instigator of change. Not only has it pioneered in developing a coordinated mode of attack upon a specific disease, but it has also introduced new concepts of fund-raising, of patient care, and of community responsibility. The mass field trials of the Salk vaccine, which the Foundation sponsored, to cite another example of innovation, were a completely new development as far as the history of immunological verification is concerned—never before has the efficacy of a newly-developed vaccine been tested on such a mass scale. It is of some interest, accordingly, to note that a considerable number of Volunteers are alert to the fact that the Foundation, in keeping with its character both as a social movement and a voluntary association, has served as a "pacesetter" in American society. . . .

Conclusions

At the time of this writing there has been no official statement by the Foundation concerning its future plans, although the organization has indicated in a number of informal ways that it is seriously considering the possibility of undertaking a new program when epidemic polio has finally been brought under control. For the present, the polio program continues to meet existing needs. Infantile paralysis still constitutes a threat to the American public; thousands of polio victims still need medical and financial assistance; sudden rises in incidence of an epidemic or near-epidemic character—in Boston in the summer of 1955, in Chicago in the summer of 1956—will probably continue to occur until a substantial proportion of the public has been given the three necessary injections of the Salk vaccine; and research is still needed in order to develop improved methods of both prevention and therapy.

Nevertheless, it is reasonable to assume on the basis of available evidence that the Foundation's major objectives will be reached within the next few years and that the organization will at that time seek to realize new goals. In the face of this situation, it is worth while to consider, on the basis of the materials presented throughout this volume, what kind of an organization it will become. What kinds of goals will it seek to obtain, what support will it have from the public and from its Volunteers, and what are its chances for success in some new venture?

Since the Foundation may fairly be said to represent majority rather than minority opinion in the United States, it is highly improbable that it will take the same course as has the Townsend Organization—dwindle in size and drift into half-hearted efforts to achieve irrelevant objectives. By the same token, given the character and accomplishments of the polio program, it is manifestly impossible for the Foundation to follow the path taken by the W.C.T.U.—limit its goals and change its strategy by aiming at a new target audience. In sharp contrast to both of these organizations, the Foundation has received social and financial support from a major segment of the American public and has had a goal which has relevance for all strata of American society.

In these respects the Foundation closely resembles the Y.M.C.A. and the Red Cross. Another point of similarity is the type of membership common to all three organizations—a membership drawn for the most part from the middle class, and from the upper middle class in the case of key positions in the national organization. In fact, the Foundation's membership is actually more representative of American society than the membership of either the Y.M.C.A. or the Red Cross, since the former is largely Protestant and the latter typically upper middle and upper-class in composition.

In terms of any criteria, accordingly, the Foundation belongs in the "big leagues" of voluntary associations; like the Y.M.C.A. and the Red Cross, it is an institutionalized aspect of American life. It is therefore highly probable that it will follow a pattern similar to that established by these organizations: it will expand its operations by adopting a goal which has even more relevance for American society than that of eliminating infantile paralysis as an epidemic disease.

Although comparisons with the Y.M.C.A. and the Red Cross serve the useful purpose of setting the topic of the future of the Foundation in a broader organizational context, they cannot by themselves be adduced as convincing evidence that the Foundation will in the years ahead make a *successful* adaptation to the achievement of its major goals. This is true in part because the Foundation's future will be determined by decisions made by specific individuals as much as it will be by those organizational forces which can now be detected. It is also true in part because both the Y.M.C.A. and the Red Cross differ from the Foundation in the specificity of their original goals. Who is to say that it is not possible "to improve the spiritual condition of young men" by giving them an opportunity to play basketball, and can the national blood program of the

Red Cross be called incompatible with the initial objective of inaugurating "such practical measures in mitigation of the suffering and for the protection of the sick and wounded as may be consistent with the objects of the Association?" The current goals of the Foundation, in contrast, are specifically concerned with problems of one disease, infantile paralysis.

It is of far-reaching importance, however, that in the course of working toward its goals the Foundation has made significant contributions in other areas. It has supported fundamental research in virology—to such an extent that William L. Laurence, Science Editor of the *New York Times*, has recently suggested that "its next goal should be to develop, with March of Dimes funds, an all-embracing multiple vaccine against all viruses attacking the nervous system." It has assisted medical schools in developing new programs of professional education; pioneered in developing improved methods of assisting in the physical, social, and vocational adjustment of disabled persons; and in a number of other ways attacked problems which are not directly linked to the problems of infantile paralysis. The very fact that the Foundation has always realized that an effective anti-polio campaign could not be carried out in isolation from other aspects of medicine and social welfare constitutes further evidence, accordingly, that the Foundation will make a successful adaptation to its post-polio program.

In the final analysis, however, the most compelling reason for predicting that the Foundation will in the future make a successful adjustment to the achievement of its major goal is that the organization has in fact *already* been transformed, in large part by its Volunteers, into something other than a special purpose association. For those Volunteers who, in spite of the fact that they may initially have been recruited as Polio Veterans or Good Citizens or Joiners, have come to regard the organization as a "social movement" or a "pacesetter" have altered not only the character of their own participation but the character of the Foundation as well. Implicit in these perceptions is the notion that the Foundation has an institutionalized status which transcends its current goals. Since the Foundation includes among its Volunteers so many who are able to conceptualize their involvement in terms of its ultimate implications (for themselves, or for society as a whole), rather than only in terms of a limited, pragmatic goal, it has already become an organization as deeply committed to its mode of operation as to its current purposes. In a word, it is an organization which is as committed to a means as it is to an end.

EIGHT

Federal Regulation and Federal Funds

The great theme of American history in the last half of the twentieth century is the expansion of the role of the federal government as the great guarantor of the rights of all citizens, regardless of wealth, age, religion, national origin, race, or gender. Many of the milestones in the expansion of federal power are household words: the Social Security Act, the G.I. Bill, the election of Catholic John F. Kennedy as president in 1960. This high point came between 1964 and 1967 with the Civil Rights Acts of 1964 and 1967 and the Voting Rights Act of 1965, the creation of Medicare and Medicaid in 1965, the Women's Movement. Less familiar now but also of great importance to nonprofits were the New Deal's Wagner Act (providing federal protection for those seeking to unionize), and the later decision to make "fringe benefits" exempt from federal tax (providing federal subsidies for employee health insurance); and the Hill-Burton Act (subsidizing "community" hospitals). The Great Society expanded the National Institutes of Health and the National Science Foundation and added federal scholarships and loans for college students.

The great expansion of the federal government reshaped nonprofit organizations in many ways. It certainly led to a great expansion of the nonprofit sector. In 1960, near the beginning of the expansion, nonprofits in Cleveland, Ohio, for example, accounted for less than 4% of the metropolitan region's payroll. By 1990, thanks in substantial part to Medicare, Medicaid, and federal student scholarships and loans, Cleveland's nonprofits had tripled in relative size: they now accounted for more than 12% of the region's payroll.

Federal funds brought new regulations as well as new resources. No nonprofit organization is required to accept federal funds, but if it does accept them it must also abide by federal rules. And even if it does not accept federal funds, a nonprofit, like any other corporation, must follow federal laws. From the New Deal on these laws have become more and more complex efforts to protect citizens from discrimination on the basis of age, religion, national origin, race, or gender; from unfair labor practices; from dangerous working conditions; and from the theft of pension funds.

Nonprofits have always received government subsidies and have always had to obey government regulation. New in the last decades is the dominant role of the federal government both in the provision of funds and as the source of regulations for American nonprofits.

The expansion of the federal role did not come easily or without controversy, and nonprofits have been in the middle of many debates and battles about its proper nature. In thinking about these controversies, it is useful to begin by recognizing that governments have always subsidized and regulated nonprofits, and that federal decisions played key roles long before the election of 1960 or the passage of Great Society legislation. For corporations the great nineteenth century Supreme Court decision came in the *Dartmouth College Case.* For African Americans that decision was overshadowed by *Dred Scott* ("the black man has no rights that the white man is bound to respect") and *Plessy v. Ferguson* ("separate but equal"), and for women by the stout opposition to woman suffrage. Federal decisions in these cases shaped nonprofit corporations just as much as they shaped other aspects of American life. In the twentieth century, an important change in direction came with the U.S. Supreme Court's decision in *Pierce v. Society of the Sisters,* which upheld the right of a private school to offer instruction to elementary students, and the right of the parents to send young children to private schools.

Nonprofit organizations not only benefited from the expansion of the federal role: true to their First Amendment origins, they helped bring it about, as key participants in the Civil Rights, Women's, environmental, and other movements. Thus they have often been in the center of controversy, as in Marian Wright's tense 1967 confrontation with Mississippi Senator John Stennis. But the expansion of federal funding for nonprofit organizations has inevitably brought with it concerns about their continued independence and about their ability to continue to perform their key roles under the First Amendment. The Filer Commission raised this concern in a particularly thoughtful and comprehensive way just after the passage of the Great Society Legislation. Steven Rathgeb Smith and Michael Lipsky, two experienced policy analysts, have examined the impact of federal funding on social service nonprofits in unusual detail and with special attention to its impact on the character of nonprofit service. The U.S. Supreme Court continues its effort to balance legislative power and First Amendment rights, even in such difficult cases as those concerning the funding of information about birth control and abortion.

37

Pierce v. Society of the Sisters, 268 U.S. 510, 1925

The "nativist," anti-foreigner, anti-Catholic and anti-Jewish movements of the early twentieth century are famous for their successful campaign to reduce and restrict immigration into the United States. Less well known, because less successful, was the nativists' parallel effort to use the powers of government to restrict and reduce the influence of parochial and other private, nonprofit schools. Laws designed for this purpose were advanced in several states. The most comprehensive law against parochial schools was enacted through referendum in Oregon in 1922. This law required that every child in the state attend public school through the first eight grades.

Oregon's anti-parochial school law never went into effect. As soon as it passed, the Society of the Sisters of the Holy Names of Jesus and Mary—the order of Catholic nuns that ran several Catholic schools and staffed others in the state—notified the state's governor that they intended to continue to operate their schools. In an effort to resolve the question before any children were directly affected, Governor Pierce sought a court order requiring the Society of the Sisters to comply with the law. Lower courts denied the governor's request, and on appeal the United States Supreme Court affirmed the denial, allowing the state's parochial and other private schools to continue.

The case of *Pierce v. Society of the Sisters* attracted national attention not only from Catholics, but from all who supported the right of religious and nonprofit organizations to sponsor schools. As William D. Guthrie and Bernard Hershkopf, attorneys for the Society of the Sisters, argued in their brief, the law applied not only to Catholics but to every group that sponsored private schools, including Episcopalians, Quakers, and Lutherans—and to those who favored military academies as well. The law not only sought to limit rights granted under the First Amendment, they argued: it also interfered with parents' right and duty to provide moral and educational guidance for their children.

WILLIAM D. GUTHRIE AND BERNARD HERSHKOPF

Brief for Private Schools

1925

. . . In substance and effect, the law requires every child between eight and sixteen years of age to be sent to a public school. It is, therefore, in necessary and intended effect, an absolute prohibition of private and parochial schools such as the appellee Society conducts and such as normal children between the ages in question have been permitted to attend from the very beginning of our Government, and even long prior thereto.

It is wholly prohibitory, and it does not even purport to regulate private or parochial schools. Indeed, the laws of Oregon already provided and still provide . . . for regulation, inspection and supervision by the state of these private or parochial schools and for adequate instruction in patriotism and civic duties. No matter how excellent and worthy the proscribed schools may be, this statute, nevertheless, practically decrees their suppression. The right of the parent to choose for his child a private or parochial school which will educate such child in the light of his own religion, or secure for the child special training in particular studies, or develop a particular aptitude, or cure a particular deficiency; the right of the child to influence its parents to the choice of a school which it instinctively prefers or desires; the right of the schools and their teachers to carry on a legitimate and lawful calling and to practise a time-honored, beneficent and noble profession—all these vital and fundamental rights are invaded and menaced with practical destruction by this enactment.

. . . all the states have compulsory school laws and . . . all such laws, except the enactment in Oregon in 1922, provide that attendance at a school other than a public school shall under prescribed conditions be compliance with the law. There are many parochial schools in the United States maintained alike by Catholics and Protestants and some maintained by Jews. The statutes of 24 states expressly provide that attendance at a parochial school shall constitute a proper substitute for attendance at a public school, viz.: Alabama, Arizona, Arkansas, Colorado, Idaho, Iowa, Kansas, Kentucky, Michigan, Mississippi, Missouri, Montana, Nebraska, New York, North Dakota, Ohio, Oregon (Section 5259 of the Oregon Laws as now in force), South Carolina, Tennessee,

Texas, Virginia, West Virginia, Wisconsin and Wyoming. The school statutes of the remaining states impliedly approve parochial schools under
the designation of private school, denominational school, or other term.
In this way freedom of education in private or parochial or other religious schools is now and has been recognized by all the states in the
Union.

In addition . . . the education laws of the various states provide for
varying degrees of regulation and control by the state of private schools,
their several curricula and teachers. Provision has, for example, been
made that representatives of the state shall inspect private schools, that
their standing under the compulsory school laws and otherwise shall
depend upon approval by the state authorities, that general standards
laid down by the state authorities shall control the curriculum of the
private school, that certain subjects inculcating patriotism shall be taught,
such as courses relating to the Constitution, civic duties, etc., that elementary courses shall be conducted in English, that the flag shall be
displayed about the schoolhouse, that teachers in private schools shall
obtain certificates from the state and be required to be citizens of the
United States or to take the oath of allegiance, that private schools shall
furnish reports and statistical data to the state authorities in connection
with the compulsory school laws and otherwise, that private schools
shall be subject to state regulation as to medical, health and sanitary
matters, and that no doctrine subversive of the authority of the state
shall be taught in private schools. In New York, *e.g.*, no license can be
granted to a private school teaching "the doctrine that organized governments shall be overthrown by force," etc. (Laws 1921, ch. 667). These
statutory provisions show how far the control of the state over private
education may reasonably extend and how unnecessary it is to suppress
all private and parochial schools in order to insure unobjectionable methods of teaching and courses of study, or the inculcation of patriotism in
the minds of American children. . . .

The appellee above-named, The Society of the Sisters of the Holy
Names of Jesus and Mary, is a branch of a large Catholic teaching order
of women who dedicate their lives to the education of children. The
Society was founded in 1844 in the Province of Quebec, Canada; and in
October, 1859, at the request of Bishop Blanchet, famous for his missionary and educational work in the Northwest and among the Indians,
twelve of these Sisters came to Portland, Oregon, after a journey by way
of the Isthmus of Panama. These Sisters at once established St. Mary's
Academy in Portland, which has attained high national repute as an
educational institution. They were followed in 1863 by twelve additional Sisters, and an academy and school were then established at Salem, the capital of the state, and other schools were soon afterwards
opened in other places throughout the state. The legislature of the State

of Oregon chartered St. Mary's Academy in 1866, and the Sisterhood was duly incorporated in 1880. . . . The Society as so incorporated has ever since and for more than forty-four years been duly conducting academies and schools in the State of Oregon for the education of youth. There are now 1,284 of these Sisters throughout the United States consecrating themselves to the holy task of teaching children, with 49 schools and 10,461 pupils.

Catholic education in the State of Oregon steadily developed, and other teaching sisterhoods were from time to time established there. In 1907 the Catholic school system received recognition from the legislature of the state . . . , and in 1910 the school laws were amended so as to give a representative of the Catholic Educational Association of Oregon a place on the State Board of Standardization. . . . These statutory provisions are still in force and effect. Moreover, since 1889, when the first compulsory education law was enacted in Oregon, the laws of the state have recognized education in parochial or other private schools as the equivalent of, and an acceptable substitution for, public school attendance. . . .

At the present time, the Society maintains in the State of Oregon sixteen elementary schools, eight secondary or preparatory schools, and one college, making a total of twenty-five educational institutions, having 96 teaching Sisters and instructing 2,636 pupils. In 1922, the Catholic elementary schools in Oregon, including those of this appellee, numbered 58, with 8,019 pupils, and the Catholic secondary schools 23 with 1,231 pupils, making a total of 9,250 pupils, mostly between the ages of eight and sixteen, with 339 teaching Sisters.

An illustrative and typical instance of devotion to the noble cause of education will be found in the services rendered by the famous Catholic teaching order of the Ursuline Sisters, who first came to Louisiana in 1727, two centuries ago. They forthwith established a school at New Orleans, and were encouraged in their educational work by the French Government, to which Louisiana then belonged. When the Spanish Government assumed control in 1769, it continued the policy of encouraging education by Catholic teaching orders. But in 1804, Spain having meantime restored Louisiana to France and Napoleon having at once ceded the territory to the United States, the Catholic teaching orders established in Louisiana became apprehensive of threatened confiscation and of hostile or oppressive laws, and they appealed to President Jefferson for protection. Few incidents in the history of education on this continent are more interesting and illuminating. James Madison was then Secretary of State. Under date of July 20, 1804, he wrote to the Superior of the Order of the Ursuline Sisters in New Orleans as follows:

I have had the honor to lay before the President your letter of the 14th of December, who views with pleasure the public benefit resulting from the benevolent endeavors of the respectable persons in whose behalf it is written. Be assured that no opportunity will be neglected of manifesting the real interest he takes in promoting the means of affording to the youth of this new portion of the American dominion, a pious and useful education, and of evincing the grateful sentiments due to those of all religious persuasions who so laudably devote themselves in its diffusion. It was under the influence of such feelings that Governor Claiborne had already assured the ladies of this monastery of the entire protection which will be afforded them, after the recent change of Government.

And a month later, on August 22, President Jefferson himself wrote the following letter:

I have received, Holy Sisters, the letters you have written to me, wherein you express anxiety for the property vested in your institution by the former Government of Louisiana. The principles of the Government and Constitution of the United States are a sure guaranty to you that it will be preserved to you sacred and inviolate, and that your institution will be permitted to govern itself according to its own voluntary rules, without interference from the civil authority. Whatever diversity of shade may appear in the religious opinions of our fellow-citizens, the charitable objects of your institution cannot be indifferent to any, and its furtherance of the wholesome purposes of society by training up its young members in the way they should go, cannot fail to insure it the patronage of the Govemrnent it is under. Be assured it will meet with all the protection my office can give it.

The attitude of Catholic parents in regard to their constitutional rights and liberties as American citizens is not at all peculiar or confined to them. Thousands of Protestant and Jewish parents are sending their children to church schools and other private schools, and these parents disapprove and condemn the principle and spirit of the Oregon Compulsory Public School Law just as emphatically as Catholic parents do. There are, for example, many Episcopal church schools, such as Groton, St. Paul's, St. Mark's, etc. The many thousands of Protestant and Jewish parents who now send their children to private church schools where religious instruction is given in the Protestant and Jewish faith respectively resent and protest against the principle of the Oregon Law just as conscientiously and ardently as Catholic parents do, for they readily realize that whilst the Oregon School Law may have been directly aimed at Catholic parochial schools, the precedent is likewise a menace to all other private schools throughout the United States.

Such drastic and extraordinary legislation is indisputably a portentous innovation in America. Private and religious schools have existed in this country from the earliest times. Indeed, the public or common school, as we know it today, dates only from 1840. For generations all Americans—including those who fought for liberty and independence in the eighteenth century, and who drafted the Declaration of Independence, the Northwest Ordinance of 1787, and the Constitution of the United States—were educated in private or religious schools, and mostly the latter. Perhaps no institution is older or a more intimate part of our colonial and national life than religious schools and colleges, both Catholic and Protestant. The private and religious schools have been the laboratories in which educational methods have been worked out and pedagogic progress accomplished from the very beginning of our History. Out of them have developed, or to them is due, our greatest colleges and universities, the most important of them to this day being private or religious institutions. In more recent times commonwealth colleges and universities have grown up. The legislation before the court manifestly carries within itself a threat, not merely to the private elementary and preparatory schools which it now practically proscribes, but to every private or religious preparatory school and every private or religious college or university in the land. If a "divided school can no more succeed than a divided nation," as the proponents and defenders of the act wrote in defense of the challenged measure when it went before the people of Oregon by initiative petition, and thus invoked the destruction of all private and parochial elementary schools, a "divided" high school or college or university would stand upon no more secure footing, and hence the doom of every private or religious institution of higher education is even now forecast and in process, if this Oregon enactment be within the constitutional powers of a state.

A learned commentator upon the police power has admonished us that

> Freedom in the pursuit of art, literature and science is, as matter of history, bound up with the freedom of religion and of speech and press, for it has practically never been opposed for other than religious or political motives (Freund on Police Power, Sec. 479).

The statute in suit is so unusual and extraordinary that it must arouse misgivings in the judicial mind upon even the slightest reflection. More than ever must it be borne in mind in judging it, as pointed out by the Chief Justice in *Wolff Co. v. Industrial Court*, that

> While there is no such thing as absolute freedom of contract and it is subject to a variety of restraints, they must not be arbitrary or

unreasonable. Freedom is the general rule, and restraint the exception. The legislative authority to abridge can be justified only by exceptional circumstances, citing *Adkins v. Children's Hospital.*

In the present case, the statute abridges the freedom of four classes closely interrelated: (1) the freedom of the private and parochial schools, (2) the freedom of teachers engaged in teaching in the private and parochial schools, (3) the freedom of parents and guardians, and (4) the freedom of children. It will, perhaps, make the true issue clear and distinct if these four categories be separately considered.

. . . .

3. This far we have considered the enactment in suit only in reference to the rights of the private and parochial schools and the teachers they employ. But there is involved in the case at bar a far more important group of individual rights, namely, the rights of the parents and guardians who desire to send their children to such schools, and the rights of the children themselves. Reflection should soon convince the court that those rights—which the statute seriously abridges and impairs—are of the very essence of personal liberty and freedom.

Children are, in the end, what men and women live for. Through them parents realize, as it were, a measure of immortality. To the parent the child represents the sum of all his hopes. One's defeated aspirations, his children may achieve; his unfulfilled ambitions, they may realize. All that we missed, lost, failed of, our children may have, do, accomplish, in fullest measure. Thus, they hold in their new, young lives the dearest and most intimate yearnings of the parent's soul. For them parents struggle and amass property and put forth their greatest efforts and strive for an honored name. In return for the enormous sacrifice they make and burden they bear, parents have the right to guide and rear their children to be worthy of them. What right could be more truly and completely of the essence of liberty? *Tillman v. Tillman,* 26 L.R.A. (n.s.) 781, 785, *et seq.* (S. Car.). Manifestly so vital and intimate a right may not be invaded by the state without the clearest justification and imperative necessity therefor: "If a state takes hold of the child, the father is no longer free, and tomorrow not a trace of liberty will be left" (Jules Simon, *L'Ecole,* p. 345).

In this day and under our civilization, the child of man is his parent's child and not the state's. Gone would be the most potent reason for women to be chaste and men to be continent, if it were otherwise. It was entirely logical for Plato, in his scheme for an "ideal commonwealth," to make women common; if their children were to be taken from them, and brought up away from them by the state for its own ends and purposes, personal morality was, after all, a secondary matter. The state-bred monster could then mean little to his parents; and such a

creature could readily be turned to whatever use a tyrannical government might conceive to be in its own interest. In such a society there
would soon be neither personal nor social liberty. "Take away from the
parents all care and concern for their children's education, and you make
a social life an impossible and unintelligible notion" (Pufendorf's *Law of
Nature and Nations*, Book VI, Ch. II, Sec. 4). It need, therefore, not excite
our wonder that today no country holds parenthood in so slight esteem
as did Plato or the Spartans—except Soviet Russia. There children do
belong to the state; as in Plato's "ideal commonwealth," "the pupils [are]
regarded as belonging to the state rather than to their parents" (Plato's
Laws, Book VII), and personal and national freedom are there at their
lowest ebb. In final analysis, it is submitted, the enactment in suit is in
consonance only with the communistic and bolshevistic ideals now obtaining in Russia, and not with those of free government and American
conceptions of liberty.

   To us in the United States, living under the blessings of free institutions and of the Constitution which guarantees them, our children mean
everything. What more natural, therefore, than that we should, as a
vital part of our own and their liberty, be tenderly solicitous about their
education and keenly zealous of our right to guide and control it? What
more natural, also, than that we should desire them to be taught our
own faith, to cherish whatever religion we accept, to hold fast to the
moral precepts taught with or in our own creed, and to learn these things
from teachers of our own choosing? Such instruction is, of course, not
to be found in the public schools. Nevertheless, to many millions, to a
very great and constantly increasing proportion of our people, it will
always seem indispensable that the education of their children should
not be merely secular; that religious and moral training should not consist merely of a short lesson every Sunday, but should be taught day by
day and every day and should accompany and, indeed, underlie and
influence all the ordinary teaching, and should be by those only who
are competent to teach religion and whose lives are dedicated to God
and His service. In such a system of training a parent may well see the
means, and perhaps the only practical means, of saving his child from
the crass materialism which more and more tends to possess the minds
and hearts of men. . . .

   It was doubtless considerations such as the foregoing which
prompted Prof. Freund to declare in his learned work on the police
power (Sec. 266),

   In one respect . . . education must be constitutionally free, namely,
   insofar as it is essential to the freedom of religon; for the free exercise of religion implies teaching as well as worship. The state could
   certainly not prescribe the religious education of children, insofar

as it would thereby establish a religion, or discriminate in favor of one; nor could it suppress all private schools, since religious denominations would thereby be prevented from inculcating their doctrines in the most effectual way.

The great French publicist Guizot pointed out that

> All rights in the matter of education do not belong to the state. There are rights which are—I do not want to say superior—but anterior to those of the state and co-exist with them. The first rights are the rights of families. Children belong to families before they belong to the state. The state has the right to furnish teaching, to supervise it, to direct it in its own establishments; it has not the basic right to impose its teaching arbitrarily and exclusively upon all families without their consent and contrary to their wishes (quoted in Bietry, Proposition de loi sur la separation des ecoles et de l'etat; session de 1910, p. 63).

President Butler of Columbia University has stated a similar doctrine, in declaring that

> In our American theory, the state steps in, not to monopolize education or attempt to cast all children in a common mold, or forcibly to deprive them of all religious training and instruction, but merely to prevent damage to itself. It offers a free opportunity to every child to receive elementary education, and usually much more than that, in tax-supported schools. But it is in no sense the business of the state, in our American political philosophy, to attempt to monopolize education or to prevent the freest choice by parents of the teachers and schools of their children.

That, we submit, is the sound and true doctrine. It is not seriously debatable that the parental right to guide one's child intellectually and religiously is a most substantial part of the liberty and freedom of the parent. In *Meyer v. Nebraska,* this court, upon full citation of authority, declared that

> While this court has not attempted to define with exactness the liberty thus guaranteed [by the Fourteenth Amendment to the Constitution], the term has received much consideration and some of the included things have been definitely stated. Without doubt, it denotes not merely freedom from bodily restraint, but also the right of the individual to contract, to engage in any of the common occupations of life, to acquire useful knowledge, to marry, establish a home and bring up children, to worship God according to the dictates of his own conscience, and, generally, to enjoy those privi-

leges long recognized at common law as essential to the orderly pursuit of happiness by free men.

In *Taylor and Marshall v. Beckham,* Mr. Justice Harlan said:

> The liberty of which the Fourteenth Amendment forbids a state from depriving any one without due process of law is something more than freedom from the enslavement of the body or from physical restraint. In my judgment the words "life, liberty or property" in the Fourteenth Amendment should be interpreted as embracing every right that may be brought within judicial cognizance, and therefore no right of that kind can be taken in violation of "due process of law."
>
> In *Allgeyer v. Louisiana,* 165 U.S. 578, 589, this court unanimously held that the liberty mentioned in the Fourteenth Amendment "means not only the right of the citizen to be free from the mere physical restraint of his person, as by incarceration, but the term is deemed to embrace the right to be free in the enjoyment of all his faculties; to be free to use them in all lawful ways; to live and work where he will; to earn his livelihood by any lawful calling; to pursue any livelihood or avocation, and for that purpose to enter into all contracts which may be proper, necessary and essential to his carrying out to a successful conclusion the purposes above-mentioned."
>
> Judge Cooley, speaking for the Supreme Court of Michigan in *People v. Hurlburt,* after observing that some things were too plain to be written, said: "Mr. Justice Story has well shown that constitutional freedom means something more than liberty permitted; it consists in the civil and political rights which are absolutely guaranteed, assured and guarded; in one's liberties as a man and a citizen—his right to vote, his right to hold office, his right to worship God according to the dictates of his conscience, his equality with all others who are his fellow citizens; all these guarded and protected and not held at the mercy and discretion of any one man or any popular majority. Story, *Miscellaneous Writings,* 620. If these are not now the absolute rights of the people of Michigan, they may be allowed more liberty of action and more privileges, but they are little nearer to constitutional freedom than Europe was when an imperial city sent out consuls to govern it."

. . . .

A reading of the authorities which have heretofore considered the meaning of the constitutional guaranty of "liberty" should, it is submitted, persuade the mind beyond doubt that the parental right herein in issue is of the very essence of the constitutional guaranty embodied in the Fourteenth Article of Amendment to the Constitution of the United States. Compared with it, the right to engage in a business, to teach, to acquire knowledge, to contract etc., which have had explicit recognition by this court as embraced within the "liberty" contemplated in the Amendment, verily shrink into relative inconsequence.

The statute in suit trespasses, not only upon the liberty of the parents individually, but upon their liberty collectively as well. It forbids them, as a body, to support private and parochial schools and thus give to their children such education and religious training as the parents may see fit, subject to the valid regulations of the state. In that respect the enactment violates the public policy of the State of Oregon and the liberty which parents have heretofore enjoyed in that state.

The highest court of that state declared in *Liggett v. Ladd* that

> The right of mankind to believe and teach such doctrines regarding religion as meet the approval of their consciences is recognized under our form of government as inherent; it is freely accorded to every sect and denomination in the land, and is so interwoven with the principles which underlie our political fabric that it cannot be taken away without the general consent or a violent revolution. The law not only tolerates the privilege, but protects everyone the enjoyment of it. The people are entitled, as an incident of such right, to form associations, adopt creeds, organize churches, and establish seminaries of learning for the advancement of their peculiar tenets of faith, and to acquire property and erect buildings to aid them in accomplishing that end.

The sound common sense which should control in the matters herein in controversy, as well as the true and patriotic rule of constitutional law upon the subject, was tersely and aptly expressed by a former distinguished Vice-President of the United States, Thomas R. Marshall:

> I have an old-fashioned notion that in a government where freedom of religion is guaranteed to the citizen, as father of a child, I have a right to train it along the lines of my own religious belief.
>
> I doubt that any officer, however gifted and high-minded he may be, can have a tenderer regard for my child than I myself possess, that he can more sincerely desire his health, happiness and success.
>
> Unless I develop into such a brute as to be unfit to take care of my child and thus warrant society in removing him permanently from my custody, I should be let alone to look after his health, care for his wants, guide his education and instill into his mind such religious views as I think will enable him to stand against the temptations of a tempestuous world.

. . . .

4. In whatever light the act in suit be regarded, it must be manifest that, in the end, it embodies the pernicious policy of state monopoly of education. Except in Soviet Russia, there has been none in modern times so poor as to do that discarded doctrine of tyrants any reverence. Courts, publicists, philosophers, pedagogues-all alike have repudiated it. The standardization of education despite the diversity of character, aptitude, inclination and physical capacity of children, which state monopolization of the training and teaching of the young renders inevitable, has found well-nigh universal condemnation. The young minds of the nation should not be cast in any such straight-jacket and their diversification and individual development dwarfed and prevented. Again, the excess of power which results to the state from such a device, clearly serves to maintain and preserve despotism and checks the normal evolution of liberty. Finally, the removal of competition with private effort offers unlimited opportunity for arbitrariness, and likewise checks experiment, innovation and progress.

The Belgian savant and statesman, Van Humbeeck, uttered this pregnant thought:

> There never was a tyrannical government—whether the tyranny was exercised by one individual or by the masses—which did not claim the right to educate the generations, to form the character of the nation; and, upon the other hand, there never was a free wintry in which public opinion did not uphold those who claimed that the individual ideas of the citizens must prevail in matters of education.

A century ago Chancellor Kent wrote in his commentaries upon the common law that

> Several of the states of antiquity were too solicitous to form their youth for the various duties of civil life, even to entrust their education solely to the parent; but this, as in Crete and Sparta, was upon the principle, totally inadmissible in the modern civilized world, of the absorption of the individual in the body politic and of his entire subjection to the despotism of the state.

Chancellor Kent's views were accepted by the courts in *Milwaukee Industrial School v. Superiors,* and *People v. Turner;* and, until the Russian Soviet system came into being in Russia, determined to destroy personal liberty, parental control and religion, and until the statute in suit was enacted in Oregon, for pernicious and intolerant purposes perhaps better left undiscussed in this court, it was doubtless true in modern times that the principle of the total absorption of the individual in the body politic and his entire subjection to the state, was everywhere in Chancellor Kent's apt words "totally inadmissible."

In his work on liberty, John Stuart Mill included a chapter on the state and education. Therein he wrote:

> That the whole or any large part of the education of the people should be in state hands, I go as far as anyone in deprecating. All that has been said of the importance of individuality of character, and diversity in opinions and modes of conduct, involves, as of the same unspeakable importance, diversity of education. A general state education is a mere contrivance for moulding people to be exactly like one another: and as the mould in which it casts them is that which pleases the predominant power in the government, whether this be a monarch, a priesthood, an aristocracy, or the majority of the existing generation, in proportion as it is efficient and successful, it establishes a despotism over the mind, leading by natural tendency to one over the body.

In a learned article on education contained in the *Encyclopedia Britannica* the following will be found (11th ed., p. 960):

> It is recognized as the duty of the state to insist upon a certain minimum of education for every future citizen. This does not necessitate a monopoly of education on the part of the state, such as was claimed by the Napoleonic despotism under the traditional influence (it would seem) of the old authoritative Gallo-Roman tradition, transformed in its outward manifestation but not in its inward spirit by the French Revolution. Such a monopoly would be plainly repugnant to the spirit of Anglo-Saxon individualism, and it is interesting to note that attempts to reassert it have in recent times been repudiated in republican France by some of the best exponents of modern thought, as an infringement of personal liberty not calculated to justify itself by any corresponding public gain.
>
> . . . .

It will, therefore, be readily appreciated why President Butler of Columbia University in a recent address on education, was moved to exclaim, in reference to the statute in suit,

> Fancy, if you can, what the future historian will say of the people of the State of Oregon, who, one hundred and thirty-five years after the adoption of the Constitution of the United States with its Bill of Rights, enact by popular vote a statute which makes elementary eduction a government monopoly. If Samuel Adams and Benjamin Franklin and Patrick Henry and Thomas Jefferson turn in their graves on learning this news, there need be no surprise.

MR. JUSTICE McREYNOLDS, DECISION OF THE
U.S. SUPREME COURT

Pierce v. Society of the Sisters

1925

These appeals are from decrees, based upon undenied allegations, which granted preliminary orders restraining appellants from threatening or attempting to enforce the Compulsory Education Act* adopted on November 7, 1922, under the initiative provision of her Constitution by the voters of Oregon (Jud. Code, Section 266). They present the same points of law; there are no controverted questions of fact. Rights said to be guaranteed by the Federal Constitution were specially set up, and appropriate prayers asked for their protection.

---

*Be it Enacted by the People of the State of Oregon: SECTION 1. That Section 5259, Oregon Laws, be and the same is hereby amended so as to read as follows:

SEC. 5259. Children Between the Ages of Eight and Sixteen Years—Any parent, guardians or other person in the State of Oregon, having control or charge or custody of a child under the age of sixteen years and of the age of eight years or over at the commencement of a term of public school of the district in which said child resides, who shall fail or neglect or refuse to send such child to a public school for the period of time a public school shall be held during the current year in said district, shall be guilty of a misdemeanor and each day's failure to send such child to a public school shall constitute a separate offense; provided, that in the following cases, children shall not be required to attend public schools:

(a) Children Physically Unable—Any child who is abnormal, subnormal, or physically unable to attend school.

(b) Children Who Have Completed the Eighth Grade—Any child who has completed the eighth grade, in accordance with the provisions of the state course of study.

(c) Distance from School—Children between the ages of eight and ten years, inclusive, whose place of residence is more than one and one-half miles, and children over ten years of age whose place of residence is more than three miles, by the nearest traveled road, from a public school; provided, however, that if transportation to and from school is furnished by the school district, this exemption shall not apply.

(d) Private Instruction—Any child who is being taught for a like period of time by the parent or private teacher such subjects as are usually taught in the first eight years in the public school; but before such child can be taught by a parent or a private teacher, such parent or private teacher must receive written permission from the county superintendent, and such permission shall not extend longer than the end of the current school year. Such child must report to the county school superintendent or some person designated by him at least once every three months and take an examination in the work covered. If, after such examination, the county superintendent shall determine that such child is not being properly taught, then the county superintendent shall order the parent, guardian or other person, to send such child to the public school the remainder of the school year.

The challenged Act, effective September 1, 1926, requires every parent, guardian or other person having control or charge or custody of a child between eight and sixteen years to send him "to a public school for the period of time a public school shall be held during the current year" in the district where the child resides; and failure so to do is declared a misdemeanor. There are exemptions—not specially important here—for children who are not normal, or who have completed the eighth grade, or who reside at considerable distances from any public school, or who hold special permits from the county superintendent. The manifest purpose is to compel general attendance at public schools by normal children, between eight and sixteen, who have not completed the eighth grade. And without doubt enforcement of the statute would seriously impair, perhaps destroy, the profitable features of appellees' business and greatly diminish the value of their property.

Appellee, the Society of Sisters, is an Oregon corporation, organized in 1880, with power to care for orphans, educate and instruct the youth, establish and maintain academies or schools, and acquire necessary real and personal property. It has long devoted its property and effort to the secular and religious education and care of children, and has acquired the valuable good-will of many parents and guardians. It conducts interdependent primary and high schools and junior colleges, and maintains orphanages for the custody and control of children between eight and sixteen. In its primary schools many children between those ages are taught the subjects usually pursued in Oregon public schools during the first eight years. Systematic religious instruction and moral training according to the tenets of the Roman Catholic Church are also regularly provided. All courses of study, both temporal and religious, contemplate continuity of training under appellee's charge; the primary schools are essential to the system and the most profitable. It owns valuable buildings, especially constructed and equipped for school purposes. The business is remunerative—the annual income from primary schools exceeds thirty thousand dollars—and the successful conduct of this requires long-time contracts with teachers and parents. The Compulsory Education Act of 1922 has already caused the withdrawal from its schools of children who would otherwise continue, and their

---

If any parent, guardian or other person having control or charge or custody of any child between the ages of eight and sixteen years, shall fail to comply with any provision of this section, he shall be guilty of a misdemeanor, and shall, on conviction thereof, be subject to a fine of not less than $5, nor more than $100, or to imprisonment in the county jail not less than two nor more than thirty days; or by both such fine and imprisonment in the discretion of the court.

This Act shall take effect and be and remain in force from and after the first day of September, 1926.

income has steadily declined. The appellants, public officers, have proclaimed their purpose strictly to enforce the statute.

After setting out the above facts the Society's bill alleges that the enactment conflicts with the right of parents to choose schools where their children will receive appropriate mental and religious training, the right of the child to influence the parents' choice of a school, the right of schools and teachers therein to engage in a useful business or profession, and is accordingly repugnant to the Constitution and void. And, further, that unless enforcement of the measure is enjoined the corporation's business and property will suffer irreparable injury.

Appellee, Hill Military Academy, is a private corporation organized in 1908 under the laws of Oregon, engaged in owning, operating and conducting for profit an elementary, college preparatory and military training school for boys between the ages of five and twenty-one years. The average attendance is one hundred and the annual fees received for each student amount to some eight hundred dollars. The elementary department is divided into eight grades, as in the public schools; the college preparatory department has four grades, similar to those of the public high schools; the course of study conform to the requirements of the State Board of Education. Military instruction and training are also given, under the supervision of an Army officer. It owns considerable real and personal property, some useful only for school purposes. The business and incident good-will are very valuable. In order to conduct its affairs long-time contracts must be made for supplies, equipment, teachers, and pupils. Appellants, law officers of the state and county, have publicly announced that the Act of November 7, 1922, is valid and have declared their intention to enforce it. By reason of the statute and threat of enforcement appellee's business is being destroyed and its property depreciated; parents and guardians are refusing to make contracts for the future instruction of their sons, and some are being withdrawn.

The Academy's bill states the foregoing facts and then alleges that the challenged act contravenes the corporation's rights guaranteed by the Fourteenth Amendment and that unless appellants are restrained from proclaiming its validity and threatening to enforce it, irreparable injury will result. The prayer is for an appropriate injunction.

No answer was interposed in either cause, and after proper notices they were heard by three judges . . . on motions for preliminary injunctions upon the specifically alleged facts. The court ruled that the Fourteenth Amendment guaranteed appellees against the deprivation of their property without due process of law consequent upon the unlawful interference by appellants with the free choice of patrons, present and prospective. It declared the right to conduct schools was property and that parents and guardians, as a part of their liberty, might direct the education of children by selecting reputable teachers and places. Also, that appellees' schools were not unfit or harmful to the public and that enforcement of the challenged statute would unlawfully deprive them of the patronage and thereby destroy appellees' business and property. Finally, that the threats to enforce the Act would continue to cause irreparable injury, and the suits were not premature.

No question is raised concerning the power of the state reasonably to regulate all schools, to inspect, supervise and examine them, their teachers and pupils; to require that all children of proper age attend some school, that teachers shall be of good moral character and patriotic disposition, that certain studies plainly essential to good citizenship must be taught, and that nothing be taught which is manifestly inimical to the public welfare.

The inevitable practical result of enforcing the Act under consideration would be destruction of appellees' primary schools, and perhaps all other private primary schools for normal children within the State of Oregon. Appellees are engaged in a kind of undertaking not inherently harmful, but long regarded as useful and meritorious. Certainly there is nothing in the present records to indicate that they have failed to discharge their obligations to patrons, students or the state. And there are no peculiar circumstances or present emergencies which demand extraordinary measures relative to primary education.

Under the doctrine of *Meyer v. Nebraska*, 262 U.S. 390, we think it entirely plain that the act of 1922 unreasonably interferes with the liberty of parents and guardians to direct the upbringing and education of children under their control. As often heretofore pointed out, rights guaranteed by the Constitution may not be abridged by legislation which has no reasonable relation to some purpose within the competency of the state. The fundamental theory of liberty upon which all governments in this Union repose excludes any general power of the state to standardize its children by forcing them to accept instruction from public teachers only. The child is not the mere creature of the state; those who nurture him and direct his destiny have the right coupled with the high duty, to recognize and prepare him for additional obligations.

Appellees are corporations and therefore, it is said, they cannot claim for themselves the liberty which the Fourteenth Amendment guarantees. Accepted in the proper sense, this is true. . . . But they have business and property for which they claim protection. These are threatened with destruction through the unwarranted compulsion which appellants are exercising over present and prospective patrons of their schools. And this Court has gone very far to protect against loss threatened by such action. . . .

Generally it is entirely true, as urged by counsel, that no person in any business has such an interest in possible customers as to enable him to restrain exercise of proper power of the state upon the ground that he will be deprived of patronage. But the injunctions here sought are not against the exercise of any *proper* power. Appellees asked protection against arbitrary, unreasonable and unlawful interference with their patrons and the consequent destruction of their business and property. Their interest is clear and immediate, within the rule approved in *Truax v. Raick, Truax v. Corrigan* and *Terrace v. Thompson,* supra, and many other cases where injunctions have issued to protect business enterprises against interference with the freedom of patrons or customers. . . .

The suits were not premature. The injury to appellees was present and very real, not a mere possibility in the remote future. If no relief had been possible prior to the effective date of the Act, the injury would have become irreparable. Prevention of impending injury by unlawful action is a well recognized function of courts of equity.

The decrees below are affirmed.

38

Senator John Stennis and Attorney Marian Wright, *Debate over a Great Society Nonprofit Organization in Mississippi,* 1967

The New Frontier, the Great Society, and the War on Poverty, associated with the presidential administrations of John F. Kennedy and Lyndon B. Johnson, greatly increased nonprofit activity in the United States. Kennedy and his associates placed great emphasis on the initiatives of individuals and of private nonprofits. In part, they drew on their experience of education and leadership in private, often nonsectarian, universities and foundations (notably the Ivy League colleges and the Rockefeller, Carnegie, and Ford foundations). In part, they drew on their extensive experience in Protestant, Catholic, and Jewish hospitals and community organizations. And in part they built on the work of the private agencies (the National Association for the Advancement of Colored People, churches and fraternal organizations, the historically Black colleges) that had supported African American life in the legally segregated south and in the practically segregated north.

The War on Poverty's use of private agencies through its Community Action Program became exceedingly controversial. In the best-known and most influential account, Daniel Patrick Moynihan (later elected to the U.S. Senate, where he still represents the State of New York) argued that this effort to use private agencies to "empower the poor" produced only acrimony and *Maximum Feasible Misunderstanding* (the title of his book, New York: Free Press, 1969). Moynihan emphasized the northern experience; other accounts of the misadventures of Community Action agencies in northern cities from Boston, New York, and Syracuse through Cleveland and Chicago to Oakland support his interpretation.

But Community Action Agencies were also designed to operate in the South, where segregationists still controlled the voting lists, the police, the courts, the city councils, and the state governments in 1967—and where segregationists employed violence and all the tactics of legal and bureaucratic delay against the civil rights movement. The struggle for civil rights for all citizens in Mississippi provided the background for a particularly striking confrontation over the proper role of private nonprofit agencies that were "independent" of local government in the Spring of 1967. At a hearing organized by a committee of the U.S. Senate in Jackson, Mississippi, John Stennis, the segregationist Democratic U.S. Senator, attacked a private, nonprofit organization, the Child Development Group of Mississippi, which had emerged as the leading provider of Head Start services in Mississippi—and which had become, thanks to federal contracts, one of the state's largest employers. Stennis found himself challenged by Democratic Senator Robert Kennedy and Republican Senator Jacob Javits, both of New York. He was also opposed by the young attorney for the Child Development Group of Mississippi, Marion Wright (later Marion Wright Edelman, the founding head of the Children's Defense Fund). Stennis laid out a very able "states' rights" case for opposition to independent nonprofit anti-poverty agencies in the South. Marion Wright countered with an eloquent defense of independent nonprofits as essential to the federal effort to redress the conditions faced by African Americans and poor people generally. Only "independent programs" run by private nonprofits, she argued, could "bypass state agencies" that enforced segregation.

Conflict and controversy over the Community Action Program has obscured the fact that the Great Society secured the passage of Medicare, Medicaid, student grant and loan programs, the expansion of the National Science Foundation and the National Institutes of Health, and the creation of the National Endowments for the Arts and for the Humanities. These programs did far more than the War on Poverty to support the expansion—probably the tripling in employment share—of nonprofits in the United States between the early 1960s and the late 1980s.

EMPLOYMENT, MANPOWER AND POVERTY SUBCOMMITTEE
U.S. SENATE LABOR AND PUBLIC WELFARE COMMITTEE

Senator John Stennis and Attorney Marian Wright, Testimony on the Child Development Group of Mississippi and the Head Start Program

Hearing in Jackson, Mississippi, April 10, 1967

CHAIRMAN [Joseph S. Clark, Democrat of Pennsylvania]. Our first witness today is one of our colleagues, Senator John Stennis, of Mississippi, appearing at his request. We are happy indeed to have him here. Senator Stennis, I want to welcome you before the subcommittee, as you have been kind enough to welcome me to Mississippi. Will you please proceed, sir, in you own way?

STATEMENT OF HON. JOHN STENNIS, A U.S. SENATOR FROM THE STATE OF MISSISSIPPI

SENATOR STENNIS [Democrat]. Mr. Chairman and members of the subcommittee, my colleagues, I want to thank you for this chance to appear here.

SENATOR CLARK. Senator, just a moment. We are going to have to have quiet over there among the television and radio people. We have got to have our concentration entirely on the witness. Will you please proceed, Senator? I know what a stickler for order you are yourself.

SENATOR STENNIS. I thank the Chair, and I thank all of you for the privilege of being here as a witness on the forthcoming bill as a Member of the Senate as well as a Mississippian with responsibility to the people of my State for what I say and do as well as responsible to you, as my colleagues, for what I say and do. . . .

PREPARED STATEMENT OF SENATOR JOHN STENNIS

Mr. Chairman, I fully realize that Mississippi is the 29th State in population, is 16th in the number of poor by OEO [Office of Economic Opportunity] standards, and stands 10th in the amount of OEO funds received.

Some good has come from these programs, of course. But the test is not just whether some benefits have been received from the more than $75 million put in Mississippi.

From my own investigation I know that a large part of the Poverty Program money has been misused, mismanaged and wasted. If the federal administration of the Poverty Program in Mississippi is typical of other states, it is the most poorly managed federal program I have encountered in 20 years as a United States Senator.

OEO area and national officers in some cases have not only approved but have insisted that responsible, local people be bypassed and top position in many local projects be filled by persons who have had no experience, little, if any, training, and who are ill-suited by nature and temperament to operate a poverty program.

Serious mismanagement and misuse of hundreds of thousands of dollars have been overlooked and in some cases the violators seemingly have been rewarded with even larger grants.

The cost of some parts of the Poverty Programs have so exceeded what OEO told Congress it would be that it is clear those in charge of the

Program at the national level had no knowledge of the facts and Congress was given inaccurate information. For instance, Congress was told by OEO in April 1965, that the Headstart Program would cost approximately $170 per child. The fact is the Headstart Program is costing in some cases over 7 times that.

One grant in this State—to the Child Development Group of Mississippi—was made on the basis of $1340 per child per year. That is almost five times the expenditure per child in the public schools of Mississippi. It is almost three times the national average for public schools and almost double the expenditure per public school student in New York City which is the highest in the nation.

I think if it had been known at the time the Poverty Program legislation was being considered in the Senate that the Federal Government was to spend three times as much per child in a kindergarten for five year olds as the average state spends per child in elementary and high schools, the Program would have been defeated overwhelmingly.

This high and unreasonable cost has resulted in a large measure from the wholesale waste and in some cases misappropriate of federal grant money. I know because I have closely followed the Headstart Program in Mississippi, particularly the CDGM project.

My views are presented here with the idea that if we are to have a Poverty Program we should make it as effective and efficient as possible. While I am in sympathy with those who want to help the poor and disadvantaged, I think the approach made through this law, particularly as it is now written, may, in fact, do more harm than good in the long run.

My suggestions today are based on three years of watching the operation of the Poverty Program in Mississippi. Some parts of it have been operated well and has done a lot of good. I have gone into some phases of the Mississippi part of it more thoroughly than others.

I have reached several conclusions which convince me that if the war on poverty is to come anywhere near to being a workable efficient program some drastic changes must be made in the law. Among other things, are the following; we must:

1. PLACE THE CONTROL AND ADMINISTRATION OF THE PROGRAM IN THE HANDS OF LOCAL RESPONSIBLE CITIZENS AND CONSTITUTED GOVERNMENTAL AUTHORITIES

The Child Development Group of Mississippi that operates a Headstart program in Mississippi counties is an outstanding example of what happens when local responsible officials are bypassed. The CDGM program was conceived and organized in 1964 by a man from New York. Many of the key employees were brought in from out of State. Despite the desire of local officials to operate Headstart programs that would have made CDGM unnecessary, the local authorities and responsible citizens were ignored to a large degree and the Headstart program in most of the State was turned over to CDGM.

In the first year of operation out of a $1.6 million grant to CDGM the OEO auditors questions over $500,000 as being improperly spent or unaccounted for. Of the $5.8 million grant the next year (1965) $600,000 was challenged by OEO for the same reason.

The flagrant misuse and waste of money by the CDGM without penalty put the entire program under suspect. Those in charge of the CDGM program knew nothing about local conditions or problems. They came into communities throughout the State ignoring the more responsible people of those communities. Many of the key personnel appeared more like beatniks and displayed little, if any, of the qualities desired for the operation of a kindergarten program for four and five year olds.

For that reason the CDGM program has never had the confidence of the more responsible element of the people. Even now the CDGM program is under the direction of a very young man from Massachusetts who is administering the present grant of $4.9 million or $7.9 million with what has been promised.

Because those in charge of CDGM program are still considered incapable of spending the federal money properly and carrying on the program as it should be conducted, the Federal Government has found it necessary in the current program to pay a Washington, D.C., management firm $144,000 a year to come to Mississippi and oversee and supervise the CDGM program. That is an unjustifiable waste of taxpayers' money.

There are local citizens and officials fully qualified to operate these Headstart programs and who are anxious to do so. CDGM, for instances, operates in Jones County. The school officials in the principal city of that county have tried for three years to obtain a Headstart grant. Each year they were told by OEO that there was no money for them but CDGM was given millions of dollars to operate in Jones County along with other counties assigned to CDGM.

It is extremely poor judgment in my opinion to pass over local officials, particularly school authorities, who are entirely capable and then put the program in the hands of persons who have to be supervised from Washington at a cost of over $12,000 per month.

2. PROVIDE WIDE AND FINAL AUTHORITY FOR THE GOVERNOR TO VETO, WITHOUT RECOURSE, ANY PROJECT HE DETERMINES NOT IN THE PUBLIC INTEREST

The success of the poverty program will be more nearly assured by making it responsible to officials who can and will avoid a situation such as that just described. The Governor of a State is in a position to know the condition in his State. He knows the people. He is closely accountable to them for the administration of programs and should have authority and control over program in his State. . . .

Should the veto be restored, the law should not contain the provision that the Governor cannot veto a community action grant, such as the CDGM Headstart Program, when it is made through an institution of higher learning. That provides a subterfuge that would make the veto meaningless. In the case of CDGM, the Appropriations Committee investigators found that Mary Holmes Junior College which actually was the grantee was used merely as a straw to avoid the possibility of a Governor's veto. . . .

If any governor should misuse his authority of veto the people have a direct remedy. They can speak loudly at the polls. Also, the influence of the local community and the needs of individuals can be brought to bear much stronger and more effectively on a local elected official than on a federal or appointed Administrator, thousands of miles away. . . .

3. STRICT REQUIREMENTS OF FISCAL CONTROL AND ACCOUNTING WITH A STATUTORY PROHIBITION AGAINST REFUNDING ANY GRANTEE THAT FAILS TO PROPERLY ACCOUNT FOR ALL GRANT FUNDS

. . . Again I cite the Child Development Group [of Mississippi]. . . . Evidence showed several hundred thousand dollars were not fully or properly accounted for in 1965 and 1966 by CDGM. In fact, the OEO director said:

"We found specifically that people were paid for work that they had not performed.

"We found that people were paid and time and attendance sheets were certified by supervisors for employees who were not even in the State of Mississippi. . . . We found a variety of conflict-of-interest matters that included people on the board of directors as well as staff members. We found cases of nepotism. We found that property paid for by the Government was used for nongovernmental purposes. Automobiles, for example, were used on weekends and at nighttimes for activities that clearly were not connected with the program. . . ."

Tremendous pressure was brought to bear on the Director of the OEO to refund this group. He finally did so. I know it is claimed that some special conditions to the grant were demanded by OEO. . . . I have examined these so-called special conditions and not a single one of them places any higher responsibility on the grantee than existed under the present provisions of the law.

In addition, one condition of the grant provides that the Presbyterian Church will stand responsible for any past, present or future claims the Government might have against CDGM. This is absolutely ridicu-

lous. First, because it is unthinkable that a church would have to underwrite the Federal Government. Second, I don't believe the President or
any other federal official who works for the President will ever sue the
Presbyterian Church or any other church....

Pressure to refund CDGM from people outside the State of Mississippi who obviously knew the least about how this program was carried
out was more than the OEO Director could stand. Over 150 lawyers
gathered at Howard University in Washington to bring legal pressure.
Hundred of ministers—misguided and uniformed though perhaps well
intentioned—picketed OEO Headquarters. National labor leaders and
other organizations mobilized to bring all of their influence and pressure upon the Director of the OEO.

The taxpayer should be protected from such pressure by a strict
provision in the law that those who do not properly account for federal
money cannot receive more money.

4. PROHIBIT THE DIRECT OR INDIRECT USE OF POVERTY PRO-
GRAM FUNDS, FACILITIES, EQUIPMENT OR OTHER RESOURCES IN
PARTISAN POLITICS

Again I cite the Child Development Group of Mississippi as a case
in point. When this group was first organized, the Board of Directors of
the Freedom Democratic Party and the Child Development Group were
interlaced. Many of the officials of the Child Development Group were
also leaders in the civil rights movement and were active in promoting
boycotts, marches, sit-ins and other demonstrations, as well as taking
an active part in partisan politics.

Evidence showed that cars leased by CDGM were used extensively
in these activities and that the leaders and sub-leaders were active in
civil rights work under the guise of community organization. The report
of the Appropriation Committee investigators last fall stated:

"The 'community organization' set up within CDGM is, in fact, a
particularly bad situation. As indicated, this segment of the organization
at the headquarters area and local levels through community gatherings
and various other methods deals with social services, including appris-
ing the colored community of their rights, how they can obtain welfare
and other federal services, furnishing pamphlets, etc. There is little doubt
but that civil rights organizational activities are being promoted within
the framework of this activity. *Patently some of this activity is not the type
which should be subsidized by federal Headstart grant funds and it is sure to
breed racial friction and possibly violence.* In some of the classrooms there
was a sign 'Black Power.' Regardless of the desirability of the parents of
these children in improving themselves and identifying them with the
Program. *The way it is seemingly being done within the framework of CDGM it
is believed to be wrong and something should be done about it. . . .*"

5. REDUCE THE DISCRIMINATION NOW GIVEN TO THE OEO DIRECTOR AND THE REGIONAL OFFICIALS AND MORE CLEARLY DEFINE AND MAKE MORE SPECIFIC THE PROVISIONS AND REQUIREMENTS FOR THE QUALIFICATION FOR A GRANT

The discretion now left in the OEO area and national administrators allows these administrators to make arbitrary and adverse decisions affecting a small political division of the community and leaves the citizens of that community without effective recourse.

I cite as a case in point the attempt by the Leflore County to organize a community action program. Two years and three days ago, in April 1965, the supervisors of that county applied for a community action program. Negotiations were conducted with OEO officials over many months and included many dozens of exchanges through correspondence, personal contacts and telephone conversations.

A résumé of the first several months of that exchange clearly shows that the broad authority of OEO administrators was used without justification to delay and evade approval of this project. Had it been approved there would have been no requirement for CDGM in that county. . . .

SENATOR CLARK. Your statement is already in, Senator. Thank you very much for a forthright and controversial statement. Senator Javits, do you have any questions?

SENATOR [Jacob] JAVITS [Republican of New York]. I have no questions for Senator Stennis, but I do believe the Senator has raised a certain number of highly controversial issues; I think the people as well as ourselves should understand that these are charges, and that those charged must have the opportunity to reply in specific detail.

The charges as I understand them, by implication at least, were that the administration of CDGM program was put in the hands of irresponsible rather than responsible people in Mississippi; that there was undue pressure on the OEO Administrator to fund the CDGM after these disclosures were made and that these disclosures represented expenditures that were "challenged" in the case of 1966, and "questioned" in the case of 1967. Well, actually whether they were improper will depend upon the facts.

We already have the report of Ernst & Ernst, which I understand reduces to a small amount of the figures which are involved, bringing them down to a few hundred or some hundreds in one case and some thousands in the other.

Finally, that there were immoral people, beatniks, et cetera, who refused to obey the Director of OEO, and the various imperfections and problems raised with respect to what was taught the children.

All of this, Mr. Chairman, I think requires the committee in basic fairness to allow those who are affected by these charges an opportunity to reply—the people in CDGM, the OEO Administrator, Mr. Shriver and any others that might be named. . . .

SENATOR JAVITS. May I say, Mr. Chairman, that we all understand we are not operating in a vacuum here. There have been tremendous tensions in this State, there have been very serious outbreaks of violence, and we know that the State for a long time has had almost an equally divided population between whites and Negroes, and there have been grave charges, many in my judgment sharply substantiated that the Negroes did not have their full participation either politically or in other ways in the activities of the State.

Now all of this has been gone into many times in the Congress but I did not believe that the record should just stand as it was even temporarily. As I said before, I am confident and the Chair has confirmed that those charged will have the full opportunity to reply and I hope that the public will be fair enough, and my colleagues I know will be fair enough to keep their minds open until both the charges and the rebuttal can be evaluated together. . . .

SENATOR CLARK. Senator Kennedy of New York.

SENATOR [Robert] KENNEDY of New York [Democrat]. . . . I have before me the report of Ernst & Ernst which made an audit of this organization and came out with some figures that are quite different in connection with the amount of money that had been misused or the amount that had disappeared . . . the report that was ultimately made which is the audited financial statement and other financial information, January 31, 1967, by Ernst & Ernst, says: "It is the opinion that the grantee, its counsel and its independent accountant that the amount, if any, ultimately disallowed by the Office of Economic Opportunity after proper consideration and evaluation of all factors pertaining to expenditures made by grantee or delegate agency under this grant will be relatively minor in amounts. . . ."

STATEMENT OF MISS MARION WRIGHT, JACKSON, MISS.

MISS WRIGHT. Thank you, Senator. . . . That the poverty program has had a major impact in the country is very clear particularly here in Mississippi from the fact that there is so much controversy. I think this controversy does show the change that is occurring. . . . [I]t has had a major impact about how people feel about themselves, again reflected by the controversy, because for the first time poor people are participating. They are making decisions, and they are insisting that they be more included in all decision-making processes of government here.

I think the greatest success story that can be told is that the number of communities at least the third largest Headstart program in the

State is being run by the poorest people out of their own pockets for 2,000 children, and this situation on a voluntary basis shows clearly that these people have been inspired by something to do things for themselves, and I think this huge volunteer operation that has gone on in the absence of Federal funds which was initiated by the poverty program where they had an atmosphere where they could do, and help their children and help themselves is a great tribute to it.

Despite this I think we see only 15 percent of the Negro children and white children in the State who are eligible for Headstart being affected. . . .

What is wrong with the poverty program and how can it be improved? I think you have heard how people feel about many of the CAP [Community Action Program] structures, and you have heard them express their desires for independent programs.

. . . I think the need for independent programs has been very strong and continues to be very strong, but in many instances we have seen these independent programs as catalytic influences to get these other elements in the community that should be involved in helping to eradicate poverty involved. As a response a lot of independent programs have started. You have had men in several communities in the State where you have now formed potentially very good CAP [Community Action Program] boards, with contented independent operation, where poor people are participating. . . . This can provide the pressure, I think, for other elements of the community to get involved. . . .

On the whole, so far, the CAP structures have not been working mainly because, I think, they are based on the thought that all elements in the community are interested in eradicating poverty. Certain preconditions must exist which do not exist in most of our communities here in the country. We are assuming one community, and we are assuming a commitment by all segments of that community, to eradication of poverty. Our experience and the history of Mississippi defies that. . . .

How do we get over that? . . . CAP boards must be representative of all elements and representatives must be chosen in open elections where people in the community have access to the information. . . . There must be openness. . . . There must be elections to insure that those people who are sitting in CAP structures are representative.

Now in terms of how much participation of poor there should be . . . [from the] President's poverty message one senses there is going to be a great move toward more control by local power structure, and I am talking about the State and local governments in this context. That would be a major tragedy for a place like Mississippi. We have documented and can document the disparate policies that these State agencies have had to the Negro and white community. Our Federal programs and our State local public agencies are not functioning as they should. . . .

If these State agencies are not going to follow those safeguards and insure participation by all elements of the community, then the Congress must preserve the right of people to participate in independent programs, and only then through the development of these independent programs are we going to move these public institutions to the posture where they should be. . . .

You must preserve these independent programs. . . .

You heard about the violence this morning and I think that while the Governor may have changed his policy it has not drifted through to many of the State highway patrol officials, and it certainly has not drifted through to many of the local officials . . . I would encourage this Congress to take stronger action in this regard so that people who do participate, white and Negro, will be protected. If the Federal Government makes it clear that it is not going to tolerate this and that people will be prosecuted, then you will have a change of atmosphere and you will have the kind of change of atmosphere where people will be freer.

Thirdly, the participation of the poor must be maintained. I think we have been shown again and again now that once they have seen, as they have in some few programs, that they can run things for themselves with dignity, they will not take less and they are going to insist that any programs that come involve them because they now understand that this is the only way in which substantial change is going to take place.

SENATOR CLARK. Let me interrupt you there to throw at you a really very difficult question. You heard Senator Stennis testify this morning, and he was about as emphatic as a man could be, that to bypass the elected public officials in this State was not only ineffective as a pragmatic matter but as a normal problem of constitutional democracy for the Federal Government to run around the State and municipal officials elected by the people, to be sure with an inadequate franchise, was just not in accordance with our American democratic system.

You are a graduate of an excellent law school. I know you studied government and constitutional history. What is your answer, what justification is there for bypassing what you call the power structure in order to give the Federal funds to these independent organizations which are either unwilling to or unable to cooperate with the elected public officials of their community?

MISS WRIGHT. Senator Clark, I would say, as a lawyer, that there are many constitutional principles and I think that one of them is that all people in this democracy are to have a chance to participate on an equal basis. This has not been done in this State. I think the State has shown again and again that it will not take care of all its citizens as it should. . . . The record of Mississippi speaks for itself. The fact that [Senator Stennis] says there is no need to bypass the State agencies I think is defied by the record in schools, the employment security commission's report, and agricultural problems documented by the Civil Rights Commission.

To talk about State control we have to also talk about State responsibility, and until Mississippi gets to the point where it can respect the law and respect the rights of all citizens it has no right to require that all these other citizens who have themselves been pushed out from the participatory process be denied benefits that the Federal Government owes to the people to make sure that they can maintain their survival—and that I think is the issue.

When Mississippi gets ready to do its job I think we will all be very, very happy to participate with them. Until that time I think the Federal Government has a clear obligation to try to bring them up to the level where they participate in the processes of government, and that hasn't come yet. . . .

SENATOR JAVITS. Miss Wright, I shall not go over the ground you have already covered, but I notice that you did not answer anything about Senator Stennis' charges against [Child Development Group of Mississippi]. Do you wish to make any comments on that?

MISS WRIGHT. He is wrong, Senator Javits, and we have been through this again and again. I hate to keep responding to trials by newspaper. CDGM has had three grants. We are in our third grant period. During our first grant period in 1965, after our OEO final audit, which we ran under a grant of $1.5 million, the amount OEO said had been misused was about $14,000, which is less than 1 percent of the total grant. That amount was made good by the Presbyterian church guarantee, and not one penny of taxpayer money was lost.

I think this is an incredibly good figure, which is again much beneath the waste generally allowed under Federal programs, and again even this 1 percent in view of the context of the number of poor people running a program with major sums of money involved, I think this is really a miraculous achievement.

The second grant was $6 million. The audit of this which has come out so far from Ernst & Ernst, which is a national accounting firm, has come out with the opinion, as Senator Kennedy stated this morning, that any disallowances which may occur will be relatively minor.

I would like to say that after the first grant where we had this 1 percent loss which we did replace through private sources, we greatly tightened up our accounting procedures, hired a first rate accountant, Ernst & Ernst, and that no expenditure was made in this program without the prior OK of our accounting firm or our independent comptroller.

In our current program, which we are operating now at a $5 million level, with the promise of an additional $3 million, we have again hired one of the leading accountants in the country.

We have also, in trying to fulfill very strenuous grant conditions to assure almost physical perfection, hired a top management firm from Washington to coordinate all administrative activities. . . .

I am proud of the administration.

Senator Stennis' testimony has no substance, and I don't think I need to say any more about it. We are open to investigation. We feel we have nothing to hide. We think we have done a fine job.

SENATOR JAVITS. The fact is that of all the programs for pre-school-age children being operated in Mississippi, this one is servicing the most children, is that not true?

MISS WRIGHT. This to this day is servicing the most children. It was the first and only Headstart initially begun.

I think its success has been reflected by the fact that when we applied to OEO for our last grant without recruitment 30,000 children had signed up to participate and it has been the single largest Headstart—not only in this State but in the country.

SENATOR JAVITS. There is no question about the fact that the poor are actually participating in this one, is there?

MISS WRIGHT. The poor control this program of CDGM. I would like to reemphasize, as some people said this morning, the local community, the board of CDGM is two-thirds poor, almost completely local, and employees in this program, quite to the contrary of Senator Stennis' program, are 98 percent local.

SENATOR JAVITS. Now, can you tell us something about the role which is being played or could be played by the private business community in respect of the matters that we have been discussing about employment, training, and education.

MISS WRIGHT. I think the private business community could play a great role if they were willing. I think in one sense the poverty program being in the State resulted in private businesses community getting a little more interested in the problems of the Negro community mainly because they have gotten something out of the poverty program too. We have found in those local communities when we decided initially that we would bank with local county banks throughout the State, as well as at a central banking location, that these businessmen who could gain from the poverty program began to see that they had something to gain too and have become a little more cooperative. Gradually, I think, with increased money, with increased intensiveness by the poor, you are going to see the business community focus a little more on these issues.

Secondly, I think the business community is beginning to understand that it cannot afford more conflict and rather than have a lot of conflict I think they are going to try to begin to work out moderate means, so in a sense these independent programs which many people attack have played a very important role in pushing people who ordinarily would not have moved into action. . . .

SENATOR JAVITS. The last question I would like to ask you, Miss Wright, to what extent is there any connection between a successful CAP that really has participation of the poor, and the extent of Negro voter registration in a particular area?

MISS WRIGHT. I think there is, Senator. I think in those areas where we have now our best CAP boards you also have a majority or a very quick potential majority of Negro voters. In Bolivar County, where Mr. Moore comes from, there are now 2,000 more Negroes registered than whites, and you have much more cooperation all of a sudden from the white public and business officials. In southwest Mississippi where Mr. Evers is involved there is a very strong registration drive and you find a much more workable CAP board. . . .

MISS WRIGHT. I don't think that more public officials should be put on CAP boards, because public officials in the past and even now are not doing their jobs properly. If they are to be put on them, there should be very specific conditions that they must meet in order to participate. . . .

SENATOR KENNEDY of New York. Part of this problem is related to the question of welfare. Could you discuss that for a moment also?

MISS WRIGHT. Welfare practices, Senator, in Mississippi, are terrible. I think we have been able to document and this committee does have . . . a welfare report which we did which shows I think the violation of Federal and State law. In hearing procedures, we found that most people in Mississippi didn't even know they had a right to a hearing; the failure of the welfare department consistently to take applications from people and people get terrible run-arounds, and we have been able to document this in county after county after county. People are not treated with dignity when they go into the welfare office, and they are not allowed to be people, and they are investigated and they are threatened, and this is a terrible kind of thing that has to be stopped.

People who have participated in civil rights have been cut off from welfare, and we have been able to document this in many counties. The whole welfare department is simply not functioning to serve the needs of the poor and particularly in the Negro community.

Secondly, even if the welfare department did function up to par, which it is not, only 31 percent is given of need [the cost of living as determined by the U.S. Department of Labor], and you cannot live on that amount of money.

Mississippi is refusing to put up the matching share which is making us lose millions of dollars in potential welfare funds a year. I think one of the things perhaps that should be thought about is to get some kind of way where a welfare department such as Mississippi is not meeting the total Federal standard and is not putting up the matching share, to see if we can't get some provision in the Federal law whereby maybe 100 percent will be given to people in situations of need such as this where the State refuses to fulfill its obligation. . . .

SENATOR KENNEDY of New York. For the reasons you discussed, first, there is widespread hunger and malnutrition, as I understand it, throughout these areas of the State, and for the reasons which you have, described, there is really not the kind of progress that needs to be made to deal with this problem. . . . Do I understand that really for many of these families it is a question of starvation or trying to leave and go to some other part of the country?

MISS WRIGHT. They are starving. They are starving, and those who can get the bus fare to go north are trying to go north. But there is absolutely nothing for them to do. There is nowhere to go, and somebody must begin to respond to them. I wish the Senators would have a chance to go and just look at the empty cupboards in the Delta and the number of people who are going around begging just to feed their children.

Starvation is a major, major problem now.

SENATOR KENNEDY of New York. I think, of course, Mr. Chairman, that this is a reflection on all of us. This country in 1967 is the most prosperous country in the world. A number of our corporations are making profits greater than 70 of the countries of the world, you would think that all of us would be able to provide for some of our citizens living in this part of the country. I think some of this testimony, Mr. Chairman, is a reflection on some of the programs and I suppose some of the officials here in the State and there might be an answer. I think it would be perhaps helpful if we at least make it possible for any of those public officials who have the responsibility either for the food stamp program or for the welfare program or for any of these other programs that have been discussed here to appear before the committee, and perhaps give their version of these events so that the committee will have all of the information possible. . . .

SENATOR [George] MURPHY [Republican of California]. . . . Now, first of all, Miss Wright, I don't know exactly whether you are a free-lance lawyer or who you represent. Would you tell me?

MISS WRIGHT. I am a member of the Mississippi bar. I am primarily engaged in civil rights law and NAACP Legal Defense and Educational Fund.

SENATOR MURPHY. Are you connected with the CDGM [Child Development Group of Mississippi]?

MISS WRIGHT. I am counsel for CDGM; yes, I am.

SENATOR MURPHY. Counsel for them. I see.

SENATOR CLARK. Senator Murphy, would you yield for a moment? The young lady is a graduate of Yale.

SENATOR MURPHY. Oh, I know that. I was a dropout. I never graduated. . . .

MISS WRIGHT. I would like to just make—I'm taking too much of the committee's time—one or two other things of the act which may have potentially dangerous implications for us here in the matching-share provision.

So far [the independent, nonprofit headstart and anti-poverty agencies] have been required to . . . put up [the] 10 percent local share [that federal law expected to be paid by local or state governments]. We have seen that we have been able to meet this with some difficulty but generally I think the volunteer response on the part of the community has been able to meet this 10 percent. If the [independent nonprofit organizations'] share goes up 20 percent, or higher, or if there is a tremendous amount of discretion to shift the amount of non-Federal share that must be made, the inevitable result [would be to] force those independent programs which cannot put up that 10 or 20 percent or anything in excess of 20 percent out of business and to have to have more local involvement of public officials, which may not be the best thing in that particular instance. I would urge that the non-Federal share, at least in independent programs or in CAP programs in communities where they are extremely poor, not be lifted because this is going to hurt a great deal. . . .

You must preserve the right of the people to participate, because only through that kind of motivation and self-help are you going to get any kind of lasting change. Else the poverty program, unless this kind of participation is practiced, is going to turn into just another form of welfareism which is just going to completely build in a horrible situation where we are going to reap terrible results, because I think each of us now has to ask ourselves, unless our institutions begin to respond to people, how long can we expect these people to continue to respond to them? What would you or I do if we had eight children and we could not feed them; what kind of action would we take?. . . .

I thank the committee. . . .

SENATOR MURPHY. You spoke about the neglect of the northern businessmen of their obligation. Do you know of the situation as pertains to the Watts area of Los Angeles and the job that has been done by the McClellan committee?

MISS WRIGHT. Vaguely, Senator Murphy.

SENATOR MURPHY. I would suggest, if I may, I would like to send you reports on what they have done, what they have accomplished, because I have worried the members of the subcommittee, I am so proud about what has happened. It is simply this, a good, sensible, civic minded, very successful businessman, who has retired, got interested and he went to work on a practical basis, and he has supplied 17,500-plus jobs for the people in Watts, and after almost a year over 80 percent of those people are still employed. They have a very high rate of staying on the job. I would think that maybe a plan of this kind might be suggested properly to some of the leaders of the business community here, and I think after examination they find it is not too complicated, it might be very productive.

MISS WRIGHT. I would hope that one could get that kind of business response in a place like Mississippi. I think we are all clear that the business community could have a major impact on change in the State. . . .

SENATOR CLARK. Thank you very much, Miss Wright. [Applause.]

39

Commission on Private Philanthropy and Public Needs (The Filer Commission), *The Third Sector,* 1974

The Great Society legislation of 1965 and 1966 greatly increased the federal government's role in fields that previously had been left to nonprofit organizations and to the states. The G.I. Bill had provided limited educational, medical, and housing benefits for veterans; the Hill-Burton Act had provided federal funds for the construction or expansion of community hospitals; and the National Institutes of Health and the National Science Foundation traced their origins to the 1940s and 1950s. But Medicare and Medicaid, federal grants for anti-poverty and community development programs, federal grants and loans to college students, and the National Endowment for the Arts and the National Endowment for the Humanities all date from 1965 and 1966. None of these Great Society programs established a new federal operating agency: they created no new hospitals, schools, or arts organizations. Instead, Great Society funds enabled existing nonprofit and state agencies to greatly expand the services they provided. Within two or three years of Richard Nixon's election in 1968, it had become clear that the Great Society's health care, aging, educational, and arts and humanities programs had quickly won wide public approval, and that the Repubican Party would not repeal them.

Most nonprofit leaders welcomed the new availability of federal funds to support the work of their organizations but recognized that federal strings would come with federal funds, and worried that if they became dependent on federal funds, nonprofits would lose their traditional independence. John D. Rockefeller 3rd, among the most prominent of the nonprofit leaders who voiced these and related concerns, took the lead in bringing together the Commission on Private Philanthropy and Public Needs in 1973 and in encouraging it to establish a thorough understanding of the nonprofit sector.

Relying exclusively on private funds during a two-year study, the Commission—which became known as the Filer Commission after its chairman, John H. Filer—carried out the most thorough study of the nonprofit sector conducted to that time. The commission emphasized the relationship between nonprofits and government, and worked closely with government officials as well as with nonprofit leaders and scholars.

Following is the opening chapter of the Commission's main report, *Giving in America*. In addition to this readable short book, the Filer Commission published five very long volumes of supporting studies and reports.

COMMISSION ON PRIVATE PHILANTHROPY
AND PUBLIC NEEDS

The Third Sector

1974

On the map of American society, one of the least charted regions is variously known as the voluntary, the private nonprofit or simply the third sector. Third, that is, after the often overshadowing worlds of government and business. While these two other realms have been and continue to be microscopically examined and analyzed and while their boundaries are for the most part readily identified by experts and laymen alike, the third sector—made up of non-governmental, nonprofit associations and organizations—remains something of a terra incognito, barely explored in terms of its inner dynamics and motivations, and its social, economic and political relations to the rest of the world. As on ancient maps, its boundaries fade off into extensions of the imagination, and a monster or two may lurk in the surrounding seas.

Yet it is within this institutional domain that nearly all philanthropic input—giving and volunteering—is transformed into philanthropic output—goods and services for ultimate beneficiaries. So the Commission has attempted to take the measure of this area, both quantitatively and qualitatively, and has examined the sector's roles and rationales, past, present and future.

The sector as a whole is most broadly defined by what it is not. It is not government—that is, its component organizations do not command the full power and authority of government, although some may exercise powerful influences over their members and some may even per-

Reprinted from *Giving in America: Toward a Stronger Voluntary Sector* (Washington, D.C.: Commission on Private Philanthropy and Public Needs, 1975) by permission of Leonard L. Silverstein, Executive Director of the Commission.

form certain functions of government. Educational accrediting organizations, for instance, exercise aspects of the governmental power of licensing. For that matter, political parties can be considered to be a part of this sector although their relationship to government is pervasive and in many cases—congressional party caucuses, for instance—inextricable.

On the other hand, the third sector is not business. Its organizations do not exist to make profit and those that enjoy tax immunities are specifically prohibited from doing so, although near the boundaries of the sector many groups do serve primarily the economic interests of their members. Chambers of commerce, labor unions, trade associations and the like hardly pretend to be principally altruistic.

THE WORLD OF PHILANTHROPY

Inside these negative boundaries is a somewhat narrower domain within which the world of philanthropy generally operates, a domain made up of private groups and institutions that are deemed to serve the public interest rather than a primarily self-benefiting one, and it is this narrower area that has been the principal focus of the Commission. This area is legally defined by laws that determine which types of organizations should be immune from income taxes and eligible to receive tax-deductible contributions from individuals and corporations. Under the Internal Revenue Code, twenty categories of organizations are exempt from federal income tax, but most of those that are eligible receive tax-deductible gifts as well as fall in one category of the code, Section 501(c)(3). To qualify for exemption under this section, whose "501(c)(3)" designation has become for the nonprofit world virtually synonymous with tax deductibility, an organization must operate exclusively for one or more of these broad purposes: charitable, religious, scientific, literary, educational. Two narrower aims are specified as well: testing for public safety and prevention of cruelty to children or animals. The code further states that no "substantial" part of such an organization's activities may be devoted to attempting to influence legislation and that the organization may not participate at all in candidates' political campaigns.

But even these boundaries, though narrower than those set by the non-government, nonprofit definition, are immensely broad and vague. What is charitable, what educational, what religious? In a time in which new and unconventional religious sects are being born, it seems, almost monthly, which are genuine expressions of the religious impulse that are legitimately protected from both taxes and governmental scrutiny? The Internal Revenue Service, for one, wishes it had an all-purpose definition of religion to work with. When is an activity educational rather than primarily propagandistic (and thus barred from tax-deductible gifts under the current laws)? Considerable litigation and administrative judgment have been devoted to answering such questions. Philosophical as well as legal arguments can be and are raised, moreover, as to whether whole groups of organizations within the tax-exempt categories are truly oriented to the public interest—their justification for tax privilege—or whether they serve primarily to further the interests of a select group.

The Commission has not attempted to establish a definition or principle by which nonprofit, nongovernmental organizations can be judged to be in the public interest and thus a proper concern of and channel for philanthropy. Others have tried to form such a definition, but none has unquestionably succeeded. In any case, a certain flexibility is seen as desirable, both philosophically and legally, in defining the public interest. One of the main virtues of the private nonprofit sector lies in its very testing and extension of any definition of public interest, so it would be counterproductive to try to establish boundaries in more than a general, expandable sense. Similarly, although this Commission has operated under the rubric of "public needs," no attempt has been made to catalogue, let alone establish any priority scale of such needs. Like the public interest, the closely related concept of public needs is itself fluid and shifting. A constant and transcendent public need by which the voluntary sector and philanthropy may perhaps be ultimately judged is how effectively they keep abreast of this shifting and how well they are deemed to meet whatever new public needs are perceived.

Likewise, no attempt has been made to attach, and certainly none has succeeded in attaching, a new, better name to the territory under examination, even though none of the existing names is universally admired. Here, and throughout the report, the terms voluntary sector, private nonprofit sector (or simply nonprofit sector for short) or third sector are used interchangeably and in all cases except where otherwise indicated are meant to exclude organizations that primarily serve the interests of their own members.

DIMENSIONS OF THE VOLUNTARY SECTOR

What are the dimensions of this sector? To the extent that they have been measured at all, the measurement has usually been only a partial one that looks at the amount of private giving and volunteer activity that goes into nonprofit organizations. Even on this incomplete scale, however, it is clear that the nonprofit sector accounts for a very large amount of time and money. According to estimates based on surveys made for the Commission, at least $25 billion annually is given to various causes and organizations, and an equal amount worth of volunteer work is devoted to philanthropic activity. Yet these figures require some subtraction, and a good deal of addition. For one, a small but significant and growing amount of private giving goes to public institutions, mainly state colleges and universities. On the other hand, a sizable share of the funding of the nonprofit sector comes from the government nowadays, and considerable additional funds come from endowment and other investment income and from operating revenues, including payments to nonprofit organizations by those who use their services—students' tuitions, medical patients' fees and the like. Government funding, endowment income and service charges must be added to the overall ledger of the voluntary sector. When they are, a rough extrapolation from available data indicated the total annual receipts of the private nonprofit sector to be in the range of $80 billion, or half as much as Americans spend on food in a year.

Another measure of the dimensions of the nonprofit sector is the employment it accounts for. Approximately 4.6 million wage and salary workers are estimated to have worked in the nonprofit sector in 1974, or 5.2 percent of the total American workforce for that year. One out of every ten service workers in the United States is employed by a nonprofit organization. The proportion of professional workers is even higher— nearly one out of six.

For a physical count of nonprofit organizations, the Commission has turned to a number of sources. The Internal Revenue Service lists, as of June, 1975, 691,627 exempt organizations, groups that have formally filed for and been accorded exemption from federal income taxes. But that number does not include a great many church organizations which automatically enjoy exemption from federal income taxes without filing, nor does it include numerous small organizations that never feel the need to file for tax exemption. On the other hand, it does include a large number of groups that fall outside the philanthropic part of the nonprofit sector, such as labor unions and fraternal organizations, and it also counts a good many groups that are only active for a short time. One Commission report calculates that a "core group" of traditional philanthropic organizations includes 350,000 religious organizations, 37,000 human service organizations, 6,000 museums, 5,500 private libraries, 4,600 privately sponsored secondary schools, 3,500 private hospitals, 1,514 private institutions of higher education, and 1,100 symphony orchestras. Some other recent calculations: There are 1,000 national professional associations. New York City alone has around 6,000 block associations. And a study of voluntary groups in the town of Arlington, Mass., identified some 350 such groups there, serving a population of around 52,000. This last finding confirms earlier estimates of proportions between community size and the number of voluntary groups, and gives support to the extrapolation that in all, counting local chapters of regional or national groups, there may be as many as six million private voluntary organizations in the United States. A purely intuitive indication that this very large number is feasible can be glimpsed in a minute sample of nonprofit groups. To name a few:

> Bedford-Stuyvesant Restoration Corporation, Phillips Exeter Academy, American Acupuncture and Herbs Research Institute, Senior Citizens Association of Wausau (Wisc.), Talmudic Research Institute, New Alchemy Institute, Aspen Institute for Humanistic Studies, Chapin School Ltd., Citizens Committee on Modernization of Maryland Courts and Justice, Bethlehem (Pa.) Public Library, Visiting Nurse Association of Milwaukee, YMCA Railroad Branch of Toledo, Chinatown (N.Y) Day Care Center, Zen Center of Los Angeles, Big Brothers of Rapid City, World Affairs Council of Syracuse, N.Y, American Parkinson Disease Association, Bethel Temple of Evansville (Ind.), Metropolitan Opera Company, Fathers Club of Mt. St. Mary's Academy (Watchung, N.J.), Mothers Club of Stanford University, Sons and Daughters of Idaho Pioneers, Family Planning Committee of Greater Fall River (Mass.).

ULTIMATE BENEFICIARIES

The arithmetic of the nonprofit sector finds much of its significance in less quantifiable and even less precise dimensions—in the human measurements of who is served, who is affected by nonprofit groups and activities. In some sense, everybody is: the contributions of voluntary organizations to broadscale social and scientific advances have been widely and frequently extolled. Charitable groups were in the forefront of ridding society of child labor, abolitionist groups in tearing down the institution of slavery, civic-minded groups in purging the spoils system from public office. The benefits of nonprofit scientific and technological research include the great reduction of scourges such as tuberculosis and polio, malaria, typhus, influenza, rabies, yaws, bilharziasis, syphilis and amoebic dysentery. These are among the myriad products of the nonprofit sector that have at least indirectly affected all Americans and much of the rest of the world besides.

Perhaps the nonprofit activity that most directly touches the lives of most Americans today is noncommercial "public" television. A bare concept twenty-five years ago, its development was underwritten mainly by foundations. Today it comprises a network of some 240 stations valued at billions of dollars, is increasingly supported by small, "subscriber" contributions and has broadened and enriched a medium that occupies hours of the average American's day.

More particularly benefited by voluntary organizations are the one quarter of all college and university students who attend private institutions of higher education. For hundreds of millions of Americans, private community hospitals, accounting for half of all hospitals in the United States, have been, as one Commission study puts it, "the primary site for handling the most dramatic of human experiences—birth, death, and the alleviation of personal suffering." In this secular age, too, it is worth noting that the largest category in the nonprofit sector is still very large indeed, that nearly two out of three Americans belong to and evidently find comfort and inspiration in the nation's hundreds of thousands of religious organizations. All told, it would be hard to imagine American life without voluntary nonprofit organizations and associations, so entwined are they in the very fabric of our society, from massive national organizations to the local Girl Scouts, the parent-teachers associations or the bottle-recycling group.

GOVERNMENT AND VOLUNTARY ASSOCIATION

Ultimately, the nonprofit sector's significance, and any measure of its continuing importance, lies in its broader societal role, as seen in the long history of voluntary association and in what signs can currently be glimpsed of new or continuing directions. To talk of the sector's role in society inevitably means looking at voluntary activity and association alongside of government. Both are expressions of the same disposition of people to join together to achieve a common end, and in much of the United States' experience they have been complementary expressions. But in global terms they often have functioned and do function as mutually competitive forces. No government tolerates all forms of voluntary association; groups that are seen as threatening a country's security or that pursue common criminal purposes are routinely suppressed. The tensions between voluntary association and government run broader and deeper in many parts of the world, however, and have done so through many periods of history.

Sociologist Robert A. Nisbet has written of the "momentous conflicts of jurisdiction between the political state and the social associations lying intermediate to it and the individual." These have been, he writes, "of all the conflicts in history, the most fateful." Such conflicts can be traced at least as far back as democratic Greece and imperial Rome, in both of which societies governments were at times hostile to voluntary association. Imperial Rome, wrote Gibbon, "viewed with the utmost jealousy and distrust any association among its subjects." The Middle Ages witnessed a flourishing in Europe of more or less autonomous groupings—guilds, churches, fiefdoms—within weak central governments. But modern history can be seen at least in part as being patterned by the return to Greek and Roman affinities for the central, dominant state, with an accompanying discouragement of nongovernmental groups. The foremost philosophers of this monism of the state in modern times were Thomas Hobbes and Jean Jacques Rousseau, and the French Revolution was one of its most exuberant expressions. Charitable, literary, educational and cultural societies were banned in the brittle course of the revolution. "A state that is truly free," declared a legislator of revolutionary France, "ought not to suffer within its bosom any association, not even such as, being dedicated to public improvement, has merited well of the country."

AMERICANS ARE FOREVER FORMING ASSOCIATIONS

In spite of this inhospitable historical and philosophical setting, "association dedicated to public improvement" found fertile territory in the New World, a land colonized far from the reach of central governments, a vast land that did not lend itself well to strong central government of its own and in frontier areas was slow to adopt even minimal local governments. As historian Daniel Boorstin has observed, America evidenced a profound tendency to rely on voluntary, nongovernmental organizations and associations to pursue community purposes "from the beginning." As this country was settled, he writes "communities existed before governments were there to care for public needs." The result was that "voluntary collaborative activities" were set up first to provide basic social services. Government followed later on.

It is no historical accident that one of the Founding Fathers is nearly as famous for his development of nongovernmental means to public ends as he is for his role in shaping and representing the fledgling republic. Benjamin Franklin's institutions outside of government compose a major portion of the index of the voluntary sector. He was the leading force in founding a library, a volunteer fire department, a hospital, a university and a research institution. An historical survey of philanthropy made for the Commission notes: "Franklin did not invent the principle of improving social conditions through voluntary association, but more than any American before him he showed the availability, usefulness and appropriateness to American conditions".

"The principle of voluntary association accorded so well with American political and economic theories," the survey observes further, "that as early as 1820 the larger cities had an embarrassment of benevolent organizations." Fifteen years later, this propensity to organize became the subject of one of Alexis de Tocqueville's most famous of many famous observations about the new nation:

> Americans of all ages, all stations in life, and all types of disposition are forever forming associations. There are not only commercial and industrial associations in which all take part, but others of a

thousand different types—religious, moral, serious, futile, very general and very limited, immensely large and very minute. Americans combine to give fetes, found seminaries, build churches, distribute books and send missionaries to the antipodes. Hospitals, prisons and schools take shape that way. Finally, if they want to proclaim a truth or propagate some feeling by the encouragement of a great example, they form an association. In every case, at the head of any new undertaking, where in France you would find the government or in England some territorial magnate, in the United States you are sure to find an association.

EVOLUTIONS WITHIN THE THIRD SECTOR

This observation applies to the United States almost as fully 140 years later. Today, in fact, private association appears to be so deeply embedded and to exist on so much broader a scale in the United States than in other parts of the world as to represent one of the principal distinguishing characteristics of American society. Yet the purposes of voluntary organization have hardly remained stationary or of the same relative significance within the voluntary sector over the years.

In a pattern of evolution that has repeated itself in different areas of society, government has taken over many services and functions of the nonprofit sector, and new focuses of nonprofit activity and organization have emerged. Schools, as de Tocqueville observed, were generally founded and run by nongovernmental organizations, often churches, in early America. But soon after de Tocqueville's observations were published in 1835, the public school system began to take hold in the United States, and today only one out of ten primary and secondary school students goes to nonpublic schools. Higher education and aid to the poor correspondingly accounted for more and more nonprofit activity as the nineteenth century progressed. Then, beginning in the late nineteenth century, many of today's giant state universities got their start, and public institutions began to challenge the primacy of private institutions in higher education as well. The private nonprofit sector was the chief dispenser of "charity" well into this century, but in recent decades this function has increasingly been absorbed by government welfare and social insurance programs.

Today we appear to be on the threshold of yet another major expansion by government in an area that until a few years ago was dominated by private nonprofit (and profit) organizations, the health field. A Commission study of philanthropy in this area anticipated that by the mid-1980's more than half of all spending on health in the United States will be accounted for by government programs, with much of the rest flowing through government-regulated private insurance plans.

UNDERLYING FUNCTIONS OF VOLUNTARY GROUPS

The end purposes of nonprofit activity have changed considerably over the course of American history, therefore, and unquestionably will continue to change. Yet certain basic functions—underlying social roles that have been characteristic of much or all nonprofit activity regardless of the particular service or cause involved—have endured throughout the changes that have taken place. This is not to say, of course, that all nonprofit organizations are performing these functions optimally or even adequately. Indeed, expert research the Commission has received and informal testimony it has listened to suggest that many organizations in the sector fall well short of their capabilities. Yet the same research and testimony is virtually unanimous in finding distinctive functions for the nonprofit sector and in asserting that these functions are today as important as they ever have been to the health and progress of American society, more important in some cases than ever. Among these basic functions are the following:

Initiating New Ideas and Processes
". . . There are critical reasons for maintaining a vital balance of public and private support for human services," asserts a Commission report by Wilbur J. Cohen, former Secretary of Health, Education and Welfare, "not the least of which is the continuing task of innovating in areas where public agencies lack knowledge or are afraid to venture. . . . The private sector is adept at innovation, and at providing the models government needs."

"A new idea stands a better chance of survival in a social system with many kinds of initiative and decision," observes a Commission study of the health field. Government undoubtedly provides the most fertile arena for certain kinds of initiative and innovation, but certain new ideas, these and other Commission reports indicate, stand a better chance of survival and growth in the nonprofit sector than in the corridors of government.

"The development of the early types of both health maintenance organizations and the physicians' assistance (paramedical aides) programs would never have surfaced if they had required prior public sector consensus and support," says the Commission's health study. Another study—on the role of philanthropy in the environmental field—finds: "The perspective of governmental agencies, even in the research only . . . agencies . . . , tends to be limited and dominated by existing and agency views of the problems and alternative strategies for "solving" the problem. . . . It is difficult to induce . . . governmental agencies . . . to undertake new directions for research and analysis." The "pioneering" role of nonprofit organizations has long been recognized. More than half a century ago, Beatrice and Sidney Webb [the British leaders of gradualist, democratic Fabian Socialism], writing on the "Sphere of Voluntary Agencies," found these agencies capable of "many kinds . . . of . . . treatment . . . the public authorities are not likely themselves to initiate." Nongovernmental organizations, precisely because they are nongovernmental and need not be attuned to a broad and diverse constituency, can take chances, experiment in areas where legislators and government agencies are hesitant to tread.

Once successfully pioneered by nonprofit groups, and having established their legitimacy and worthiness, new ideas and processes can be, and often have been, supported and expanded by government. Birth-control technology, to take a relatively recent example, was pioneered by the nonprofit world in its more controversial beginnings and today is heavily underwritten by many governments throughout the world.

Developing Public Policy
Standing outside of government, voluntary organizations not only can try out new ideas, initiate services that may be too controversial for government bodies to deal with at early stages, but can exercise a direct influence on shaping and advancing government policy in broad areas in which the government is already involved. Groups specializing in certain policy areas are continually producing research and analysis, information and viewpoints, especially on long-rage policy matters, that may be lacking at times in government circles themselves, preoccupied as they often are with day-to-day operating concerns. A major function of nonprofit groups in public policy development has been to help clarify and define issues for public consideration, both at local and regional levels, as the Regional Plan Association does through its studies and proposals for the New York metropolitan area, or as The Brookings Institution does at the national level. Privately sponsored special commissions and boards of inquiry have been frequently formed at both levels to focus analysis and attention on issues as diverse as hunger, cable communication and legalized gambling.

Supporting Minority or Local Interests
For many of the same reasons the nonprofit world can experiment with new ideas less cautiously than government, voluntary groups can support causes and interests that may be swept aside by majoritarian priorities or prejudices. The civil rights movement grew out of the initiatives of nonprofit organizations such as the NAACP; the consumer and environmental movements, once the concerns of only a few perceptive or single-minded people, also found their early nourishment in private groups. But the causes need not be—or may not ever come to be regarded as so large and socially significant. William S. Vickrey, an econo-

mist at Columbia University [and winner of the Nobel Memorial Prize in Economics in 1996], has written of the "cumbersomeness of public agencies in dealing with relatively small-scale activities," of the impediments facing "high-level decision-making bodies on matters of small magnitude in which they have relatively little basis for judgment." More specialized private agencies may be able to operate efficiently and intelligently within their spheres, may be more sensitive to small-scale problems than government. In the health field, for example, a Commission report notes that nonprofit organizations "can assist in support of health programs for religious and ethnic groups, migratory workers, and racial minority groups which the public sector cannot often address. . . . Private philanthropy will be needed in the future to even out some of the inequities which will invariably occur between different communities, and to respond to the health needs of groups too culturally different to gain adequate public support."

Providing Services That the Government Is Constitutionally Barred from Providing

In the United States, the government is proscribed from entering the broadest area of the nonprofit sector, religion. So there is simply no alternative to the nonprofit sector if religious functions are to be filled at all in this country. Similarly, the Council on Foundations points out in its report to the Commission, the establishment in 1973 of a private nonprofit National News Council to oversee the news media "is an experiment that, if not totally off limits to the government because of the First Amendment, is clearly not the kind of function that it should or would undertake."

Overseeing Government

Alongside government's constitutional inhibitions are its institutional ones. Despite its own internal checks and balances, government can hardly be counted on to keep a disinterested eye on itself. In his historical perspective on philanthropy written for the Commission, historian Robert H. Bremner observes: "A marked tendency of American philanthropy has been to encourage, assist and even goad democratic government—and democratic citizens—toward better performance of civic duties and closer attention to social requirements." The Nathan Committee, which looked at philanthropy in Great Britain a quarter century ago, saw much the same role for voluntary groups. "They are able to stand aside from and criticize state action, or inaction, in the interest of the inarticulate man-in-the-street." As government's role in many areas formerly dominated by nongovernmental groups grows even larger, and the voluntary role grows correspondingly smaller, the monitoring and influencing of government may be emerging as one of the single most important and effective functions of the private nonprofit sector.

Overseeing the Market Place

While most of the third sector's activity relates more closely to government than to the business sector because of the nonprofit, public-interest common denominator of government and voluntary organizations, the sector does play a role, and perhaps a growing one, in relation to the business world. In some areas, voluntary organizations provide a direct alternative to, and a kind of yardstick for, business organizations. Nonprofit hospitals and research organizations, for instance, operate in competition with close commercial counterparts. A number of nonprofit groups makes it their business to keep a critical gaze on business, including labor union activity, as well. Potentially freer from the influence of powerful economic interests, nonprofit groups can act as detached overseers of the market place in ways that government agencies and legislators are often restrained from doing.

Bringing the Sectors Together

Nonprofit organizations frequently serve to stimulate and coordinate activities in which government or business or both interact with voluntary groups to pursue public purposes. Organization for community development is one example of this synergistic role. Another is the practice by a group such as The Nature Conservancy of enlisting the help of industry in the form of low-interest loans to buy land for preservation and conservation purposes, land that may eventually be turned over to government ownership. The fact that voluntary organizations have neither commercial interests to pursue nor official status often makes them best suited to act as intermediary or coordinator in activities involving government and business.

Giving Aid Abroad

In a time of heightened nationalistic sensitivities, especially where official American actions abroad are concerned, nonprofit organizations have been able to offer aid in situations where government help would be politically unacceptable. Workers for the American Friends Service Committee, for instance, were able to remain behind in Da Nang during the North Vietnamese takeover of that city and were able to help war victims there even though the United States government was considered hostile by the city's occupiers. As a Ford Foundation annual report observed a few years ago: . . . "Our welcome in sensitive areas often derives from the fact that we are not a government."

Furthering Active Citizenship and Altruism

While the previous categories deal mainly with the important roles nonprofit organizations serve for the society as a whole or for certain beneficiary segments of the society, one of the broadest and most important functions voluntary groups perform derives not so much from what they do for beneficiaries as what they do for participants. Voluntary groups serve as ready and accessible outlets for public-spirited initiative and activity-for philanthropy broadly defined. In a complex urbanized and suburbanized society, the individual acting alone can hope to make little impress on community or national problems, is often at a loss to find and help those who need help. Many government agencies have highly structured work arrangements and cannot or do not readily receive the assistance of public-spirited citizens. But those so minded can usually join or can help form a voluntary organization as an effective vehicle for altruistic action, and this possibility itself serves as a constant encouragement to altruism, to an active involvement in public causes, which is of the very essence in a healthy democratic society.

NEW FRONTIERS AND AN AGELESS RATIONALE

These vital roles for voluntary organizations continue to serve and influence areas of society that have traditionally been the concern of the nonprofit sector. In addition, many new or greatly expanded concerns of voluntary activity have emerged in recent years as challenging new frontiers of the sector and of its particular capabilities. "Over the past 20 years," observes Pablo Eisenberg, head of the Center for Community Change, "hundreds if not thousands of new local organizations have been created to deal with issues such as ecology, consumer problems, economic and social self-determination, public-interest law, poverty and neighborhood revitalization . . . groups with different purposes and structures and, in some cases, constituencies." Indeed, a recent survey indicates that possibly as many as 40,000 environmental organizations alone have sprung up throughout the country, mostly in the last few years. And in a Commission study of philanthropy in five cities, one major conclusion is that "nonprofit, tax-exempt organizations continue to grow in each of the cities studied."

For all the absorptions by government and despite severe financial difficulties of many voluntary organizations, it would appear, in other words, that the impulse to associate is still very strong. Indeed, there are social currents in motion that should be adding fresh impetus and vitality to this ageless expression of man's community with man.

One current is the sense of alienation that modern men and women are viewed as experiencing in the face of giant, impersonal institutions or government and business. The generally smaller size and more perceptible humanity of voluntary groups—be they block associations, local chapters of the American Legion or women's rights organizations— would appear to offer at partial antidote to any contemporary malaise stemming from feelings of ineffectiveness or unidentity. As Richard W. Lyman, president of Stanford University, wrote recently in an essay entitled "In Defense of the Private Sector," "People everywhere are yearning for the chance to feel significant as individuals. They are yearning for institutions built on a human scale, and responsive to human needs and aspirations. Is this not precisely what we have believed in and worked for, long before it became so popular to do so?"

In addition to responding to an existential yearning, the voluntary sector should appeal more than ever today in terms of its bedrock grounding in the spirit and political philosophy of pluralism—in the idea that society benefits from having many different ways for striving to advance the common weal. The federal government's unavailing efforts to control the economy follow many frustrating social programs of the Great Society and both add to the evidence of our senses that in our increasingly complex society there is no one body, one governing structure, that holds the answers to society's problems, is equipped to find the answers by itself or could put them into effect if it did. In the wake of Watergate, moreover, we are probably less persuaded than ever to stake our destiny totally on the wisdom or beneficence of centralized authority. This sorry and sordid chapter in recent history has dramatically demonstrated the virtues of diffusion of power and decentralization of decision making in public affairs, and it has demonstrated the correlative virtues of a vigorous public-minded and independent sector. The sector ideally should not compete with government so much as complement it and help humanize it, however. Nor because of institutional inertia or self-protectiveness should it or parts of it stand in the way of proper extensions of government into areas where, because of the demands of scale or equity, the private sector simply cannot fill a collective want. The sector should not be at odds with government, in other words, so much as outside of it and in addition to it.

In furtherance of its own role of serving the public interest, government at the same time should actively encourage a large and vigorous voluntary sector that can help carry the burdens of public services. For to operate effectively, and humanely, government must take care not to overload its own mechanisms by attempting to bring every public purpose directly under its direction and control.

The late Walter Lippmann recognized this central importance to government, and to American society at large, of nongovernmental organization. American democracy, he wrote a number of years ago, "has worked, I am convinced, for two reasons. The first is that government in America has not, hitherto, been permitted to attempt to do too many things; its problems have been kept within the capacity of ordinary men. The second . . . is that outside the government and outside the party system, there have existed independent institutions and independent men . . ." His observation describes the ultimate rationale for a "third" sector in American society, a rationale that applies as fully for today and tomorrow as it did for yesterday.

40

Steven Rathgeb Smith and Michael Lipsky, *The Political Economy of Nonprofit Revenues,* 1993

The extraordinary expansion of federal spending for social and health care services brought about by Lyndon Johnson's Great Society and Richard Nixon's New Federalism profoundly reshaped the nonprofit sector. The federal government played almost no role in funding nonprofit organizations before the mid-1960s. Local and state governments provided many municipal services to tax-exempt nonprofits of all kinds, as well as significant cash funding to organizations that cared for orphans and the elderly, and to some hospitals. But local and state governments offered very little in the way of direct financial support to nonprofits that provided other kinds of services. The federal innovations of the late 1960s and early 1970s changed all this. By the mid-1970s, as this reading shows, it was possible to identify three large groups of nonprofits: "traditional agencies" that had been transformed by the availability of federal funds; "government-sponsored agencies" created in response to the concerns of government officials and almost exclusively dependent on federal funds; and "new community agencies" set up by ordinary citizens but supported almost entirely by federal money. In the later 1970s and 1980s many state and local governments added funds of their own to the federal flow.

Steven Rathgeb Smith and Michael Lipsky provide the most complete overview of these developments yet available. In later chapters of their important book, they explore the consequences for many nonprofits of the shift from local, charitable, and limited funding to large-scale but unstable federal funding.

STEVEN RATHGEB SMITH AND MICHAEL LIPSKY

The Political Economy of Nonprofit Revenues

1993

Government subsidies to private colleges and hospitals predate the founding of the American Republic. In this light some of the most influential analysts of nonprofit activities have maintained that the contemporary rise in government funding of nonprofit agencies is part of a typical American tradition of using private agencies and groups, rather than government, to address public problems. They see the wave of contracting over the last 30 years as evidence of continuity with the past. Our emphasis is different. We argue that the unprecedented scope, pervasiveness, and diversity of the present contracting regime does indeed represent an important break with previous practices. . . .

THE POSTWAR YEARS

In the early postwar period the federal government slowly increased its role in funding social services, either through subsidies to state and local government welfare agencies or through direct grants to nonprofit organizations. These allocations tended to be for research and demonstration projects rather than for subsidies to ongoing activities. For example, Baden Street Settlement House of Rochester, New York, coordinated social services to poor persons in its neighborhood under a grant from the New York State Youth Commission.

Overall, public subsidies to social services came primarily from state and local governments. In 1953–54 the federal government spent $124.1 million on social services, primarily for vocational rehabilitation, child welfare, school lunches, and institutional services. By contrast, state and local governments spent $605 million. The bulk of this money was spent on institutional support for such state institutions as hospitals for the

Excerpts from chapter 3 of Smith and Lipsky, *Nonprofits for Hire: The Welfare State in the Age of Contracting* (Cambridge: The President and Fellows of Harvard College, 1993), pp. 46, 50–71. Reprinted by permission of Harvard University Press.

mentally ill, schools for the developmentally disabled, and training schools for juvenile delinquents.

Most nonprofit agencies did not receive any significant public funding. Judge Baker Guidance Center of Boston, one of the premier child guidance clinics in the country, received no public funds in 1950: 47 percent of its revenues came from investment income on its endowment. Likewise, Worcester (Mass.) Children's Friend Society, also lacking public funds, relied on private fees for 40 percent of its revenue in 1948.

Absence of public funding of nonprofits remained the norm throughout the 1950s. However, in some service categories such as child welfare, government funding of nonprofit agencies was more prevalent. A 1960 study of 23 urban centers found that "payments to private agencies represented 28.5 percent of all public expenditures for institutional care of dependent children, 8 percent of all public expenditures for family services and foster care, 13.4 percent in the case of institutional care for aged persons, and 100 percent of the maternity home care provided from public funds."

Nonetheless, public funds to nonprofit agencies tended to be concentrated in the more urban states with large numbers of providers such as New York, New Jersey, and Pennsylvania. In 1957 public expenditure for foster care to nonprofit child welfare agencies as a percentage of total public expenditures was less than 25 percent in 35 states. In only three states (New York, North Dakota, and Pennsylvania) was the percentage greater than 50 percent. Moreover, even in these states, most nonprofits depended upon private donations from endowments and the Community Chest and investment income. At this time, few agencies existed which were funded primarily by government. The reliance of most nonprofit agencies on private funding at this time is confirmed in examining the income streams in 1960 of 13 New England agencies we selected for intensive analysis.

When government did provide funding, it usually did not cover the full cost of service. St. Mary's Home for Children in North Providence, Rhode Island, charged $20 per week for board and an additional six dollars for clothing and other incidentals for each child in 1962. (It was $10 total in 1955!) This was the fee that the Rhode Island Department of Child Welfare paid for its wards. However, St. Mary's director reported that the actual cost of yearly care was $5,000 per child. State government kept rates to nonprofit agencies deliberately low, expecting these agencies to make up the shortfall from their private revenues and fees from clients. (St. Mary's Home cared for poor children, so fees did not generate much income.)

Traditional agencies depended heavily on investment income generated by the endowment, private contributions, and United Way contributions. Investment income was limited by the return on the endowment principal. Private contributions were generally bequests and donations from wealthy individuals who were often affiliated with the agency. The broad-based fundraising campaigns by individual agencies characteristic of the 1980s were not then in evidence. The Community Chest, the predecessor organization of the United Way, distributed funds from a pot of money which grew very slowly from year to year. Fees were used extensively, but this source of revenue was limiting because fees came directly from individuals in this period, not from insurance companies as is frequently the case today. Thus many agencies were dependent upon the small group of clients with adequate means. Most agencies were unwilling to raise fees substantially to subsidize public clients for fear of further restricting their already narrow client base. As a result of the incremental and self-limiting character of these revenue streams, agencies were hard-pressed to keep up with rising service costs and demands.

Because of the constraints on private revenues, most agencies operated at a deficit or with only a small surplus. To compensate for deficits, agencies dipped at times into their endowment principal, in effect subsidizing the cost of service to agency clients or consumers. Partly as a result, endowments grew very slowly or were stagnant; sometimes they actually declined. In a pinch, wealthy board members simply made up for agency deficits on their own.

Remarkably, agency losses apparently failed to alarm their boards of directors. Spending the endowment principal was an accepted practice, partly because losses tended to be modest, but largely because board members regarded their agencies' missions as having priority over the integrity of the endowment. Out-of-balance financial statements neither precipitated major service cuts nor staff changes, as they would today.

The traditional agencies dominated the universe of social service agencies. These agencies usually controlled the distribution of Community Chest allocations and the modest public funding available. Consequently, agencies without access to these private and public funds tended to be small. Friendly House, a settlement house founded in 1922 in Worcester, Massachusetts, was this sort of small community-based agency which offered a variety of recreational and social services to neighborhood residents. It struggled along on modest cash and in-kind donations from year to year. The Worcester Area Association of Retarded Citizens (WAARC) was not even legally incorporated as a nonprofit organization; it was just a loose collective of parents who struggled to provide services to their retarded children.

THE ADVENT OF EXTENSIVE FEDERAL FUNDING

During the 1950s standards of care in some of the traditional service areas started to come under criticism. State mental institutions came under attack, for example, as did systems of adoption placement dependent upon sectarian community agencies. Child abuse as a societal problem was introduced onto the political agenda during this period. Social welfare advocates attacked the larger traditional agencies for neglecting the needs of the poor and racial and ethnic minorities. Meanwhile, government officials exerted greater regulatory oversight over private social programs, especially on public safety and staffing issues.

While criticism of private social service agencies increased, public financial support for their activities was slow to materialize. Even in the mid-1960s nonprofit agencies were still overwhelmingly reliant on private funds. A study by the Family Service Association of America in 1965 found that public funds accounted for only eight percent of agencies' income. For the same year, a survey of health and welfare agencies in 13 urban areas found that public funding in all fields only accounted for six percent of revenues. For this period a study of over 800 service organizations found that 80 percent did not receive public funds.

The broad disenchantment with existing state and local and private nonprofit services and their financing led to many new initiatives. The Gray Areas Project of the Ford Foundation represented a private effort in selected cities to provide catalytic funding that would mobilize existing community resources to address problems experienced by poor people in New Haven and a dozen or so other cities. Several federal programs emerged from the community mobilization model pioneered by Gray Areas activities: the 1962 amendments to the Social Security Act; the Community Mental Health Centers Act of 1963; the Community Action component of the Economic Opportunity Act (1964); and a sharp increase in federal spending on social services for discretionary programs and research and demonstration grants. The Office of Economic Opportunity (OEO), established in 1964 to administer the War on Poverty, was also instrumental in developing new services. Some of this federal money was channeled to state and local governments, which then distributed it to public and private agencies. In the case of community action programs, the federal government essentially created new agencies to provide services to the poor.

These several initiatives led to a sharp rise in federal expenditures for social welfare services. Federal expenditures for social welfare services almost tripled between 1965 and 1970, from $812 million to $2.2 billion. (Expenditures on special OEO and other poverty related service programs rose from $51.7 million in 1965 to $752 million in 1970.) State and local expenditures rose only modestly, from $1.2 billion to $1.8 billion, during this same five-year period.

The federal role continued to expand throughout the 1970s. By 1980 the federal funds comprised 65 percent of total government spending at all levels on social welfare services, compared to 37 percent in 1960. Total federal spending (in current dollars) rose from $1.14 billion in 1960 to $13.5 billion in 1980. Per capita spending (in constant 1988 dollars) rose from $23 in 1960 to $84 in 1980.

A big percentage of the increase in public funding of social services was expended through nonprofit agencies. This development was due in large part to new federal policies. Faced with public pressure to expand social services, particularly for the poor, Congress enacted the 1967 Amendments to the Social Security Act (commonly called Title IV-A) which specifically encouraged states to enter into purchase-of-service agreements with private agencies.

These amendments contained a novel provision that allowed states to increase social services by obtaining from the federal government triple the amount contributed by public or private local sources. A nonprofit agency could "donate" $25,000 to the state and receive a public match of $75,000 for a total contract amount of $100,000. Since the $75,000 came from the federal government, a state could either increase services without any cost to its treasury or shift the cost of existing services to the federal government and private sources. The provision about donated services tended to favor contracting with the traditional agencies because they had access to private funds that could be designated as donations. A common practice was for the traditional agencies to assign a portion of their annual United Way allocation for their private match. An agency could receive a contract essentially at no cost.

Predictably, federal spending under Title IV-A rose rapidly: from $281 million in 1967 to $1.6 billion in 1972. A 1972 study predicted that expenditures would reach $4.7 billion by 1973 if the program were left unchecked. Alarmed at the rapid rise of federal spending, Congress enacted an expenditure ceiling of $2.5 billion in 1972.

A 1971 study indicated that 25 percent of state spending on social services was for purchased services. By 1976 this expenditure had risen to 49 percent. A 1978 study by the Urban Institute found similar results. The services provided by nonprofit agencies funded through Title XX (the successor program to Title IV-A) included daycare, homemaker/chore, substitute care, counseling, protective services, health services, family planning, legal services, and services for the developmentally disabled. The financial incentives to combine mostly federal funds with some state monies proved so attractive that states such as Oklahoma, which had hardly ever before purchased social services from private agencies, developed contracting systems.

In 1977, 25 states used half or more of their state human service expenditures for purchase-of-service contracts. In the Massachusetts Department of Public Welfare, the dollar amount of purchase of service contracts with private nonprofit service agencies more than doubled, from $36 million (and 380 contracts) to $84 million (and over 1,000 contracts), between 1977 and 1981. Many state agencies relied almost exclusively on nonprofit agencies to provide services, especially new and innovative services such as community residential programs, respite care, and day treatment.

While these figures reflect substantial growth in government contracting for social services, they still understate the increase in contracting in several key respects. First, they miss federal block grant funds that were originally allocated by the lead state agency to a public agency subcontractor (and thus were officially recorded as "public purchase" of services), but then went to private contractors providing services to the subcontracting public agency. For example, the lead state agency for Title XX funds (usually the state Department of Public Welfare) would contract with another state agency such as the Department of Youth Services (DYS) for adolescent care. But these state agencies would often contract with private child welfare agencies as subcontractors. Consequently, the actual level of federal funding of purchased services from private agencies under Title XX was much higher than reported in these studies (probably closer to 60 percent or more).

Second, the calculations do not include the new federal programs such as community mental health centers, community action agencies, Head Start, neighborhood health clinics, drug and alcohol treatment, runaway shelters, and child and adult protective services. These categorical programs spent hundreds of millions of dollars a year, largely through nonprofit service agencies. For example, federal spending for special OEO and ACTION programs, which included funding for community action, rose from $51.7 million in 1965 to $2.3 billion in 1980. The federal Head Start program alone spent $735 million in fiscal year 1980, with a majority of these funds going to nonprofit agencies. Federal funding on community mental health centers rose from $143 million in 1969 to $1.4 billion in 1979.

Third, these amounts did not include the hundreds of millions of dollars spent by the federal government on research and demonstration grants. Thousands of social service agencies such as rape crisis centers, battered women shelters, and child protective services received such grants in the 1960s and 1970s. In many cases these were short-term grants for operating expenses. After the expiration of their research and demonstration grants, many agencies obtained state and local public funds to continue their services.

Fourth, these studies do not include state spending on purchased services that is not related to Title XX. This and other federal programs spurred state governments to increase their own social service spending, especially through purchases from private agencies. For example, the deinstitutionalization of state hospitals, state training schools, and in some cases public juvenile detention centers was under way in earnest during this period. Deinstitutionalization meant transferring services from the public sector to the nonprofit sector. But now funds went to community-based counseling, training, and residential services rather than large public institutions. Overall, state spending on social welfare services (both public and private agencies) almost doubled between 1975 and 1980: from $2.6 billion to $4.8 billion.

IMPACT AT THE SERVICE DELIVERY LEVEL

Broad national trends in government contracting with nonprofit agencies were reflected in dramatic changes in their revenue mix. The specific effect tended to vary depending upon the type of nonprofit service agency.

Traditional Agencies

Traditional agencies tended to take a very cautious approach to the growth of federal funding. Many executives of traditional agencies worried that government funding would compromise and undermine their mission. Harking back to Progressive Era counterparts, Bertram M. Beck, a leading nonprofit executive in New York City, expressed his view of this danger: "Truly voluntary associations are desperately needed for the revitalization of the democratic process, but they cannot be supported by government funds since governmental funding immediately contaminates their nature and is self-defeating." With Beck, many executives of the traditional agencies saw their mission as distinctly private and separate from the public sphere. Executives of traditional agencies were hardly in the forefront of the extensive changes in public support for community action and reform of various treatment regimes. Nonetheless, they expressed concern that the advocacy role of nonprofits would be constrained by government funding.

Government funding of traditional agencies tended to grow slowly during the early and mid-1960s. In part this reflected the principled objections of critical actors in the sector. In part it was the result of lags between the initiation of key programs and the development of contracting relationships at the grassroots.

As the demands for social services burgeoned with the mobilization and social ferment in American cities in the 1960s, traditional agencies experienced pressures from within and without to expand their activities. At first, following policies whose continuation would have placed them in financial jeopardy, the agencies drew from their endowments and began to borrow to meet the new demands. Boston Children's Service Association (BCSA) lost hundreds of thousands of dollars in the late 1960s and early 1970s as it expanded services to the poor without adequate financing. BCSA essentially miscalculated its capacity to generate adequate revenue. The agency suffered financially for many years as it "worked off the deficit." It was only in the late 1970s with the infusion of hundreds of thousands of government dollars that the agency stabilized financially.

Federal funding, particularly through Title IV-A and later Title XX, pushed up revenues throughout the sector. The revenues of one traditional agency, the Massachusetts Society for the Prevention of Cruelty to Children (MSPCC), increased almost five-fold between 1970 and 1980.

The growth of government funding clearly bailed out many financially troubled traditional agencies. Recognizing his debt to government funding, the executive director of MSPCC exclaimed in 1974, "Title IV-A has been a financial lifesaver in arresting increasing deficits."

With these public funds agencies entered into a new relationship to government. Agencies which for decades had relied on private contributions or small government subsidies were now primarily dependent on government funds. Most of this funding was federal (often administered by the state), although by 1980 many states were contributing their own funds. Settlement houses, initially reluctant to accept government support, were especially attractive funding targets for public officials because they were usually located in low-income neighborhoods and offered governments the opportunity to respond quickly to social problems associated with poverty. Many settlement houses across the country received community action funds from OEO, grants to establish neighborhood health clinics, Head Start funds, and subsidized daycare funds through Title IV-A and Title XX.

Friendly House of Worcester is a good example of this transformation. It was designated a community action agency in the mid-1960s and received government funds for daycare services for abused and neglected children in the 1970s. By 1980 government was providing 49 percent of the agency's total revenues of $677,000. In the late 1970s the wealthy board members who had provided the bulk of financial support for the agency throughout its history resigned; they were succeeded by individuals more comfortable with the substantial dependence of the agency on government funding.

As government funding rose, private funding from the United Way, fees, private contributions, and investment income usually rose in absolute terms but declined sharply as a percentage of total revenues.

Government funding of traditional agencies had other major implications for the balance between public and private provision. First, such funding represented a transfer of the costs of social services from clients (and their families), private donors, and the United Way to the federal government, and to a lesser extent to state government. Second, the reduction in agencies' reliance on client fees permitted them to give more needy individuals access to services.

Third, government funding freed these agencies from the incrementalism dictated by dependence on private funding sources and fees. Under the old system the agencies could not undertake new initiatives or meet unexpected obligations without running sizable deficits. Government funding through contracting permitted rapid growth and the introduction of new services which sometimes represented substantial policy departures. Nonincremental growth permitted some heady experimentation in agencies often regarded as stodgy. But innovativeness and quick growth were to show their shortcomings during later periods of government contraction. The traditional agencies had now become instrumentalities of government funding, expanding beyond the niches supported by private funds. The transformation in the scale of these agencies meant that they would be less able to cover shortfalls in funding with private contributions or endowment income.

Government-Sponsored Agencies
Many of the agencies in this category represent an effort by government officials in cooperation with social welfare advocates and professionals to create new nonprofit service programs that would provide alternatives to the existing public and private agencies. Community action agencies were to be an alternative to the state social service bureaucracies. Community mental health centers would be community-based alternatives to the public state hospitals. New community programs for the developmentally disabled and juvenile delinquents were conceived as more humane and effective programs than the existing state schools and training schools. Spending on these programs rose sharply from 1965 to 1980.

As federal funding emerged to support these initiatives, the new government-sponsored agencies grew rapidly. Coastal Community Counseling Center (CCCC) was founded in 1968 with seed money from a federal grant. Total revenues were $296,000, with government funding providing 64 percent of this amount. By 1980 agency revenues had reached $2.27 million, and revenue from private sources had disappeared. While its total dependence on government funding makes CCCC an unusual case, most community mental health centers were heavily reliant on government funds.

The Community Action Program (CAP) of the federal Office of Economic Opportunity showed similar growth. Prospect House in Worcester, Massachusetts, was founded in 1968 through an OEO grant under the CAP program. In 1975 its budget was approximately $74,000. By 1980 annual revenues had reached $259,000, with 89 percent derived from government.

Youth agencies also increased in size. Youth Opportunities Upheld, Inc. (Y.O.U.), another Worcester agency, was started with a small private grant and a sizable federal grant in 1972. Annual revenues were $100,000. By 1980 revenues had reached $995,000, with government funding contributing 90 percent. Other types of service agencies in this category include drug and alcohol treatment, neighborhood health services, homemaker/chore services, and daycare.

New Community Agencies
The agencies we include in this category were created on an all volunteer basis and originally depended on small cash and in-kind donations. They include organizations for retarded citizens, emergency shelters for youth, battered women shelters, and rape crisis centers. The well-known drug program, Phoenix House, started in this fashion. According to a 1972 Phoenix House report, the founders of the organization were "five addicts, straight out of a hospital detoxification ward and desperate to stay free from heroin. They pooled their welfare checks for rent and food, scrubbed and scoured their rooms, and cadged paint and furniture to make a real home. . . . Out of a common need to reclaim their lives, they had bonded together."

These and similar agencies focused on other social concerns experienced explosive growth in the late 1960s and 1970s, owing to the sharp increase in contracting. Phoenix House grew from nothing in 1967 to a $4.7 million program in 1972, with 48 percent from government contracts and an additional 22 percent from the residents' public assistance payments. The Minute Man Association of Retarded Citizens (MMARC) of Concord, Massachusetts, is another good example. Organized in 1958 by 21 people interested in providing more services for the developmentally disabled, its first year budget was only $3,263.29. It did not hire an executive director (half-time) until 1975. Before that, the agency's only paid staff was a secretary who worked a few hours a week. In the late 1970s the agency entered an organizational "take-off" stage. In 1978 its budget was $98,750; by 1982 revenues had reached $693,000, fueled by $563,000 in government contracts (81 percent of total revenues).

This rapid growth in funding was typical of many community agencies. The Ecumenical Social Action Committee (ESAC) of Jamaica Plain, a neighborhood in Boston, was founded in the late 1960s by local clergy concerned about neighborhood youth. Its revenue jumped from $92,000 in 1971 to over $1.1 million in 1980. Government funding accounted for 70 percent of revenues.

In short, the new community agencies expanded in tune with the dramatic growth in federal and state revenues during the 1970s. Many of these agencies were transformed from relatively small community-based organizations reliant upon private donations, volunteer labor, and in-kind assistance to much larger agencies dependent primarily on public funds.

THE REAGAN ERA AND A CHANGING FEDERAL ROLE

In the first year of his presidency, Ronald Reagan successfully pressed for the enactment of the Omnibus Budget Reconciliation Act. The major budget cutting legislation of the President's first term in office included provisions that affected social services and government funding of nonprofit agencies.

- •Title XX, renamed the Social Service Block Grant (SSBG), was cut approximately 20 percent.
- •New federal regulations allowed states more discretion in their funding decisions.
- •Matching requirements for federal funding of Title XX were eliminated.
- •The Comprehensive Employment and Training Act (CETA), which provided funding to nonprofits such as child welfare agencies and battered women shelters as well as job training programs, was abolished.
- •Federal funding for social service programs such as community action agencies and neighborhood health clinics was reduced significantly.

Other social programs, ostensibly supported by the Reagan administration, received only modest increases, inadequate to keep pace with inflation. The Bush administration largely continued the policies initiated in Reagan's first term.

The impact of Reagan administration policies on public social expenditures is evident in the shifting obligations of the federal and state governments. Total federal spending on social welfare services through the Social Services Block Grant (SSBG) and other grant programs declined from $8.8 billion in 1980 to $8.1 billion in 1988.

The SSBG declined in real terms (1990 dollars) from $4.4 billion in 1980 to $2.6 billion in 1991. To compensate for declining federal assistance and rising service demand, state and local spending on social welfare services increased from $4.8 billion in 1980 to $7.3 billion in 1988. Total expenditures from federal, state, and local sources increased from $13.6 billion in 1980 to $15.24 billion in 1988. (These figures understate federal and state funding on social services, since they exclude funding through public health programs such as Medicaid and Medicare.) Federal expenditures as a percentage of total social welfare service expenditures declined from 64.6 percent in 1980 to 52.4 percent in 1988.

Child Welfare Services

Despite the overall decline of the federal role in social services, federal funding of some services increased. Federal child welfare expenditures through Title IV-B of the Social Security Act rose from $163.6 million in fiscal year 1981 to $273.9 million (estimated) in fiscal year 1991. Title IV-E expenditures for foster care increased even more sharply: from $308.8 million in fiscal year 1981 to $1.8 billion (estimated) in fiscal year 1991.

The continued growth in government funds for child welfare services was reflected in a survey of member agencies of the Child Welfare League of America. From 1979 to 1986 median agency revenues from government rose from $453,000 to $1,032,000. Overall, government revenues represented 59 percent of total revenues for the 238 member agencies, down from 62 percent in 1980 but still more than double the 28 percent of total revenues for 1960. A 1988 study by Family Service America concluded that the proportion of total revenues from government sources was 34 percent in 1979, 30 percent in 1982, and 37 percent in 1986. Overall revenue growth from 1982 to 1986 was 23 percent, outpacing the four-year inflation rate of 13 percent.

The Homeless

Other service categories received increased government funding. Congress passed the Stewart B. McKinney Homeless Assistance Act on June 30, 1987. This legislation augmented funding authority for already existing federal programs to help the homeless and hungry. In addition, the act established two new programs under the authority of the Department of Housing and Urban Development to help the homeless find permanent housing. The act authorized $1 billion in federal funding for fiscal years 1987 and 1988.

A General Accounting Office (GAO) study reported that in 1988, 9,000 shelters and other agencies planned to use funds from the Federal Emergency Management Agency (FEMA) to provide 80 million meals and nearly 14 million nights' lodging to the needy, as well as rental, mortgage, and utility assistance. Small providers relied heavily upon FEMA funds for operating expenses. Over one-fifth of the service providers who responded to a GAO survey had operating budgets of

$10,000 or less. These organizations, on average, received 63 percent of their operating funds from the Emergency Food and Shelter (EFS) program administered by FEMA. For 10 percent of these organizations, EFS funds were their only source of revenue.

State spending on homeless programs also increased, although the amounts varied across the country. Expenditures on homeless single men and women in New York City, where homelessness was perhaps most acute, rose from $8 million in 1978 to $100 million in 1985. The city also spent $100 million on homeless families in 1985.

Drug and Alcohol Treatment

Public funding of drug and alcohol treatment increased substantially. New York State expenditures rose from $309 million in 1985 to $504 million in 1988. During the same period, expenditures in California rose from $202 million to $261 million and in Minnesota expenditures rose from $5.6 million to $46 million. While many social welfare advocates complain about the adequacy of current government expenditures on drug programs, present spending is nonetheless substantially higher than just a few years ago. The revenues of drug treatment agencies from client fees and insurance companies also escalated very sharply. Fee income rose from $21.3 million in 1980 to $157.3 million in 1987, while private insurance payments rose from $20 million to $348.1 million.

Nonetheless, total public and private spending on drug treatment programs is only just beginning to approach the level of 1976 spending in real terms. Total spending in 1987 dollars fell from $1.5 billion in 1976 to $1.3 billion in 1987. Demonstrating the sharp decline in the federal portion in the early years of the Reagan administration, federal spending for drug treatment as a percent of total public and private revenues dropped from 42.5 percent in 1976 to 19.5 percent in 1987. During this same period, state and local funding as a percent of total public and private revenues also dropped, though much less sharply than the federal share, reflecting the growing role of state and local governments in funding drug treatment during the 1980s.

A large portion of the public and private treatment funds for alcohol and drug abuse is spent by nonprofit agencies. Nationwide, 65 percent of alcohol treatment units were nonprofit agencies in 1982. The increase in spending on treatment for alcoholism has attracted competition from for-profit providers. However, nonprofit providers still served 58 percent of all clients in alcohol treatment programs in 1987.

Drug treatment programs are characterized by a sharp distinction between programs serving private and public clients. Private clients tend to be middle class and upper class and to have private insurance. In 1987, 63 percent of the providers serving these clients were hospitals, both for-profit and nonprofit. Public clients, by contrast, tend to be indigent, often with criminal records. In 1987 these clients were served primarily by outpatient programs (63 percent), which were principally provided by nonprofit organizations. In that year four-fifths of the $800 million that went to serve 650,000 clients in drug treatment nationwide came from public sources, including government contracts and Medicaid reimbursement, with the states carrying most of the funding burden.

Services for the Mentally Retarded

During the last 15 years, deinstitutionalization has continued to reduce dependent populations in state institutions and increase the clients of private providers. In 1977, 155,000 155,000 mentally retarded resided in state institutions, compared to only 93,000 in private facilities and specially licensed foster homes. From 1977 to 1986 deinstitutionalization continued at a rate of about 5,000 per year. By 1986, 129,000 people with mental retardation resided in private facilities and 19,000 in specialized foster homes, compared to 105,000 in state institutions. In New York State over 25,000 people lived in public institutions in 1975. By 1987 fewer than 10,000 people lived in public institutions, and community programs had been developed for 17,000 people previously residing in the institutions or at home.

This shift to the community is reflected in the spending data. Total state and federal commitments to mental retardation and developmental disabilities programs increased from $3.5 billion in 1977 to $11.7 billion in 1988. In inflation-adjusted 1988 dollars, this represents an increase of 72 percent during this period. Spending for community services advanced much more rapidly than for institutional service.

A 1986 nationwide survey of providers of services for the mentally retarded found that about half of the providers were nonprofit agencies. (Only seven percent were for-profit.) In that year 79 percent of revenues came from government sources, and another 10 percent was contributed from federal income maintenance programs such as Supplemental Security Income (SSI) and Social Security Disability Income (SSDI).

The shift to community-based programs has been facilitated by federal income support programs for the developmentally disabled. The federal government has also assumed the cost of care for the developmentally disabled (and to a lesser extent for the seriously mentally ill) through Medicaid's Intermediate Care Facility-Mental Retardation (ICF-MR) program, which allows the handicapped to live in small community settings. In 1988, 27,304 persons were served in public or private ICF-MR facilities of 15 or fewer beds. Total federal commitment (excluding the state match) was $543 million. This represents an increase of 56 percent in unadjusted terms from 1986. These programs are especially attractive to state governments because they permit shifting the cost of coverage for the developmentally disabled (and chronic mentally ill), who previously resided in state institutions at state expense, to small-scale residences subsidized substantially by the federal government.

In summary, in the 1980s the federal government reduced expenditures in some social services areas but increased them in others. State governments assumed responsibility for many services started in the 1970s by federal grants, and increasingly spent funds to purchase services from nonprofit agencies. As state economies recovered from the recession of the early 1980s, state funding rose significantly in many service areas. Consequently, nonprofit agencies remained substantially dependent upon government funds throughout the 1980s.

DIFFERENTIAL IMPACTS AND
THE SEARCH FOR ALTERNATIVES

Federal policy changes of the 1980s had differential impacts on individual agencies. However, this decade also demonstrated that government has influenced nonprofit service agencies through means other than contract funds, including Medicaid (the public health insurance program for the poor) and income maintenance payments such as SSI, as nonprofit agencies searched for alternatives to federal funding.

In the early 1980s many nonprofits primarily dependent on federal funding were forced to cut their budgets and curtail services. Consolidated Neighborhood Services, Inc. (CNSI) of St. Louis, Missouri, a multi-service agency, lost $750,000 of its $2 million budget almost overnight. Other agencies grew apace.

Agencies with substantial reliance on federal programs that were cut, such as job training and placement, experienced declining revenues in the early 1980s. This was the case with the Center for Human Development (CHD), the FCAC, Jobs For Youth, Boston, Inc. (JFY), and the Key Program. ESAC suffered even more severely.

Despite a drop in federal funding, these agencies were able to increase their revenues after the early 1980s because they switched to state-funded contracts or other federal programs. FCAC picked up the federal cheese-and-butter distribution program and fuel assistance. CHD received substantial increases in Medicaid funding. Other agencies primarily dependent on state funding or a combination of State funding with secure federal funding, such as The Harbor Schools (THS), were able to weather the change in federal social policy without setbacks. They expanded in the 1980s in tune with the expansion of state funding for child welfare services.

New sources of contract income are not available to all. With the decline in federal revenues, and with fiscal stresses affecting even states which tried to replace federal funds, nonprofit service organizations are trying to develop other income sources including Medicaid, fees-for-service, community fundraising campaigns such as the United Way, and income producing activities such as technical assistance.

MEDICAID

Medicaid is a particularly attractive new funding source because, as an entitlement program, it is still growing. Total spending (in current dollars) on Medicaid more than doubled from 1980 to 1988, going from $27.3 billion to $60.5 billion.

As noted, Medicaid is an important source of funds for many nonprofit agencies providing group care for the mentally ill and developmentally disabled. The Medicaid ICF-MR program fueled the growth of agencies for the developmentally disabled across the country. The annual revenues of the St. Louis Association of Retarded Citizens (SLARC) rose from $4 million in 1985 to $5.9 million in 1988. ICF-MR funds comprised 42 percent of its revenues in 1988.

Many nonprofit mental health and family service programs have tapped Medicaid for reimbursement for counseling and therapy. The Worcester Children's Friend Society (WCFS), the MSPCC, and the Judge Baker Guidance Center received over 60 percent of their fee income from Medicaid in the late 1980s. Fee income for these agencies rose substantially from 1980 to 1988.

Other agencies such as Family Services of Greater Boston relied more heavily on reimbursement from private health insurers. However, this shift to private reimbursement does not necessarily indicate a shift in clientele, since many traditional agencies prior to the 1980s were not primarily involved in serving the poor. The increase in fees from private insurers represents refinancing of services whereby services previously subsidized by federal and state funds, by individuals, or by private charities are shifted to private insurers.

The transfer of costs to Medicaid and private health insurers has implications for policy. To qualify for reimbursement from Medicaid or private insurers, an agency that offers mental health services needs to be certified as a mental health clinic. Clinic status requires that social service agencies use the standard medical classification system (contained in the compendium known as DSM-III) and adjust their practices to conform to medical diagnostic procedures and treatment approaches. This shift to a certain extent results in the "medicalization" of social work and counseling practice. Problems previously regarded as situational are now placed in medical illness categories. Consequently, a social worker's focus may move away from the community or support network or the circumstantial source of a person's difficulty to an individual pathology.

The rising importance of mental health clinic status to agencies is contributing to the consolidation of providers and the winnowing out of small agencies. The clinic application process is expensive and time consuming. Approval is only granted to agencies that meet fairly substantial professional staffing levels. The newer agencies, which tend to be undercapitalized, find it difficult even to apply.

Public and private health insurers are not the only source of fees. Many agencies receive payments directly from individuals. Residential programs, for example, often ask residents to pay their room and board from their SSI or General Assistance payments. Thus SLARC received 16 percent of its income from program fees in FY 1988, but most of this fee income was resident SSI payments in that year. The importance of SSI payments for these programs grew during the 1980s, because these payments (a primarily federal program) continued to increase in real terms while other sources of revenue declined.

Despite the search for fee income for public and private sources, fees remain a relatively small percentage of agency budgets. A 1991 survey of over 300 Massachusetts agencies found that client fees accounted for only six percent of all revenue. An Arizona survey concluded that client fees represented 13 percent of agency income with less than half of the almost 200 surveyed agencies reporting any income from client fees. Further, many fee-dependent services are losing money because of reimbursement limits by public and private insurers, which fail to pay the full cost of service.

Private charity has also failed to keep pace with rising costs and demand and has not been able to substitute for lost federal or state funding. Charitable donations climbed in the 1980s, but haltingly. Giving to the United Way rose from $1.7 billion in 1981 to an estimated $3.2 billion in 1991, but the latest year-to-year increase failed to keep pace with inflation. Philanthropic giving to all human services agencies rose by less than four percent in 1990, a drop of one percent in real terms. A 1988 survey of the CWLA agencies concluded that the United Way share of total agency expenditures was up slightly, from nine percent in 1980 to 10.4 percent in 1987. The median percent of total income from contributions rose from two to five. Many social welfare organizations find the recent experience of the Holy Family shelter in Indianapolis typical. Public funds for homelessness helped increase the capacity of the shelter, as the *Wall Street Journal* reported, but capacity still falls far short of keeping pace with the rising demand for shelter. United Way funding has fallen and community volunteers are sorely lacking.

Overall, United Way funding is a relatively small source of total revenues for nonprofit service agencies. A 1991 survey of over 350 Massachusetts service agencies found that United Way funding comprised four percent of agency income, compared to 52 percent from state contracts and 17 percent from nonstate contract government funding such as SSI and Medicaid. A majority of agencies do not receive any United Way funding, because the United Way allocation process is resistant to change. United Way agencies tend to be organizations previously affiliated with Community Chest, long before the explosion of government-sponsored and new community agencies. Only one of the government-sponsored or community agencies we surveyed received any United Way funding in 1988.

In sum, by the early 1990s, despite changes in the mix of federal and state support, nonprofit service providers still depended heavily upon government contracts. Unable to diversify because of undercapitalization, staff limitations on fundraising, and lack of access to private charity, the newer agencies still receive most of their funds from contracts.

The picture for the traditional agencies is more mixed, but on the whole it shows the strong continuing influence of contracting. The only traditional agencies whose total revenues declined substantially were Children's Friend and Service (CFS) and WCFS: they lost substantial government contracts. In response, these agencies aggressively tried to raise more private funds, but with only partial success.

Even the agencies with significant revenue growth from government experienced severe fiscal distress, because their costs rose faster than their revenue. Several factors pushed up costs during the 1980s: more demanding government regulations, increases in wages, payroll taxes and insurance, and programming for a more needy client population. In addition, agencies reliant upon contracts were persuaded to accept responsibilities that were not entirely matched by contract reimbursements, as they sought to maintain their programs rather than close shop.

CONCLUSION

The changing revenue mix of nonprofit service organizations heralds little noticed but profound changes in American social policy. Prior to the 1960s nonprofit agencies were primarily dependent upon endowment income, and in-kind assistance upon private donations, This situation reflected prevailing social policies that emphasized a minimal federal role in funding social services, a circumscribed state role, and voluntarism. Private charity was the primary provider of social services, except for traditional concerns such as institutional care of juvenile delinquents, the mentally ill and mentally retarded, and child protection, in which state and local governments played critical roles. This decentralized and largely private structure of responsibility for social services produced incremental change and a limited service system.

During the 1960s and 1970s the federal government undertook to overcome the historical limits of state and local governments and private charity in meeting social service needs. Nonprofit agencies became agents of government in the expansion of the American welfare state.

The Reagan administration reversed course by cutting federal spending on most social services and halting the growth of the federal role. It initiated an extensive reallocation of funding responsibilities between levels of government (federal to state) and rearranged some responsibilities between government programs (social service to health). Nonprofit agencies once again became more dependent on state and local funding. Private charity was asked to do more. The cutbacks of the Reagan and Bush administration were also "absorbed" by nonprofit workers whose salaries declined in real terms, and by clients who are no longer served, have to wait longer, or receive poorer service.

The decentralization of many social programs to the states makes the financial health of nonprofit agencies highly dependent on the fiscal health of the states. In the 1980s the capacity of state governments to increase their funding to nonprofit service agencies grew with their growing economies. But as state economies slump, nonprofit agencies are increasingly squeezed as states try to hold down social spending. The result is further consolidation among nonprofit agencies, and staff and service cutbacks. In 1990 Prospect House, an agency founded as a community action agency in the 1960s, declared bankruptcy. In 1991 the WAARC took over the government contracts of three other faltering service providers. Social services are now more dependent on state economies that are more vulnerable to shifting economic tides. And, like other state welfare expenditures, social services are now caught in the grip of a federal logic in which states compete with each other to keep taxes low.

41

Rust v. Sullivan, U.S. Supreme Court Decision by Chief Justice William Rehnquist, 1991

The expansion of federal funding for health, education, social service programs, and the arts after the mid-1960s set the stage for many disputes. In most cases, federal, state, and local governments rely on nonprofit organizations rather than government agencies or for-profit business firms to provide and deliver services. Private nonprofits (and private business firms as well) enjoy a variety of rights established under the U.S. Constitution, including the rights to freedom of speech, freedom of religion, and to "petition the government for a redress of grievances." Under the *Dartmouth College Case*, as we have also seen, the trustees of nonprofits were left free to set the policies of their organizations. There have always been questions, however, about the conditions that legislatures could impose on organizations that receive public funds or enjoy special tax benefits.

Nonprofits have, of course, always been required to obey the laws, including laws designed to protect the rights of employees and clients. During the nineteenth century and the first two-thirds of the twentieth century nonprofits received much of their funding from municipal, county, and state governments: and in that era each nonprofit that received government funds had to meet the requirements imposed by local and state governments, or seek redress in the state courts. On occasion, as in the case of *Pierce v. the Society of the Sisters* (a case that involved not a subsidy but the sheer right to use a service that was provided by a nonprofit), nonprofits successfully appealed state regulations to the federal courts.

The large-scale introduction of federal funding after 1965 raised the question of government regulation of nonprofit organizations to the national level. The Civil Rights movement succeeded at the same time, and the Civil Rights Acts of 1964 and 1969 required more equal treatment of people of color and also of women. Hence the expansion of federal support for a wide variety of social, health care, educational, and cultural purposes provided additional resources to those who sought to advance the civil rights agenda. Over the next twenty years, debates over the implementation of civil rights principles—and then over other divisive questions such as abortion—grew more and more intense. Federal regulations, accordingly, grew longer and more complex, and encountered increasing criticism and resistance.

The U.S. Supreme Court resolved many of these battles, establishing rules that govern the options open to nonprofits that accept federal funds. In the case of *Rust v. Sullivan,* the court held that Congress could insist, as a condition of receiving federal funds, that an organization set up programs exactly in accordance with rules enacted by Congress, and that they keep activities derived from their First-Amendment-protected right to free speech and petition "separate and distinct" from the programs supported by federal funds.

CHIEF JUSTICE WILLIAM REHNQUIST

U.S. *Supreme Court Majority Opinion*

RUST v. SULLIVAN

1991

These cases concern a . . . challenge to Department of Health and Human Services (HHS) regulations which limit the ability of Title X fund recipients to engage in abortion-related activities. The United States Court of Appeals for the Second Circuit upheld the regulations, finding them to be a permissible construction of the statute as well as consistent with the First and Fifth Amendments of the Constitution. We granted certiorari to resolve a split among the Courts of Appeals.[1] We affirm [the ruling of the U.S. Court of Appeals of the Second District, which rejected the challenge to the Department of Health and Human Services regulations].

In 1970, Congress enacted Title X of the Public Health Service Act (Act) . . . which provides federal funding for family planning services. The Act authorizes the Secretary to "make grants to and enter into contracts with public or nonprofit private entities to assist in the establishment and operation of voluntary family planning projects which shall offer a broad range of acceptable and effective family planning methods and services." Grants and contracts under Title X must "be made in accordance with such regulations as the Secretary may promulgate." Section 1008 of the Act, however, provides that "[n]one of the funds appropriated under this subchapter shall be used in programs where abortion is a method of family planning." That restriction was intended to ensure that Title X funds would "be used only to support preventive family planning services, population research, infertility services, and other related medical, informational, and educational activities."

In 1988, the Secretary promulgated new regulations designed to provide "'clear and operational guidance' to grantees about how to preserve the distinction between Title X programs and abortion as a method of family planning." The regulations clarify, through the definition of the term "family planning," that Congress intended Title X funds "to be used only to support preventive family planning services." Accordingly, Title X services are limited to "preconceptual counseling, education, and general reproductive health care," and expressly exclude "pregnancy care (including obstetric or prenatal care)." The regulations "focus the emphasis of the Title X program on its traditional mission: The provision of preventive family planning services specifically designed to enable individuals to determine the number and spacing of their children, while clarifying that pregnant women must be referred to appropriate prenatal care services."

The regulations attach three principal conditions on the grant of federal funds for Title X projects. First, the regulations specify that a "Title X project may not provide counseling concerning the use of abortion as a method of family planning or provide referral for abortion as a method of family planning." Because Title X is limited to preconceptional services, the program does not furnish services related to childbirth. Only in the context of a referral out of the Title X program is a pregnant woman given transitional information. Title X projects must refer every pregnant client "for appropriate prenatal and/or social services by furnishing a list of available providers that promote the welfare of the mother and the unborn child." The list may not be used indirectly to encourage or promote abortion, "such as by weighing the list of referrals in favor of health care providers which perform abortions, by including on the list of referral health care providers whose principal business is the provision of abortions, by excluding available providers who do not provide abortions, or by 'steering' clients to providers who offer abortion as a method of family planning." The Title X project is expressly prohibited from referring a pregnant woman to an abortion provider, even upon specific request. One permissible response to such an inquiry is that "the project does not consider abortion an appropriate method of family planning and therefore does not counsel or refer for abortion."

Second, the regulations broadly prohibit a Title X project from engaging in activities that "encourage, promote or advocate abortion as a method of family planning." Forbidden activities include lobbying for legislation that would increase the availability of abortion as a method of family planning, developing or disseminating materials advocating abortion as a method of family planning, providing speakers to promote abortion as a method of family planning, using legal action to make abortion available in any way as a method of family planning, and paying dues to any group that advocates abortion as a a method of family planning as a substantial part of its activities.

Third, the regulations require that Title X projects be organized so that they are "physically and financially separate" from prohibited abortion activities. To be deemed physically and financially separate, "a Title X project must have an objective integrity and independence from prohibited activities. Mere bookkeeping separation of Title X funds from other monies is not sufficient." The regulations provide a list of nonexclusive factors for the Secretary to consider in conducting a case-by-case determination of objective integrity and independence, such as the existence of separate accounting records and separate personnel, and the degree of physical separation of the project from facilities for prohibited activities.

Petitioners are Title X grantees and doctors who supervise Title X funds suing on behalf of themselves and their patients. Respondent is the Secretary of the Department of Health and Human Services. After the regulations had been promulgated, but before they had been applied, petitioners filed two separate actions, later consolidated, challenging the facial validity of the regulations and seeking declaratory and injunctive relief to prevent implementation of the regulations. Petitioners challenged the regulations on the grounds that they were not authorized by Title X and that they violate the First and Fifth Amendment rights of Title X clients and the First Amendment rights of Title X health providers. After initially granting the petitioners a preliminary injunction, the District Court rejected petitioners' statutory and constitutional challenges to the regulations and granted summary judgment in favor of the Secretary.

A panel of the Court of Appeals for the Second Circuit affirmed . . . that the regulations were a permissible construction of the statute that legitimately effectuated Congressional intent. . . .

Petitioners also contend that the restrictions on the subsidization of abortion-related speech contained in the regulations are impermissible because they condition the receipt of a benefit, in this case Title X funding, on the relinquishment of a constitutional right, the right to engage in abortion advocacy and counseling. Petitioners argue that "even though the government may deny [a] . . . benefit for any number of reasons, there are some reasons upon which the government may not rely. It may not deny a benefit to a person on a basis that infringes his constitutionally protected interests—especially, his interest in freedom of speech."

Petitioners' [assertion here] is unavailing, however, because here the government is not denying a benefit to anyone, but is instead simply insisting that public funds be spent for the purposes for which they were authorized. The Secretary's regulations do not force the Title X grantee to give up abortion-related speech; they merely require that the grantee keep such activities separate and distinct from Title X activities. Title X expressly distinguishes between a Title X grantee and a Title X project. The grantee, which normally is a health care organization, may receive funds from a variety of sources for a variety of purposes. The grantee receives Title X funds, however, for the specific and limited purpose of establishing and operating a Title X project. The regulations govern the scope of the Title X project's activities, and leave the grantee unfettered in its other activities. The Title X grantee can continue to perform abortions, provide abortion-related services, and engage in abortion advocacy; it simply is required to conduct those activities through programs that are separate and independent from the project that receives Title X funds.

In contrast, our "unconstitutional conditions" cases involve situations in which the government has placed a condition on the recipient of the subsidy rather than on a particular program or service, thus effectively prohibiting the recipient from engaging in the protected conduct outside the scope of the federally funded program. *In FCC v. League of Women Voters of California*, we invalidated a federal law providing that noncommercial television and radio stations that receive federal grants may not "engage in editorializing." Under that law, a recipient of federal funds was "barred absolutely from all editorializing" because it "is not able to segregate its activities according to the source of its funding" and thus "has no way of limiting the use of its federal funds to all noneditorializing activities." The effect of the law was that "a noncommercial educational station that receives only 1% of its overall income from [federal] grants is barred absolutely from all editorializing" and "barred from using even wholly private funds to finance its editorial activity." We expressly recognized, however, that were Congress to permit the recipient stations to "establish 'affiliate' organizations which could then use the station's facilities to editorialize with nonfederal funds, such a statutory mechanism would plainly be valid." Such a scheme would permit the station "to make known its views on matters of public importance through its nonfederally funded, editorializing affiliate without losing federal grants for its noneditorializing broadcast activities."

Similarly, in *Regan v. Taxation with Representation of Wash*[2] we held that Congress could, in the exercise of its spending power, reasonably refuse to subsidize the lobbying activities of tax-exempt charitable organizations by prohibiting such organizations from using tax-deductible contributions to support their lobbying efforts. In so holding, we explained that such organizations remained free "to receive deductible contributions to support . . . nonlobbying activit[ies]." Thus, a charitable organization could create, under [Section] 501(c)(3) of the Internal Revenue Code of 1954, an affiliate to conduct its nonlobbying activities using tax-deductible contributions, and at the same time establish, under [Section] 501(c)(4), a separate affiliate to pursue its lobbying efforts without such contributions. Given that alternative, the Court concluded that "Congress has not infringed any First Amendment rights or regulated any First Amendment activity [it] has simply chosen not to pay for [appellee's] lobbying." We also noted that appellee "would, of course, have to ensure that the 501(c)(3) organization did not subsidize the . . . 501(c)(4) organization; otherwise, public funds might be spent on an activity Congress chose not to subsidize." The condition that federal funds will be used only to further the purposes of a grant does not violate constitutional rights. "Congress could, for example, grant funds to an organization dedicated to combating teenage drug abuse, but condition the grant by providing that none of the money received from Congress should be used to lobby state legislatures."

By requiring that the Title X grantee engage in abortion-related activity separately from activity receiving federal funding, Congress has, consistent with our teachings in *League of Women Voters* and *Regan*, not denied it the right to engage in abortion-related activities. Congress has merely refused to fund such activities out of the public fisc, and the Secretary has simply required a certain degree of separation from the Title X project in order to ensure the integrity of the federally funded program.

The same principles apply to petitioners' claim that the regulations abridge the free speech rights of the grantee's staff. Individuals who are voluntarily employed for a Title X project must perform their duties in accordance with the regulation's restrictions on abortion counseling and referral. The employees remain free, however, to pursue abortion-related activities when they are not acting under the auspices of the Title X project. The regulations, which govern solely the scope of the Title X project's activities, do not in any way restrict the activities of those persons acting as private individuals. The employees' freedom of expression is limited during the time that they actually work for the project; but this limitation is a consequence of their decision to accept employment in a project, the scope of which is permissibly restricted by the funding authority.[3]

This is not to suggest that funding by the Government, even when coupled with the freedom of the fund recipients to speak outside the scope of the Government-funded project, is invariably sufficient to justify government control over the content of expression. For example, this Court has recognized that the existence of a Government "subsidy," in the form of Government-owned property, does not justify the restriction of speech in areas that have "been traditionally open to the public for expressive activity,"[4] or have been "expressly dedicated to speech activity."[5] Similarly, we have recognized that the university is a traditional sphere of free expression so fundamental to the functioning of our society that the Government's ability to control speech within that sphere by means of conditions attached to the expenditure of Government funds is restricted by the vagueness and overbreadth doctrines of the First Amendment.[6]

It could be argued by analogy that traditional relationships such as that between doctor and patient should enjoy protection under the First Amendment from government regulation, even when subsidized by the Government. We need not resolve that question here, however, because the Title X program regulations do not significantly impinge upon the doctor-patient relationship. Nothing in them requires a doctor to represent as his own any opinion that he does not in fact hold. Nor is the doctor-patient relationship established by the Title X program sufficiently all-encompassing so as to justify an expectation on the part of the patient of comprehensive medical advice. The program does not provide postconception medical care, and therefore a doctor's silence with regard to abortion cannot reasonably be thought to mislead a client into thinking that the doctor does not consider abortion an appropriate option for her. The doctor is always free to make clear that advice regarding abortion is simply beyond the scope of the program. In these circumstances, the general rule that the Government may choose not to subsidize speech applies with full force.

NOTES

1. Both the First Circuit and the Tenth Circuit have invalidated the regulations, primarily on constitutional grounds. See *Massachusetts v. Secretary of Health and Human Services*, 899 F. 2d 53 (CA1 1990); *Planned Parenthood Federation of America v. Sullivan*, 913 F. 2d 1492 (CA10 1990).

2. *Regan v. Taxation with Representation of Wash.*, 461 U. S. 540 (1983), the government has no obligation to subsidize even the exercise of fundamental rights, including "speech rights." The court also held that the regulations do not violate the First Amendment by "condition[ing] receipt of a benefit on the relinquishment of constitutional rights" because Title X grantees and their employees "remain free to say whatever they wish about abortion outside the Title X project." 889 F. 2d, at 412.

3. Petitioners also contend that the regulations violate the First Amendment by penalizing speech funded with non-Title X monies. They argue that since Title X requires that grant recipients contribute to the financing of Title X projects through the use of matching funds and grant-related income, the regulation's restrictions on abortion counseling and advocacy penalize privately funded speech.

We find this argument flawed for several reasons. First, Title X subsidies are just that, subsidies. The recipient is in no way compelled to operate a Title X project; to avoid the force of the regulations, it can simply decline the subsidy. See *Grove City College v. Bell*, 465 U. S. 555, 575 (1984) (petitioner's First Amendment rights not violated because it "may terminate its participation in the [federal] program and thus avoid the requirements of [the federal program]"). By accepting Title X funds, a recipient voluntarily consents to any restrictions placed on any matching funds or grant-related income. Potential grant recipients can choose between accepting Title X funds—subject to the Government's conditions that they provide matching funds and forgo abortion counseling and referral in the Title X project—or declining the subsidy and financing their own unsubsidized program. We have never held that the Government violates the First Amendment simply by offering that choice.

Second, the Secretary's regulations apply only to Title X programs. A recipient is therefore able to "limi[t] the use of its federal funds to [Title X] activities." *FCC v. League of Women Voters of Cal.*, 468 U. S. 364, at 400 (1984). It is in no way "barred from using even wholly private funds to finance" its pro-abortion activities outside the Title X program. Ibid. The regulations are limited to Title X funds; the recipient remains free to use private, non-Title X funds to finance abortion-related activities.

4. *United States v. Kokinda*, 110 S. Ct. 3115, 3119 (1990); *Hague v. CIO*, 307 U. S. 496, 515 (1939) (opinion of Roberts, J.).

5. *Kokinda*, supra, 110 S. Ct., at 3119; *Perry Education Assn. v. Perry Local Educators' Assn.*, 460 U. S. 37, 45 (1983).

6. *Keyishian v. Board of Regents*, 385 U. S. 589, 603, 605–606 (1967).

David C. Hammack is Hiram C. Haydn Professor of History and Chair of the Committee on Educational Programs of the Mandel Center for Nonprofit Organizations at Case Western Reserve University. Previously he taught in the City University of New York and at Princeton University. Hammack has held a Guggenheim Fellowship and was a Resident Fellow at the Russell Sage Foundation. His research has also been supported by grants from the American Council of Learned Societies and the Aspen Institute Nonprofit Sector Research Fund. Hammack is the author of *Power and Society: Greater New York at the Turn of the Century* and *Social Science in the Making: Essays on the Russell Sage Foundation, 1907–1972,* and is the editor, with Dennis R. Young, of *Nonprofit Organizations in a Market Economy.* He is currently Vice President for Meetings of the Association for Research on Nonprofit Organizations and Voluntary Action and serves on the editorial boards of *Nonprofit Sector and Voluntary Sector Quarterly, Urban Affairs Review,* and the American Historical Association–sponsored H-State internet discussion list on the American Welfare State.